Arthur Cox
Employment Law
Yearbook 2014

Arthur Cox
Employment Law
Yearbook 2014

Bloomsbury Professional

Published by
Bloomsbury Professional
Maxwelton House
41–43 Boltro Road
Haywards Heath
West Sussex
RH16 1BJ

Bloomsbury Professional
The Fitzwilliam Business Centre
26 Upper Pembroke Street
Dublin 2

ISBN 978 1 78043 693 7

© Arthur Cox

British Library Cataloguing-in-Publication Data
A catalogue record for this book is available from the British Library

Typeset by Marie Armah-Kwantreng, Dublin, Ireland
Printed and bound in the United Kingdom by CPI Group (UK) Ltd,
Croydon, CR0 4YYL

INTRODUCTION

This is the fourth volume of the *Arthur Cox Employment Law Yearbook* which is designed to set out the latest developments and information on areas that affect employment law in Ireland in 2014. The *Yearbook* is a unique resource for lawyers, human resource professionals, management, public and private sector employers, employees and trade unionists, for whom keeping up to date in employment law is an ever-present challenge.

The 2014 *Yearbook*, as before, is available as an ebook and readers are given instant access to the cases and materials from 2014 in employment law, data protection, freedom of information, pensions and taxation which have been selected and described by experienced lawyers in these fields.

The scope of the 2014 *Yearbook* covers: Irish law, legislation and decisions of the Superior Courts, the Labour Court, the Equality Tribunal and the Employment Appeals Tribunal; English law so far as relevant; and EU law, decisions of the Court of Justice of the European Union, the European Court of Human Rights, and relevant European legislative developments.

The opening chapter of the *Arthur Cox Employment Law Yearbook* is a mini-version of the *Yearbook* itself. It outlines in sequence the content which follows in subsequent chapters, and is intended to assist the reader by providing a synopsis of the 2014 content with brief comments thereon. The *Yearbook* is intended to be as user-friendly as possible. It has been produced with a detailed schedule of contents, in alphabetical format and with subjects cross-referenced to lead the reader to their area of interest without difficulty.

The 2014 *Yearbook* includes a number of new chapters on whistleblowing, freedom of information, injunctions, wages, immigration, and the proposed reforms in the Workplace Relations Bill. In addition, we are delighted to include a contribution on employment mediation from our colleague and leading academic and practitioner in this field, Dr Mary Redmond.

The line for inclusion in the 2014 *Yearbook* was drawn as of December 2014. Where we are aware that cases are being appealed, this is noted in the text. Work on the fifth *Arthur Cox Employment Law Yearbook* is already in progress.

Among those deserving special thanks are Amy Hayes of Bloomsbury Professional, whose encouragement and support was much valued, as ever, Tessa Robinson BL for editing, Andrew Turner for indexing, and Marie Armah-Kwantreng for typesetting and tabling. Sincere thanks also to all those in Arthur Cox who contributed to the 2014 *Yearbook*, in particular to Therese Broy and Niamh Hanratty, in the Arthur Cox Library, for their assistance.

Elaine Mettler, Arthur Cox Editor

February 2015

PRACTICE AREAS INVOLVED IN THE ARTHUR COX EMPLOYMENT LAW YEARBOOK 2014

Employment and Industrial Relations

Séamus Given

Kevin Langford

Cian Beecher

Gill Woods

John O'Dwyer

Dr Mary Redmond

Elaine Mettler, Arthur Cox Editor

Michael Doyle

Louise O'Byrne

Jacqueline Ho

Deborah Delahunt

Sarelle Buckley

Zelda Cunningham

Grace Gannon

Michelle Maloney

Fran Moran

Pensions

Declan Drislane

Philip Smith

Catherine Austin

Sarah McCague

Orla Ormsby

Katherine Hayes

Taxation

Conor Hurley

Caroline Devlin

Fintan Clancy

Ailish Finnerty

Anne Corrigan

Edel Hargaden

Aisling Burke

David Kilty

Orlaith Kane

Aoibhin O'Hare

Diyu Wu

Patricia McCarvill

Clodagh Power

Technology and Innovation

John Menton

Rob Corbet

Pearse Ryan

Colin Rooney

Bob Clarke

Iseult Mangan

Olivia Mullooly

Chris Bollard

Claire O'Brien

Joanne Neary

Contents

Contents

Contents

Contents

TABLE OF CASES

C

D

G

H

I

S

T

U

V

W

X

Y

Z

TABLE OF STATUTES

TABLE OF STATUTORY INSTRUMENTS

TABLE OF EUROPEAN LEGISLATION

TABLE OF CONSTITUTIONS

Chapter 1

INTRODUCTION: 2014 IN OUTLINE

CHAPTER 1: 2014 IN OUTLINE

[1.01] 2014 has been a busy and fascinating year for employment law. There have been significant legislative developments, specifically the Protected Disclosures Act 2014, the Employment Permits (Amendment) Act 2014 and the Workplace Relations Bill. The body of significant case law has continued to grow in each of the employment fora and a selection of those notable decisions have been included in this *Yearbook*.

The structure of **CHAPTER 1** mirrors the structure of the *Yearbook* and follows the same sequence. The idea is to provide a snapshot of each chapter and to whet the reader's appetite for the substantive case summary.

CONTRACT OF EMPLOYMENT

Employment status: contract for services or contract of service

[1.02] The question of employment status and whether an individual is an employee or an independent contractor/consultant continues to generate decisions across all employment fora and in the context of a variety of claims. In *Football Association of Ireland v Hand,*[1] the Labour Court considered whether the complainant was an employee of the respondent on a succession of fixed-term contracts of employment, in the context of a claim that his 'employment' transmuted to one of indefinite duration. The Labour Court also looked at whether the complainant was estopped from denying his status as a self-employed contractor by the doctrine of promissory estoppel.

[1.03] The UK Court of Appeal reiterated the control test in *White and Another v Troutbeck SA*[2] to determine whether an individual is a contractor or an employee. This case concerns a claim for unfair dismissal by two caretakers/housekeepers of a country estate. The Court of Appeal held as significant the fact that there was a written employment agreement but noted that this of itself would not always be determinative, and all the facts must be considered.

[1.04] In *Kelly v Charles Kelly Ltd,*[3] the EAT considered whether the claimant, a shareholder, statutory director and joint owner, was also an employee of the respondent company such as to be able to bring a claim for unfair dismissal. In *Murphy v Grand Circle Travel,*[4] the High Court was asked to overturn a finding of the Circuit Court (on

---

1. *Football Association of Ireland v Hand* FTD 143.
2. *White and Anor v Troutbeck SA* [2013] EWCA Civ 1171.
3. *Kelly v Charles Kelly Ltd* MN341/2012, UD394/2012.
4. *Murphy v Grand Circle Travel* [2014] IEHC 337.

1

appeal) that the claimant was employed by the respondent such that she could bring an unfair dismissal claim. The High Court overturned the Circuit Court finding and upheld the decision of the EAT that the claimant was an independent contractor. In *Hassett v Údarás na Gaeltachta*,[5] the EAT analysed the facts in accordance with the Code of Practice for Determining Employment or Self-Employment Status and concluded that the claimant scored 11 out of 13 factors as an employee.

Restrictive covenants

[1.05] Apart from one noteworthy Irish High Court case, the cases of note this year come from the UK.

In *Levinwick Ltd v Hollingsworth*,[6] the High Court considered the enforceability of a restraint of trade/non-solicitation clause in the contract of employment of a pharmacy manager. In his decision, McGovern J restated the test, ie whether the clause protects a legitimate business interest and is no wider than is reasonably necessary for the protection of that interest.

[1.06] In *Coppage and Another v Safety Net Security Ltd*[7], the UK Court of Appeal considered the reasonableness of a non-solicitation clause and set out several general principles which apply to restrictive covenants. In *JM Finn & Co Ltd v Holliday*,[8] the English High Court was asked to discontinue an injunction, which was imposed on the defendant, an investment manager in a stockbroking firm, preventing him from taking up new employment with a competitor until the expiry of his contractual 12-month garden leave. The High Court refused to discontinue the injunction. The High Court drew a distinction between post-termination restrictions and garden leave clauses and noted that, where an employer seeks an injunction to enforce a garden leave clause, the Court must apply the doctrine of restraint of trade in determining whether the garden leave provisions are more than what is reasonably necessary to protect the legitimate interest of the employer. In *Merlin Financial Consultants Ltd v Cooper*,[9] the English High Court considered whether restrictive covenants contained in a goodwill agreement and employment agreement, relating to the defendant's employment in the financial services sector, were enforceable. The Court noted the distinction between covenants in employment contracts and covenants in business sale agreements, because of the differences that may exist in the nature of the relationship and bargaining power between the parties. The degree to which non-solicitation provisions in the contract of employment of a recruitment consultant were enforceable was considered by the English High Court in *East England Schools CIC (T/A 4myschools) v Palmer*.[10] A feature of this case was the consideration by the Court of the educational market and the fact that

---

5.   *Hassett v Údarás na Gaeltachta* UD659/2012, MN490/2012.

6.   *Levinwick Ltd v Hollingsworth* [2014] IEHC 333.

7.   *Coppage v Safety Net Security Ltd* [2013] EWCA Civ 1176.

8.   *JM Finn & Co Ltd v Holliday* [2013] EWHC 3450 (QB).

9.   *Merlin Financial Consultants Ltd v Cooper* [2014] EWHC 1196.

10.   *East England Schools CIC (T/A 4myschools) v Palmer* [2013] EWHC 4138.

prospective schools and candidate teachers used many different employment agencies. The Court noted that there was little loyalty by schools or teachers to a particular consultant or employment agency. The Court further considered whether certain clauses could be blue pencilled to make them enforceable.

[1.07] In *Prophet plc v Huggett*,[11] the English Court of Appeal overturned a decision of the High Court in which the High Court decided to add words to a restrictive covenant to give the plaintiff employer protection. In *Elsevier Ltd v Munro*[12], the defendant chartered accountant handed in his notice and attempted to work as a CFO with one of the plaintiff's competitors one month later, notwithstanding that he had a 12-month notice period. The plaintiff sought an injunction to prevent him from working for a competitor. The English High Court considered whether the defendant was still bound by his contract of employment or whether he had been constructively dismissed and, if he was still bound by the contract, what terms should be enforced by injunction. The Court granted the injunction sought until the end of the defendant's notice period.

Duty of fidelity

[1.08] In *Thompson Ecology Ltd and another v APEM Ltd & Ors*,[13] the English High Court considered whether the third defendant, an operations manager employed by Thompson Unicomarine, had broken his duty of fidelity in failing to inform his employer of the threat from its competitor and by his actions in assisting that competitor to recruit Unicomarine staff.

Duty of confidentiality

[1.09] In *Warm Zones v Thurley and another*,[14] the plaintiff sought interim relief on the grounds that the defendants had used or disclosed confidential information contained within the plaintiff's consumer database without authorisation in breach of the express and implied terms of their contracts. The English High Court granted the mandatory injunction for imaging and inspection of computers/electrical devices.

Job abandonment

[1.10] In *Maher v Panache Lingerie Ltd*,[15] the EAT considered the concepts of job abandonment and frustration of contract. The employee in this case immediately went on sick leave following performance discussions and cited work-related stress, and subsequently there was a complete lack of engagement on the part of the claimant. The

---

11.   *Prophet plc v Huggett* [2014] EWCA Civ 1013.
12.   *Elsevier Ltd v Munro* [2014] EWHC 2648 (QB).
13.   *Thompson Ecology Ltd v APEM Ltd* [2014] IRLR 184.
14.   *Warm Zones v Thurley* [2014] EWHC 988 (QB), [2014] IRLR 791.
15.   *Maher v Panache Lingerie* UD1158/2012.

EAT held that it was reasonable of the employer to conclude that the claimant had abandoned his job and had frustrated his contract of employment.

Imposition of a retirement age

[1.11] In *Kane v Dublin Stevedores Ltd*,[16] the EAT considered the termination of the claimant's employment by reason of retirement. The EAT held that the imposition of retirement on the claimant, where there was no express contractual retirement age in his employment documents, was an unfair dismissal.

Mobility clauses

[1.12] The ability to relocate employees was considered in *Noonan Services Group Ltd v A Worker*.[17] The Labour Court held that the employer was entitled to rely on a mobility clause in the contract of employment to move the claimant employee from one client site to another. See **[22.01]**.

Calculation of damages for breach of contract

[1.13] In *Brown v Iarnród Éireann Irish Rail (No 2)*,[18] the High Court considered whether, in circumstances where an employer is guilty of a breach of contract as it has wrongfully refused to honour an early retirement package offered to the plaintiff, the plaintiff could recover the contract debt as the full measure of his compensation.

Contractual disciplinary procedures

[1.14] In *McMillan v Airedale NHS Foundation Trust*,[19] the English Court of Appeal considered whether the power to increase a disciplinary sanction on appeal could be implied into a contractual disciplinary procedure which is silent on the issue. The Court concluded that it could not.

The right to suspend

[1.15] In *McEneaney v Cavan and Monaghan Education & Training Board and O'Brien*,[20] the High Court considered whether a decision to place the applicant teacher on administrative leave was void in circumstances where a significant number of complaints were made about the applicant's teaching performance. The Court concluded

---

16.   *Kane v Dublin Stevedores Ltd* UD197/2012.
17.   *Noonan Services Group Ltd v A Worker* AD1419.
18.   *Brown v Iarnród Éireann/Irish Rail (No 2)* [2014] IEHC 117.
19.   *McMillan v Airedale NHS Foundation Trust* [2014] EWCA Civ 1031.
20.   *McEneaney v Cavan and Monaghan Education & Training Board and O'Brien* [2014] IEHC 423.

that the placing of the applicant on administrative leave was good administration in the circumstances of this case.

[1.16] However, *McMahon v The Irish Aviation Authority and the Irish Parachute Club*[21] provides a contrast. Here, the High Court considered the impact of the paid suspension of the applicant from his post as club chief instructor with the Irish Parachute Club. The Court referred specifically to the impact of the suspension on the applicant's good name and was critical of the fact that the period of suspension had continued beyond 12 months without a full disciplinary hearing. High Court concluded that the suspension had become invalid and was no longer operative.

DATA PROTECTION
Relevant Legislation

[1.17] The remaining un-commenced sections of the Data Protection Acts 1988 and 2003 (the DPA) were brought into force by the Minister for Justice and Equality with effect from 18 July 2014.[22]

Case law

[1.18] In *Data Protection Commissioner v MCK Rentals Ltd, Stuart and Martin*,[23] the Data Protection Commissioner successfully brought the first prosecution under s 22 of the DPA. A private investigation firm was charged with 23 counts of breaches of s 22 of the DPA, which states that it is an offence to obtain access to personal data without the prior authority of the data controller or data processor by whom the data is kept, and to subsequently disclose this data to another person.

References for a preliminary ruling – CJEU – concept of personal data – scope of the right of access of a data subject

[1.19] In July 2014, the CJEU gave a preliminary ruling that a requester who submits a data access request is not entitled to the entire document in which his or her personal data is contained, as the data that is subject to release only extends to personal data. See *YS v Minister voor Immigratie, Integratie en Asiel*[24] and *Minister voor Immigratie, Integratie en Asiel v M and S*.[25]

The decision is of assistance to employers who are faced with an increasing volume and scope of requests from employees and former employees who seek access to their personnel files and other data by reference to the DPA. The decision permits employers

---

21.   *McMahon v The Irish Aviation Authority and the Irish Parachute Club* [2014] IEHC 431.
22.   SI 337/2014 and SI 338/2014.
23.   *Data Protection Commissioner v MCK Rentals Ltd & Ors* (6 October 2014) Bray DC.
24.   *YS v Minister voor Immigratie, Integratie en Asiel* (Case C–141/12).
25.   *Minister voor Immigratie, Integratie en Asiel v M and S* (Case C–372/12).

to extract personal data from documents and it is not required that the original document (or a 'redacted' version of the document) be produced in response to a data access request.

Relevant case studies of the Office of the Data Protection Commissioner (ODPC)

[1.20] In 2013, five case studies relevant to the workplace were published by the ODPC in its 25th Annual Report.

Case Study 8 of 2013 concerned the unlawful transmission of CCTV images of staff member to third parties.

Case Study 9 of 2013 concerned the use of CCTV by a data controller in disciplinary proceedings and serves as a reminder that the use of CCTV should be limited to the purposes for which it was installed, and it is important that the employees are made aware of these purposes, particularly in circumstances where it may be used in disciplinary procedures.

[1.21] In *Case Study 10 of 2013*, the ODPC considered separate complaints concerning the alleged unfair processing of personal data from two former employees of a hotel in Dublin in relation to similar incidents which occurred six months apart. The complainants worked as night porters and were dismissed for allegedly sleeping on duty. In both cases, the evidence used to ground the disciplinary proceedings were photographs taken by the assistant night manager on his personal mobile phone.

[1.22] In *Case Study 11 of 2013*, the ODPC has again issued a reminder to employers as to the scope of s 4(4A) of the DPA, which exempts from release in response to a data access request, an expression of opinion given in confidence or on the understanding that it could be treated as confidential.

Case Study 15 of 2013 concerns a client list taken by an ex-employee to a new employer and a subsequent complaint about unsolicited correspondence received. This case study highlights the importance of ensuring that, when an employee departs his or her position of employment, security measures are in place to ensure that he or she does not remove personal data, for which the employer is the data controller, as such an action constitutes a data breach. Similarly, employers who hire an employee from a competitor must ensure that the client list which he may bring to the new employer has not been procured in breach of the DPA, as the new employer will not have consent to the processing of personal data that was provided by those clients to the previous employer, particularly in relation to direct marketing activities.

Guide to audit process

[1.23] The ODPC has revised its 2009 Guide to Audit Process (the Guide), which is designed to assist organisations selected for audit by the ODPC.

New Data Protection Commissioner

[1.24] In September 2014, the government announced the appointment of a new Data Protection Commissioner, Ms Helen Dixon.

EMPLOYMENT EQUALITY
Preliminary issues
Extensions of time limits

[1.25] Whether the time limit for bringing a valid complaint of discrimination or victimisation should be extended by the Director of the Equality Tribunal for reasonable cause, was considered in *Complaint by a teacher against a school board of management*[26] and *Complaint by retail assistant against an employer.*[27]

Compromise agreement

[1.26] In *An Employer v A Worker,*[28] the Labour Court considered an appeal of a decision of an Equality Officer where the complaint has been dismissed as misconceived in circumstances where the issues between the parties had been the subject of a compromise agreement and where the agreed payment was delayed but ultimately paid to the complainant. The Labour Court held that the complainant was not entitled to continue her complaint of sexual harassment in circumstances where she accepted the delayed payment in full and final settlement of all claims.

Protected Grounds
Gender

[1.27] In *Rafferty v National Educational Welfare Board,*[29] the Equality Tribunal held that the complaints of discrimination and victimisation were out of time but the time limits did not apply to the equal pay claim. The Equality Tribunal found that there were grounds other than gender for the differences in pay and that the decisions to award or refuse incremental credit were not influenced by gender. On appeal to the Labour Court,[30] the Court upheld the complaint. The complainant had established a prima facie case and the respondent could not rely on its own incomplete response to two Government departments on objective justification.

Time limits were again a feature of the Labour Court's decision in *Department of Justice Equality and Law Reform v A Worker.*[31] The complainant claimed she had been

---

26.   *Complaint by a teacher against a school board of management* DIR–E2014–002.
27.   *Complaint by retail assistant against an employer* DIR–E2014–001.
28.   *An Employer v A Worker* EDA1423.
29.   *Rafferty v National Educational Welfare Board* DEC–E2014–013.
30.   EDA 1438.
31.   *Department of Justice Equality and Law Reform v A Worker* EDA1422.

discriminated against on grounds of gender, marital status, age and race in relation to a civil service post. Her allegations of gender discrimination concerned a competition which occurred in 2008, which the Labour Court ruled to be statute barred as it was outside the six-month time limit. The complainant's claims were not upheld by the Labour Court.

In *Parfums Chanel Ltd & Chanel Ltd v Cappello*,[32] the Labour Court considered whether the reaction of the complainant's manager to the news that she was pregnant, and the subsequent treatment of her, was less favourable treatment on grounds of gender, marital status and family status. Complaints of harassment and victimisation were not upheld. The Labour Court acknowledged that certain comments made in the course of the conversation between the complainant and her manager may have been indiscreet and improper but they were not unlawful.

[1.28] An internal competition for a promotional post was considered by the Equality Tribunal in *Sheehy Skeffington v National University of Ireland, Galway*.[33] The complainant asserted that the selection process indicated a bias against female candidates. The Tribunal held that the implementation of the respondent's system of promotion fell short of best practice. The Tribunal noted that the application form required candidates to indicate whether they had availed of maternity or other unpaid leave, and held that this drew attention to caring responsibilities and disadvantaged female applicants. The complainant was awarded redress of €70,000 and the respondent was ordered to promote her with backdated effect.

In *Mullen v BCon Communications (In liquidation)*,[34] a complaint of discriminatory treatment and harassment on grounds of gender, pregnancy, and family status, the Equality Tribunal considered whether the definition of dismissal in the Employment Equality Acts extends to constructive dismissal.

In *Mentel v Top Heights Ltd T/A Foys Bar & Lounge*,[35] the Equality Tribunal considered whether the complainant was harassed, discriminated against, and victimised on grounds of race and gender. There was also a claim for equal pay on the basis of a hypothetical comparator. The Tribunal also considered whether the complaints were *res judicata* as the same facts had already been relied upon to ground a claim for constructive dismissal.

In *An Employee v An Employer*[36] the complainant asserted that he was subjected to unfair treatment once he commenced a reduced working week in a parental leave arrangement. The Equality Tribunal referenced the obligation on an employer to make arrangements in respect of an employee's workload where that employee avails of parental leave.

---

32.   *Parfums Chanel Ltd and Chanel Ltd v Cappello* EDA1434.
33.   *Sheehy Skeffington v National University of Ireland Galway* DEC–E2014–078.
34.   *Mullen v BCon Communications (In liq)* DEC–E2014–007.
35.   *Mentel v Top Heights Ltd T/A Foys Bar & Lounge* DEC–E2014–017.
36.   *An Employee v An Employer* DEC–E2014–022.

In *Nowakowska v Noel Recruitment (Ireland) Ltd and Rottapharm Ltd*[37] the Equality Tribunal concluded that the complainant was discriminated against and dismissed on the ground of gender by reason of her pregnancy.

Equal pay/gender

[1.29] In *Kenny v Department of Justice, Equality & Law Reform, Department of Finance and the Commissioner of An Garda Síochána*,[38] the complainants, who held administrative posts, and were not members of the force, sought equal pay with members of An Garda Síochána whose remuneration was higher, and claimed that the differential constituted indirect gender discrimination. The High Court referred a number of questions to the CJEU which gave guidance to the Court on the establishment of objective justification. It is noteworthy that the CJEU accepted that good industrial relations could be taken into consideration as one factor, amongst others, in the Court's assessment of whether differences in pay are due to objective factors.

Civil status

[1.30] *Parris v Trinity College Dublin & Ors*[39] concerned age, sexual orientation and civil status. The complainant sought to have his civil partnership recognised by the respondent in 2009, prior to the enactment of the Civil Partnership and Certain Rights and Obligations of Co-habitants Act 2010. The Equality Tribunal noted that the 2010 Act did not have retrospective effect and ruled against the complainant. This case is under appeal.

In *Hay v Credit Agricole Mutuel de Charente-Maritime et des Deux-Sévres*,[40] the CJEU considered whether a collective agreement which provided for days of special leave and a salary bonus to employees on the occasion of their marriage, and which did not apply to employees who entered into a civil solidarity act (civil partnership agreement), was discrimination on the grounds of sexual orientation.

Family status

[1.31] In *Coakley v Department of Social Protection*[41] the Equality Tribunal determined that the Department was the correct respondent in circumstances where it wholly controlled the complainant's eligibility for the particular employment scheme, as well as providing funding for the salaries of participants under the scheme. The Tribunal did not uphold the claim of discrimination on grounds of family status in terms of access to

---

37. *Nowakowska v Noel Recruitment (Ireland) Ltd and Rottapharm Ltd* DEC–E2014–074.
38. *Kenny v Department of Justice, Equality & Law Reform, Department of Finance and the Commissioner of An Garda Síochána* [2014] IEHC 11.
39. *Parris v Trinity College Dublin & Ors* DEC–P2013–004.
40. *Hay v Credit Agricole Mutuel de Charente-Maritime et des Deux-Sévres* (Case C–267/12).
41. *Coakley v Department of Social Protection* DEC–E2014–011.

employment and noted that, regardless of the complainant's family status, she would not have been eligible to participate in the scheme

Age

[1.32] In *Sefidvash v Institute of Art, Design & Technology*[42] the Labour Court was asked to consider whether the complainant, a mature student, had been less favourably treated than other students on the basis of his age, arising from an alleged remark made by his lecturer, a difference in treatment when accused of plagiarism and a consequent refusal to award him a degree, an alleged lack of transparency in the assessment process, and a refusal to allow the complainant to log minutes of a disciplinary meeting. The Labour Court decided against referring the question as to the vocational nature of the course within the meaning of the Employment Equality Acts, to the CJEU. The Court was satisfied that the complainant had not substantiated his claims and that evidence suggested that the complainant had not reached the required standards to be able to graduate.

[1.33] In *Wilson v Diageo (Scotland) Ltd*,[43] the Scottish Employment Tribunal considered whether a cap on ex gratia redundancy payments, which had an indirectly discriminatory effect on older employees with longer service, could be objectively justified. The Employment Tribunal upheld the claim and held that the respondent was unable to demonstrate a real need to introduce the cap.

A contrast can be seen in the Equality Tribunal's decision in *Hanlon & Ors v Lake Communications Ltd*,[44] where it was claimed that a cap on ex gratia redundancy payments indirectly discriminated against the complainants on grounds of their ages. The Equality Tribunal accepted the respondent's reliance on s 34(3)(d) of the Employment Equality Acts and held that, as the redundancy cap was based on service and not age, it was not discriminatory.

In *MacNamara and Seven Named Complainants v Electricity Supply Board*,[45] the Equality Tribunal was asked to consider whether the manner in which the pensions levy was applied to the respondent's defined benefit pension scheme amounted to discrimination on grounds of age. The respondent asserted that the claims were frivolous, vexatious, misconceived and statute barred. The Equality Tribunal accepted the respondent's position, holding that the claims were statute barred but were also taken against the incorrect respondent. In circumstances where the decision to reduce the pensions was taken by the trustees, the claims ought to have been brought against them.

In *Lett v Earagail Eisc Teoranta*[46] the Equality Tribunal considered the objective justifications put forward by the respondent for its decision to compulsorily retire the

---

42. *Sefidvash v Institute Of Art, Design & Technology* EDA 1334.
43. *Wilson v Diageo (Scotland) Ltd* S/4100153/13.
44. *Hanlon & Ors v Lake Communications Ltd* DEC–E2014–062.
45. *MacNamara and Seven Named Complainants v Electricity Supply Board* DEC–P2014–001.
46. *Lett v Earagail Eisc Teoranta* DEC–E2014–076.

complainant at the age of 66. The Tribunal also considered whether a forced reduction in hours to a three-day week prior to retirement was discrimination on grounds of age.

Disability

Could obesity come within the definition of disability?

[1.34] In *Kaltoft v Kommunernes Landsforening (KL), acting on behalf of the Municipality of Billund*,[47] an opinion of the Advocate General indicated that, in his view, obesity can amount to a 'disability' under art 1 of Directive 2000/78. The CJEU affirmed this in December 2014.

The definition of disability

[1.35] The broad definition of 'disability' is evident from *Byrne v Sea and Shore Safety Services Ltd*,[48] where the Labour Court accepted that the complainant, who was suffering from anxiety and post-traumatic stress due to ongoing exposure to rodents at her place of work, was suffering from a disability. The Labour Court upheld the complaints of harassment and discriminatory dismissal. The Court noted that the reasonable accommodation sought was the institution of an effective plan to deal with the rodent problem. The Labour Court noted that professional management of the problem would have been inexpensive and easy, and upheld the claim that the respondent had failed in this regard.

In *Stobart (Ireland) Ltd v Beashel*,[49] the Labour Court considered whether the complainant's condition (depression) constituted an illness or disability such as to give him *locus standi* to bring the claim and concluded it was a disability. The Labour Court was critical of the respondent's lack of engagement with the complainant and failure to make medical enquiries regarding the nature of his condition and any reasonable accommodation he might need.

Reasonable accommodation

[1.36] The requirements of employees to be near adequate toilet facilities because of their disabilities were considered by the Labour Court in two separate cases. In *A Public Service Employer v A Worker*,[50] the Labour Court concluded that the respondent had failed to provide the complainant with a suitable place of work having regard to her requirements during a three-year period. From 2010 onwards, the Labour Court noted that the respondent did all that was reasonably open to it to accommodate the complainant and its response was a model as to how an employer should respond. In *H v*

---

47. *Kaltoft v Kommunernes Landsforening (KL), acting on behalf of the Municipality of Billund* (Case C–354/13).

48. *Byrne v Sea and Shore Safety Services Ltd* EDA 143 and EDA 1435.

49. *Stobart (Ireland) Ltd v Beashel* EDA1411.

50. *A Public Service Employer v A Worker* EDA 1410.

A Multinational Retailer[51] both the Equality Tribunal and the Labour Court were critical of the respondent's failure to provide appropriate measures, to include facilitating the claimant's request to be able to sit for some of her working day and to use a wheelchair accessible toilet on site. It was held that the cost of providing a disabled toilet in the respondent's store was not a disproportionate burden for the respondent, a large multinational company.

In *Limerick and Clare Education and Training Board v Cotter*,[52] the complainant teacher agreed to go on sick leave following complaints about his conduct by parents of pupils. The Labour Court upheld part of the complainant's case when it held the respondent failed to reasonably accommodate him when he was subsequently certified as fit to return to work. The Labour Court noted that the respondent's actions in refusing a return to work were based on a medical report which was 12 months old, and held there was a statutory obligation on the respondent to at least investigate the nature of the accommodation sought and to make a decision as to whether it could or could not accommodate the complainant based on its investigation.

The treatment of an employee on his return from a serious workplace accident was considered in *O'Rourke v Brennan Convenience Foods Ltd T/A Food Partners (in liquidation)*.[53] It was claimed that there was an ongoing failure to reasonably accommodate the complainant in light of his ongoing injuries, which culminated in his dismissal. The claims were upheld.

In *London Borough of Southwark v Charles*,[54] the complainant's disability precluded him from being able to attend or engage in an administrative meeting. The complainant was subsequently dismissed by reason of redundancy. The UK EAT held that the respondent had failed to make reasonable accommodation for the claimant in the course of the redundancy/redeployment process.

In *A Worker v A Company (in receivership)*,[55] the Equality Tribunal considered whether the respondent's refusal to allow the complainant to work on a part-time basis constituted a failure to provide reasonable accommodation. The Equality Tribunal concluded that the dismissal of the employee due to his inability to work full-time hours was a discriminatory dismissal.

[1.37] In *General Dynamics Information Technology v Carranza*,[56] the UK EAT held that the respondent employer's failure to disregard a final written warning previously issued to the complainant when deciding to dismiss the complainant was not unfair or a failure to make 'reasonable adjustments'.

The obligations on an employer where an employee developed a psychological injury as a result of being a victim of a criminal action at work were considered in *McDonald v Road Safety Operations Ireland Ltd T/A Go Safe*.[57] The Equality Tribunal held that,

---

51.   *H v A Multinational Retailer* Dec–E2014–030.
52.   *Limerick and Clare Education and Training Board v Cotter* EDA1417.
53.   *O'Rourke v Brennan Convenience Foods Ltd T/A Food Partners (in liq)* DEC–E2014–058.
54.   *London Borough of Southwark v Charles* UK EAT/0008/14/RN.
55.   *A Worker v A Company (in receivership)* DEC–E2014–066.
56.   *General Dynamics Information Technology v Carranza* UKEAT/0107/14/KN.
57.   *McDonald v Road Safety Operations Ireland Ltd T/A Go Safe* DEC–E2014–069.

although the employer had obtained two medical assessments of the complainant, they had not made any enquiries of the complainant or otherwise as to what, if any, measures could be taken to facilitate the complainant's return to work. The Equality Tribunal was satisfied that the decision to dismiss the complainant was influenced by his disability, his absence and his inability to return to his position.

In *Wozniak v Tuleya*[58] the Equality Tribunal considered whether the complainant was dismissed because of her disability or family status and concluded that the dismissal was directly related to the complainant's disability and sick leave and was discriminatory.

Associative disability

[1.38] The concept of associative disability was considered by the English Court of Appeal in *Hainsworth v Ministry of Defence*,[59] where the appellant claimed a right to an adjustment to her employment to accommodate her disabled daughter's needs. This was not upheld.

Refusal of surrogacy leave

[1.39] The leave entitlements of mothers, who have a baby through surrogacy arrangements, were considered by the CJEU in *Z v A Government Dept and the Board of Management of a Community School*[60] and *CD v ST*.[61] The CJEU considered that a refusal of maternity or adoptive leave did not constitute discrimination on grounds of disability or gender.[62]

Race and nationality

[1.40] In *Conrad Hotel v Jurksa*,[63] the Labour Court considered whether the complainant was less favourably treated in an internal recruitment process. The Labour Court held that the complainant had failed to establish any connection between his nationality and the failure to offer him the role, and had not identified a comparator to demonstrate unfavourable treatment.

The fee structure in third level education was considered by the Labour Court in *Dublin Institute of Technology v Awojuola*.[64] The complainant, a Nigerian national, asserted that the fact she was charged fees at the non-EU rate was indirectly discriminatory of her on grounds of her race. The Labour Court considered whether there was a recognised racial group located in or referable to the EU but concluded there

58. *Wozniak v Tuleya* DEC–E2014–049.

59. *Hainsworth v Ministry of Defence (Respondent) and Equality and Human Rights Commission (Intervener)* [2014] EWCA Civ 763.

60. *Z v A Government Dept and the Board of Management of a Community School* (Case C–363/12).

61. *CD v ST* (Case C–167/12).

62. See **[20.02]**.

63. *Conrad Hotel v Jurksa* EDA1333.

64. *Dublin Institute of Technology v Awojuola* EDA1335.

was not. The Labour Court accepted the respondent's contention that the criteria which determined which fees were payable depended on residency or citizenship of the EU and were wholly unrelated to race.

In *Gajdos v Securikey Ltd,*[65] the Labour Court upheld a complaint of victimisation and discriminatory dismissal. The Court accepted the evidence that, in response to the complainant's allegations of unfavourable treatment, he was required to travel long distances to work assignments and was subsequently dismissed without discussion or engagement.

[1.41] The treatment and remuneration of hourly paid bar staff was considered by the Equality Tribunal in two cases brought by Chinese nationals. Both asserted less favourable treatment in terms of their conditions of employment and both asserted that their rates of pay were less favourable compared to identified Irish colleagues who performed like work. In *Xin Wei v Drew International Ltd (in Receivership),*[66] the Tribunal upheld the complaint of equal pay and ordered that arrears be paid. In *Ying Ying Sun Summer v McGraths Pub T/A Dawn Taverns Ltd,*[67] the Tribunal upheld the complaint of discriminatory dismissal and awarded compensation.

[1.42] Where a complainant is an agency worker and alleges less favourable treatment during the course of the placement, then who is the correct respondent: the employment agency or the end user company? The Equality Tribunal considered this in *Wszotek v Moduslink and O'Reilly Recruitment Ltd.*[68] In circumstances where the complaint referred to actions of the staff of the end user company, it was the correct respondent. The complainant failed to establish a prima facie case on the facts. The Tribunal took a similar approach in *Spyra v Ryanair Ltd,*[69] where the end user company was held to be the correct respondent. The complainant asserted that the termination of her agency work assignment constituted a discriminatory dismissal on grounds of her Polish nationality in circumstances where Irish nationals subsequently continued in employment. The Tribunal noted that, because of a seasonal downturn in business, it was necessary for the respondent to withdraw work from several long-term agency staff including the complainant. The Tribunal noted that, of the agency staff that were kept on, seven were Polish, one was Estonian and one was Irish. The Tribunal held that the complainant was selected because of her performance and her nationality was not a factor. This was affirmed on appeal by the Labour Court.[70]

[1.43] In *Kulasza v California White Services Ltd,*[71] the Equality Tribunal considered whether the complainant, a Polish dental nurse, was treated less favourably in respect of

65.   *Gajdos v Securikey Ltd* EDA1317.
66.   *Xin Wei v Drew International Ltd (in Receivership)* DEC–E2014–003.
67.   *Ying Ying Sun Summer v McGraths Pub T/A Dawn Taverns Ltd* DEC–E2014–064.
68.   *Wszotek v Moduslink and O'Reilly Recruitment Ltd* DEC–E2014–002.
69.   *Spyra v Ryanair Ltd* DEC–E2013–195.
70.   *Spyra v Ryanair Ltd* EDA1428.
71.   *Kulasza v California White Services Ltd* DEC–E2014–052.

her conditions of employment. The Tribunal did not consider the complainant's workload to be excessive and noted that she had been provided with other employment benefits that were inconsistent with less than favourable treatment. There was no evidence of victimisation or discriminatory dismissal.

Equal pay/race

[1.44] In *Marzec v Billy Purcell Plant Hire Ltd (in liquidation)*,[72] the Equality Tribunal upheld a claim for equal pay and held that the complainant, a Polish national, performed like work with his team members, one of whom (an Irish national) received a higher wage. The Tribunal concluded that there was no objective basis for any difference in pay, and the respondent had discriminated against the complainant on grounds of his race.

Victimisation

[1.45] The Equality Tribunal awarded compensation equivalent to three years' salary in *Wach v Travelodge Management Ltd T/A Travelodge Waterford*[73] for the discrimination of the complainant on grounds of her gender and race and for the victimising conduct of the respondent in threatening the complainant with false disciplinary charges after she had raised a complaint of discrimination. The question whether acts of alleged victimisation committed against a former employee are covered by the Equality Act 2010 was considered by the English Court of Appeal in *Jessemey v Rowstock Ltd and Another*.[74] This case arose from the respondent's provision of a very poor reference for the complainant because he had brought proceedings against the respondent for unfair dismissal and age discrimination on termination of his employment.

EMPLOYMENT-RELATED TORTS

Bullying and harassment

[1.46] 2014 has seen three significant developments in the case law relating to bullying and harassment. In *Becton Dickinson v A Worker*,[75] the Labour Court was asked to determine whether an independent investigation should be carried out in circumstances where complaints of bullying, harassment, victimisation and intimidation were made and already investigated internally. In this case, excessive delay was conceded by the employer. The Labour Court recommended that a review be carried out by an independent person with a view to deciding a process of resolution for the parties.

---

72. *Marzec v Billy Purcell Plant Hire Ltd (in liq)* DEC–E2014–014.
73. *Wach v Travelodge Management Ltd T/A Travelodge Waterford* DEC–E2014–055.
74. *Jessemey v Rowstock Ltd* [2014] EWCA Civ 185.
75. *Becton Dickinson v A Worker* Labour Court Recommendation No LCR20696.

[1.47] A stark contrast can be seen between the High Court decisions in *Ruffley v The Board of Management of St Anne's School*[76] and *Glynn v Minister for Justice, Equality and Law Reform, Ireland and the Attorney General.*[77] Both cases concerned claims for damages for bullying and harassment arising from alleged events in the workplace. In *Ruffley*, significant damages (an award of €255,276) were awarded to the plaintiff, a special needs assistant in a national school, for the unfair and inappropriate treatment of her, in the course of her employment.

In contrast, the claims of Ms Glynn were not upheld by the High Court. This case is significant for the distinctions drawn by Kearns P between occupational stress, workplace stress and bullying, and for his application of an objective test to the claim of bullying.

Vicarious liability

[1.48] In *Elmontem v Nethercross Ltd T/A Roganstown Golf and Country Club and Usi,*[78] the High Court considered whether an employer was vicariously liable for a tort committed by one of its employees against another, which resulted in significant physical injuries to the plaintiff. Herbert J considered the 'close connection' test for the imposition of vicarious liability and the extent to which an employer is liable under statute and common law for the safety of its employees.

EUROPEAN UNION LAW

[1.49] In *Hernández v Reino de España (Subdelegación del Gobierno de España en Alicante),*[79] the CJEU considered an employer's right to compensation from a Member State in respect of the remuneration paid to an employee beyond the 60th working day after the action challenging that employee's dismissal is brought. The CJEU held that there was no right to compensation in the case of invalid dismissal.

[1.50] An opinion of the Advocate General in *United Kingdom of Great Britain and Northern Ireland v The European Parliament of the Council of the European Union*[80] would refuse an application by the United Kingdom which sought to annul certain articles of the CRD IV Directive[81] and the Capital Requirements Regulations[82] relating

---

76. *Ruffley v The Board of Management of St Anne's School* [2014] IEHC 235.

77. *Glynn v Minister for Justice, Equality and Law Reform, Ireland and the AG* [2014] IEHC 133.

78. *Elmontem v Nethercross Ltd T/A Roganstown Golf and Country Club and Usi* [2014] IEHC 91.

79. *Hernández v Reino de España (Subdelegación del Gobierno de España en Alicante)* (Case C–198/13).

80. *United Kingdom of Great Britain and Northern Ireland v The European Parliament of the Council of the European Union* (Case C–507/2013).

81. Directive on access to the activity of credit institutions and the prudential supervision of credit institutions and investment firms.

82. Regulation EU 575/13 of the European Parliament, a credential requirement for the credit institutions and investment firms.

to the setting of ratios between the fixed and variable components of the remuneration payable to employees of credit institutions and investment firms and which require disclosure of certain information pertaining to remuneration.

CHAPTER 6 also sets out the key provisions of three new European Council Directives that relate to employment:

(i)   Directive of the European Parliament and the Council on the Enforcement of Directive 96/71/EC (The Posted Workers Enforcement Directive);[83]

(ii)   Directive of the European Parliament and of the Council on the conditions of entry and stay of third-country nationals for the purpose of employment as seasonal workers;[84]

(iii)   Directive of the European Parliament and of the Council on the conditions of entry and residence of their country nationals in the framework of an intra-corporate transfer.[85]

FIXED-TERM WORK

Contract of indefinite duration and objective grounds

[1.51] Most fixed-term cases concern an asserted entitlement to a contract of indefinite duration. Central to each of the cases that feature in this Yearbook is an analysis by the Labour Court of whether there are objective grounds to justify the continuing employment of the complainant on a fixed-term basis. In each of the cases the Labour Court has referenced the decision of the CJEU in *Angelidaki & Ors v Organismos Nomarchiaki Autodioikisis Rethymnis*[86] where the CJEU distinguished between the temporary needs of the employer, for which successive fixed-term contracts could be legitimately used and the permanent needs of an employer for which fixed-term contracts are not appropriate beyond the four-year time limit.

[1.52] In *Márquez Samohano v Universitat Pompeu Fabra*,[87] the CJEU held that the Framework Agreement on Fixed-Term Work[88] did not preclude national rules which allow universities to renew successive fixed-term employment contracts concluded with associate lecturers, with no limitation as to the maximum duration and the number of renewals of those contracts where such contracts are justified by an objective reason.

---

83.   Directive 2014/67/EU.
84.   Directive 2014/36/EU.
85.   Directive 2014/66/EU.
86.   *Angelidaki & Ors v Organismos Nomarchiaki Autodioikisis Rethymnis* (Cases C–378/07 to C–380/07).
87.   *Márquez Samohano v Universitat Pompeu Fabra* (Case C–190/13).
88.   Council Directive 1999/EC/70.

In *National University of Ireland Galway v Welford,*[89] the Labour Court examined the nature of the research project that the complainant was undertaking and held that it was part of a period of temporary or transient need and did not form part of the respondent's continuing or permanent research requirements such that there were objective grounds to justify the renewal of the complainant's fixed-term contract.

[1.53] In *White v Dun Laoghaire VEC*[90] the Labour Court did not accept that covering for employees on career breaks or on statutory leave over a long term was an objective justification for fixed-term renewal. The complainant was entitled to a contract of indefinite duration.

In *HSE West v Ismael,*[91] the Labour Court held that the complainant's contract of employment, which clearly stated that his appointment was to provide cover for a named consultant undertaking clinical director duties, did fulfil a temporary requirement of the respondent and was based on objective grounds.

In *National University of Ireland v O'Keefe,*[92] the Labour Court upheld the respondent's claim that the replacement of an identified employee on sabbatical leave by the complainant on a fixed-term contract was objectively justified.

[1.54] By contrast, in *National University of Ireland v Benson,*[93] the Labour Court held that the respondent had failed to establish that the complainant's third contract was concluded for the purpose of providing cover for the duration of the temporary absence of another person.

In *Gorey Community School v Wildes,*[94] the Labour Court accepted that keeping a position open for a permanent employee who has a right to return can be a legitimate objective which an employer is entitled to pursue; however, the employer must show that the absent person is actually returning to his/her duties.

In *Board of Management of St Joseph's School for Deaf Boys v Grehan,*[95] the Labour Court concluded that the respondent's failure to provide written objective grounds for the renewal of a fixed-term contract inferred that the objective grounds relied upon were not the operative grounds for the impugned decision. The Court noted that no satisfactory contemporaneous objective grounds had been put forward and upheld the claim to a contract of indefinite duration. The Labour Court ordered reinstatement with effect from a date two years prior to the dismissal.

[1.55] In *Dublin Institute of Technology v Scott,*[96] the complainant accepted a further 'specified purpose contract' after he became entitled to a contract of indefinite duration.

---

89. *National University of Ireland Galway v Welford* FTD1325.
90. *White v Dun Laoghaire VEC* FTD1329.
91. *HSE West v Ismael* FTD141.
92. *National University of Ireland v O'Keefe* FTD1411.
93. *National University of Ireland v Benson* FTD1412.
94. *Gorey Community School v Wildes* FTD1419.
95. *Board of Management St Joseph's School for Deaf Boys v Grehan* FTC1416.
96. *Dublin Institute of Technology v Scott* FTD1417.

The Labour Court held that the respondent employer could not rely on its own errors (in allowing the complainant's service to continue) to deny his claim. The Court ordered reinstatement without loss of income from the date of termination of employment.

In *University of Limerick v Arbuckle*,[97] the Labour Court accepted the respondent's use of fixed-term contracts to meet a specific temporary need, which was the completion of a specific defined project, and held this was a legitimate objective of the respondent.

Breaks between fixed-term contracts

[1.56] In *Abbott v Department of Education & Skills*,[98] the Labour Court held that a civil servant, who was employed under a fixed-term contract by one Governmental Department and was subsequently employed by another (notwithstanding that she had resigned between employments) did have continuity of employment for a period exceeding four years and, in the absence of objective grounds, the complainant was entitled to be reinstated. In *Athlone Institute of Technology v McManus*,[99] the Labour Court considered whether a break between two fixed-term contracts of employment constituted a period of layoff, and concluded that the ending of the first contract without its renewal had all the appearances of a dismissal. However the immediate re-employment of the complainant 10 days after the termination of the first contract did, in the view of the Labour Court, preserve her continuity of service.

The extent to which a break in service may disentitle an employee to a contract of indefinite duration was considered by the High Court in *HSE v Sallam*.[100] The complainant had over eight years of employment under successive fixed-term contracts which contained two separate breaks between the various contracts; the first being a period of 15 days and the second being 21 days. The Labour Court held these periods could not 'provide a sufficient basis' to render the employment non-continuous. While accepting this part of the Labour Court's analysis, the High Court found that the Labour Court did not deal with the question of justification correctly and concluded that the Labour Court's finding may have been made on a hypothetical basis and did not form part of its decision on the facts.

Locus standi

[1.57] Whether the complainant had *locus standi* to bring a complaint under the Protection of Employees (Fixed-Term Work) Act 2003 was considered by the Labour Court in *Frobel College of Education v Raftery*.[101] The complainant, a primary school teacher with a permanent contract of employment, was seconded to work in a fixed-term capacity with the respondent. The Court concluded that the complainant was a

---

97. *University of Limerick v Arbuckle* FTD1420.
98. *Abbott v Department of Education & Skills* FTD1331.
99. *Athlone Institute of Technology v McManus* FTD1410.
100. *HSE v Sallam* [2014] IEHC 298.
101. *Frobel College of Education v Raftery* FTD144.

permanent employee of the school, whose employment was never at risk during the period of secondment. She therefore did not enjoy the protection of the 2003 Act.

Comparators

[1.58] The circumstances where one can look outside the employee's organisation for a comparator was considered by the Labour Court in *A University v A Worker*.[102] The complainant asserted that she was treated less favourably than comparable permanent employees when she was not paid an ex gratia redundancy payment over and above statutory redundancy terms. The complainant wished to rely on s 5(1)(c) of the 2003 Act to identify comparable permanent employees within the higher educational sector, as there were no proper internal comparators within the meaning of s 5(1)(a) and (b) of the 2003 Act. The Labour Court was satisfied that there was at least one appropriate internal comparator treated in the same manner as the complainant and hence there was no necessity to examine s 5(1)(b) or (c).

Unfair dismissals claim arising out of a termination of employment and failure to provide a contract of indefinite duration

[1.59] In *Cunning v Dublin Institute of Technology*[103] the claimant challenged her employer's failure to provide her with a contract of indefinite duration under s 9 of the Protection of Employees (Fixed-Term Work) Act 2003 by way of an unfair dismissals claim in the EAT, which claim was upheld by the EAT.

National exclusions from the statutory entitlements

[1.60] In *Fiamingo & Ors v Rete Ferroviaria Italiana SpA*,[104] the CJEU confirmed that the Framework Agreement on Fixed-Term Work did apply to seafarer's contracts of employment and thus Italian legislation as contained, in the navigation code, was permitted.

FREEDOM OF INFORMATION

The Freedom of Information Act 2014

[1.61] CHAPTER 8 details the key provisions of the Freedom of Information Act 2014, the most significant development in freedom of information (FOI) law in Ireland in over a decade.

The Act represents a major overhaul of the current legislation, the Freedom of Information Act 1997, as amended by the Freedom of Information (Amendment) Act

---

102. *A University v A Worker* FTD142.
103. *Cunning v Dublin Institute of Technology* UD1006/2012.
104. *Fiamingo & Ors v Rete Ferroviaria Italiana SpA* (Joined Cases C–362/13, C–363/13, and C–407/13).

2003 and the scope of FOI has been expanded to include almost all public bodies (including a number of high profile public bodies), as opposed to the specific schedule of prescribed bodies subject to the terms of the previous Act.

Relevant case law/Information Commissioner case studies

[1.62] In *Minister for Health v The Information Commissioner & Ors*,[105] the High Court allowed an appeal from the decision of the Commissioner and determined that the Minister for Health was not entitled to grant access to documents which had been lodged for safe keeping with the Department of Health by Smyth J as part of an inquiry into practices at Our Lady of Lourdes Hospital, Drogheda.

[1.63] *Westwood Club v Information Commissioner and Bray Town Council*[106] was a successful High Court challenge to a decision of the former Commissioner, Emily O'Reilly, to affirm Bray Town Council's refusal to grant Westwood Club access to the financial records of a competitor, Bray Swimming Pool and Sports Leisure Centre Ltd (trading as 'Shoreline').

Courts service publishes judges' names in relation to expenses

[1.64] On 16 October 2014, the Courts Service released a breakdown by name of judicial expense claims, following a decision in August 2014 by the current Information Commissioner that the Irish Courts Service was not justified in withholding the names of individual judges when releasing expenses information.

New Information Commissioner

[1.65] In December 2013, the government announced the appointment of Mr Peter Tyndall as Information Commissioner.

HEALTH AND SAFETY

Penalisation

[1.66] In *Bus Éireann v Browne*,[107] the Labour Court considered whether the claimant had been penalised for having raised a complaint of bullying and harassment. The Court noted that certain of the alleged detriments complained of, a relocation of the claimant, removal of flexitime; and failure to notify her of a promotional post, all post-dated her complaint of penalisation. The claimant did not establish a nexus between the detriments complained of and her original complaints.

---

105. *Minister for Health v The Information Commissioner & Ors* [2014] IEHC 231.
106. *Westwood Club v Information Commissioner and Bray Town Council* [2014] IEHC 375.
107. *Bus Éireann v Browne* HSD1317.

[1.67] In *Stobart (Ireland) Driver Services Ltd v Carroll*,[108] an appeal on a point of law, the High Court was asked to consider whether the Labour Court had erred in concluding that the dismissal of the respondent from his employment with the appellant constituted penalisation under the Safety, Health and Welfare at Work Act 2005 and in its award of reinstatement. The High Court set out the principles governing an appeal on a point of law and stated a reluctance to interfere with the finding of a specialist tribunal, such as the Labour Court, unless there was no evidence to support it. In this case, the High Court upheld the finding of the Labour Court that penalisation had taken place and that reinstatement was a permitted remedy under the 2005 Act. The matter was remitted to the Labour Court[109] so that the respondent's loss of earnings could be calculated.

HUMAN RIGHTS

[1.68] The joined UK cases of *Benkharbouche v Embassy of the Republic of Sudan* and *Janah v Libya*,[110] each of which involve employment law claims against employer embassies, are significant. In its ruling, the UK EAT held itself bound by EU law to disapply domestic law. The UK EAT recognised the applicability of the Charter of Fundamental Rights of the European Union in the UK and of the principle of horizontal effect. The impact of this decision is that even where the Human Rights Act 1998 does not allow the disapplication of a statutory provision, EU law requires a court or tribunal to disapply primary legislation where it concerns the material scope of EU law.

[1.69] In *Mba v Mayor and Burgesses of the London Borough of Merton*,[111] the English Court of Appeal considered whether a requirement to work on Sundays, in circumstances where the claimant was a practising Christian who believed Sunday was a day of worship and not for work, were grounds justifying constructive dismissal and amounted to indirect religious discrimination against her. The Court held it was legitimate for an Employment Tribunal to consider the belief that treating Sunday as a day of rest was a 'core component of the Christian faith' in circumstances where the right to freedom to manifest religion under art 9 of the European Convention of Human Rights was invoked.

[1.70] In *Matúz v Republic of Hungary*,[112] the European Court of Human Rights held that the dismissal of the applicant (a television journalist employed by the state broadcaster) for divulging confidential information and documents was a breach of his right to freedom of expression and in particular the right to impart information.

---

108. *Stobart (Ireland) Driver Services Ltd v Carroll* [2013] IEHC 581.
109. *Stobart (Ireland) Driver Services Ltd v Carroll* HSD045.
110. *Benkharbouche v Embassy of the Republic of Sudan; Janah v Libya* UK EAT/0401/12/GE, UK EAT/0020/13/GE.
111. *Mba v Mayor and Burgesses of the London Borough of Merton* [2013] EWCA Civ 1562.
112. *Matúz v Republic of Hungary* 73571/10 [2014] ECHR 1112.

IMMIGRATION

[1.71] In *Hussein v Minister for Justice and Equality*,[113] an application for judicial review, the High Court considered the decision of the Minister for Justice and Equality to refuse an application for 'long term residence with exemption from work permit conditions', also referred to as a five-year 'Stamp 4 permission', on the basis of a minor road traffic offence, which the applicant had openly admitted. In this case, an order of *certiorari* was made, quashing the Minister's decision.

Significant changes to Ireland's immigration regime were introduced on 1 October 2014, by the Employment Permits (Amendment) Act 2014 and two separate Regulations thereunder. A detailed analysis of all of the changes is set out in **CHAPTER 11**.

INDUSTRIAL RELATIONS
Trade Union recognition

[1.72] In *Waterford Co Co v A Group of Workers, PNA (Irish Fire & Emergency Service Association)*[114] the Labour Court considered a claim for recognition by the Irish Fire & Emergency Association, which was a branch of a trade union already recognised by the employer. The Court had to consider whether an employer was obliged to recognise a trade union for collective bargaining in circumstances where that employer already has established arrangements in place with authorised trade unions. The Labour Court found the claim should not be conceded.

The Labour Court was critical of the employer in *Unilever Ireland v SIPTU*,[115] which related to a refusal by management to engage with the union in relation to proposed redundancies, notwithstanding 30 years of collective bargaining history between the parties. The Court recommended that the parties' relationship resume immediately.

[1.73] In *Cavan and Monaghan Community Area Services v SIPTU*,[116] the Court recommended that the respondent employer, which was supported by public funds, should enter into negotiations with the relevant union which was seeking recognition.

Bias in an internal selection procedure

[1.74] In *A University v A Worker*,[117] the Labour Court considered the handling of a grievance resulting from an internal selection process in a university, and allegations of bias which were raised by the candidate after the process had concluded.

---

113. *Hussein v Minister for Justice and Equality* [2014] IEHC 34.
114. *Waterford Co Co v A Group of Workers, PNA (Irish Fire & Emergency Service Association)* LCR20726.
115. *Unilever Ireland v SIPTU* CD/14236, LCR20826.
116. *Cavan and Monaghan Community Area Services v SIPTU* LCR20838.
117. *A University and A Worker* AD1411.

Ability of the Labour Court to investigate post-retirement disputes

[1.75] In *Health Service Executive v A Worker*[118] the Labour Court was asked to consider whether it had jurisdiction to hear a claim in circumstances where the claimant had retired from employment and the issue was not referred to the LRC, or the Labour Court, prior to her retirement. The Labour Court relied on an opinion from the Attorney General to decline jurisdiction to hear the claim.

Concept of normal ongoing change

[1.76] The joined cases *An Post v CPSU*[119] and *An Post v PSEU*[120] concerned a dispute between the respondent employer and two of the respondent's recognised trade unions in relation to the proposed introduction of an online attendance reporting system. The Labour Court considered whether the proposed changes constituted 'normal ongoing change' and concluded that they did.

Unilateral amendments to collective agreements

[1.77] In *Tesco Ireland Ltd v Mandate and SIPTU*,[121] the Labour Court was asked to consider whether the employer acted unilaterally to alter the terms of collective agreements governing workers' sick pay arrangements. The Court concluded that applying a notional social welfare deduction from employees' sick pay on the fourth, fifth and sixth days of absence was a breach of the terms of the agreed sick pay schemes.

New Boliden Tara Mines v SIPTU[122] concerned the decision of the respondent to unilaterally alter an arrangement whereby an individual worker was paid extra for shifts. The Labour Court affirmed the decision of the Rights Commissioner and accepted the respondent's submission that it reserved the right to manage its workers and the ending of this windfall benefit did not merit any compensation.

Injunction to restrain industrial action

[1.78] In *Dublin Airport Authority v SIPTU*,[123] the High Court considered an application to restrain industrial action in the form of a proposed work stoppage at Cork and Dublin airports. The proposed secret ballot conducted by SIPTU and its compliance with s 19 of the Industrial Relations Act 1990 was the central issue in this case.

---

118.   *Health Service Executive v A Worker* LCR20771.
119.   *An Post v CPSU* LCR20805.
120.   *An Post v PSEU* LCR20806.
121.   *Tesco Ireland Ltd v Mandate and SIPTU* LCR20808.
122.   *New Boliden Tara Mines v SIPTU* AD1450.
123.   *Dublin Airport Authority plc v SIPTU and Ryanair Ltd v SIPTU* [2014] IEHC 644.

INJUNCTIONS

[1.79] In 2014 the High Court has continued to apply the well-established three-pronged test as originally espoused in *Campus Oil v Minister for Industry and Energy*[124] and modified by the Supreme Court in *Maha Lingham v Health Service Executive.*[125] Details are in CHAPTER 13.

Restrain a dismissal

[1.80] In *Hartnett v Advanced Tyre Co Ltd T/A Advanced Pitstop*[126] Keane J held that the employer had committed a number of procedural breaches when investigating alleged serious misconduct, to include the failure to present the principal witness for cross-examination by the plaintiff's representatives. However he declined to grant the injunction and held that the plaintiff by his actions (in failing to disclose receipt of an alleged gratuity from a witness until the appeal) had failed to satisfy the balance of convenience test.

[1.81] In *Bradshaw v Murphy & Ors,*[127] Finlay Geoghegan J refused to grant an order restraining the defendant from terminating or purporting to terminate the employment of the plaintiff, in circumstances where the defendant provided an undertaking to the Court that the plaintiff would not be dismissed by reason of misconduct. Finlay Geoghegan J noted that the plaintiff had not shown a serious issue to be tried as to the employer's entitlement at common law to terminate the employment of the plaintiff in accordance with the relevant contractual provisions.

[1.82] In *Hughes v Mongodb Ltd,*[128] Keane J considered the plaintiff's submission that an employer's right to rely on a contractual notice provision to terminate employment is dependent on the reason for dismissal being 'good'. The Court did not accept that a dismissal for 'poor performance' (rather than misconduct) gives rise to the entitlement to fair procedures that is to be implied into every contract of employment.

Restrain suspension of sick pay/disciplinary proceedings

[1.83] In *Elmes & Ors v Vedanta Lisheen Mining Ltd & Ors,*[129] Ryan J refused to grant any form of injunction to restrain proposed disciplinary proceedings and noted the Court's reluctance to interfere with the internal affairs of a company. He further refused to grant a mandatory order to direct that a proposed investigation be carried out by an independent investigator. Ryan J did, however, acknowledge the custom and practice of

---

124. *Campus Oil v Minister for Industry and Energy* [1983] 1 IR 88.
125. *Maha Lingham v Health Service Executive* [2006] 17 ELR 137.
126. *Hartnett v Advanced Tyre Co Ltd T/A Advanced Pitstop* [2013] IEHC 615.
127. *Bradshaw v Murphy & Ors* [2014] IEHC 146.
128. *Hughes v Mongodb Ltd* [2014] IEHC 335.
129. *Elmes & Ors v Vedanta Lisheen Mining Ltd & Ors* [2014] IEHC 73.

paying sick pay in the company and determined that sick pay should be continued for a further six months, after which the plaintiffs could apply for further sick pay, to be determined on the merits of the case at that time.

Restrain a disciplinary process until the determination of criminal proceedings

[1.84] In *Rogers v An Post,*[130] the High Court was asked to restrain any further steps in a disciplinary process relating to the plaintiff until the determination of criminal proceedings in the Circuit Criminal Court. Keane J refused the application and held that the grant of an interlocutory injunction on the terms sought would not be appropriate as a means of maintaining the status quo. He noted the plaintiff's implied acceptance that the grant of the injunction would determine the issue in the main action in his favour. Keane J held that to grant the injunction would be an injustice as there was a very great likelihood that this would effectively preclude the defendant from the opportunity of having its rights determined at a full trial.

Restrain the operation of the Public Service Management (Sick Leave) Regulations 2014 pending the outcome of Judicial Review Proceedings

[1.85] In *Garda Representative Association v Minister for Public Expenditure and Reform,*[131] Peart J refused an application for an interlocutory injunction to restrain the Minister from operating the Public Service Management (Sick Leave) Regulations 2014 (SI 124/2014) to respective members of An Garda Síochána pending the determination of judicial review proceedings. See para **[21.08]**.

Costs

[1.86] Liability for the plaintiff's interlocutory injunction costs was considered in *Irish Bacon Slicers Ltd v Weidemark Fleischwaren GmbH & Co.*[132] A delay on the part of the defendant in proffering an undertaking resulted in the granting of an interim injunction and the subsequent application for an interlocutory injunction. The High Court awarded the plaintiff its costs.

INSOLVENCY

[1.87] In *Tracey v Game Stores Group Ltd,*[133] the EAT held that the joint administrator of the respondent was required to attend before the EAT in order to make its submission that the EAT did not have jurisdiction to hear the case.

---

130.   *Rogers v An Post* [2014] IEHC 412.
131.   *Garda Representative Association v Minister for Public Expenditure and Reform* [2014] IEHC 237.
132.   *Irish Bacon Slicers Ltd v Weidemark Fleischwaren GmbH & Co* [2014] IEHC 293.
133.   *Tracey v Game Stores Group Ltd* UD1632/2011.

See also *Phelan v REL Refrigeration Group Ltd*[134] in **[22.28]**, a redundancy case in which the EAT extended the time limit for bringing a claim because of false assurances provided by the liquidator of the respondent to the complainant.

LEGISLATION

Selected Acts

[1.88] The following Acts, which have a relevance to employment law, were enacted in 2014:

(i)   Irish Human Rights and Equality Commission Act 2014;

(ii)   Friendly Societies and Industrial and Provident Societies (Miscellaneous Provisions) Act 2014;

(iii)   Court of Appeal Act 2014;

(iv)   Social Welfare and Pensions Act 2014;

(v)   Health Identifiers Act 2014;

(vi)   Local Government Reform Act 2014;

(vii)   Employment Permits (Amendment) Act 2014;

(viii) Protected Disclosures Act 2014;

(ix)   Competition and Consumer Protection Act 2014;

(x)   Industrial Development (Forfás Dissolution) Act 2014;

(xi)   Health (General Practitioners Service) Act 2014;

(xii)   National Treasury Management Agency (Amendment) Act 2014; and

(xiii) Public Health (Sunbeds) Act 2014.

Selected Bills

[1.89] The following Bills, which have relevance to employment law, were proposed in 2014:

(i)   Workplace Relations Bill 2014;

(ii)   Public Service Management (Transparency of Boards) Bill 2014;

(iii)   Education (Miscellaneous Provisions) Bill 2014;

(iv)   Roads Bill 2014;

(v)   Equality (Amendment) Bill 2014;

(vi)   Employment Equality (Abolition of Mandatory Retirement Age) Bill 2014;

(vii)   Immigration Reform for US Citizens Living in Ireland Bill 2014;

---

134.   *Phelan v REL Refrigeration Group Ltd* RP411/2013.

(viii)   Immigration (Reform) (Regularisation of Residency Status) Bill 2014;

(ix)   Intellectual Property (Miscellaneous Provisions) Bill 2014;

(x)   Defamation (Amendment) Bill 2014;

(xi)   Higher Education and Research (Consolidation and Improvement) Bill 2014;

(xii)   Adoption (Identity and Information) Bill 2014;

(xiii) State Boards (Appointment) Bill 2014;

(xiv)   Thirty-fourth Amendment of the Constitution (Right to Personal Autonomy and Bodily Integrity) Bill 2014;

(xv)   Industrial Relations (Amendment) Bill 2015

Selected statutory instruments

[1.90] The following statutory instruments which have relevance to employment law were made in 2014:

(i)   Public Service Management (Sick Leave) Regulations 2014 (SI 124/2014);

(ii)   Employment Permits Regulations 2014 (SI 432/2014);

(iii)   Employment Permits (Amendment) Regulations 2014 (SI 506/2014);

(iv)   Education Acts 1998 (Unregistered Persons) Regulations 2014 (SI 32/2013);

(v)   Civil Partnership (Recognition of Registered Foreign Relationships) Order 2014 (SI 212/2014);

(vi)   Protected Disclosures Act 2014 (Section 7(2)) Order 2014 (SI 339/2014); and

(vii)   Protection of Young Persons (Employment) (Exclusion of Workers in the Fishing and Shipping Sectors) Regulations 2014 (SI 357/2014).

Joint Labour Committee Orders

[1.91] The Minister for Jobs and Enterprise and Innovation, Richard Bruton TD, has signed six statutory orders to effect recommendations of the Labour Court Review of the Joint Labour Committee system.

LITIGATION
Whether proceedings should be dismissed for want of prosecution

[1.92] In *Vernon v AIBP Ltd*,[135] the High Court considered whether the plaintiff's personal injury proceedings (following a workplace accident) should be dismissed for want of prosecution. The Court held that, while the delay in progressing the proceedings was inordinate, it could have regard to the socio-economic background of the plaintiff

---

135.   *Vernon v AIBP Ltd* [2014] IEHC 98.

and apply a less rigorous standard when considering whether there was inexcusable delay is. The Court noted that the plaintiff had suffered ill-health and a variety of personal and family misfortunes during the time in question. The proceedings were allowed to continue.

Can a party be compelled to continue an appeal they wish to withdraw?

[1.93] The Labour Court concluded in *Tansey Transport Ltd v Sauter*[136] that it could not compel a party to continue an appeal that they had withdrawn and no longer wished to pursue when the other side had not availed of the opportunity to put in an appeal. In the Court's view this would be contrary to public policy and a waste of court time.

Judgment in default of defence

[1.94] In *Monaghan v United Drug plc*,[137] the High Court was asked set aside a judgment that was obtained in default of defence. The Court considered whether the interests of justice required that the consequences of the defendant's insurance company's actions or inactions be visited on the plaintiff, whose advisors had complied with every rule of procedure and extended every professional courtesy. The High Court held that the judgment in default of defence should not be set aside.

Should constructive dismissal proceedings be stayed to permit related High Court personal injury proceedings to run their course?

[1.95] In *Hickey v Bloomfield House Hotel and Bloomfield Hotel Co Ltd*,[138] the EAT considered whether its hearing of constructive dismissal proceedings should be postponed to allow High Court personal injury proceedings instituted by the claimant to run their course. The EAT declined to postpone the hearing and proceeded to hear the substantive case.

Can EAT proceedings be recorded on a mobile phone?

[1.96] The question as to whether employees should be allowed to record EAT proceedings on a mobile phone was the subject of a preliminary application before the EAT in *Przesmycki v Thomas Farrell & Sons (Garage) Ltd T/A Tramore Services Station*.[139] In its determination, the EAT held it was under no legal obligation to permit

---

136. *Tansey Transport Ltd v Sauter* DWT1417.
137. *Monaghan v United Drug plc* [2014] IEHC 183.
138. *Hickey v Bloomfield House Hotel and Bloomfield Hotel Co Ltd* UD384/2012.
139. *Przesmycki v Thomas Farrell & Sons (Garage) Ltd T/A Tramore Services Station* UD1066/2012, MN688/2012.

the recording and set out the reasons for its conclusion that such recording was undesirable.

It should be noted that a preliminary application to have a hearing held *in camera* was refused by the EAT in *Monnickendam v Limerick County Council.*[140] See **[27.42]**.

Costs

[1.97] In *DTT Fuels Ltd T/A Econ Fuels v Cullen-Raleigh,*[141] the employer did not attend its own appeal of a decision of a Rights Commissioner. In ruling that the appeal must fail for want of prosecution, the EAT took the unusual step of making an award of costs to the respondent employee in the amount of €1,250 exclusive of VAT.

Fitness to participate in the proceedings

[1.98] In *Riley v Crown Prosecution Service*[142] the English Court of Appeal upheld a decision of the UK EAT and held that, in light of the medical evidence that suggested the claimant would not be in a position to engage for at least two years, it was not possible for either party to have a fair trial in the foreseeable future. The Court referenced the entitlement of both parties to have matters dealt with justly and expeditiously without reasonable expense, a right enshrined in art 6 of the European Convention on Human Rights.

Personal Injuries Assessment Board

[1.99] In *PR v KC Legal Representative of the Estate of MC Deceased,*[143] the High Court considered, whether the plaintiff's claim was a personal injuries action or a claim for damages for assault and trespass. Baker J considered the requirement to obtain authorisation under the Personal Injuries Assessment Board Act 2003 and the classes of action excluded from the 2003 Act.

PART-TIME WORK

[1.100] *University College Cork v Noonan*[144] was an appeal of a decision of a Rights Commissioner and concerned the question whether the claimant, a part-time library assistant, who was engaged in work of equal value with two full-time senior library assistants, was entitled to equal pay to these comparators. The Labour Court considered whether the differences in pay were objectively justified by the respondent's grading system, the terms of the Public Service Stability (Haddington Road) Agreement, and the

---

140. *Monnickendam v Limerick County Council* UD765/2012, MN569/2012.
141. *DTT Fuels Ltd T/A Econ Fuels v Cullen-Raleigh* PW44/2013, TE23/2013.
142. *Riley v Crown Prosecution Service* [2013] EWCA Civ 951.
143. *PR v KC Legal Personal Representative of the Estate of MC Deceased* [2014] IEHC 126.
144. *University College Cork v Noonan* PTD141.

terms of the Financial Emergency Measures in the Public Interest (No 2) Act 2009, and followed the High Court in concluding that cost was not capable of being an objective ground justifying less favourable treatment or unequal pay.

PARTNERSHIP LAW

Non-discrimination/equality/age discrimination/the Seldon saga continues

[1.101] CHAPTER 18 looks at recent developments in *Seldon v Clarkson Wright & Jakes (No 2)*.[145] This UK case was the subject of an extensive note in the *Arthur Cox Employment Law Yearbook 2013*, para 22.01.

The claimant's appeal against the Employment Tribunal decision (following remittal from the Supreme Court) was the subject of a determination by the UK EAT, which dismissed the appeal.

Whistleblowing – Is a partner a 'worker'?

[1.102] In *Bates van Winkelhof v Clyde & Co LLP*,[146] the UK Supreme Court considered whether the claimant, an equity partner in the respondent law firm, qualified as a 'worker' for the purposes of the UK statutory whistleblowing protection. In a decision that has been interpreted as having considerable implications for UK limited liability partnerships, the Supreme Court held that the claimant did fall within the definition of worker.

PENSIONS

Budget 2015

[1.103] CHAPTER 19 sets out the pensions-related measures contained in Budget 2015, which was published on 14 October 2014, including discontinuance of the 0.6% pension levy from 31 December 2014 and elimination of top slicing relief on termination payments to €2 million.

The Social Welfare and Pensions Act 2014

[1.104] The Social Welfare and Pensions Act 2014 amends the Pensions Act 1990 to clarify provisions relating to the notification to the members of a defined benefit (DB) scheme regarding the restructure of scheme benefits as a result of a unilateral direction of the Pensions Authority under s 50 or s 50B (wind-up) of the Pensions Act.

---

145. *Seldon v Clarkson Wright & Jakes (No 2)* [2014] IRLR 748.
146. *Bates van Winkelhof v Clyde & Co LLP* [2014] ICR 703.

Occupational Pension Schemes (Sections 50 and 50B) Regulations 2014

[1.105] The Occupational Pension Schemes (Sections 50 and 50B) Regulations 2014, made on 2 September 2014, set out the procedure to be followed when the Pensions Authority is making a direction under s 50 of the Pensions Act to restructure the benefits of a pension scheme or a direction under s 50B to wind up a pension scheme.

Legislative updates – Europe

[1.106] A number of European legislative developments, which affect pensions, including obligations under the European Market Infrastructure Regulation (EMIR) and the draft IORP II Directive, are discussed in detail in **CHAPTER 19**.

Pensions Authority

[1.107] There were a number of Pensions Authority developments throughout 2014, including the issuance of statutory guidance regarding applications to the Authority under ss 49 and 50 of the Pensions Act, statutory guidance in relation to transfer payments and guidance notes in relation to Family Law Acts. Additionally, the Pensions Authority published financial management guidelines for defined benefit schemes and a series of model disclosure documents[147] on disclosure of information requirements. These developments are discussed in more detail in **CHAPTER 19**.

The Pensions Board Annual Report[148] for 2013 was published in June 2014 and was the final report to be published under the old structures of the Pensions Board. The report noted, inter alia, that there was a fall of 12,249 in active membership of defined benefit schemes.

The Pensions Board continued to prosecute cases for failure to remit pension contributions throughout 2014.

Pensions Ombudsman – Annual Report 2013

[1.108] The focus for the Pensions Ombudsman in 2013 was on resolving older cases and shortening the duration of investigations.

Updated Revenue Pensions Manual

[1.109] In May 2014 the Revenue Commissioners updated the Revenue Pensions Manual. The changes are discussed in detail in **CHAPTER 19**.

---

147.   Available at www.pensionsauthority.ie.
148.   Available at www.pensionsauthority.ie.

Case law – pensions

Element six

[1.110] The decision of the High Court in *Greene & Ors v Coady & Ors*[149] confirms that the Courts will not lightly entertain a challenge to trustee decisions where they have acted honestly, in good faith and on professional advice.

The Court found that 'wilful default' is something more than an intentional breach of trust and rejected the argument that an intentional breach of trust amounted to wilful default. The importance of this decision is that where trustees, as a result of unforeseen circumstances, are faced with two unpalatable decisions, each of which are arguably in breach of a duty, the fact that the trustees must choose one of the courses of action does not amount to an actionable breach of trust where that choice has been made properly, honestly and in good faith. The decision confirms that the hurdle faced by members attempting to demonstrate bad faith is a high one.

The Court noted that the threats of closure of the company in this case did appear to be serious and that trustees were entitled to take those threats and the potential loss of employment into account when considering whether to issue a contribution demand to the company.

Omega pharma

[1.111] The decision in *Holloway & Ors and Damianus BV & Ors*[150] was a landmark one for Irish defined benefit pension schemes, and is likely to be the catalyst for significant change to the manner in which defined benefit pension schemes are viewed and treated in Ireland. The case centred on two key issues. The first necessitated technical interpretation as to when the employers' contribution liability terminated. The second issue, the more important, was whether trustees are entitled to make a contribution demand in excess of the statutory Minimum Funding Standard (MFS).

The High Court concluded that the trustees had come to a reasonable decision as to the amount of the contribution demand in the absence of any engagement by the employers. The Court found in favour of the trustees. It was satisfied that the contribution demand was not one which no reasonable body of trustees would have made, and it directed the employers to pay the amount of the contribution demand plus interest and costs to the trustees on behalf of the scheme. The employers appealed the High Court judgment to the newly established Court of Appeal. On 20 November 2014, the Court of Appeal unanimously dismissed the appeal, affirming the decision of the High Court.

Overseas transfer of PRSA funds

[1.112] The High Court in *O'Sullivan v Canada Life Assurance (Ireland) Ltd*[151] clarified the rules relating to the overseas transfer of PRSA funds. While the full implications of

---

149. *Greene & Ors v Coady & Ors* [2014] IEHC 38.
150. *Holloway & Ors and Damianus & Ors* [2014] IEHC 383.
151. *O'Sullivan v Canada Life Assurance (Ireland) Ltd* [2014] IEHC 217.

the decision are as yet unclear, the judgment provides guidance to pension scheme administrators on the approach to be taken in dealing with a request to transfer a PRSA fund to an overseas pension administrator.

It is important to note that since the judgment was delivered, there has been some controversy surrounding overseas pensions transfers. The Revenue Commissioners have confirmed that where an individual transfers their PRSA to another jurisdiction, they may face an automatic tax claw back of up to 52% of the amount they have paid to the PRSA. While no formal update has been issued by the Revenue in relation to this statement, there is some concern amongst industry experts that this would be in contravention of EU rules relating to free movement of goods and services.

Employer duty of good faith

[1.113] In *IBM United Kingdom Holdings Ltd v Dalgleish*,[152] the English High Court found that an employer had breached its implied duty of good faith in the way that it went about closing its defined benefit (DB) schemes to the future accrual of benefits. The reasonable expectations of pension scheme members as to their employer's intentions for the future were noted. It is envisaged that the decision may be persuasive in the event that a similar case were to arise in Ireland. The case demonstrates that employers need to approach any pension change, and the rationale for such change, with care, before embarking on member consultation or communication. Proposals for future benefit changes will need to be carefully formulated, and thought will need to be given to what reasonable expectations members are likely to have as a result of previous communications. The business justifications for any proposed change will need to be carefully considered, and employers proposing to make changes to schemes will need to ensure that there is a robust business case for such change. This justification should also be shared with trustees, and the employer should be prepared to assist with any queries arising. Decisions should never be taken in advance of an open and transparent consultation process. Finally, employers proposing changes should think through timescales carefully, particularly where changes have been made in recent years.

The judgment does not deal with the implications for IBM or its scheme's members and there will be a further hearing to determine what remedies will be applied. At the time of writing, IBM has announced its intention to appeal the decision.

[1.114] CHAPTER 19 also includes an appraisal of *Briggs v Gleeds*[153] on trust law requirements for the execution of deeds, and also a decision of the UK Pensions Ombudsman[154] which found that past practices are not sufficient to give rise to reasonable expectations.

---

152.   *IBM United Kingdom Holdings Ltd v Dalgleish* [2014] EWHC 980 (Ch).

153.   *Briggs v Gleeds* [2014] EWHC 1178 (Ch).

154.   *Thompson* PO–1203.

PROTECTIVE LEAVE

Surrogacy

[1.115] In *Z v A Government Dept and the Board of Management of a Community School*[155] *and CD v ST,*[156] the CJEU considered whether the refusal of paid leave, equivalent to maternity leave or adoptive leave, constitutes discrimination contrary to the Pregnant Workers Directive, or whether it constitutes discrimination on grounds of gender or of disability. The case was remitted to the Equality Tribunal which followed the CJEU decision and held that the respondent did not discriminate against the complainant by refusing to grant her maternity leave or adoptive leave following the birth of her daughter through a surrogacy arrangement.

Exclusion of women on maternity leave from a training course

[1.116] In *Napoli v Ministero della Giustizia-Dipartimento dell' Amministrazione Penitenziaria,*[157] the CJEU held that the exclusion of the claimant, who was on maternity leave, from a training course required for the acquiring the status of a public official, was discriminatory.

Entitlements of an employee who was dismissed whilst on (part-time) parental leave and thus a reduced salary

[1.117] In *Lyreco Belgium NV v Rogiers,*[158] the CJEU considered whether it was contrary to the Framework Agreement for a protective award, payable to a worker who is unilaterally dismissed whilst on part-time parental leave, to be determined on the basis of the reduced salary earned at the date of dismissal.

Can an employer unilaterally withdraw the provision of paid maternity leave?

[1.118] In *Red Ribbon Project v A Worker,*[159] the Labour Court considered whether an employer was entitled to unilaterally withdraw the provision of paid maternity leave in circumstances where the employee has a contractual right to same.

---

155. *Z v A Government Dept and the Board of Management of a Community School* (Case C–363/12).
156. *CD v ST* (Case C–167/12).
157. *Napoli v Ministero della Giustizia-Dipartimento dell' Amministrazione Penitenziaria* (Case C–593/12).
158. *Lyreco Belgium NV v Rogiers* (Case C–588/12).
159. *Red Ribbon Project v A Worker* AD1420.

Do persons unable to work because of physical constraints in the late stages of pregnancy retain the status of 'worker'?

[1.119] In *Saint Prix v Secretary of State for Work and Pensions*,[160] the CJEU held that EU law and in particular art 42 of the Treaty on the Functioning of the European Union and art 7 of Directive 2004/38 were to be interpreted as meaning that a woman who gives up work or seeking work, because of the physical constraints of the late stages of pregnancy and the aftermath of childbirth, retains the status of worker within the meaning of those articles.

Failure to offer suitable alternative employment upon a return from maternity leave

[1.120] In *Cahill v Focus Suites Ireland Ltd (In Liquidation) T/A Focus Suites*,[161] the EAT upheld a claim of unfair dismissal as the claimant was not offered suitable alternative employment upon her return from maternity leave. The EAT was also critical of the respondent employer's lack of consultation with the claimant.

PUBLIC SERVANTS

Public Service Stability Agreement 2013 to 2016 (Haddington Road Agreement)

[1.121] The Labour Court has considered alleged breaches of the Haddington Road Agreement. In *Health Service Executive v Irish Medical Organisation*[162] it was submitted that a proposed reduction in working time of non-consultant hospital doctors was a cost-increasing claim, and in *South Dublin Co Co v SIPTU*[163] the Court considered whether the cessation of a 'working in the rain' allowance was a breach of the Agreement.

Outsourcing

[1.122] In *Personal Injuries Assessment Board v Public Services Executive Union & Ors*[164] the Labour Court held that the outsourcing of the preparation of files for statutory assessors without prior consultation was a breach of the Public Services Agreement.

---

160. *Saint Prix v Secretary of State for Work and Pensions* (C–507/12).
161. *Cahill v Focus Suites Ireland Ltd (In Liquidation) T/A Focus Suites* UD723/2013.
162. *Health Service Executive v Irish Medical Organisation* LCR20671.
163. *South Dublin Co Co v SIPTU* LCR20713.
164. *Personal Injuries Assessment Board v Public Services Executive Union & Ors* LCR20820.

Public Service Agreement 2010–2014 (Croke Park Agreement)

[1.123] In *Department of Education and Skills v SIPTU/IMPACT/TUI/IFUT/UNITE,*[165] the Labour Court considered proposals for the harmonisation of annual leave arrangements for non-academic staff.

In *National University of Ireland Galway v IFUT,*[166] the Labour Court held that a decision to make a researcher redundant following the termination of a research grant was a breach of the Croke Park Agreement. The Court held the claimant came within the employment protection measures set out in the Croke Park Agreement. The entitlement of a worker to an ex gratia redundancy payment was considered by the Labour Court in *National University of Ireland Galway v Irish Federation of University Teachers.*[167] The Court held that where the redundancy was not in dispute, the enhanced redundancy payment terms set out in the agreement must apply.

Moratorium on recruitment and promotions in the public sector

[1.124] The effect of the Moratorium on Recruitment and Promotions in the Public Sector on a local employment agreement was considered by the Labour Court in *Teagasc v A Worker.*[168]

Public Service Management (Sick Leave) Regulations 2014

[1.125] In *Garda Representative Association v Minister for Public Expenditure and Reform,*[169] the High Court declined to grant an application for an interlocutory injunction to restrain the Minister from applying the Public Service Management (Sick Leave) Regulations 2014 (SI 124/2014) to An Garda Síochána pending the determination of judicial review proceedings.

In the substantive hearing *The Garda Representative Association and Bourke v the Minister for Public Expenditure and Reform*[170] the President of the High Court considered whether the Regulations should apply to members of An Garda Síochána and held that they should, rejecting the applicants' claims.

---

165. *Department of Education and Skills v SIPTU/IMPACT/TUI/IFUT/UNITE* LCR10679.

166. *National University of Ireland Galway v IFUT* LCR20742.

167. *National University of Ireland Galway v Irish Federation of University Teachers* LCR20772.

168. *Teagasc v A Worker* AD13102.

169. *Garda Representative Association v Minister for Public Expenditure and Reform* [2014] IEHC 237.

170. *The Garda Representative Association and Bourke v the Minister for Public Expenditure and Reform* [2014] IEHC 457.

Financial Emergency Measures in the Public Interest (No 2) Act 2009/Reductions in pay

[1.126] In *Nic Bhradaigh v Mount Anville School*,[171] the EAT considered, in the context of a payment of wages claim, whether employees of privately funded schools fall within the definition of public servants for the purposes of Financial Emergency Measures in the Public Interest (No 2) Act 2009 (FEMPI) and concluded that because the claimant worked for a recognised school, she was deemed to be a public servant.

Judicial review

[1.127] In *Gormley & Scott v Minister for Agriculture, Food and Marine (No 2)*,[172] the High Court considered a challenge to the Minister's decision to exclude applicants from certain internal competitions. The Court restated the applicable test (as *per* Fennelly in *Mallak v Minister for Justice*) of *bona fides*, factual sustainability and a showing that the decision made was not unreasonable.[173]

REDUNDANCY

Changing the place of work and mobility clauses

[1.128] The reliance on mobility clauses and whether an employee is entitled to a redundancy payment when their place of work changes are considered in a number of cases in **CHAPTER 21**.

In *Murphy & Ors v Orbit Security Ltd*,[174] the EAT upheld the entitlement to a redundancy payment and noted that the alternative locations (in the Donegal region) were too far away for the claimants (who were based in Mayo). In *Fitzpatrick v Greenberry Ltd*,[175] the EAT noted the requirement on employers to act reasonably and responsibly in the operation of a mobility clause. The claimant was entitled to a redundancy payment in respect of a proposal to move her place of employment from Carlow to Waterford. In *Heavey v Casey Doors Ltd*[176] the EAT considered whether the decision of the claimant not to move location from Baldoyle to Balbriggan was reasonable and held that the claimant was entitled to a redundancy payment. The EAT noted that it was required to consider the employee's subjective view of what was being proposed.

---

171. *Nic Bhradaigh v Mount Anville School* PW244/2012.
172. *Gormley & Scott v Minister for Agriculture, Food and Marine (No 2)* [2013] IEHC 459.
173. *Mallak v Minister for Justice* [2012] IESC 59.
174. *Murphy & Ors v Orbit Security Ltd* RP597/2012, RP598/2012, RP599/2012.
175. *Fitzpatrick v Greenberry Ltd* UD893/2012, RP703/2012.
176. *Heavey v Casey Doors Ltd* RP1040/2013–759/2013.

Consultation requirements in a collective redundancy

[1.129] In *Brian Tangney and 27 others v Dell Products Limerick*,[177] an appeal was brought to the High Court on a point of law against a decision of the EAT, which dismissed the complaints under s 9 of the Protection of Employment Act 1977 and found that the respondent had not commenced its collective consultation process when redundancies were contemplated and before they were decided on. The High Court held that a point of law had not been identified to provide a basis for overturning the EAT decision.

Entitlement to consultation and representation in an individual redundancy

[1.130] The extent to which an employee has a right to be consulted and represented in advance of a redundancy was considered by the EAT in *Nigrell v Graham*.[178] The EAT concluded that a lack of representation or consultation does not cause a genuine redundancy to become an unfair dismissal.

A contrast in the EAT's approach can be seen in *Murtagh v Galmere Freshfoods Ltd*,[179] where it held that the claimant was unfairly selected for redundancy. The EAT was critical of the respondent's failure to consider alternatives to redundancy and its lack of meaningful engagement or consultation with the claimant. In *Murray v Ridgeway International Ltd (in Receivership) T/A Toughers Restaurant*,[180] the EAT set out very clear reasons as to why the redundancy was not fair by reference to the process adopted by the employer.

Cross border employment

[1.131] The extent to which a period of continuous employment in Northern Ireland could be taken into account to determine eligibility to receive a statutory redundancy payment under the Redundancy Payments Acts 1967 to 2014 was considered in *Meehan v College Freight Ltd T/A Target Express*.[181] The EAT noted s 25(3) of the Acts and held the service could be taken into account.

Entitlement to a redundancy payment on cessation of participation in a community employment scheme

[1.132] The question of whether a participant in a community employment scheme is entitled to a redundancy payment on cessation of his employment was considered by the

---

177. *Tangney and 27 others v Dell Products Limerick* [2013] IEHC 622.

178. *Nigrell v Graham* UD690/2013.

179. *Murtagh v Galmere Freshfoods Ltd* UD493/2013.

180. *Murray v Ridgeway International Ltd (in Receivership) T/A Toughers Restaurant* UD1321/2012.

181. *Meehan v College Freight Ltd T/A Target Express* RP347/2013.

EAT in *Donohoe v The Dunboyne Area Community Employment Co Ltd.*[182] The EAT held that the claim failed as the employment was not insured under the Social Welfare Acts for the purposes of a redundancy payment.

Unfair selection

[1.133] Fairness of selection for redundancy continues to be a subject of dispute in the EAT, which has awarded large amounts of compensation to employees who have been unfairly selected.

In *Barrett v GEA Farm Technologies (Ireland) Ltd,*[183] while the EAT accepted the validity of the redundancy situation, it found the claimant to have been unfairly selected. The decision to make her role redundant was made before the commencement of the consultation process and none of the options put forward by her with regard to alternative roles was adequately considered by the employer. The EAT criticised the employer for the speedy confirmation of the redundancy, which came after a short recess in a meeting. Compensation of €45,000 was awarded. In *Andreucetti v Spark Glade Ltd,*[184] the EAT considered whether the claimant was unfairly selected for redundancy in circumstances where her employer did not appear to realise that what was being proposed was a collective redundancy with obligations to engage in a statutory consultation process and notification process, to which the employer did not adhere. The claimant was not told how she was selected for redundancy, no selection criteria were articulated, nor did the claimant have an opportunity to make submissions on her behalf. Compensation of €32,000 was awarded.

[1.134] In *Duffy v National University of Ireland Galway,*[185] the EAT awarded €30,000 in compensation and noted there was no proper consultation or discussion with the claimant about the proposed redundancy and there was a failure to justify reasons for redundancy. *Brady v Home Lee Beddings (1975) Ltd*[186] was a case where the respondent decided to deviate from 'last in first out' as a method of selection for redundancy, which it had used previously. The claimant, who was employed since 1978, was informed that he was being dismissed and no alternatives were offered to him, nor was he given an opportunity to put forward alternatives. The EAT awarded him compensation of €30,000 in addition to his statutory redundancy entitlement.

In *Anderson & Ors v Ascension Lifts Ltd,*[187] the EAT accepted that there was a genuine redundancy situation due to the economic downturn. It was proposed by the respondent that two redundancies would be made on the basis of 'last in first out', which approach was agreed. However the respondent then decided to do a full restructure and

---

182. *Donohoe v The Dunboyne Area Community Employment Co Ltd* RP1006/2012.
183. *Barrett v GEA Farm Technologies (Ireland) Ltd* UD106/2012, RP75/2012, MN55/2012, WT26/2012.
184. *Andreucetti v Spark Glade Ltd* UD29/2012.
185. *Duffy v National University of Ireland Galway* UCD1387/2012.
186. *Brady v Home Lee Beddings (1975) Ltd* UD941/2012.
187. *Anderson & Ors v Ascension Lifts Ltd* UD570/2013, UD569/2013, UD568/2013.

to make three redundancies and the respondent unilaterally proposed a new job title, a new rate of pay and some altered employment conditions. When the claimants refused to accept this proposal, they were dismissed. The EAT upheld their claims of unfair selection and unfair dismissal.

[1.135] In *Kennedy v Edmar Golf Ltd*,[188] the EAT concluded that the selection of the claimant for redundancy was unfair, in circumstances where the respondent acknowledged that it did not carry out a cost analysis of retaining the role, no selection matrix was created, and there was no consideration of alternative roles for the claimant. The EAT was not satisfied that the claimant had mitigated his loss and it awarded compensation of €10,000. In *Merity v Dolan and Garvey practising as DCA Accountants*[189] the EAT concluded that the claimant was unfairly selected for redundancy in circumstances where the decision was neither impersonal nor objective and where the claimant appeared to have been replaced by another colleague. The EAT awarded compensation of €43,941.67, less statutory redundancy already received.

[1.136] In *McCarey v Hugh Lennon and Associates Ltd*,[190] the claimant was advised that she was being made redundant on her first day back after maternity leave. The EAT was not satisfied that there was a genuine redundancy situation and held that the respondent had not acted fairly or reasonably. The EAT noted the absence of selection criteria and the fact that there had been no engagement with the claimant and concluded that the claimant was unfairly selected for redundancy and there was no meaningful discussion with her about alternatives. She was awarded compensation of €25,000 in addition to her statutory redundancy entitlement. In *McCann v CIL Precision Ltd*,[191] the EAT accepted that a reduction in workload and income justified the respondent's decision to effect redundancies. As the roles of the four engineers, to include the claimant, were interchangeable and there were no differences in their skillsets, selection for redundancy should have been on the basis of 'last in first out'. The EAT was critical of the respondent for failing to consider alternatives such as voluntary redundancies, pay cuts, reduced hours or other cost-cutting measures. The claimant was awarded compensation of €30,000 in addition to his statutory redundancy entitlement.

[1.137] *Ryan v Signature Flight Support Shannon Ltd T/A Signature Flight Support*[192] is an example of a case where an employer's process of selection was upheld by the EAT. The EAT accepted that the respondent was entitled to restructure, and the process whereby the two affected managers were invited to interview for the newly created position was not unfair. The EAT did not accept the claimant's assertion that 'last in first out' should have been used instead of an interview-based selection process. The EAT

---

188. *Kennedy v Edmar Golf Ltd* UD1102/2012.
189. *Merity v Dolan and Garvey practising as DCA Accountants* UD814/2013.
190. *McCarey v Hugh Lennon and Associates Ltd* UD909/2012 – [27.12] – parallel claims.
191. *McCann v CIL Precision Ltd* UD1619/2012, TE259/2012.
192. *Ryan v Signature Flight Support Shannon Ltd T/A Signature Flight Support* UD1638/2012. Note: this case is under appeal to Circuit Court.

held that the claimant's refusal to engage in the interview process was not a reasonable course of action and thus his dismissal was not unfair.

The use of selection matrices

[1.138] In a redundancy situation, there is no statutory guidance for employers as to how they might implement a selection process, save that the selection must be fair and objective and collective agreements and custom and practice must be followed where relevant and applicable. A tool commonly used by employers is a selection matrix. This year has seen cases which have examined how selection matrices have been used. In *Goodison v Rigney Dolphin*[193] the EAT upheld the claim of unfair dismissal and noted that the employer failed to adequately explain the redundancy process and the criteria for selection to the claimant. In this case, the scoring matrix was not made available to the claimant and incomplete records were kept by the employer in relation to the selection process.

[1.139] In *Mulqueen v Prometric Ireland Ltd T/A Prometric,*[194] the EAT examined the decision to terminate the claimant's employment by reason of redundancy and in a particular the selection matrix used by the respondent, and concluded that the procedures used were flawed. The question of what selection criteria should be used in a compulsory redundancy was considered by the Labour Court in *DLRS Group Security Concepts v SIPTU.*[195] The Labour Court was willing to look at factors such as service and attendance as part of a redundancy matrix.

Short time or redundancy?

[1.140] In *Nolan v Nolan T/A Tivoli Dry Cleaners*[196] the EAT considered whether a reduction of hours constituted short time or whether there was a redundancy situation thus entitling the claimant to a redundancy payment. The EAT found the claimant was not put on short time and thus he was not allowed to trigger a redundancy by serving a RP9 form.

Entitlement to a cooling off period

[1.141] In the context of an unfair dismissal claim arising from the claimant's redundancy, the EAT was critical of the respondent in *McFarland v Stanley Security Ltd*[197] for placing immediate and, what it concluded was, unfair pressure on the claimant to accept a redundancy package. The EAT noted the failure to afford the claimant a 'cooling off' period to consider the redundancy offer made.

---

193. *Goodison v Rigney Dolphin* UD1475/2012.
194. *Mulqueen v Prometric Ireland Ltd T/A Prometric* UD1259/2012.
195. *DLRS Group Security Concepts v SIPTU* LCR20819.
196. *Nolan v Nolan T/A Tivoli Dry Cleaners* RP523/2013.
197. *McFarland v Stanley Security Ltd* UD2323/2011, PW519/2011.

Enhanced ex gratia redundancy payments

[1.142] The entitlement to an ex gratia redundancy payment was considered by the Labour Court under the Industrial Relations Acts 1946 to 2012 in *Alzheimer's Society of Ireland v Four Workers*.[198] The fact that the employer organisation was a not-for-profit organisation substantially funded by the HSE was noted by the Court, which recommended, in line with the provisions of the Public Service Agreement 2010–2014, that the workers should receive an ex gratia payment of three weeks' pay per year of service, in excess of the statutory redundancy payment already paid.

Knowledge of right to appeal

[1.143] In *Brody v Bradley & Doyle practising under the style and title of Malcomson Law*[199] the EAT held that the claimant, a qualified solicitor, ought to have known that she had a right to appeal a redundancy decision.

Attempts to break an employee's continuous service

[1.144] An attempt by an employer to break an employee's continuous service and a subsequent selection of that employee for redundancy on the basis of 'last in first out' was held to be an unfair dismissal by the EAT in *Moloney v Keg Securities Tralee Ltd*.[200]

Time limits

[1.145] Claims for a statutory redundancy payment under the Redundancy Payments Acts 1967 to 2014 must be submitted within 12 months of the date of termination. In *Phelan v REL Refrigeration Group Ltd*,[201] the EAT granted an extension of the time for lodging a claim for a redundancy payment, on the basis of false assurances made by the liquidator of the respondent company.

Validity of a settlement/compromise agreement

[1.146] In *Healy and Healy v Bia Ganbreise Teoranta*,[202] the claimants asserted their right to receive a statutory redundancy payment in circumstances where the respondent employer refused the payments as the claimants had signed a waiver of claims, to include claims for a redundancy payment and they did not have requisite 104 weeks' service. The EAT noted that the document signed did not specify the employment legislation under which the claimants may have waived claims, nor did it make clear that

---

198. *Alzheimer's Society of Ireland v Four Workers* LCR20827.
199. *Brody v Bradley & Doyle practising under the style and title of Malcomson Law* UD1703/2012.
200. *Moloney v Keg Securities Tralee Ltd* UD870/2012.
201. *Phelan v REL Refrigeration Group Ltd* RP411/2013.
202. *Healy and Healy v Bia Ganbreise Teoranta* RP493/2012.

the claimants were notified of the specific claims they were waiving. The EAT upheld its jurisdiction to hear the substantive case on the basis that the subject matter of the complaints were not matters contemplated by the employees at the time the settlement waiver was signed.

Entitlement to a redundancy payment following a business transfer where TUPE not applied

[1.147] In *Striuogaitiene v Noonan Services Group Ltd*,[203] the EAT considered whether the claimant was entitled to a redundancy payment in circumstances where the work done by the claimant was brought in-house by the respondent's client and the claimant's employment did not transfer, under TUPE or otherwise.

Can a refusal of part-time work constitute a redundancy?

[1.148] A refusal of part-time work to a full-time employee who was returning to university did not constitute a redundancy in *Tuczynski v Students Union Áras Na Mac Leinn*.[204]

REFORM

[1.149] The Workplace Relations Bill 2014 was presented to the Oireachtas by the Minister for Jobs, Enterprise and Innovation on 28 July 2014 as part of a broader reform programme.

     CHAPTER 23 sets out the key reforms envisaged by the Bill in its current form.

TAXATION RELATING TO EMPLOYMENT

Budget 2015: USC and Income Tax

[1.150] Budget 2015 was announced on 23 October 2014 (Budget Day 2014). Income tax bands, rates and credits have all been changed to benefit workers. USC rates and bands have also undergone changes, with reductions in the USC rate for workers earning below €70,000.

Foreign earnings deduction

[1.151] Finance Act 2014 extended the scheme to 2017 and modified the conditions under which relief can be sought. The scheme provides for relief from taxation on

---

203.   *Striuogaitiene v Noonan Services Group Ltd* RP747/2013.

204.   *Tuczynski v Students Union Áras Na Mac Leinn* RP1257/2012.

certain emoluments of individuals who are tax resident in Ireland but who spend a significant amount of time working in certain countries.

Special assignee relief programme

[1.152] Finance Act 2014 extended the Special Assignee Relief Programme to 2017, and made other improvements to the scheme. The scheme incentivises companies to locate high value employees in Ireland.

Relevant contracts tax

[1.153] The hybrid fixed penalty/outstanding tax regime has been replaced by a penalty based on the percentage of outstanding tax.

Employment Incentive and Investment Scheme

[1.154] Subject to Ministerial commencement and EU approval, the EII scheme is being enlarged to provide greater incentives to invest in qualifying SMEs for a substantive period of time. This scheme provides income tax relief to investors who subscribe for shares in qualifying SMEs.

TEMPORARY AGENCY WORK

Selected Labour Court decisions

[1.155] In *O'Reilly Recruitment Ltd v Zaremba & Ors,*[205] the Labour Court upheld a claim by eight complainants, who were agency workers. The complainants asserted they performed the same or similar work as the directly hired employees who were paid €10.08 per hour. The complainants were paid €8.65 per hour. The Labour Court ordered that the complainants' rates of pay be adjusted to €10.08 per hour.

This can be contrasted with the outcome in *MK Human Resources Ltd T/A Temple Recruitment v Messrs Jacek & Ors*[206] where the Labour Court held that the complainants' pay claim was not well founded.

Meaning of 'temporary' in the UK Agency Work Regulations 2010

[1.156] As the volume of published cases on temporary agency work remains low in Ireland, *Moran v Ideal Cleaning Services Ltd and Anor*[207] is noted. The UK EAT was asked to consider whether the claimants, who had been placed with the second respondent for up to 25 years, could be regarded as 'temporary' agency workers. In so

---

205. *O'Reilly Recruitment Ltd v Zaremba & Ors* AWD41.
206. *MK Human Resources Ltd T/A Temple Recruitment v Messrs Jacek & Ors* AWD48.
207. *Moran v Ideal Cleaning Services Ltd and Anor* UKEAT/0274/13/DM.

doing, the EAT considered the meaning of the word 'temporary' in the UK Agency Workers Regulations 2010 (SI 2010/93) and the intended effect of the Temporary Agency Workers Directive. The EAT concluded that, as the concept of 'temporary' in the 2010 Regulations and the Directive meant 'non-permanent', the Employment Tribunal did not err in concluding the claimants were outside the scope of the Regulations.

TRANSFER OF UNDERTAKINGS

Change in security/cleaning contractors

[1.157] *An Employee v An Employer and An Employer*[208] is a rare consideration of the European Communities (Protection of Employees on Transfer of Undertakings) Regulations 2003 by the EAT. The EAT looked at whether a transfer of an undertaking had taken place and concluded that as there had been no asset transfer, it did not amount to a 'transfer' within the meaning of the Directive. The decision is noteworthy for the emphasis on the fact that the economic entity had retained its identity and for the EAT's application of the principles in *Ayse Süzen*.[209]

Interaction of Directive 2001/23/EEC with Member States' law to like effect

[1.158] In *Amatori & Ors v Telecom Italia SPA and Anor*,[210] the CJEU considered whether the Directive precluded national legislation which, on the transfer of part of the undertaking, permits the transferee to take over the employment relationship from the transferor if that part of the undertaking does not constitute a functionally autonomous economic entity existing before the transfer. The CJEU further considered whether the Directive precluded national legislation which enables a transferee to take over the employment relationship, if, after the transfer of part of the undertaking concerned, the transferor exercises extensive and overriding powers over the transferee.

Change in warehouse and distribution contractor

[1.159] In *Bligh & Ors v Stobart Ireland Driver Services Ltd*,[211] the EAT considered whether a transfer of undertakings occurred when a contract for the operation of a chilled and frozen foods warehouse and national distribution centre was transferred from company K to the respondent.

---

208. *An Employee v An Employer and An Employer* RP2097/2010, MN1500/2010, WT660/2010.
209. *Ayse Süzen v Zehnacker Gebäudereinigung GmbH Krankenhausservice* (Case C–13/95).
210. *Amatori v Telecom Italia SpA and Anor* (Case C–458/12).
211. *Bligh & Ors v Stobart Ireland Driver Services Ltd* TU29–TU46/2011.

Post share acquisition – de facto merger

[1.160] In *Jackson Lloyd Ltd and Mears Group v Smith*,[212] the UK EAT considered whether the claimants had transferred under TUPE after the transferee (ML) purchased all the shares of the transferor (JL). The EAT found that TUPE was triggered in the aftermath of a share acquisition and that there had been a transfer of an undertaking from JL to MG following and in the context of the share sale to ML. The EAT noted that the share purchase effectively provided the means by which the parent company MG gained control of JL.

Loss of a service contract

[1.161] In *Cavan Industrial Cleaning Services Ltd v Germanaviciene*,[213] the EAT was asked to consider whether there was a transfer of undertaking in circumstances where there had been a loss of a service contract. The EAT considered whether any assets, tangible or intangible, were transferred in its finding that there was a transfer of an undertaking to which the 2003 Regulations applied.

UNFAIR DISMISSAL

Preliminary issues

[1.162] A wide variety of preliminary issues have been raised by parties before the EAT in 2014.

Time limits

[1.163] Section 8(2) of the Unfair Dismissals Acts provides that the six-month time limit for bringing claims can be extended in exceptional circumstances. The EAT's approach has varied.

Settlement negotiations

[1.164] In *O'Connor v McInerney Holdings plc*,[214] the EAT did not accept that the fact that parties were engaged in settlement negotiations was reason to extend the time limit for making a claim.

---

212. *Jackson Lloyd Ltd and Mears Group v Smith* UKEAT/0127/13/LA.

213. *Cavan Industrial Cleaning Services Ltd v Germanaviciene & Ors* TU29–TU36/2013.

214. *O'Connor v McInerney Holdings plc* UD688/2011.

Medical grounds

[1.165] The EAT has been willing to extend the time limits on medical grounds provided the medical evidence clearly supports the contention. *Hayes v Cork Education Support Centre*[215] is an example where the medical report furnished by the claimant did not state that her medical issues had prevented her from lodging a claim within the prescribed time period and the EAT declined to extend the time limits. A contrasting outcome can be seen in *Keenan v The Governor and the Company of the Bank of Ireland*[216] where the EAT accepted the medical evidence established that the claimant was medically diagnosed with depression and was under treatment for depression for at least six months after the date of dismissal. The EAT noted the claimant's evidence as to the debilitating and disabling effects of the illness on her and found exceptional circumstances did exist such that the time limit was extended

Taking up new employment

[1.166] In *O'Dwyer v Blackstar Ltd,*[217] the claimant argued that her employment did not end until the conclusion of an appeal process. However the EAT noted that she had taken up new employment shortly after her dismissal and concluded that the act of taking up new employment constituted acceptance of the dismissal date, and accordingly there were no exceptional circumstances preventing her from bringing a claim.

Insufficiency of legal advice

[1.167] The EAT was unwilling to extend the time limits on grounds of the insufficiency of legal advice in *Higgins v Superquinn Ltd T/A Musgrave Operating Partners Ltd.*[218]

Does a P45 terminate employment?

[1.168] The preliminary issue of when employment ends and whether the sending of a P45 is definitive was considered in *Vasilveca v Maybin Sports Services (Ireland) Ltd T/A Momentum Support.*[219]

Where claim filed before alleged date of dismissal

[1.169] Where an employee files an unfair dismissal claim before the actual dismissal takes effect, does the EAT have jurisdiction?

---

215. *Hayes v Cork Education Support Centre* UD254/2014.
216. *Keenan v The Governor and the Company of the Bank of Ireland* UD1574/2012.
217. *O'Dwyer v Blackstar Ltd* UD952/2012.
218. *Higgins v Superquinn Ltd T/A Musgrave Operating Partners Ltd* UD498/2013.
219. *Vasilveca v Maybin Sports Services (Ireland) Ltd T/A Momentum Support* UD1655/2012, RP421/1012, MN436/2012.

In *Brady v Employment Appeals Tribunal and Bohemians Football Club (Notice Party)*,[220] the High Court held that it would be absurd, where the EAT had notice of the claim at the commencement of and throughout the six-month period, that the applicant should be denied the opportunity to bring his claim because the EAT, through no fault of the applicant, may have also have had notice of the claim immediately prior to the applicable six-month period.

A different approach was taken by the EAT in *Barry v Newbridge Silverware Ltd*[221] where the claimant submitted her T1A too early and prior to the expiry of her notice period. The EAT declined jurisdiction on the basis that the claim of unfair dismissal was brought in the course of the claimant's ongoing employment.

Locus standi

[1.170] In *O'Farrell v County Dublin VEC*,[222] the EAT rejected the contention that the claimant was an office holder of the VEC and therefore precluded from the protection afforded by the Unfair Dismissals Acts 1977 to 2007, relying on s 23 of the Vocational Education Act 1930.

Application for a postponement pending the outcome of High Court proceedings

[1.171] The EAT has shown a reluctance to postpone its hearing of a claim in deference to contemporaneous High Court proceedings.

In *O'Doherty v Independent Newspapers (Ireland) Ltd*,[223] the EAT refused to stay the claimant's unfair dismissals case pending the outcome of her High Court defamation proceedings which were brought against the same respondent.[224]

In *Hickey v Bloomfield House Hotel and Bloomfield Hotel Co Ltd*,[225] the EAT decided that the claimant's constructive dismissal claim could proceed despite the fact that she had parallel High Court personal injury proceedings.

Parallel claims

[1.172] The application of s 101(2) of the Employment Equality Acts 1998 and 2012, where a claimant has brought parallel claims of discriminatory dismissal and unfair dismissal, was considered by the EAT in *McCarey v Hugh Lennon & Associates Ltd*.[226] See **[22.17]** for the EAT decision.

---

220. *Brady v Employment Appeals Tribunal and Bohemians Football Club (Notice Party)* [2014] IEHC 302.
221. *Barry v Newbridge Silverware Ltd* UD1517/2012.
222. *O'Farrell v County Dublin VEC* UD114/2012, MN60/2012, RP87/2012, WT29/2012.
223. *O'Doherty v Independent Newspapers (Ireland) Ltd* UD234/2014.
224. Note this EAT unfair dismissals case settled between the parties in December 2014.
225. *Hickey v Bloomfield House Hotel and Bloomfield Hotel Co Ltd* UD384/2012.
226. *McCarey v Hugh Lennon & Associates Ltd* UD909/2012.

Whether there has been a dismissal

[1.173] The EAT has been asked to adjudicate whether a dismissal actually took place in order to determine whether a claim for unfair dismissal can proceed.

In *Cullen v Argos Distributors (Ireland) Ltd*,[227] the EAT held that the claimant had not resigned from employment in clear and unambiguous terms and concluded that her actions whilst absent, including the submission of medical certificates and a grievance and having discussions about an alternative position, were not actions of a person who had in fact resigned.

Where an employee continues in employment

[1.174] In *Schonfeld v Centre for Effective Services Ltd*[228] the EAT declined jurisdiction to hear the claim as the claimant continued in the employment of the respondent on the same terms of employment, but in a different position, for some time after the claim was submitted.

Admissibility of evidence

[1.175] In *White v Dawn Meats Group T/A Dawn Meats*,[229] the EAT considered two preliminary issues: whether a collection of photos should be before the EAT at the outset of the hearing and the admissibility of certain witness evidence.

Where a recommendation has already issued under s 13 of the Industrial Relations Acts 1946 to 2012

[1.176] Can the EAT hear a claim for unfair dismissal where the claimant had already received a recommendation from a Rights Commissioner in a claim under s 13 of the Industrial Relations Acts 1946 to 2012? In *McGuire v Sleedagh Farms Ltd*,[230] the EAT noted that the Rights Commissioner recommendation was in respect of a claim regarding a contractual entitlement to an enhanced redundancy payment and was not in relation to the dismissal per se.

Fixed-term contracts

[1.177] In *Walshe v Department of Arts, Heritage and Gaeltacht*,[231] the EAT considered whether it had jurisdiction to hear a claim where the claimant was employed under a

---

227. *Cullen v Argos Distributors (Ireland) Ltd* UD23/2013.
228. *Schonfeld v Centre for Effective Services Ltd* UD233/2013.
229. *White v Dawn Meats Group T/A Dawn Meats* UD852/2012.
230. *McGuire v Sleedagh Farms Ltd* UD1320/2012.
231. *Walshe v Department of Arts, Heritage and Gaeltacht* UD569/2012, MN430/2012.

series of fixed-term contracts from 2002 to 2011 and where there was a gap of four months between each contract every year.

[1.178] In *Kemmy v Amgen Technology (Ireland)*,[232] the EAT upheld the validity of a clause in a fixed-term contract which provided for the non-application of the Unfair Dismissals Acts 1977 to 2007 on the expiry of a fixed term.

Notice entitlement and continuous service

[1.179] The inclusion of an employee's notice entitlement when calculating service was the preliminary issue in *Viel v Mongodb Ltd.*[233] The EAT held that the claimant's entitlement to one month's notice could be aggregated with his accrued 11 months' service to bring him within the scope of the Unfair Dismissals Acts.

Validity of a release

[1.180] In *Browne v AA Ireland Ltd,*[234] the EAT declined jurisdiction to hear unfair dismissals claim where the claimant accepted an enhanced redundancy payment and had signed a release in respect of any potential claims.

Failure to return from a career break

[1.181] An employee who went on a career break and failed to return was the subject of *McDonagh v Enterprise Ireland*[235] where the EAT found that there was no dismissal and the claim for unfair dismissal failed.

Where the respondent company is a dissolved entity

[1.182] In *Devine v GE Grainger Enterprises Ltd T/A Stephen Grainger*[236] the EAT held that, despite the fact that the respondent company was dissolved at the date of hearing, a decision could be made against an entity that no longer existed.

Does the EAT have jurisdiction where the employer is in UK administration?

[1.183] In *Tracey v Game Stores Group Ltd*[237] the EAT was critical of the respondent's UK joint administrator who raised a jurisdictional issue in writing but did not attend before the EAT in person. The EAT held that the respondent was required to attend

---

232. *Kemmy v Amgen Technology* (Ireland) UD1079/2013, MN563/2013, WT187/2013.
233. *Viel v Mongodb Ltd* UD1772/2012.
234. *Browne v AA Ireland Ltd* UD191/2013.
235. *McDonagh v Enterprise Ireland* UD2179/2011, RP2789/2011, MN2214/2011.
236. *Devine v GE Grainger Enterprises Ltd T/A Stephen Grainger* RP265/2013, MN185/2013.
237. *Tracey v Game Stores Group Ltd* UD1632/2011.

before it in order to submit its case that the EAT did not have jurisdiction to hear the case. The EAT proceeded to hear the substantive unfair dismissals claim and awarded compensation of €30,000 to the claimant.

Dismissals on grounds of conduct

[1.184] Dismissals on grounds of conduct continue to make up the largest body of cases that are considered for this Yearbook. What is clear is that employers need to be extremely careful not to rush to terminate employment when faced with unacceptable conduct. The EAT continues to place considerable importance on the proportionality of the sanction and is generally cautious when asked to uphold summary dismissals for gross misconduct. What is interesting is that employers are continuing to create procedural flaws. The selected cases in **CHAPTER 27** are guidance to employers contemplating disciplinary action for conduct reasons.

Fair procedures

Obligations on an employer when dismissing for misconduct

[1.185] The factual background to *Bentley v Tesco Ireland Ltd*[238] was unusual in so far as the claimant was dismissed for gross misconduct for an apparent breach of an honesty policy for failing to disclose the fact of an overpayment over a number of months. It transpired in the disciplinary process that the claimant's wife was aware of the overpayment but had not disclosed it to him. The EAT was critical of the procedures used and of the proportionality of the sanction. The EAT set out the obligations on an employer when dismissing for misconduct.

Suspension without pay

[1.186] The decision to suspend the claimant without pay before establishing the employee's account of what occurred and the subsequent dismissal, without giving the claimant adequate time to consider the allegations, were held by the EAT in *Morrissey v Central Garage Clonmel Ltd*[239] to be a breach of procedures and an unfair dismissal.

Failure to comply with reasonable procedures

[1.187] In *Reilly v O'Reilly Ledwith Consultants Ltd T/A O'Reilly Ledwith Consultants Ltd*,[240] the EAT held that the respondent had failed to comply with fair procedures leading up to dismissal of the claimant. The EAT was also critical of the claimant's failure to engage in an appeals process leading up to dismissal. No award was made as

---

238.   *Bentley v Tesco Ireland Ltd* UD818/2012.
239.   *Morrissey v Central Garage Clonmel Ltd* UD1039/2012.
240.   *Reilly v O'Reilly Ledwith Consultants Ltd T/A O'Reilly Ledwith Consultants Ltd* UD347/2013, MN189/2013.

the claimant was on disability benefit and not available for work and also had admitted to engaging in paid child-minding during this time.

Defective disciplinary procedures

[1.188] In *Fox v National Gallery of Ireland*,[241] the EAT was critical of the respondent's disciplinary procedures and noted that the investigator had made conclusions on the claimant's guilt at fact-finding stage which were then acted upon by the decision maker.

The importance of an impartial unbiased decision-maker was reiterated by the EAT in *Farnan v KM Healthcare Enterprises Ltd T/A Castleross*[242] where the person investigating allegations of misconduct had, in a previous employment also, dismissed the claimant and where the dismissal was found to be unfair.

In *Maher v Allied Irish Banks plc*,[243] the EAT accepted the claimant's submission that a disciplinary process was flawed in circumstances where the decision to dismiss was based on a 'final' investigatory report of uncertain authorship. The respondent's subsequent holding of an independent appeal, which did not rely on this report and was a full *de novo* hearing, was not sufficient to cause the decision to dismiss to be fair.

Dismissal for breaches of policy/procedure

[1.189] **CHAPTER 27** includes a number of cases involving dismissals for alleged breaches of policy/procedure. It is noteworthy that almost all of these cases occur in a retail/manufacturing background when trust and adherence to procedures are paramount and where employers are more likely to take a 'zero tolerance' approach. It is striking that the proportionality of the sanction of dismissal is criticised in a great many of the cases featured.

Breach of mark down sales procedure

[1.190] In *Bermingham v Marks & Spencer (Ireland) Ltd*,[244] the EAT ordered that a dismissal for a breach of the respondent's mark down sales procedure was unfair and ordered re-engagement.

Breach of policy on reserving sale items

[1.191] In *McCrann v Marks & Spencer Ireland Ltd*,[245] the EAT held that the summary dismissal of the claimant for a breach of the respondent's policy on reserving sale items was unfair, disproportionate and unreasonable.

---

241. *Fox v National Gallery of Ireland* UD950/2012.
242. *Farnan v KM Healthcare Enterprises Ltd T/A Castleross* UD847/2012.
243. *Maher v Allied Irish Banks plc* UD2189/2011.
244. *Bermingham v Marks & Spencer (Ireland) Ltd* UD601/2011, MN639/2011.
245. *McCrann v Marks & Spencer (Ireland) Ltd* UD3/2013.

Breach of sales and refunds policy

[1.192] In *O'Callaghan v Dunnes Stores*, the EAT considered whether the employer was justified in dismissing the claimant, a store manager, following breaches by him of the respondent's sales and refunds procedure and his instructions to junior staff to carry out false sales and refund transactions, and the EAT held that this was gross misconduct in the circumstances. The EAT noted the seriousness of the claimant's actions, especially given his managerial role, and held that he had by his actions destroyed the relationship of trust and confidence between him and his employer.

Breach of staff purchasing policy

[1.193] In *O'Brien v Dunnes Stores*[246] the EAT was critical of the procedural flaws which led to the dismissal of the claimant, who took and wore a tie whilst working and later brought it home. The EAT noted the respondent's failure to consider options other than dismissal.

A similar approach can be seen in *McNally v Olhausens Ltd (in receivership)*[247] where the dismissal of the claimant for breaches of staff purchasing procedure was held to be unfair. The willingness of the EAT to award compensation in respect of the loss of a potential redundancy payment under the hearing of 'financial loss' should be noted.

Dismissal for alleged misrepresentation, forgery and fraud

[1.194] In *Preston v Dunnes Stores*,[248] which related to the dismissal of a retail manager for misrepresentation, forgery and fraud (all of which were admitted by her), the EAT held that the sanction of dismissal was disproportionate. The fact that it was the claimant's first disciplinary infraction and occurred at a time of great personal difficulty for her were mitigating factors that ought to have been taken into account.

Selling alcohol to a minor during a test purchase

[1.195] A decision to dismiss the claimant for gross misconduct for selling alcohol to a minor, who was acting on behalf of the gardaí for test purchasing, was held by the EAT to be procedurally unfair and disproportionate in *Fitzpatrick v Dunnes Stores*.[249]

Breach of staff purchasing procedure

[1.196] In *Meade v Adelphi Carlton Ltd T/A Cineworld*,[250] the EAT criticised the respondent's automatic conclusion of gross misconduct for the claimant's breach of

---

246. *O'Brien v Dunnes Stores* UD1133/2012.
247. *McNally v Olhausens Ltd (in receivership)* UD701/2013.
248. *Preston v Dunnes Stores* UD517/2012, RP385/2012, MN396/2012.
249. *Fitzpatrick v Dunnes Stores* UD196/2012, MN150/2012.
250. *Meade v Adelphi Carlton Ltd T/A Cineworld* UD892/2012.

company policy on staff purchasing from the cinema shop. The EAT noted the failure of respondent to take into account the claimant's innocent mistake and held that the sanction was disproportionate.

Dismissal for tampering with stock

[1.197] A zero tolerance policy in relation to stock was examined by the EAT in *Boyne v Keelings Logistics Solutions* and *Moran v Keelings Logistics Solutions.*[251] The EAT held that the claimants' evidence was not credible and that on balance they did tamper with a packet of jam tarts. The EAT found that the disciplinary process was fair and objective and the sanction was proportionate and reasonable in light of the employer's policy.

Dismissal for the removal of money and stock and the use of IOUs

[1.198] In *Murphy v Cara Pharmacy,*[252] a majority of the EAT held that the dismissal of the claimant for the removal of money and stock without authorisation and the utilisation of IOUs, until the money and items were refunded or replaced, was unfair.

Breach of health and safety rule – use of mobile telephone

[1.199] *Burczy v Tesco Ireland Ltd*[253] concerned the dismissal of an employee for breaching a health and safety rule in using his mobile phone whilst operating a mechanical handling equipment vehicle. Notwithstanding that the conduct was admitted and the respondent employer followed its own disciplinary procedure, the EAT's view was that the sanction was disproportionate in circumstances where other employees may have been treated differently.

Dismissal following findings of harassment and sexual harassment

[1.200] The fact that there may be findings of misconduct against an employee arising from an internal investigation does not of itself remove the requirement of fair procedures and/or natural justice in any subsequent disciplinary process.

In *Sheridan v Ampleforth Ltd T/A The Fitzwilliam Hotel,*[254] the claimant was dismissed on grounds of gross misconduct arising from allegations of harassment, to include sexual harassment. The EAT found that there were procedural flaws in both the investigation and the disciplinary procedures, and made the decision to award reinstatement, notwithstanding the wishes of both parties.

---

251. *Boyne v Keelings Logistics Solutions* and *Elton John Moran v Keelings Logistics Solutions* UD829/2013, UD828/2013.
252. *Murphy v Cara Pharmacy* UD871/2012.
253. *Burczy v Tesco Ireland Ltd* UD618/2012.
254. *Sheridan v Ampleforth Ltd T/A The Fitzwilliam Hotel* UD273/2010.

A contrast in approach can be seen in *Monnickendam v Limerick County Council*,[255] which concerned the dismissal of the claimant for gross misconduct following an investigation which upheld complaints of harassment and sexual harassment against him. The EAT upheld the disciplinary procedure used by the employer and held that the dismissal was not unfair.

Reliance on CCTV

[1.201] Employers are increasingly turning to technology for safety, security and surveillance in the workplace. As a consequence, reliance on CCTV footage to establish misconduct on the part of employees has become commonplace. **CHAPTER 27** contains a number of cases where employers have relied upon CCTV as part of a disciplinary process and subsequent unfair dismissals claim. In *Deegan v Dunnes Stores*,[256] the respondent employer relied on covert CCTV footage in a disciplinary process to dismiss the claimant for having consumed food from the hot delicatessen without payment. The EAT held that the dismissal was unfair, notwithstanding that the claimant by her conduct had contributed to her dismissal. This was overturned by the Circuit Court on appeal, where Judge Linnane held that there were substantial grounds justifying the company's decision to dismiss the respondent employee, along with seven other members of staff.

In *Hayes v Kinsella T/A Kinsella's of Rocklands*,[257] the EAT considered the dismissal for theft of an employee who worked in the retail sector, in reliance on CCTV footage. The EAT held that it was of concern that the decision to dismiss was based on a subjective analysis of a vast amount of CCTV footage, and in its decision the EAT was critical of the way in which the CCTV footage was presented to the claimant and the fact that it was not independently scrutinised.

A confrontation between staff at a Christmas party formed the basis for the dismissal of the claimant in *Graham v Newlands Cross Hotel T/A Bewley's Hotel Dublin Airport*.[258] Central to the evidence relied upon by the respondent at the disciplinary hearing, and before the EAT, was the CCTV footage of the evening in question. The EAT noted that, the footage was not completely conclusive and did not provide the EAT with any clear or accurate evidence of what occurred. The EAT held that the decision to dismiss was unfair in the circumstances and noted that the claimant was the only individual disciplined following the incident.

In *Murtagh v TLC Health Service Ltd*,[259] which concerned the dismissal of the claimant as a result of his conduct in the respondent's nursing home, the EAT noted that amongst the procedural failings, there was reliance on CCTV footage which was not shown to the claimant during the disciplinary process. The EAT further criticised the

---

255. *Monnickendam v Limerick County Council* UD765/2012, MN569/2012.
256. *Deegan v Dunnes Stores* UD202/2012, MN152/2012.
257. *Hayes v Kinsella T/A Kinsellas of Rocklands* UD690/2012, WT211/2012, TE80/2013.
258. *Graham v Newlands Cross Hotel T/A Bewley's Hotel Dublin Airport* UD886/2012, MN625/2012.
259. *Murtagh v TLC Health Service Ltd* UD1425/2012,MN821/2012.

respondent's reliance on witness statements of parties who were not present when the conduct of concern took place and its failure to have regard to witness statements that exonerated the claimant. The respondent had further failed to verify the legitimacy of the allegations.

Criminal convictions

[1.202] Whether an employer is entitled to dismiss an employee who is convicted of a criminal offence was considered by the EAT in *Moore v Tesco Ireland Ltd.*[260] The claimant was dismissed when he was convicted and received a suspended sentence for an offence relating to the supply of drugs with intent to sell. The respondent determined that the conviction brought the respondent company into disrepute and constituted serious misconduct. The EAT held that the dismissal was unfair and noted that the claimant had previously a good record at work and had at all times kept the respondent appraised of the criminal proceedings. The respondent's procedures for considering the case were inadequate and it could not demonstrate that it had considered alternative sanctions.

Forcing open a locker

[1.203] In *Occipital Ltd v Wojtun*,[261] the EAT held that the dismissal of the claimant for gross misconduct for forcing open a locker (in the company of the locker owner) was a disproportionate sanction in all of the circumstances.

The sale of illegal cigarettes in the workplace

[1.204] In *Maslova v Golden Mushrooms Ltd*,[262] the decision to dismiss the claimant for gross misconduct was reasonable in circumstances where she was selling illegal cigarettes in the workplace during working hours.

Being untruthful

[1.205] The importance of truthfulness in the workplace can be seen in *Lynott Thomas v Atlantic Homecare Ltd.*[263] In that case, the EAT upheld the decision to summarily dismiss the claimant for gross misconduct where she was found to have told a deliberate lie to her line manager whilst taking a day of sick leave when she was not genuinely sick. The EAT held that the telling of a lie by an employee is a breach of the bond of trust which must exist between employer and employee, and rendered the dismissal fair.

---

260. *Moore v Tesco Ireland Ltd* UD2423/2011.
261. *Occipital Ltd v Wojtun* UD283/2013 TE44/2013.
262. *Maslova v Golden Mushrooms Ltd* UD18/2012.
263. *Lynott Thomas v Atlantic Homecare Ltd* UD1671/2012.

Call centre/customer service dismissals

[1.206] The requirements of and expectations on staff in call centres are distinctive in that employers require high standards of conduct relating to the way in which employees engage with and handle customer calls over the telephone. Allied to this is the fact that these calls are recorded and can then be scrutinised by employers. However, employers in this environment need to proceed with care when dealing with conduct or competence issues as the overriding right to fair procedures and natural justice will apply.

In *McCaffrey v Telefonica Ireland Ltd*,[264] the EAT considered the dismissal of a customer service agent as a result of the frequency and duration of her line hanging and voicemail manipulation activities. The EAT set out the obligations on an employer in gross misconduct cases. The EAT held that the employer had overreacted to the claimant's alleged shortcomings and moved too quickly to a disciplinary process. The sanction of dismissal was disproportionate, undeserved and unreasonable.

A further example of where an employer utilised unfair procedures and imposed a disproportionate sanction is *Mooney v Oxyien Environmental*.[265] This case concerned a dismissal for gross misconduct by reason of inappropriate language used in telephone conversations and for poor handling of a customer phone call. The claim for unfair dismissal succeeded.

Childcare workers

[1.207] From those who work with children, the highest standards of conduct are expected. **CHAPTER 27** contains three contrasting cases where concerns about the conduct of childcare workers were raised and dismissals followed. In *Burke v Egan T/A Little Sunflowers Crèche & Montessori*[266] a dismissal of a crèche worker for misconduct was upheld and the EAT noted that whilst there were flaws in the procedures used, they were not so flawed as to render the dismissal unfair. A contrast can be seen in *Fox v Clevercloggs Full Day Care Nursery Ltd*[267] which also concerned the dismissal of a crèche worker for misconduct following incidents where children under her supervision had left the room unaccompanied on more than one occasion. The EAT was critical of the respondent employer and noted that it had failed to ensure that there were adequate door closing mechanisms in place. The EAT viewed the decision to dismiss as a disproportionate sanction in circumstances where the parents of the children were not informed about the incidents of concern suggesting that they were not serious incidents.

In *McNulty v Ballyheane Community Sports Club Ltd*[268] the claimant was dismissed from her position as childcare worker in circumstances where she had been accused of inadequacy in the care of children. The EAT held that its role was to consider whether

---

264. *McCaffrey v Telefonica Ireland Ltd* UD1668/2011, MN1725/2011, WT662/2011.
265. *Mooney v Oxigen Environmental* UD1525/2012, MN866/2012.
266. *Burke v Egan T/A Little Sunflowers Crèche & Montessori* UD902/2012.
267. *Fox v Clevercloggs Full Day Care Nursery Ltd* UD49/2012.
268. *McNulty v Ballyheane Community Sports Club Ltd* UD26/2012.

the decision reached by the respondent was a reasonable one in light of the facts, and in this case the decision to dismiss was upheld.

Dismissal for lack of engagement in grievance or disciplinary procedure

[1.208] Where a claimant refuses to engage in a grievance and/or disciplinary procedure and is subsequently dismissed, is this unfair?

In *Finegan v PhoneWatch Ltd,*[269] the EAT upheld the decision to dismiss the claimant for his failure to attend work on the introduction of a new working rota, and his subsequent refusal to engage in grievance or disciplinary procedures and to comply with reasonable requests.

The circumstances behind a refusal to engage must be considered by an employer before disciplinary action is taken. In *Healy v United Cinemas International Ltd T/A Castletroy Cinemas*[270] the EAT held that the decision to dismiss the claimant following his refusal to engage with the disciplinary process was unreasonable in circumstances where failure to engage was attributable to his severe and debilitating stress and anxiety.

Dismissal for internet usage whilst on duty

[1.209] In *Adeagbo v Mitie Facilities Management Ltd*[271] the EAT considered the dismissal of the claimant, a security guard, for time spent by him on the internet and for falsification of documents. During the time in question, a burglary had taken place. The EAT held that this was neglect of his fundamental duties and his subsequent attempts to cover up the incident did amount to gross misconduct.

Alleged falsification of manufacturing records

[1.210] In *Haughey v Becton Dickinson Penel Ltd,*[272] the EAT held that a dismissal for the falsification of manufacturing records was procedurally unfairand ordered re-instatement.

Disruptive and unacceptable conduct

[1.211] *Myers v Direct Fuels Ltd*[273] is an example of a case where the claimant was dismissed for being disruptive and for his unacceptable conduct. The EAT concluded that the decision to dismiss was reasonable in all of the circumstances.

---

269. *Finegan v PhoneWatch Ltd* UD749/2012.
270. *Healy v United Cinemas International Ltd T/A Castletroy Cinemas* UD1256/2011, RP1655/2011, MN1354/2011.
271. *Adeagbo v Mitie Facilities Management Ltd* UD692/2013.
272. *Haughey v Becton Dickinson Penel Ltd* UD65/2012.
273. *Myers v Direct Fuels Ltd* UD2412/2011, MN2423/2011.

In *Feery v Oxigen Environmental T/A Oxigen,*[274] the claimant behaved in an unacceptable manner in the course of a telephone call with management, where he was advised that he would not be paid for his sick leave, and was subsequently dismissed. The EAT noted that the respondent had no regard for the claimant's previous record or his current financial circumstances and that the dismissal was unfair.

Must an employer accept the decision of an internal appeal panel that had overturned the initial decision to dismiss?

[1.212] In *Kisoka v Ratnpinyotip T/A Rydevale Day Nursery,*[275] the UK EAT considered summary dismissal for gross misconduct in circumstances of suspected involvement in arson. An independent appeal had overturned the original decision to dismiss on procedural grounds. However the respondent decided not to implement the appeal decision and dismissed the claimant. The UK EAT concluded that the employer was not obliged to accept the appeal outcome. The EAT found that the Employment Tribunal was entitled to take into account that the respondent was responsible for the welfare of children and was concerned not to re-employ a member of staff in circumstances where it still considered there were reasonable grounds that the appellant was involved in arson.

Alleged dishonesty

[1.213] In *Vesey v MBNA Ltd,*[276] the EAT considered that the respondent went beyond the allegations put to the claimant in the disciplinary process (relating to the submission of incorrect action codes) by making a finding of 'dishonesty'. The EAT noted that the claimant had not been in the role for a significant period and that he was experiencing teething problems. Thus the decision to dismiss him was unreasonable.

Disclosure of sensitive confidential information

[1.214] Where an employee discloses sensitive confidential information belonging to her employer, is a subsequent dismissal fair?

In *Jessup v Power Home Products Ltd,*[277] the EAT concluded that the dismissal of the claimant for sharing sensitive confidential information by email in an alleged breach of confidence was procedurally unfair.

---

274.   *Feery v Oxigen Environmental T/A Oxigen* UD184/2013.

275.   *Kisoka v Ratnpinyotip T/A Rydevale Day Nursery* UKEAT/0311/13/LA.

276.   *Vesey v MBNA Ltd* UD953/2012.

277.   *Jessup v Power Home Products Ltd* UD346/2013.

Dismissals for unauthorised absence

[1.215] In *Rutkowski v Café Nestors Ltd T/A Abrakebabra Ennis and Goodblend Catering Ltd T/A Abrakebabra Ennis,*[278] the claimant's request to take holidays during the Christmas period was refused and he was subsequently dismissed for failing to attend work over the Christmas period. The EAT held that there was a procedural deficit and concluded that the dismissal was unfair in the circumstances. In *Jordan v Mainway North Road Ltd*[279] the EAT held that a dismissal for unauthorised absence, and alleged failure to adhere to the respondent's sick leave procedures, was unfair. The EAT held that the claimant's failure to exhaust internal appeal procedures was not fatal to the unfair dismissal claim and held there was an obligation on the employer to take into account the circumstances of the employee's absence.

Refusal of employee to return to previous working arrangements

[1.216] Where an employee refuses to revert to her previous working arrangements, as set out in her employment contract, a consequential dismissal was held by the EAT to be fair in *Hooper v Philpot & Malone T/A Kudos Hairdressing.*[280]

Dismissals on grounds of incapacity

[1.217] In *London Central Bus Co Ltd v Manning*[281] the UK EAT examined whether a dismissal on grounds of ill-health was unfair. The EAT held that the withholding of information relating to unsuitable vacancies at appeal stage did not cause the dismissal to become an unfair dismissal and this procedural failing could not displace the fairness of the original decision to dismiss.

The Scottish case *BS v Dundee City Council,*[282] which concerned the termination of employment for long-term sickness absence, is noteworthy for the Court of Session's detailed analysis of the factors to be considered when dismissing on grounds of incapacity.

In *Farrell v Kepak Group (Meat Division) T/A Kepak Longford,*[283] the EAT noted that the claimant had been dismissed for the provision of inconsistent statements in relation to a workplace injury and for misrepresenting his ability to work, which were considered by the employer to be serious misconduct which damaged the relationship of trust and confidence between the parties. The EAT held that dismissal was a disproportionate, unfair and unreasonable sanction.

---

278. *Rutkowski v Café Nestors Ltd T/A Abrakebabra Ennis and Goodblend Catering Ltd T/A Abrakebabra Ennis* UD285/2013, MN146/2013,WT30/2013.

279. *Jordan v Mainway North Road Ltd* UD1741/2012.

280. *Hooper v Philpot & Malone T/A Kudos Hairdressing* UD834/2013.

281. *London Central Bus Co Ltd v Manning* UKEAT/0103/13/DM.

282. *BS v Dundee City Council* [2013] CSIH 91.

283. *Farrell v Kepak Group (Meat Division) T/A Kepak Longford* UD1202/2013.

Competence and performance management

[1.218] To terminate employment fairly on grounds of competence/performance requires an employer to apply patiently a process of performance management and fair procedures.

Failure to work to a new sales model and accept a change in work practice

[1.219] In *Citti v Apple Distribution International T/A Apple Computer,*[284] the claimant was dismissed following a process of performance management in relation to his failure to work to a new sales model. The EAT noted that the respondent had made a reasonable request of the claimant and had utilised fair procedures in dealing with him. His claim of unfair dismissal was not upheld.

A procedurally unfair dismissal on competency grounds

[1.220] In *Berthold v Google Ireland Ltd,*[285] the EAT determined that the dismissal of the claimant for competency reasons, following a performance management process, was procedurally unfair and the EAT awarded compensation of €110,000.

Use of mystery shopper as an assessment tool

[1.221] In *Maxi Zoo Ireland Ltd v Caffrey,*[286] a case involving a dismissal of a sales assistant for performance and conduct reasons, the EAT was not satisfied that the process of assessment by a mystery shopper was in accordance with fair procedures.

Other substantive grounds

[1.222] In *Veronko v James Kelly & Sons,*[287] the EAT held that the dismissal of the claimant for her failure to work the hours required by the employer was justified on other substantive grounds, in circumstances where the employer's actions were objectively justified in light of the needs of the business and were provided for in the contract of employment.

Dismissal in community employment schemes

[1.223] In *Goold v Cashel Heritage and Development Trust Co Ltd*[288] the EAT considered the claimant's participation in a community employment scheme and, in

---

284. *Citti v Apple Distribution International T/A Apple Computer* UD994/2013.
285. *Berthold v Google Ireland Ltd* UD2147/2011, MN2174/2011.
286. *Maxi Zoo Ireland Ltd v Caffrey* UD83/2013.
287. *Veronko v James Kelly & Sons (Wexford) Ltd* UD624/2012, RP460/2012, MN475/2012.
288. *Goold v Cashel Heritage and Development Trust Co Ltd* UD1031/2011.

particular, whether the operation of a 10% discretionary retention option was reasonable in all of the circumstances. The EAT noted the requirements on a publicly funded body when exercising a discretion. The EAT held that the respondent had failed to afford the claimant an opportunity to make a case for her retention in employment in circumstances where she was not aware of the retention option and the criteria for its exercise.

Pre-employment background checks

[1.224] The legitimacy of a pre-employment background check was considered by the EAT in *Deegan v United Parcel Service of Ireland Ltd*[289] where the respondent employer was required by a European Directive to complete background checks on all prospective and current employees. The dismissal of the claimant for his failure to provide details about apparent gaps in his employment was found to be unfair in all of the circumstances.

Constructive dismissal

[1.225] CHAPTER 27 contains a selection of cases where employees have claimed that they were justified in bringing their employment to an end and that they were constructively dismissed.

Extreme working conditions and severe underpayment

[1.226] The plight of three domestic migrant workers was highlighted by the EAT in *Calderon & Ors v Nasser Rashed Lootah and Metad Alghubaisi*[290] In finding that the claimants were constructively dismissed by their employers, the EAT noted their extreme working conditions, that they had been severely underpaid and had been physically and verbally mistreated. Each claimant was awarded €80,000 compensation.

Lack of engagement with employer

[1.227] In *McDonnell v Dublin Airport Authority plc*[291] the EAT refused to uphold a claim of constructive dismissal and pointed to the lack of engagement on the part of the claimant, in particular his refusal to attend meetings without a family member present and his refusal to attend occupational health services.

---

289. *Deegan v United Parcel Service of Ireland Ltd* UD894/2012.
290. *Calderon & Ors v Nasser Rashed Lootah and Metad Alghubaisi* UD1219/2013, UD1220/2013, UD1221/2013.
291. *McDonnell v Dublin Airport Authority plc* UD1899/2011, RP2481/2011.

Delay on the part of an employer in dealing with a complaint

[1.228] In *Shannon v Pat the Baker*[292] the EAT held that delay on the part of the employer in progressing the grievance/complaint procedure was not of such magnitude or order that the claimant could reasonably have no confidence in the procedure itself.

Resignation under duress

[1.229] In *Canon v Black Bros Ltd*,[293] the EAT considered whether the claimant had been forced to resign under duress where there were complaints of misconduct pending against the claimant. In its determination, the EAT set out the obligations on an employer when investigating alleged misconduct. The EAT held it was not remotely fair or reasonable to arrange for the claimant to sign a letter of resignation in a car park and that what occurred was a forced resignation. In *O'Farrell v Board of Management of St Brigid's School*,[294] the EAT held that the requirement placed on the claimant to constantly supervise a teacher (who the claimant had previously sought permission to dismiss) was irrational and put the claimant in an impossible position and had the effect of undermining the employment relationship. The claim of constructive dismissal was upheld.

Changes to sales territory and imposition of new sales targets

[1.230] In *Beglan v Scanomat Ireland Ltd*,[295] the EAT noted that there were changes to the claimant's sales territory and customer base and but held that the new sales targets that were imposed on him without consultation were unrealistic. The EAT was critical of the respondent's failure to engage with the claimant. The EAT upheld the claim of constructive dismissal and awarded compensation of €70,000.

Excessive disciplinary sanctions

[1.231] In *McGinty v Gallagher T/A Hillcrest Nursing Home*,[296] the EAT held that the claimant was constructively dismissed following an investigation of a verbal altercation with a colleague. The EAT noted that no full and fair investigation was ever carried out and there was at all times an unreasonable presumption that the claimant was the instigator.

---

292. *Shannon v Pat the Baker* UD1840/2011.
293. *Canon v Black Bros Ltd* UD2116/2011.
294. *O'Farrell v Board of Management of St Brigid's School* UD2199/2011; MN2238/2011; WT905/2011.
295. *Beglan v Scanomat Ireland Ltd* UD688/2012.
296. *McGinty v Gallagher T/A Hillcrest Nursing Home* UD501/2012.

Refusal to accept an employer's solutions to grievance

[1.232] The conduct of a claimant will be examined carefully by the EAT, as can be seen in *Jarzab v OCS One Complete Solution Ltd.*[297] The EAT held that the claimant's refusal to consider solutions offered by the respondent to resolve a difficult situation and her subsequent decision to resign were unreasonable.

Failure to investigate complaints

[1.233] In *Hegarty v Clare Civil Engineering Co Ltd and Clare Civil Engineering Ltd*[298] the claimant's decision to resign was deemed reasonable in light of the complete failure of the respondent to deal with complaints made by her against a colleague.

A similar approach can be seen in *O'Connor v Dairy Master*[299] where the EAT considered whether the claimant was constructively dismissed in circumstances where he resigned due to alleged bullying and harassment on the part of his supervisor towards him. The EAT noted the respondent's failure to train its employees in respect of its bullying and harassment policy, the failure of management to take any action and the unreasonable behaviour of the respondent in failing to address the complaints made.

Resignation prior to the outcome of bullying/harassment investigation

[1.234] The EAT held that the respondent employer did not have sufficient opportunity to resolve the claimant's complaints prior to her resignation (in dissatisfaction at the way in which a complaint raised by her had been handled) in *Zaino v SAP Service and Support Centre (Ireland) Ltd.*[300]

Excessive workload

[1.235] In *Kelly v Charlie Shiels Ltd,*[301] the EAT accepted that the claimant's position within the workplace was not such that she had no alternative other than to tender her resignation. The EAT noted that as soon as the respondent knew that the claimant was not coping with her workload, it agreed to get her assistance and a recruitment process commenced which culminated in the arrival of another employee two to three days after the claimant had resigned.

---

297. *Jarzab v OCS One Complete Solution Ltd* UD1188/2012.
298. *Hegarty v Clare Civil Engineering Co Ltd and Anor* UD2093/2011, RP2672/2011, MN2115/2011, WT838/2011.
299. *O'Connor v Dairy Master* UD351/2012.
300. *Zaino v SAP Service and Support Centre (Ireland) Ltd* UD583/2011, MN621/2011.
301. *Kelly v Charlie Shiels Ltd* UD707/2013.

Requirement to show situation at work is untenable

[1.236] In *Ronan v Wyse Transport Ltd*[302] and *Wyse Transport Ltd v Ronan*,[303] the EAT held that a claim for constructive dismissal requires that the claimant prove his situation had become so untenable that he had no choice but to leave his employment, and that in this case the claimant had not established this.

Change in working hours

[1.237] In *Robinson v Johnston Logistics Ltd*,[304] the EAT considered whether a change in working hours, from morning to evening work, rendered the claimant's working conditions untenable. The EAT concluded that the claimant's failure to engage with the respondent's proposed compromise was unreasonable and his claim for constructive dismissal failed.

The fact that the claimant in *Maher v Health Service Executive*[305] was assigned to care for a particular client under a specified purpose contract meant that notwithstanding that there was a reduction in her working hours, the respondent had complied with its contractual obligations to her and she was not constructively dismissed.

Failure to facilitate a return to work

[1.238] In *Carrick v Dublin Stevedores Ltd*,[306] the EAT examined the conduct of the respondent towards the claimant, as a consequence of a dispute between original shareholders (including the claimant's father). The EAT found that the respondent's failure to facilitate the claimant's return to work after sick leave did amount to a constructive dismissal.

Raising concerns about financial practices

[1.239] In *Baldwin v Ace Compaction Systems Ltd (in liquidation)*[307] the EAT held that the claimant was constructively dismissed as a consequence of raising concerns about financial practices in the respondent company and the respondent's failure to deal with the matter.

Imposition of compulsory retirement age

[1.240] See *Kane v Dublin Stevedores Ltd*[308] at **[1.11]**.

---

302. *Ronan v Wyse Transport Ltd* UD1435/2012.
303. *Wyse Transport Ltd v Ronan* PW667/2012, TE217/2012, WT348/2012, UD1425/2012.
304. *Robinson v Johnston Logistics Ltd* UD821/2013.
305. *Maher v Health Service Executive* UD1185/2013.
306. *Carrick v Dublin Stevedores Ltd* UD831/2013.
307. *Baldwin v Ace Compaction Systems Ltd (in liq)* UD1314/2012.
308. *Kane v Dublin Stevedores Ltd* UD197/2012.

Unfair dismissals claim brought under the Industrial Relations Acts 1969

[1.241] *Kavanagh's Pharmacy v A Worker*[309] is an example of an unfair dismissals claim brought to the Labour Court under s 20(1) of the Industrial Relations Act 1969. The Court considered whether the worker was unfairly dismissed and held there was a denial of fair procedures and natural justice, and recommended that compensation of €25,000 be paid.

WAGES

Time limits

[1.242] In *Moran v The Employment Appeals Tribunal and the Health Service Executive*[310] the High Court was asked on appeal to consider whether the EAT had incorrectly applied s 6(4) of the Payment of Wages Act 1991 in respect of time limits applicable to the bringing of the appellant's complaint and had incorrectly held that the complaint was time-barred. The High Court dismissed the appeal and held that the appellant did not as a matter of fact present a complaint in relation to the contravention of the 1991 Act on any specific day or dates within six months of 17 May 2002.

[1.243] In *Health Service Executive v McDermott*,[311] the High Court considered the interpretation of s 6(4) of the Payment of Wages Act 1991 and held that the reference to 'contravention to which the complaint relates' meant that every distinct and separate breach of the Payment of Wages Act 1991 amounts to a contravention of the 1991 Act. Thus the time for referring a claim ran from the date of the contravention to which the complaint relates. The High Court distinguished *Moran v Employment Appeals Tribunal*[312] and noted that the claims in that case related to unlawful deductions in 2010 and therefore the claim was statute-barred.

Exceptional circumstances

[1.244] In *Cork Rape Crisis Centre Ltd v Knott & Ors*[313] the EAT considered whether the fact that the parties were in negotiations and took part in an LRC conciliation process constituted exceptional circumstances so as to extend the time limits in accordance with s 6(4) of the Payment of Wages Act 1991.

---

309. *Kavanagh's Pharmacy v A Worker* LCR20828.
310. *Moran v The Employment Appeals Tribunal and the Health Service Executive* [2014] IEHC 154.
311. *Health Service Executive v McDermott* [2014] IEHC 331.
312. *Moran v The Employment Appeals Tribunal and the Health Service Executive* [2014] IEHC 154.
313. *Cork Rape Crisis Centre Ltd v Knott & Ors* PW397/2011, PW398/2011, PW399/2011 and PW400/2011.

Employer estopped from removing applicants from payroll

[1.245] In *Fuller & Ors v Minister for Agriculture, Food and Forestry,*[314] the Supreme Court accepted that the Minister for Agriculture was estopped from pleading a different reason for the removal of the applicants from the payroll than had been previously pleaded in a different case. The Supreme Court accepted this argument and granted a declaration that the applicants were entitled to be paid a salary as if they had continued to work between the respective dates on which they were removed from the payroll and when they returned to work following the resolution of the underlying industrial relations dispute.

Entitlement to wages during a period of layoff

[1.246] An issue which has repeatedly arisen in 2014 is whether there is an entitlement to wages during a period of layoff. **CHAPTER 28** contains five such determinations of the EAT, on appeal from a Rights Commissioner, under the Payment of Wages Act 1991, all of which are similar in their conclusion, that there is notorious custom and practice in Ireland that employees will not be paid during a period of layoff.

The EAT decisions are: *McDonough v Shoreline Taverns Ltd T/A Daly's of Donore;*[315] *Racyla v Sheridan;*[316] *Strzelecki v Zahir Ltd (in liquidation);*[317] *Stanisevskaja v Office and Industrial Cleaners Ltd;*[318] and *Matenko v Bocnara Ltd.*[319]

Non-payment of increments

[1.247] The question as to whether the non-payment of an increment is an unlawful deduction contrary to s 5 of the Payment of Wages Act 1991 has arisen frequently in 2014. It is notable that the EAT has been consistent in its application of the High Court decision in *McKenzie v The Minister for Finance,*[320] which is authority for the proposition that the 1991 Act has no application to reductions in wages as distinct from 'deductions'.

The EAT decisions are: *Eucon Shipping and Transport Ltd v Hynes & Ors;*[321] *Irish Ferries Ltd v Murtagh & Ors;*[322] and *Byrne v Clare County Council.*[323]

---

314. *Fuller & Ors v Minister for Agriculture, Food and Forestry* [2013] IESC 52.
315. *McDonough v Shoreline Taverns Ltd T/A Dalys of Donore* PW674/2012.
316. *Racyla v Sheridan* PW379/2012.
317. *Strzelecki v Zahir Ltd (in liq)* PW664/2012.
318. *Stanisevskaja v Office and Industrial Cleaners Ltd* PW239/2011.
319. *Matenko v Bocnara Ltd* PW340/2011.
320. *McKenzie and Anor v The Minister for Finance & Ors* [2010] IEHC 461.
321. *Eucon Shipping and Transport Ltd v Hynes & Ors* PW222–225/2013.
322. *Irish Ferries Ltd v Murtagh & Ors* PW222–PW225/2013.
323. *Byrne & Ors v Clare Co Co* PW263/2012, PW264/2012, PW 265/2012, PW266/2012, PW 267/2012.

Reductions in pay/allowances

[1.248] In *Byrne and Kelly v Dublin 12 Congress Centre Ltd*,[324] the EAT considered whether a reduction in pay constituted an unlawful deduction contrary to the 1991 Act. The EAT noted that the reductions in wages were made across the board, following an instruction from FAS, and that the respondent had no discretion. The EAT applied the decision in *McKenzie* and concluded that the 1991 Act had no application to reductions in wages.

In *B&Q Ireland Ltd v Masters & Ors*[325] *and B&Q Ireland Ltd v Cleary*,[326] the EAT concluded that the removal of a seasonal bonus was provided for in the appellants' contracts of employment and therefore the withdrawal of same came within s 5(1)(b) of the Payment of Wages Act 1991. The removal of the zone allowance was a 100% reduction and as such was not a deduction from wages. On this basis, the EAT concluded that the 1991 Act had no application.

Suspension with and without pay

[1.249] The distinction between a suspension with and without pay was considered by the EAT in *Hanuszewicz v Strand Security Ltd (In Liquidation)*.[327] The appellant had been suspended without pay for a period of six months during which time no disciplinary process took place. The EAT noted that there was no provision for suspension without pay in the appellant's contract of employment and thus the EAT held there was a breach of the Payment of Wages Act 1991.

Requirements of s 7(2) of the Payment of Wages Act 1991 when lodging an appeal

[1.250] In *Ó Gógáin v Bord na Móna plc*,[328] the EAT restated the strict obligations on a party who wished to appeal a decision of a Rights Commissioner in accordance with s 7(2) of the 1991 Act. The EAT noted that two acts must be completed within six weeks – a notice in writing must be issued to the EAT, and the appealing party must issue a copy of the notice to the other party concerned; otherwise the EAT has no jurisdiction.

Implied contractual entitlement to equal allowances on the basis of legitimate expectation

[1.251] In *Malanaphy v Minister of Transport, Tourism and Sport*[329] the EAT considered whether a term could be implied into the claimant's contract of employment entitling

---

324.   *Byrne and Kelly v Dublin 12 Congress Centre Ltd* PW257/2011.
325.   *B&Q Ireland Ltd v Masters & Ors* PW474/2013, PW475/2013 and PW476/2013. This case is
       currently under appeal to the High Court.
326.   *B&Q Ireland Ltd v Cleary* PW777/2012.
327.   *Hanuszewicz v Strand Security Ltd (In Liq)* PW317/2013.
328.   *Ó Gógáin v Bord na Móna plc* W234/2013.
329.   *Malanaphy v Minister of Transport, Tourism and Sport* PW655/2012.

him to equal allowances and benefits to those received by his predecessor, on the basis of a legitimate expectation created by the respondent, notwithstanding the fact that the claimant's contract was silent on the issue and the position had been given a new title in the interim.

Payment of wages during sick leave

[1.252] The entitlement to wages during sick leave was considered in *Gallagher v Department of Arts, Heritage and the Gaeltacht.*[330] It was noted that the claimant had failed to attend a scheduled medical appointment and was subsequently removed from the payroll. The EAT, by majority, accepted that the respondent could remove the claimant from its sick pay scheme for non-compliance.

Whether an unlawful deduction from wages was a penalty clause and was unenforceable

[1.253] In *Cleeve Link Ltd v Bryla*[331] the UK EAT considered whether a deduction from wages (by way of recoupment of certain costs) which was provided for in the contract of employment, had the effect of a penalty clause. The EAT concluded that the clause in issue was one for liquidated damages and there was a reasonable relationship between the amount that could be recovered in a common law action for damages and the sum stipulated in the agreement, so the deduction, which was a genuine pre-estimate of loss, was lawful.

Contractual entitlement to a pay increase

[1.254] In *Thorne & Ors v House of Commons Commission*[332] the English High Court considered whether the claimants had a contractual right (either express or implied) to annual pay increases.

National Minimum Wage Act 2000 as amended

Whether the monetary value of 'board' can be included in determining an hourly rate of pay

[1.255] In *Skuja v Slieve Russell Hotel Property Ltd,*[333] the Labour Court noted the definition of pay in the National Minimum Wage Act 2000 and that Sch 1 of the 2000 Act set out what constituted reckonable components of pay and included 'the monetary value of board with lodgings, or board only or lodgings only, not exceeding the amount,

---

330. *Gallagher v Department of Arts, Heritage and the Gaeltacht* PW32/2013.

331. *Cleeve Link Ltd v Bryla* UKEAT/0440/12/BA.

332. *Thorne & Ors v House of Commons Commission* [2014] EWHC 93 (QC).

333. *Skuja v Slieve Russell Hotel Property Ltd* MWD143.

if any, prescribed for the purposes of this item.' The Court accepted the inclusion of monetary value of 'board' provided to the claimant when determining her hourly rate of pay and noted that the rate exceeded €8.65 per hour.

Requirement of s 28 of the National Minimum Wage Act 2000 to have requested a statement of average hourly rate of pay

[1.256] In *Abcom Security Ltd v Ejaz*,[334] the fact that the claimant had not requested a statement of average hourly rates of pay in accordance with s 23 of the National Minimum Wage Act 2000 meant that the claim could not be heard by a Rights Commissioner under s 24(2)(a) of the 2000 Act. That request was a precondition to the claim being heard by the Rights Commissioner and by the Labour Court on appeal.

WHISTLEBLOWING

[1.257] The most significant legislative development in employment law in 2014 occurred in July 2014 with the enactment and coming into force of the Protected Disclosures Act 2014.

CHAPTER 29 provides a detailed analysis of the new Act. A flowchart is included which summarises the channels of disclosure and the tests that determine the circumstances in which each can be used.

WORKING TIME

Time limits

[1.258] Section 27(4) of the Organisation of Working Time Act 1997 provides that a complaint must be lodged with a Rights Commissioner within six months, beginning on the date of the alleged contravention to which the complaint relates. A Rights Commissioner may extend the time under s 27(5) if it can be shown that the complaint was not presented during the time limit because of reasonable cause.

In *E Smith School T/A The High School v McDonnell*[335] the Labour Court referenced the well-established test for deciding if reasonable cause has been shown and the requirement that a claimant must explain and afford an excuse for the delay. The Labour Court accepted that the claimant had queried his entitlement to public holidays with his employer three years previously and was told at that time that he had no such contractual entitlement and it was on that basis that he did not pursue the claim further. The Labour Court held that this both explained the delay and afforded a justifiable excuse for the delay.

---

334. *Abcom Security Ltd v Ejaz* MWD1418.
335. *E Smith School T/A The High School v McDonnell* DWT1411.

In *Sword Risk Services Ltd v O'Dwyer*,[336] the Labour Court accepted that the claimant had suffered from emotional upset by reason of his partner's difficult pregnancy and his daughter's health problems. However the Court did not accept that these factors explained the claimant's failure to pursue a claim or that they excused the delay. The claimant was not prevented from bringing a claim in time but chose not to do so.

Exceptional circumstances/emergency – a narrow defence for employers

[1.259] In *Nurendale Ltd T/A Panda Waste v Suvac*,[337] the Labour Court considered whether s 5 of the 1997 Act offered a complete defence to the respondent in circumstances where there had been a fire which had destroyed a major part of the plant and this necessitated the quick rebuilding of the facility. The Labour Court outlined the narrow circumstances where the derogation s 5 will apply.

The provision of rest facilities on site

[1.260] In *Stasaitis v Noonan Services Group Ltd and the Labour Court*,[338] the High Court considered whether the Labour Court erred in law in its decision that the respondent had complied with s 12 of the Organisation of Working Time Act 1997 and the Organisation of Working Time (General Exemptions) Regulations 1998 (SI 21/1998). The central issue was whether the respondent was in breach of its statutory obligations where it did not schedule rest breaks but instead provided facilities in a security hut for an employee to take breaks during periods of inactivity.

Rest breaks

[1.261] In *HSE National Ambulance Service v O'Connor*[339] the Labour Court considered whether the employer was in breach of ss 11 and 12 of the Organisation of Working Time Act 1997 and whether the claimant was afforded adequate compensatory requirements in respect of s 11 of the Act. The Court noted that the right to an 11-hour break is a fundamental right in EU law and that there was a requirement on employers to justify each failure to provide a break of 11 hours between shifts on objective grounds.

Point of law appeals on quantum

[1.262] The High Court considered two appeals (held jointly) under s 28(1) of the Organisation of Working Time Act 1997 where it was asked to consider whether the amount of compensation awarded in both cases by the Labour Court was inadequate and

---

336.   *Sword Risk Services Ltd v O'Dwyer* DWT1410.
337.   *Nurendale Ltd T/A Panda Waste v Suvac* DWT1419.
338.   *Stasaitis v Noonan Services Group Ltd and the Labour Court* [2014] IEHC 199.
339.   *HSE National Ambulance Service v O'Connor* DWT1484.

whether the Labour Court departed from legal principles binding upon it. The High Court further examined whether the Labour Court failed to have regard to and apply the principles of effectiveness, deterrence and proportionality as derived from European law and in particular the judgment of *Von Colson and Kamann*.[340]

These cases were *Bryszewski v Fitzpatricks and Hanleys Ltd T/A Caterway and the Labour Court (Notice Party)*[341] and *Ruskys v Genpact Ltd and another*.[342]

Mobile road transport activities

[1.263] The very specific requirements on employers who operate mobile road transport activities can be seen in *First Direct Logistics Ltd v Stankiewicz*,[343] where the Labour Court considered and upheld certain of the complaints under the relevant Regulations.[344]

Zero-hour contracts

[1.264] The obligations of an employer under s 18 of the Organisation of Working Time Act 1997 in respect of zero-hour contracts of employment were considered by the Labour Court in *Ticketline T/A Ticketmaster v Mullen*.[345]

'Sleep in' night shifts

[1.265] In *Esparon T/A Middle West Residential Care Home v Slavikovska*,[346] the UK EAT considered whether the claimant was entitled to be paid in accordance with the national minimum wage in circumstances where she was required to work a number of 'sleep in' night shifts at a residential care home. The UK EAT concluded that the time spent by the claimant during the night shift amounted to working time for which she was entitled to be appropriately remunerated.

Entitlement to receive commission payments while on annual leave

[1.266] The CJEU held in *Lock v British Gas Trading Ltd*[347] that employees who receive commission payments as part of their normal pay are entitled to have these taken into account when calculating their normal pay for periods of annual leave.

---

340. *Von Colson and Kamann v Land Nordrhein Westfalen* (Case C–14/83).
341. *Bryszewski v Fitzpatricks and Hanleys Ltd T/A Caterway and the Labour Court (Notice Party)* [2014] IEHC 263.
342. *Ruskys v Genpact Foods Ltd and Labour Court* [2014] IEHC 262.
343. *First Direct Logistics Ltd v Stankiewicz* RTD141.
344. European Communities (Road Transport) (Organisation of Working Time of Persons Performing Mobile Road Transport Activities) Regulations (SI 36/2012).
345. *Ticketline T/A Ticketmaster v Mullen* DWT1434.
346. *Esparon T/A Middle West Residential Care Home v Slavikovska* [2014] UK EAT 0217/12.
347. *Lock v British Gas Trading Ltd* (Case C–539/12).

Entitlement to paid accrued but untaken annual leave on death

[1.267] In *Bollacke v K+K Klaas and Kock BV & Co AG*,[348] the CJEU considered whether Directive 2003/88/EC precludes national legislation which provides that the entitlement to accrued paid annual leave is lost where an employee dies whilst in employment. The CJEU concluded that the Directive could not be interpreted as meaning that the entitlement to accrued annual leave may be lost on death.

Accrual of annual leave during sick leave

[1.268] The Workplace Relations Bill 2014,[349] as at report stage, contains a proposed amendment to the Organisation of Working Time Act 1997, such that employees can accrue annual leave whilst on certified sick leave and that accrued annual leave can be taken within 15 months of the end of that leave year.

---

348. *Bollacke v K+K Klaas and Kock BV & Co AG* (Case C–118/13).
349. See **CH 23**.

Chapter 2

CONTRACT OF EMPLOYMENT

EMPLOYMENT STATUS – CONTRACT FOR SERVICES OR CONTRACT OF SERVICE

[2.01] *Football Association of Ireland v Hand[1] – Labour Court – Protection of Employees (Fixed-Term Work) Act 2003, s 15(1) – Industrial Relations Acts 1946 to 2012 – appeal of Rights Commissioner decision – whether complainant was an employee of respondent employed on series of fixed-term contracts of employment – whether complainant's employment transmuted to one of indefinite duration – whether complainant engaged as consultant under contract for services or employment contract – whether complainant estopped from denying status as self-employed contractor*

This was an appeal of a Rights Commissioner decision by the Football Association of Ireland. The complainant was a fixed-term employee, employed on a succession of fixed-term contracts which the Rights Commissioner determined had transmuted to one of indefinite duration by operation of s 9(3) of the Protection of Employees (Fixed-Term Work) Act 2003. The complainant contended that he was a fixed-term employee within the statutory meaning of the term, providing services to the respondent in various capacities with various titles from 1999 to 2012. The Labour Court heard significant witness evidence over two days. The Labour Court set out the history of the complainant's engagement with the respondent and summarised the various documents reviewed. The complainant was first engaged as a youth career advisor and following this, a further agreement was put in place which designated him as a career guidance officer. Further negotiations took place which resulted in an extension of the agreement, and revised terms were agreed. At that point, the complainant was known as a careers officer. Further agreements were entered and the terms amended in April 2004, May 2005 and in May 2008 the arrangement was extended for a further four years until April 2012. On the expiry of the 2008 contract, the contract was not renewed.

The Court noted that a meeting took place between the respondent's HR manager and the complainant in or about August 2007 to discuss matters relating to his engagement, and the Court noted that the specific matter of the complainant's retirement was discussed. It appears that at that meeting, the complainant suggested some form of payment be made to him upon retirement. The witness on behalf of the respondent recollected that both parties understood the contract would not be further renewed on its expiry. However, the complainant's recollection on this point was that he had not decided to retire in 2012, but it was a possibility.

---

1. *Football Association of Ireland v Hand* FTD 143.

Subsequent meetings took place and ultimately, in January 2012, the complainant wrote to the CEO of the respondent setting out a proposal for his continued involvement with the respondent. The Court noted that the complainant, in the penultimate paragraph of this letter, stated: 'Should the FAI wish to avail of my continued services, I feel sure that an acceptable consultancy fee can be negotiated. I am confident that all will benefit and would appreciate if you would give due consideration to the foregoing at your earliest convenience.' Ultimately, the complainant was told that the board of the respondent had decided not to renew his contract and the decision was final.

The complainant wrote to the CEO, asserting that the association had employed him on a series of fixed-term contracts and that his employment was one of indefinite duration under the 2003 Act. The Labour Court stated its satisfaction that this was the first occasion on which the complainant had asserted the status of his engagement with the respondent as one of employment. The Court considered the basis upon which the complainant was engaged by the respondent. The Court noted that, between 1999 and 2002, the arrangements in place between the parties were relatively informal and the payments made to the complainant were modest. The complainant had other commercial interests including commercial involvement with RTÉ as a contributor on football-related matters, as well as an annual retainer with a sports management company. The Court noted the complainant's engagement with RTÉ continued during the currency of his engagement with the respondent and that he was paid fees by RTÉ as a sole trader between 2000 and 2004. The Court noted that in 2002 the arrangements with the respondent were put on a more formal footing and the amounts paid to him increased substantially. Evidence was given that the complainant was being paid a gross fee for professional services and that the mode of payment involved him raising invoices each month for an amount equal to 1/12 of the agreed annual fee, together with agreed expenses. Evidence was given by the respondent's head of finance that concerns arose about the classification of the complainant by the Revenue Commissioners as an employee. The complainant was made aware of those concerns and was advised that unless he could obtain clearance from the Revenue Commissioners that he should properly be classified as self-employed, it was proposed to treat him as an employee, payable through payroll.

The Court noted that in response to these concerns, correspondence was exchanged between the complainant's accountant and the Revenue Commissioners. In the course of these dealings, the accountant advanced the case that the complainant was engaged on a contract for services and that he should be liable as self-employed under Sch D of the Taxes Consolidation Act 1997. The Court stated its satisfaction that the complainant and the respondent were at all times aware of the nature and implications of the case being advanced on his behalf with the Revenue Commissioners. Evidence was given by the respondent that, if the arrangements were allowed to continue by the Revenue Commissioners, the complainant would be required to charge VAT for his services. As the respondent was not registered for VAT, this would increase the cost of his services to the respondent by the applicable rate of VAT. The Court noted that the complainant had sought and obtained advice from his accountant on the implications for him of a ruling by Revenue that he was an employee. The Court noted the contents of a letter from the accountant to the complainant in May 2002 as being significant. It was pointed out to the complainant in this letter that one consequence of a change to employee status would be the availability of employment protection legislation. The Court noted that the complainant appeared to have been separately advised by a solicitor in that regard. However, notwithstanding this advice, the accountant's instructions were to continue to make representations to the Revenue Commissioners seeking to have the complainant designated as self-employed. Representations were made to the Revenue Commissioners by both the accountant and the complainant seeking to have his status as self-employed accepted. The Inspector of Taxes then confirmed that the Revenue Commissioners were prepared to accept that the complainant continue to be regarded as self-employed for tax purposes.

The Court was satisfied both parties proceeded on the basis that the relationship was that of consultant and client. The Court noted that two arguments were advanced. Firstly, whether the complainant was employed by the respondent under a contract of service, or whether his employment was under a contract for services. The second issue raised by the respondent was that the complainant was estopped from denying his engagement was as a self-employed consultant by operation of the doctrine of promissory estoppel. The respondent relied on the representations made to the Revenue Commissioners when consenting to the respondent having his status recognised as one for services.

The Court set out the applicable law in determining employment status and noted the respondent had exercised day-to-day control over the complainant and while this was not itself a decisive consideration, it did not leave the complainant free to organise his work in a manner that suited his own circumstances. He did not have any set or fixed hours of work and payments that he received were not linked to or dependent on the time he spent rendering services to the respondent. The Court noted the other commercial interests and his freedom to organise his work in a way that maximised opportunities to generate income from other sources. The Court further noted the complainant was paid 'consultancy fees' on foot of invoices on which he charged. It was significant that the complainant did not join the respondent's pension scheme and that, while other employees of the respondent suffered reductions in pay, the complainant suffered no such reduction. He was also not subject to any performance appraisal process. The Court did note that the service the complainant provided was personal and he was not contractually entitled to delegate any of the duties, and while there was some suggestion that he could delegate, it was clear he never did.

The Court concluded that there were factors of the relationship that pointed in each direction. However, on viewing the nature and history of the relationship between the parties in totality, the Court concluded that the complainant was properly classified as a consultant engaged on a contract for services.

The Court noted that promissory estoppel, or estoppel by representation, can arise if a person, by words or by conduct, makes a representation of existing fact upon which the person to whom the representation is made relies to their detriment. In these circumstances, the person making the representation will not be allowed to act inconsistently with the representation made. The Court noted that the respondent had intended to treat the complainant as an employee in or around 2002 and, had they proceeded to do so, the complainant would have accrued rights under various employment statutes to include the 2003 Act. However, the complainant, having been fully advised of the legal implications of so doing, successfully made out a case that he was not an employee. The Court held that this entailed an undertaking by the complainant that he would not subsequently claim the benefits that flow from a contract of employment. In the circumstances it would seem unconscionable for the complainant to be allowed to deny that which he previously asserted.

[2.02] *White and Anor v Troutbeck SA*[2] *– Court of Appeal of England and Wales – Employment Rights Act 1996 – contractor v employee – control test – unfair dismissal*

The workers were engaged by the appellant as caretakers/managers of a house and small farm estate, responsible for undertaking duties which included estate management, maintenance of the house and grounds and housekeeping. An agreement to this effect was signed by the parties, which included a provision allowing the workers to work for another person as long as that work would not diminish their responsibilities under the agreement. A 30-day notice period was specified and in March 2010, notice to terminate was given. A dispute arose and the matter came before the Employment Tribunal.

The Employment Tribunal found that the respondents were workers, but not employees. It held that there was a contract under which they were required to work, they were entitled to be paid for that work and there was mutuality of obligation. On the issue of control, the Employment Tribunal found that the owner had specifically divested day-to-day control to the workers and that there was never any suggestion that control was exercised by the owners.

The decision of the Employment Tribunal was overturned by the Employment Appeals Tribunal; and that decision was appealed to the UK Court of Appeal. The Court of Appeal found that the EAT had been entitled to find that the respondents were employees of the appellant.

The Court of Appeal held that the Employment Tribunal had erred in law in finding that the level of day-to-day control over the workers by the appellant precluded the respondents from asserting an employment relationship.

The Court examined the agreement that was in place between the parties. The respondents were referred to as employees and their relationship with the appellant was described in terms of an employment relationship. The Court of Appeal concluded that there was an intention on the part of the parties to create a legally binding agreement. The Court noted that the employment agreement was preceded by a previous oral agreement between the parties. The relationship had been formalised at the appellant's request. The appellant was not therefore in a position to deny an intention to create a legally binding contract.

The Court of Appeal held that, notwithstanding that there was an agreement in place, an agreement in writing would always not be determinative of whether an employer/ employee relationship existed, as all the prevailing facts should be considered. In this case, it was noted that the respondents were required to live on the appellant's farm and carry out maintenance work as required. They were paid a personal allowance of £600

---

2.   *White and Anor v Troutbeck SA* [2013] IRLR 949.

annually, but did not pay tax on this. It was also noted that the respondents were entitled to annual leave, which demonstrated compliance with employee protection legislation.

The Court of Appeal concluded that the respondents' relationship to the appellant could not be described as that of independent contractors. It stated it would be highly unusual for an independent contractor to be required to remain and reside on the premises of its customer. The fact that the respondents had worked in other premises did not preclude them from asserting that they were employees of the appellant.

Finally, the Court of Appeal noted that the level of control exerted by the appellant over the respondents was consistent with an employer/employee relationship. While the respondents had some autonomy on the farm on a day-to-day basis, the overall control was held by the appellants. The Court of Appeal upheld the decision of the EAT, finding that the Employment Tribunal had erred in law in its finding.

[2.03] *Kelly v Charles Kelly Ltd[3] – Employment Appeals Tribunal – Minimum Notice and Terms of Employment Acts 1973 to 2005 – Unfair Dismissals Acts 1977 to 2007 as amended – employment status – whether claimant, a shareholder, statutory director and joint owner, was employee of respondent company*

The claimant and the managing director of the respondent were siblings. This claim arose in the context of litigation relating to the company which was taken as far as the Supreme Court. The EAT noted that if the claimant were found to be an employee of the respondent, his claim would succeed as no evidence to justify dismissal had been provided by the respondent, whereas, if he were not, it would fail.

The EAT held that whether or not a person is an employee is a question which must be decided on the individual circumstances of each case. The EAT noted that there are often mixed questions of fact and law. However, some factors were common to many of the decided cases in this area. Reference was made to *Henry Denny & Sons v Minister for Social Welfare*[4] where the Supreme Court, in deciding whether a person is employed under a contract of service or contract for services, held that each case must be determined in light of its particular facts. In general, a person will be regarded as being employed under a contract of service and not as an independent contractor where he or she is performing a service for another person and not for himself or herself. The EAT also noted the Supreme Court decision in *Castleisland Cattle Breeding Society Ltd v Minister for Social and Family Affairs.*[5]

In this case, the claimant had been a substantial shareholder in and director of the respondent company. The claimant and the managing director of the respondent each had three different roles in relation to the company over the years: firstly as an employed executive or self-employed director of the company; secondly as shareholders of the company jointly owning almost all of the issued share capital; and thirdly as directors of

---

3.   *Kelly v Charles Kelly Ltd* MN341/2012, UD394/2012.
4.   *Henry Denny & Sons (Ireland) Ltd v Minister for Social Welfare* [1998] 1 IR 34.
5.   *Castleisland Cattle Breeding Society Ltd v Minister for Social and Family Affairs* [2004] IESC 42.

the company for which they were paid directors' fees. Evidence was given that prior to 1992 others held shares, but the managing director's evidence was that effectively he and the claimant made all direct decisions jointly. Subsequently, they each held 49.99% of the company, with the balance held by a relative.

The EAT noted that the High Court had made an order that the claimant must resign as a director of the company. The claimant was claiming he was dismissed as of that date. The EAT noted that the claimant and the managing director had each been paid under two separate PRSI numbers in an apparent effort to distinguish directors' fees from wages. PRSI had been deducted at the employee rate A. Evidence was given by the respondent that attempts were sought to regularise the position in 2008 and to apply the directors' rate of PRSI and this was successful. However the claimant appealed this to the Department of Social Protection and obtained a decision from the Department that he was an employee for PRSI purposes. The EAT stated that this determination was only one factor for it to take into account in reaching its decision.

The EAT concluded that the claimant and the managing director were joint owners and directors of the company and, even if they had previously held the status of employees, they were not now employed by the company, but were office-holders. Neither worked under the control or direction of the other. Each set their own hours and took holidays and days off as it suited them. Neither had a written contract specifying them to be an employee. The operation of dual payment methods and separate PRSI numbers was not a factor supporting the contention that the claimant was an employee as it seemed to the EAT that the wages paid were effectively payments on account of directors' fees, with the second payment made at a later stage to make up the total payment for the year. The EAT noted that each was entitled to equal shares in the profits of the company. The Tribunal concluded that in all respects, save as to the rate of PRSI paid by the claimant, they were self-employed and thus the EAT found that the claimant was not an employee and his unfair dismissal claim failed.

[2.04] *Murphy v Grand Circle Travel[6] – Unfair Dismissals Acts 1977 to 2007 (as amended) – High Court – Moriarty J – appeal of decision of Circuit Court – unfair dismissals claim – whether plaintiff employee or independent contractor*

The claimant's contract as a program director with the respondent's Irish tourism operations was terminated and the claimant brought an unfair dismissal claim to the EAT. The preliminary issue that arose was whether the claimant's retention was as an employee or an independent contractor. The EAT found that the claimant was not an employee. The claimant appealed to the Circuit Court and, following a hearing before Judge Keenan Johnson, the claimant's appeal was upheld – the effect of which was to find that the claimant was entitled to bring a claim under the Unfair Dismissals Act in respect of the termination of her employment, had been unfairly dismissed and was entitled to compensation in the sum of €50,900 plus costs.

---

6.   *Murphy v Grand Circle Travel* [2014] IEHC 337.

The respondent appealed to the High Court.

Moriarty J noted that counsel for the respondent acknowledged that certain of the documents referred to 'employment' and that the level of control exercised by the respondent over the claimant was 'comparatively high'. Moriarty J also noted the evidence adduced by the respondent which indicated that the relationship was not of the employment kind, namely the formal document executed by the claimant which was expressly designated as an 'Independent Contractor's Agreement' and contained terms that accorded with that description of the engagement. Despite the fact that the claimant gave evidence that her signing of the formal document was effectively thrust upon her by her senior supervisor, a considerable time after her engagement commencing and in circumstances in which she had no adequate opportunity to consider the full content, or take independent legal advice, Moriarty J stated that:

> I do not readily see a lady who has sturdily asserted her rights before the defendant and the legal system meekly assenting to the signed endorsement of a document expressly purporting to commit her to a regime fundamentally at variance with her perception of her engagement already then over several months. It seems to me that she must have been aware of the nature of the engagement to which she was signifying her commitment.

Moriarty J also placed considerable emphasis on the documentation which related to the claimant's remuneration which appeared 'clearly referable to the status of an independent contractor'. Moriarty J, having regard to the decisions in *Denny and Sons Ltd v Minister for Social Welfare*[7] and *Castleisland Cattle Breeding Society Ltd v Minister for Social and Family Affairs*,[8] determined that, while engaged by the respondent, the claimant's work 'involved a degree of engagement by tourism entities other than the respondent in excess of the small incidence she referred to in evidence [which] warrant a finding that the relationship was that of an independent contractor'.

[2.05] *Hassett v Údarás na Gaeltachta*[9] *– Employment Appeals Tribunal – Minimum Terms and Notice of Employment Acts 1973 to 2005 – Unfair Dismissals Acts 1977 to 2007 (as amended) – whether claimant engaged under contract for services or contract of service*

The claimant claimed he was employed by Údarás na Gaeltachta for a period of over nine years before being dismissed in February 2012. The respondent considered the claimant to be self-employed and engaged as a sub-contractor under a contract for services. The claimant informed the EAT that he regarded himself as an employee of the respondent and was always given that impression by the respondent. As no evidence to

---

7.   *Denny and Sons Ltd v Minister for Social Welfare* [1998] 1 IR 34.
8.   *Castleisland Cattle Breeding Society Ltd v Minister for Social and Family Affairs* [2004] 4 IR 150.
9.   *Hassett v Udaras Na Gaeltachta* UD659/2012, MN490/2012.

justify the dismissal was offered by the respondent, the case turned on the employment status of the claimant.

The EAT heard that the claimant applied annually to the Revenue Commissioners for a Form C2 and was responsible for his own taxation and social welfare affairs. Furthermore, a signed contract of employment did not exist. The EAT noted that '[t]he authorities are clear that mere wording cannot overbear the actuality of employment' and that each case must be determined in light of its particular facts. The EAT referred to the judgment of Geoghegan J in the Supreme Court in *Castleisland Cattle Breeding Society Ltd v Minister for Social and Family Affairs*[10] as follows:

> ... the decider must look at how the contract is worked out in practice as mere wording cannot determine its nature. Nevertheless the wording of a written contract still remains of great importance. It can, however, emerge that the working arrangements between the parties are consistent only with a different kind of contract or at least are consistent with the expressed categorisation of the contract'. The EAT also noted the comments of Mr Justice Edwards in the case of *Minister for Agriculture v Barry*,[11] who noted that 'in general a person will be regarded as being employed under a contract of service and not as an independent contractor (a contract for services) where he or she is performing service for another person and not for himself or herself'.

In that regard, the EAT considered the nature and day-to-day practice of the claimant's work. The claimant was instructed to work 39 hours per week (ie eight hours per day Monday to Thursday and seven hours on Friday) by a manager of the respondent. He was paid an hourly rate and paid at the end of each month. The respondent refunded the claimant for fuel costs incurred for using his personal vehicle for work. The respondent paid for any equipment and materials required to carry out the work. The claimant would seek approval to do certain tasks outside of his regular scope. Similarly, if a contractor was required to carry out such tasks, the claimant would first seek approval to obtain a quote from a contractor and the respondent would ultimately decide whether or not to accept the quote. The claimant did not receive holiday pay, but always sought prior approval for holidays and would accrue holiday hours by undertaking extra work at other times. The claimant never engaged a replacement while he was on holidays or if he was missing for any other reason. The EAT heard that the claimant never considered himself as eligible to work for anyone else during this period and was never informed otherwise by the respondent.

The EAT referred to the Code of Practice for Determining Employment or Self-Employment Status of Individuals, noting that the claimant scored 11 out of 13 factors as an employee. The EAT accepted the claimant's evidence that he was unaware that signing up for a C2 tax clearance meant that he was self-employed. The EAT found that

---

10. *Castleisland Cattle Breeding Society Ltd v Minister for Social and Family Affairs* [2004] IESC 42.

11. *Minister for Agriculture v Barry* [2008] IEHC 2016.

the claimant was an employee in all but name and it had jurisdiction to determine that a contract of employment existed between the parties.

The EAT held that that the claimant's dismissal was unfair and awarded the claimant €20,000 in compensation. The claimant was also awarded €1,879.80 under the Minimum Notice and Terms of Employment Acts 1973 to 2005.

RESTRICTIVE COVENANTS

[2.06] *Levinwick Ltd v Hollingsworth[12] – High Court – contract of employment – enforceability of restraint of trade/non-solicitation clause – whether clause satisfies test of protecting legitimate business interest and is no wider than reasonably necessary for protection of that interest*

The plaintiff operates a chain of pharmacies, including Blakes Pharmacy in Celbridge, Co Kildare. The defendant worked as pharmacy manager at Blakes Pharmacy from August 2007 until March 2013. After that period he was employed by two other employers before commencing employment with Chemco Pharmacy as pharmacy manager. That pharmacy began trading in Celbridge, Co Kildare in January 2014. When the defendant commenced employment with Chemco, the plaintiff sought to enforce the terms of the contract of employment dated 7 August 2007 (the contract) which contained the following non-solicitation clause:

> You undertake that during the term of your employment but for a period of 24 months after the termination of your employment, for any reason, you will not be employed or engaged by, do locum work, manage, own or part-own, a pharmacy or other retail business which trades in cosmetics or gifts or which provides photography services within a two-mile radius of the Pharmacy, you will not solicit in competition with the Pharmacy the business of any person, firm or company who is at the time of termination of your employment or was during the preceding 12 months a customer of the Pharmacy and you will not, in competition with the Pharmacy, solicit any person who was during your employment with the Pharmacy employed or engaged by the Pharmacy within 12 months prior to the termination of your employment, and who by means of such employment, is likely to be in possession of confidential information relating to the Pharmacy or its business.

> You agree that all of the above restrictions are reasonable in all the circumstances and are no more than is necessary for the protection of the interests of the Pharmacy.

> You agree that, in the event that any of the above restrictions is held to be unreasonable by reason of the area, duration or type or scope of the service covered by such restriction, then effect will be given to such restriction in such reduced form as may be decided by any Court of competent jurisdiction.

---

12. *Levinwick Ltd v Hollingsworth* [2014] IEHC 333.

McGovern J noted that the issue was one of the enforceability of a covenant in restraint of trade and that such covenants are, prima facie, unenforceable at common law. They are, however, enforceable if they:

(a)   protect a legitimate business interest; and

(b)   are no wider than are reasonably necessary for the protection of that interest.

McGovern J stated that, in determining the reasonableness of a covenant between the parties, the burden of proving reasonableness lies on the person who seeks to rely on the covenant. He noted the reasoning of Clarke J in *Murgitroyd & Co Ltd v Purdy*[13] where Clarke J stated 'the test seems to be, therefore, as to whether in all of the circumstances of the case both the nature of the restriction and its extent is reasonable to protect the goodwill of the employer'. McGovern J also noted the distinction identified in that case by Clarke J between covenants by employees and covenants given on the sale of a business, and Clarke J's observation in respect of covenants by employees that 'they might be upheld only where the employee might obtain such personal knowledge of, and influence over, the customers of his employer as would enable him, if competition were allowed, to take advantage of his employer's trade connection.'

The plaintiff contended that, by virtue of the defendant's position as pharmacy manager, the defendant had a particular degree of contact with the customers of Blakes Pharmacy, such that many customers would follow him if he worked for another pharmacy in the Celbridge area. The defendant contended that the plaintiff had exaggerated the level of personal relationship which he, as pharmacy manager, had built up with the plaintiff's customers and he had not commenced working for another pharmacy until 10 months after his employment with the plaintiff had terminated.

McGovern J noted that, in assessing whether the restrictions in the contract are necessary to protect the legitimate business interests of the plaintiff and are no wider than are reasonably necessary for the protection of that interest, it was necessary to analyse the role of the defendant while he was working with Blakes Pharmacy, his current role and the extent to which he interacted with the customers of Blakes Pharmacy. The defendant was the only person who gave evidence in this regard. The defendant's evidence was that when he commenced employment in Blakes Pharmacy in 2007, there were three pharmacies in Celbridge. Three further pharmacies had opened since 2011. His role as pharmacy manager primarily involved the dispensing of prescription medicines and he had responsibility for purchasing and making payments to suppliers. The defendant had converted one upstairs room in the premises to an office and the defendant gave evidence that the majority of his 40-hour week was worked in that office as opposed to on the pharmacy floor. There were two full time pharmacists (one of whom was the defendant but he also had many administrative duties) and also part-time locum pharmacists who covered weekends and did back-up work. The main role of the other full-time pharmacist was to run the dispensary, and the defendant stated

---

13.   *Murgitroyd & Co Ltd v Purdy* [2005] 3 IR 12.

that she had a higher level of personal contact with customers than the defendant did. There were two dispensing technicians and eight or nine counter retail assistants who handled the bulk of customer transactions, although these would have been dealing with non-prescription items. The defendant did not see himself as 'the face of the pharmacy' and in his view issues which draw people to a pharmacy are proximity to their home or to their doctor and the availability of parking facilities. The defendant argued that it would be unusual that people would follow a pharmacist to another pharmacy.

The Court considered evidence from a chartered accountant who provided services to the plaintiff. McGovern J accepted the evidence that various State agencies had cut charges for pharmaceutical products which had led to a progressive reduction in prescription fees for pharmacies and there was an increasing competition in the market. Evidence was given that there was a decline in the business at Blakes Pharmacy, and the witness attributed 75% of that decline to the defendant's move as the customers were following the defendant. The witness stated that the 24-month restriction in the defendant's contract would protect the goodwill of the pharmacy.

The Court also heard evidence from a different accounting firm who had carried out a review of the financial statements of the plaintiff from 2008 to 2013, together with copies of VAT returns for certain periods and the projected losses for 2014 and 2015. The evidence was that since 2009 sales started to decline at Blakes Pharmacy and continued thereafter. McGovern J accepted this evidence and stated that it was clear therefrom that sales had been declining for the greater part of the defendant's tenure at Blakes Pharmacy. Other factors which McGovern J noted were the increasing number of pharmacies in the Celbridge area and the reduction in prescription fees.

McGovern J concluded that the evidence fell a long way short of establishing that the defendant represented 'the face' of Blakes Pharmacy and that he was identified by customers as such. McGovern J said he must consider other relevant factors, such as the fact that there were a substantial number of employees at Blakes Pharmacy and whether it was likely that a particular pharmacist (the defendant) would have built up such a special relationship with customers as claimed by the plaintiff. Of relevance was the fact that the defendant, as pharmacy manager, needed to carry out a large number of administrative duties which required him to spend a considerable amount of time in an office on the premises.

McGovern J concluded that the particular clause in the defendant's contract was a restraint of trade and therefore it was only enforceable if it protected a legitimate business interest of the plaintiff and was no wider than is reasonably necessary for the protection of that interest. McGovern J accepted the submissions of the defendant that both the nature of the restriction and its extent must be reasonable to protect the goodwill of the employer if the clause is to be enforceable. McGovern J found that the plaintiff had failed to establish that the nature of the defendant's position and his work in Blakes Pharmacy gave rise to such a personal connection with customers of the pharmacy and that the restriction imposed was necessary to protect the goodwill of the plaintiff. Therefore, the plaintiff was not entitled to the injunctive relief or damages or any other relief claimed in the statement of claim.

[2.07] *Coppage and Anor v Safety Net Security Ltd[14] – Court of Appeal of England and Wales – restrictive covenants – terms of employment – reasonableness of non-solicitation clauses – senior employees*

The appellant was employed as the business development director of the respondent security company, which provided security guards and door supervisors in the Birmingham area. The appellant's contract contained a restrictive covenant which stated as follows:

> It is a condition of your employment that for a period of six months immediately following termination of your employment for any reason whatsoever, you will not, whether directly or indirectly as principal, agent, employee, director, partner or otherwise howsoever approach any individual or organisation who has during your period of employment been a customer of ours, if the purpose of such an approach is to solicit business which could have been undertaken by us.

Following a redundancy consultation, the appellant resigned from the respondent by email in April 2012. Following his resignation, a trainee electrician and part-time door supervisor, Mr Hadley, also resigned. The appellant and Mr Hadley then formed a company called Freedom Security Solutions Ltd (FFS). Following his resignation, over the next month the appellant contacted five customers of the respondent. Those customers terminated their contracts with the respondent and became customers of FFS.

The respondent brought a claim against the appellant for breach of the non-solicitation clause and for breach of his fiduciary duty, and was awarded £50,000 damages. The appellant appealed the decision, asserting that the non-solicitation clause was not reasonable because it ought to have been restricted to the non-solicitation of current customers of the respondent, being customers of the respondent within the six or perhaps twelve months prior to the termination of the appellant's contract.

The appellant submitted that, because the contract could have been drafted in a less restrictive way, and because as drafted it afforded the employer a greater protection than was necessary to protect its legitimate interest, the Court should find the restrictive covenant overreaching and unenforceable. The appellant also argued that, as the respondent had a 'stable customer base', there was no need for any protection beyond the last 12 months of the appellant's contract. The appellants also argued that the non-solicitation clause was unreasonable because it envisaged a situation whereby the appellant could not have any dealings with any customer who, at any point during his six-year employment with the respondent, was a customer of the respondent.

The Court of Appeal found that there had been no error in judgment by the Employment Tribunal and the restrictive covenant did not fail the test of reasonableness. The Court of Appeal stated the following general principles which apply to restrictive covenants:

(i)   post-termination restraints are enforceable if they are reasonable and restrictive covenants in employment contracts are more jealously viewed that in other commercial contracts;

---

14.   *Coppage and Anor v Safety Net Security Ltd* [2013] EWCA Civ 1176.

(ii)   an employer must be able to demonstrate that a particular clause is required to protect its proprietary interests;

(iii)   customer lists are proprietary interests;

(iv)   non-solicitation clauses are more favourably viewed than non-competition clauses;

(v)   the question of reasonableness of a restrictive covenant should be ascertained at the outset of the contract looking forward, and generally should not take into account events that have subsequently taken place, save in certain circumstances;

(vi)   the validity of restrictive covenants should not be tested by hypothetical matters;

(vii)   a clause which is unreasonable in terms of space and time will be unlikely to be enforced; and

(viii) on the whole cases in this area turn so much on their facts that a precedent is not generally of assistance.

The Court of Appeal's decision focused on the fact that this was clearly a non-solicitation clause and that the restraint was only to be in place for six months, which was reasonable in the circumstances. The Court was also persuaded by the fact that the appellant was a key employee of the respondent and had power to influence customers with whom he came into contact, which he had done in respect of the five customers who ended their contracts with the respondent having been approached by the appellant.

The Court was satisfied that the respondent had demonstrated the reasonableness of the non-solicitation clause given the time limit and scope of the clause. The Court also examined the provision in the non-solicitation clause which specifically limited the scope of the clause to restrict the appellant from approaching customers where the purpose of the approach was to solicit business that could have been undertaken by the respondent. The Court determined that this was not just a reference to a theoretical possibility, but rather to a commercially practical reality. The non-solicitation clause did not refer, for example, to ex-customers who had left the respondent on bad terms where there was a limited or no prospect of the respondent's recovering that business, it referred to existing customers of the respondent who left the respondent only because they were approached by the appellant.

The Court also examined the appellant's contention that the effect of the contract meant that anyone who was a customer of the respondent at any point during the six years during which the appellant was an employee of the respondent could not be approached by the appellant. The Court stated that this was an example of a theoretical argument and could not be accepted as a basis to find the restrictive covenant was unenforceable. The Court rejected the appellant's appeal.

[2.08] *JM Finn & Co Ltd v Holliday[15] – High Court of England and Wales – contract of employment – garden leave – restrictive covenants – circumstances constituting repudiatory breach – engineering constructive dismissal – injunction to enforce restrictive covenants*

This was an appeal by a former employee against an injunction which prevented him from taking up a new position with a competitor until the expiry of the 12-month garden leave clause in his contract of employment.

The plaintiff employer was an investment management and stockbroking firm. The defendant was a stockbroker. His contact of employment contained a 12-month notice period with a discretionary garden leave clause.

As part of its know-how system, the plaintiff collated broker opinions and market opinion from a variety of financial press and circulated this information as a daily digest. Following the introduction of a new dealing operating system, the defendant tendered his resignation and accepted an offer of employment with a competitor. The plaintiff advised the defendant that under his contract of employment, he was being placed on garden leave for a 12-month period and was precluded from taking up new employment until the expiry of that period.

The defendant requested that the daily digests prepared by the plaintiff be forwarded to him during his garden leave to ensure that he did not lose his market knowledge. The plaintiff refused to supply the defendant with this information.

The defendant then wrote to the plaintiff stating that the failure of the plaintiff to comply with this request had repudiated his contract of employment. He advised the plaintiff that he had decided to accept that with immediate effect. On that basis, he contended that he was no longer bound by the restrictive covenants contained in his contract.

The plaintiff was granted an interim injunction prohibiting the defendant from commencing his employment with the competitor or any rival organisation until judgment. The terms of the injunction mirrored the contractual restrictive covenants.

The defendant appealed to the High Court to have the injunction discontinued. He contended that the imposition of a 12-month garden leave was a restraint of trade and the plaintiff failed to demonstrate that this limitation was no more than what was reasonably necessary to protect its legitimate needs. The defendant contended that the restraint of trade clause damaged his reputation and that the High Court had the authority to reduce the duration of the garden leave clause.

The High Court declined to discontinue the injunction, determining that the defendant had not been constructively dismissed. The Court held that the plaintiff's refusal to supply the daily digests was not a repudiatory breach of contract and the defendant had overstated the importance of the digests to engineer a constructive dismissal and that, when assessed objectively, while the absence of the daily digests was inconvenient, it could not be said to be something which would deprive the defendant of his skills or constitute a breach of the implied term of trust and confidence. In the

---

15.   *JM Finn & Co Ltd v Holliday* [2013] EWHC 3450 (QB).

circumstances, the High Court found that the plaintiff had reasonable and proper cause justifying the withdrawal of the digests.

The High Court then examined the distinction between post-termination restrictions (which necessarily arise after the cessation of employment) and garden leave clauses, which apply while the employee is still employed. The High Court held that the doctrine of restraint of trade does not apply when the employee continues to be employed and that it is not necessary for an employer to justify any restriction during employment, including during garden leave. However, where an employer seeks an injunction to enforce garden leave, the High Court must apply the doctrine of restraint of trade in determining whether the garden leave provisions forming the subject matter of the application are more than what is reasonably necessary to protect the employer's legitimate interest. The High Court stated that the fact that an employee has agreed to the contractual garden leave clause is not the primary factor in determining whether to grant the injunction, and the High Court must consider the public policy of granting such injunctions in light of the fact that employers may seek to abuse the garden leave and unjustly restrict their employees from entering new employment.

When seeking an injunction to enforce a garden leave clause, the employer must justify the imposition of an injunction by demonstrating that it has a legitimate interest to protect, that the injunction will go no further than reasonably necessary to protect that interest and that the employer will endure damage if the garden leave clause is not enforced.

The High Court also stated that when dealing with post-termination restrictions, it is bound by the provisions in the contract; however, in respect of obligations during the employment period, the High Court has authority to intervene to reduce garden leave periods. The High Court has discretion to imply shorter garden leave periods if justified in the circumstances.

In this case, given the nature of the work of the defendant, the long period it took to develop client relationships and the strong risk that the defendant could attract his customers away from the plaintiff, the 12-month restriction was not unjustified. The High Court further commented that garden leave clauses did not cause any repudiatory restrictions, as had been contended by the defendant.

[2.09] *Merlin Financial Consultants Ltd v Cooper[16] – High Court of England and Wales – whether restrictive covenants contained in goodwill agreement and employment agreement relating to the respondent's employment in financial services sector were enforceable*

The defendant employee was employed as a financial adviser for the plaintiff company. On joining, it was agreed that he would receive a capital payment for the goodwill arising from the transfer of his client's funds (estimated as approximately £44,000). This was reflected in a goodwill agreement that was executed between the parties. This contained a non-complete provision for a duration of 12 months post-termination. Subsequently, a side letter was agreed whereby the parties agreed a claw back provision

---

16.   *Merlin Financial Consultants Ltd v Cooper* [2014] EWHC 1196.

in the event that the defendant's employment ended within four years of the commencement date and if income arising from the clients did not remain with the plaintiff.

Separately, the parties entered into a contract of employment which also contained provisions regarding a duty of fidelity and restrictive covenants for a six-month duration.

The defendant employee began taking steps to leave employment after the four-year period envisaged in the goodwill agreement had expired. He and a former employee of the plaintiff set up a limited company to provide financial advice. Certain changes in the sector meant that the defendant would have to pass certain exams to continue to practice, and because of his dyslexia the plaintiff engaged with him as to what steps could be taken to assist him to continue practising to include a buddy type system, whereby a suitably qualified person could work with him. However, the defendant employee indicated that he did not wish to go down this route and suggested he may sell his clients or set up on his own. In a subsequent meeting, the defendant announced he was leaving, no date was fixed for his departure and he was not put on garden leave. He was allowed to continue to deal with his clients.

The defendant challenged the validity of the restrictive covenants contained in the goodwill agreement. It was asserted that the plaintiff had informed the defendant that he could take his clients with him. He had originally asserted that he had not read the provisions of the goodwill agreement (although it was signed by him) because of his dyslexia. However, during the trial, he had conceded that he had in fact read the agreement and this was subsequently abandoned by him. The High Court noted that the defendant employee was not a credible or reliable witness. The Court concluded he had been told that if he left employment he could take his clients with him; however, this was in the context of his employment contract and before any discussions had taken place about paying him the goodwill payment in respect of his client base. The Court found that the goodwill agreement was a relatively short formal document and the defendant could not be in any doubt that it contained restrictive covenants. The Court found that there was consideration for the payment to the defendant for the purchase of the goodwill in the clients, who became clients of the plaintiff. The Court made reference to the well-established principle that it was not concerned with the adequacy of the consideration save to the extent that it may be a relevant factor in deciding whether a restraint clause was reasonable or not.

It was argued on behalf of the defendant that the Court should consider the enforceability of the restrictive covenant in the goodwill agreement from the standpoint that it formed part of an arrangement to provide the defendant with employment rather than as an intrinsic part of a business agreement to acquire goodwill.

The Court noted that the law distinguishes between covenants in employment contracts and covenants in business sale agreements, because of the differences that may exist in the nature of the relationship and bargaining power between the parties. The Court noted the recent decision of the Court of Appeal in *Beckett Investment Management Group Ltd v Hall*[17] where the Court upheld covenants which restrained the

---

17.   *Beckett Investment Management Group Ltd v Hall* [2007] EWCA Civ 613.

defendants, for 12 months after the termination of employment from supplying advice to any client of the company of a type provided by it in the ordinary course of business. The Court also noted the case of *Croesus Financial Services Ltd v Bradshaw & Bradshaw*[18] where from the evidence before it about the strength of the relationship between the adviser and the client, the pattern of contact and the fact that 12 months appeared to be industry standard, the Court decided that 12 months was reasonable both for non-solicitation and non-dealing having regard to the interests of the parties and the interests of the public.

The High Court concluded that the plaintiff did have a legitimate interest to protect and the defendant had an important asset which the plaintiff was keen to acquire and secure for itself. In return for the capital payment to acquire his client base, they wanted protection were he to leave and try to take his clients with him. The Court concluded that the goodwill agreement was a bargain, fairly entered into between parties of comparable bargaining power. The plaintiff had a legitimate interest to protect and the restrictions imposed for one year were reasonable between the parties and in the public interest.

[2.10] *East England Schools CIC (T/A 4myschools) v Palmer and Anor*[19] *– High Court of England and Wales – whether restrictive covenants in contract of employment of recruitment consultant enforceable – whether certain clauses could be blue pencilled to make them enforceable*

The plaintiff, a recruitment agency in the education sector, matches teacher applicants with schools that have both short and long term vacancies. At the relevant time, it had 13 staff including the first defendant, a recruitment consultant. The first defendant's contract of employment contained restrictive covenants not to solicit or deal with candidate teachers and client schools with whom she dealt in her 12 months prior to termination for six months following termination. These covenants extended to any actions by her in any capacity.

The first defendant decided to leave her employment and accepted an offer with the second defendant, another educational sector recruitment agency. On expiry of her notice period, the first defendant commenced her new job, covering the same area in Essex that she had previously covered for the plaintiff. The plaintiff became aware that the first defendant was possibly breaching her obligations by having contact with candidate teachers and schools with whom she had dealt whilst employed by it. Correspondence was exchanged where the plaintiff sought undertakings from the defendants. The first defendant acknowledged two contacts in a personal capacity with individuals at schools who were clients of both the plaintiff and second defendant. She rejected the various undertakings sought as too widely drawn to be legally enforceable. Further correspondence threatening legal action was exchanged, which led to the first defendant offering various undertakings; however, the plaintiff did not accept these. An

---

18. *Croesus Financial Services Ltd v Bradshaw & Bradshaw* [2013] EWHC 3685.
19. *East England Schools CIC (T/A 4myschools) v Palmer and Anor* [2013] EWHC 4138.

application for an interim injunction was made and at hearing the parties agreed certain undertakings and the matter was listed for a full trial.

The trial judge considered whether there was a proprietary interest for the plaintiff employer and noted the submission of the first defendant that all relevant details were in the public domain because of increasing use of social media and the internet. The first defendant further submitted that neither schools nor teachers have any loyalty to any particular agency and each goes to whichever of the many agencies in the market that can meet their immediate need for placement. The trial judge concluded that the market was candidate driven, there were more vacancies than teachers, and much of the relevant information was available publicly. Candidates sign up to and use multiple agencies and there was little loyalty owed by schools or teachers toward any particular consultant or agency.

The judge concluded the plaintiff did have a proprietary interest that it was entitled to protect in the business connections the first defendant would be likely to make whilst employed by the plaintiff. The reasons were that the first defendant's job was to represent the plaintiff to its Essex secondary school clients and candidates. She was the person who visited the schools and spoke to them over the phone representing the plaintiff. She was the person who met and spoke with candidate teachers. The establishment and development of relationships with schools and teachers was an integral part of her role. The trial judge noted that, even though schools may ultimately use whichever agency has the right candidate, they have a choice about which agency to contact first. Whilst that choice may be influenced by a number of factors, the relationship between the consultant and the school could be the deciding factor, not as to which agency will ultimately be used to fill the vacancy, but as to which will have the first chance to do so. To be a school's first choice and having a good pool of candidate teachers are valuable assets for an agency like the plaintiff. Likewise the trust built up between a candidate teacher and the consultant may also be influential in persuading that candidate to stay with a particular agency.

With regard to social media and the internet, although identities, addresses and other contact details may be publicly available, the first defendant would have acquired other valuable information about schools and candidates such as information about the personalities involved, their likes, dislikes and foibles and about their special requirements. The judge concluded that it was reasonable for the plaintiff to envisage when the contract of employment was put in place, that the first defendant would, on leaving employment, be in a position to use the relationships she had built up and confidential information she had acquired to influence the choice of an appreciable number of schools and teachers away from the claimant to her new employer. The judge noted that the fragility of the relationships between schools, teachers and the plaintiff agency made it more necessary and legitimate for the employer to have sought to protect it because it made the prospect of a successful solicitation more likely.

Regarding the non-dealing covenant, it was submitted that they extended to actions carried out, not just by the first defendant on her own account, but 'as a principal, partner, shareholder, director, employee, consultant or in any capacity whatsoever' which made them unreasonably wide. Thus the example was offered that the first defendant would have fallen within the prohibition by becoming a minority shareholder in a competing company, even if she played no active part in that business. The trial judge noted the parts of the covenants which required the first defendant not to 'canvass or solicit business or custom from any client or prospective client in relation to services' and noted that this required a positive act on her part. The judge concluded that the restrictions in the non-solicitation covenants were not wider than had been reasonably necessary for the protection of the legitimate proprietary interest. However the same was not true for two sub-clauses within the covenants which required the first defendant 'not to be concerned with the supply to any Client or Prospective client of services ...'.

The judge found that it was possible that this could be infringed by the mere ownership of a minority shareholding in a competing company. On that basis, he considered whether they were capable of remedy by blue pencilling and concluded that they were. He further concluded that the duration of the restrictive covenants was reasonable and noted that relationships with schools and teachers took time to build up.

Finally, the judge concluded that the second defendant was, from the start, sufficiently aware of the restrictive covenants binding the first defendant to make the second defendant liable for procuring the breaches that she committed. He concluded that the second defendant was liable jointly and severally with the first defendant to pay compensatory damages of £7,040 (a figure measured by the Court on the basis of the agreed list of placements) to the plaintiff, plus interest from the date of each placement to the date of judgment.

[2.11] *Prophet plc v Huggett[20] – Court of Appeal of England and Wales (CD) – breach of restrictive covenant and interpretation thereof – injunction – non-compete*

This case was an appeal against a decision of the High Court to grant an injunction restraining an employee from working for a competitor of the respondent. The employee was a sales manager who had worked for the respondent which developed and sold computer software for use in the fresh produce industry. The employee was subject to a restrictive covenant following the termination of his contract of employment. The first sentence of the restrictive covenant would have been unenforceable on its own as an unreasonable restraint of trade as it would have restricted the employee from working for a company providing software systems unrelated to the types of system with which he would have been involved while working at the plaintiff company. It would also restrict the employee from working for a company that supplied software systems to a sector of the fresh produce industry other than that served by the plaintiff.

However, the restrictive covenant was followed by a proviso that limited the restraint to preventing the employee from working for competitors who provided computer software which the employee had worked on during the course of his employment with the plaintiff. The whole point of this proviso was to narrow down the nature of the post-employment clause, thereby ensuring that the covenant was not an unreasonable restraint of trade. This had little practical effect as the plaintiff was the only company which actually supplied the relevant software.

---

20. *Prophet plc v Huggett* [2014] EWCA Civ 1013; [2014] IRLR 797.

The High Court held that the clause, read literally, would give the respondent no protection. The Court stated that it was necessary to add the words 'or similar thereto' at the end of the proviso so that the restrictive covenant would extend to products that were similar to those the employee had been involved with. The employee appealed on the grounds that the High Court had misinterpreted the covenant and had gone wider than was reasonably necessary for the plaintiff's protection.

The Court of Appeal concluded that the language of the proviso was not truly ambiguous. It stated that this was not a case of where something had 'gone wrong' with regard to the drafting as had been asserted by the High Court. The Court of Appeal referred to the case of *Chartbrook Ltd and Anor v Persimmon Homes Ltd and Anor*[21] in which Lord Hoffmann stated that the courts do not 'easily accept that people have made linguistic mistakes, particularly in formal documents', and that it 'clearly requires a strong case to persuade the Court that something must have gone wrong with the language'. Furthermore, the Court relied on *East v Pantiles (Plant Hire) Ltd*[22] in which Lord Hoffmann stated that it must also 'be clear what correction ought to be made to cure the mistake'.

The Court of Appeal stated that 'a Court should be very cautious before finding and correcting supposed mistakes in a restriction' and that the Court should 'err on the side of enforceability rather than voidness'. The Court stated that to widen the language of the proviso would offend public policy as it would give the respondent wider protection than was reasonably necessary. The Court concluded that the meaning of 'any products' in the context of the restrictive covenant simply referred to those products that the employee had been involved with while he was employed at the plaintiff and that the Court did 'not regard that conclusion as being capable of much elaboration'.

The appeal was allowed and the injunction was set aside.

[2.12] *Elsevier Ltd v Munro*[23] – High Court of England and Wales – non-compete covenants – notice requirements – constructive dismissal – injunctions – mutual trust and confidence

The defendant was a former employee of the plaintiff who had worked as a chartered accountant. Before working for the plaintiff, he had been employed for a number of years by the plaintiff's parent company. Following a re-organisation in January 2014, the defendant was moved from his position as CFO of one sub-division to a similar position in another sub-division, to which he had reluctantly agreed. In April 2014 the defendant handed in notice of his resignation and sought to commence work as a CFO of one of the plaintiff's competitors at the end of the following month. The plaintiff rejected this on the grounds that the defendant's contract of employment required that he give the plaintiff 12 months' notice. The plaintiff asked that the defendant stay working with the plaintiff until January 2015 in accordance with his notice period. The defendant refused to do so, and, after a number of exchanges, left the plaintiff as he considered his

---

21.   *Chartbrook Ltd and Anor v Persimmon Homes Ltd and Anor* [2009] 1 AC 1101.

22.   *East v Pantiles (Plant Hire) Ltd* [1981] 263 EG 61.

23.   *Elsevier Ltd v Munro* [2014] EWHC 2648 (QB); [2014] IRLR 766.

employment as ended. The plaintiff then sought an injunction to prevent the defendant from working with the competitor.

The defendant asserted that the plaintiff had breached his contractual right to be provided with work of a type appropriate to his original post and that this conduct had undermined his trust and confidence in his employer. The defendant also argued that an injunction was unnecessary as the alleged competitor was not a significant competitor and the plaintiff would suffer no real harm.

The issues before the Court were: (i) whether the defendant was still bound by his contract of employment or whether he had been constructively dismissed; and (ii) if he was still bound by his contract, whether its terms should be enforced by an injunction.

The Court held that the defendant had not been constructively dismissed. The Court held that an employer could only be in breach of its obligation of trust and confidence if its conduct was calculated to, or was likely to, destroy or seriously damage the relationship between it and the employee without reasonable cause. By continuing in his new role, the defendant had affirmed his contract in the new role. The Court stated that the defendant had given notice of his resignation rather than resigning straight away when he would have been aware of the features of his new role that he later argued amounted to a repudiatory breach of contract. The Court held this amounted to an affirmation of the contract rather than repudiation. Furthermore, the Court stated that it was of the opinion that the defendant had decided he wanted to leave the plaintiff's employment because he found the job on offer at the competitor more attractive.

The Court stated that an injunction could be granted without proof that an employee would misuse his employer's confidential information where such a move by an employee would cause unquantifiable damage to the employer. The Court pointed out that this was not such a case. However, the Court did state that while the defendant would not deliberately misuse the information which was of value to the plaintiff, there was a real risk that he could do so unconsciously with reference to the confidential information he retained by memory. If he did so, there was a real risk of substantial damage to the applicant for which monetary compensation would not be an adequate remedy. The Court held that this was sufficient to justify an injunction to prevent the defendant from working for the competitor for his notice period.

The fact that the defendant would continue to be paid during his notice period, whether or not he was working for the plaintiff, did not mean the Court should exercise its discretion in light of the principles developed in the garden leave cases. The Court stated that restraint of trade considerations would need to be taken into account as there was a public policy against the atrophy of skills. However, the Court acknowledged that the plaintiff had asked the defendant to continue to work until January 2015 and that having declined to do so, the defendant could not complain that the idleness which he had chosen for himself amounted to a breach of his contract of employment.

The Court concluded that the plaintiff's claim for an injunction to restrain a breach of duty of good faith was unsound, as the wording was too vague and uncertain. The Court granted an injunction to prohibit the defendant from working for the specific competitor until the end of his contractual notice period.

DUTY OF FIDELITY

[2.13] *Thompson Ecology Ltd and Anor v APEM Ltd and Ors[24] – High Court of England and Wales – whether third defendant (Hall) had broken his duty of fidelity by failing to inform his employer, Unicomarine, of threat from its competitor and by assisting competitor to recruit Unicomarine staff – application for summary judgment – whether duty of fidelity applied during period of garden leave*

This case involved a biologist (H) employed as an operations manager by Thompson Unicomarine at a marine biology laboratory. H was the most senior employee and had overall charge of the operation with an obligation to manage it and to report to the operations team on a fortnightly basis on matters concerning the business. H was also obliged to oversee senior staff in the maintenance of client relationships and to represent the company in a positive light to staff. In early November 2012, he signed an employment contract with APEM Ltd, a competitor of Unicomarine, and on 22 November 2012, he gave notice to that effect to his employer. He was put on garden leave for his four-week notice period. H commenced working for APEM on 2 January 2013. Another 17 biologists left Unicomarine and some or all of them started to work for APEM shortly thereafter.

Unicomarine and its parent company brought claims against APEM and H claiming H and APEM had acted together to effect a whole sub-transplantation of Unicomarine's business to APEM, to include the transfer to APEM of a substantial section of the workforce. This application was for summary judgment against H on the basis that he had broken his contractual duty of fidelity.

There were two areas of concern – the fact that H had not told the claimants of the threat to Unicomarine's business and staff from the competitor and his active assistance to APEM to identify and recruit Unicomarine's staff, including discussions with APEM as to how they might go about recruiting interested Unicomarine staff and the compatibility of salaries and grades. Furthermore, it was alleged that he had: informed Unicomarine staff that APEM was looking to recruit; provided APEM with a list of Unicomarine staff who might contact them, and provided details of salaries to expedite the making of offers.

It was acknowledged by H that he had not informed Unicomarine about APEM's ambitions or that Unicomarine staff had contacted him about working with APEM.

The High Court held that H had broken his duty of fidelity in failing to inform Unicomarine of the threat from its competitor and in assisting that competitor. The Court noted that H was under an obligation to report to his superiors the existence of a threat to the business or staff. As operations manager, he was required to report on a fortnightly basis and his job description contained express obligations. The Court concluded that he must have been expected to report matters relating to the business that were relevant to his superiors, including how the business or staff were performing. The Court also concluded that H could not have properly discharged his reporting obligations without alerting his superiors to the developing threat to the business.

---

24.   *Thompson Ecology Ltd and Anor v APEM Ltd and Ors* [2014] IRLR 184.

Furthermore, H was under an obligation to oversee senior staff, the maintenance of Unicomarine's client relationships and to present Unicomarine in a positive light to staff. This implied an obligation to do nothing to disrupt Unicomarine's relationship with its staff. The Court concluded that it was not consistent with his duty of fidelity for H to assist an actual or potential competitor to entice away the employer's staff.

The Court noted however that telling other staff members of his decision to join APEM before he had told the plaintiff was not necessarily a breach of the duty of fidelity. The Court noted the context in which the information had been imparted to the other employees was likely to be determinative of the question of whether or not a breach of duty was involved and this could not be concluded or determined on a summary judgment application.

The High Court then considered the extent to which H's obligation of fidelity was affected by the fact that he was not required to work out his notice period. The Court noted that whilst it was obvious he would not have been expected to carry out the majority, if indeed any, of the tasks described in his job description, nevertheless he remained employed during garden leave and the employer was entitled to expect his continued loyalty. H was, in the view of the Court, obliged to report that he was assisting APEM to recruit and that assistance itself was a breach of his duty. The Court noted the judgment of Popplewell J in *Imam-Sadeque v Bluebay Asset Management (Services) Ltd*:[25]

> To some extent it is right to say that the content of the duty of fidelity is attenuated when an employee is put on garden leave; he is relieved of the duty to carry out the work activities for which he was employed and owes no duty to pursue those activities loyally or indeed at all...but the same cannot be said of the obligations which are imposed by the duty of fidelity and/or of relevance in this case, which are obligations to refrain from acting in a particular way. Such negative obligations remain part of his duties for so long as he is employed. During garden leave, the employee has the benefit of being paid in full without having to carry out any positive work obligations. The employer is paying for the continued right to insist upon the employee performing his negative obligation. Moreover, one of the common purposes of putting an employee on garden leave is to secure his loyalty to the current employer during the notice period, and to delay the transfer of his loyalty to a new employer until after its expiry. An employer may thereby legitimately seek to restrict the impact of any competitive activity by the employee and protect the integrity of the employer's workforce. There is no reason in principle or authority why the aspects of the duty of loyalty which touch upon competitive activity or the enticing away of employees should be attenuated so as to interfere with these legitimate purposes of garden leave.

The High Court concluded that the effect of H's admitted actions was to deprive the plaintiff of an opportunity to prepare for the competition by APEM and to retain the loyalty of staff. The Court noted that the plaintiff perceived that a judgment to that effect might enable it to influence the marketplace in its favour and so recover some of the

---

25. *Imam-Sadeque v Bluebay Asset Management (Services) Ltd* [2013] IRLR 34. See *Arthur Cox Employment Law Yearbook* 2013, para [4.26].

ground lost due to H's activities but if it had to wait for such judgment until after a trial, it would be too late to have any commercial effect. The Court concluded that the plaintiff was entitled to a prompt judgment in circumstances where it had established that there were no reasonable prospects of H defending at least some of its claims. The Court granted summary judgment to the plaintiff and held that H had broken his duty of fidelity. Separate orders were sought in respect of unrelated commercial aspects of the case.

DUTY OF CONFIDENTIALITY

[2.14] *Warm Zones v Thurley and Anor*[26] *– High Court of England and Wales – breach of contractual duty of confidentiality – disclosure of confidential information to competitor during course of employment – balance of convenience – least risk of injustice – mandatory injunction granted for imaging and inspection of computers/ electrical devices*

The first defendant was employed as a zone director and the second defendant as an IT and project manager of the plaintiff employer. The second defendant reported to the first. Both defendants had regular access to the plaintiff's database in order to discharge their duties. The first defendant was involved in both the strategic and day-to-day management of the company's operations in the North Staffordshire and Cheshire West areas. She operated with significant autonomy and responsibility in carrying out her duties.

The defendants' employment contracts contained identical clauses prohibiting them from disclosing the plaintiff's confidential information both during and after their employment with the plaintiff. There were no restrictive covenants contained within either defendant's employment contract.

In November 2012 the first defendant was suspended and in March 2013 she was dismissed on grounds of gross misconduct. In March 2013 the second defendant resigned. The plaintiff became aware that the first defendant had found employment with a competitor (RES) and that both defendants had been involved in business dealings with RES while they were still employed with the plaintiff. In February 2013, while the first defendant was suspended, she sent a document to RES which stated that she had information that would provide opportunities for business development for RES. Furthermore, after her employment with the plaintiff had ended, she had offered to provide a 'tender file' to RES. Additionally, while the second defendant was still employed with the plaintiff, he sent an email to RES that referred to the first defendant and offered to provide a list of business leads that were taken from a much larger set of data. He stated that the leads were based on information gathered over the previous four years which was when he was working for the plaintiff.

The plaintiff showed that the information disseminated by the defendants constituted approximately 20 years of work. The information consisted of details of large numbers of householders and had been developed by the plaintiff through the devotion of

---

26.   *Warm Zones v Thurley and Anor* [2014] EWHC 988 (QB), [2014] IRLR 791.

substantial time, effort and money. The plaintiff was unique within the sector in the way it collected, maintained and used its data. A witness stated that the information was not only commercially sensitive, but also confidential, not publicly available, and certainly not publicly available in such a convenient and accessible form. Therefore, the database contained important, unique confidential information and property belonging to the plaintiff.

The plaintiff applied for interim relief on the grounds that the defendants had used or disclosed confidential information contained within the plaintiff's consumer database without authorisation, which was in breach of the express and implied terms of their contracts. The order which the plaintiff sought provided for the imaging and inspection of the defendants' computers or other electronic storage devices by a computer specialist, who would then provide the information to an independently instructed solicitor nominated by the defendants but at the expense of the plaintiff.

The second defendant alleged that the plaintiff did not genuinely want to know whether and to what extent its confidential information had been used or disclosed; rather, he submitted that it was a campaign to harass the defendants and to persecute the first defendant at a critical point in her Employment Tribunal proceedings. Both defendants denied using or disclosing the plaintiff's confidential information to RES and asserted that the information was in fact the property of Stoke-on-Trent City Council and that the relevant information was publicly available.

The High Court cited the principles set out by Chadwick J in *Nottingham Building Society v Eurodynamics Systems*[27] (as approved by the Court of Appeal in *Zockoll Group Ltd v Mercury Communications Ltd*[28]) that the overriding consideration was what course of action would involve the least risk of injustice if it ultimately transpired that the course chosen by the Court proved wrong, citing *Films Rover International Ltd v Cannon Film Sales Ltd*[29] in this regard.

The Court referred to *Coco v AN Clark Engineers*[30] in stating that in order to constitute a breach of confidence or an unauthorised use of confidential information, the information in question:

> must have the necessary quality of confidence about it. It must have been communicated in circumstances importing an obligation of confidence, and there must have been an unauthorised use of the information to the detriment of the party communicating it … the preservation of its confidentiality must be of significant concern to the claimant.

The Court stated that, in the absence of a restrictive covenant, an ex-employee could only be restricted from using information which is a trade secret or akin to a trade secret. However, the Court said that the question as to which category the information fell into did not need to be resolved at the hearing.

---

27. *Nottingham Building Society v Eurodynamics Systems* [1993] FSR 468 at 474.
28. *Zockoll Group Ltd v Mercury Communications Ltd* [1998] FSR 3.
29. *Films Rover International Ltd v Cannon Film Sales Ltd* [1986] 3 All ER 772.
30. *Coco v AN Clark Engineers* [1969] RPC 41.

The Court held that:

- there was a serious issue to be tried in that the plaintiff company had confidential information that it was entitled to protect;

- there was cogent prima facie evidence of misuse by the defendants of the plaintiff's database;

- the Court had a high degree of assurance about the strength of the applicant's claim;

- regarding the balance of convenience, damages were rarely an adequate remedy in cases of this kind and this case was no exception;

- it was relevant that the plaintiff was not seeking to restrain the defendants from working in their chosen fields, whether in competition with the plaintiff or not – both defendants were free to do so; and

- the order sought was a focused one, designed simply to secure the return, protection and security of the plaintiff's confidential information.

The Court concluded that the balance of convenience lay firmly in favour of granting the imaging and inspection order sought. There was a strong, objectively justified basis for the plaintiff's suspicion in respect of the defendants' conduct. There was nothing to support the defendants' assertions that the action was being taken merely to harass or persecute them or that the information was not the property of the plaintiff. Therefore, the least risk of injustice was to make the order sought.

JOB ABANDONMENT

[2.15] *Maher v Panache Lingerie Ltd[31] – Employment Appeals Tribunal – Unfair Dismissal Acts 1977 to 2007 (as amended) – performance concerns raised by employer – immediate absence on sick leave in response citing work related stress – lack of engagement on part of claimant – whether respondent entitled to regard claimant as having frustrated his contract of employment – job abandonment*

The claimant was the sole employee of the respondent in Ireland. Following an audit into the claimant's workload, he was approached informally by the HR manager and the director of sales who presented the claimant with an audit report and their comments. A follow-up invitation to attend an investigation meeting was then sent to the claimant. At this meeting, the respondent claimed that the claimant had acknowledged he was not doing his job the way it should be done. The following day, the respondent received a medical certificate from the claimant's doctor, stating he was unfit for work. The claimant's solicitor also wrote to the respondent, requesting that all correspondence be directed to his office.

---

31.   *Maher v Panache Lingerie Ltd* UD1158/2012.

The claimant claimed he was suffering from stress due to the way the respondent was treating him and an assessment with an occupational health physician was arranged. The medical opinion was that the claimant was suffering from an adjustment reaction disorder relating to his perceived stress in the workplace. An extended period then followed where there was no engagement, from either the claimant or his solicitor with the respondent. The solicitor informed the respondent that the claimant would not be returning to employment. The respondent wrote to the claimant directly indicating its intention to issue him with a P45 unless he confirmed otherwise. In the absence of any further correspondence from the claimant a P45 was issued; however, the respondent indicated that it was willing to withdraw the document under certain defined conditions.

The EAT determined that the claimant's lack of direct engagement with the respondent from early on ill-served him. In particular, the EAT noted that the claimant, by depending entirely on his solicitor to conduct his affairs, had damaged his position. The EAT noted that the respondent's handling of the case was generally fair, patient, tolerant and understanding given, there was approximately a six-month period where there was no engagement by the employee including no updated medical certs, etc. Accordingly, the EAT found the employer was justified and reasonable in concluding that the claimant had frustrated his contract of employment and had effectively abandoned his employment. The claim for unfair dismissal failed.

IMPOSITION OF A RETIREMENT AGE

[2.16] *Kane v Dublin Stevedores Ltd[32] – Employment Appeals Tribunal – Unfair Dismissals Acts 1977 to 2007 (as amended) – termination of employment by reason of retirement – imposition of retirement where no express contractual retirement age*

This case arose from the termination of the claimant's employment by reason of retirement in February 2011. Evidence was given that the claimant had worked as a clerk in and around the docks in Dublin since 1962. The claimant had previously worked from 1992 to 2003 for a company in which the respondent held a significant shareholding. In 2003, the operations of that company transferred to the respondent and another company. The respondent employed the claimant from 2003. The claimant wrote to the managing director of the respondent in August 2003 setting out matters relating to his employment, and both parties accepted that this letter represented the claimant's contract of employment and that there were no other documents relating to such matters. This letter did not make any reference to retirement age. While subsequent pension arrangements were put in place for the claimant and the claimant accepted that he had signed relevant paperwork associated with the pension scheme, he asserted he did not fill out the forms and was not involved in the wrong date of birth being put on the forms. Ultimately, in November 2010, the managing director of the respondent wrote to the

---

32.   *Kane v Dublin Stevedores Ltd* UD197/2012.

claimant to advise that his retirement date was in February 2011. The claimant challenged the termination of his employment and claimed that it was unfair.

In determining this matter, the EAT noted that the contractual arrangement between the parties was represented by the letter between the claimant and the managing director of the respondent company from August 2003 and the terms of the letter did not specify a retirement age. The EAT found that the claimant had assumed he could work after the age of 65 despite having signed pension documentation on which a retirement age was specified. The EAT noted that the provisions of the Employment Equality Act 1998, as amended, prohibit discrimination on grounds of age, but also noted that it is open to an employer to specify a retirement age for staff in accordance with legislation.

The EAT determined that the respondent imposed retirement on the claimant in circumstances where his contract of employment did not provide for it and his dismissal was unfair. The EAT in assessing compensation, noted that respondent was operating in challenging economic times, that all employees had been placed on a reduced working week and measured the award at €17,500.

MOBILITY CLAUSES

[2.17] *Noonan Services Group Ltd v A Worker*[33] – *Labour Court – Industrial Relations Act 1969, s 13(9) – appeal of Rights Commissioner's recommendation – whether employer entitled to rely on mobility clause in contract of employment to move employee from one client site to another*

This was an appeal of a Rights Commissioner recommendation, which found against the employee's original claim. The claimant employee was on sick leave from January 2010 and sought to return to work in August 2011, but was informed that his position as a static guard at the University of Limerick was no longer available and he was being assigned elsewhere. The claimant refused to work in another location and sought an immediate return to his role at the University of Limerick and compensation for loss of earnings he had sustained in the interim.

The employer informed the Labour Court that changes in its contract with the University of Limerick had resulted in a reduction in contracted hours and the numbers employed on site. Other security officers were moved off site and reassigned to other contracts in the Limerick area. The claimant had refused offers of other sites within a reasonable distance of his home.

The Labour Court noted the mobility clause contained in the claimant's contract of employment which stated: 'It is a condition of employment that you agree to work at any of the company's contract assignments within reasonable travelling distance from your home to suit the needs of the business and its customers.'

The Labour Court accepted that mobility was an integral part of the claimant's terms and conditions of employment, and indeed of security officers in general within the industry and accordingly the Court could not find in favour of the claimant. The Court

---

33.   *Noonan Services Group Ltd v A Worker* AD1419.

recommended that the claimant should accept positions assigned to [...] in accordance with his contractual requirements, which could incluc [...] University of Limerick site.

CALCULATION OF DAMAGES FOR BREACH OI [...]

[2.18] *Brown v Iarnrod Éireann/Irish Rail (No 2)[34] – High Court – employer guilty of breach of contract – wrongful refusal to honour early retirement package offered to plaintiff – whether plaintiff could recover contract debt to which he said he was entitled as full measure of his compensation – how are damages to be calculated?*

This case is linked to a previous judgment of Hogan J in *Brown v Iarnrod Éireann*[35] where Hogan J held that the defendant, Iarnrod Éireann, was guilty of a breach of contract by wrongfully refusing to honour an early retirement package which it had previously offered the plaintiff, a longstanding employee of the company, and which he had accepted.

Hogan J noted that the plaintiff, who was aged 62 at the time of his first judgment, found himself compelled by economic circumstances to return to work and he continued in that position until September 2009 whereupon he retired, having reached the compulsory retirement age. Hogan J noted that had the plaintiff retired as part of the early retirement package in September 2006, he would have received a voluntary severance offer of €148,157 together with a payment of €2,174 per month. In this case the plaintiff claimed that latter sum plus the voluntary severance payment for a period of three years up to retirement being €78,249 together with interest as a contract debt.

Hogan J stated that the case presented was a difficult one in terms of the assessment of damages for breach of contract. He noted that the well-established distinction between a debt on the one hand and an action for damages for breach of contract on the other. Hogan J noted the decision of the House of Lords in *White and Carter (Councils) v McGregor*[36] but stated that he was unpersuaded by its reasoning. Hogan J stated that:

> I cannot think that an action for debt is so sacrosanct that the ordinary rules as to mitigation do not apply to a breach of their own obligation of the kind at issue in the present case just as much as they do in the case of an action for damages for breach of contract.

He held that if the House of Lords decision was followed without at least a significant qualification, it might result in an over compensation of the plaintiff. Hogan J noted that in *White and Carter* it was striking that the plaintiff company was in the fortunate position that it could perform the contract without any assistance from the defendant whatsoever. In the majority judgment in that case Lord Reid acknowledged this unusual

---

34. *Brown v Iarnrod Éireann/Irish Rail (No 2)* [2014] IEHC 117.
35. *Brown v Iarnrod Éireann* [2013] IEHC 620.
36. *White and Carter (Councils) v McGregor* [1962] AC 413.

ure of the litigation, noting that in most cases 'by refusing co-operation the party in breach can compel the innocent party to restrict his claim to damages'.

Hogan J noted that in the case before him, the plaintiff's capacity to perform his side of the contractual bargain, that is to take early retirement, was entirely dependent on the willingness of the respondent to accept the state of affairs. In the circumstances, the respondent was not so willing, even though by refusing it was wrongfully repudiating the contractual offer which the plaintiff had already accepted. The Court noted that at that point the plaintiff had an option, namely to accept the repudiation and to sue for damages for breach of contract, or to refuse to accept it and if necessary to sue to enforce the subsisting contract. Effectively he could accept the repudiation and return to work whilst later suing for damages or he could refuse to return to work and insist that the early retirement contract was still in force and effect. Hogan J noted that this was not an easy choice to make and stated that it was hardly a surprise that the plaintiff had elected to carry on working despite his most profound misgivings. Hogan J concluded that the plaintiff must be regarded as having accepted the repudiation by then returning to work and indeed continuing to work for three further years. In so doing, he forfeited his right to sue in debt for the liquidated sum promised by the early retirement package so his remedy, was in the judgment of Hogan J, confined to damages for breach of contract.

Hogan J then went on to consider what, if any, was the plaintiff's loss and noted that he did not suffer any direct financial loss as a result of working three extra years and in fact his lump sum and final retirement pension were all enhanced by virtue of the fact that he did indeed work for those years. The plaintiff's loss was summarised by Hogan J as being a different loss, namely being deprived of his right to take early retirement after long years as an exemplary employee. Hogan J noted that the law endeavoured to compensate for the disappointment associated with an unsatisfactory holiday[37] and the inconvenience suffered by a home owner resulting from the defective construction of a residential dwelling[38] and stated the same could be said, by analogy, in respect of the disappointment which the plaintiff suffered in September 2006 when he was compelled to return to work. The Court considered that the type of loss and inconvenience suffered by the plaintiff was undoubtedly intangible and very difficult to measure but it was nevertheless real. Hogan J stated that the loss can be regarded as a form of inconvenience and lost expectation in as much that the plaintiff was deprived of an important benefit, a restful and less stressful life associated with the early retirement contract. Hogan J stated that the measurement of the loss in monetary terms was in many ways all but impossible but stated that the yardstick should be that any damages awarded should be tangible and significant without being excessive or generous. He decided to award the plaintiff a sum of €20,000 for each of the three years he was obliged to work by way of damages for breach of contract making a total award of €60,000.

---

37.   *Jarvis v Swan Tours Ltd* [1973] 2 QB 233.
38.   *Johnson v Longly Properties Ltd* [1976–1977] ILRM 93.

CONTRACTUAL DISCIPLINARY PROCEDURES

[2.19] *McMillan v Airedale NHS Foundation Trust*[39] – *Court of Appeal of England and Wales – whether power to increase disciplinary sanction on appeal can be implied into contractual disciplinary procedure which is silent on issue*

The was an appeal from the High Court against a permanent injunction restraining the respondent employer from reconvening an appeal panel to consider the issue of sanction or any further matters after the claimant had withdrawn her appeal.

The claimant, a consultant obstetrician and gynaecologist, was given a final written warning under the Trust's contractual disciplinary procedure for misconduct following internal disciplinary proceedings arising from an allegation that she had provided inconsistent accounts of an adverse incident.

On internal appeal, the charges against the claimant were upheld and the appeal panel proposed to reconsider the appropriate sanction, which could lead to the potential termination of the claimant's employment. Before the panel reconvened, the claimant lodged High Court proceedings and obtained an injunction restraining the Trust from reconsidering the sanction.

The two issues which came before the High Court were:

1. Whether, on the claimant's appeal against sanction, the appeal panel was permitted under her contract of employment to impose a sanction which was more severe than the final written warning imposed by the first instance panel, and in particular whether it could terminate her employment; and

2. Whether, the claimant, having at least purported to withdraw her appeal, the appeal panel could proceed to consider sanction consistently with her contract of employment.

The High Court found against the respondant on both issues and granted a permanent injunction. The respondent appealed.

The Court of Appeal dismissed the respondant's appeal. It concluded that the right of internal appeal was for the employee's benefit (as a safeguard against a capricious employer) and it is not intended to be a continuation of the disciplinary procedure. The Court noted that the ACAS guide emphasises this point in stating that an 'appeal must never be used as an opportunity to punish an employee for appealing a decision and it should not result in any increase in penalty that may deter individuals from appealing'.

The respondent's disciplinary policy expressly stated that the appeal was the final stage and the Court of Appeal held it would be contrary to natural justice (and guidance about the management of internal disciplinary procedures) if a warning were to be increased to a dismissal on appeal without this possibility being spelt out in the policy.

The Court stated that because the only practical purpose of the reconvened hearing to consider sanction would be to increase it, the High Court was justified in granting the injunctive relief to the claimant. The Court concluded that the claimant's contract of employment provided her with an appeal which could not result in an increase in

---

39. *McMillan v Airedale NHS Foundation Trust* [2014] EWCA Civ 1031.

sanction. That position was not affected by the procedural agreements reached in the course of the disciplinary process. These arrangements did not amount to a binding variation of the claimant's contract. The imposition of an increased sanction on appeal would amount to a breach of the respondent's contract with the claimant.

THE RIGHT TO SUSPEND

[2.20] *McEneaney v Cavan and Monaghan Education & Training Board and O'Brien[40] – High Court – judicial review – whether decision to transfer applicant was valid – whether decision to place her on administrative leave was null and void where significant number of complaints about applicant's performance – whether applicant had legitimate expectation that procedures set out in Circular 59/2009 would be applied in determining complaints about her competence*

By way of background, Kearns P noted that the applicant had been appointed as a member of staff of County Monaghan VEC under the powers conferred by s 20 of the Vocational Education (Amendment) Act 2001. The Court noted that by Circular 59/2009, the Department of Education and Science had notified VECs that new procedures had been agreed for dealing with the suspension and dismissal of teachers. In summary, the circular set out procedures and provide for an informal process and a formal process relating to teachers experiencing professional competency issues. The applicant had commenced work with Co Monaghan VEC in Largy College in 1999 and her appointment was made permanent in 2002. In early 2013, she was the subject matter of five complaints made by parents and pupils. On receipt of the complaints, the applicant was supplied with a copy of Circular 59/2009 and was informed that this would apply to the complaints.

Kearns P set out the aspects of the relevant process relating to professional competence issues. He noted that the applicant had contended that the procedures, although commenced, were not followed in her case. The Court noted that the applicant was referred for medical assessment by an occupational specialist to determine if she was fit for work and it was submitted that this was an attempt to 'medicalise' an issue that should have been dealt with under the procedures and Circular. On confirmation that the applicant was medically fit to teach and fit to engage with the school management in the normal way, a meeting took place with the applicant who was accompanied by her trade union representative. In the course of this meeting, it appears that the applicant's representative suggested she engage in team teaching, which was something the respondent was happy to accept. However, the applicant was unwilling to accept this proposal and noted it was not an option contemplated by Circular 59/2009. The Court noted that the applicant became extremely distressed during this meeting and advised her trade union representative that she was feeling suicidal. The process came to a halt. The applicant was then certified unfit by her own doctors for a period of time and subsequently the respondent's own doctor also certified her as being unfit.

---

40.   *McEneaney v Cavan and Monaghan Education & Training Board and O'Brien* [2014] IEHC 423.

The applicant sought a transfer from Largy College with the intention that if the transfer proceeded, it would dispose of all complaints against the applicant. In an email to the applicant on 27 June 2013, the CEO stated he was actively seeking a transfer for her, but in the meantime, it was necessary to plan for her return to Largy College. The CEO asked her what supports she would require. In a further medical report, an occupational specialist concluded that it was no longer necessary or tenable for him to certify the applicant to be medically disabled for employment. The doctor noted that, whilst a transfer option might not address all concerns that had arisen, it might offer the applicant a fresh start in a new environment, allowing her to leave historic issues behind her. The Court noted that events took a peculiar turn when the applicant subsequently withdrew her application for the transfer. The Court noted that the respondent continued to press the applicant to accept a transfer and it was made clear to her at a meeting in August 2013 that she had two options; first, to return to Largy College and have a full investigation into the complaints, or second, to accept the transfer to another school where she would be teaching a smaller class. The applicant confirmed in writing that she did not wish to transfer and noted that a return to Largy College would mean she would have to address the complaints that had been made. Further correspondence was exchanged where the applicant confirmed again that she did not wish to transfer and wished to resume her duties.

In an email to the applicant in mid-August 2013, the CEO informed the applicant that he had decided to transfer her to St Mogue's post-primary school with immediate effect. In making the transfer decision, the respondent relied on s 20.1 of memo V7 and characterised the transfer as a 'change in headquarters' for the applicant, the power to exercise which did not depend on Circular 59/2009. The solicitors for the applicant wrote to the CEO calling on him to rescind the decision and, when he declined to do so, proceedings issued and the applicant obtained leave for judicial review from Laffoy J on 23 August 2013. As part of the Court's order, the proposed decision to transfer the applicant was stayed until the determination of the application for judicial review.

The respondent's legal advisors advised the applicant in September 2013 that if the applicant continued to insist on a return to Largy College, she would be placed on administrative leave with pay pending the final outcome of proceedings. The Court noted that this was what occurred and the applicant had, up to and including the date of the hearing, remained on administrative leave with pay. Clarification was provided in writing to the applicant that this was a required step, it was not a penalty. The respondent submitted that the legal effect of placing the applicant on administrative leave was to ensure she could continue to draw her full salary without the necessity for her to perform under her contract of employment. The applicant contended that all aspects of the dispute were subject to the terms of Circular 59/2009 and, whilst the Circular did not have statutory force, the applicant was entitled to expect that where a Circular lays down a manner in which a public employer will act in a given set of circumstances, that Circular will apply until varied or altered. Furthermore, reliance was placed on the judgment of Fennelly J in *McGrath v Minister for Defence*[41] in which Fennelly J held that the plaintiff was entitled to invoke the doctrine of legitimate expectation.

---

41.   *McGrath v Minister for Defence* [2010] 1 IR 560.

Kearns P stated that it was quite clear that by its conduct in supplying the applicant with a copy of Circular 59/2009 and in stating that it would apply Circular 59/2009, the VEC did create the expectation, at least at the outset, that the various stages of Circular 59/2009 would be applicable in her case. However, Kearns P noted that in this case, the process never got beyond the informal stage and this was a result of the applicant's own conduct, decisions and changes of mind. The Court noted that the meeting in February 2013 was proceeding towards an informal solution of the applicant's problems when she collapsed the process. The Court noted that in furnishing a note to her trade union representative to say she felt suicidal and later disavowing her willingness to engage in the form of teaching under discussion, she, albeit unintentionally, exacerbated the difficulties faced by the respondent, who had an unusually high number of complaints to deal with insofar as this teacher was concerned. Thereafter, the applicant sought and obtained a transfer to another school and after careful consideration the respondents agreed to facilitate the applicant by arranging a transfer for her to a smaller school, which it was felt would provide her with an opportunity to make a fresh start. The Court stated it was unfortunate that the applicant resiled from her decision, bringing about a situation where the current stalemate arose. The Court noted that the respondents were left with an unresolved significant problem where the competence of the applicant had been called into question and where numerous complaints remained to be resolved. Instead of returning to the processes contained in Circular 59/2009, the respondents opted to place the applicant on administrative leave with full pay.

The Court said it was safe to say at this stage that the informal processes in Stage 1 of the Circular had failed. The Court noted that the respondent had found itself in an extremely unusual situation in August 2013, where it had genuine concerns regarding the mental health of the applicant and the impact it was having on the operation and functioning of the school and her competence in that regard. The Court noted that the school chaplain had received a number of informal expressions of concern from the applicant's colleagues regarding her mental health.

The Court stated that it was necessary to consider the validity of the two decisions by the respondent which the applicant sought to impugn. Firstly, the Court noted that the applicant has complained that the decision to transfer her should be construed as meaning that the complaints against her were made out and amounted in the circumstances to a penalty. The Court noted that the decision was prompted by the applicant's own request and noted the terms of memo V7, which permitted the headquarters of a teacher to be changed from one centre to another. Kearns P noted that the power had been exercised and the applicant did not challenge the decision on the basis that her terms and conditions of employment had not been adhered to by virtue of an absence of notice or consultation. Kearns P stated it was not open to him to determine as a point of appeal whether the decision was the correct one in the particular circumstances.

The Court caveated that the view could be taken that a 'pass the parcel' solution to a problem of this nature may be open to question and made reference to recent Church scandals which led to the relocation of persons with particular difficulties. The Court noted it did not have to make any merit based adjudication on the decision, but confirmed it had heard no evidence to suggest that the plaintiff's remuneration, pension or other entitlements would suffer any reduction by virtue of any such transfer and so it altogether failed to understand how the particular decision could be construed as a penalty having regard to the fact that it was the solution proposed by the applicant herself. Whilst holding that the terms of the Circular did not apply to the latter stages of this matter, the Court held that it was clear from the general principles therein that the placing of a teacher on administrative leave with full pay, pending an investigation, is permissible where the circumstances warrant. The Court was satisfied that the circumstances of this case warranted, and mandated, such a decision. The Court noted it would have been quite unrealistic to allow the applicant to return to teaching duties without a full resolution of the complaints. The interests of the school, its students and more particularly the applicant herself, required no less.

The Court noted that the placing of an employee on administrative leave does not depend on any particular circular, nor does it amount to a punitive decision. The applicant's suspension was not initially resorted to by the respondent. It was only when the applicant had insisted on returning to her role in Largy College that it became necessary and was stated at the time clearly as being non-punitive in nature. The Court was satisfied that the applicant was at all material times fully aware of the reasons for her being placed on paid administrative leave. The Court noted its decision in *Morgan v Trinity College*[42] where it had to consider whether suspension was punitive in nature. Kearns P considered his own judgment in that case and stated that the considerations in that case must apply where the interests of parents and children in a teaching context are concerned. The suspension or the placing of persons such as the applicant on administrative leave in such a case is merely done by way of good administration. A situation had arisen in this case that demanded something be done and the applicant could not be allowed to resume teaching duties as though nothing had happened.

The Court held against the applicant on both grounds and noted that it was a great pity that she had not availed of the solution offered to her. The Court noted the applicant had suffered significantly from depression and other difficulties involving a considerable amount of medical intervention. While the medical evidence appeared to have shown that the applicant was recovering from her psychological difficulties, the Court held that any resumption of her teaching duties at Largy College could only occur or be allowed once the complaints against her had been resolved appropriately. The Court noted that in this regard, the provisions of the Circular seemed singularly inappropriate to address the particular facts of this case, but noted that any investigation undertaken would have to afford fair procedures to the applicant and conform with the principles of natural and constitutional justice.

[2.21] ***McMahon v The Irish Aviation Authority (respondent) and the Irish Parachute Club (notice party)*[43] *– High Court – judicial review – whether suspension of applicant from his post as club chief instructor with the Irish Parachute Club by officials of the***

---

42. *Morgan v Trinity College Dublin* [2003] 3 IR 159.
43. *McMahon v The Irish Aviation Authority and the Irish Parachute Club* [2014] IEHC 431.

Irish Aviation Authority valid – duration of suspension and impact on applicant's good name

The applicant in these proceedings held the position of club chief instructor with the Irish Parachute Club Ltd ('IPC') prior to his suspension from that post by officials of the Irish Aviation Authority. The club chief instructor is the person primarily responsible for ensuring the general safety of both participants in the sport of parachuting and also the general public.

Hogan J noted that IPC was a limited company authorised by the Irish Aviation Authority to conduct a parachute operation under a statutory instrument. One of the conditions attached to the licence deals with the position of post-holders and stipulated a series of important safety and operational requirements, to include the reporting of any incident or accident involving injury to any party involved in a parachuting operation to the Air Accident Investigation Unit of the Department of Transport and the Flight Operations Department of the Irish Aviation Authority. Hogan J noted that the respondent was responsible for the management of Irish controlled airspace, the safety regulation of Irish Civil Aviation and the oversight of the Civil Aviation Security. Article 7.1 of the Irish Aviation Authority (Rules of the Air) Order 2004[44] prohibits descent by parachute, save in cases of an emergency, without the appropriate permission from the authorities.

The IPC was granted permission by the respondent to permit individuals to drop from aircraft in various forms of parachuting subject to strict conditions.

The event that gave rise to these proceedings arose in July 2012. An experienced parachutist was injured following a hard landing. The individual sustained a broken ankle and torn ligaments in his left leg requiring hospitalisation and surgery. He originally made a complaint to the chairman of the Parachute Association of Ireland. The essence of his complaint was that he was due to jump with three other wingsuit jumpers on the fifth load. However, jumping was delayed due to bad weather conditions. After a delay, the fourth load took off, at which point the applicant came to the jumpers as they left the hangar and told them bad weather was approaching. The injured party (Mr de Khors) gave evidence in a detailed narrative which is set out by Hogan J in his judgment to the effect that there was a clear sky when the plane took off. He noted that the applicant did not stand down the load. The non-winged jumpers exited the aircraft, as is normal practice. The wingsuit jumpers continued on to be dropped further from the spot for a normal freefall. In a detailed narrative, Mr de Khors set out that he prepared to do a parachute landing fall because he anticipated a hard landing. He felt pain in his ankle on impacting the ground.

Hogan J noted that a parachute landing fall was a safety technique used by parachutists to cushion the effect of a hard landing by spreading the shock across the body. Hogan J noted that the rest of the complaint was directed to the suggestion that the response time of 45 to 55 minutes before an ambulance was called was too long. It was asserted by Mr de Khors that the applicant had failed in his duties and was in breach of the operations manual of the Parachute Association of Ireland in a number of material

---

44.   Irish Aviation Authority (Rules of the Air) Order 2004 (SI 72/2004).

respects. In a detailed letter, the applicant responded and noted that he had conveyed the worsening weather forecast to the wingsuiters before they boarded the aircraft to enable them to make a better decision as to how they wished to proceed with their intended jump. Hogan J noted that, for reasons that were unclear, the complaint was not processed by the Parachute Association of Ireland. In any event, Mr de Khors subsequently contacted the respondent in early 2013 and made a complaint regarding this incident. Hogan J stated that while the focus of the complaint was directed at the response time of the applicant and the time it took for the ambulance to arrive, the Irish Aviation Authority's investigators were ultimately more exercised by the operations and other features of the applicant's decision-making and judgment.

In his complaint, Mr de Khors attached his earlier correspondence with both the respondent and the Parachute Association of Ireland regarding his earlier complaint. He also made reference to another incident which he maintained was of similar character which happened in August 2012. Following receipt of the correspondence, an aeronautical officer attached to the respondent wrote to the applicant asking for his response to the complaints. He drew attention to the incidents involving both individuals and enquired whether these matters were under investigation by the Parachute Association of Ireland. Attention was also drawn to the reporting obligations in IPC's operating licence.

Hogan J noted the response of the applicant, which acknowledged the failure of IPC to report the incidents and contained an apology for the omissions. The applicant provided a response as regards both incidents and noted that there had been a rule change since the incident where parachutists were now required to carry mobile phones and to identify their location if they landed off the drop zone.

The applicant and the chairperson of the Safety & Training Committee of the Parachute Association of Ireland were invited to meetings with the Irish Aviation Authority on 19 February 2013, which occurred separately and in sequence. Hogan J noted that, by this time, the Irish Aviation Authority had received information to the effect that there had been a low flying incident at the IPC's airfield in January 2013, together with a photograph of this incident. The Irish Aviation Authority had concluded that this incident amount to flying an aircraft in a reckless manner, contrary to art 2 of the Irish Aviation Authority (Rules of the Air) Order 2004.[45] Hogan J noted that this incident was put to the applicant in the course of the meeting, although he had no previous notice of the complaint and his response was that he was unaware of it, even though he accepted he was at the airfield on the day in question.

A decision was taken to suspend both the applicant and another person, following which the applicant requested a meeting with the directors of the respondent. At that meeting, the directors were informed that applicant had been suspended from his position as club chief instructor, the practical effect of which was that IPC could not operate parachuting operations with its existing permission, as one of the conditions of that permission was that the applicant act as club chief instructor. IPC also learned that the respondent was investigating certain complaints concerning the way in which tIPC was conducting its operations. An emergency meeting of IPC was convened and Hogan

---

45.   Irish Aviation Authority (Rules of the Air) Order 2004 (SI 72/2004).

J noted that the directors were very exercised by the manner in which the suspensions had been imposed, but the IPC could not comply with the terms of its permission in the absence of its nominated chief pilot and its club chief instructor, the applicant. A few days later, IPC received a letter from the respondent to the effect that it was prohibited from conducting parachuting operations without appointing a chief pilot and a temporary club chief instructor acceptable to the respondent. Hogan J noted that this presented IPC with a considerable dilemma. He further noted that IPC had held both men in the highest regard and it gave serious consideration as to whether it should commence judicial review proceedings against the respondent. However, it reluctantly yielded to the realities of the situation and a new chief pilot and new chief club instructor were then nominated by IPC, which were approved by the respondent in March 2013. Hogan J noted that the respondent was confronted with three separate incidents in considering the decision to suspend; the de Khors complaint, the previous injury and the low flight incident, which together with the reporting failures all gave rise to concerns.

Hogan J noted that the actual permission which had been issued by the respondent provided that it was operative unless varied, suspended or revoked. The first schedule to the permission designated the applicant as the club chief instructor. Paragraph 15 of the permission provided that the permission might be suspended, varied or revoked at any time. Hogan J held there was no doubt that the the the respondent enjoyed the power of suspension in respect of the identity of the club chief instructor post-holder. As with any statutory power of this kind, the discretion conferred had to be exercised in a manner which respected the *East Donegal* principles.[46] Hogan J summarised that this meant that the respondent must generally respect fair procedures and ensure that its decisions are: (1) *bona fide*; (2) factually sustainable; and (3) not unreasonable. Hogan J stated that the extent to which a person is entitled to fair procedures prior to the imposition of a suspension will generally depend on the overall circumstances and the context in which the action has been taken. He held that the necessity for urgent action, the nature of the suspension, its implications for the good name of the person concerned and above all, its duration, were critical factors. He further noted that if the suspension is in the nature of a purely holding suspension, which has been imposed to enable an urgent enquiry to take place, then any obligation to abide by fair procedures prior to its imposition may be attenuated or may even not apply at all. Hogan J noted that in some sporting situations, a suspension might not be regarded as having particularly serious implications for the suspended person. In this regard, he referenced Kearns J in *Morgan v Trinity College Dublin*[47] when he observed that 'a professional footballer might not regard a suspension, even a lengthy one, as being particularly detrimental or damaging to career reputation'.

Hogan J distinguished that from the present case where the suspension was of an altogether different character, even if it also concerned the operation of a sporting organisation. Hogan J held that it was much more akin to a suspension imposed in an employment context than the type of routine, everyday suspensions in the sporting arena of the kind to which Kearns P alluded in *Morgan*. The impact of the suspension meant

---

46.   *East Donegal Co-Operative Livestock Mart Ltd v Attorney General* [1970] IR 317.
47.   *Morgan v Trinity College Dublin* [2003] IEHC 167.

that the applicant was obliged to stand down from a prestigious position which meant everything to him and that position had to be filled. His prospects of being appointed to that post again could not be regarded as high. Hogan J further noted that this type of suspension had considerable implications for the good name of the person affected. He noted that many might reasonably think that this suspension had been implemented because of concerns that the applicant had taken a casual or even irresponsible attitude to the vital question of air safety or that he improperly yielded to commercial pressures in allowing flights to take off where the weather conditions were doubtful or hazardous. However, Hogan J also acknowledged that the complaint placed the respondent in a difficult position, as parachuting was a hazardous sport where there was little room for error. The Court held that any consideration of the fair procedures question must be coloured by this general background. In the case of a hazardous activity, such as parachuting, the regulatory authority must be allowed the widest possible degree of flexibility when it came to taking urgent action in the interests of safety.

Hogan J held the respondent was presented with three serious complaints and if these complaints were ultimately substantiated, then those who participated in parachute jumping at the IPC site may face unacceptable risk. He held that the need to take urgent action to investigate these complaints, and above all to ensure air safety was not compromised meant that the State's obligation to fully protect and vindicate the applicant's right to a good name was circumscribed in the first instance. He stated it was probably sufficient to say that even if there was an obligation to hold a hearing prior to the imposition of the initial suspension, the respondent complied with that basic obligation having regard to the fact that it must be allowed to take urgent action in the first instance.

Hogan J was critical of the hearing that did take place in February 2013 and stated it was less than perfect. The Court held that if action such as suspension was under consideration, fair procedures would normally have required that the applicant be given advance notice in writing of the specific grounds of complaint or concern so he would know in broad terms the case which he had to meet. The Court made specific reference to the low-flying incident and stated that if this was of fundamental concern to the respondent, then fair procedures would normally dictate that advance notice be given of this, rather than simply introducing it for the first time at the meeting. However, Hogan J concluded that in view of the fact that the respondent must have the necessary freedom to take urgent action in the interests of public safety and having regard to the hazardous nature of the activities which it regulates, it was entitled in the first instance, in line with the comments of O'Higgins CJ in *The State (Lynch) v Cooney*,[48] to take urgent action and suspend the applicant in these circumstances.

The Court then considered the duration of the suspension and noted that, had it lasted days or perhaps a matter of weeks, then no objection could have been taken to the attenuated fashion in which fair procedures had been followed in this case. However, he noted that this is not what had occurred. The suspension had lasted from February 2013 until the date of the hearing in June 2014. Hogan J stated that, viewed objectively, a

---

48. *The State (Lynch) v Cooney* [1982] IR 337 at 380: 'The time was short and a decision was urgent, there was no opportunity for debate or parley.'

suspension of this duration could not realistically be regarded as a purely holding mechanism, not least given that the underlying facts were not – at least so far as the question of whether the applicant was fit to remain in his position as club chief instructor is concerned – unduly complex. He noted that there was clear authority to the effect that a lengthy suspension would be rendered invalid, especially if that delay is prejudicial to the applicant.[49] Hogan J concluded that the delay had been considerable, stretching well beyond any period necessary to get to the bottom of the basic facts of the matter so as to allay any possible safety concerns. He noted the suspension had some financial implications for the applicant, but most of all it had the effect of seriously affecting the applicant's constitutional right to a good name and dashing a cherished ambition of his, which were matters prejudicial in and of themselves.

Hogan J also noted that the reasons given for suspension have to be factually sustainable. He noted that the respondent was clearly unwilling to accept the applicant's explanations regarding the failure to keep a proper documentary record of safety incidents or to report these to the respondent and it was similarly likewise unimpressed by the applicant's explanations regarding the low-flying incident. He stated that it could not be said that these particular reasons were not factually sustainable in the context of a holding suspension, pending a fuller hearing with adequate notice and an opportunity to call evidence. However, he noted that one of the key reasons for the suspension was not factually sustainable, at least in the present form. He observed that the question of whether the applicant gave the appropriate warning to the pilot and to the jumpers was of critical importance in the respondent's assessment of whether a suspension was necessary. Hogan J concluded that the respondent's reasoning and conclusions could not stand for the following reasons. It was implicit that the respondent doubted whether the applicant had given the appropriate warnings regarding the weather. Hogan J noted that Mr de Khors himself had acknowledged that such a warning had been given. There was no evidence which could justify the respondent's conclusion that the applicant's decision not to ground the flight may have been influenced by commercial consideration. Hogan J further noted that none of these matters was put to the applicant. While it may have been that the weather conditions were so generally unsuitable that the respondent considered the flight should not have been permitted to take off, this was never put to the applicant.

In conclusion, Hogan J stated that the respondent's decision to suspend could not be impugned on the grounds that fair procedures were not perfectly observed. Given the obvious importance of aviation safety, the obligation to ensure fair procedures had to yield, in the first instance, to the respondent's necessary entitlement to take urgent action in aid of the fundamental objectives. However, this could not justify a lengthy suspension. It was to be expected that the respondent would act with all due speed to ensure that complaints are investigated fully, promptly and fairly. The Court concluded that this did not happen here given that the reasons for the suspension so obviously affected the good name of the applicant and the suspension itself has lasted for well over a year.

---

49.   *Flynn v An Post* [1987] IR 68.

Hogan J concluded that whilst the respondent was entitled to act in a summary fashion in order to protect public safety, as happened in this case, if it so acts by suspension then it is obliged to ensure that there is a fuller hearing which complies with the requirements of fair procedures (including adequate notice to all concerned), within a relatively short space of time. The proper protection of the constitutional right to a good name demands no less. Hogan J concluded that this did not happen in the present case and for that reason the suspension had become invalid.

Chapter 3

DATA PROTECTION

INTRODUCTION

[3.01] The year 2014 has been an interesting one for data protection. The post-Snowden controversy in respect of transfers of personal data from the European Union to the United States and in respect of the alleged unfettered access by US state entities to the data of EU citizens has continued. This controversy is likely to also have had a bearing on the two most important decisions for data protection that have been issued in recent years, ie the decisions of the CJEU in the Google 'right to be forgotten' case and on the illegality of the laws obliging telecommunications companies to retain all communications traffic data for a period of two years. The Irish High Court has also considered the adequacy of Safe Harbor as a mechanism to legitimise transfers of personal data from the European Union to the United States and has requested that the CJEU consider the issue. This will form part of the wider European Commission review of the use of 'Safe Harbor', and companies that rely upon this mechanism to effect the transfer of employee data to the United States may see some changes to this mechanism over the coming year, albeit likely in the form of its revision rather than its abolition.

The CJEU has also issued a decision on the scope of personal data under data access requests that will be of interest to employers in the context of data access requests made by employees and former employees.

Overall, 2014 has seen the roles of arts 7 and 8 of the Charter of Fundamental Rights of the European Union, on data protection and privacy rights, as human rights in EU law, as firmly established in the CJEU case law on data privacy. Once again, the concepts of proportionality and transparency have been identified as important principles for data protection compliance. These concepts are particularly important in an employment context, where consent, the generally relied upon 'legitimiser' for the processing of personal data, is considered by the Office of the Data Protection Commissioner as an inappropriate basis upon which to process employee data. In circumstances where employee privacy rights are potentially prejudiced, adherence to these principles will be of paramount importance.

RELEVANT LEGISLATION
Enforced subject access now an offence

[3.02] The remaining un-commenced sections of the Data Protection Acts 1988 and 2003 (the DPA) were brought into force by the Minister for Justice and Equality with effect from 18 July 2014.[1]

---

1. SIs 337/2014 and 338/2014.

The effect of SI 338/2014 was to commence the operation of the s 4(13) of the DPA. This provision makes it unlawful for employers to require employees or applicants for employment to make an access request seeking copies of personal data which is then made available to the employer or prospective employer. This provision also applies to any person who engages another person to provide such a service. While the section was on the statute books for many years without being commenced, the offence has now been established, reflecting the fact that enhanced Garda vetting laws and procedures are now available under the National Vetting Bureau (Children and Vulnerable Persons) Act 2012.

CASE LAW

[3.03] *Data Protection Commissioner v MCK Rentals Ltd, Stuart and Martin – Bray District Court, 6 October 2014 – first successful prosecution under s 22 and s 29 of DPA – accessing personal data without prior authority of data controller – personal conviction of directors*

On 6 October 2014, the Data Protection Commissioner successfully brought the first prosecution under s 22 of the DPA. A private investigation firm, MCK Rentals Ltd (trading as MCK Investigations), was charged with 23 counts of breaches of s 22 of the DPA, which states that it is an offence to obtain access to personal data without the prior authority of the data controller or data processor by whom the data is kept, and to subsequently disclose this data to another person.

The two directors of MCK Rentals Ltd were separately charged in the District Court with 23 counts of breaches of s 29 of the DPA. Section 29 provides for the prosecution of company directors where an offence by a company is proved to have been committed with the consent or connivance of, or to be attributable to any neglect on the part of the company directors or other officers.

The data controllers of the personal data in question were the Department of Social Protection and the Health Service Executive (HSE). The defendants had been engaged by credit unions to unearth the new addresses of credit union debtors who were in arrears. To assist the defendants in this, the credit unions disclosed personal data of the debtors, including PPS numbers and dates of birth, to the defendants. The defendants then contacted employees of the Department of Social Protection and the HSE to obtain the new addresses using 'blagging' techniques. The defendants then passed this personal data to their credit union clients.

MCK Rentals Ltd pleaded guilty to five sample charges for offences under s 22 of the DPA. The District Court convicted the company in respect of each of the five charges and imposed a fine of €1,500 per offence. The directors both pleaded guilty to one sample charge for an offence under s 29 of the DPA. The Court convicted them both and imposed fines of €1,500 for those offences. This is the first occasion where individual company officers have been found to be criminally liable for breach of the DPA.

[3.04] *YS v Minister voor Immigratie, Integratie en Asiel[2] and Minister voor Immigratie, Integratie en Asiel v M and S[3] – References for preliminary ruling – CJEU – concept of personal data –scope of right of access of data subject*

On 17 July 2014, the CJEU gave a preliminary ruling that a requester who submits a data access request is not entitled to the entire document in which his or her personal data is contained, as the data that is subject to release only extends to personal data. In this instance, legal analysis contained within a document was held to not constitute personal data and did not fall within the scope of the request.

The requests for preliminary ruling concerned the interpretation of arts 2(a), 12(a) and 13(1)(d),(f) and (g) of Directive 95/46/EC on the protection of individuals with regard to the processing of personal data and on the free movement of such data and of arts 8(2) and 41(2)(b) of the Charter of Fundamental Rights of the European Union.

The claimants, who were asylum seekers in the Netherlands, had made a request to the Immigration and Naturalisation Service (INS) for a copy of the internal memorandum which explained the reasoning behind each draft decision of an INS case officer on an application for residence. Generally minutes contain personal information relating to a residence applicant, including name, date of birth, nationality, gender, ethnicity and religion, as well as the legal provisions which are applicable and a legal analysis of the assessment of the application in light of these legal provisions. The INS had provided the individuals with a summary of the personal data contained in the minutes but had refused to disclose the full minutes or legal analysis.

The CJEU ruled that, whilst the legal analysis contained personal data under art 2(a) of Directive 95/46/EC, such as applicant's name, date of birth, nationality, gender, ethnicity, religion and language, the legal analysis itself is not personal data. The CJEU held that extending the right of access to that legal analysis would serve the purpose of guaranteeing a right of access to administrative documents, which is not covered by Directive 95/46/EC and would not guarantee the protection of the applicants' right to privacy with regard to the processing of data relating to them.

The CJEU gave guidance on what information data controllers are obliged to provide in response to data access requests. It held that as long as the response is 'intelligible', in other words it allows the data subject to become aware of the data and to check that they are accurate and processed in compliance with Directive 95/46/EC, an organisation will satisfy its duty. The CJEU reiterated that art 12(a) of the Directive and art 8(2) of the Charter of the Fundamental Rights of the European Union do not grant the data subject a right to obtain a copy of the document of the original file in which the data appears.

CASE STUDIES OF THE OFFICE OF THE DATA PROTECTION COMMISSIONER (ODPC)

[3.05] Five case studies relevant to the workplace were published by the ODPC in its 25th Annual Report. Two of these related to the use of CCTV in the workplace. In

---

2. *YS v Minister voor Immigratie, Integratie en Asiel* (Case C–141/12).
3. *Minister voor Immigratie, Integratie en Asiel v M and S* (Case C–372/12).

addition to the decisions discussed below, employers should be mindful of the Guidance Note issued by the ODPC and available on its website[4] in respect of the use of CCTV in the workplace generally and the importance of proportionality and transparency in its use.

[3.06] *Case Study 8 of 2013 – CCTV images of staff member unlawfully transmitted to third parties – security of CCTV data*

The complainant was an employee of a Spar store and brought a complaint to the ODPC concerning the alleged further processing of her personal data, as contained in CCTV footage captured in her place of work. CCTV footage of the complainant sustaining an injury at the workplace was accessed by another staff member, copied and circulated to third parties. The complainant contended that this was a breach of s 2(1)(c)(ii) of the DPA, as the use of CCTV within the shop was for security purposes.

On investigation, Spar admitted this action constituted a breach of store policy, for which the relevant employees were disciplined. Spar acknowledged the error and issued an apology.

The ODPC was satisfied that this action on the part of the employees was a clear contravention of s 2(1)(c)(ii) of the DPA when CCTV footage was accessed, copied and circulated by staff for a purpose unrelated to those purposes for which the data was obtained. The ODPC noted that data controllers should be constantly vigilant to ensure that CCTV footage of individuals is processed only for its intended purpose, is restricted from access by staff who have no business need to access it and that all managerial staff handle such footage with the level of care that is expected for the processing of personal data generally.

[3.07] *Case Study 9 of 2013 – data controller legitimately uses CCTV in disciplinary proceedings – legitimate interests*

The ODPC received a complaint, which included an allegation that the complainant's employers viewed three weeks of CCTV footage to ground disciplinary charges against the complainant relating to alleged irregularities in the cash management process in the store. The store's policy on CCTV was to 'protect against inventory loss by criminal actions'.

In order to ensure that the CCTV was not overwritten, the CCTV footage in question had been removed by its authorised contractor to a regional distribution centre for inspection, where it was securely held and only reviewed by employees appointed to conduct the investigation. The employer informed the ODPC that the contents of CCTV footage were explained verbally to the complainant to allow him to explain the irregularities in the cash handling process. Furthermore, the complainant was afforded the opportunity to view the entire footage in line with fair HR policies and proceedings.

Although the CCTV footage did not of itself determine the outcome of the disciplinary process, which found that the employee had not engaged in fraudulent or

---

4.   www.dataprotection.ie.

criminal behaviour, the complainant maintained that the amount of CCTV footage viewed was excessive and disproportionate. The employer maintained that this was necessary due to the 'complex and serious nature' of the irregularities in question.

The key issue that arose for consideration under the DPA was whether the supermarket acted in accordance with the requirements of the DPA when it processed CCTV footage containing images of the complainant. The ODPC referred to s 2A(1)(d) of the DPA, which provides that a data controller should not process personal data unless:

> the processing is necessary for the purposes of the legitimate interests pursued by the data controller or by a third party or parties to whom the data are disclosed, except where the processing is unwarranted in any particular case by reason of prejudice to the fundamental rights and freedoms of the data subject.

The ODP10C considered that when the supermarket viewed the CCTV footage, it did so in the pursuit of its own legitimate interests and that this was *not* unwarranted by reason of prejudice to the fundamental rights and freedoms or legitimate interests of the data subject, and thus the ODPC was unable to conclude that a contravention of the DPA took place in this instance.

[3.08] *Case Study 10 of 2013 – breaches by hotel in use of photographs of employees in dismissal cases – use of clandestine techniques in processing personal data*

The ODPC received separate complaints concerning the alleged unfair processing of personal data from two former employees of a hotel in Dublin in relation to similar incidents which occurred six months apart. The complainants worked as night porters and were dismissed for allegedly sleeping on duty. In both cases, the evidence used to ground the disciplinary proceedings were photographs taken by the assistant night manager on his personal mobile phone.

In response to an enquiry from the ODPC, the hotel stated that it did not request or condone any employee taking photographs of another employee without their knowledge. Although the hotel admitted that the photograph had been provided to the director of operations and the human resources officer, the hotel specified that the findings of the investigation were based on the report of the assistant night manager and not on the photograph, and that the complainant had given a statement and did not deny the allegation. In any event, the ODPC believed that this photograph was likely unfairly obtained by the hotel, and requested that the photograph be destroyed and that the employer make no use of it in the disciplinary proceedings against the employee concerned.

It subsequently transpired that an electronic version of the photograph had been seen by other members of staff and was used against a complainant and recorded in the minutes of the investigative hearing. The ODPC formed the opinion that the personal data (the photograph of each complainant) was unfairly obtained and unfairly processed by the hotel in contravention of s 2(1)(a) of the DPA.

[3.09] *Case Study 11 of 2013 – incorrect application of s 4(4A) to restrict access to personal data – expressions of opinion given in confidence*

In this case study, an employee of a media organisation complained that that he had not been provided with a copy of all of his personal data as the organisation had withheld some personal data, in this case, an email, citing s 4(4A) on the basis that it considered that the data consisted of an expression of opinion given in confidence. Section 4(4A)(a) provides as follows:

> Where personal data relating to a data subject consists of an expression of opinion about the data subject by another person, the data may be disclosed to the data subject without obtaining the consent of that person to the disclosure ...

but this is subject to s 4(4A)(b)(ii) of the DPA which dis-applies the right of access if the expression of opinion was 'given in confidence or on the understanding that it could be treated as confidential'.

The ODPC issued a reminder that an opinion given in confidence or on the understanding that it will be kept confidential 'must satisfy a high threshold of confidentiality'. In particular, the ODPC has warned that simply placing the word 'confidential' on the document or communication in question will not automatically render the data confidential. The ODPC has noted that in situations in which this exemption is relied upon, it will assess the data in its context and will need to be satisfied that the data would not otherwise have been given but for this understanding. Of particular relevance to employers is the reiteration of the ODPC's position that supervisors and managers will not normally be able to rely on s 4(4A) to restrict access as 'it is an expected part of their role to give opinions on staff which they should be capable of standing over'. The ODPC has also stated however that 'a colleague who reports a matter relating to an individual in confidence to a supervisor or manager could be expected to be protected by the confidentiality provision'. However, the exemption only covers the actual opinion.

In this instance, the ODPC found that, while the opinion did not issue from the complainant's manager, it did issue from someone in a position of authority and the email was sent in the context of that position. In that regard, the ODPC advised that the data in question must be released.

[3.10] *Case Study 15 of 2013 – client list taken by ex-employee to new employer – fair use of personal data – client consent to direct marketing*

The ODPC received a complaint from an individual in relation to receipt of unsolicited correspondence to her home address from a company with whom she had no business relationship. This arose from a new employee of that company having taken the personal and financial details of his or her previous employer's clients to the new employer.

The ODPC found that the new employer did not have consent, as required by the DPA and reg 13 of SI 336/2011,[5] to send direct marketing communications to this client

---

5. European Communities (Electronic Communications Networks and Services) (Privacy and Electronic Communications) Regulations 2011 (SI 336/2011).

list. As a result of this finding, the client list was subsequently destroyed by the new employer. The previous employer sent a data breach notification to the ODPC in respect of the removal of this client list by its former employee in accordance with the ODPC's Data Breach Code of Practice.

This case study highlights the importance of ensuring that, when an employee departs his or her employment, security measures are in place to ensure that he or she does not remove personal data, for which the employer is the data controller, as such an action constitutes a data breach. Similarly, employers who hire an employee from a competitor must ensure that the client list which he or she may take to the new employer has not been procured in breach of the DPA, as the new employer will not have consent to the processing of personal data that was provided by those clients to the previous employer, particularly where the new employer sends direct marketing communications to individuals on the client list. Any such actions could give rise to a prosecution of the new employer and it is important to ensure that all databases in use for direct marketing are the subject of a valid marketing consent to receive communications from that sender.

GUIDE TO AUDIT PROCESS

[3.11] The ODPC has revised its 2009 Guide to Audit Process (the Guide) which is designed to assist organisations selected for audit by the ODPC. The Guide, published in August 2014, has been updated to take account of legislative developments since 2009 and to reflect changes in the approach of the ODPC to the audit process. This should be consulted by companies in preparation for an audit.

DATA PROTECTION COMMISSIONER

[3.12] In September 2014, the Government announced the appointment of Ms Helen Dixon as Data Protection Commissioner. Ms Dixon has succeeded Mr Billy Hawkes, who has retired.

Chapter 4

EMPLOYMENT EQUALITY

PRELIMINARY ISSUES

Extensions of time limits

[4.01] *Complaint by a teacher against a school board of management[1] – direction under Employment Equality Acts 1998 to 2011, s 77(5) – Equality Tribunal – whether time limits for bringing valid complaint of discrimination or victimisation should be extended for reasonable cause*

The claimant referred a complaint to the Equality Tribunal on 29 January 2013 alleging that the respondent discriminated against her on gender grounds on or before 25 June 2012 by having improperly failed to offer her teaching hours to which she was entitled. The complainant had originally submitted a complaint on 24 December 2012 naming the Department of Education and Skills as her employer. She stated she had been misled by the Tribunal's online form, which she claimed stated that her employer was the entity that produced her P60. The Department returned correspondence from the Tribunal in January 2013 stating that the employer was the principal of the school, and the Equality Tribunal confirmed this in writing to the complainant on 24 January 2013. The complainant responded with a withdrawal of the original complaint on 25 January 2013 and the subsequent complaint which was received on 29 January 2013.

The Equality Tribunal noted the requirements imposed by s 77(5)(b) of the Acts that where reasonable cause can be shown, the Director may extend the period in which the complainant may refer a complaint to the Tribunal. The Equality Tribunal noted the views of the High Court on extending time where there is 'good reason to do so' in *O'Donnell v Dun Laoghaire Corporation.*[2] The Equality Tribunal also noted the Labour Court decision in *Elephant Haulage Ltd v Juska*[3] that:

> in considering if reasonable cause existed it is for the Claimant to show that there are reasons which both explain the delay and offer and excuse for the delay. The explanation must be reasonable that is to say it must make sense, be agreeable to reason and must not be irrational or absurd.

The Equality Tribunal noted that the complaint was referred over four weeks outside the time limit and concluded that the delay was entirely due to an administrative error on the part of the complainant in naming the wrong employer in the original complaint. The Equality Tribunal noted that this error arose as the complainant had mistakenly complied with an information guide note attached to the complaint form which suggested that, in order to correctly identify an employer, the complainant should check

---

1.   *Complaint by a teacher against a school board of management* DIR–E2014–002.
2.   *O'Donnell v Dun Laoghaire Corporation* [1991] ILRM 301.
3.   *Elephant Haulage Ltd v Juska* EET082.

their P45 and/or P60 tax certificate for the correct employer name. The Equality Tribunal noted that the complainant had acted promptly to issue a new claim form as soon as she became aware there was an issue with the party she had named as her employer. It was further noted that the four-week delay between issuing of the two complaints was mostly due to the Christmas period falling during that time and thus the Equality Tribunal held that the complainant had showed reasonable cause and extended the time limit.

[4.02] *Complaint by retail assistant against an employer[4] – Equality Tribunal – direction under Employment Equality Acts 1998 to 2011, s 77(5) – whether time limits for bringing valid complaint of discrimination or victimisation should be extended for reasonable cause – complainant medically certified to be suffering from depression and anxiety which impacted on her ability to make claim during required period*

This complaint was one of harassment and it was received on 2 September 2013. The date of the most recent occurrence of the alleged discriminatory action was stated to be 28 February 2013, outside the six months stipulated in the Acts. Evidence was given by the complainant, including medical certification from the complainant's doctor that the complainant was suffering from depression and anxiety from February to August 2013:

> This impacted significantly on her ability to make decisions and to concentrate and therefore she would have been medically not in a position to make a claim of unfair dismissal.

Further evidence was given by the complainant that she had been on sick leave for an extended period and that the termination of her employment had worsened her medical conditions and left her unable to comprehend her rights at the time. Correspondence was received from the respondent contesting many of the points raised.

The Equality Tribunal concluded that the original complaint was referred six days outside the time limit and that the complainant's reason for the delay was due to a mental health issue as she was impeded by the pressure and anxiety allegedly caused by the respondent's actions. The Equality Tribunal noted that the complainant had produced medical certification to confirm that she was not medically in a position to make a claim during the required period, and thus concluded that the complainant had shown reasonable cause and extended the time limit.

Dismissal of claim for being misconceived

[4.03] *An Employer v A Worker[5] – Labour Court – Industrial Relations Acts 1946 to 2012 – Employment Equality Acts 1998 to 2011, s 77(a)(2A) – appeal of decision of Equality Officer where case dismissed for being misconceived – issues between parties subject of settlement agreement where agreed payment delayed but ultimately*

---

4.   *Complaint by retail assistant against an employer* DIR–E2014–001.
5.   *An Employer v A Worker* EDA 1423.

paid – whether complainant entitled to bring claim of sexual harassment on grounds of gender in circumstances where she accepted the delayed payment in full and final settlement of all claims

The complainant brought a claim of sexual harassment against the respondent. In separate proceedings the parties, with the assistance of a Rights Commissioner, reached agreement on settlement terms, to include this complaint under the Employment Equality Acts. In return for withdrawing those proceedings, the respondent agreed to pay the complainant €4,000 within four weeks of the date of agreement. The respondent delayed the payment beyond the agreed period and the complainant's representative wrote to the respondent seeking payment of the agreed sum. The payment was made to the complainant subsequently within five working days and she cashed the cheque six days later. The complainant then sought to continue with the complaint before the Equality Tribunal on grounds that the settlement payment was not made within the agreed four-week period specified in the agreement. The Equality Tribunal dismissed the complaint on the basis that it was misconceived, and this was appealed by the complainant to the Labour Court.

A formal hearing took place at which the complainant stated that, as the settlement agreement had not been strictly complied with by the respondent, she was not bound by the terms limiting her capacity to pursue the complaint to the Tribunal. The respondent acknowledged that the payment had been delayed. However, it argued that the complainant had ultimately accepted the payment and the matter now being pursued had therefore been settled between the parties and there could be no cause of action.

The Labour Court found that the complainant had entered into an agreement to settle the matter before the Court and that that agreement was complied with in all material respects. Once the late payment was drawn to the attention of the respondent, it immediately made good on its obligations under the agreement and the complainant accepted the monies offered in discharge of the obligations of the respondent under the agreement. The Court concluded that it was not now open to the complainant, having taken the benefit of the agreement, to seek to avoid her obligations under the agreement. Accordingly the Labour Court upheld the decision of the Equality Officer.

Protected grounds

Gender

[4.04] *Rafferty v National Educational Welfare Board[6] – Equality Tribunal – Labour Court Appeal – Employment Equality Acts 1998 to 2011 – whether discrimination on grounds of gender in relation to conditions of employment and remuneration – time limits – reasons other than gender for differences in pay*

The complainant was employed by the respondent as an educational welfare officer (EWO). She claimed that she was discriminated against by her employer in relation to

---

6. *Rafferty v National Educational Welfare Board* DEC–E2014–013; *Rafferty v National Educational Welfare Board* EDA Report 38.

conditions of employment on the grounds of gender, that she was victimised by her employer, and that she was entitled to equal remuneration for performing like work with named comparators.

The complainant alleged she was treated differently to six male comparators whose previous experience was recognised and who were accordingly awarded incremental credit. She claimed that the respondent should have recognised her previous experience of providing home tuition to students with behavioural problems and awarded her incremental credit.

The respondent could appoint EWOs above the minimum salary and award incremental credit under two mechanisms. The first mechanism operated by way of a derogation set out in a Department of Finance Circular. This Circular applied to public and civil servants promoted or recruited through internal or external competitions. These employees could be appointed to pay equivalent to their existing pay, plus an additional increment for those promoted internally. The second mechanism applied to appointees who were not previously public or civil servants but who had experience that was considered suitable for the post of EWO. Having considered this prior experience, the respondent could then make a submission to the Department of Education and Science for a sanction to appoint above the minimum salary. This was then forwarded for consideration to the Department of Finance.

The complainant applied for incremental credit under the second mechanism. Her application was rejected by the Department of Finance on 3 November 2009. In April 2011, she became aware that one of her comparators (Mr C) had been placed above the minimum salary. She wrote to the respondent asking not to be treated less favourably than Mr C. The respondent replied on 13 April 2011 confirming 'they could do nothing further'.

The Equality Tribunal decided that the claims of discrimination in relation to conditions of employment and of victimisation were outside of the six-month time limit under s 77(5)(a) of the Employment Equality Acts 1998 to 2011. The Equality Tribunal noted the approach of the UK Court of Appeal in *Cast v Croydon College*.[7] In that case the Court of Appeal stated that:

> a further decision can constitute a separate act of discrimination even though it is made on the same facts as a previous decision, providing that there has been a further consideration to the matter and has not merely reiterated or referred back to the earlier decision.

The Equality Tribunal held that the alleged discrimination and victimisation occurred on 3 November 2009. The claim was therefore outside of the six-month time limit. The reply of 13 April 2011 was a reiteration of the earlier decision rather than a separate occurrence of discrimination and victimisation.

The time limit does not apply to claims for equal remuneration, and so the Equality Tribunal considered the substantive aspects of this claim. The Tribunal emphasised that it was investigating whether the process that led to decisions to award, and refuse, incremental credit was tainted, and not any person's entitlement to such credit.

---

7.   *Cast v Croydon College* [1998] IRLR 318.

The complainant gave evidence of six male comparators who received incremental credit on their appointment. The respondent gave evidence that 67 EWOs were appointed between 2003 and 2009, 54 of whom were female, and 31 of this group were appointed above the minimum salary.

The Equality Tribunal rejected the claim and concluded there were reasons other than gender for the differences in pay between the complainant and her comparators. The Tribunal found no evidence that decisions to award or refuse incremental credit were influenced by gender. While the Tribunal accepted that the respondent did not apply its own guidelines consistently, especially in respect of their interpretation of 'public service', there was no evidence that this inconsistency was influenced by the complainant's gender.

Labour Court Appeal

In a subsequent appeal to the Labour Court, a different outcome was reached.

The Labour Court held that the complainant had established the fact that she had prior service in the amount of 385 days as a teacher in Northern Ireland that she could have expected to have credited to her for the purposes of assimilation to the pay scale. The complainant also established that one of her cited comparators was allowed credit for previous public service. The Labour Court found that there was a presumption that there was discrimination on grounds of age and the burden shifted onto the respondent to prove otherwise.

The Court noted the respondent's reliance on a letter from the Department of Finance in support of its case but held it was not a definitive answer to the questions raised.

If the respondent wished to rely on its statutory requirement to have Departmental sanction to apply additional increments in any individual case, then it must do all that is necessary to bring all relevant facts to the attention of the decision makers, when making an application for permission. Its failure to do so in this case rendered it liable for the consequences of its decision not to provide the relevant information to the relevant Department. The Court noted that the respondent was aware that Mr W, one of the comparators, had been given incremental credit for prior public service, and did not explicitly so advise the Department when requested to do so. The Court held that the respondent could not rely on its incomplete response as objective justification for the decision it took. The Labour Court upheld the appeal and found the complaint to be well founded.

It ordered the respondent to put the complainant on the fourth point of the EWO scale with effect from her appointment and to thereafter progress her through the relevant scale. The Equality Tribunal decision was set aside.

[4.05] *Department of Justice Equality and Law Reform v A Worker[8] – Labour Court – appeal of decision of Equality Tribunal – Industrial Relations Acts 1946 to 2012 –*

---

8. *Department of Justice Equality and Law Reform v A Worker* EDA1422.

Employment Equality Acts 1998 to 2011 – discrimination on grounds of gender, marital status, age and race

The complainant claimed she was discriminated against on grounds of gender, marital status, age and race in relation to the post of 'Overseas Visa Officer' within the Civil Service. She applied for the post on four occasions over a five-year period and was unsuccessful each time.

The complainant submitted that the discrimination at issue was a form of continuing discrimination under the Employment Equality Acts.

The complainant was born in Ireland but spent half of her life in Canada and retained a Canadian accent. She contended that some Irish people found her accent 'irritating'. The complainant submitted that the assumption of Canadian nationality raised a presumption of discrimination. On grounds of age, the complainant contended that she was discriminated against as out of 22 candidates, 18% were over 50 years old and only 13% of the successful candidates were over 50 years old.

On grounds of gender, the complainant submitted that in the February 2008 competition, three candidates were deemed suitable, herself and two male colleagues. The two male colleagues were successful and the claimant submitted that it was not credible that two younger male candidates were more suitable than her given her experience and positive assessments. On grounds of marital status, the complainant submitted that in respect of the July 2008 competition, 80% of the successful candidates were single and the complainant had stated her family status as divorced on her application.

The complainant contended that the pattern of rejection for the competitions at issue was influenced by discriminatory prejudice against her on grounds of race, age, gender and marital status.

The Labour Court found that the competitions were independent of each other and the alleged discrimination relating to the 2008 competitions was statute barred as it was outside the six-month time limit (s 77(5) of the Employment Equality Acts).

The advertisement for the job vacancy included the following advice:

> Officers should give careful consideration to their personal and family circumstances before applying under this competition, and only those with a committed interest should forward their names for consideration.

The respondent justified this statement as being for the purpose of alerting potential candidates to the social, political, health and education conditions involved. The respondent wanted to ensure that potential candidates were aware of the potential lifestyle changes involved in relocating to foreign locations. The Court found that the job advertisement was badly phrased but was not designed to nor did it have the effect of discriminating against the complainant on any of the protected grounds. The Court found that the inclusion of the need for a person to consider their personal and family circumstances before relocating to a developing country was reasonable in the circumstances. The Court also found that the interviewers overplayed the importance of teamwork in its selection criteria but this was irregular and not discriminatory. The decision was not found to be discriminatory on any of the grounds contended for in the case.

The Court found the statistical evidence to be distorted. If one more candidate aged fifty or over had been successful, then 75% of the candidates in that age bracket would have been successful. Taking all the evidence into account, the Court found the nationality, marital status, family status or age of the complainant not to be factors that consciously or unconsciously influenced the panel in its decision. The Court found that the complainant was unsuccessful due predominantly to the manner in which she addressed questions that were put to her during the interview. Accordingly, the appeal failed.

[4.06] *Parfums Chanel Ltd & Chanel Ltd v Cappello[9] – Labour Court – Industrial Relations Acts 1946 to 2012 – Employment Equality Acts 1998 to 2011 – appeal of decision of Equality Tribunal – pregnant sales assistant – alleged discrimination on grounds of gender, marital status and family status – alleged harassment and victimisation*

During the course of a telephone conversation, the complainant had told her direct manager that she was pregnant. The manager had asked the complainant if it was planned or unplanned and how she felt about the pregnancy. The manager denied asking the complainant if she was going to 'keep' the baby.

The complainant stated that the manager had asked her to cover up matters and not to disclose the information to the assistant manager. The complainant said this made her feel that pregnant workers were not welcome in the shop and that her job was in jeopardy.

The manager said that the complainant had been certified unfit for work and that she was following up to ascertain when the complainant would be returning to work so that she could arrange her rosters. The manager said that at no point did she indicate to the complainant that her job was in jeopardy or that she was not welcome to return to work.

The Labour Court found that, given the significance of the event in the complainant's life, the complainant would have had reason to recall the conversation in greater detail than the respondent. The manager conceded that her recollection of the conversation was not as clear as that of the complainant. Ultimately, the Court found the manager's evidence plausible and consistent with the exchange that took place. The Court was not persuaded that the conversation was designed to create a hostile atmosphere for the complainant or to try to discourage her from returning to work. The Court accepted that the manager was trying to be supportive on the one hand but also trying to establish the complainant's intentions regarding her return to work.

Regarding the manager's statement that they should keep the conversation private, the Court accepted that the manager's statement was said out of respect for the complainant's right to manage the timing of any announcement regarding the pregnancy.

Regarding the complainant's complaint that the manager had asked her if the pregnancy was planned or unplanned and had asked her how comfortable she was with the pregnancy; the respondent explained to the Court that she had a very good relationship with the complainant and that she was talking to the complainant as both a

---

9.   *Parfums Chanel Ltd and Chanel Ltd v Cappello* EDA1434.

friend and as an employer. She said that not everyone was happy when they are told they are pregnant. She said she was not passing comment or forming any judgment. The complainant acknowledged her friendly relationship with the manager but claimed that the statements were addressing her marital status and were inappropriate and unlawful.

The Labour Court held that the conversation did not in any way compromise the complainant's terms and conditions of employment or her employment itself because of her pregnancy or her family status. The Court stated that the conversation may or may not have been indiscreet or improper, but it was not unlawful. Therefore, the Court did not accept the assertions of the complainant.

As regards the comment as to whether the complainant was going to 'keep' the baby, the Court concluded that that conversation did not adversely impact on the complainant's employment. The Court stated that there was no evidence to the contrary.

The complainant claimed that the manager had called her to ask about her medical certificates and that this amounted to an invasion of her privacy and to unfavourable treatment under the Acts. The Court held that there was nothing unusual in this and that no element of the manager's actions could be interpreted as adverse treatment. The Court concluded that the respondent's actions were reasonable and proportionate in this regard.

The complainant stated that there was a delay in providing her with her contract of employment when she requested it. The respondent stated that it acted quickly when it received the request and that a contract was provided to her when she commenced her employment and then copied for her from the London office when she requested it, which took a short time as it had to be retrieved from storage. The complainant filed a grievance and requested that her complaint be investigated. The investigator sought to arrange a meeting with the complainant; however, she declined to meet him.

The Court held that the respondent had acted with reasonable speed to initiate the investigation. It held that the respondent was willing and anxious to conduct an investigation into the grievances raised but was frustrated in doing so by the conduct of the complainant herself. The complainant was either not medically fit to participate in the investigation or, when fit, refused to do so unless she was legally represented in that process. The Court found that she had no entitlement to legal representation and that the respondent made a number of efforts to accommodate the complaints but she refused them. Accordingly, the Court found that the delay in investigating the complainant's grievances was occasioned by her own behaviour.

The Court held that the complainant presented no evidence of victimisation within the meaning of s 74(2) of the Acts. It found that the respondent engaged reasonably with the complainant and took no action that could amount to victimisation against her.

The Court concluded that the respondent did not discriminate against the complainant on grounds of gender, family status or marital status, did not harass her and did not victimise her. The appeal was rejected.

[4.07] *Sheehy Skeffington v National University of Ireland Galway*[10] – *Employment Equality Acts 1998 to 2011, ss 8(1)(d) and 22 – gender – discrimination regarding*

---

10.   *Sheehy Skeffington v National University of Ireland Galway* DEC–E2014–078.

promotion – indirect discrimination – selection process – gender imbalance – drawing attention to caring responsibilities – awarded €70,000 in compensation – promotion backdated to 1 July 2009 – review policies and procedures

The complainant alleged that she was discriminated against on the grounds of gender regarding access to promotion to senior lecturer grade. The complainant became eligible to apply for promotion to senior lecturer when she reached the top point of the college lecturer scale. She was not shortlisted for the first competition she applied for but she accepted that she did not expect to succeed on her first attempt as the standard was high. She applied again in 2001/2002 and was not shortlisted. In the 2006/2007 competition she was shortlisted and interviewed but did not get on the panel. The complainant submitted that she felt compelled to complain about the 2008/2009 competition when only one woman was promoted.

The complainant pointed to a number of aspects of the selection process which she submitted indicated a bias against female candidates. There was only one woman on the interview panel. Interviewers did not hold a pre-meeting before the interview to discuss the candidates and what questions should be asked. The complainant submitted that there was a 'funnel effect' against women once they hit the age group where they traditionally have caring responsibilities.

She submitted that four of the candidates were ineligible for promotion as they had not reached the maximum point on the college lecturer scale. She submitted that there is an over emphasis on research in the assessment of candidates to the detriment of teaching which she claimed was 'deeply gendered.' The complainant also cited inconsistencies in the scoring of the candidates.

The complainant also submitted that she was indirectly discriminated against. She submitted that men spend more time on research than women. Women care more about student welfare than men and are given the biggest teaching burden. She claimed that men get management roles on a 'nod and a wink' basis.

The respondent claimed that its process was fair and transparent. The respondent pointed out, and the complainant accepted, that no discriminatory questions were asked at interview. The respondent denied that any extra weight was given to the research portion of the assessment.

The Equality Tribunal was satisfied that, although on paper the system of promotion in the respondent university appeared to be fair, its implementation fell short of best practice. There was no training for the interviewers on the panel, there had been no pre-meeting to discuss the candidates, the suggestions of the external interviewer were ignored and the composition of the selection board lacked gender balance.

The Equality Tribunal was also critical of the fact that the Registrar, who heard the complainant's appeal, had served on the selection board.

With reference to the claim of indirect discrimination, the Tribunal pointed to the fact that the application form asked people to disclose whether they had been on maternity leave or other unpaid leave. Male applicants left this blank. The complainant had referred to time off for the care of her mother in the 1990s. While the question was legitimate, in that it intended to make allowances for employees for period of non-availability for work, its effects were discriminatory. The Tribunal found that the act of drawing attention to caring responsibilities 'disadvantaged female applicants.'

The Tribunal ordered that the respondent carry out a review of its policies and procedures concerning the selection of academics for promotion to senior lecturer posts. The Tribunal also awarded the complainant €70,000 in compensation and instructed the respondent to promote the complainant to the post of senior lecturer, with the promotion backdated to 1 July 2009.

[4.08] *Mullen v B Con Communications (In Liquidation)[11] – Employment Equality Acts 1998 to 2011, ss 6 and 14A – discriminatory treatment – harassment – gender – pregnancy – family status – maternity leave – whether definition of dismissal in Employment Equality Acts extends to constructive dismissal – whether Equality Tribunal entitled to consider incidents which occurred outside six-month time limit but were connected to allegations within the time limits – compensation of €80,000 awarded*

This case concerned a complaint of less favourable treatment, harassment and discriminatory dismissal on grounds of the complainant's gender and family status.[12] The complainant gave evidence that she was appointed financial controller of the respondent company in September 2007 and on informing the respondent's managing director she was pregnant with her third child in November 2009, attitudes towards her changed significantly. She alleged that that she was subjected to a number of comments regarding the fact of her pregnancy occurring closely after a miscarriage and also in relation to the fact that she had become pregnant again with her third child. In this regard, the complainant gave two examples of specific comments made towards her by the respondent's managing director which she cited as less favourable treatment. Evidence was given by the complainant that she was directed by the managing director to return to work shortly after a road traffic collision notwithstanding that her medical team had advised her to rest for a week. The complainant stated that she complied with this instruction because she felt intimidated by the respondent's managing director and was fearful of losing her job. She also cited a meeting where the managing director made reference to the fact that the complainant might not return to work (after maternity leave) because she would have three small children to look after. The complainant said she was shocked by this comment as she had never done or said anything which might lead to this conclusion. The complainant stated she made it perfectly clear that she intended to continue to work and would be returning after maternity leave.

In support of her claim, the complainant referenced a decision of the respondent not to top up maternity leave by the full amount to bring her to full salary but to agree a top up of payment of €150 per month. She also cited their requirement that she transfer her mobile telephone to her own name and to also return the company car for the duration of her leave as examples of less favourable treatment. When the complainant was in a

---

11.   *Mullen v BCon Communications (In liq)* DEC–E2014–007.

12.   It should be noted that prior to the hearing of this matter the Equality Tribunal was advised that the respondent company had gone into liquidation and that the appointed liquidator did not intend to attend or defend the claim on the company's behalf. Thus the Equality Tribunal heard evidence only from the complainant.

position to return to work she attempted to make contact with the respondent to agree a return date but initially there was no response from the managing director.

Ultimately a meeting did take place in which the complainant was advised that her role as financial controller no longer existed, that she was redundant and she was offered an alternative position which she claimed involved additional hours work per week, a 40% cut in her salary and a more junior and less responsible position. A series of negotiations took place, as a result of which the respondent agreed to restore the complainant's pre-maternity hours and terms and conditions, to include pay but the respondent was unwilling to consider a reversion to the financial controller role which it claimed no longer existed. The complainant was not satisfied with the revised proposal as it involved debt collection only, which had been about 10% of her previous job, and all other functions were removed from her. She rejected in its entirety any assertion that her role was redundant and noted that all other tasks previously performed by her were continuing to be performed by her (maternity leave) replacement, who was based in her office. Extended correspondence took place between the parties wherein the complainant reiterated her opinion that what she was being offered was a demotion and she repeatedly sought to return to the role which she previously occupied. Ultimately she received an email from the respondent's new technical director advising her that her views were being rejected and that the role most recently offered remained open for 14 days. A further response was sent by the complainant which restated her position and asked to return to her original role. The respondent's managing director finally wrote to her on 15 February 2011 rejecting all of her arguments and advising that as she had not yet reported for duty, the respondent considered her to have resigned.

Evidence was given for the complainant that three months after her employment had terminated, the respondent's website named her (maternity leave) replacement as its financial controller. She claimed that the actions of the respondent amounted to discriminatory dismissal of her, constructive or otherwise on grounds of her gender and family status.

The Equality Tribunal dealt with the allegation of dismissal and noted that it was the only alleged incident to have occurred within the six-month period described at s 77(2) of the Acts. The Tribunal noted that the complainant had sought to exercise her statutory right to return to the post she had held immediately before her maternity leave. Having considered all of the evidence, the Tribunal found that the revised role was a demotion and that the respondent had unilaterally attempted to change the complainant's basic terms and conditions of employment. It further found that the post of financial controller had remained in existence and that the replacement employee was performing this role. The Tribunal noted that nowhere in any of the correspondence issued to the complainant did the respondent state that she had been dismissed and thus her claim would be addressed as one of constructive discriminatory dismissal on the grounds advanced. The Equality Tribunal noted the definition of dismissal in s 2(1) of the Acts and further noted the approach of the Labour Court in *An Employer v A Worker (Mr O No 2)*[13] where the Court addressed the issue of constructive dismissal under employment

---

13. *An Employer v A Worker (Mr O No 2)* EED0410.

legislation and noted that the tests for constructive dismissal as developed under the Unfair Dismissals Acts[14] were the applicable tests under the Employment Equality Acts.

The Equality Tribunal stated that it was satisfied that the respondent had acted in a manner which is consistent with the intention not to be bound by the essential terms of the original contract between it and the complainant and in those circumstances the contract of employment was brought to an end. The complainant was entitled to consider herself dismissed in terms of the definition of dismissal at s 2 of the Employment Equality Acts. The Equality Tribunal found that the termination of the complainant's employment was inextricably linked to her pregnancy and maternity, given the nexus of her dismissal to her attempts to return to work following the expiry of a protected period in respect of those matters. The Tribunal stated that it was further satisfied that the fact that the complainant had three young children at the time acted as more than a trivial influence on the actions of the respondent and that the complainant had raised a prima facie case that she was dismissed in circumstances amounting to discrimination on grounds of gender and family status contrary to s 8 of the Employment Equality Acts. The Tribunal noted that the respondent had failed to discharge the burden and thus the complainant was entitled to succeed with this element of her complaint.

The Equality Tribunal then considered the alleged incidents of January 2011 to see if they were sufficiently connected to the incident which had occurred within the six-month period (the dismissal) so as to make them part of a chain of interlinked acts of discrimination. The Equality Tribunal found that the first comment by the managing director that the complainant did not 'hang around' in becoming pregnant demonstrated a profound insensitivity to the complainant's past experience of miscarrying some months before, but the Equality Tribunal held that it did not on its own amount to unlawful harassment of her on either gender or family status grounds, contrary to the Acts. The Tribunal noted however that it may have a probative value in terms of displaying a certain disposition as regards other incidents encompassed by the complaints.

The Equality Tribunal then considered a subsequent comment made by the same manager whilst the complainant was talking to two of the respondent's clients and advised them that she was pregnant. The comment was 'Yes, and to be honest lads I'm not too happy about this. She was meant to stop after her first two and now I have been informed that she is having a third.' The Equality Tribunal found that this comment, having regard to the previous comment made by the same person, amounted prima facie to the harassment of the complainant on grounds of her gender and family status as it had the effect of creating an offensive, humiliating and degrading environment for her in terms of her pregnancy and the fact that she had children at the time.

The Equality Tribunal noted that when the complainant sought to raise her objection to this comment the managing director was dismissive of her. Thus the respondent was unable to avail of the defence in s 14(A)(2) of the Acts and the complainant was entitled to succeed with this element of her complaint as regards an allegation of harassment.

---

14. Unfair Dismissals Acts 1977 to 2007 as amended.

With regard to the issue of the treatment of the complainant after her road traffic accident, the Equality Tribunal noted the complainant's evidence that she complied with the direction to return to work because she felt intimidated by the managing director and was fearful of her losing job and that she had formed this opinion because she was aware that the managing director had a tendency to dismiss people in such circumstances. The Equality Tribunal stated it appeared that the managing director would on balance have behaved in a similar fashion in respect of another employee who found himself or herself in the same situation and for that reason the complainant was not able to demonstrate a prima facie case that his actions amounted to less favourable treatment to her on discriminatory grounds.

The Equality Tribunal found that the comment made by the managing director, in the course of the interview for the complainant's maternity leave replacement, that he was not sure whether she would coming back to work as she would have three children to look after, was harassment of the complainant on the grounds of gender and family status. The Equality Tribunal noted that this comment, regardless of the managing director's misguided opinion, created concern and fear for the complainant in terms of her job and had the effect of producing an intimidating working environment for the remainder of her period of employment before she commenced maternity leave especially as it was made in front of the candidate who was replacing her during that absence. Again the Equality Tribunal noted that the respondent's managing director did nothing to allay her fears in this regard when she raised it with him and thus was unable to avail of the defence available at s 14(A)(2).

The Equality Tribunal noted that an employee on maternity leave does not have any statutory entitlement to payment of salary and other benefits during that leave and that an employer had discretion as to whether or not it continues to provide such benefits and/or pay during that leave. On that basis, the Equality Tribunal was unable to hold that the respondent's actions in requiring the complainant to return her company car and discharge her mobile phone costs, as well as their decision not to pay full salary, was not less favourable treatment of the complainant or harassment of her on either of the grounds advanced. In this regard the Equality Tribunal distinguished the decision of the Equality Tribunal in *O'Brien v Persian Properties T/A O'Callaghan Hotels*[15] as in that case the non-payment of the complainant's salary and the removal of benefits was found to amount to victimisation of the complainant.

The Equality Tribunal concluded that the respondent did harass the complainant on grounds of her family status and gender and did dismiss her in circumstances amounting to discrimination on grounds of family status and gender. The Equality Tribunal awarded the complainant €80,000 as compensation.

[4.09] *Mentel v Top Heights Ltd T/A Foys Bar & Lounge*[16] *– Equality Tribunal – Employment Equality Acts 1998 to 2011 – whether complainant discriminated against regarding conditions of work on grounds of race and gender – victimisation – culture*

---

15.   *O'Brien v Persian Properties T/A O'Callaghan Hotels* DEC–E2012–010.

16.   *Mentel v Top Heights Ltd T/A Foys Bar & Lounge* DEC–E2014–017.

of harassment – whether complaints res judicata as the same facts had already been relied upon to ground claim for constructive dismissal – complaint of equal pay on basis of hypothetical comparator

The complainant, a Polish national, worked for the respondent on two separate occasions from August 2008 to June 2009 and from September 2009 to September 2010. She claimed that she was discriminated against as she was not given a contract of employment, was not provided with breaks or annual leave in accordance with Organisation of Working Time Act 1997 nor was she properly paid for Sundays and public holidays under that Act. The complainant submitted she was required to work extra hours without pay and in an unsafe and unhealthy environment.

The complainant stated that management fostered a culture of harassment and discrimination against her. She claimed that she was constantly summoned back to work during her breaks and expected to be at everyone's 'beck and call'. The complainant claimed she was threatened with dismissal if she refused to work extra hours and was never paid for them. It was claimed that her request for pay slips was met with a derogatory comment by the respondent and her hours were then reduced to eight per week. She claimed that on one occasion management accused her of stealing. The complainant complained that she was put down constantly by colleagues: for example her cleaning materials were hidden from her and floors she had just cleaned were deliberately dirtied soon after.

The complainant claimed she was victimised when, following a successful Rights Commissioner case, she received three post-dated cheques directly from the respondent's solicitor, who requested her to accept and sign same in full and final settlement of all her complaints against the respondent. The complainant claimed that as the document enclosing the cheques was in English she was not in a position to fully understand it.

The respondent did not attend the hearing and advised in advance that he had a funeral to attend on that date. Despite being requested to do so the respondent submitted no documentation to support this and the hearing proceeded in his absence. The respondent's representative argued the complaints raised were *res judicata* on the basis that the complainant was relying on the same facts in this case as she had already relied on in her claim for constructive dismissal at the EAT. The respondent acknowledged that while legislation did not preclude this, the person hearing the case must look at the facts and decide if an award has already been made on those facts. It was submitted the victimisation complaint related to alleged incidents that occurred almost a year after the complainant's employment had terminated and so the respondent's duty of care had ceased towards her. The Equality Tribunal considered the *res judicata* issue and held that it had jurisdiction to examine the complaint in relation to harassment on grounds of race and gender.

The Equality Tribunal held that the complaints of non-provision of contracts, rest breaks and annual leave and non-payment for Sundays and public holidays had been examined in the EAT and redress was provided to the complainant. With regard to the complaint of harassment, the Equality Tribunal found the complainant had established a prima facie case of discrimination which, in the absence of any evidence, the respondent had failed to rebut.

With regard to the claim of victimisation, the Equality Tribunal found that the cheques were in full and final settlement in respect of the Rights Commissioner matter only. The complainant contacted her representative when she received this correspondence and so the Equality Tribunal was satisfied that she did not suffer any adverse treatment. The Equality Tribunal held it was not possible to ground a claim of equal pay by reference to a hypothetical comparator.

The complainant was awarded €2,500 for distress suffered as a result of the discrimination.

[4.10] *An Employee v An Employer[17] – Equality Tribunal – Employment Equality Acts 1998 to 2011 – discrimination on grounds of gender, family status and disability regarding conditions of employment – harassment and victimisation – failure to provide reasonable accommodation – obligation on employer to make arrangements in respect of employee's workload where employee avails of parental leave*

The complainant claimed that he was subjected to unfair treatment once he commenced a reduced working week by virtue of a parental leave arrangement. The complainant's workload increased and he complained, but no action was taken. The complainant claimed that he was subjected to undermining behaviour, humiliation and harassment by Mr A and that he gave up one day of parental leave in response to pressure from Mr A who, at a sales meeting, referenced complaints from the sales team about orders not being completed. The complainant experienced dizzy spells in 2011 which were confirmed as stress related by a cardiologist and he took sick leave from January 2011 to November 2011 sparked by alleged verbal abuse from Mr A. Evidence was given that, in a return to work meeting with the CEO, the complainant requested not to work with Mr A. Afterwards, the complainant made an official complaint against Mr A but, following an internal investigation and appeal, it was not upheld. The complainant returned to work in November 2011 with one day of parental leave per week.

The complainant was loaned money pending his application to the insurers and, when this was unsuccessful, the respondent asked for the money back. The complainant alleged that this was done in an aggressive way. The complainant also submitted that, at a meeting with the CEO and another manager, he was told his equality claim was making his reintegration into the workplace more difficult. Some months later, the complainant took up a role in the stores department, where he received the same salary and worked a four-day week. The complainant claimed that the CEO stated he understood the case before the Equality Tribunal would be withdrawn now this position had been offered.

The respondent claimed that no pressure was placed on the complainant to give up parental leave and, when he was asked to reduce his leave, he agreed. The respondent claimed that the complainant did not work long hours and, in his appraisal for 2010, there was no mention of workload. The respondent claimed that no issues about Mr A were raised to the CEO until the formal complaint. The respondent claimed that the complainant accepted the stores job on the basis of a four-day week at the same pay as

---

17.   *An Employee v An Employer* DEC–E2014–022.

his previous job. The respondent argued that they had no knowledge of any disability as the only doctor's certificate submitted did not refer to stress, nor was any accommodation requested by the complainant prior to him returning to work.

The Equality Tribunal found the claim of harassment to be out of time and so it failed.

The Tribunal drew attention to the fact that parental leave is unpaid. Thus, the respondent achieved savings as a result of the shorter week and had scope to make arrangements to cope with the additional workload. The Tribunal found they had chosen not to do this. The respondent's failure to make appropriate arrangements would not have occurred to a female taking parental leave and this was found to be discriminatory treatment on the grounds of gender.

The Tribunal held that the respondent was not aware that the complainant had a disability within the meaning of the Acts when he returned to work and so the respondent was under no obligation to consider whether the complainant needed any reasonable accommodation. The complainant had only ever submitted one medical certificate which stated he was under cardiac investigation and would not be fit to return to work for one month.

Finally, with regard to the claim of victimisation, the Tribunal held that, in the absence of any evidence of adverse treatment, the complainant's claim failed. The Tribunal stated that a disagreement as to how the money was to be repaid did not amount to victimisation, nor did mere questions as to whether the complainant would withdraw his equality claim.

In light of the above, the respondent was ordered to pay €7,000 in compensation to the complainant for the discriminatory treatment suffered.

[4.11] *Nowakowska v Noel Recruitment (Ireland) Ltd and Rottapharm Ltd[18] – Equality Tribunal – Employment Equality Acts 1998 to 2011 – whether complainant discriminated against on ground of gender by reason of her pregnancy or family status contrary to s 6(2A) – whether complainant dismissed because of her pregnancy*

The complainant was employed as a general operative at Rottapharm and was placed there by Noel Recruitment, an employment agency. Rottapharm managed the complainant's training and working arrangements and Noel Recruitment paid her. In January 2011, the complainant advised her manager at Rottapharm that she was pregnant and she also advised Noel Recruitment of her pregnancy by email. In March 2011 the complainant was asked by Rottapharm to work a three-cycle shift involving night shift work. She said that she was unable to do so and provided a medical certificate advising that she should not undertake night shifts. It was alleged that the complainant was repeatedly asked to work the three-cycle shift, even though Rottapharm were aware that she could not do so on medical advice. She alleged to the Equality Tribunal that her requests to be assigned to day shift work only were refused. On 1 April 2011 Noel Recruitment contacted the complainant to advise her that she was no longer required by

18.   *Nowakowska v Noel Recruitment (Ireland) Ltd and Rottapharm Ltd* DEC–E2014–074.

Rottapharm because of a downturn in business. As Noel Recruitment did not succeed in securing another placement for her, she requested her P45.

The complainant alleged that she had been discriminated against and dismissed on grounds of her pregnancy. She submitted that the close proximity of these events to the announcement of her pregnancy was a sufficient coincidence to discharge her burden of proof. Rottapharm submitted that it was advised of significant changes to the forecast volumes of its key markets. The net effect of these changes was a reduction of 43 million sachets in 2011, equivalent to 12% of total sachet production. Rottapharm gave evidence that it commenced a programme of reduction of agency workers and the complainant was neither the first nor the last agency worker to be phased out under this process. The numbers of workers was reduced depending on the line that staff were working on, their experience and in line with the volume adjustments and demands. It was submitted by Rottapharm that the complainant was not dismissed but rather she was one of a number of agency staff at the time whose services were discontinued.

The Equality Tribunal concluded that, while Noel Recruitment was technically the employer of the complainant, it was satisfied that the agency had no role or part in the decision to lay off the complainant in April 2011. The Equality Tribunal noted the complainant's assertion that there was no clear and fair procedure followed and that other agency workers with less service than her were retained after she was let go. The Tribunal noted that the complainant had provided a list of names of other workers at Rottapharm who she stated had a shorter period of service and less experience than her but who were retained following her redundancy. The Tribunal noted that, at the hearing, it was established that two of the workers on the list were agency workers who had also been recruited through Noel Recruitment and both were retained. The Equality Tribunal noted that Rottapharm had not disputed at the hearing that the complainant was the first of the agency workers to be phased out because of the downturn.

The Equality Tribunal accepted there was a downturn in Rottapharm's business and this necessitated the phasing out of the use of agency workers; however the Equality Tribunal held that Rottapharm did not show any objective rationale for terminating the complainant's employment prior to that of other less experienced workers. The Tribunal concluded that the complainant's pregnancy must have been a consideration to terminate her assignment. The Equality Tribunal did however accept that the complainant would have been laid off in due course, regardless of whether or not she was pregnant, and noted that all of Rottapharm's agency workers were subsequently laid off due to the downturn.

The Equality Tribunal concluded that Rottapharm did not rebut the inference of discrimination and its selection process lacked transparent objectivity.

The Tribunal concluded that it was unlawful to dismiss a pregnant person at any stage of employment for any reason that is linked with pregnancy. Rottapharm had failed to discharge the burden to show there were exceptional circumstances justifying the dismissal of the complainant. The Tribunal ultimately concluded that the complainant was discriminated against on ground of her gender by Rottapharm. The Equality Tribunal ordered Rottapharm to pay the complainant compensation of €20,000 for the effects of the unlawful discriminatory treatment. The Equality Tribunal noted that this award was appropriate in light of the phasing out of the use of agency work by

Rottapharm which was objectively justified and that all of the agency workers engaged by Rottapharm were subsequently laid off due to the downturn.

Equal pay/gender

[4.12] *Kenny v Department of Justice, Equality & Law Reform, Department of Finance and the Commissioner of An Garda Síochána[19] – High Court – McCarthy J – referral to Court of Justice of the European Union for preliminary ruling – remittance of case back to Labour Court – subsequent appeal on point of law – Employment Equality Acts 1998 to 2011 – right to equal pay for like work – indirect gender discrimination – choice of comparators – objective justification for difference in pay – whether good industrial relations can constitute objective justification for difference in pay*

This was an appeal on a point of law from a determination of the Labour Court under s 90 of the Employment Equality Acts. The claimants were established civil servants, and in particular clerical officers, and their claim was for equal pay with members of An Garda Síochána whose remuneration is higher, claiming that the differential constitutes indirect gender discrimination. This was rejected by the Labour Court.

Section 19 of the Acts provides for equal pay for like work and indirect discrimination is provided for in s 9(4), which provides that:

> indirect discrimination occurs where an apparently neutral provision puts persons of a particular gender ... at a particular disadvantage in respect of remuneration compared with other employees of their employer ... unless the provision is objectively justified by a legitimate aim and the means of achieving the aim are appropriate and necessary.

The burden of proof is on a claimant to establish that an apparently neutral provision puts him or her at a disadvantage in respect of remuneration compared to other employees, and it is then a matter for the employer to show that the differential in remuneration can be objectively justified by a legitimate aim and the means of achieving the aim were appropriate and necessary.

The High Court noted that there are a number of gardaí who also carry out clerical duties in addition to the claimants and that these fall into three distinct groups:

(i)   gardaí who are assigned to similar duties as the claimants and carry out 'pure clerical duties';

(ii)   other gardaí required to undertake duties which, although clerical in nature, must be performed by gardaí;

(iii)   gardaí who perform clerical duties in addition to what is described as 'normal police duties' – their clerical work is accordingly part time.

---

19.   *Kenny v Department of Justice, Equality & Law Reform, Department of Finance and the Commissioner of An Garda Síochána* [2014] IEHC 11.

The claimants identified Group (i) – the gardaí who perform pure clerical duties – as their comparators.

The High Court held that, in a claim of this kind, the Labour Court should first address the issue of identity of those with higher remuneration who are chosen for the purposes of comparison by the claimants. This was done, on the basis that the parties agreed at the outset that the work of the claimants and the chosen comparators was 'like work'. Twelve persons were chosen from amongst the gardaí engaged in purely clerical duties. Despite agreeing to the comparators who were chosen initially, the respondent subsequently stated that the comparators were drawn from too narrow a class and ought to have been drawn from the generality of gardaí involved in clerical duties. The respondent also relied upon the justification that it was an operational necessity for the deployment of gardaí to clerical posts on the assumption that, as such deployment was justified, the differential was justified. The respondent also sought to rely upon industrial relations considerations as part of the justification for deployment to clerical duties.

McCarthy J referred the following questions to the CJEU for a preliminary ruling:

(1) In circumstances where there is prima facie indirect gender discrimination in pay, in breach of Article 141 EC ... and Council Directive [75/117], in order to establish objective justification, does the employer have to provide:

(a)   Justification in respect of the deployment of the comparators in the posts occupied by them;

(b)   Justification of the payment of a higher rate of pay to the comparators; or

(c)   Justification of the payment of a lower rate of pay [to the appellants in the main proceedings]?

(2) In circumstances where there is prima facie indirect gender discrimination in pay, in order to establish objective justification does the employer have to provide justification in respect of:

(a)   The specific comparators cited by the [appellants in the main proceedings]; and/or

(b)   The generality of comparator posts.

(3) If the answer to question 2(b) is in the affirmative, is objective justification established notwithstanding that such justification does not apply to the chosen comparators?

(4) Did the Labour Court, as a matter of Community law, err in accepting that the 'interests of good industrial relations' could be taken into account in the determination of whether the employer could objectively justify the difference in pay?

(5) In circumstances where there is prima facie indirect gender discrimination in pay, can objective justification be established by reliance on the industrial relations concerns of the respondent? Should such concerns have any relevance to an analysis of objective justification?

The Court of Justice of the European Union answered these questions as follows:

–   Employees perform the same work or work to which equal value can be attributed if, taking account of a number of factors such as the nature of the work, the training requirements, and the working conditions, those persons can be considered to be in comparable situation, which it is a matter for the national court to ascertain;

–   In relation to indirect pay discrimination, it is for the employer to establish objective justification for the difference in pay between the workers they consider that they have been discriminated against and the comparators;

–   The employer's justification for the difference pay, which is evidence of a prima facie case of gender discrimination, must relate to the comparators who, on account of the fact that their situation is described by valid statistics which cover enough individuals, do not illustrate purely fortuitous or short term phenomena and which, in general, appear to be significant, have been taken into account by the referring court in establishing that difference; and

–   The interest of good industrial relations may be taken into consideration by the national court as one factor among others in its assessment of whether differences between the pay of two groups of workers are due to objective factors unrelated to any discrimination on grounds of sex and are compatible with the principle of proportionality.

The High Court also considered the decision of the Supreme Court in *National University of Ireland Cork v Ahern.*[20] This case involved persons engaged in security work who, it was alleged, were treated differently in pay from certain part-time switchboard operators, who had once been full-time but because of family commitments were permitted to work on a part-time basis. The Labour Court had concluded that the work of such part-time telephonists and the claimants was like work, on the basis of the claimants' comparators. The Supreme Court noted that the Labour Court ought to have looked at the position of the comparators, not only in isolation, but also in the context of other persons in the same grade who had not been chosen as comparators, ie the full-time telephonists. The Supreme Court held that the Labour Court had not dealt with the question of whether the relationship between the comparators and other full-time switchboard operators remained the same, when part-time work was introduced for family reasons.

In this case, the High Court held that, contrary to what was submitted on behalf of the claimants, the choice of comparators made in this instance was not a valid or lawful choice. The High Court noted that the comparators should be drawn from the generality of those engaged in clerical duties among the Garda Síochána. McCarthy J stated that his reasons for this conclusion included the following:

(i)   gardaí and clerical officers are all performing clerical duties connected with policing;

(ii)   there is plainly a great deal of overlap in work between gardaí who fill posts where garda membership or expertise is essential of their nature and that of clerical officers;

---

20.   *National University of Ireland Cork v Ahern & Ors* [2005] 2 IR 577.

(iii) the number of persons in the chosen comparators' class is unknown but on any view of the evidence it is a modest proportion of the generality and an even smaller proportion of the total number of those involved in clerical work;

(iv) the class from which the claimants' comparators are insufficient in themselves to be of significance for valid comparison;

(v) the choice pays no or no proper regard to rationally relevant principles which have been elaborated above.

The Court noted that a perfectly coherent argument could be advanced that the comparators should be drawn from the force as a whole, since the reality of the case is that parity of remuneration is sought with all gardaí even if, superficially, it was confined to those engaged in pure clerical duties.

On the issue of objective justification, the Court noted that the fact that the Commissioner of An Garda Síochána had chosen, for whatever reason, to assign gardaí to these tasks, cannot justify a differential in pay; it is merely the reason why a differential which has always existed between gardaí and clerical workers has been highlighted. McCarthy J stated that the objective justification for a differential should not be confused with the practical reasons which have led to it. On the issue of good industrial relations, the Court noted that the concern for good industrial relations cannot of itself constitute the only basis justifying a discrimination in pay, but the interests of good industrial relations may be taken into consideration by the national court as one factor among others in its assessment of whether differences in pay between two groups of workers are due to objective factors unrelated to any discrimination.

McCarthy J held that the case should be remitted to the Labour Court and set out the approach to be adopted for the rehearing of the matter namely: (i) choosing valid comparators; (ii) addressing the issue of whether like work is performed; and (iii) addressing whether or not the difference in pay is objectively justified.

Civil status

[4.13] *Parris v Trinity College Dublin &Ors[21] – Equality Tribunal[22] – Pensions Acts 1990 to 2012 – discrimination in rules of occupational pension scheme – age – sexual orientation – civil status – combination of grounds – defence – ultra vires – Civil Partnership and Certain Rights and Obligations of Cohabitants Act 2010*

The complainant was a retired senior lecturer in Trinity College Dublin who had been employed since 1972 until his retirement on 31 December 2010. He asserted that he was discriminated against by the respondents on grounds of age, sexual orientation and civil status in terms of s 66(2) of the Pensions Acts 1990 to 2012 (as amended) (the Acts) and contrary to ss 70 and 78 of the Acts, in the operation of the rules of the occupational pension scheme.

---

21. *Parris v Trinity College Dublin & Ors* (DEC-P2013–004).
22. This decision is under appeal to the Labour Court.

Under the pension scheme there were certain benefits associated with an employee being married before a certain age or prior to a certain date. On 22 April 2009, the complainant sought to have his status for the purposes of his membership of the pension scheme changed from single to married, following his partnership under the UK Civil Partnership Act 2004.

The first-named respondent informed him that it was not in a position to recognise his civil status, on the basis that there was no equivalent legislation recognising civil partnerships under Irish law. The complainant could not therefore benefit from the favourable treatment for married members of the pension scheme.

The Equality Tribunal considered whether or not there had been discrimination in relation to the pension scheme on the basis of civil status, sexual discrimination and age. It was noted that the complainant was first required to show a *prima facia* case, and the respondent would then be required to rebut the inference raised.

Firstly, the Equality Tribunal examined the complaint that the complainant had been discriminated against on grounds of age. It referred to Council Directive 2000/78/EC[23] which established a general framework for equal treatment in employment and occupation and introduced the concept of discrimination on age and sexual orientation into Irish law which was given effect in the Acts. It was noted that the Directive was without prejudice to national laws on marital status and benefits dependent thereon.

The Equality Tribunal referred to *Maruko v Versorgungsanstalt der deutshen Buhnen*[24] where the CJEU held that German regulations that treated people in life partnerships differently to married people with regard to a widower's pension were directly discriminatory on the grounds of sexual orientation. The CJEU held in that case that the life partners were treated less favourably than surviving spouses as regards entitlement to survivors benefit, and this was direct discrimination. The Equality Tribunal considered the *Maruko* case, and noted that it reiterated the Directive's intention that each Member State would determine what constituted marriage in each territory. Additionally it was noted that Germany had introduced civil partnership prior to the *Maruko* decision, and that in finding the relevant German regulations to be directly discriminatory, the CJEU was not giving retrospective effect to any determination.

In this case, the Equality Tribunal noted that, until the Civil Partnership and Certain Rights and Obligations of Cohabitants Act 2010 (the 2010 Act), Ireland did not give equal status to same-sex couples as it did to opposite sex couples in respect of pension entitlements. The respondents' pension scheme was put in place prior to the enactment of the 2010 Act and was therefore not discriminatory at the time. As the 2010 Act did not have retrospective effect the pension scheme could not be read in light of the Act. On that basis, the Equality Tribunal held that, although the complainant had established he was treated differently on civil status grounds before civil partnership was recognised by the State, it was not satisfied that any such treatment was encompassed in the

---

23. Council Directive 2000/78/EC of 27 November 2000 establishing a general framework for equal treatment in employment and occupation.

24. *Maruko v Versorgungsanstalt der deutshen Buhnen* (Case C–267/06).

definition of discrimination under both the Acts and the Directive. Accordingly, his claim on the ground of civil status was dismissed.

In respect of the sexual orientation ground, the Equality Tribunal concluded that the complainant's claim was in relation to his entitlement to recognition of his civil partnership rather than any restriction or denial of an entitlement based on his sexual orientation *per se*. The Equality Tribunal stated that both the Directive and the Acts made a clear distinction between sexual orientation as a ground of discrimination and civil status ground of discrimination, and therefore the matter was dealt with in respect of civil status.

In assessing the discrimination on grounds of age argument, the Equality Tribunal noted that it was accepted that the complainant was treated differently to other members of the pension scheme who had married or established civil partnerships prior to their 60th birthday. The respondent asserted that it was neither discriminatory nor unlawful to fix an age to qualify for an entitlement under the Acts. It referred to s 72(1)(c) of the Pensions Acts which states that it should not constitute a breach of the principle of equal pension treatment on the age ground for a scheme to '... fix age or qualifying service, or a combination of both for entitlement to benefit under the scheme'.

The Equality Tribunal noted that the complainant was not allowed to join the pension scheme because he was over 50 when he was recruited by the first-named respondent and the pension scheme rules prohibited members joining over the age of 50. The complainant asserted that respondent did not provide an objective reason for the age restriction in the pension scheme, and that funding and financial implications in relation to the pension were not objective reasons for denying access to a scheme (as stated in *Catholic University School v Dooley and Scannell*).[25] On this basis, financial grounds were not a legitimate defence to a claim of discrimination. The respondents stated that s 72 of the Acts permits the employer to set an age limit for entry to the scheme, and this by way of objective justifications; the respondent submitted that the rules and the eligibility requirements as regards the age of entry to the pension scheme are contained in SI 242/1945[26] and any changes to the pension scheme would have to be agreed by CIE, the trade unions and the Minister for Transport, Tourism and Sport. Any increase to the upper age limit for entry to the scheme would have serious funding implications given that the same pension is paid to retiring staff irrespective of service and the contribution made to the scheme.

The Equality Tribunal stated that it was satisfied that under s 76 of Acts that the complainant had established that he was treated less favourably than a person who was recruited between the ages of 20 and 49 and, therefore, the respondent was required to rebut the inference of discrimination. The respondent referred to s 72 of the Acts and it was noted that subs (a) and (b) provided a full defence to the complainant's claim that the fixed age was discriminatory in effect. Section 72(1) of the Pensions Acts provides it shall not constitute a breach of the principle of equal pension treatment on the age

---

25. *Catholic University School v Dooley and Scannell* [2010] IEHC 496.
26. Córas Iompair Éireann Pension Scheme for Regular Wages Staff (confirmed by the Córas Iompair Éireann Superannuation Scheme for Regular Wages Staff (Confirmation) Order 1945 (SI 242/1945)).

ground for a scheme to fix an age or qualifying service, or to fix different ages for qualifying service, or a combination of both, as conditions or criteria for admission to the scheme for employees or groups or categories of employees.

The Tribunal then considered whether the respondent was required to justify the rules regarding admission to the scheme. The Equality Tribunal stated that the requirement to objectively justify the age was only required when it related to the accrual of rights of a member. Applying statutory interpretation, the Equality Tribunal stated that it does not apply to claims in respect of gender discrimination and concluded that although the complainant established he was less favourably treated on the grounds of age, the respondent was entitled to rely on the defence contained in s 72(1)(c) of the Pensions Acts. The complainant's claim accordingly failed.

The complainant also sought redress on the combined grounds of civil status, sexual orientation and age for indirect discrimination. The Equality Tribunal stated that it was satisfied that the complainant had established that the impact of the introduction of the 2010 Act, combined with the limit placed on his ability to regularise his civil status as a homosexual in an ongoing relationship prior to that point, placed him at a particular disadvantage with respect to his pension against, for example, a heterosexual man of similar age who entered into a regularised heterosexual relationship at a younger age.

The Equality Tribunal noted that the 2010 Act did not have retrospective effect, and that any decision in favour of the complainant on this basis would have the effect of conferring retrospective effect on the 2010 Act. The Equality Tribunal stated that as the legislature did not see it as necessary to include retrospective effect in the 2010 Act, having regard to the purpose of the Directive, it could not find in favour of the complainant on this basis, either on national or European legislation. The complainant's claim failed.

[4.14] *Hay v Credit Agricole Mutuel de Charente-Maritime et des Deux-Sévres[27] – CJEU – request for preliminary ruling – Directive 2000/78 establishing a general framework for equal treatment in employment and occupation – whether collective agreement which provided days of special leave and salary bonus to employees on occasion of their marriage and but did not apply to employees who entered into civil solidarity pact (civil partnership agreement) was discriminatory on grounds of sexual orientation*

A national collective agreement made provision for special paid leave granted in circumstances where a permanent employee marries, where a child of the employee marries or where a sibling of the employee marries. In addition, the collective agreement provides for a marriage bonus payable to employees at the time of their marriage. The claimant, an employee of the respondent in France, entered into a civil solidarity pact with his partner of the same sex and applied for special leave and the marriage bonus in accordance with the agreement. These were refused on grounds that under the collective agreement, they were granted only upon marriage. He brought an action to a labour tribunal to obtain payment of the marriage bonus and compensation for the days of

---

27.   *Hay v Credit Agricole Mutuel de Charente-Maritime et des Deux-Sévres* (Case C–267/12).

special leave, which was refused. His action was appealed to the Court of Appeal in Poitiers which upheld that judgment on the basis that the civil solidarity pact differed from marriage in respect of the formality of governing its celebration, the possibility that it may be entered into by two individuals of full age of different sexes or of the same sex, the manner in which it may be broken, and in respect of their reciprocal obligations under property law, succession law and the law in relation to parenthood.

The claimant brought a further appeal and alleged that the refusal to grant him the days of special leave and the marriage bonus provided for under the national collective agreement constituted discrimination based on his sexual orientation contrary to the relevant French Labour Code and Directive 2000/78/EC and the European Convention on Human Rights.

The French Court decided to stay proceedings and refer the following question to the CJEU – must art 2(2)(b) of Directive 2000/78 be interpreted as meaning that the choice of the national legislature to allow only persons of different sexes to marry can constitute a legitimate appropriate and necessary aim such as to justify indirect discrimination resulting from the fact that a collective agreement which restricts an advantage in respect of pay and working conditions to employees who marry, thereby necessarily excluding from the benefit of that advantage same sex partners who have entered into a civil solidarity agreement?

The CJEU noted the question referred was based on the premise that the collective agreement gave rise to indirect discrimination based on sexual orientation within the meaning of art 2(2)(b) of Directive 2000/78 and concerned the issue of whether such discrimination can be justified. The Court said it was appropriate to consider the issue of whether a collective agreement gave rise to direct or indirect discrimination within the meaning of art 2(2) of the Directive and thus the preliminary reference must be interpreted as asking whether the Directive must be interpreted as precluding a provision in the collective agreement such as the one at issue in the main proceedings under which an employee who concludes a civil solidarity pact with a person of the same sex is not allowed to obtain the same benefits, such as days of special leave and a salary bonus, as those granted to employees on the occasion of their marriage, where the national rules of the Member State concerned do not allow persons of the same sex to marry.

As to whether there is direct discrimination, art 2(2)(a) of Directive 2000/78 provided that direct discrimination is to be taken to occur when a person is treated in a less favourable manner than another person in a comparable situation, on one of the grounds listed in art 1 thereof, to include sexual orientation. As regards the days of paid leave and the bonus which the provisions at issue in the main proceedings grant to employees on the occasion of their marriage, the Court determined it necessary to examine whether persons who enter into a marriage and persons who, being unable to marry a person of their own sex, enter into a civil solidarity pact are in comparable situations. The CJEU noted that a civil solidarity pact must be the subject of a joint declaration registration with the registry of the court within whose jurisdiction the persons concerned established their common residence and constitutes, like marriage, a form of civil union under French law, which places the couple within a specific legal framework containing rights and obligations in respect of each other and vis-a-vis third parties. Although the civil solidarity pact may also be concluded by persons of different sexes and although there may be general differences between the systems governing marriage and the civil solidarity pact arrangement, the latter was, at the time of this case, the only possibility under French law for same sex couples to procure legal status for the relationship which could be certain and effective against third parties. Thus the Court concluded, as regards benefits in terms of pay or working conditions (such as days of special leave and a bonus like those at issue granted at the time of an employee's marriage, which is a form of a civil union), persons of the same sex who cannot enter into marriage and therefore conclude a civil solidarity pact are in a situation which is comparable to that of couples who marry.

The CJEU noted that the differences between marriage and the civil solidarity pact noted by the referring court in respect of the formalities, the possibility that it may be entered into by two individuals of different sexes or of the same sex, the manner in which they may be broken and the reciprocal obligations under property succession law and the law relating to parenthood, were irrelevant to the assessment of an employee's right to benefit in terms of pay or working conditions such as those at issue in the main case. The Court noted that the collective agreement granted those benefits on the occasion of marriage irrespective of the rights and obligations arising from marriage which was confirmed by the fact that the agreement granted leave not only on the occasion of a permanent employee's marriage but also on the occasion of the marriage of that employee's children, brother or sister. The CJEU held the fact that the civil solidarity pact is not restricted to homosexual couples was irrelevant and in particular did not change the nature of the discrimination against homosexual couples who, unlike heterosexual couples could not, on the date of the claim, legally enter into marriage. The difference in treatment based on the employee's marital status and not expressly on their sexual orientation is still direct discrimination because only persons of different sexes may marry and homosexual employees are therefore unable to meet the condition required for obtaining the benefit claimed. The CJEU concluded that the answer to the question referred is that Directive 2000/78 must be interpreted as precluding a provision in a collective agreement, such as the one at issue, under which an employee who concludes a civil solidarity pact with a person of the same sex is not allowed to obtain the same benefits, such as days of special leave and a salary bonus as those granted to employees on the occasion of their marriage where the national rules of the Member State concerned do not allow persons of the same sex to marry.

Family status

[4.15] *Coakley v Department of Social Protection*[28] *– Equality Tribunal – Employment Equality Acts 1998 to 2011 – whether alleged discrimination on grounds of family status in terms of access to employment – whether respondent is correct respondent where it wholly controlled the complainant's eligibility for her employment, as well as providing funding for salaries of participants under scheme*

The complainant applied for a position as a supervisor on an employment scheme administered on behalf of State body Pobal. The relevant place of employment was the

---

28.   *Coakley v Department of Social Protection* DEC–E2014–011.

West Cork Development Partnership. Shortly before the complainant was due to commence employment, she received a phone call from the West Cork Development Partnership to say that it needed to withdraw the offer of employment due to the intervention of the respondent. The respondent had determined that she did not meet the necessary criteria for participation in the scheme.

It was alleged by the complainant that, as she was a recipient of the one parent family payment and not jobseekers allowance, she was deemed ineligible to participate in the scheme as the respondent had ruled out recipients of the one parent family payment for participants and she claimed this constituted discrimination on grounds of her family status. The respondent initially submitted that it was not the employer or prospective employer of the complainant and in this instance it explained that the rules of the relevant scheme were that applicants had to be in receipt of jobseekers benefit or jobseekers allowance and fully unemployed as the aim of the scheme was to provide quality work opportunities for people affected by long-term unemployment.

The Equality Tribunal noted that the respondent wholly controlled the complainant's eligibility for her employment with the West Cork Development Partnership and also provided the funding for the salaries for participants under this scheme. The Tribunal noted there was a potential tripartite employment relationship between the complainant, the West Cork Development Partnership and the respondent. Reference was made to the judgment of Dunne J in *Catholic University School v Dooley and Scannall*.[29] In that case, Dunne J held that the employment relationship is analogous to legislation applicable to agency workers, ie the person paying the worker was for the purpose of that legislation, the employer. Dunne J concluded that the Department of Education had to be viewed as the employer of the chosen comparators for the purpose of the legislation.

In this case, the Equality Tribunal concluded that the Department of Social Protection was the appropriate respondent for the complaint where it is alleged that conditions of access to a particular labour activation scheme, which it solely determines, are indirectly discriminatory for a person who enjoys the protections of the Employment Equality Acts. Ultimately, the Equality Tribunal found that the complainant had not established a prima facie case of discrimination on family status grounds and noted that, regardless of the complainant's family status, she would not have been eligible for the position for reasons wholly unrelated to her family status.

Age

[4.16] *Sefidvash v Institute of Art, Design & Technology*[30] – *Labour Court – Industrial Relations Acts 1946 to 2012 – Employment Equality Acts 1998 to 2011, s 83 – appeal of decision of Equality Tribunal to dismiss claim – appeal limited to claim of discrimination on grounds of age – requirement to establish prima facie case – lack of*

---

29. *Catholic University School v Dooley and Scannall* [2010] IEHC 496.
30. *Sefidvash v Institute of Art, Design & Technology* EDA 1334.

substantiation of claim – whether necessary to refer question as to vocational nature of course to CJEU

The complainant was a student of the respondent institution and alleged that the respondent discriminated against him on the grounds of age, race and religion in failing to award him a degree and failing to permit him to backdate his degree if he later succeeded in passing his examinations. The complainant failed to appear at the Equality Tribunal hearing and on that basis the Equality Tribunal dismissed his claim. He appealed the Equality Tribunal's dismissal of his claim to the Labour Court and proceeded with a claim of discrimination on the grounds of age only.

In the preliminary hearing, the Labour Court stated that it would be obliged to make a preliminary reference to the CJEU regarding the 'vocational' status of the course in question, within the meaning of the Employment Equality Acts but it would reserve making this reference unless and until it found that the complainant was discriminated against.

The complainant cited a number of situations where he alleged that he had been treated less favourably than other students on the basis of his age, including his treatment in relation to a project with which he admitted that he had received 'help', and the subsequent plagiarism investigation by the respondent in respect of the project. The Labour Court summarised the complainant's allegations of discriminatory treatment as follows:

(i)   an alleged remark made by his lecturer in January 2006 regarding his duty as a mature student in his fifties to take a leadership role for younger students;

(ii) a difference in treatment because of his age when he was accused of plagiarism and the respondent's refusal to award him a degree as a result;

(iii) an alleged lack of transparency in the assessment process, resulting in significant drop out rates by mature students;

(iv) an alleged failure to allow the complainant to log minutes of the disciplinary meeting regarding his plagiarism, thereby omitting his allegation of ageism from the record of the meeting.

Following his eventual exoneration from plagiarism allegations in respect of his project, the respondent nevertheless did not allow him to graduate.

The Labour Court referred to the statutory requirement on the complainant to establish facts from which discrimination may be inferred. The Labour Court referred to the test in *Mitchell v Southern Health Board*[31] which stated that the facts presented must be of sufficient significance to raise the presumption of discrimination and mere speculation or assertions, unsupported by evidence, cannot be elevated to a factual basis upon which an inference of discrimination can be drawn. The Labour Court stated that where a prima facie case of discrimination has been made out, the onus of proof shifts to the respondent to establish that its conduct was not based on discriminatory grounds,

---

31.   *Mitchell v Southern Health Board* [2001] ELR 201.

either consciously or unconsciously (as was stated in *Nagarajan v London Regional Transport*).[32]

The Labour Court stated that, in cases where discrimination is alleged, it is not the function of the Labour Court to assess the merits of a decision, but rather to ensure that the decision-making process was not tainted by unlawful discrimination.

During the course of its submission, the respondent contended that the complainant's claims were statute-barred, as the alleged conduct occurred over six months before the claim was initiated. The Labour Court held the complainant could only rely on matters that occurred within the six-month time limit.

Regarding the substantive issues which allegedly occurred within the statutory timeframe, the Labour Court found that it had not been presented with any facts to suggest that the complainant met the requisite academic standards and was nevertheless prevented from graduating due to his age. On the contrary, the Labour Court concluded that the facts presented support the position that the complainant did not reach the required standards but was afforded every opportunity and encouragement by the respondent to do so. Evidence was given that the respondent's registrar wrote to the complainant setting out the procedure for the complainant to present his updated project, how the new assessment process would work, and that if he was successful in passing the assignment, it would be in time for his degree conferral. The complainant was permitted to bring a friend to his assessment if he wished and the registrar also offered to sit in on the assessment panel as an observer if he so required. From this evidence, the Labour Court was satisfied that the complainant had not been treated in a discriminatory fashion by the respondent in respect of his assessment, or in respect of his grades in other subjects required to meet the degree standard.

The Labour Court found that the complainant could not substantiate any of his claims of discrimination by reference to facts from which discrimination could be inferred, and found that the complainant failed to establish a prima facie case of discrimination. The complainant's appeal was rejected.

[4.17] *Wilson v Diageo (Scotland) Ltd[33] – Employment Tribunal Scotland – age discrimination – whether cap on ex gratia redundancy payments amounted to indirect discrimination on ground of age*

The appellant brought a claim of age discrimination on the basis that a change to the respondent's redundancy policy to cap service related ex gratia payments at a maximum of 24 months' pay disadvantaged older employees with longer service. The respondent had conceded that the cap did have an indirectly discriminatory effect but asserted that same was objectively justified.

The redundancy arose because the site, on which the appellant was employed, was due to close and production was due to cease. It was decided that ex gratia redundancy payments to such employees of the claimant's category would be capped at a maximum of 24 months. There were other categories of employees on the relevant site and it was

---

32.   *Nagarajan v London Regional Transport* EOR87A.

33.   *Wilson v Diageo (Scotland) Ltd* S/4100153/13.

decided that the new policy would not apply to these employees as the respondent's view was that this group had already been through significant changes and therefore to impose a cap would be 'one step too far'. The new policy was to apply to employees of the claimant's category in order to align the level of redundancy payments across the Diageo Group in the UK. The ultimate aim at the time was to subsequently move to full consistency in respect of all employees.

The respondent gave evidence that the main driver for change, ie imposition of the cap, was a desire to standardise policies across the constituent companies which formed Diageo plc. The respondent confirmed that a benchmarking process had been carried out and that a cap of 24 months was seen as a generous scheme. A further objective was that the employees would be able to enjoy freedom of movement within the respondent's UK business, secure in the knowledge that they will be treated fairly and consistently through a robust and transparent set of employment policies. It was accepted by the respondent that the provision of the Scotland redundancy policy indirectly discriminated the category of employees affected and particularly placed those in the age group of 40 plus at a disadvantage. However, the respondent submitted that the legitimate aim at the time when the cap was imposed was to have a generous, fair and consistent scheme and to draw a line for that employee population in Scotland, taking into account all the relevant circumstances. It was submitted that the legitimate aim centred on what the respondent considered the appropriate and fair allocation of its financial resources in a redundancy situation having regard in particular to the position of the affected employees. Notwithstanding that the respondent could afford it, it was submitted that the cap was reasonably necessary as otherwise the legitimate aim of standardisation would have been defeated.

The Scottish Employment Tribunal concluded that the reason why the respondent sought to change the redundancy policies was its desire to simplify the position and bring together all the schemes into one consistent policy. In circumstances where a number of companies came together to form the respondent, the desire to review the various policies and put in place one consistent policy was a legitimate aim.

The Tribunal considered the question of proportionality and whether the means adopted to achieve this aim were proportionate. The Tribunal inferred that there was a desire to make available a comparably generous scheme, but with some limit imposed on the payment. The respondent's submission was that it was proportionate to cap the redundancy payments of the affected employees as they had higher rates of pay and bonus payments and the more highly skilled managers were better able to find alternative employment. However, the Tribunal found difficulty with the submission as the decision to introduce the cap was taken in London and it was a decision to cap all employees' redundancy payments regardless of category. The Tribunal felt that this undermined the respondent's submission and therefore there was no need to have regard to factors such as rate of pay and bonus payments. The Tribunal also found that no consideration was given as to why it was proportionate for the new policy to apply only to one category of employees. In this regard, the Tribunal found that there was no evidence to demonstrate that the means chosen for achieving the objective corresponded to a real need on the part of the respondent to introduce a cap on redundancy levels. There was likewise no evidence to explain why the imposition of a cap was necessary to achieve a consistent policy, applicable to all employees, which was generous and fair. The Tribunal found the respondent had been unable to demonstrate a real need to introduce the cap. The Tribunal also took into account the fact that there was no evidence to suggest that the respondent considered whether the legitimate aim could be achieved by other means. The Tribunal upheld the claim and ordered the respondent to pay to the appellant the sum of £58,267, ie the difference between the capped and uncapped redundancy payments.

[4.18] *Hanlon & Ors v Lake Communications Ltd[34] – Equality Tribunal – Employment Equality Acts 1998 to 2011 – discrimination in relation to conditions of employment on grounds of age – whether cap on ex gratia redundancy payments indirectly discriminated against complainants on grounds of age – redundancy cap based on service not age*

The claims arose from a decision towards the end of 2010 by the respondent to transfer the hardware development and support function carried out in Ireland to Arizona and to make corresponding redundancies in Ireland owing to the considerable losses at the multi-national group of which the respondent was part. The complainants were made redundant and were paid their statutory redundancy entitlement plus an ex gratia payment. They claimed that the cap on their redundancy payments was indirectly discriminatory against them as each complainant received proportionately less ex gratia payment per year of service. The Labour Court concluded in separate proceedings under the Industrial Relations Acts that the complainants had been unfairly treated and recommended that the respondent enter into dialogue with the complainants. However, the respondent refused to do so due to its financial circumstances.

The respondent submitted that the matter was *res judicata* as the Labour Court had made a final judicial decision on the same facts and that the equality claim should be estopped as the matter could not be re-litigated. Furthermore, the respondent asserted that the complainants had failed to establish a link between their ages and their treatment as the calculation of the redundancy payments had no connection to the complainant's age.

The respondent submitted that a full and proper consultation process was carried out. It explained that no cap was imposed on the redundancies made in 2008 as the respondent's financial position was vastly different. It submitted that the cap was not discriminatory as it applied to all employees and was fair and reasonable in light of the financial circumstances. The respondent relied on *Hospira v Mary Roper & Ors[35]* in which the Labour Court stated that it was reasonably and objectively justifiable to provide for different treatment where the underlying rationale is that workers close to retirement are in a substantially different position than those who have longer periods in which they could have expected to remain in the active labour force. The respondent further submitted that the complainants had provided no comparators who received different treatment.

---

34.   *Hanlon & Ors v Lake Communications Ltd* DEC–E2014–062.
35.   *Hospira v Roper & Ors* EDA1315.

The respondent cited s 34(3)(d) of the Acts which provides, *inter alia*, that providing different severance payments based on the age of employees does not constitute age discrimination.

The Equality Tribunal found that the recommendation of the Labour Court was not 'a final judicial decision' and that there was nothing in the recommendation that indicated that the matter was considered as an age discrimination issue. The Equality Tribunal stated that, although the facts of the claims were largely similar, they were being investigated in different contexts; the Labour Court had considered the matter as an industrial relations issue, while the Equality Tribunal was considering it as a claim of discrimination.

The Equality Tribunal stated that the cap was imposed on the basis of service with the respondent and was not directly related to their closeness to retirement. The complainants:

> did not receive a lesser payment but less recognition of their service ... The cap did not mean that anyone approaching retirement age was paid less. No one was paid less; those with more service were paid the same as each other and more than those with less than ten years' service.

Therefore, the amount the complainants were provided with depended on service. Age was not a primary factor in their different treatment. The Equality Tribunal concluded that the redundancy cap imposed by the respondent did not amount to discrimination on the grounds of age.

[4.19] *MacNamara and Seven Named Complainants v Electricity Supply Board[36] – Equality Tribunal – Pension Acts 1990 to 2012, s 66, 70 and 81(E) – equal pension treatment – age – frivolous, vexatious and misconceived*

The complainants were all retired employees of the respondent and in receipt of pension benefits from the ESB defined benefit pension scheme. The complainants submitted that, as a consequence of the manner in which the pension levy was applied to the scheme, the respondent discriminated against them on grounds of age contrary to the Pensions Acts 1990 to 2012.

The complainants stated that membership of the scheme was compulsory under their conditions of employment with the respondent and that contributions to the scheme were made, by both the respondent and staff, on a ratio of 2:1. The complainants further stated that previous funding shortfalls in the scheme were generally addressed by increased funding by both the respondent and employees. They submitted that the respondent had an obligation to contribute all, or a significant element, of the cost of pension levy. The trustees wrote to the respondent seeking financial assistance towards payment of the pension levy and the respondent refused to do so. The trustees then decided to reduce retired members' benefits by 0.6% to discharge the pension levy costs. The complainants submitted that the decision to reduce the retired members' benefits amounted to discrimination against them on grounds of age.

---

36.   *MacNamara and Seven Named Complainants v Electricity Supply Board* DEC-P2014–001.

The respondent submitted that the complainants' claims were frivolous, vexatious and misconceived. The respondent argued:

(a) that the claims were time barred;

(b) that it was a stranger to the claims, which should properly lie against the trustees of the scheme of which the complainants are members; and

(c) that the claims did not relate to a rule of the scheme.

The respondent argued that as per s 81E(5) of the Pensions Acts, claims must in the first instance be referred to the Equality Tribunal within six months of the termination of the relevant employment. This may be extended to a maximum of 12 months. The respondent noted that all of the complainants had ceased employment more one year before the claim was referred to the Equality Tribunal.

The complainants argued that the time limits prescribed by the Employment Equality Acts, rather than the Pension Acts, should be applied to the present case. The pension levy was only introduced in 2011 and therefore could not have been contemplated by pension legislation. They noted that the decision to fund the levy by reducing their benefits from the scheme was only communicated to them in November 2012 and they made the complaint within a month or so, well within the time limits.

The complainants argued that the ESB was the correct respondent as it was responsible for appointing several key members of the board of trustees and provides administrative assistance to the Scheme.

The Equality Tribunal found that the Pensions Acts 1990 to 2012 applied and therefore the claims were statute barred.

However, in the interest of completeness the Equality Tribunal also noted that the decision to reduce the complainants' pension was made by the trustees alone and therefore the claims taken were against the incorrect respondent. The Equality Tribunal was also satisfied that in reaching that decision the trustees were not applying or operating any 'rule' of the scheme as per the definition of that word at s 65 of the Pensions Acts 1990 to 2012.

[4.20] *Lett v Earagail Eisc Teoranta*[37] *– Equality Tribunal – Employment Equality Acts 1998 to 2011 – whether complainant discriminated against on grounds of age in relation to his dismissal and in relation to his conditions of employment by being forced to retire at age 66 and by being forced to work part-time prior to that retirement*

The respondent company was previously owned and controlled by the complainant and his family, before being taken over in April 2007. It was accepted, that whilst the complainant had been in control of the respondent, he only became an employee of the respondent in April 2007 when the takeover was complete. The complainant was offered a two-year fixed-term contract of employment which was subsequently renewed until it eventually became a contract of indefinite duration. In March 2010 the complainant received a document purporting to relate back to March 2009 and suggesting that his

---

37.   *Lett v Earagail Eisc Teoranta* DEC–E2014–076.

employment would terminate in September 2011 on his 66th birthday. In February 2011, the complainant was informed that, as part of a restructuring, his position might be superfluous to ongoing requirements. In the same correspondence, he was advised that as there was no current requirement for his position to be carried out on a full time basis, he would be on a three-day week until his retirement date in September 2011.

The complainant submitted that he had to be on call seven days a week 24 hours a day to liaise with trawler men and sellers of products. He stated that the February letter was the first time he had been advised of any alleged retirement date and noted that at least one other staff member had worked with the respondent up to the age of 70. It was submitted by the respondent that the complainant was well aware of the company's retirement age (65), however this was denied by the complainant, who stated that prior to the takeover there were no uniform or structured HR practices and the company handbook had only been developed in 2006.

The Equality Tribunal concluded that the complainant had not received a copy of the handbook as part of his contract and thus may not have been aware of the clause which provided that 65 is the mandatory retirement age for employees. The Equality Tribunal noted s 34(4) of the Acts and noted it has been the practice of the Equality Tribunal to interpret s 34(4) in a harmonious way with art 6(1) of the Equal Treatment Directive. The Tribunal therefore concluded that where the complainant had established a prima facie case of discriminatory dismissal the respondent, even as a private employer, must provide the Equality Tribunal with an objective justification for the discriminatory treatment.

The Equality Tribunal considered the objective grounds put forward by the respondent, including workforce planning, ensuring a high quality of service and ensuring continued competence, having an age balanced work force and intergenerational fairness or sharing job opportunities amongst the generations, avoiding disputes with older employees about their fitness to work, contributing to a pleasant workplace and protecting the dignity of the older workforce by not requiring them to undergo performance management procedures, and ensuring that the company is perceived as fair and decent by retaining employees in so far as is possible until they can avail of the statutory and private pension arrangements, thereby ensuring any drop in living standards is minimised.

The Tribunal noted two of the reasons advanced by the respondent, namely workforce planning and having an age balanced workforce, and intergenerational fairness, and held that while such reasons have, in the past, been accepted in principle as amounting to objective justification – in the instant case the complainant was never replaced. The Tribunal found that it was clear that the complainant's job was not used as an internal promotion opportunity for junior staff but instead it was advertised externally.

The Tribunal also noted that the post had not yet been filled. The Tribunal queried the necessity for the complainant to retire at 65 if the job was not given to anyone else. The Tribunal concluded that the respondent had provided no evidence to support the claim that this aim was necessary and gave no evidence that valuable staff could be lost if no promotional opportunities were provided. The Tribunal also noted the cited justification 'avoiding disputes with older employees about their fitness to work'. The

Tribunal noted that the respondent had not raised an issue in respect of the complainant's ability to perform the job and further did not relate the ability to perform the job with any attributes or characteristics requiring the incumbent to be 65 or under. The reasons advanced by the respondent appeared to be more general reasons and were not in any way specific to its staff. The Tribunal was critical of the respondent for taking a one-size-fits-all approach for the setting of a retirement age at 65.

The Tribunal noted that employers were entitled to set a mandatory retirement age but noted that this requirement should be capable of being justified on objective and reasonable grounds.

The Equality Tribunal concluded that the respondent had failed to show that its decision to apply the retirement age was objectively justified this time. The Tribunal further concluded that the respondent discriminated against the complainant on grounds of age in respect of his dismissal.

The Equality Tribunal noted the respondent's decision that the complainant's job could be done on a three-day week basis and the fact that this had been decided on foot of a restructuring of the respondent's activities. The Tribunal noted that no evidence of such restructuring or any evidence to show that the job could be done on a three-day week basis was submitted. The Tribunal held that the respondent had arrived at this conclusion without any consultation or discussion with the complainant, which would appear in the view of the Tribunal to be necessary before arriving at the conclusion the role could be carried out over a three-day week. The Tribunal noted that subsequently the respondent advertised the position as a full time position. The Equality Tribunal upheld the complaint of discrimination on grounds of age in relation to conditions of employment and also in relation to the complainant's dismissal.

In considering redress, the Equality Tribunal noted that the respondent had kept the complainant on after the takeover and the complainant had agreed the terms of the contract days before the takeover. The respondent had inherited a company handbook which imposed a mandatory retirement age of 65 which it was then unable to objectively justify. The Tribunal also noted the decision to reduce the complainant's hours to three days a week prior to his retirement and concluded that the complainant's assertion that he had continued to do the job on a full time basis despite being only paid for three days a week was implausible. The Equality Tribunal awarded compensation of €24,000.

DISABILITY

Could obesity come within the definition of disability?

[4.21] *Kaltoft v Kommunernes Landsforening (KL), acting on behalf of the Municipality of Billund[38] – opinion of Advocate General – equal treatment in employment and occupation – discrimination on grounds of disability – whether EU fundamental rights law includes general prohibition of discrimination in labour*

---

38. *Karsten Kaltoft v Kommunernes Landsforening (KL), acting on behalf of the Municipality of Billund* (Case C–354/13).

market covering discrimination on grounds of obesity – scope of application of EU Charter of Fundamental Rights – whether obesity can amount to 'disability' under Directive 2000/78, art 1

The plaintiff was a childminder who, during the course of his 15 years of employment, was obese. He was dismissed by the respondent, who informed the plaintiff that there had been a decline in the number of children requiring childminding. The plaintiff weighed 25 stone and had a body mass index of 54 at the time of his dismissal. He alleged that he was unlawfully discriminated against because of his obesity and sought compensation.

The Advocate General considered whether EU fundamental rights law includes a general prohibition of discrimination in the labour market and covered discrimination on grounds of obesity.

The Advocate General noted that the concept of 'disability' is not defined by the Directive, and nor does the Directive refer to the laws of the Member States for its definition (which was also noted in the *Chacon Navas*[39] case).

The Advocate General cited the *Z* case in which it was held that the notion of 'disability' for the purposes of the Directive must be understood as referring to limitations which result, in particular, from:

(i)   long-term;

(ii) physical, mental or psychological impairments;

(iii) which in interaction with various barriers;

(iv) may hinder;

(v)   the full and effective participation of the person in professional life;

(vi) on an equal basis with other workers.[40]

While the Advocate General acknowledged that there is nothing in the Directive to suggest that workers are protected by the prohibition of discrimination on grounds of disability as soon as they develop any type of sickness, he pointed out that it is established in the case law that 'if a curable or incurable illness' entails a limitation corresponding with the definition above, such an illness can be covered by the concept of 'disability' within the meaning of the Directive, if medically diagnosed, and the limitation is a long term one. Furthermore, he highlighted that the Court has held that it 'would run counter to the very aim of the directive, which is to implement equal treatment, to define its scope by reference to the origin of the disability'.

The Advocate General stated that taking into account that the objective of the Directive is to enable a person with a disability to have access to or participate in employment, the concept of disability must be understood as referring to a hindrance to the exercise of professional activity, not only to the impossibility of exercising such

---

39.   *Chacon Navas v Eurest Colectividades SA* [2006] ECR 1–6467.

40.   *Z v A Government Dept and the Board of Management of a Community School* (Case C–363/12), para 80, and *Commission v Italy* (Case C–213/11), para 56, citing *HK Danmark* (Case C–335/11), paras 38 and 39.

activity. He pointed out that the UN Convention on Human Rights acknowledges in recital (e) that:

> disability is an evolving concept and that disability results from the interaction between persons with impairments and attitudinal and environmental barriers that hinders their full and effective participation in society on an equal basis with others.

The Advocate General stated that it is sufficient that a long-term condition causes limitations in full and effective participation in professional life in general on equal terms with persons not having that condition. No link has to be made between the work concerned and the disability in issue before the Directive can apply.

He noted that recital 17 of Directive 2000/78 imposes no obligation to maintain in employment an individual who is not competent to perform the essential functions of the post concerned, but this is without prejudice to the obligation appearing in art 5 of Directive 2000/78 for reasonable accommodation to be provided in order to guarantee compliance with the principle of equal treatment in relation to persons with disabilities. This means that employers are to take appropriate measures, where needed in a particular case, to enable a person with a disability to have access to, participate in, or advance in employment, unless such measures result in the imposition of a disproportionate burden on the employer.

The Advocate General stated that the applicability of the concept of disability depends on the concrete circumstances of the work in question, not abstract medical or social insurance classifications concerning the degree of the impairment as such, ie what is decisive is the 'obstacles' a person encounters when they come into contact with that environment.

In conclusion on this point, the Advocate General stated that it need not be impossible for Mr Kaltoft to carry out his work as a childminder with the Municipality of Billund before he can rely on the disability discrimination protection afforded by the Directive. The case law merely requires him to meet the notion of disability set out in the Directive and as set out above.

The Advocate General noted that obesity is usually measured with reference to body mass index. The WHO ranks obesity into three classes by reference to the BMI. Persons with a BMI of 30.00 to 34.99 are obese class I, persons with a BMI of 35.00 to 39.99 are obese class II, and persons with a BMI in excess of 40.00 are obese class III, which is sometimes referred to as severe, extreme or morbid obesity. The Advocate General noted that obesity has been considered to be a disability under the law of the United States of America.

The Advocate General noted that classification of obesity as an illness by the World Health Organisation is not sufficient to render it a disability for the purposes of the Directive.

He concluded that in cases where the condition of obesity has reached such a severe degree that it, in interaction with attitudinal and environmental barriers as mentioned in the UN Convention, plainly hinders full participation in professional life on an equal footing with other employees due to the physical and/or psychological limitations that it entails, it can be considered to be a disability. However, he stated that 'mere' obesity in the sense of WHO class I obesity is insufficient to fulfil the criteria in the Court's case law on 'disability' under the Directive.

A concern was raised at the hearing that admitting obesity in any form as being a disability would lead to intolerable results because alcoholism and drug addiction could then, as serious illnesses, be covered by that notion. The AG stated that this concern was misplaced because while these are diseases, an employer would not be required to tolerate an employee's breach of contract by reference to these diseases.

On 18 December 2014[41] the CJEU handed down its judgment in this case. The CJEU held that EU law must be interpreted as not laying down a general principle of non-discrimination on grounds of obesity as regards employment and occupation. The CJEU held that the Framework Directive must be interpreted such that obesity of a worker constitutes a disability within the meaning of that directive where it entails a limitation resulting in particular from long-term physical, mental or psychological impairments which, in interaction with various barriers, may hinder the full and effective participation of the person concerned in professional life on an equal basis with other workers. The CJEU confirmed that it was for the national court to determine whether, in the main proceedings, those conditions are met.

The definition of disability

[4.22] *Byrne v Sea and Shore Safety Services Ltd[42] – Labour Court — appeal of decision of Equality Tribunal – Employment Equality Acts 1998 to 2011 – whether anxiety and post-traumatic stress due to ongoing exposure to rodents came within definition of disability – reasonable accommodation – discriminatory treatment – harassment – victimisation – valid redundancy or discriminatory dismissal*

The complainant claimed that in May 2008 she saw a mouse in the small timber-framed office where she worked, which was adjacent to the proprietor's home. It was established in evidence that there had previously been no issue of rodents in the workplace but that in 2008 major works commenced associated with the development of a retail centre on adjacent lands. This resulted in the increased presence of rodents in the workplace of the complainant. The complainant brought the sighting of the mouse to the attention of the general manager of the respondent, who installed mouse traps to deal with the problem. A number of days later the complainant saw a mouse on the desk in front of her. The complainant left the office and informed the managing director of the respondent that she could not return to work until the rodent problem was resolved. The complainant wrote to the directors of the respondent in June 2008 advising that she had been unhappy, stressed and nervous about coming into work because of rodents. In this letter the complainant noted that she had suggested that the respondent acquire the services of a pest removal company in order to rid the workplace of rodents, but that the respondent instead had relied on plug-in sonar devices. The complainant stated that for her

---

41.   *Karsten Kaltoft v Kommunernes Landsforening (KL), acting on behalf of the Municipality of Billund* (Case C–354/13).

42.   *Byrne v Sea and Shore Safety Services Ltd* EDA 143.

employer to expect her to work in such an environment was putting undue stress and pressure upon her. The complainant had previously sent a letter to the directors of the respondent explaining her phobia with regard to rodents.

The directors of the respondent subsequently wrote to the complainant in which they stated that they had laid mouse traps in the office and that these would be re-baited and checked regularly. The respondent had also purchased a powerful ultrasonic rodent repellent and installed this in the office and in the barn area. With regard to the complainant's absence from work, the respondent offered her a combination of annual leave (which had already been pre-booked) and paid leave so that she would not return to work until August 2008. The complainant duly returned on this date.

In July 2010 the complainant submitted that she encountered a rat in the office which resulted in her becoming hysterical as she has a phobia with regard to rodents, and rats in particular. The complainant was unable to enter the premises and took some belongings and files with her in order to work from home. The complainant wrote to the managing director requesting that the situation be addressed as a matter of urgency. The complainant reminded the respondent of her phobia and stressed the seriousness of the problem for her. The complainant set out the elements of a preventive plan that she sought by way of accommodation of her phobia, to enable her to return to work. This plan included implementing a pest prevention strategy carrying out a risk assessment of the work environment and monitoring that the strategy was working correctly. On the complainant's return to work on 3 August 2010, there was an unpleasant smell in the workplace and the complainant was informed that poison had been laid to deal with the infestation, and the smell was that of dead rodents. The complainant submitted that the director of the respondent was entirely unsympathetic to her in relation to this and shouted at her to open a window. The director also stated that the smell had been caused as a result of laying poison for the complainant's 'little friends'. The complainant stated that she could not cope with the conditions at this point and left work until the situation was resolved.

The general manager of the respondent wrote to the complainant in August 2010 and stated that a number of steps had been undertaken to eliminate any possible risks in relation to the rodent problem. This letter also informed the complainant that the respondent had paid her full pay while she was absent from work since July, and that with effect from 13 September 2010 the respondent would discontinue payment in respect of sick leave.

The complainant's solicitor wrote to the respondent on 2 September 2010 putting the respondent on notice that the complainant's rights under the Acts had been infringed by failing to provide her with reasonable accommodation to undertake her work. This letter also offered for the complainant to meet with the respondent accompanied by her representative.

As a result of the downturn in the market, the directors of the respondent asked the general manager to conduct a review of the financial costs of the respondent and to report on the current position and the option to either: (a) reduce the respondent's expenditure; or (b) market the respondent's services in order to increase its income. The accounts for the year ended 31 December 2009 showed that the respondent had traded at a loss in 2009. The general manager presented his report to the directors of the respondent on 5 October 2010, and recommended that the complainant be made redundant. The directors sanctioned this on 6 October 2010.

The complainant received a letter from the general manager of the respondent on 7 October 2010 advising that her employment would terminate by reason of redundancy with effect from 5 November 2010.

The Labour Court noted that there were four points to be determined in relation to the complainant's appeal:

(i)   Was the complainant suffering from a disability within the meaning of the Acts, and if so, was the complainant afforded reasonable accommodation to perform her work in light of her disability?

(ii) Did the complainant suffer harassment in relation to her disability?

(iii) Was the complainant victimised as a result of making a complaint/asserting her rights under the Acts?

(iv) Was the complainant's redundancy a valid redundancy or was her dismissal related to her complaint under the Acts?

The Labour Court noted that s 2 of the Employment Equality Acts 1998 to 2011 includes the following in the definition of disability:

> ... a condition, illness or disease which affects a person's thought process, perception of reality, emotions or judgement or which results in disturbed behaviour, and shall be taken to include a disability which exists at present or which previously existed but no longer exits, or which may exist in the future or which is imputed to a person.

The Labour Court noted that the complainant had submitted a medical report in which it was stated that she was suffering from 'excess anxiety and post-traumatic stress due to ongoing exposure to rodents at her place of work'. On the basis of the uncontested medical evidence before it, the Labour Court found that the complainant had a disability within the meaning of s 2(e) of the Acts.

The Labour Court then addressed the issues of whether the complainant had been afforded reasonable accommodation in order to perform her work.

The Labour Court noted that the reasonable accommodation sought by the complainant was for the respondent to develop and institute a coherent and effective plan to deal with the rodent problem. While the complainant suggested the use of a professional pest extermination company for this purpose, the respondent refused this on the basis of its cost. Instead the respondent engaged in *ad hoc* measures to address the problem as and when it was brought to its attention. The complainant was not communicated with in the development of a plan to address the issue and there were no detailed measures established to address the issue. The Labour Court also noted that no evidence was presented that the respondent at any time carried out a risk assessment of the work environment. The Labour Court found that the facts revealed that the professional management of the problem would have been inexpensive and easy to document had the respondent done so. The Labour Court determined that the respondent failed to provide the complainant with reasonable accommodation within the meaning of the Acts.

In relation to the claim of harassment, the Labour Court noted that s 14(a)(7)(a) of the Employment Equality Acts 1998 to 2011 defines harassment as:

> any form of unwanted conduct related to any of the discriminatory grounds ... being conduct which in either case has the purpose or effect of violating a person's dignity and creating an intimidating, hostile, degrading, humiliating or offensive environment for that person.

The complainant submitted that she had been harassed on 3 August 2010 when the director shouted at her regarding the smell of dead rodents. The director did not contest the complainant's evidence that he had referred to the rats as her 'little friends'. The Labour Court found that the respondent's director had created a hostile and intimidating environment through his behaviour towards the complainant, and this hostile environment was connected with the rodent problem raised by the complainant and was therefore connected with her disability. The Labour Court noted that the incident lead to the complainant leaving work to which she never returned thereafter. The Labour Court found that the claim in relation to harassment was well founded.

In relation to the claim of victimisation for making a complaint to the respondent regarding a breach of the Acts, the Labour Court noted, that in the letter to the complainant of 25 August 2010, the respondent indicated to her that it would have to place her on unpaid sick leave and gave her two weeks' notice of this. The Labour Court noted that the real purpose of this letter was to threaten the complainant with the removal of sick pay. The Labour Court noted that the respondent had failed to engage with the complainant and the letter of 25 August 2010 was a device to compel her to return to work without any effort to assess or accommodate her disability. The Labour Court found that the actual removal of the complainant from sick pay on 13 September 2010 was influenced by the complainant's solicitor's letter of 2 September 2010, and accordingly the complaint was well founded.

In respect of the redundancy issue, the Labour Court found that the justification for redundancy could not be separated from the events that were taking place in the respondent at the time. The Labour Court found, on the balance of probabilities, that the respondent had decided to dismiss the complainant as a means of dealing with the issues under the Act which had been raised. The Labour Court noted that the respondent did not engage either with the complainant or with her representative and instead it took the opportunity presented by the respondent's trading position to terminate the complainant's employment. The Labour Court found that the complaint in this regard was well founded.

The Labour Court determined that the decision of the Equality Tribunal be set aside and ordered the respondent to pay the complainant compensation of €20,000.

[4.23] *Stobart (Ireland) Ltd v Beashel[43] – Labour Court – Industrial Relations Acts 1946 to 2012 –Employment Equality Acts 1998 to 2011, s 83 – appeal of Equality Tribunal decision – whether complainant dismissed on grounds of disability –*

---

43. *Stobart (Ireland) Ltd v Beashel* EDA 1411.

whether complainant's condition constituted an illness or disability such as to give
him locus standi to bring claim – obligations of employer

Evidence was given that the complainant had accrued 23 days of absence, all bar two
days of which were certified. He had suffered from a variety of issues, to include sinus
trouble, a back injury and, following the loss of his father in December 2008, he was
diagnosed with suffering from depression in May 2010 and required some time off. He
was medically certified unfit for work for a two-week period at this time. On returning
to work he was interviewed by the respondent's operations manager and was informed
that if he needed more time off this could be arranged. He then returned to work. One
week later he was instructed by human resources to attend a meeting with another
manager. He was given no details of the purpose of the meeting and at the meeting was
informed that he was being dismissed with immediate effect.

The parties differed as to the reasons given for the dismissal. It was alleged by the
complainant that he was absent for 23 days and this was why he was dismissed. However
the respondent stated that he was told that the reason for his dismissal was a
combination of his absence levels and his poor performance. The complainant asserted
that he was suffering from depression, a medically diagnosed disability, and that written
evidence of this had been provided to the respondent on his return to work. It was
submitted that the proximity of his declaration of disability, and the subsequent decision
to dismiss him summarily, raised a prima facie case of discriminatory dismissal. It was
also submitted that no reasonable accommodation was offered to him to enable to him to
discharge his duties.

The respondent asserted that the complainant was suffering from an illness but not a
disability and therefore did not have *locus standi* to bring the claim. The respondent
placed reliance on the decision of the CJEU in *Chacon Navas*[44] where it was held:

> for limitation of the capacity to participate in professional life to fall within the
> concept of disability it must be probably that it would last for a long time.

The respondent submitted that the complainant was not prescribed any further
medication and that he appeared to have recovered within a very short time and
therefore the test set out in *Chacon Navas* was not met.

The Labour Court referred to the evidence provided by the manager who made the
decision to dismiss that he was not advised by human resources of any reason why he
should not proceed to dismiss the complainant and specifically he was not aware that the
complainant was suffering from depression or had been offered time off by his other
manager. Notably the decision maker admitted in evidence that, had he had the
information to hand, he would not have dismissed the complainant but would have made
accommodation to enable the complainant to manage his depression. The Labour Court
did not accept the respondent's reliance on the decision of the CJEU in *Chacon Navas*
and the assertion that the complainant's case was not long term in nature. The Labour
Court noted that the complainant had been medically diagnosed with depression and
that the respondent had noted this and the manager who had met with him had offered to
accommodate him with time off should he need it to cope with this disability. It was

---

44.   *Chacon Navas v Eurest Colectividades SA* [2006] ECR 1–6467.

further noted that human resources was copied with medical certificates and the manager's reports and observations. The Labour Court concluded that the respondent, whilst aware of the condition, made no enquiries to determine the likely prognosis for it. The Labour Court further noted the complainant's evidence that he still suffers from periods of depression. The Court took the view that the respondent had kept itself ignorant of the complainant's prognosis, and having done so, could not seek to rely on subsequent events to excuse its failure to establish his medical condition at the time it decided the issue.

The Court held that the obligation on the respondent was to establish whether the complainant's condition was likely to be long or short term, either by engaging with the complainant directly or through his or the company's own medical advisors. It was not sufficient that it made no enquiries and sought to rely on subsequent events to justify its decision. The Court concluded that the complainant was suffering from a disability within the meaning of the Acts. The Court then considered whether the decision to dismiss the complainant was influenced by his disability. It noted that the complainant did have a history of absence from the time his employment started and that the acceptable level of absenteeism had been exceeded by the complainant before he was diagnosed with depression. The Court however noted that human resources had not flagged to the decision maker the complainant's high level of absenteeism until after it received the medical cert diagnosing depression and the original manager's report on the return to work discussion he had with him. The Court noted that, when the human resources department did flag the high level of absenteeism, they did not disclose the medical diagnosis or the return to work report.

The Labour Court concluded that the complainant had established a prima facie case that his dismissal may have been influenced by his disability. It gave particular weight to the evidence of the decision maker that he would have come to a different decision had he been aware of the information that had been submitted to human resources. The Court accepted the complainant's contention that depression was a long-term condition that may not be ever present but may affect a person from time to time. The Court noted that the respondent had made no medical enquiries as to the nature of the complainant's depression or as to the frequency or extent it might impair his capacity to work, nor did it engage with the complainant to determine the reasonable accommodation he might require when suffering bouts of depression. The Court concluded that the respondent had discriminatorily dismissed the complainant on grounds of his disability and that the respondent had failed to provide appropriate measures to allow the complainant to continue in his employment. The complainant was awarded €12,000 compensation.

Reasonable accommodation

[4.24] *A Public Service Employer v A Worker*[45] *– Labour Court – appeal of decision of Equality Tribunal – Industrial Relations Acts 1946 to 2012 – Employment Equality Acts 1998 to 2011 – whether complainant discriminated against by respondent on disability grounds – whether respondent had breached its duty to provide complainant*

---

45. *A Public Service Employer v A Worker* ADE/13/43.

with reasonable measures to accommodate her disability to include suitable place of work having regard to her requirements to be near toilet facilities – time limits and concept of continuing discrimination – award of €65,000

The complainant worked as a medical secretary, originally located in a hospital under the control of the respondent. It was accepted that the complainant suffered from a medical condition that required her to visit the toilet frequently. Originally she worked with one other person in an office adjacent to a toilet. The respondent then decided to relocate the complainant and all of her colleagues to another part of the hospital. The complainant did not believe this location to be suitable because of its distance from the toilet facilities and given it required office sharing. The complainant provided her manager with a medical report on her condition and it was accepted that she should not be relocated at that particular time.

She remained in situ until July 2007, when she was instructed by a different manager to relocate to a multi-person office occupied by the other secretaries. The complainant went on sick leave, and, apart from a return to work for a short period in the interim, she remained on sick leave. The complainant's doctor and an independent occupational health physician both concurred with the medical opinion that the complainant would be able to return to work if she was provided with a room on her own, adjacent to toilet facilities. The complainant's trade union became involved in trying to resolve the problems faced by her and in 2008 she was offered a number of different positions all of which were considered unsuitable by the complainant because of their requirement that she have direct contact with the public and/or work out of hours. Ultimately the complainant was appointed to an upgraded post in primary care in December 2009, which she accepted, subject to suitable office accommodation being provided.

From May 2010, there was direct engagement with her as to the work facilities where she would be located. The complainant was brought on a visit to the primary health centre and showed the facilities, and when alterations were requested by the complainant to the layout of the centre, these were undertaken. The complainant began working at that location in June 2010 but shortly thereafter she went on sick leave as she referenced that she had a problem in dealing with the public. Further arrangements were made whereby the complainant could work elsewhere on the day that was open to the public on a weekly basis. The complainant was also advised to contact the respondent's support office to discuss her difficulties with them. However, the Labour Court noted that the complainant did not take up this advice. Further evidence was given as to different proposals that were made to the complainant regarding a number of different alternative assignments that were offered to her. Evidence was given by the complainant of the various reasons for rejecting the offers of alternative employment made by the respondent.

The second limb of the complaint was that the respondent advertised a competition to upgrade the type of post in which the complainant was employed and following an application process, she was placed 51st on a panel. The complainant asserted that the first 50 candidates were appointed to an upgraded post but she was not upgraded and subsequently the person placed number 54 was upgraded. It was noted however that the complainant was ultimately upgraded to the post in December 2009.

The Labour Court firstly considered the issue of time limits as it was contended by the respondent that this complaint was outside the limits specified at s 77(5) of the Employment Equality Acts. It was submitted by the complainant that this was a case of continuing discrimination arising from the respondent's failure to provide the complainant with an appropriate place of work. The Labour Court made reference to *Hurley v County Cork VEC*[46] *Robertson v Bexley Community Centre*[47] and the decision of the Court of Appeal for England and Wales in *Cast v Croydon College.*[48] The Labour Court concluded that the 'gravamen' of the complainant's case was that the respondent failed to provide her with a place of work that adequately took account of her disability which involved a claim that the respondent had failed to fulfil its statutory duty to provide her with reasonable accommodation. The Court stated its satisfaction that, for as long as the complainant remained in the respondent's employment, that duty subsisted. It appeared to the Court, 'that a failure to fulfil that duty amounted to the keeping in force of a discriminatory regime, rule, practice or principle which has had a clear and adverse effect on the complainant'. The Court also noted that, from the evidence before it, the respondent had continued to review the decision on where to locate the complainant over an extended period. With reference to *Cast v Croydon College*, the Court concluded that this could also prevent time from running against the complainant in relation to the original decision.

The Court noted that it was not clear as to the circumstances in which the complainant came to be moved from the office she originally occupied, but found that the decision to relocate the complainant was not because of her disability but it was to meet a requirement of the respondent. In this regard, the Court noted that she was treated no differently from others who were similarly required to relocate. However, the Court noted its findings in *Campbell Catering v Raseq*[49] where the Court stated 'discrimination can arise where similar situations are treated differently and where different situations are treated similarly'. The Court concluded that in order to continue in employment the complainant needed special arrangements in relation to the facilities available to her during the course of her employment. The Labour Court did find that the witnesses that engaged with the complainant after May 2010 did all that was reasonably open to them to accommodate her. They consulted with her and her trade union on what was required and they responded to any request she had made. The Court noted that their response was a model of how an employer should respond to the type of situation with which they were presented.

The Labour Court noted that the accommodation provided to the complainant at the primary healthcare centre in May 2010 met all of her identified needs and fulfilled the respondent's duty to provide her with reasonable accommodation. It was noted that the respondent continued to offer her alternative places of work which met her requirements. However the complainant had rejected all of them. The Court stated that she had no justifiable grounds for so doing. The Labour Court concluded that, from

---

46. *Hurley v County Cork VEC* EDA1124.
47. *Robertson v Bexley Community Centre* [2003] IRLR 434.
48. *Cast v Croydon College* [1998] IRLR 318.
49. *Campbell Catering v Raseq* [2005] 15 ELR 310.

June 2010, the respondent had fulfilled its duty to provide the complainant with reasonable accommodation and did not discriminate against her thereafter.

However, the Court said there was no evidence offered by the respondent as to what, if anything, was done to accommodate her until the matter was taken up at national level by the general secretary of her union and the deputy director of human resources and in the interim she was unable to continue her employment and was required to avail of sick leave. The Court concluded that the respondent had failed to provide the complainant with a suitable place of work having to regard to her disability between July 2007 and June 2010 and had discriminated against her between those dates.

The Labour Court determined that the complainant was not treated any less favourably in relation to the upgrading of posts and therefore had failed to raise an inference of discrimination as is required.

The Court noted the award of €70,000 compensation made by the Equality Tribunal for the discrimination that was found to have occurred. The Court noted its difference in finding that the complainant had not suffered discrimination in relation to the filling of the upgraded post. The Court concluded that the appropriate award was €65,000. The Court noted that the Equality Tribunal had made an ancillary order directing the type and location of office accommodation with which the complainant should be provided and the duties to which she should be assigned, and the Court determined it was appropriate not to uphold that ancillary order and varied the findings of the Equality Tribunal on that basis.

[4.25] *Ms H v A Multinational Retailer[50] – Equality Tribunal – Employment Equality Acts 1998 to 2011 – discrimination on grounds of disability – failure to provide appropriate measures to include facilitating complainant's request to be able to sit for some of her working day and having access to a wheelchair accessible toilet on site – failure of occupational health report to consider certain of the complainant's disabilities – whether respondent had financial resources available to be able to install required toilet facility*

The complainant had worked for the respondent since 1975 and spent the last 30 years at the customer service desk. She underwent a colectomy (removal of the colon) in 2001 and had two knee replacements in 2005 due to osteoarthritis. The complainant claimed that, after her operations, she had difficulty using the store's toilet facilities as they were too low and located upstairs (there was no lift in the building). She therefore used the facilities in another store in the shopping centre. The respondent had no disabled toilet and she submitted that she was given many various excuses over the years as to why it was not installed. She had suggested that one be installed during a proposed store refurbishment.

The complainant had further health issues in that she suffered a broken leg in 2009 and was confined to a wheelchair for six months. Two further operations followed in 2010. She was medically certified as fit to return to work in July 2011 subject to three

---

50.   *Ms H v A Multinational Retailer* Dec–E2014–030.

conditions: a phased return to work, that she could sit for periods of time during her working day, and that she had access to a disabled toilet.

The respondent facilitated her phased return, and whilst she would have no chair at the proposed kiosk position, it did state that she would be facilitated with a role at the checkout, where a seat would be provided. The complainant was further advised that she would been given extra time to use the shopping centre's disabled toilet as the planned store refurbishment was not going ahead. A formal grievance was raised by the complainant but was not upheld.

It was submitted that, at no stage did the respondent carry out an assessment on what appropriate measures could be provided to allow the complainant to continue in the role she enjoyed so much. The complainant submitted that the respondent had ignored her disabilities since 2005 and failed in their duty of care towards her. The respondent denied this. The complainant had been absent from work since June 2009.

In July 2009, the complainant met with the personnel manager and informed her that the recovery period advised by her doctor was six to nine months. The respondent claimed that, at another return to work meeting in October 2010, the personnel manager advised the complainant that she was outside her support period (a reference to the respondent's absence procedures) and recommended that she attend the company doctor. The doctor recommended that the complainant should not return to work for three months.

The occupational health advisor advised returning to work on reduced hours and, as the respondent pointed out, did not recommend a seat for the complainant. The respondent submitted that, prior to her accident in 2009, a suggestion was put to the complainant to convert a shower in the staff toilets to a disabled toilet but this was rejected as it would still be upstairs. The respondent submitted that in the complainant's two-year absence the customer service desk role had changed and was now more sales focused.

The respondent, at the request of the Equality Tribunal, submitted a builder's estimate of the cost of installing a disabled toilet at €22,670.70 accompanied by a report from the respondent's technical manager. The report cited reasons why chairs are not provided at desks in the store. These included insufficient space; the chairs themselves would be a health and safety hazard; and ergonomic reasons.

The Equality Tribunal considered the complainant to have two disabilities within s 2 of the Employment Equality Acts 1998 and 2011: a colectomy, one of its consequences being pouchitis, and osteoarthritis, which had the consequence of reduced mobility.

The Equality Tribunal noted that disability can be a causative factor in not retaining a person as an employee. It considered s 16 of the Employment Equality Acts 1998 to 2011 which provides that there is no obligation to recruit or retain an individual if they are not fully competent to carry out the duties attached to that position. However, this section must be read in conjunction with s 16(3) which provides that a person with a disability is regarded as fully competent if 'reasonable accommodation' is the only difference between that person being able to do the job and not being able to do the job. Thus the Equality Tribunal had to consider whether the respondent failed to provide reasonable accommodation (or appropriate measures) to allow the complainant to continue to be employed by them.

The Tribunal noted that the respondent had no difficulty facilitating a return to work on a phased basis and the current store manager's admission that the height of the desk had not changed and occasionally a stool is provided for pregnant women. The Tribunal accepted the role had changed but noted the complainant had not objected at any stage to taking on new responsibilities. The Tribunal noted that the health and safety report did not address the complainant's specific health and safety issues nor was her doctor consulted.

The Tribunal, in considering the language of the report, held that business reasons should not be confused with health and safety concerns. The Equality Tribunal found the suggested accommodation of working at a checkout unreasonable, as it would involve the complainant lifting heavy weights, something she was medically restricted from doing. Thus the Tribunal found the respondent had not explored the request of allowing the complainant to sit for some of her working day thoroughly enough.

The Tribunal held that the use of the toilet facilities in the shopping centre was not a long-term solution. It noted that the legislative requirement to provide a wheelchair accessible toilet could not be relied on where its provision would place a disproportionate burden on an employer. However, as the respondent's revenue in Ireland was £2.3m (sterling) at the last reported period, the Tribunal held the respondent had the financial resources to install the toilet.

The Tribunal held that the occupational health advisor's report was cursory in that it only dealt with the complainant's broken leg and was silent in respect of her other disabilities. The Tribunal considered the grievance and subsequent internal appeal to be 'a mere tick the box exercise' and did not demonstrate engagement by the respondent of real attempts to provide reasonable accommodation. The Tribunal held compensation was the appropriate form of redress and awarded €30,000 to the complainant (the approximate equivalent of one year's salary), which was appealed – see [4.26].

[4.26] *A Multinational Employer v A Worker*[51] – *Labour Court – appeal of the decision of the Equality Tribunal – Employment Equality Acts 1998 to 2011, s 83 – failure to provide complainant with reasonable accommodation in provision of toilet facilities*

The Labour Court noted that the statutory duty to provide reasonable accommodation was not just directed at allowing a disabled person to exercise the right to work (which is a human right and fundamental freedom) but to allow them to do so on an equal basis with others. That duty is limited only by what is proportionate and reasonable, and the issue of cost was one factor that goes to this question on the facts of each case. The Court held that this suggested that any detriment that a disabled person may suffer in employment relative to a person without a disability should be eliminated, provided the means of so doing remained within the bounds of what is reasonable and proportionate.

There was no doubt that the complainant had particular needs arising from her disability, including a need to use the toilet with a degree of frequency and urgency that is different to that of others who do not suffer from a similar disability. This

---

51.   *A Multinational Employer v A Worker* EDA1435.

manifestation of her disability placed the complainant at a particular disadvantage relative to workers without that disability. The complainant's situation was compounded by her knee injury, which restricted her mobility, and meant that the use of an upstairs toilet was not suitable for her.

The Labour Court held that the question that arose was whether the course of action proposed by the respondent discharged its statutory duties. The Court took into account the evidence tendered by the complainant that the shopping centre was visited regularly by other disabled people from a local care facility and thus the disabled toilet had frequent and lengthy queues. The Court noted that the complainant had described the consequences of this for her in light of her disability and this evidence was not contradicted.

The Court was satisfied that the only toilet facilities available for the complainant were not suitable to her needs. The Court was further satisfied that the respondent's failure in this regard prevented the complainant from having access to employment on the same terms as others. The duty to provide a person with reasonable accommodation was limited by what was reasonable and that included cost. The Court had regard to s 16(3)(c) of the Employment Equality Acts and the estimated cost of providing a disabled toilet in the store, which was €22,000. The Court referenced the fact that the respondent was a large multinational company and held that expenditure of €22,000 could not, by any standard, be regarded as imposing a disproportionate burden. The Court concluded that the respondent had failed to discharge its duty to provide the complainant with reasonable accommodation in accordance with s 16(3)(b) of the Employment Equality Acts and affirmed the decision of the Equality Tribunal. The appeal was disallowed.

[4.27] *Limerick and Clare Education and Training Board v Cotter[52] – Labour Court – Industrial Relations Acts 1946 to 2012 – Employment Equality Acts 1998 to 2011, s 83 – appeal of decision of Equality Tribunal by complainant – alleged discrimination on grounds of gender, sexual orientation and disability – where complainant agreed to go on leave following complaints by parents – whether reasonable accommodation was provided when complainant subsequently certified as fit to return to work*

The complainant was employed as a secondary school teacher and had been employed for some years when an incident arose in a class when a student questioned the complainant about his sexuality. Around the same time, the principal of the school had received four complaints from parents relating to the complainant's management of the class. Following this, a meeting took place at which the parties agreed that the complainant would take administrative leave on full pay and the complainant was asked and agreed to attend a consultant psychiatrist for psychiatric assessment. The psychiatrist confirmed the complainant was suffering from depression and that his illness would be exacerbated were he to return to work. The complainant was further confirmed by the same psychiatrist in 2006 to be unfit to return to work and was placed on sick leave, commencing May 2007. In July 2007, the complainant attended another

---

52. *Limerick and Clare Education and Training Board v Cotter* EDA1417.

psychiatrist for assessment and treatment and subsequently submitted medical certification that he was fit to resume work.

The respondent sought advice from the psychiatrist who had previously examined the complainant on two occasions. He was unwilling to advise the respondent without further details of the complainant's condition, but the complainant's psychiatrist declined to further engage in any process. The respondent then arranged for its chief executive to meet with the complainant in January 2008. However, the chief executive, due to illness, was unavailable to meet in January as scheduled and no further meetings took place prior to this complaint being submitted to the Equality Tribunal in April 2008.

The first issue complained of was that the respondent's response to the incident, which occurred in class in February 2005, and as a result of which he was placed on administrative/sick leave and referred for a psychiatric assessment, discriminated against him on grounds of gender and sexual orientation. The second issue raised was that the refusal by the respondent to allow him to return to work on a phased basis amounted to a refusal to offer him reasonable accommodation within the statutory meaning of that term. The complainant further claimed that he was victimised because he had successfully taken an earlier claim under the Act against the respondent and that he had filed a separate and distinct claim of age discrimination, which was scheduled for hearing in April 2008.

The Labour Court noted that the placement of the complainant on administrative or sick leave was a standalone issue and was agreed by all as he was unfit for work. The Court said that there was no question of victimisation or a failure to provide reasonable accommodation in this regard. The Court found that the complainant was unfit to work until 5 October 2007 and in those circumstances there was no continuation between the initial placement of the complainant on administrative leave by agreement and subsequently on sick leave following medical certification and his complaint that when fit he was not accommodated with a phased return to work. The Court found the first part of the complainant's complaint to be statute-barred.

The Court then considered the obligations on the respondent employer under s 16(3) of the Employment Equality Acts, which require that reasonable accommodation be made. The complainant asserted that the respondent's refusal of permission for him to return to work until further details were supplied to its medical advisor was entirely inappropriate and did not constitute reasonable accommodation of his disability. The Court noted the complainant's case, which was that the time he was certified fit for work, there was an obligation under s 16(3) on his employer to take such appropriate measures as might be required to enable him to undertake his duties on a phased basis as he was not fit for an immediate return to full-time working. He stated that this incapacity was the result of the manner in which he had been treated by the respondent, and having been so certified, the respondent was aware of his disability and of the accommodation he was seeking to facilitate a return to work. He submitted that the respondent did not engage with him in that context, rather it sought to deny that he was fit to return to work and placed obstacles in his way. It was asserted by the complainant that these actions constituted discrimination against him on the grounds of sexual orientation and disability. He stated that discrimination on the sexual orientation ground occurred because the decision to refuse him permission to return to work was influenced by the respondent's hostility to the gender identity issues it imputed to him. He stated that discrimination on the disability ground occurred because of the respondent's failure to engage with him to establish the accommodation he sought to facilitate his return to work following a period of illness which it diagnosed as depression, which amounts to disability within the meaning of the Acts.

The respondent stated that at all times it had acted in accordance with its statutory duties and its general duty of care to its employee. It removed the complainant from a stressful environment and sought professional advice as to his capacity to continue work. That advice was that he was not fit to return to work. The respondent argued that it had no alternative but to act on that advice. The certificate of fitness to return to work was signed by the complainant's doctor, but its own medical advisor stated that he required further information before he could advise. It was the complainant that failed to elicit the additional information required.

The Labour Court noted that the Acts prohibit discrimination on grounds of disability and, where a person suffers from a disability, the Acts place an obligation on an employer to make reasonable accommodation to enable a person with a disability to return to work. The Court noted that it was common case that the complainant was diagnosed as suffering from a disability and was placed on sick leave in May 2007. The Court noted that the sequence of events where the complainant's doctor refused to cooperate further and stood over his certification and the respondent's doctor refused to give advice without further information, placed the respondent in a difficult position. The Court stated that the question was whether, by allowing this state of affairs to continue, the respondent took all appropriate measures to ensure that the complainant, as a person with a disability, could with reasonable accommodation be fully competent and capable of returning to his duties. The Court noted that the respondent's medical advisor had not seen the complainant for almost 12 months and further noted that the certificate provided by the complainant stated that his own doctor had been reviewing him over several months and was happy that he was fit for work, initially on a phased basis.

It was noted by the Court that the respondent did not refer the claimant at that point to its medical advisor for an updated examination so that its subsequent actions were based on a report that was 12 months old and that could not be deemed current. The only current information available to the respondent was that the claimant was fit for work. The Labour Court stated that the respondent had a number of options open to it. It was quite entitled to take medical advice as to whether the complainant was or was not fit to return to work on a phased or full-time basis or at all. It was also entitled to refer the complainant for a further assessment by its own medical advisor in order to establish his current medical condition. It was also entitled to seek to agree an independent medical expert to resolve any conflict between the two medical advisors. However, the Court noted that the respondent did none of these. Instead, it asked the complainant to return to his doctor to query the certificate he had issued. The Court noted that the respondent at that point had the option of conducting its own assessment of the complainant's capacity to return to work, but it did not do so, or at least delayed in doing do. The Court further noted that the proposed meeting between the complainant and the chief executive did not go ahead as planned and subsequent to this, this meeting was not rearranged or otherwise progressed in any way. The Court concluded that the respondent was unsure how to proceed in the best interests of both the complainant and the children it was charged with educating. The Court found the appropriate step to take was to engage with the complainant in a timely manner to establish his medical condition, by way of either a medical examination by its own doctors or by an agreed independent qualified medical specialist. The Court noted the effect of the respondent's actions in neither arranging for a medical assessment nor accepting the psychiatrist's certificate was to cause a delay in dealing with the matter.

The Court held that the statutory obligation on the employer was to at least investigate the nature of the accommodation sought and to make a decision as to whether it could or could not accommodate the complainant based on the findings of its investigations. The Court was critical of the respondent as no such investigation took place and the Court found that the complainant was denied reasonable accommodation for a period of up to six months when he commenced the current proceedings. The Court stated that it was satisfied that the respondent's responses related to the nature of the complainant's disability and it was also satisfied that it would not have treated a person suffering from a different disability in such a fashion. In the normal course of business, the respondent would have either referred the complainant for a medical examination to its medical advisor or have accepted its certificate and engaged with him regarding a phased return. The Court noted that the respondent was acting out of concern for the complainant and for the children he would be assigned to teach and was at a loss as to how to deal with the issue. However, the Court held that the motivation of the respondent, whether benign or otherwise, did not negative the effect of the discrimination on disability grounds.

The Court upheld the complaint of discrimination on grounds of disability and awarded the complainant compensation in the amount of €7,500, thereby varying the Equality Tribunal decision.

[4.28] *O'Rourke v Brennan Convenience Foods Ltd T/A Food Partners (in liquidation)[53] – Equality Tribunal – Employment Equality Acts 1998 to 2011 – alleged discrimination on grounds of disability – failure to reasonably accommodate claimant in light of ongoing injuries – alleged discriminatory dismissal – denial of previous assurances provided to complainant*

Evidence was given by the complainant that he was employed by the respondent as a van driver and delivery sales representative. In May 2011, he suffered a serious accident while loading his van and suffered significant soft tissue and muscular injuries to his back, shoulder and neck area. He was certified unfit to work for eight weeks due to the injuries. When he sought to return to work on lighter duties on the advice from his physiotherapist, he was given two hours' of office work on the first day, but then was required to pack fridges, causing him pain in his neck, shoulder and back. The complainant stated that he was accommodated with office duties for about four weeks,

---

53.   *O'Rourke v Brennan Convenience Foods Ltd T/A Food Partners (in liq)* DEC–E2014–058.

but was then requested to resume his old delivery route despite the continuing pain in his back, shoulder and neck. He was promised an assistant, but this did not materialise. The pattern of requests for doing deliveries made of the complainant caused him to experience pain and need time off work which was then followed by a brief period of office duties followed by another request for doing deliveries and this continued until September 2011 when he was summoned to a meeting with no warning whatsoever and was dismissed.

The complainant stated that he was the only employee of the respondent who was dismissed at the time and the driver who had covered his route during his period of sick leave was retained. The complainant submitted that this amounted to failure to provide him with reasonable accommodation, was discriminatory treatment and constituted a discriminatory dismissal within the meaning of the Acts. The Equality Tribunal noted that the complainant had submitted medical reports detailing his injuries and stated that even three years after the accidents, he was still experiencing back and neck pain when lifting things or reaching overhead. The Equality Tribunal was satisfied that the injuries complained of rendered the complainant disabled within the meanings of s 2(C) of the Employment Equality Acts. The Equality Tribunal found that the complainant was a credible witness and accepted his submissions that, when he started to work for the respondent in 2009, he was self-employed and then from August 2010 to September 2014 he was employed as a PAYE worker.

The complainant stated that, two weeks prior to his accident, intimations had been made to him that he could revert to a self-employed status on his route if he was interested. However, these assurances were denied by the respondent by the time he was dismissed, even though the complainant stated the respondent denied that this was anything to do with his disability. The complainant submitted that he believed that had he not experienced disability, he would have been able to work on his route as a self-employed driver.

The Equality Tribunal found that, the respondent's denial of its previous assurances was linked to his disability and would not have occurred had the complainant retained his health and it was satisfied that this constituted less favourable treatment on grounds of his disability. The Equality Tribunal held that the respondent had failed in its duty to provide the complainant with reasonable accommodation. The Equality Tribunal noted that the respondent had 10 office-based staff and there was considerable office-based work in the business and that a solution to accommodate the complainant could probably have been found if the respondent had made any effort to meet its legal obligations towards him. The complainant was entitled to succeed in his complaint concerning lack of reasonable accommodation.

The Equality Tribunal concluded that the complainant had adduced sufficient evidence to show that his dismissal was not a redundancy and that the respondent had never met its obligations towards the complainant under the Acts in a manner which would enable it to rely on the provisions of 16(1) of the Acts with regards to the complainant's dismissal. Thus the Tribunal found that the complainant was discriminatorily dismissed because of his disability. The respondent was ordered to pay the complainant €25,000, being nine months' pay.

[4.29] *London Borough of Southwark v Charles[54] – UK Employment Appeal Tribunal – Equality Act 2010 – dismissal by reason of redundancy – whether claimant discriminated against by reason of his disability – claimant's disability an inability to attend administrative meetings – failure of respondent to make reasonable accommodation for claimant in course of redundancy/redeployment process*

The respondent local authority employed the claimant as an environmental enforcement officer. Following a reorganisation, the claimant's post was abolished and he was dismissed by reason of redundancy. The Employment Tribunal found that his dismissal was by reason of redundancy and that the procedure was fair. However, the Tribunal found that the claimant, to the knowledge of the respondent, suffered from a disability, namely an inability to attend administrative meetings. The Tribunal concluded this would include interviews for new jobs in a redeployment process and thus the respondent had both discriminated against him by requiring the claimant to attend such an interview and had also failed to make reasonable adjustments by not dispensing with the need for such an interview. In consequence, the Employment Tribunal found that the claimant was placed at a substantial disadvantage by being dismissed and that the respondent was in breach of its duties under the UK Equality Act 2010.

The UK EAT set out the facts of this case and noted that, whilst the claimant was in the redeployment pool, there had been a confirmation of his medical unfitness and also his inability to attend administrative meetings. Nevertheless, the respondent's human resources team continued to make contact by way of email with the claimant with regard to the redeployment process. The UK EAT concluded that the Employment Tribunal was plainly entitled to find that the practice of the respondent in requiring those in the redeployment pool to attend for interview for the post for which they were applying was a practice, even though it may not have been a criterion or provision. The Tribunal was also entitled to find that it put the claimant at a substantial disadvantage because he could not attend an interview, so following upon the respondent's practice, he could not demonstrate to them that he was qualified for any of the jobs for which he might have applied, and in particular the job of noise support officer, for which he had applied and been unsuccessful and in respect of which he had indicated a qualified expression of interest.

The UK EAT found that the Tribunal was entitled to find that the claimant suffered from a significant disability, being an inability to attend management meetings and interviews, and was entitled to find that the respondent knew that he suffered from that disability. Accordingly, all of the ingredients of the obligation to make a reasonable adjustment were present. The UK EAT found that the respondent had imposed a requirement on the complainant to attend for interviews and so treated the claimant unfavourably because of something arising in consequence of his disability and no attempt was made to justify the differential treatment. The UK EAT did offer one caveat in terms of the Tribunal finding. It did not agree with the suggestion made by the Tribunal at the initial hearing that had the claimant been appointed to the noise support officer role without the need for an interview, the disadvantage would have been

---

54.   *London Borough of Southwark v Charles* UK EAT/0008/14/RN.

avoided. The UK EAT noted that it was not the disadvantage that the Tribunal found should have been subject of a reasonable adjustment.

The UK EAT stated that if the reasonable adjustment which should have been made was that the claimant should not have been subjected to a formal interview process, but that his suitability should have been assessed by some other means, it does not follow automatically that he would have been appointed to the post of noise support officer. The UK EAT stated that these were matters that should be the subject of further submissions and made subject of further evidence by either side. The UK EAT decided to dismiss the appeal.

[4.30] *A Worker v A Company (in receivership)*[55] *– Equality Tribunal – Employment Equality Acts 1998 to 2011, ss 8(6) and 16 – disability – whether respondent employer's refusal to allow complainant to work on part-time basis constituted failure to provide reasonable accommodation within meaning of s 16 – whether dismissal of employee due to his inability to work full time hours constituted discriminatory dismissal within meaning of s 8(6) – €40,000 awarded*

The complainant commenced employment as a general operative in the respondent's quarrying business. In November 2009, the complainant underwent surgery for a brain tumour. The operation was successful and the complainant made a full recovery. In October 2010, the complainant's doctor confirmed that he was fit to return to work for 20 hours per week, and the complainant recommenced work on this basis.

In December 2010, the respondent's operations manager informed the complainant that he would have to return to work full-time or he would lose his job, notwithstanding the medical evidence that he was not capable of working full-time. In January 2011, the complainant went on sick leave as the respondent would no longer accommodate him with a 20-hour work week. In June 2011, the complainant underwent a medical assessment with a doctor approved by the respondent which confirmed that the complainant could not resume full-time work. On 5 August 2011 the complainant was dismissed on the basis that the respondent could not offer him a 20-hour work week on an ongoing basis. The complainant appealed this dismissal internally, but the appeal was unsuccessful.

On 1 December 2011 the complainant referred a complaint to the Equality Tribunal. The complainant alleged that the respondent had failed in its duty to provide him with 'reasonable accommodation' on his return to work in accordance with its obligations under s 16 of the Acts and that he been discriminatorily dismissed on the grounds of his disability, contrary to s 8(6) of the Acts. The respondent did not furnish a written submission to the Tribunal.

With regard to the preliminary issue of whether the complainant's brain tumour constituted a 'disability' within the meaning of the Acts, the Tribunal found that it did, stating that it was 'satisfied that a serious, lengthy illness such as a brain tumour, even if successfully treated, does constitute a disability within the meaning of the Acts'.

---

55.   *A Worker v A Company (in receivership)* DEC – E2014 – 066.

The Tribunal then proceeded to consider the question of whether the respondent had failed in its duty to provide 'reasonable accommodation' to the complainant within the meaning of s 16 of the Acts.

As a preliminary point, the Tribunal stated that an employer's obligation to make reasonable accommodation for an employee with a disability exists notwithstanding the fact that the employee may be receiving disability benefit from the Department of Social Protection.

Examining the steps actually taken by the respondent to address the complainant's return to work, the Tribunal noted that the medical examination arranged with a company doctor on 5 August 2011 did not lead to discussions or plans on how to accommodate the complainant, but rather to his dismissal, and that the respondent never seriously considered offers by the complainant to split his responsibilities with his son (and so make up the full time hours).

Stating 'it is settled law that permitting part-time work is one way in which reasonable accommodation can be provided', the Tribunal found that:

> while some degree of accommodation was provided to the complainant on his initial return to work, the respondent never seriously assessed the complainant's situation in the light of its obligations to provide reasonable accommodation under the Employment Equality Acts.

Accordingly, it was found that the respondent had failed to fulfil its obligation under s 16 of the Acts.

The Tribunal then proceeded to consider whether the subsequent dismissal of the complainant could be considered discriminatory. It was noted that complainant was issued with a P45 when the company doctor confirmed that he was only fit to work 20 hours per week. Accordingly, the Tribunal found that the complainant's dismissal was directly related to both his disability and to the respondent's failure to offer reasonable accommodation for such, and constituted a discriminatory dismissal within the terms of s 8(6) of the Acts. The respondent was ordered to pay €40,000 to the complainant (the maximum award available).

[4.31] *General Dynamics Information Technology v Carranza*[56] *– UK Employment Appeal Tribunal – Equality Act 2010, s 20(3) – whether respondent employer's failure to disregard final written warning previously issued to complainant when deciding to dismiss complainant constituted failure to make 'reasonable adjustments' – whether decision to dismiss complainant rendered 'procedurally unfair' by virtue of respondent's failure to reconsider propriety of final written warning at time of dismissal*

The complainant was employed as a customer services advisor for London Borough of Lambeth from 2 May 2008 until his employment was transferred to the respondent by virtue of the Transfer of Undertakings (Protection of Employment) Regulations 2006 (SI 2006/246) in 2011.

---

56.   *General Dynamics Information Technology v Carranza* UKEAT/0107/14/KN.

Since childhood, the complainant had suffered from stomach adhesions, a disability within the meaning of the UK Equality Act 2010.

The complainant's former employer, Lambeth, had made adjustments such as extra breaks and time off to attend medical appointments to accommodate this disability. Nevertheless the complainant had very substantial periods off work. Lambeth held informal meetings and discussions with the complainant, following which the complainant was issued with a written warning on the basis of his excessive absences.

Following receipt of occupational health advice, Lambeth held a sickness panel hearing in September 2011. At this point, the complainant had, in the past three years, taken a total of 206 days (41.5 weeks) off work. These absences were mainly due to his stomach adhesions, but there were also absences for a sprained ankle (six days), a viral illness (nine days) and flu (a total of seven days). By letter dated 16 September 2011, the complainant was issued with a final written warning. This written warning stated that the complainant had failed to follow Lambeth's sickness policy on two occasions during his absence, and that his illness was severely impacting on the business unit and had cost Lambeth £22,000.

In December 2011, the complainant's employment was transferred to the respondent under TUPE. Shortly after the complainant's transfer to the respondent, the complainant took two periods of absence due to his disability. The respondent did not take any action in relation to these periods as they were short in duration. The respondent continued to offer the complainant support at work and to make adjustments for him. However, in July 2012 the complainant injured his shoulder while rolling over in bed. Due to this injury, the complainant took three months off work, from 30 July to 9 November 2012. The respondent sought the advice of an occupational health specialist on 28 November 2012, who advised the respondent that due to the complainant's disability, his attendance at work in the future was 'likely to mirror the attendance he has been able to achieve in the last few years'. On 18 December 2012, a formal sickness hearing was held following which the complainant was dismissed. The complainant initially accepted his dismissal and stated that he had felt supported by the respondent. However, the complainant later appealed the decision to dismiss him but the appeal was not upheld. The UK EAT noted that at the appeal hearing, the complainant did not suggest that his previous absences should not have been considered in the context of this review.

Following his unsuccessful internal appeal, the complainant brought a claim to the Employment Tribunal. The complainant alleged that the respondent, in failing to disregard the final written warning when deciding whether to dismiss the employee or not, was in breach of its duty to make 'reasonable adjustments' for him in accordance with its obligation under s 20(3) of the Act. The complainant also alleged that his dismissal constituted an unfair dismissal within the meaning of the Act. The Employment Tribunal found for the complainant on both points.

The respondent appealed this decision to the UK EAT who allowed the appeal. With regard the question of 'reasonable adjustments', the UK EAT looked at what 'step', if any, would have been reasonable for the respondent to make to avoid the complainant's disadvantage. The UK EAT found that the mental process of disregarding the final written warning imposed on the complainant by Lambeth could not be considered a 'step' for the purposes of s 20(3) of the Equality Act 2010. Further, the fact that the respondent had shown leniency in not dismissing the complainant for two relatively short periods of absence following the final written warning, provided no basis in itself for alleging that the respondent should have shown this leniency again following the complainant's longer period of absence. The respondent's aim of ensuring consistent attendance at work was a legitimate one. The final written warning issued to the complainant was a proportionate way of achieving this legitimate aim. Accordingly the respondent had not failed in its duty to make reasonable adjustments for the complainant.

With regard the question of whether the respondent's failure to consider, at the time of dismissal, whether the final written warning had been justified or not rendered the decision to dismiss 'procedurally unfair', the UK EAT found that it did not. The UK EAT found that:

> there are limits to the extent to which an employer can be expected to revisit what took place at an earlier stage of a [disciplinary] process ... if the earlier warning was allegedly issued in bad faith, manifestly improper or issued without any prima facie grounds an earlier stage of a process may require revisiting; but otherwise an employer is entitled to proceed on the basis of what has already been decided.

Accordingly, the respondent's decision to dismiss, without reconsidering the propriety of the previously issued warning, was not unfair.

[4.32] *McDonald v Road Safety Operations Ireland Ltd T/A Go Safe[57] – Equality Tribunal – whether complainant discriminated against on grounds of his disability in terms of s 6(2)(G) and contrary to s 8 of the Employment Equality Acts 1998 to 2011 in relation to his dismissal – whether failure to reasonably accommodate complainant – complainant developed psychological injury as result of criminal act which took place whilst he was at work*

The complainant was employed as a speed monitoring/surveying operator and carried out his duties working alone in a mobile speed survey van, and his duties involved the monitoring of speed of vehicles on public roads. An incident occurred where two individuals threw petrol over the van in which the complainant was working and set it alight, burning the van. Whilst the complainant was not physically injured in the incident, he suffered severe psychological injury, depression, anxiety, sleep disturbance and he was on sick leave for several months and was paid sick pay by the respondent. The complainant was placed on medication and was referred for counselling and psychological therapy by his GP. The respondent's occupational health consultants examined the complainant in June 2011 and subsequently in October 2011.

The October 2011 medical report stated that the complainant was adamant he would never go back to working as a speed monitor operator. A decision was taken to dismiss the complainant from employment on 24 October 2011. He appealed against the dismissal but it was upheld and confirmed by letter on 7 November 2011. The claimant asserted that he wished to continue working with the respondent company and might have been able to do so, had the respondent been willing to provide reasonable

---

57.   *McDonald v Road Safety Operations Ireland Ltd T/A Go Safe* DEC–E2014–069.

accommodation to enable him to do so. The complainant further claimed that there had been no consultation with him or his medical advisors regarding what reasonable accommodation might be possible.

The respondent claimed that the complainant's employment was terminated solely due to his inability to work in the capacity for which he had been trained and employed, and there was no less favourable treatment of the complainant as there was no position for which he was trained or indeed no other position within the organisation which would have been comparable. The respondent further submitted that the complainant did not dispute the results of the medical assessment by an occupational therapist some seven months after the event. The occupational assessment revealed that the complainant was not fully confident or capable of performing duties for which he was employed.

The Equality Tribunal noted that the parties had accepted that the complainant has a disability for the purpose of the Acts. In considering whether the complainant was subject to discriminatory dismissal the Equality Tribunal noted that, after the incident, the complainant was unable to attend work but kept the respondent appraised of his condition through regular phones calls and also submitted medical certificates on a weekly, fortnightly, and then on a monthly basis.

The Equality Tribunal noted the evidence of the respondent that the decision to terminate the complainant's employment was based on the October 2011 medical report and that the respondent had wanted the complainant to come back to work, was anxious to get him back to work and had contacted him on a number of occasions between March and October seeking his return. This was not disputed by the complainant, who stated that he had received about eight or nine phone calls asking how he was and asking when he thought he would be back to work.

The respondent stated that the medical report indicated that the complainant was adamant that he would not return to work as a monitoring operator. The respondent advised the Equality Tribunal that the complainant's position could not be kept open indefinitely, and that the medical report clearly stated that the complainant was not fit to return to work as a monitoring operator. The Equality Tribunal stated that, although it was the respondent's contention that the complainant was dismissed due to his health and due to his inability to return to his position, it was clear that the complainant's absence and his inability to return to work were due to his disability and thus it followed that the complainant's disability contributed to or was the reason for his dismissal.

The Equality Tribunal was satisfied that the decision to dismiss the complainant was influenced by his disability and his absence and by his inability to return to his position. The Equality Tribunal thus concluded that the complainant had established a prima facie case of less favourable treatment on grounds of disability in relation of his dismissal. The Equality Tribunal noted the obligation under s 16(3) of the Acts to take appropriate measures where needed to enable a person with a disability to have access to participate in or advance in employment. The Equality Tribunal stated that the respondent, once armed with the knowledge that a contributory factor to the complainant's absence from and inability to return to work related to his disability, was at that point obliged to make a proper and adequate assessment of the situation before taking the decision to dismiss.

The Tribunal took note of s 16(1)(b) of the Employment Equality Acts which provide an employer with a complete defence to a claim of discrimination if it can be shown that the employer had a *bona fide* belief that the complainant is not fully capable to perform the duties for which he was employed.

The Equality Tribunal noted the decision of the Labour Court in *A Health and Fitness Club v A Worker*[58] which was upheld on appeal to the Circuit Court by Judge Dunne. The Equality Tribunal noted that the Labour Court had interpreted s 16 as placing an obligation on an employer to embark on a process of ascertaining the real reasons for the employee's inability to do the job, taking appropriate expert advice, consulting with the employee concerned and considering with an open mind what special treatment or facilities could realistically overcome any obstacles to the employee doing the job for which he or she is otherwise competent and accessing the actual cost and practicality of providing that accommodation.

In applying this Labour Court approach, the Equality Tribunal held that it was clear that there was an obligation on the respondent in the first instance to ascertain the level and extent of the complainant's disability. In requesting a medical assessment in June 2011 and October 2011, the respondent had complied with its obligation to make these enquiries. However the respondent, following receipt of the October 2011 report, when it became aware that the complainant was unable to return to work, was then obliged to make further enquiries as to what, if any, special measures could be taken to assist the complainant in returning to work. It was noted by the Equality Tribunal that the evidence from the complainant was that he was not at any point engaged in a discussion or consultation about any alternative roles.

The Equality Tribunal noted the evidence of the respondent that huge improvements had been made to prevent a repeat of the incident that happened to the complainant, to include the installation of CCTV cameras in all vehicles, the installation of DVD recorders to record everything that happened, as well as a speaker system on vans and warning beacons on the vehicles. It was acknowledged by the respondent at the hearing that the complainant was not consulted about these improvements. The respondent had stated that the complainant was not fully capable and, even with the installation of special treatment or facilities, he would not return to that type of work. However the Equality Tribunal noted that this conclusion was arrived at without consultation with the complainant, and the complainant was never asked whether or to what extent special measures could be taken to enable him to return to work. The Equality Tribunal held that there was a clear obligation on the respondent, when it became aware that the complainant was unable to return to his duties due to his disability, to consult with him to look at suitable measures and accommodation which would enable him to return to work, as well as to discuss with him and evaluate certain employment alternatives before concluding there was no suitable alternative for him. The respondent was then obliged to inform the complainant that, having concluded there were no suitable measures or accommodation which would enable him to return to his position and as there was no suitable alternative employment for him, he was being considered for dismissal. The Equality Tribunal stated it was clear that the respondent did not bring any of these issues

---

58. *A Health and Fitness Club v A Worker* EED037.

to the attention of the complainant prior to taking the decision that it could no longer retain him in employment.

As a consequence, the complainant was not afforded any opportunity to participate in or influence the decision-making process which resulted in his dismissal. The Equality Tribunal stated that it was satisfied that the respondent did make appropriate enquires to ascertain the extent of the complainant's condition but failed to consult with him on the advice received before it came to the conclusion that he was incapable on the grounds of his disability of performing the duties for which he was employed. The Equality Tribunal stated that it was satisfied that the respondent could not rely on s 37(3) of the Employment Equality Acts in the first instance as the position of monitoring operator in the respondent company does not fall within the definition of 'employment in the An Garda Síochána, prison service or any emergency service as provided for in s 37(3)'. The Equality Tribunal found that the respondent dismissed the complaint in circumstances amounting to discrimination on grounds of his disability in terms of s 6(2) of the Acts and contrary to s 8 of those Acts and failed to provide him with reasonable accommodation within the meaning of s 16 of the Acts. The Equality Tribunal determined that an award of compensation in the sum of €28,000 was just and equitable in all of the circumstances.

[4.33] *Wozniak v Tuleya*[59] *– Equality Tribunal – Employment Equality Acts 1998 to 2011, ss 6 and 8 – family status and disability – discriminatory dismissal – compensation of €12,000 awarded*

The complainant began work with the respondent in late 2010. On 17 October 2011, the complainant was diagnosed with a hernia of the spine and a dislocated disc. She informed the respondent's partner that she had to leave for Poland for an operation on 19 October 2011. She had the operation on 26 October and returned for assessment on 15 November when she was told that she could not return to work until 31 December 2011. She informed the respondent's partner of this and offered to produce a medical certificate to that effect. The husband of the complainant gave evidence that he dropped his wife's medical certificate into her workplace. The respondent denied receiving this.

The respondent gave evidence that the complainant contacted him on 16 November 2011 to explain that she would not be fit to work until January 2012 and that she wanted to be let go. It was the complainant's evidence that she was not made aware of her dismissal while she was on sick leave. Her first knowledge of her dismissal was when her husband visited the salon and saw that the respondent had recruited another employee. She submitted that she received a letter from the respondent explaining her dismissal and the recruitment of a new employee. The translation reads; 'with this employee we have no problems, he does not have a family and he can come to work whenever I phone him.'

The Equality Tribunal accepted that the letter indicated that the complainant's lack of flexibility was a factor in her dismissal but did not find that there was a case of discriminatory dismissal on the grounds of family status. However, the Equality

---

59.　*Wozniak v Tuleya* DEC–E2014–049.

Tribunal accepted the evidence of the complainant that a medical certificate had been delivered to the respondent. It found the evidence of the respondent and his partner to be unreliable and did not accept that there was a misunderstanding over whether the complainant wished to leave her job. The Tribunal found that the respondent recruited a permanent replacement for the complainant even though it knew she was on sick leave and had given no indication that she was resigning her position. The dismissal was directly related to her disability and was therefore discriminatory. The complainant was awarded €12,000 in compensation.

Associative disability

[4.34] *Hainsworth v Ministry of Defence*[60] – *Court of Appeal of England and Wales (CD) – appeal of decision of Langstaff J, President of the Employment Appeal Tribunal – whether Directive 2000/78,*[61] *art 5 gave appellant right to an adjustment to her employment to accommodate her disabled daughter's needs – associative disability and reasonable accommodation*

The respondent employed the appellant as a civilian employee attached to the British Armed Forces. From 2004 onward she was employed as an inclusion support development teacher. The appellant's daughter at the time of the case was 17 years old, had Down's syndrome and was regarded as a disabled person within the meaning of s 6 of the Equality Act 2010. The respondent, through an agency, provided facilities for the education of children of service and civilian personnel serving away from the United Kingdom, to include education and training for such children at an Army base in Germany. However the respondent did not provide any special schools or training facilities for children in Germany, nor did it provide for children who have more significant needs. Non-disabled children of service and civilian personnel, and those whose needs could be easily met within mainstream provision, were schooled at the respondent's facilities in Germany. However, owing to her disability, the appellant's daughter could not be schooled there.

The appellant was required to provide the services required of her within a British enclave in Germany. In August 2011 she submitted a formal request to be transferred to a location within the United Kingdom in order to be able to meet the special needs of her daughter. However this was rejected. Her case before the Court was that it would have amounted to a reasonable adjustment to the PCP (provision, criteria or practice) for the respondent to have allowed the appellant's application for a compassionate transfer and to transfer her employment to the United Kingdom and alternatively to have transferred her to a role within the Ministry's organisation in the United Kingdom.

The Court of Appeal noted that PCP is an acronym for 'provision, criterion or practice', an expression appearing in s 20(3) of the Equality Act 2010 which dealt with

---

60.   *Hainsworth v Ministry of Defence (Respondent) and Equality and Human Rights Commission (Intervener)* [2014] EWCA Civ 763.

61.   Council Directive 2000/78/EC of 27 November 2000 establishing a general framework for equal treatment in employment and occupation.

an employer's duty to make reasonable adjustments for disabled persons. Laws LJ on behalf of the Court concluded that this case principally turned on the proper interpretation of art 5 of Council Directive 2000/78/EC.

Article 5 provides:

> In order to guarantee compliance with the principle of equal treatment in relation to persons with disabilities, reasonable accommodation shall be provided. This means that employers shall take appropriate measures, where needed in a particular case, to enable a person with a disability to have access to, participate in or advance in employment or undergo training unless such measures would impose a disproportionate burden on the employer.

In the UK, the implementing provisions of the Equality Act 2010 relating to disability discrimination are set out in three requirements at s 20 of the 2010 Act. The first requirement is given by s 20(3) of the 2010 Act as follows:

> The first requirement is a requirement, where a provision, criterion or practices of A's puts a disabled person at a substantial disadvantage in relation to a relevant matter in comparison with persons who are not disabled to take such steps as it is reasonable to have to take to avoid the disadvantage.

A in this provision is the person upon whom the duty to make reasonable adjustment falls.

Laws LJ noted that it had been denied by the appellant and conceded before the Employment Appeal Tribunal that on a purely literal approach to the provisions of the Equality Act, an employer owes a duty to make reasonable adjustments only in respect of a disabled person who is either an applicant for employment with the employer or already in his employ.

The Court of Appeal noted that, on that approach to the Equality Act, the appellant's daughter would not be included as a potential beneficiary for the material provisions. However, the Court of Appeal noted that the appellant's case was that the right to claim an adjustment to her employment in order to accommodate her disabled daughter's needs is given to her by the terms of art 5 of the Directive. If that is right, the appellant asserts that the Equality Act, notwithstanding its ordinary meaning, should be interpreted or read so as to give effect to her EU rights in accordance with the well-known principle enunciated in *Marleasing*[62] and later cases – or, in the alternative, if the language of the Equality Act rules out that recourse, then the appellant has asserted she is entitled to rely directly on art 5 against the respondent which is an emanation of the State.

Laws LJ, having considered art 5 and also recitals 16, 17, 20 and 27 of the Directive, concluded that the obvious entire focus of art 5 is upon provisions to be made by an employer for his disabled employees, prospective employees, and trainees. Law LJ concluded that it is not possible to read art 5 so as to confer upon that provision a meaning which it simply cannot bear. Moreover once it is postulated that the disabled beneficiary of art 5 may be a person other than an employee, Laws LJ noted that the article gave no 'clue' as to who that other person might be and noted it would be entirely

---

62. *Marleasing SA v La Comercial Internacional de Alimentacion SA* [1990] ECR 1–4135.

an open question. This would leave art 5 hopelessly uncertain. The Court noted the arguments of the appellant that a person associated with the employee would qualify, as of course the appellant's disabled daughter is associated with her. However, the Court noted that the concept of association is of itself vague and open-ended.

The Court then considered *Colman v Attridge Law,*[63] in which the claimant had given birth to a disabled child and, having taken voluntary redundancy, claimed unfair constructive dismissal citing that she had been treated less favourably than other employees because she was the primary carer of a disabled child. The Employment Tribunal referred a preliminary issue to the CJEU to ask whether the Directive had to be interpreted as prohibiting direct discrimination only in respect of an employee who is himself disabled, or whether the prohibition applied equally to an employee, who was not himself disabled but who was treated less favourably by reason of the disability of his child. The CJEU answered the question in favour of the claimant and indicated that the principle of equal treatment which the direct discrimination provisions were designed to safeguard, was not:

> limited to people who themselves have a disability within the meaning of the Directive. On the contrary the purpose of the Directive as regards employment and occupation is to combat all forms of discrimination on grounds of disability. The principle of equal treatment enshrined in the Directive in that area applies not only to a category of persons but by reference to the grounds mentioned in Article 1.

However, the CJEU in *Colman* went on to contrast art 5 of the Directive with art 1 and noted that the Directive included a number of provisions which applied only to disabled people. The CJEU held that art 5 provides that:

> in order to guarantee compliance with the principle of equal treatment in relation to persons with disabilities, reasonable accommodation is to be provided. That means that employers must take appropriate measures, where needed in a particular case, to enable a person with a disability to have access to, participate or advance in employment or undergo training unless such measures would impose a disproportionate burden on the employer.

Laws LJ stated that the contrast was plain. Article 5 is limited so as to require measures only for the assistance of disabled employees and prospective employees of the employer. He concluded that *Colman* supports this straightforward interpretation of art 5. The Court of Appeal noted that the fact that the disabled person in *Colman* was the employee's child, not the employee herself, does not offer a read-across to art 5 upon which the appellant could reply. The Court noted that in *Colman* the claimant was herself the victim of discrimination, her child's disability was simply the cause of it. Hence, their exact relationship was in those circumstances not critical to proof of the cause. However, in this case the appellant has to assert a duty upon the respondent to act effectively for the benefit of her child. The proximity of the relationship between the appellant and the disabled person, here her daughter, therefore becomes critical. However, art 5, as noted by the Court, gives no assistance as to what degree of proximity might be required. That is, the Court concluded, why the CJEU in *Colman* said that the

---

63.   *Colman v Attridge Law* [2008] All ER (EC) 1105.

art 5 measures 'would be rendered meaningless or could prove disproportionate if they were not limited to disabled persons only.'

By way of conclusion, Laws LJ stated that the short and conclusive point was that neither the UN Convention on the Rights of Persons with Disabilities, nor the EU Charter of Fundamental Rights nor the European Social Charter, all of which were relied on, qualified the plain and inescapable meaning of art 5 of the Directive. The Court dismissed the appeal and stated that the appellant's interpretation of art 5 required an open ended and unspecific approach to the identity of the disabled person and was unsustainable. But even if is the appellant were correct, the open ended and unspecific approach remains, thus leading the Court to the conclusion that art 5 upon that interpretation was insufficiently precise to permit its application by way of direct effect.

The appeal was dismissed and Tomlinson and Greggs LJJ concurred.

REFUSAL OF SURROGACY

[4.35] *Z v A Government Dept and the Board of Management of a Community School[64] and CD v ST[65] – CJEU – whether mothers who have had a baby through surrogacy agreements entitled to maternity leave or its equivalent – Council Directive 92/85/EEC of 19 October 1992 on the introduction of measures to encourage improvements in the safety and health at work of pregnant workers and workers who have recently given birth or are breastfeeding – Directive 2006/54/EC of the European Parliament and of the Council of 5 July 2006 on the implementation of the principle of equal opportunities and equal treatment of men and women in matters of employment and occupation – whether refusal of paid leave equivalent to maternity leave or adoptive leave constitutes discrimination contrary to the Pregnancy Workers Directive, or whether it constitutes discrimination on grounds of gender or of disability*

See [**20.02**].

RACE AND NATIONALITY

[4.36] *Conrad Hotel v Jurksa[66] – Labour Court – appeal of decision of Equality Tribunal – Employment Equality Acts 1998 to 2011 – discrimination on grounds of race – internal recruitment process – establishing prima facie discrimination*

The complainant unsuccessfully applied for a position in the respondent hotel's laundry room, a position for which he felt he was highly qualified. The complainant asserted that the only reason that he was unsuccessful was his as a result of his race, stating that the person interviewing for the role was African and so was one of the successful applicants.

---

64. *Z v A Government Dept and the Board of Management of a Community School* (Case C–363/12).
65. *CD v ST* (Case C–167/12).
66. *Conrad Hotel v Jurksa* EDA1333.

The Labour Court stated that it was not its function to look behind a decision unless there is clear evidence of unfairness in the selection process or a manifest irrationality in the result. The Labour Court referred to *O'Halloran v Galway City Partnership*[67] and affirmed that its role was not to choose the selection criteria for a role, and it would intervene only where the chosen criteria are applied inconsistently between candidates or where an unsuccessful candidate is clearly better qualified than the successful candidate against the chosen criteria, resulting in an inference of discrimination.

The Labour Court stated that it is settled law that a mere difference in treatment of candidates having different protected characteristics is insufficient to give rise to an inference of discrimination. In this case, the complainant failed to establish any possible connection between his nationality and the respondent's failure to offer him employment and he did not refer to a comparator within the respondent to demonstrate unfavourable treatment. The complainant's appeal was dismissed.

[4.37] *Dublin Institute of Technology v Awojuola*[68] *– Labour Court – appeal of decision of Equality Tribunal – Industrial Relations Acts 1946 to 2012 – Employment Equality Acts 1998 to 2011, s 83 – definition of 'vocational training' – whether requirement to pay third-level fees at non-EEA national rate discriminatory on grounds of race – categorisation of comparators*

The complainant sought to challenge the decision of the respondent to charge her the rate of fees applicable to non-EU nationals on the basis that the rate of fees was discriminatory on the ground of race. The Equality Tribunal rejected her complaint and she appealed the decision to the Labour Court.

The Labour Court determined that it would only address the interpretation of the term 'vocational training' if the outcome of the case depended on that question, and this would only arise if the Labour Court came to the conclusion that the decision to charge the complainant the non-EU scale fees was considered indirect discrimination.

The respondent justified the decision to charge the complaint the non-EU rate of fees on the basis that the criteria determining which fees were payable depended on residency or citizenship of the EU and were wholly unrelated to race. The Labour Court accepted that the provisions were neutral on their face; however, the complainant argued that this was indirect discrimination, as it placed persons of her ethnic origin (Nigerian) at a disadvantage relative to persons of a different racial origin. The complainant stated that the comparators should be all those who were neither residents nor citizens of the EU, which formed for the purpose of this case a separate race. The Labour Court was therefore asked to consider whether there could be a recognised racial group located in or referable to the European Union, and, by exclusion, whether all other persons are a separate racial group.

In determining whether EU/EEA nationals could be considered a separate race within the meaning of the Employment Equality Acts 1998 to 2011 the Labour Court utilised the criteria set out in the UK House of Lords decision in *Mandla v Lee*.[69] The

---

67.   *O'Halloran v Galway City Partnership* EDA077.

68.   *Dublin Institute of Technology v Awojuola* EDA1335.

69.   *Mandla v Lee* [1983] 1 ICR 385.

Labour Court applied what Lord Fraser in that case had referred to as 'the essential distinguishing characteristics' of a people. In examining the origins and cultures included in the EU, the Labour Court found that there was no identifiable ethnic group, shared history, common language or culture in the EU, and therefore nationals of the EU could not be considered a 'racial group'. Nor could all other people in the entire World be considered a racial or ethnic group on the basis that they were not nationals of the EU.

The complainant also asserted that she was a member of a racial group, which was encompassed in the definition of 'national origin'. However, the Labour Court found that it was difficult to envisage how a claim of indirect discrimination on grounds of national origin (hers being Nigerian) could succeed when a claim on ground of nationality (which was also Nigerian) was unsustainable. For the purposes of interpreting the Irish legislation, 'national origin' and 'nationality' meant the same thing.

The Labour Court also rejected the complaint of indirect discrimination on the basis of colour. The Labour Court held that, when establishing a pool for determining whether indirect discrimination had occurred, it was insufficient for the complainant to demonstrate that more black people would potentially be affected by the non-EU rate of fees, but rather she would be required to demonstrate that that there was a significant imbalance in racial make-up, as defined by reference to colour between those actually charged the EU rates of fees compared to those charged the non-EU rate. As the complainant adduced no such evidence, her argument was unsuccessful.

The Labour Court determined that the decision to charge the complainant the non-EU rate of fees was based on nationality which, by virtue of the Act, fell outside the purview of the anti-discrimination provisions of the Act. The Labour Court was satisfied that the intention of the Oireachtas was clearly set out in the drafting of the legislation, and therefore, it could not construe s 12(7) of the Employment Equality Act 1998 so as to produce a result which, in its practical application, would undermine the intention of the Oireachtas.

The complainant's appeal was rejected.

[4.38] *Gajdos v Securikey Ltd[70] – Labour Court – appeal of decision of Equality Tribunal – Industrial Relations Acts 1946 to 2012 – Employment Equality Acts 1998 to 2011, s 83 – discrimination on grounds of nationality/race – discriminatory dismissal – victimisation – compensation of €7,500 awarded*

The respondent employed the complainant, a Slovakian national, as a security guard from August to December 2009. He claimed that he was discriminated against on grounds of race/nationality, victimised for making a complaint and subsequently dismissed. The Equality Tribunal found that his complaint was not well founded. The complainant appealed this decision to the Labour Court.

---

70. *Gajdos v Securikey Ltd* EDA1317.

In respect of his claim of discrimination on grounds of race, the complainant argued that the unfavourable treatment took the form of:

(i)   not being provided with sufficient time to review his contract of employment;

(ii) not being provided with his payslips in a timely manner; and

(iii) a failure of the respondent to provide him with a copy of his employment contract.

He also claimed that, when his solicitor set out his complaints and requested a copy of his contract from the respondent, his work placements became erratic and he was required to travel long distances for assignment. The complainant further claimed that following a further letter from his solicitor to the respondent, he was dismissed. The respondent submitted that the complainant was dismissed during his probationary period for being unable to meet his roster requirements and being unavailable for work on two week-long occasions due to his own sick leave and his partner's sick leave.

The Court examined whether the complainant had received less favourable treatment on the basis of his race. Section 85A of the Employment Equality Acts 1998 to 2011 provides that once a complainant establishes facts from which an inference of discrimination arises, the onus of proof shifts to the employer to establish that no discrimination took place. If the complainant in this case could not discharge the initial probative burden required of him, his case would not succeed. The Court heard conflicting evidence from the parties in relation to the time afforded to the complainant to review his contract of employment prior to signing it, and found that on the balance of probabilities, given the complainant's standard of English, he understood the terms of his contract relating to travelling to work assignments. It also found that the respondent did not provide a copy of the contract to the complainant. However, the complainant failed to adduce any evidence that he received less favourable treatment on the basis of his race or nationality compared to other employees of the respondent.

The Labour Court noted that the complainant had the opportunity under s 76 of the Acts to seek information from the respondent regarding the manner in which it had dealt with any or all other workers, but the complainant had failed to do so. The Labour Court referred to its decision in *Valpeters v Melbury Developments Ltd*[71] and found that 'mere speculation' on the part of the complainant that the basis of his treatment was due to his race or nationality was not sufficient to discharge the burden of proof to the respondent. The complainant's claim of discrimination was dismissed.

The Labour Court examined the complainant's allegation of victimisation following his complaint of unfavourable treatment by the respondent. It was noted that his solicitor's letter specifically referred to the fact that their client was making a complaint, which was a necessary element to establish that victimisation could have occurred. The complainant's job description provided that he would work on assignments either in Waterford, New Ross (which was 20km from the complainant's home) or Clonmel (which was 50km from his home). The Labour Court accepted evidence that, following his request to see his contractual documentation, pay slips, etc the complainant was

---

71.   *Valpeters v Melbury Developments Ltd* EDA0917.

assigned frequently to Clonmel, whereas prior to his raising complaints, he was rarely sent on assignments to Clonmel. The Labour Court found that this amounted to an inference of victimisation, and in the absence of the respondent providing a reasonable explanation for the change in the complainant's assignments, it concluded that victimisation had occurred.

In respect of the complainant's claim for discriminatory dismissal, the Labour Court found that he had established that, through his solicitor, he had made a complaint of discrimination and, on the following day, he was dismissed. This amounted to an inference of discrimination, shifting the burden of proof to the respondent.

The respondent attempted to rebut the inferences by submitting that the complainant had been dismissed for his unwillingness to work in any of the locations in which the respondent operated and due to the number of days lost due to his sick leave. The Labour Court found that the respondent did not adduce evidence to suggest that the complainant was unwilling to work and found that the complainant had acted reasonably in his request to be provided with a copy of his contract. It was noted that, following the raising of concerns by the complainant, he was dismissed without discussion or engagement. The Court also found that as the decision to dismiss the complainant occurred before he took sick leave, the respondent could not use this ground to justify his dismissal. Finally, the Court did not accept that the respondent was justified dismissing the complainant because he was on probation.

The Court upheld the complaint of victimisation through dismissal and awarded the complainant compensation of €7,500.

[4.39] *Xin Wei v Drew International Ltd (in Receivership)[72] – Equality Tribunal – whether complainant was discriminated against on ground of race contrary to Employment Equality Acts 1998 to 2011, ss 6 and 8 – alleged failure to adequately pay complainant or formally promote him – equal remuneration for 'like work' – no reason other than race for differences in pay*

The complainant, a Chinese national working as a waiter/bartender since April 2002, submitted that he was expected to perform duties in addition to the duties of waiter/bartender and became a de facto assistant manager. These extra duties were not in the complainant's official job description and he was not paid accordingly. The complainant submitted that, by not formally being appointed to the role of assistant manager, he was discriminated against in relation to promotion and conditions of employment.

The complainant also complained that he was paid less than Irish workers who were performing similar tasks with similar responsibilities, and specifically a named comparator who commenced employment with the respondent in February 2009. The complainant was paid €10 per hour, and received tips of €15 to €20 per shift. The respondent submitted that the named comparator was recruited just before the respondent went into receivership in 2009 in an effort to increase bar trade by engaging with customers and being responsible for the music and television in the bar. He was paid €12 per hour and also received tips. The respondent submitted that any difference

---

in pay between the comparator and the complainant had nothing to do with race as the complainant and the comparator were doing different jobs.

The Equality Tribunal noted that the complainant undertook cashing up and locking when the bar manager was not on duty, and otherwise these were duties of the bar manager. The Equality Tribunal accepted that there was not a promotional vacancy available in relation to the role of assistant manager, and consequently there was no such role which could have been offered to the complainant. The Equality Tribunal found no evidence to substantiate a claim of discrimination in relation to conditions of employment.

In relation to the claim for equal remuneration for 'like work', the Equality Tribunal noted that both the complainant and the comparator worked as bartenders, and the only differences in their duties that could be identified were the extra responsibilities carried out by the complainant. The respondent provided no evidence of the nature of the duties of the comparator that raised his work above that of the complainant, nor that he had previous relevant experience. The Equality Tribunal concluded that the complainant and the comparator performed like work and there was no reason other than race for any difference in pay. The Equality Tribunal ordered that the respondent pay to the complainant arrears of pay of €2 per hour for 20 hours per week from February 2009 until 1 July 2011 (€4,960), in accordance with s 82(1)(a) of the Employment Equality Acts.

[4.40] *Miss Ying Ying Sun Summer v McGraths Pub T/A Dawn Taverns Ltd*[73] *– Equality Tribunal – Employment Equality Acts 1998 to 2011, s 8 – whether complainant, a part-time weekend worker, discriminated against on grounds of race in relation to her conditions of employment, remuneration and in relation to her dismissal.*

The complainant, a Chinese national, was employed by the respondent on a part-time basis and worked weekends from February 2002 to January 2011. She submitted that her hourly rate of €15.00 per hour was suddenly, without explanation, reduced to €10.00 per hour in June 2010. Thereafter, the complainant's hours were reduced without explanation. She continued to work and be paid at this rate until 27 December 2010, after which she received no hours at all. She made contact with the respondent on a number of occasions and was told that there was no more work for her at the time. The complainant claimed that another staff member, who was male and Irish, was taken on after her and continued to work there after the complainant was told there were no more hours for her. The complainant submitted that her identified comparator was also employed on a part-time basis and normally worked weekends, the same as herself. The complainant further claimed that she was awarded a lump sum payable under the Redundancy Payments Acts by the Employment Appeals Tribunal but claimed that the respondent had refused to comply with this award. The complainant further advised at the hearing that during the time period in question she was the only female member of

---

73.   *Miss Ying Ying Sun Summer v McGraths Pub T/A Dawn Taverns Ltd* DEC–E2014–064.

staff and whilst other females had worked in the respondent's pub from time to time, they were either related to the owner, or family friends.

The respondent did not provide a submission to the Tribunal in relation to these matters and did not attend the hearing.

The Equality Tribunal initially addressed the question as to whether the complainant's claim was validly within time. It was noted that the complaint was submitted to the Tribunal on 4 July 2011. The Tribunal noted that the last date actually worked by the complainant was 27 December 2010 and thus the complaint, on its face, was out of time. However, the Equality Tribunal accepted the complainant's evidence that she was not advised or aware that 27 December 2010 was her last day at work. She had telephoned the respondent on a number of occasions in January 2011 and was told that there were no hours for her at the time but that they would be in contact again as hours arose. The complainant did not receive any official documentation that her employment had come to an end and was unaware that her employment had ended on the last day that she had been rostered to work.

The Equality Tribunal noted of s 77(6) of the Employment Equality Acts which provides for the circumstance where an employee submits a late claim due to a misrepresentation on the part of the respondent. In view of the Equality Tribunal, this case fell into the category provided for because the complainant in this case was unaware, due to misrepresentation on the part of the respondent, that she would not be rostered to work any more hours after 27 December 2010. The Equality Tribunal further noted that had the complainant received her four-week notice entitlement, her date of termination would have been 27 January 2011 as cited on her complaint forms. The Equality Tribunal concluded that the complaint was submitted within the six-month time limit set out in s 77(5) of the Acts.

In her evidence before the Tribunal the complainant named a male colleague as the comparator whom she was paid less than. However she was unable to confirm to the Tribunal how much he was being paid or whether he was being paid more or less than her. The complainant stated she was not aware of these details and conceded that hers was not an equal pay claim for the purposes of the Acts. The complainant stated to the Tribunal that her issue with her pay was the fact that her wages were reduced without warning or reason in June 2010.

The Equality Tribunal decided to look at this aspect of the complaint under conditions of employment. The complainant advised the Equality Tribunal that she only realised her hourly rate had been reduced when she received her pay slip and did not receive any warning or discussion in relation to the reduction. When she queried it with the respondent, she was told that that was all the respondent could pay her. She asked the respondent to show her some documentation to indicate the reason for the reduction. However the respondent did not provide any documentation to indicate the reason for the reduction in her salary. The complainant submitted that she was the only staff member whose wages were reduced at the time and stated her belief that this was due to the fact that she was Chinese and female. She was the only non-Irish person working for the respondent during the time in question and also the only female. Wage cuts were introduced for other staff members months later, but these were agreed with staff members and the respondent with the involvement of the staff union.

The Equality Tribunal was satisfied that the complainant had established a prima facie case of discrimination on grounds of race and gender, which the respondent had failed to rebut. With regard to the alleged discriminatory dismissal, the complainant advised the Tribunal that her hours began to be reduced in late 2010 until eventually she was not rostered for any hours at all. Her identified comparator who was male and Irish, was taken on after her and continued to work there after she was told there were no more hours for her. Her evidence was that she and her comparator did the same job. The Equality Tribunal again found that the complainant had established a prima facie case of discriminatory dismissal on grounds of race and gender which the respondent had failed to rebut.

The Equality Tribunal considered that any award of compensation should be proportionate, effective and dissuasive. In making its award the Tribunal was mindful of the remuneration which the complainant was in receipt of at the relevant time and the length of time she was employed by the respondent. It awarded the complainant compensation of €10,000.

[4.41] *Wszotek v Moduslink and O'Reilly Recruitment Ltd[74] – Equality Tribunal – Employment Equality Acts 1998 to 2011 – alleged discrimination on grounds of race – promotion – training – conditions of employment – harassment – race – agency workers*

The complainant stated that he worked at Moduslink from October 2008 to 23 March 2011 and that he was discriminated against in relation to selection for work and was treated differently to Irish workers. He alleged that he received verbal insults, he was given more difficult work than Irish workers and he was denied cigarette breaks. The complainant submitted that there was a selection process every Friday for agency workers to be called back the following week, in which Irish workers were always called back first, and this resulted in the complainant having less job security, being assigned less hours and being paid less than Irish workers. The complainant stated that his employer informed him that they had a report from Moduslink that they should not give him any more work.

Moduslink submitted that it was not the correct respondent as the complainant was supplied to it through an employment agency. The Equality Tribunal noted that s 8(1) of the Acts states that:

> a provider of agency work shall not discriminate against an agency worker', and that s 8(2) of the Acts states that 'a provider of agency work shall be taken to discriminate against an agency worker unless (on one of the discriminatory grounds) that agency worker is treated less favourably than another agency worker is, has been or would be treated.

The Equality Tribunal noted that s 14A of the Acts refers to harassment 'at a place where the employee is employed ... by a person who is employed at that place by the same employer'. As the allegations by the complainant referred to the actions of staff of

---

74.   *Wszotek v Moduslink and O'Reilly Recruitment Ltd* DEC–E2014–002.

Moduslink, the Equality Tribunal concluded that Moduslink was the correct party to whom the claim of harassment should be addressed.

Moduslink submitted that it used agency staff as and when required and the level of usage depended on the needs of the business. The complainant was assigned to work for Moduslink between October 2008 and March 2011, depending on its operational requirements, and during this period he worked a total of 52 weeks. On his initial assignment he received its standard induction programme, which includes a reference to the bullying and harassment and grievance procedures. Moduslink claimed that, in March 2011, the complainant was responsible for a serious quality failure. As a result of this quality failure, a direction was given to the second respondent, the agency, not to place the complainant back on site. Two other workers were also deemed unsuitable arising from the same incident: one was Irish and the other Polish. Moduslink submitted that from 23 October 2010 to 23 March 2011, 23 agency workers were deemed not suitable for future assignments. Of these 12 were Irish and 11 were of various other nationalities. In relation to the selection process on Friday for agency staff, Moduslink submitted that the complainant attended an initial induction course and provided evidence that the induction day included a presentation on the 'Review Process – Temp Staff' which set out that, where temporary employees were required to be laid off due to a decrease in capacity/business requirements, selection would be based on:

(i)   time and attendance;

(ii)   flexibility with regard to hours/duties/overtime/shift, etc;

(iii)   attitude to team leaders/supervisors/other team members;

(iv)   performance;

(v)   quality and attention; and

(vi)   ability to follow instruction.

Moduslink claimed that these were the criteria used when selections were made on a Friday in respect of agency workers being called back to work.

The Equality Tribunal considered whether the complainant had established a prima facie case of discrimination in order to shift the burden of proof to Moduslink as set out by the Labour Court in *Valpeters v Melbury Developments Ltd.*[75] Noting that the complainant had made assertions, rather than provide more concrete evidence of the alleged discrimination, the Equality Tribunal decided that the complainant had failed to establish a prima facie case of discrimination in relation to access to employment or conditions of employment. The Equality Tribunal noted that s 14A(2) of the Employment Equality Acts 1998 to 2011 gives an employer a defence against harassment if it can prove that it took such reasonable steps as are practicable to prevent the harassment. The Equality Tribunal found that Moduslink had a procedure in place for investigating harassment, but was unaware of any issues relating to the complainant

---

75.   *Valpeters v Melbury Developments Ltd* EDA0917.

as the complainant had not brought this to its attention. The Equality Tribunal decided that the complainant had failed to establish a prima facie case of harassment.

[4.42] *Spyra v Ryanair Ltd*[76] *– Equality Tribunal – Labour Court Appeal – Employment Equality Acts 1998 to 2011 – whether complainant discriminated against on grounds of her nationality or race in terms of discriminatory dismissal – preliminary issue – whether complainant, an agency worker, could be regarded as being employed by respondent, the provider – whether ceasing agency work is dismissal within meaning of Acts*

The complainant began working for the respondent as an agency worker from 1 October 2007 in a customer services role. Her employment was terminated on 31 October 2011 along with three other employees – one of whom was Irish, one Polish like herself and one Lithuanian. It was claimed by the complainant that the Irish worker was subsequently taken back and the complainant asserted that this amounted to discriminatory dismissal of her on the grounds of race.

The respondent contended that it did not have a contract of employment with the complainant and it did not pay her and thus was not her employer. With regard to the substantive issue, the respondent asserted that the complainant and 13 other staff had their assignments ended because of a downturn in business and subsequently four positions had become available in its reservations department, but the offer for the complainant was subsequently withdrawn following an unfavourable reference. The employment agency was also party to these proceedings, as parallel proceedings were brought against it. It asserted that assignments were discontinued, 11 of whom were Irish and three of whom were non-nationals and that subsequently five non-Irish nationals were placed with the respondent again. The agency therefore disputed that nationality was a factor in the staff fluctuations.

The Equality Tribunal considered whether the cessation of the provision of agency work was a dismissal within the meaning of the Acts. In considering s 8(3) of the Acts, the Equality Tribunal concluded that the agency was properly described as a provider of agency workers to the respondent. The Equality Tribunal noted the Labour Court decision in *Citi Bank v Ntoko.*[77]

The Equality Tribunal noted that the complainant was under the respondent's day-to-day control as to how she carried on her work and she was subject to performance appraisals by the respondent. The Tribunal noted that nobody had denied that the respondent was paying the employment agency, which had placed the complainant with it for her work which passed to the complainant as her salary. Evidence was submitted by the employment agency, stating that the agency had no part in the complainant's daily management or in the complainant's formal appraisals and this was not contested. The Equality Tribunal noted the intention of the Oireachtas to protect agency workers

---

76. *Spyra v Ryanair Ltd* DEC–E2013–195; *Spyra v Ryanair Ltd T/A Ryanair* EDA142.
77. *City Bank v Ntoko* EED045.

against discrimination, to include discriminatory dismissal. The Equality Tribunal stated that it was taking this to mean that agency work may be withdrawn from agency workers by a provider of agency work only by reason of the exigencies connected with the use of agency work on the part of an undertaking or because of issues of personal conduct of an agency worker, but not for one of the characteristics which are protected within the Acts. The Equality Tribunal further concluded that:

> an implied contract of employment within the meaning of Section 2 of the Acts existed between the complainant and the respondent which came to an end when the respondent withdrew agency work from the complainant, thereby amounting to a dismissal within the meaning of the Acts.

The Equality Tribunal, having determined that it had jurisdiction to investigate whether work was withdrawn from the complainant because of her Polish nationality, ie because of a discriminatory reason, then went on to consider whether the complainant had established a prima facie case. Evidence was given that a seasonal downturn in business necessitated withdrawing work from certain long-term agency staff who had previously been accommodated with part-time work during the winter months, including the complainant. In order to facilitate the decision-making process, performance appraisals were carried out with all check-in agents, to include the complainant who had never before been appraised for her performance. The complainant had scored second from bottom but an Irish worker, who had scored one point lower than the complainant, was nevertheless reinstated. Evidence was given by the respondent that the Irish worker had considerable potential, whereas the complainant with her long service should have been a better worker at the time of her appraisal. The Equality Tribunal stated that the complainant was entitled in response to raise the point as to whether bias in the assessment process in favour of her Irish comparators may have influenced the decision to withdraw work from her but to reinstate an Irish worker who had scored lower than herself. The Equality Tribunal noted the decision of the Labour Court in *Portroe Stevedores v Nevins, Murphy and Flood*[78] where the Labour Court held that:

> discrimination is usually covert and often routed in the subconscious of the discriminator. Sometimes a person may discriminate as a result of inbuilt and unrecognised prejudice of which he or she is unaware. Thus a person accused of discrimination may give seemingly honest evidence in rebuttal of what is alleged against them. Nonetheless the Court must be alert to the possibility of unconscious or inadvertent discrimination and mere denial of a discriminatory motive, in the absence of independent corroborative, must be approached with caution.

The Equality Tribunal referenced other performance appraisal documents from the respondent in respect of one of the four workers amongst the five top scorers who were Polish nationals. This was evidence (as well as the respondent's uncontroverted evidence that, of the workers that were kept on during the winter, seven were Polish, one was Estonian and only two were Irish) meant that the respondent had successfully rebutted

---

78.   *Portroe Stevedores v Nevins, Murphy and Flood* EDA051.

the presumption that its worker assessments may have been influenced by conscious or unconscious bias in favour of Irish workers. The Equality Tribunal concluded that it was satisfied that when the respondent needed to withdraw agency work from a number of long-term agency staff, the complainant was selected because of her mediocre performance and that her Polish nationality played no part in this and thus the complaint of discriminatory dismissal failed.

Labour Court Appeal

The decision of the Equality Tribunal was appealed by the complainant to the Labour Court.

The Labour Court accepted that the seasonal downturn in the airline industry was more acute than normal in 2013 and that special measures were required to bring the supply and demand for staff into balance. The Labour Court noted that unusually that year the respondent decided to develop and apply an assessment matrix by which to select staff for layoff. The Court observed that this procedure may or may not have been fair, but held that the only issue for consideration by the Court was whether the system introduced and applied by the respondent amounted to a result of discrimination on grounds of national origins.

The Court noted that some of the factors used in the assessment were transparent and subject to empirical verification, however some were more subjective in so far as they consisted of assessment by supervisory staff of qualitative rather than quantitative performance. The Court reviewed the outcome of the procedure to determine whether it affected people of different nationalities to different degrees and the Court found the respondent's evidence did not disclose differential outcomes for staff of different origins. The Court then considered the complainant's argument that the lowest ranked employee, an Irish national, was exempt from the selection procedure and whether this gave rise to a presumption of discriminatory treatment.

Whilst finding merit in that argument, the Court considered the respondent's position that the worker that scored the lowest number of points out of the assessment process was a recent recruit and was making constant progress at an acceptable pace, and should not be judged by the same standards as long standing workers like the complainant. The Court summarised that it was not required to decide if this was a fair procedure but only had to decide whether it was discriminatory in design or outcome giving rise to discrimination on the grounds of national origin. In that context the Court found that it was not.

The Court noted the composition of the respondent's workforce, specifically that it was multi-racial and the supervisory structure reflected that. It further noted the outcome of the assessment, namely that foreign national workers were placed in four of the top five positions. The Court found that those figures did not indicate an inherent adverse bias in the design or conduct of the exercise against non-Irish workers and neither did it disclose or suggest a bias against non-Irish workers in the outcome of the exercise.

The Court held that the complaint was not well founded and the decision of the Equality Tribunal was affirmed.

[4.43] *Kulasza v California White Services Ltd*[79] – *Equality Tribunal – Employment Equality Acts 1998 to 2011 – discriminatory treatment – harassment – alleged discriminatory dismissal on grounds of race – victimisation*

The respondent employed the complainant, a Polish national, as a dental nurse, from January 2008 to March 2010. Initially, she was one of two dental nurses at the practice. However, the second dental nurse left in May 2009 and, as a result, the complainant's workload increased substantially. She stated that she was required to do this work without any assistance. She raised this as a complaint with the respondent and was informed that a replacement would be found within two or three weeks but she was later informed that there would be no replacement. She raised this complaint a number of times but it was rejected. A second dental nurse was hired in December 2009. She was assigned to work with one of the two dentists at the practice. This nurse was of Irish nationality.

The complainant contended that she was treated less favourably in terms of her conditions of employment. She submitted that she was assigned an excessive workload when she was the sole dental nurse at the practice and later that her workload was excessive in comparison to the second nurse that was subsequently hired. The Equality Tribunal noted that, while the complainant's workload increased, the tasks she was asked to complete were ones which she would have expected to perform as a dental nurse and were nothing out of the ordinary. It also noted the evidence of the respondent that it was normal practice to have only one dental nurse and this practice continued after the complainant had ceased employment with the respondent. The Equality Tribunal was satisfied that the decision not to recruit a replacement was a normal management decision and that the complainant had failed to adduce any evidence that it was influenced by her Polish nationality. The Equality Tribunal also noted that the complainant was given other benefits, such as Friday afternoons off and annual leave before Christmas, which were inconsistent with allegations of less favourable treatment. The complainant also made several allegations about the behaviour of one of the dentists at the practice. She submitted that his actions, which included shouting at her and telling her not to look at patients, constituted harassment on the grounds of her nationality. The Equality Tribunal was satisfied that the behaviour complained of was a result of the respondent's frustration with the complainant for arguing with him and, whilst his behaviour was brusque and rude and was clearly intimidating and humiliating to the complainant, it was not linked to her Polish nationality. The complainant accepted that the respondent never used any racially derogatory language towards her.

The Equality Tribunal found that the complainant had failed to establish a prima facie case that she was harassed by the respondent on grounds of race. The complainant's claim for victimisation also failed. There was no evidence to suggest that she had been dismissed, rather she left of her own accord.

---

79.   *Kulasza v California White Services Ltd* DEC–E2014–052.

Equal pay/race

[4.44] *Marzec v Billy Purcell Plant Hire Ltd (in liquidation)[80] – Equality Tribunal – Employment Equality Acts 1998 to 2011 – whether discrimination on grounds of race in relation to conditions of employment and remuneration*

The respondent employed the complainant, a Polish national. He was not provided with a written contract of employment or job description and was not given a job title. He was part of a three-person team, whose duties involved driving out in a van, digging trenches and manholes for laying cables and telephone boxes, laying bricks to house the boxes and connecting pipes and cables to the boxes.

He claimed he was discriminated against by the respondent on grounds of race in relation to his conditions of employment and remuneration. Neither the respondent nor the liquidator made a submission to the Equality Tribunal prior to the hearing and neither gave evidence during the hearing. After the hearing, the liquidator provided information to the Equality Tribunal, which included a statement from a director of the respondent.

The first claim of discrimination concerned conditions of employment under s 8 of the Employment Equality Acts and referred to a redundancy payment that was not paid. The Equality Tribunal rejected this claim because the complainant failed to provide evidence that he was treated any differently to other employees with respect to redundancy payments. The second claim concerned an entitlement to equal remuneration under s 29 of the Employment Equality Acts. The complainant gave evidence that the Irish team member (comparator A) received a higher wage than both the complainant and his Polish colleague.

The Equality Tribunal accepted that the complainant earned less than comparator A at all times. The complainant's evidence stated that this was so despite the fact all team members carried out 'like work'. The director's statement sought to justify the wage differential in terms of qualifications held by the Irish employee. He said he considered comparator A to be the Team Foreman, given his qualifications to operate digging machinery, whereas the complainant, who did not hold such qualifications, was considered a general operative. The complainant countered that he and his Polish colleague carried out more work than comparator A in terms of driving and laying bricks. He also stated that as the respondent was a subcontractor to eircom, the team worked equally and were instructed and supervised by, and answerable to, the eircom employee on site.

Having considered the limited evidence available, the Equality Tribunal accepted that the three team members did carry out 'like work' in accordance with the definition in s 7(1) of the Employment Equality Acts. The Tribunal concluded there was no objective basis for any difference in pay, and the respondent had discriminated against the complainant on grounds of race.

The Equality Tribunal ordered the respondent to pay arrears of remuneration to the complainant, ie the difference between the complainant's gross pay and the gross pay of

---

80.   *Marzec v Billy Purcell Plant Hire Ltd (in liq)* DEC–E2014–014.

complainant A, from three years before the claim was made until the complainant left employment. As the award constituted remuneration it was subject to PAYE/PRSI deductions.

VICTIMISATION

[4.45] *Wach v Travelodge Management Ltd T/A Travelodge Waterford[81] – Equality Tribunal – Employment Equality Acts 1998 to 2011 – discrimination on grounds of gender, family status and race – whether complainant victimised contrary to s 74(2) – reduced hours on return from maternity leave – complainant's fluency in English queried – false disciplinary charges threatened after complainant raised complaint of discrimination – compensation awarded equivalent to three years' salary*

Evidence was given that the complainant, a Polish national, was working from September 2008 as a receptionist and worked shifts averaging 42.9 hours per week. She went on maternity leave from March 2011 to September 2011 and, on her return, she found her hours reduced and also found that the respondent had brought in a staff member from Cork to do shifts when the complainant would have been available. When she raised concerns about this with the HR manager, her manager expressed annoyance. Her manager further advised her that her contract was only for 24 hours and that was all she was entitled to. The complainant claimed that the 24 hours referenced in her contract were minimum hours and with prior agreement with the previous manager, she had been working full-time for the previous three years. The complainant stated that her manager told her that her English was not good enough to work day shifts. She asserted that she had been working days for three years with no complaints. A written complaint was furnished by the complainant in October 2011 to her manager, following on from which there was a meeting attended by the complainant, one of her colleagues and a staff member from human resources. At this meeting, the complainant stated that she felt discriminated against. Following on from this meeting, the complainant claimed that her manager threatened her in that he would look through CCTV footage for any possible wrongdoing by her and use it against her. A number of days after her internal appeal against the outcome of her grievance was rejected in January 2012, the complainant was called into a disciplinary meeting with her manager where he raised an allegation that she had been selling alcohol to non-residents of the hotel. This allegation ultimately was dropped as the manager was unable to adduce any evidence that the persons the complainant sold the alcohol to were not guests of the hotel.

The Equality Tribunal noted from the evidence that the complainant was fluent in written and spoken English. The Equality Tribunal concluded that the complainant was a credible witness and that she had returned from maternity leave to less favourable working conditions than she had enjoyed before. The Equality Tribunal attached particular importance to the fact that the staff member who covered for the complainant during maternity leave was left in place. The Equality Tribunal noted previous findings of the Tribunal that assigning undesirable shifts to workers with protected characteristics

---

81.　*Wach v Travelodge Management Ltd T/A Travelodge Waterford* DEC–E2014–055.

and more favourable shifts to other workers can be considered as less favourable treatment. The Equality Tribunal did not accept the complainant's manager's evidence with regard to the complainant's proficiency in English and did not accept his reasoning for not assigning her day shifts.

The Equality Tribunal then considered the complainant's complaint of victimisation and noted that she had raised a formal written complaint against her manager in which she had raised a possible issue of discrimination and also enclosed a copy of the respondent's equality policy. The Equality Tribunal concluded that these facts made her complaint a protected action within the meaning of s 74(2)(a) of the Acts. The Equality Tribunal noted the evidence from the complainant that her manager was incensed at the complaint and said to her that he would look through the hotel's CCTV footage for disciplinary infractions on her part. The Tribunal noted that the purported disciplinary matter was dropped when the complainant was able to show that the customer in question was a hotel guest who bought alcohol and then took it offsite. The Equality Tribunal concluded that the actions of the complainant's manager did constitute adverse treatment of her and that she was entitled to succeed with her complaint of victimisation.

In its decision the Equality Tribunal upheld the complaints made by the complainant and held that she had been less favourably treated in her terms and conditions of employment contrary to s 8 of the Acts on grounds of gender and race and had been victimised contrary to s 74(2) of the Act. In terms of redress, the Equality Tribunal ordered that the respondent pay the complainant: (1) €22,100 (equal to one year's salary prior to the reduction of her hours); and (2) €42,000, the equivalent of two years' salary in compensation for the effects of victimisation. The Equality Tribunal noted the seriousness of the finding that the complainant found herself immediately threatened with false disciplinary charges when she exercised her right of complaint under the respondent's own policy.

[4.46] *Jessemey v Rowstock Ltd[82]– Court of Appeal of England and Wales – Underhill LJ – respondent provided claimant with very poor reference because he brought proceedings against respondent for unfair dismissal and age discrimination*

This was a joined appeal[83] on a point of law as to whether the Equality Act 2010 prohibited acts of victimisation committed against former employees.

The Court of Appeal noted that the claimant had been employed by the first respondent, a small car sales and repair business, and was dismissed on the ground that he was aged over 65. He brought a claim for unfair dismissal and age discrimination and sought the help of an employment agency to find another job. When they approached

---

82.   *Jessemey v Rowstock Ltd* [2014] EWCA Civ 185.

83.   This appeal arose in the context of decision of the EAT which held it did not. However, in a subsequent case, *Onu v Akwiwu* [2014] EWCA Civ 279, the EAT held that it did. The Court of Appeal noted that this issue was of practical importance because claims by former employees that their employer had acted to their prejudice following the termination of their employment typically, though by no means only, by giving a bad or no reference, are not uncommon. The Court noted that the appeals in both cases were listed on the same occasion but that it was agreed by all parties that the present case should be treated as the lead.

the owner of the respondent, he gave the claimant a very poor reference by reason of the fact that the claimant had brought proceedings and the claimant presented a further claim alleging victimisation contrary to the Equality Act 2010.

An Employment Tribunal, upholding the claim of unfair dismissal, found as a matter of fact that the reason for the bad reference provided for the claimant was that he was pursuing Employment Tribunal proceedings. However, it was held that post-employment victimisation was not unlawful under the 2010 Act. The same conclusion was reached by the UK EAT whose decision was the subject of the appeal to the Court.

The Court of Appeal considered the provisions of the Equality Act 2010 and noted that it was intended to give effect in UK law to the requirements of a number of EU Directives. The Court of Appeal made reference to the CJEU decision in *Coote v Grenada Hospitality Ltd*[84] where the CJEU decided that a reference from the UK EAT in the case of an alleged discrimination of a former employee who had brought a claim of sex discrimination meant that Member States were required to ensure that employees making claims of sex discrimination were protected against being victimised on that account and this was the case whether the victimisation occurred during employment or subsequently.

The Court of Appeal noted that this had been authoritatively determined by the House of Lords in a number of joint appeals reported as *Rhys-Harper v Relaxion Group plc*[85] where the House of Lords held that the statutory language was indeed capable of applying in certain circumstances to discrimination against (or victimisation of) former employees. The Court noted that at the time the 2010 Act was drafted, it was well established that post-employment discrimination due to victimisation was unlawful.

The Court of Appeal noted that on a natural reading of the relevant provisions of the 2010 Act, post-termination victimisation is not prohibited. The Court of Appeal concluded that the apparent failure of the statute to prescribe post termination victimisation was a drafting error and the Court further concluded that it was possible to imply words into the 2010 Act to achieve that result. The Court concluded that post termination victimisation is prohibited by the 2010 Act and the Court allowed the appeal accordingly. The Court held that in light of the finding of the Employment Tribunal the respondent gave the reference because the claimant was pursuing Tribunal proceedings, the victimisation claim must succeed and thus the case must be remitted to the Tribunal for assessment of compensation.

---

84. *Coote v Grenada Hospitality Ltd* (Case C–185/1997) [1999] ICR 100.
85. *Rhys-Harper v Relaxion Group plc* [2003] ICR 867.

Chapter 5

EMPLOYMENT-RELATED TORTS

BULLYING AND HARASSMENT

[5.01] *Becton Dickinson v A Worker[1] – Industrial Relations Act 1969, s 20(1) – Labour Court – whether independent investigation should be carried out in circumstances where complaints of bullying, harassment, victimisation and intimidation made and already investigated internally – delay*

This claim arose from a complaint of bullying, harassment, victimisation and intimidation by the claimant and the subsequent investigation of same by the respondent. It was contended by the claimant that management did not follow its own procedures in relation to the investigation and there was excessive delay. The claimant sought an independent investigation. It was submitted by the respondent that the investigation was carried out in line with policies and procedures, although delay was conceded. The Labour Court concluded that there were remaining issues that needed to be resolved in an efficient and expeditious manner so that the parties could resume normal working relations and proceed with their respective roles in a productive manner.

The Court recommended that an independent person, as nominated by the Court, should, in consultation with and with the full cooperation of both parties, 'carry out a review of the situation to date within a period of four weeks from the commencement of such review'. The Court held that the purpose of this review was to 'enable the independent person to make a recommendation to the parties as to how matters should be resolved including a process to bring final resolution to the matters in dispute'. The Court did confirm, however, that it was not recommending a new investigation into the allegations made.

[5.02] *Ruffley v The Board of Management of St Anne's School[2] – High Court – O'Neill J – significant damages for bullying and harassment which occurred in course of plaintiff's employment as special needs assistant in primary school and arising from disciplinary process – unfair and inappropriate treatment of plaintiff*

The plaintiff was employed as a special needs assistant in a national school that caters exclusively for children with physical or intellectual disabilities between the age of 4 and 18. One of the services offered to pupils was a sensory room, which was used to develop the sensory perception of pupils by exposing them to a variety of sensory experiences such as music, vibration, movement, light and colour. Pupils who used the sensory room had an individualised programme designed by the occupational therapist

---

1.   *Becton Dickinson v A Worker* LCR20696.
2.   *Ruffley v The Board of Management of St Anne's School* [2014] IEHC 235.

and this was carried out by at least one if not two special needs assistants, depending on the pupil in question. In general only one pupil at a time was accommodated in the sensory room and the High Court noted that it was normal for the door of the sensory room to be left closed while a pupil was inside, to minimise distraction or disruptions. O'Neill J noted that the room had a lock on the inside, of the door which could be operated by twisting the lock to either open or close it. In this case a central issue arose as to whether it was common practice for the plaintiff and her colleagues to lock the door whilst a pupil was going through his or her programme in the sensory room.

An incident occurred when the plaintiff was in the sensory room with a student who fell asleep. As this was unusual for the particular pupil, the plaintiff went to the telephone outside the room a short distance away and telephoned the class teacher for further instructions. The teacher instructed the plaintiff to allow the pupil to continue to sleep for a further period of 20 minutes before returning him to class and, in the meantime, the teacher rang the principal and asked her to check the situation. On approaching the sensory room, the principal found the door locked and on her third attempt to gain entry, the door was opened by the plaintiff who readily accepted that the door had been locked.

A meeting took place the next day where the plaintiff was advised by the principal that the matter was to be handled in the context of a disciplinary procedure as the plaintiff had locked the door with the pupil inside. A statement was given by the plaintiff that she was shocked at this development, as it was her evidence, which was corroborated by other special needs assistants, that it was common practice to lock the sensory room door whilst conducting the occupational therapy program and no instruction had ever been given around this practice. The Court noted that, in the course of the meeting, the plaintiff had accepted that she had locked the sensory room door and had explained the reason for doing this was to prevent other children from entering the room while she was conducting a session with the pupil, and also to prevent the particular pupil from running out of the room whilst the programme equipment was being set up. The meeting then moved on to consider the suitability of the programme for the child who was asleep the previous day. O'Neill J noted that the notes of the meeting made no mention at all of a complaint about the plaintiff, of any inadequacy in her training or use of the sensory room and/or the need for any further training in that regard. The school principal gave evidence that after this meeting a process of training was set up which required the plaintiff to fill out a form indicating the activities accomplished by the child in the sensory room, and at the end of a four-week period there would be a review. A letter issued to the plaintiff confirming this, however it went on to state: 'if the required improvement is not made or if there is any such breach of discipline in any aspect of your work performance, this may result in disciplinary action'.

The Court noted that, at the subsequent review meeting, the plaintiff sought to correct an error on the form (by her) so as to ensure it accurately reflected the activities completed by the child. The teacher however refused her to allow her to do this and recorded the result on the review of the plaintiff's performance as a miscommunication by her. O'Neill J noted that it was difficult to comprehend this refusal on the part of the teacher, given that what was being recorded were the activities accomplished by the child in question. The Court noted that, in the course of these discussions and review periods there was no reference at all to any threat to the plaintiff, disciplinary or otherwise, and that the concern was focused on getting the child's programme right. The Court noted that the evidence of the school principal was to express dissatisfaction with the outcome of the review process conducted over the four-week period and specifically with the plaintiff's performance during that time. From this, the principal concluded that there had been no improvement and that the inaccurate completion of the form by the plaintiff, which the principal characterised as 'falsification' of the form, was an additional disciplinary issue such that the disciplinary procedure needed to be revived. The Court noted that this evidence was strange in circumstances where the student had advanced in his program and was now accomplishing more than had been the case at the start of the four-week program. The Court further noted that the description of the plaintiff's request to change the content of the forms so as to make them more accurately reflect the reality as being 'falsification', could only be said to be extreme, and 'utterly removed from what right thinking people would consider to be a reasonable conclusion'. The Court noted that this type of form was not normally used by the special needs assistants and the plaintiff was entirely unfamiliar with it.

The disciplinary process was revived and ultimately, arising from a board of management meeting, the plaintiff was issued with a Part 4 final warning. The Court noted that, at no stage, had the principal of the school done anything to investigate the plaintiff's contention that other colleagues locked the door of the sensory room and that it was common practice to do so. O'Neill J stated that he would accept that it was reasonable of the defendant, both for health and safety and for child protection reasons, to insist on a prohibition on locking the sensory room door. However he noted that, notwithstanding a comprehensive safety statement in place, no one had addressed the locking of this door or the presence of a lock on the inside of the door, whether in the context of health and safety or child protection issues, and because no one had considered the matter no instruction was given either to lock the door or not to lock it and the matter was simply overlooked by the defendant. The Court noted, however, that the daily task of carrying out programmes with the children in the room fell to the special needs assistants and they had to cope with the problem of intrusions by other children and also by individual children who needed to be restrained from running out of the room. The Court noted that the principal and the chairperson of the board gave evidence of what transpired at the board meeting. The Court noted that, whilst the plaintiff's conduct and what the appropriate sanction should be, was being discussed during the meeting, at no stage was the identity of the plaintiff ever revealed to the board and it was known only to the principal and the chairperson. The Court suggested that it was a matter of probability that the account given by the principal to the board of the history of this matter was almost certainly untrue, highly biased, coloured and grossly and unfairly damnifying of the plaintiff. The Court noted that what the board was being asked to consider was the gross misconduct of a single special needs assistant as distinct from a common practice amongst many staff, albeit one that was unacceptable.

The Court noted that the plaintiff knew nothing in advance of this meeting and was given no opportunity to represent herself in any way. The Court further noted that the representation given of her by the principal was in fact a gross misrepresentation. The plaintiff was ultimately advised just before Christmas that she was getting a Part 4 final warning which would be given to her formally in the New Year. Initially, when the plaintiff inquired how long it would be on record, she was informed that it would be on the record for six months. However, in January she was formally advised that the warning would be on her file for 18 months. The Court concluded that the plaintiff had been subject to a disciplinary sanction of a severe kind which was unmerited. The offence of locking the sensory room door, which the defendant was entitled to regard as unacceptable, was undoubtedly a common practice amongst the special needs assistants. Had the defendant, and in particular the principal, carried out the appropriate enquiries after the incident took place, this would undoubtedly have been readily ascertainable. As a consequence, the picture presented to the board in November 2009 was of individual misconduct on the part of the plaintiff. Had the board been told the true position, whilst they might well have been shocked that such a practice existed and directed steps to prohibit it, they could not single out the plaintiff to suffer punishment for it alone.

O'Neill J concluded that it was unfair to impose a severe disciplinary sanction on the plaintiff for doing something that, in the circumstances in which it was done, had practical merits, and where no instruction was given not to do it. The Court further noted that the manner in which the disciplinary process with regard to the locking of the door was handled by the principal of the school was grossly unfair to the plaintiff and denied her the benefit of her constitutional right to natural justice and fair procedures. The Court concluded that the conjuring up by the principal of an additional offence of failing to improve during a review process, and of the falsification of review forms, was at best irrational in the sense of there being a complete lack of any real basis for such conclusions. The Court concluded that the treatment of the plaintiff throughout this process by the principal was entirely inappropriate within the meaning of the definition of bullying within the workplace. The Court noted the definition in para 5 of the LRC Code of Practice.[3]

The plaintiff appealed to the board, and the Court noted that the board did not give any meaningful consideration to the case being made by the plaintiff, namely that the locking of the door was a common practice. The Court noted that the plaintiff's appeal to the board, insofar as it could be said to be an appeal in the normal sense, as the appeal was to the same decision maker as made the decision appealed against, demonstrably offended the maxim *nemo iudex in causa sua*,[4] and therefore fell on deaf ears.

The Court found that the defendant's apparent reliance on the safety statement was curious, given it was entirely silent on any health and safety aspects relating to the locking of the sensory room doors. From March 2010 onwards there was no doubt that the board was clearly alerted to the plaintiff's case and was also aware that several other staff members also occasionally locked the sensory room door. The Court was critical of the board's conduct in rejecting the plaintiff's appeal in May 2010 without any

---

3.   Industrial Relations Act 1990 (Code of Practice Detailing Procedures for Addressing Bullying in the Work Place) (Declaration) Order 2002 (SI 17/2002).

4.   'No man shall be the judge in his own cause'.

meaningful consideration of the merits of her case and in its subsequent failure or refusal to reconsider the merits of the case, on receipt of correspondence from the plaintiff's solicitor. This refusal, when the board members were aware of the impact that their now erroneous and unjust decision was having on the plaintiff, was, in the view of O'Neill J, a persistence by them in their unfair and inappropriate treatment of the plaintiff.

O'Neill J concluded that the plaintiff had demonstrated to his satisfaction that the inappropriate behaviour of the defendants was not merely an isolated incident but was persistent over a period of in excess of one year and that this behaviour had wholly undermined the plaintiff's dignity at work. O'Neill J then considered whether the plaintiff, as a result of the conduct of the defendant, suffered an identifiable psychiatric injury as per the judgment of Fennelly J in *Quigley Complex Tooling and Moulding Ltd.*[5] The Court noted that the plaintiff had suffered from a significant anxiety and depressive disorder since late 2010 and that this continued to affect her. Prior to 2009 the plaintiff did have two previous episodes of depression, one of which was a post-partum depression, and the other a reaction to bereavement. The Court noted the evidence from the plaintiff's GP and her psychiatrist that the plaintiff had suffered an anxiety and depressive disorder resulting from her reaction to what had happened to her in the school from September 2009 to September 2010 causing a high state of anxiety, low mood, loss of confidence and self-esteem, and an inability to cope with everyday life. The Court noted that the plaintiff was incapable of returning to work at the defendant's school and all of that, together with her fear that she would not have a good reference inhibited her from seeking employment elsewhere and thus she had not worked since 27 September 2010.

O'Neill J concluded that the plaintiff had suffered an identifiable psychiatric injury from which she still continued to suffer significantly and would continue to do so for some time into the future. In terms of compensation for her pain and suffering, O'Neill J determined that the appropriate sum to compensate the plaintiff for her psychiatric injury to date was €75,000 and the appropriate sum to compensate her for her injury into the future was €40,000 making a total for general damages of €115,000. The Court noted the plaintiff's loss of earnings up to 6 March 2014 was agreed in the sum of €93,276.39 and, in light of the conclusion that it was probable that with appropriate treatment the plaintiff would be fit for some employment in the relatively near future, the Court decided to award her half that sum in respect of future loss of earnings, namely €47,000 making a total of €140,276 in respect of loss of earnings past and future. Accordingly, judgment was entered for the plaintiff in the sum of €255,276.

[5.03] *Glynn v Minister for Justice, Equality and Law Reform, Ireland and the AG*[6] – *High Court – Kearns P – claim for damages for alleged bullying and harassment – distinction between occupational stress and work related stress and bullying –*

---

5. *Quigley v Complex Tooling and Moulding Ltd* [2009] 1 IR 349.
6. *Glynn v Minister for Justice, Equality and Law Reform, Ireland and the AG* [2014] IEHC133.

application of objective test for bullying – restatement of practical propositions in Hatton v Sutherland[7] – failure of plaintiff to disclose prior medical history of depression

The plaintiff was employed since 1979 as a civil servant, performing clerical duties at a garda station in Co Galway. She claimed damages arising from events which she alleged occurred when she was required by the superintendent of the garda station to complete monthly accounts for the garda station in the district office of the station. She alleged that she suffered significant stress as a result of being hounded and harassed by the superintendent in relation to the need to complete the task quickly, and in relation to an issue of an individual cheque which the superintendent had drawn in respect of his expenses.

The plaintiff gave evidence as to her dissatisfaction back in 1996 with her working conditions when she was based in a portacabin along with another colleague, with whom she did not get on. She asserted that she was very 'stressed' by these circumstances and was absent on sick leave for a six-month period, after which she returned on a three-day week. In the course of this absence, she met with the superintendent to discuss the issue she was having. It was noted by Kearns P that the plaintiff compared this meeting to having been held captive and the length of the meeting was unfair. Subsequent to this meeting, she was contacted by the superintendent on three occasions in a single day, which she felt was harassment as she was absent from work on certified sick leave at the time. She attended her GP who subsequently rang the superintendent in her presence and asked him to cease calling her. Evidence was given that the plaintiff returned to work in May 1997 and worked until she went on maternity leave in October 1997. On return in March 1998, her desk was switched to the sergeant's office where she was no longer working with her colleague and her workplace difficulties appeared to cease. It should be noted that the plaintiff herself conceded that no significant problems occurred for her in the period between her return to work in March 1998 and 2005.

In 2004, the plaintiff applied for a promotion to the position of finance officer and was successful. However, as her colleague continued to perform the finance duties, she was advised that she could not take up the position until he retired or left. This case concerned events that occurred on 9 May 2005 when she was asked to complete monthly accounts for the garda station, in the absence of her colleague who was out of the office. She stated that she was unhappy with this task which she stated came out of the blue, and she complained that it required a return to her previous office with her colleague and could not be completed at her own desk in the sergeant's office. In the course of preparing these accounts, she noted a cheque for expenses drawn by the superintendent in his own favour, which had been inserted in the records on a day prior to the date upon which the station cheque was sent to Killarney for reimbursement, which was not in accordance with the practice in the station. The plaintiff contacted the accountant in Garda Headquarters to seek guidance on what she could do. She subsequently discussed this with the superintendent and she gave evidence that he informed her that she was

---

7.   *Sutherland v Hatton, Somerset Co Co & Ors* [2002] EWCA Civ 76.

making a big deal out of it. She then went on sick leave from this time, returning in July 2006, after which she worked consistently.

Kearns P noted that, up until the hearing of this matter and in the course of pleadings, the plaintiff had not revealed that she had any prior psychological history and/or had suffered from depression in the past. However, the Court noted that when she was cross-examined in respect of her GP records, the plaintiff conceded that she had had some difficulties with depression for which she was prescribed medication. She had conceded that in 1996 she did not file any complaint of bullying, and whilst she had contact with the Employment Assistance Programme of the Department of Justice, she had not made any complaint to that service, nor had she attended a meeting that had been arranged with a local representative of that service.

The Court heard medical evidence from various treating doctors. The defendant employer gave evidence that the plaintiff had raised issues about the fact that a colleague was on a higher rate of pay than her. The plaintiff had made no complaints about bullying, harassment or indeed about the inability to open windows, insufficient heat in winter or being followed. The intention behind telephone calls to the plaintiff at home were part of a process to ensure that staff were properly supported and helped and that there was an interest in knowing when the plaintiff would be coming back to work. On the request to perform the accounts, the defendant felt that the plaintiff was well capable of performing the accounting task as she previously had the function of completing the books from which the accounts were drawn before her colleague arrived at the station. Evidence was given by the superintendent that the plaintiff had more than enough experience to perform this function, but because her office was not a secure location, she was requested to move upstairs to the district office to complete the work there.

In his judgment, Kearns P stated that bullying was one of the more 'obnoxious' traits in human behaviour because it involved a 'deliberate and repeated course of action designed to humiliate and belittle the victim'. He noted that bullying, workplace stress and occupational stress are all things which, conceptually at least, are quite different from each other, although on occasion they can overlap and coincide. He noted that occupational stress is not actionable, given that occupational stress is something that every employed person may experience at some stage of his/her working life and can occur for reasons quite distinct from and unrelated to bullying. He noted that workplace stress, on the other hand, may be actionable if certain legal criteria are met. It can be the result of behaviour falling short of bullying, the result of negligence where excessive demands are made of an employee, or where complaints about shortcomings in the workplace go unheeded. Kearns P stated that work-related stress lacked the degree of deliberateness that is the hallmark of bullying.

Kearns P stated that the first question that must be asked in every bullying case is whether the behaviour complained of, by reference to an objective test, imports that degree of calibrated inappropriateness and repetition which differentiates bullying from workplace stress or occupational stress. He noted the legal definition of bullying[8] as recommended by the report of the Taskforce on Prevention of Workplace Bullying that was set out in the LRC Code of Practice.[9] Kearns P noted that this definition required an objective test to determine if bullying had occurred, as any other form of test would leave a defendant vulnerable to allegations of bullying purely on subjective perceptions on the part of the plaintiff, who might contend that straightforward situations at work or otherwise were construed by him or her as amounting to bullying.

Kearns P noted the conclusion of the Supreme Court in *Quigley v Complex Tooling and Moulding Ltd*[10] that, when defining bullying and harassment at work, there was no need to go further that the statutory definition. Kearns P further noted that, whilst the plaintiff in this case also complained of workplace stress, the genesis of that particular aspect of the case lay in events which transpired in 1996/1997 which were not the subject matter of the present claim for compensation. Kearns P stated that the current claim was one in which the plaintiff had alleged in her pleadings that she was repeatedly hounded and harassed by the superintendent over a four-day period in May 2005 in relation to the preparation of monthly accounts and the need to complete the task quickly and in relation to the issue of the irregular payment to him. The Court noted the reliance that had been placed by counsel on the decision of Herbert J, in *Sweeney v Board of Management of Ballinteer Community School*,[11] to argue that the legal test for bullying was a two-pronged test, the second part of which is to enquire whether the activities complained of were such as to meet a test of reasonable foreseeability that the particular claimant had suffered harm or damage. Kearns P stated that such a test is more appropriate to cases where it is alleged an employer failed to alleviate workplace stress which they knew, or should have known, was likely to cause injury to the employee.

In this case, Kearns P chose to reiterate the legal principles derived from the practical propositions set out by Hale LJ in *Sutherland v Hatton, Somerset Co Co & Ors*[12] as restated by the Irish Supreme Court in *Berber v Dunnes Stores*.[13] Kearns P concluded that there were two issues greatly exercising the plaintiff: firstly, the sense of injustice that she, as a civilian employee, was not being paid the same rate for same work; and secondly, that her working conditions were unsatisfactory. He found that these facts fell far short of substantiating an allegation of bullying by her colleague or anyone else.

The Court was critical of the plaintiff and stated that there was no acceptable explanation for her failure to disclose her prior history of depression to either her own medical expert and/or by way of reply to particulars. The Court found that in a case of this nature an omission or failure of this sort was enormously significant, given that so much turns on the credibility of the witnesses on both sides. The Court was critical of the plaintiff's non-cooperation with the Employment Assistance Programme and, in

---

8. 'Repeated inappropriate behaviour, direct or indirect, whether verbal, physical or otherwise, conducted by one or more persons against another or others at the place of work and/or in the course of employment, which could reasonably be regarded as undermining the individual's right to dignity at work. An isolated incident of the behaviour described in this definition may be an affront to dignity at work but, as a once off incident, it is not considered to be bullying.'

9. The Industrial Relations Act 1990 (Code of Practice Detailing Procedures for Addressing Bullying in the Workplace) (Declaration) Order 2002 (SI 17/2002).

10. *Quigley v Complex Tooling and Moulding Ltd* [2009] 1 IR 349.

11. *Sweeney v Board of Management of Ballinteer Community School* [2011] IEHC 131.

12. *Sutherland v Hatton, Somerset Co Co & Ors* [2002] EWCA Civ 76.

13. *Berber v Dunnes Stores* [2009] ELR 61.

particular, her failure to attend a scheduled meeting without explanation. The Court noted that the superintendent was perfectly entitled to make a phone call to the plaintiff at her home as a concerned senior officer in the station, given that he wished to enquire as to when she might be returning to work and whether he could help in any way, but on making the call the plaintiff had hung up the phone. The Court found as a fact there was no bullying or harassment of the plaintiff in 1996/1997. With regard to the request to complete the accounts, the Court stated that the superintendent was entitled to ask the plaintiff to complete the accounts in her colleague's absence and, whilst it may have come as a surprise to the plaintiff, she was well capable of performing the task and should not have adopted the unwilling disposition which she did adopt in relation to the task. The Court concluded that it could not see anything in the behaviour of the colleague or superintendent constituting bullying or harassment.

The Court noted that, when the plaintiff was moved to an office in which she wished to work in 1998, all her complaints ceased and only resurfaced when she was asked to do something she was unwilling to do. Kearns P stated that the length of this interval was remarkable in the context of this case because, far from supporting a complaint of bullying, it indicates that in reality the plaintiff had a workplace issue and her complaints and stress went away once she moved to a different environment within the station. Kearns P stated that the events upon which the plaintiff tried to mount her claim turned on the events of a few short days in May 2005, a time span more identifiable with a once-off or single incident, rather than the kind of repetitive and inappropriate conduct which constitutes the wrong of workplace bullying and harassment. The Court noted that no other member of the garda station offered evidence to suggest there was any culture of workplace bullying and harassment, nor was there a single witness to corroborate the plaintiff's complaint in any way. Kearns P dismissed the claim insofar as it was consistent with an allegation of bullying. Kearns P found that the plaintiff had not made out a case of workplace stress causing or contributing to foreseeable injury or damage. He noted that she had no complaint of workplace stress for the eight years between 1997 and 2005 and that her workplace conditions were not markedly altered when she was asked to perform a straightforward task for which she was qualified. The claim was dismissed on this ground also.

The Court stated that, even if it was mistaken on these issues, the plaintiff had failed to demonstrate that her stress was attributable to the matter she complained of. She had a prior history of stress and depression which was not disclosed until discovered through the pre-trial discovery process and Kearns P stated his belief that any subsequent stresses suffered by the plaintiff were attributable to life events and to occupational stress only. The claim was dismissed.

VICARIOUS LIABILITY

[5.04] *Elmontem v Nethercross Ltd T/A Roganstown Golf and Country Club and Usi[14] – High Court – Herbert J – whether employer vicariously liable for tort committed by one of its employees against another which resulted in significant*

---

14. *Elmontem v Nethercross Ltd T/A Roganstown Golf and Country Club and Usi* [2014] IEHC 91.

physical injuries being sustained – consideration of 'close connection' test for imposition of vicarious liability – extent to which employer is liable under statute and common law for safety of its employees

This case arose from an incident at the defendant's clubhouse when the second defendant, the head chef, went to the office of the plaintiff, the financial controller, and raised a grievance. Evidence was given that, in the course of this discussion, matters became heated and the second defendant became increasingly aggressive. Ultimately, there appears to have been a violent physical assault on the plaintiff by the second defendant, which left him with significant injuries. This assault took place in the presence of another employee who was working at a desk in the same office as the plaintiff. The plaintiff was brought initially to a medical clinic and then to a garda station where a complaint was made. Herbert J noted the fact that the second defendant had pleaded guilty to criminal charges arising out of this matter.

The plaintiff claimed that the first defendant was vicariously liable for the assault by the second defendant. In the alternative the plaintiff also claimed that the first defendant was negligent and in breach of its duty in failing to provide him with a safe place of work. Herbert J considered the 'close connection' test for the imposition of vicarious liability as set out by Fennelly J in *O'Keeffe v Hickey.*[15] Herbert J concluded that the fact that the opportunity to commit the act would not have arisen but for the second defendant's access to the plaintiff's office by reason of his employment, was not enough to establish close connection between his employment and the tortious act. Herbert J expressed a concern that to hold the first defendant vicariously liable for the tort of the second defendant would, on the facts, amount to imposing absolute liability on the employer. To alter the law to this extent would require, in his view, a clear act of the legislature. Herbert J concluded that the first defendant was not vicariously liable for the assault and then proceeded to consider the common law and statutory duties on an employer to take all reasonable precautions for the safety of employees and not to expose them unnecessarily to foreseeable risk of injury.

Evidence was given that the first defendant's general manager had been involved (in previous employment) in the dismissal of the second defendant from his previous employment and therefore was aware that the second defendant had, on a previous occasion, lost his temper and caused physical injury to a colleague. Herbert J concluded that that general manager 'knew or ought to have known that there was a very real risk, not a mere possibility, that this could occur again if for any reason the second defendant's temper became aroused, and that this exposed his fellow employees including the plaintiff to a risk of physical injury'.

Herbert J noted that a real risk of occurrence remained, and while it was not a risk that could be entirely eliminated, it was, in his judgment, one which could 'have been adequately controlled without grossly disproportionate or expensive measures'. Herbert J noted that the first defendant had taken no care to put in place measures to prevent a reoccurrence of such improper conduct or behaviour on the part of the second defendant. There was no safety statement or notified policy which identified conduct or

---

15.　*O'Keeffe v Hickey* [2009] 2 IR 302.

behaviour in the workplace which would not be tolerated such as verbal abuse or physical violence to other workers. There was no evidence that the general manager had warned the second defendant in writing that any physical violence towards any other employee would not be tolerated and would result in a dismissal for gross misconduct. Furthermore, Herbert J noted that the evidence had not established that the first defendant had security staff or CCTV monitoring at the complex which might have had an initial deterrent effect on the second defendant. The High Court concluded that the plaintiff should succeed in this part of his claim and that the first defendant and second defendant were jointly liable to the plaintiff for the injuries suffered by him. The Court awarded damages in the sum of €28,000 for pain and suffering and special damages in the sum of €5,984.

Chapter 6

EUROPEAN UNION LAW

SELECTED CASE LAW

[6.01] *Hernández v Reino de España (Subdelegación del Gobierno de España en Alicante)[1] – CJEU, Fifth Chamber – Directive 2008/94/EC – employer's right to compensation from Member State in respect of remuneration paid to employee during proceedings challenging that employee's dismissal beyond 60th working day after action challenging that employee's dismissal brought – no right to compensation in case of invalid dismissal – subrogation of employee to right to compensation in event of employer's provisional insolvency – discrimination against employees who are subject of invalid, as distinct from unfair, dismissal – Charter of Fundamental Rights of the European Union – scope of art 20*

This preliminary reference arose from proceedings in the Spanish Courts and concerned a number of provisions of Spanish law, specifically art 56(1) of the Workers Statute, which provides that where a dismissal is deemed unfair, the employer may reinstate the worker or *inter alia* pay to the worker: '(b) an amount equal to the sum of remuneration unpaid between the date of dismissal and the date on which notice of the judgment declaring the dismissal to be unfair is served …'.

Article 57(1) of the Workers Statute also provides that where a judgment declaring a dismissal of an employee to be unfair is delivered more than 60 working days after the date on which the action was brought, the employer may claim the payment of the economic benefit which the employee receives from the state.

Article 116(2) of the consolidated text of the Law on Employment Procedure provides:

> In the event of the employer's provisional insolvency the worker may claim directly from the State any remuneration as referred to in the preceding paragraph which has not been paid by the employer.

On 16 December 2008, the applicants in the main proceedings brought an action against their employers before the Social Court in Benidorm challenging their dismissals. On 2 October 2009, the Social Court declared that the dismissals had been invalid and directed two of the companies to pay the outstanding remuneration owed since their dismissal (up to the date of the judgment) and compensation for the dismissal. The Court also ordered the Wage Guarantee Fund (Fogasa) to guarantee the payment of those sums within statutory limits in accordance with EU obligations as implemented by national law.

On 11 June 2010, those companies were declared insolvent. The applicants applied to Fogasa seeking payment of the amounts owed under the judgment of 2 October 2009.

---

1.   *Hernández v Reino de España (Subdelegación del Gobierno de España en Alicante)* (Case C–198/13).

They also subsequently sought from the *Subdeleación* (government) the payment of remuneration which had become due after the 60th working day from the day their action had been brought until the judgment. The applicants' request was rejected on the grounds that their dismissal had been declared invalid as opposed to unfair.

The applicants brought an action before the Social Court in Benidorm seeking an order directing the *Subdeleación* to pay that sum. The Court noted that the principal beneficiary of art 57(1) is the employer. The rationale being that an employer should not have to bear the consequences of delays in court proceedings. Only in the event of employer insolvency, by subrogation, can an employee seek payment from the state. Since an employer cannot seek payment from the state where there is an invalid dismissal, neither can an employee.

The Social Court referred a number of questions to the CJEU for preliminary ruling concerning, *inter alia*, the compatibility of a national law which discriminates between an invalid and an unfair dismissal with art 20 of the Charter of Fundamental Rights of the European Union which provides: 'Everyone is equal before the law.'

The CJEU noted that the provisions of Spanish law can be assessed under art 20 of the Charter for Fundamental Rights of the European Union only to the extent that they come within EU law namely, in this case, Directive 2008/94/EC (the Directive) on the protection of employees in the event of the insolvency of their employer.

In order to determine this, the CJEU stated that it must consider the nature of the legislation at issue and whether it pursues objectives other than those covered by EU law, even if it is capable of indirectly affecting EU law; and also whether there are specific rules of EU law on the matter or rules which are capable of affecting it.

As regards objective, the CJEU found that the objective of the national legislation at issue was to compensate employers for adverse consequences suffered as a result of judicial proceedings which last for more than 60 working days. The objective was not to provide employees with any supplemental protection. The objective of Directive 2008/94/EC is to guarantee a minimum protection for employees in the event of the employer's insolvency. Therefore the CJEU determined that the national legislation could not be examined for compatibility with the Charter for Fundamental Rights of the European Union.

The referring Court alluded to art 11 of Directive 2008/94/EC in its order for reference. Article 11 provides: '[the Directive] shall not affect the option of Member States to apply or introduce laws, regulations or administrative provisions which are more favourable to employees.' The referring Court stated that this does not provide the Member States with an option of legislating by virtue of EU law, but merely recognises the power which the Member States enjoy under national law to provide for more favourable provisions outside the framework established by the Directive.

The CJEU ruled that national legislation, such as that at issue in the main proceedings, according to which an employer can request from the Member State concerned payment of remuneration which has become due during proceedings challenging a dismissal after the 60th working day following the date on which the action was brought, and according to which, where the employer has not paid that remuneration and finds itself in a state of provisional insolvency, the employee concerned may, by operation of legal subrogation, claim directly from that state the payment of that remuneration, does not come within the scope of Directive 2008/94/EC on the protection of employees in the event of the insolvency of their employer and cannot, therefore, be examined in the light of the fundamental rights guaranteed by the Charter of Fundamental Rights of the European Union and, in particular, of art 20 thereof.

[6.02] *United Kingdom of Great Britain and Northern Ireland v The European Parliament of the Counsel of the European Union[2] – Opinion of Advocate General Jaaskinen – action seeking annulment of certain articles (arts 94(1)(g), 94(2), 162(1), (3)) of the Directive 2013/36/EU[3] and arts 450(1)(d), (i) and (j) and 521(2) of the Capital Requirements Regulation)[4] – CRD IV package – setting of ratios between fixed and variable components of remuneration payable to employees of credit institutions and investment firms whose professional activities have material impact on institution's risk profile – disclosure of certain information pertaining to remuneration*

This case was brought by the United Kingdom seeking the annulment of certain articles of the CRD IV Directive and certain articles in the Capital Requirement Regulation.

The United Kingdom objected to these provisions insofar as they contained provisions indexing variable remuneration with respect to individuals whose professional activities impacted on the risk profile of the credit institutions and investment firms. The Advocate General said that he preferred that this arrangement be described as a maximum fixed ratio for variable remuneration rather than a cap on banker's bonuses. The United Kingdom also challenged the provisions relating to compulsory disclosure of remuneration ratios by financial institutions in certain circumstances.

The Advocate General noted that Directive 2013/36/EC provides that the variable component of remuneration shall not exceed 100% of the fixed component of the total remuneration for each individual and they also contained some additional rules, to include an option permitting Member States to allow shareholders to increase the ratio by up to 200%, subject to certain conditions. The Directive also provides for compulsory disclosure by financial institutions of the ratios between variable remuneration and the number of individuals being remunerated over a certain threshold. It also requires disclosure by the financial institutions of remuneration on demand from the Member States or competent authorities concerning the total remuneration for each member of the management body or senior management.

The United Kingdom raised six pleas in this case – that the legal basis for the contested measures was incorrect, a challenge based on the principles of proportionality and subsidiarity, a plea based on legal certainty, a plea that the conferral of powers on

---

2.   *United Kingdom of Great Britain and Northern Ireland v The European Parliament of the Counsel of the European Union* (Case C–507/2013).

3.   Directive on access to the activity of credit institutions and the prudential supervision of credit institutions and investment firms.

4.   Regulation 575/13/EU of the European Parliament, a credential requirement for the credit institutions and investment firms.

the European Banking Authority was *ultra vires*, that art 450(1)(j) of the Regulation offended the right to privacy and legal principles governing the protection of personal data, and in its sixth plea, it was asserted that to the extent to which art 94(1)(g) of the CRD IV Directive is required to be applied to employees of institutions outside of the EEA, it infringes the principle against extraterritoriality under customary public international law.

The Advocate General set out the background to the CRD IV Directive and the Capital Requirements Regulation and addressed each plea in detail. With regard to the concerns raised as to the compatibility of the articles with the right to privacy and EU data protection law, the Advocate General stated it was relevant that the impugned provisions were not applicable to all so-called material risk takers but only to management or senior management and they did not lead to any automatic disclosure of protected personal data. The Advocate General noted that art 450(1)(j) of the Capital Requirements Regulation imposed no automatic obligation to require such disclosure. It simply vested the Member States or competent authority with discretion to do so. The Advocate General noted the recital of the Capital Requirements Regulation also binds Member States to comply with the EU data protection legislation when considering any demand for such information.

The Advocate General opined that, contrary to arguments made by the United Kingdom, art 94(1)(g) of the CRD IV Directive did not impose a cap on variable remuneration, which was evident from the fact that no limit was imposed on the amount of fixed remuneration individuals can earn, so that the 100% ratio can attach to any sum of money which a financial institution is prepared to pay by way of fixed salary. The absence of any capping effect resulting from the ratio from variable remuneration was further underscored by art 91(1)(g)(ii) of the CRD IV Directive which, in any event, furnished a mechanism for the ratio to be increased to 200% and at the same time allows for members states to fix the maximum ratio at a lower maximum percentage.

In the opinion of the Advocate General, art 94(1)(g) of the CRD IV Directive, and the limit on variable remuneration that it contains, does not impact directly on the level of pay of persons falling within its scope. It merely establishes a ratio between the fixed and variable element, without affecting the level of remuneration as such. The Advocate General concluded that this article did not impose any limit on the level of pay, it only established a structure for remuneration, in the form of a ratio between the fixed level of remuneration and the variable remuneration, in order to avoid excessive risk taking. The Advocate General concluded that in his view this constituted a legitimate objective to ensure the freedom of establishment of financial institutions and free provision of financial services on the basis of single authorisation and home country control and can function safely in the EU and internal markets.

The Advocate General concluded that the conferral of powers on the European Banking Authority was valid given that proposals from that Authority have no legal effect. The United Kingdom contended the principle of legal certainty was breached as a result of the stipulation that the Directive should apply retrospectively to employment contracts concluded before the Directive was adopted. However, the Advocate General pointed out that the financial institutions received notice concerning further legislation on remuneration well in advance of the transposition dates contained in the Directive.

The Advocate General concluded that the key provision on bonuses should not be annulled as was requested by the United Kingdom and he recommended that the action be dismissed.

SELECTED 2014 DIRECTIVES

The Posted Workers Enforcement Directive

[6.03] The Posted Workers Enforcement Directive[5] was agreed in May 2014. The Directive aims to increase the protection of workers temporarily posted to Member States within the EU by improving the supervision and enforcement of the rules relating to posted workers under Directive 96/71/EC. The deadline for implementation of the Directive is 18 June 2016.

The Directive seeks to establish a general framework of appropriate provisions, measures and control mechanisms necessary for an improved and more uniform implementation, application and enforcement of Directive 96/71/EC, including measures to prevent and sanction any abuse and circumvention of the applicable rules, without prejudice to the scope of the Directive 96/71/EC. The Directive requires Member States to appoint competent authorities and liaison offices to deal with and manage posted workers within a Member State. The competent authorities will be engaged in obtaining and processing factual elements related to the service provider who intends to post workers in the Member State, including details of their establishment in their Member State of origin and details in relation to the posting of the worker.

There is a strong emphasis on access to information in relation to posted workers. The Directive provides for an online portal to enable service providers to access information in a clear and accessible way in relation to the standards of employment in that Member State.

The Directive also envisages administrative cooperation between Member States and sets out the general principles to be complied with by Member States, in terms of coordination of posted workers. With regard to national control measures for posted workers, the Directive provides that Member States may only impose such administrative formalities or control measures which are reasonably required to protect posted workers' rights, and such measures should go no further than is reasonably necessary to achieve this objective.

Member States will also be required to implement rules in relation to inspections of records, and other employment-related documents in respect of posted workers within their territory.

The Directive includes extensive provisions regarding the enforcement of rights of posted workers, and the penalties that may be imposed on service providers in breach of the employment rights and Directive 96/71/EC. In particular, the Directive states that employees of subcontractors may hold the contractor, of which their direct employer is the subcontractor, liable in addition to, or in place of, their employer in respect of any

---

5.   Directive 2014/67/EU.

matters regarding workers' rights including any outstanding net remuneration corresponding to the minimum rate of pay in the Member State.

The National Employment Rights Authority (NERA) shall be the competent authority in Ireland entrusted with enforcing the requirements regarding the provision of information on posted workers to Ireland and overseeing the administrative obligations on the sending organisations. The Department of Jobs, Enterprise and Innovation has stated that the functions required of Member States under the proposed Directive will greatly enhance the role of NERA in ensuring vulnerable workers are not exploited and that Irish employment law is fully respected by service providers posting workers to Ireland. The Department stated that Irish companies will benefit from the Directive in that they will be protected from unfair competition on the domestic market by ensuring foreign service providers are not permitted to unfairly undercut nationally determined terms of employment.

Seasonal Workers Directive

[6.04] On 26 February 2014, the European Parliament and the Council passed Directive 2014/36/EU (the Seasonal Workers Directive) on the conditions of entry and stay of third country nationals for the purpose of employment as seasonal workers. The deadline for implementation for this Directive is 30 September 2016.

The Directive aims to contribute to the effective management of migration flows for the specific category of seasonal temporary migration and to ensure decent working and living conditions for seasonal workers, by setting out rules for admission and stay. The Directive defines the rights of seasonal workers, while at the same time providing for incentives and safeguards to prevent overstaying or to prevent a temporary stay from becoming permanent.

A 'seasonal worker' is defined in art 3 of Directive 2014/36/EU as a third country national who retains his or her principal place of residence in a third country and stays legally and temporarily in the territory of a Member State to carry out an activity depending on the passing of the season, under one or more fixed-term work contracts concluded directly between that third-country national and the employer established in that Member State.

The Directive provides for a flexible entry system based on demand and objective criteria. Member States are permitted to require that the employer seek to fill the vacancy from the national workforce at first instance. Applicants will be required to produce a valid work contract or a binding job offer. Applicants will also be required to provide evidence of having or applying for sickness insurance and evidence that they will have adequate accommodation in the Member State.

Member States must determine a maximum stay for seasonal workers of between five and nine months in any twelve-month period. Seasonal workers who are already in an EU Member State will have the possibility of extending their work contract or changing their employer at least once, provided they fulfil the entry conditions and no grounds for refusal apply.

Seasonal workers are entitled to equal treatment with nationals of the host Member State in respect of terms of employment, including the minimum working age, working conditions, including pay and dismissal, working hours, leave and holidays, and health and safety requirements at the workplace.

Intra-corporate Transfer Directive

[6.05] On 15 May 2014 the European Parliament and the Council passed Directive 2014/66/EU (the Intra-corporate Transfer Directive) on the conditions of entry and residence of third country nationals in the framework of an intra-corporate transfer. The deadline for transposition is 29 November 2016.

The Directive aims to facilitate the mobility of intra-corporate transferees within the European Union and to reduce the administrative burden associated with working in several Member States. The Directive establishes a simplified procedure for admission of intra-corporate transferees, based on common definitions and harmonised criteria.

The Directive sets up a specific intra-EU mobility scheme whereby the holder of a valid intra-corporate transferee permit issued by a Member State is allowed to enter, to stay and to work in one or more Member States. The maximum duration of one transfer to the Union including mobility between Member States should not exceed three years for manager and specialist occupations and one year for a trainee employee, after which they should leave for a third country unless they obtain a residence permit on another basis.

The Directive requires that intra-corporate transferees enjoy equal treatment with nationals occupying comparable positions as regards the remuneration during the transfer.

Article 5 of the Directive provides that the host entity and the undertaking in the third country must be part of the same undertaking or group of undertakings. The applicant must have completed a minimum period of employment with the company prior to the transfer. The applicant will also be required to produce a contract of employment or if necessary an assignment letter setting out the basic terms of employment.

'Intra-corporate transfer' is defined in art 3 of the Directive as the temporary secondment, for occupational or training purposes, of a third country national who, at the time of application for an intra-corporate transferee permit, resides outside the territory of the Member States, from an undertaking established outside the territory of a Member State and to which the third country national is bound by a work contract prior to and during the transfer, to an entity belonging to the undertaking or to the same group of undertakings which is established in that Member State, and, where applicable, the mobility between host entities established in or several second Member States.

'Intra-corporate transferee' means any third-country national who resides outside the territory of the Member States at the time of application for an intra-corporate transferee permit and who is subject to an intra-corporate transfer.

Chapter 7

FIXED-TERM WORK

CONTRACT OF INDEFINITE DURATION AND OBJECTIVE GROUNDS

[7.01] *Samohano v Universitat Pompeu Fabra[1] – CJEU – whether Framework Agreement on Fixed-term Work[2] precluded national rules which allow universities to renew successive fixed-term employment contracts concluded with associate lecturers, with no limitation as to maximum duration and number of renewals of those contracts where such contracts justified by objective reason – concept of objective reason*

This was a request for a preliminary ruling on the interpretation of cls 3 and 5 of the Framework Agreement on Fixed-term Work in the context of proceedings between the complainant and his employer, the respondent university, concerning the classification of employment contracts between them.

The complainant was employed as a part-time fixed-term associate lecturer from September 2008, which contract was renewed on three occasions. He was informed on 29 June 2012 that his duties would end on 28 July 2012. In his last employment contract, he was contracted to work six hours per week. He sought an annulment of his dismissal (or alternatively a finding that the dismissal was unfounded) on the basis that his employment contract, and the subsequent renewals of that contract, were unlawful and were entered into in circumvention of the law because the legal requirements for his employment as an associate lecturer were not met and because the circumstances stipulated by national law for the conclusion of fixed-term employment contracts were not present.

It should be noted that unlike general rules applicable to fixed-term employment contracts in Spain, the rules applicable to universities by way of art 53 of Law 6/2001[3] did not lay down, in respect of employment of associate lecturers, any equivalent legal measure to prevent the abusive use of successive fixed-term contracts. Nor did those rules require objective reasons justifying the renewal of such contracts and they imposed neither a maximum total duration nor a limit on the number of renewals of those contracts.

The CJEU noted that it was common ground that the rules applicable to the applicant, in particular the constitution of the university, include no equivalent legal measure within the meaning of cl 5(1) of the Framework Agreement and impose no limitation as to both the maximum total duration and number of renewals of fixed-term

---

1. *Samohano v Universitat Pompeu Fabra* (Case C–190/13).
2. Council Directive 1999/EC/70.
3. Framework Law 6/2001 on Universities (Ley Organica 6/2001 de Universidades) as amended by Framework Law No 7 of 2007.

contracts entered into by universities and associate lecturers. The CJEU stated that in those circumstances it must examine to what extent the renewal of such contracts may be justified by an objective reason within the meaning of cl 5(1)(a) of the Framework Agreement. The CJEU noted the case law, which requires that that the concept of objective justification must be understood as referring to precise and concrete circumstances characterising a given activity which are therefore capable in that particular context of justifying the use of successive fixed-term contracts. The CJEU stated that it was clear from the national rules at issue in the main proceedings that the conclusion and renewal by universities of fixed-term contracts with associate lecturers, such as the complainant, are justified by the need to introduce specialists with recognised competence who exercise a professional activity, otherwise than in a university, with the performance, on a part-time basis, of specific teaching tasks, so that those specialists can bring their knowledge and professional experience to the university, thus establishing a partnership between university teaching circles and professional circles.

The CJEU noted the provision in the rules that an associate lecturer must have exercised a paid professional activity on the basis of a diploma obtained by that associate lecturer for a minimum period of several years in the course of a specific period preceding his employment by the university. Furthermore, the employment contracts in question are entered into and renewed on the condition that the conditions relating to the exercise of the professional activity remain in place and those employment contracts must be terminated when the associate lecturer concerned reaches the age of retirement.

The CJEU stated that those rules lay down the precise and concrete circumstances in which fixed-term employment contracts may be concluded or renewed for the purpose of the employment of associate lecturers and that they respond to a genuine need. The CJEU determined that such temporary contracts appear to be capable of achieving the objective pursued namely in enriching university teaching in specific areas with the experience of recognised specialists, because those contracts allow the development of the competencies of the persons concerned and the areas concerned and allow the needs of the universities to be taken into account. The CJEU noted that fixed-term contracts are a feature of employment in certain sectors and/or in certain occupations or activities.

In light of the fact that, to be recruited as an associate lecturer, the person in question must necessarily exercise the professional activity outside the university and may perform his teaching tasks only on a part-time basis, it did not appear that such a fixed-term employment contract was capable of undermining the purpose of the Framework Agreement which is to protect workers against job instability.

However, the mere fact that the fixed-term employment contracts concluded with associate lecturers are renewed in order to cover a recurring or permanent need of the relevant universities and that such a need can be met within the framework of a contract of indefinite duration are not, however, such as to preclude the existence of an objective reason within the meaning of cl 5(1) of the Framework Agreement because the nature of the teaching activity at issue and the inherent characteristics of that activity can justify the use of fixed-term employment contracts in the context in question.

The CJEU found that the need in terms of employment of associate lecturers remains temporary in so far as that lecturer is supposed to resume his professional activity on a full-time basis at the end of his contract. The CJEU contrasted fixed-term employment contracts in the main proceedings, which could not be renewed, with fixed term contracts for the purpose of a performance in a fixed or permanent manner, even on a part time basis, of teaching tasks which normally came under the activity of ordinary teaching staff. The CJEU concluded that it was for the authorities of the Member State concerned to include the national court, to ensure that cl 5(1)(a) of the Framework Agreement is complied with, by ascertaining that the renewal of successive fixed-term employment contracts or relationships concluded with associate lecturers is intended to cover the temporary needs and that a provision such as that at issue in the main proceedings is not in fact being used to meet fixed and permanent needs of the universities in terms of employment of teaching staff.

The CJEU concluded that cl 5 of the Framework Agreement must be interpreted as not precluding national rules such as those at issue which allowed universities to renew successive fixed-term employment contracts concluded with associate lecturers, with no limitation as to the maximum duration and the number of renewals of those contracts, where such contracts are justified by an objective reason within the meaning of cl 5(1)(a) which is a matter for the referring court to verify. The CJEU held that the second and third questions by the referring court were inadmissible.

[7.02] *National University of Ireland Galway v Welford[4] – Labour Court – Protection of Employees (Fixed-Term Work) Act 2003 – appeal of Rights Commissioner decision that complainant entitled to contract of indefinite duration – whether objective grounds justifying continued employment of complainant on fixed-term basis – temporary nature of research project – whether work for which complainant was employed came within fixed and permanent needs of respondent or whether part of period of temporary or transient need*

The respondent employed the complainant on a series of fixed term contracts and her claim was that she became entitled to a contract of indefinite duration. The Rights Commissioner had found for the complainant on this point and the respondent appealed.

The complainant commenced employment with the respondent on 13 April 2005, under a fixed-term contract, as a lecturer in nursing studies. That contract was expressed to run until 12 April 2006. On expiry of that contract, it was extended to 12 April 2007. By letter dated 3 April 2007 the complainant's employment was further extended for a fixed-term commencing on 13 April 2007 and expiring on 31 August 2008. During the period of the final fixed-term contract, funding was received from the Health Research Board to undertake a research study. The complainant was to undertake the study and this contract commenced on December 2007 running to 30 November 2010. Funding was in fact extended to 31 December 2010 and the complainant's fixed-term contract was extended accordingly. Subsequently the complainant obtained a further fixed-term contract, commencing on 1 January 2011 and ending on 21 August 2011, as a lecturer in

---

4.   *National University of Ireland Galway v Welford* FTD1325.

general nursing. This was for the purpose of providing maternity leave cover. Finally, the complainant's employment was continued on a fixed-term contract as the part-time teaching assistant in the school of nursing and midwifery from 1 September 2011 to 30 June 2012. The purpose of this fixed-term contract was to provide temporary cover pending the permanent filling of the post.

The complainant claimed that on or about 12 April 2009 her fixed-term contract was transmuted to one of indefinite duration by operation of law. However, the respondent contended that there were objective grounds justifying the continued employment of the complainant on a fixed-term basis and these grounds related to the temporary nature of the research project for which she was employed on the contract commencing 1 December 2007 which was also limited by the finite nature of the funding.

The Labour Court held that s 9(3) of the Protection of Employees (Fixed-Term Work) Act 2003 would have operated to transmute the contract to one of indefinite duration from the date of its commencement. In particular, the Labour Court referred to the CJEU judgment in *Angelidaki*,[5] where the CJEU drew a distinction between work undertaken for the purposes of meeting the fixed and permanent needs of the employer and work for the purpose of meeting some temporary transient need. Work in the former category should normally be undertaken on permanent contracts of employment and temporary or fixed-term contracts would normally be suitable for work in the latter category. Accordingly, the Labour Court found that the net question for determination was whether the work for which the complainant was employed under the contract of 1 December 2007 should be determined as coming within the fixed and permanent needs of the respondent or whether it was part of a period of temporary or transient need.

The Court accepted that conduct of research *per se* is part of the core functions of an academic and forms part of the fixed and permanent needs of a university. However, the Court concluded that the issue in this particular case was whether the study which the complainant was contracted to undertake in December 2007 could properly be classified as forming part of its fixed and permanent needs or whether it fulfilled a temporary or transient need. Having considered the evidence, the Labour Court held that the project in question had the nature of a standalone undertaking, rather than forming part of a continuing sequence of similar projects which could be required as meeting the respondent's permanent needs. The project was to last for a defined period of three years and this was recognised by the complainant in a letter. It was also of significance that the funding for the project was arranged by the complainant herself and was part of the PhD programme that she was undertaking.

The Labour Court held that the research project which the complainant was undertaking was of a temporary or a transient need and did not form part of the respondent's continuing or permanent research requirements. In those circumstances, the Court concluded that there were objective grounds justifying the renewal of the complainant's employment for a fixed-term for this specific project and accordingly s 9(3) did not apply to this renewal.

---

5.   *Angelidaki & Ors v Organismos Nomarchiakis Autodioikisis Rethymnis* [2009] ECR 1–3071.

[7.03] *White v Dun Laoghaire VEC[6] – Labour Court – appeal of decision of Rights Commissioner – Industrial Relations Acts 1946 to 2012 – Protection of Employees (Fixed-Term Work) Act 2003, s 15(1) – preliminary issue – whether appeal in time as wrong form lodged – successive specific purpose fixed-term contracts – contract of indefinite duration – whether objective grounds justifying renewal of fixed-term contract – covering for employees on career breaks or on statutory leave*

The respondent employed the complainant as a fixed-term teacher from February 2003. The complainant claimed that she was continuously employed on a series of fixed-term contracts and became entitled to a contract of indefinite duration under s 9 of the 2003 Act in September 2007. The respondent contended that the complainant was engaged on a specific purpose contract to fill a particular need of the institution, ie filling-in for employees on career breaks or statutory leave – which amounted to an objective justification permitting the renewal of the fixed-term contract.

As a preliminary point, the respondent argued that the complainant's claim should be rejected on the basis that she lodged her appeal to the Labour Court on the incorrect form, and, by the time she lodged the correct form, her appeal was statute barred. The complainant sought to appeal a decision of the Rights Commissioner, but, in making her appeal, she used the wrong Labour Court form. While the initial incorrect form was lodged with the Labour Court within the six-week deadline, the subsequent (and correct) form was lodged outside the time limit.

The Labour Court noted that s 15 of the Protection of Employees (Fixed-Term Work) Act 2003 (the Act) specified what was required to appeal a decision of the Rights Commissioner, namely:

(i)   that an appeal must be made in writing to the Labour Court;

(ii)   the notice of appeal shall contain any particulars that are determined by the Labour Court; and

(iii)   it shall state the intention of the party to appeal against the decision.

On reviewing the original appeal notice lodged, the Labour Court was satisfied that, notwithstanding the fact that the appeal was submitted on the incorrect form, it complied with all of the requirements of s 15 and therefore the appeal was properly before the Labour Court.

In the substantive claim, the complainant asserted that she was entitled to a contract of indefinite duration under the Act on the basis of her being engaged on a series of successive fixed-term contracts by which she covered employees' statutory and contractual leave, as well as teaching courses. The complainant argued that her work represented a fixed and permanent need of the school. The respondent claimed that the complainant was only ever engaged to fill in where its employees were on statutory/ contractual leave and that it had a statutory obligation to ensure those employees could return to work after such leave. The respondent argued that this amounted to an objective justification for the issue of fixed-term contracts as opposed to a contract of indefinite duration.

---

6.   *White v Dun Laoghaire* VEC FTD1329.

The Labour Court examined the complainant's fixed-term contract of employment with the respondent. It noted that the contract itself did not refer to the complainant replacing a teacher on a career break. It then looked at the actual work undertaken by the complainant. It was noted that the teacher for whom she purportedly was covering was contracted to work 18 hours per week. However, the complainant was contracted to work 22 hours per week. Further, it transpired that the complainant only covered 12 hours of classes of the employee on a career leave, and that she was allocated a further 10 hours of classes that the employee on a career break had not taught. The respondent sought to argue that the differences between the complainant's contract and that of the employee on the career break were due to administrative flexibility in the respondent. However the Labour Court noted that the respondent did not adequately explain the discrepancy in hours and that there was a significant difference between the work of the complainant and the work of the employee on a career break.

In assessing the law on objective grounds justifying the renewal of a fixed-term contract, the Labour Court stated that the relevant grounds should be assessed by reference to the circumstances pertaining at the commencement of the contract in question. In order to permit the employer to rely on the defence of objective justification, it must demonstrate that there was a real need for the renewal of the fixed-term contract (which denied the fixed-term worker access to a level of permanency in his role), and that the less favourable treatment of fixed-term workers was necessary to meet that need. The respondent must also demonstrate that the less favourable treatment is proportionate, and balances the detriment to the employee to the need of the employer, and that there were no alternate means by which the objective could be achieved which were less detrimental to the employee.

The Labour Court accepted that there were social policy reasons justifying career breaks for employees and that, for this purpose, it was often necessary to engage a fixed-term worker to cover the period of that employee's absence. It further noted that the employer was obliged to facilitate the return of that employee to the workplace. However, an employer must show that a person is employed on a series of fixed-term contracts of employment because another member of staff has availed of a career break, and it must be shown that the fixed-term worker was so employed for the purpose of filling in for the employee on a career break. The respondent failed to satisfy the Labour Court that the employee was so employed, as there were significant differences between the nature of the work carried out by the complainant on one hand and the employee on the career break on the other hand. On this basis, the objective justification for the fixed-term contract, ie filling in for an employee on a career break, failed.

The Labour Court found that the complainant was entitled to a contract of indefinite duration and as the complainant was already employed by the respondent, it should pay her compensation of €6,500 for infringements of her rights under the Act.

[7.04] ***HSE West v Ismael*[7] *– Labour Court – appeal of Rights Commissioner decision – Protection of Employees (Fixed-Term Work) Act 2003 – entitlement to contract of indefinite duration – whether complainant's contract of employment, which***

---

7.   *HSE West v Ismael* FTD141.

facilitated a named consultant to undertake clinical director duties, fulfilled temporary requirement

The complainant, a consultant plastic surgeon, had previous service with the respondent between July 2002 and June 2008. However, the substantive issue in this case concerned a contract which was entered into by him in September 2008 until July 2011. The contract stated that his employment was 'for the purpose of cover for Mr. [named consultant] Friday, Thursday, from 5pm of each week, and Friday, Saturday and Sunday each fourth week'. That named consultant retired on or about May 2010 and the respondent set about filling the vacant post through the Public Appointments Service. In the interim, the complainant covered the vacancy in a fulltime capacity, but declined to apply for the post. The person subsequently appointed to the permanent post took up appointment in July 2011 and the complainant's appointment terminated.

The complainant asserted that he was entitled to a contract of indefinite duration. The Labour Court concluded that in September 2008 there were objective grounds justifying the respondent's decision to fill the specific post on a fixed-term contract, rather than one of indefinite duration. They also noted that the complainant was in effect seeking a permanent appointment to a post that had ceased to exist. The Labour Court highlighted the provisions of ss 7(1) and 9 of the Protection of Employees (Fixed-Term Work) Act 2003 (the Act) and also the concept of objective grounds as determined by the CJEU in *Angelidaki & Ors*[8] and specifically the distinction that was drawn in that case between contracts the purpose of which are to meet needs which are temporary in nature and those which in reality are intended to cover the fixed and permanent needs of the employer. The Labour Court concluded that the September 2008 contract was to facilitate the named consultant in undertaking the duties of clinical director of the hospital. That was a temporary requirement that would only last for so long as the named consultant continued to undertake those duties. On the retirement of the named consultant and his eventual replacement by a consultant to perform the full range of duties attaching to the post, the position that the complainant held under the contract of 22 September 2008 ceased to exist.

The Labour Court found that it 'could not be held that in September 2008 the requirements of the post that the claimant [sic] filled formed a part of the fixed and permanent needs of the respondent.' The Court concluded that in these circumstances the fixed-term contract was a proportionate means of achieving the legitimate objective of the respondent in seeking to accommodate its need to provide cover for the period during which the clinical director was performing the duties of that post. The Labour Court stated itself to be guided by the decision of the High Court in *An Post v Monaghan and Ors,*[9] where Hedigan J held that 'a court should ask itself if the impugned measures (in this case employing the complainant for a fixed-term) was the minimum unfavourable treatment necessary to enable the employer to obtain the objective.'

The Labour Court concluded that it could not see how else the respondent could have provided for what was undoubtedly a purely temporary need. The conclusion of the Court was that there were objective grounds justifying the complainant's employment

---

8.   *Angelidaki & Ors v Organismos Nomarchiakis Autodioikisis Rethymnis* [2009] ECR 1–3071.
9.   *An Post v Monaghan & Ors* [2013] IEHC 404. See *ACELY 2013* at 11.21.

for a fixed-term to provide cover for the named consultant on the days in question and so he could not succeed in his claim.

[7.05] *National University of Ireland v O'Keefe[10] – Labour Court – appeal of decision of Rights Commissioner – Protection of Employees (Fixed-Term Work) Act 2003 – whether replacement of identified employee who is out on leave constitutes objective grounds justifying fixed-term contract*

The complainant worked for the respondent as an assistant lecturer in politics on a succession of five fixed-term contracts from September 2008 until June 2013. In an email to the respondent dated 1 October 2012, the complainant claimed that she was entitled to a contract of indefinite duration by reason of the duration of her continuous fixed-term employment up until that date. On 28 February 2013, the complainant referred two claims to a Rights Commissioner alleging that the respondent had contravened ss 6 and 9 of the Protection of Employee (Fixed-Term Work) Act 2003 (the Act).

The Rights Commissioner found that both claims were well founded and held that under s 9 of the Act, the complainant was entitled to a contract of indefinite duration with effect from 31 August 2012.

The respondent appealed, claiming that each of the complainant's fixed-term contracts was to meet a temporary need of the university. The respondent submitted that it was constrained by the Employment Control Framework in that the number of academic posts it could maintain was fixed. The respondent contended that each vacancy the complainant had filled arose from the temporary absence of another lecturer. The duration of her employment corresponded to the duration of time for which the other lecturer was absent and her employment came to an end when the permanent holder of the position returned.

The respondent claimed that it was precluded by the Employment Control Framework from creating additional permanent posts without the sanction from the Department of Education and Skills. It also contended that it was required to fill by open competition any post leading to a permanent increase in its headcount. This open competition was to involve an interview process as to ascertain the best candidate. The respondent therefore claimed that the complainant could not be appointed to a permanent post by converting her fixed-term contract into one of indefinite duration and bypassing the open competition process.

The complainant's trade union did not accept that the complainant was employed to replace an identified permanent member of staff. Instead, the trade union submitted that the real and substantial reason for the continued employment of the complainant on a fixed-term rather than indefinite duration basis was to adhere to the Employment Control Framework. The complainant contended that this was a 'general' Government policy which contravened the rights of fixed-term employees under the Act.

The interpretation of the term 'objective ground' was central to the judgment. The Labour Court pointed to the decision of the CJEU in *Angelidaki & Ors v Organismos*

_____

10.   *National University of Ireland v O'Keefe* FTD1411.

Nomarchiaki Autodioikisis Rethymnis[11] where the concept of 'objective reasons' was held to refer to:

> precise and concrete circumstances characterising a given activity ... in particular from the specific nature of the tasks for the performance of which such contracts have been concluded and from the inherent characteristics of those tasks or, as the case may be, from pursuit of a legitimate social-policy objective of a Member State.

In order to make out a plea of objective justification, the respondent had to first establish a legitimate objective to which the impugned measure was referable. It had to then show that the means chosen were appropriate and necessary in order to achieve that objective. The Court noted that in *An Post v Monaghan & Ors*[12] Hedigan J, in considering if a ground relied upon was an objective ground, held that there must be the minimum unfavourable treatment necessary to enable the employer to obtain its objective.

The Labour Court noted that it has been held, in situations that the fixed-term contract has been justified on objective grounds where a worker is engaged on a fixed-term contract to perform work which corresponds to the fixed and permanent needs of the employer, but the primary purpose of their employment is to provide temporary cover for an absent employee.

The Court considered *Kucuk v Land Nordrhein-Westfalen*[13] where the temporary replacement of employees on sick, maternity, parental or other leave constituted an objective reason.

The respondent claimed that it could not circumvent the Act by translating the complainant's fixed-term contract into a contract of indefinite duration. The Labour Court noted that in *Ahmed v Health Service Executive*[14], the requirement to fill certain posts by way of open competition could not be relied upon to defeat the entitlement to a contract of indefinite duration under the 2003 Act. However in contrast, the later decision of Hedigan J in *Health Service Executive, Dublin North East v Umar*[15] a claimed objective ground, using an open competition process in order to find 'the best available person', was upheld. The respondent therefore submitted that Government policy requiring the post to be filled by way of open competition prevented the appointment of the complainant to the post without such a competition.

The evidence indicated that the complainant in fact continued in employment because a temporary vacancy arose from an identified lecturer's absence on sabbatical leave. In considering whether the work undertaken amounted to a genuine replacement for that performed by an absent permanent employee, the Court held that '[t]he fundamental test will always be whether he or she is occupying a freestanding post which corresponds to the fixed and permanent needs of the employer'.

---

11. *Angelidaki & Ors v Organismos Nomarchiaki Autodioikisis Rethymnis* [2009] ECR 1–3071.
12. *An Post v Monaghan & Ors* [2013] IEHC 404. See *ACELY 2013* at 11.21.
13. *Kucuk v Land Nordrhein-Westfalen* (Case C–586/10).
14. *Ahmed v Health Service Executive* [2006] IEHC 245 *per* Laffoy J.
15. *Health Service Executive, Dublin North East v Umar* [2011] 22 ELR 229.

The Court was satisfied that the complainant's employment was renewed for the purpose of replacing an identified lecturer. The Court accepted in these circumstances that the complainant's employment on a fixed-term contract was both appropriate and necessary to achieve the legitimate objective of providing tuition for the duration on that sabbatical. The Court therefore held that the renewal of the complainant's fixed-term contract for a further fixed-term was saved by s 9(4) of the Act.

The respondent's appeal was allowed and the decision of the Rights Commissioner was set aside.

[7.06] *National University of Ireland v Benson[16] – Labour Court – appeal by respondent of decision of Rights Commissioner – Protection of Employees (Fixed-Term Work) Act 2003[17] – entitlement to contract of indefinite duration*

The complainant was a lecturer employed by the respondent in the Department of Sociology from February 2007 until 30 June 2013 by way of five consecutive fixed-term contracts. On expiry of the fifth contract, the complainant was made redundant and she subsequently asserted a right to a contract of indefinite duration.

The Labour Court suggested to the parties that, given the combined effect of s 9(2) and (3) of the Protection of Employee (Fixed-Term Work) Act 2003 (the Act), the third contract was the relevant contract for the purposes of the appeal. The third contract was to fill a vacancy that arose for a post of assistant lecturer in the respondent's Department of Sociology. This post was expressed to be for a three-year period. The complainant applied for the post and took part in a competition, which included six other candidates. The complainant was successful and the three-year fixed-term contract commenced on 1 September 2008. At the time of the commencement of the contract, the complainant had already accrued 18 months of continuous fixed-term employment with the respondent. The conclusion of the three-year contract extended the aggregate duration of her fixed-term employment beyond four years. The respondent therefore had to prove that the renewal for the further fixed-term was justified on objective grounds in order to defeat the claim for a contract of indefinite duration.

Similar to its position in *O'Keeffe v NUI,*[18] the respondent claimed that the purpose of the contract was to provide cover for the temporary absence of a colleague. Evidence, in the form of an email from the relevant head of department, stated that the claimant was not a direct replacement for any individual. However, the author of this email was not available to give evidence and therefore the Court could not speculate that they meant something other than what was stated.

Other emails suggested that the complainant was replacing an identified member of staff who was out on leave. However this correspondence related to budgetary allocations and the Court interpreted the emails as meaning at best, that funding had become available to the respondent and it was used to meet costs associated with the complainant's employment.

---

16. *National University of Ireland v O'Keefe* FTD1412.
17. Appeal heard in conjunction with *National University of Ireland v O'Keefe* FTD1411.
18. *National University of Ireland v O'Keefe* FTD1411, see **[7.05]**.

The fact that the complainant remained in her post after the expiry of the third contract and that the identified lecturer did not return to teach in the department on the expiry of that contract suggested that the post was intended to meet a permanent or core need of the respondent.

The complainant had been offered a contract of indefinite duration in June 2012 but the offer was subsequently withdrawn. The Court accepted that this did not indicate what considerations were in the minds of the relevant decision makers in August 2008. This was important as objective grounds for the renewal of a fixed-term contract are judged by reference to the circumstances prevailing at the commencement of the contract.[19] What the previous offer of the contract of indefinite duration did show however was that in June 2012 at least, there was some reason to believe that the post occupied by the claimant was a continuing need of the respondent.

The Court referred to the decision of the CJEU in *Angelidaki*[20] to stress that the jurisprudence of the CJEU highlights that the fixed and permanent needs of an employer should normally be fulfilled by the use of permanent employment relationships. The Court also accepted that a fixed and permanent need of an employer can be performed by fixed-term contracts and that this can be objectively justified, especially where temporary cover for an absent colleague is needed.

The Labour Court ultimately found that there was 'no firm or clearly discernible connection between the absence of the identified lecturer and the employment of the claimant so as to establish that the latter was a replacement for the former'.

The respondent therefore failed to establish that the complainant's third contract was concluded for the purpose of providing cover for the duration of the temporary absence of another person. The Court disallowed the respondent's appeal and affirmed the decision of the Rights Commissioner.

[7.07] *Gorey Community School v Wildes*[21] *– Labour Court – appeal of Rights Commissioner decision – Industrial Relations Acts 1946 to 2012 – Protection of Employees (Fixed-Term Work) Act 2003 – objective grounds justifying renewal of fixed-term contract – temporary needs of employer and permanent needs of employer*

The complainant was a maths and science teacher who was employed by the respondent under continuous successive fixed-term contracts from 2007 to 2012. The complainant unsuccessfully argued before the Rights Commissioner that her continued employment on fixed-term contracts contravened s 9(2) of the Protection of Employees (Fixed-Term Work) Act 2003 (the Act). She argued that by operation of s 9(3) of the Act, she was entitled to a contract of indefinite duration and that the respondent had not provided her with acceptable objective grounds of justifying the renewal of a fixed-term contract. She appealed the Rights Commissioner's finding.

The Labour Court found that due to the complainant's length of service as of 2011, prima facie, there was a contravention of s 9(2) of the Act and therefore, the respondent

---

19. *Russell v Mount Temple Comprehensive School* [2009] IEHC 533.
20. *Angelidaki & Ors v Organismos Nomarchiaki Autodioikisis Rethymnis* (Cases C–378/07 to C–380/07).
21. *Gorey Community School v Wildes* FTD1419.

would be required to demonstrate that the 12-month fixed-term contract entered into between the respondent and the complainant in 2011 was objectively justified.

The respondent relied on three objective grounds to justify the renewal of the complainant's fixed-term contract, namely:

(i)   the complainant's hours were available only because two teachers in the respondent school were on career break and eight teachers were job-sharing;

(ii)   the Department of Education and Skills had advised the respondent that its staffing allocation was in a 'supernumerary position' and therefore the respondent was precluded from making permanent appointments; and

(iii) the complainant's position was not viable in the long term as enrolments to the school and teacher allocations were decreasing (on the basis that a new secondary school had opened in Gorey).

In his evidence, the principal of the respondent explained that although the complainant was not directly replacing teachers on reduced hours/career breaks, one of the teachers on reduced hours could teach the subjects taught by the complainant. He also gave evidence that 11 teaching hours of the teachers on leave were allocated to the complainant.

In reaching its decision on the complainant's entitlement to a contract of indefinite duration, the Labour Court considered the decision of the CJEU in joined cases *Angelidaki*.[22] In those cases, the CJEU held that 'objective reasons' relied on to justify the renewal of a fixed-term contract must be 'precise and concrete circumstances characterising a given activity'. The CJEU held that objective reasons could be established by reference to the specific nature and inherent characteristics of the tasks involved in the fixed-term contract, and, as the case may be, from the pursuit of a legitimate social-policy objective of a Member State. The CJEU distinguished between the temporary needs of the employer, for which successive fixed-term contracts could legitimately be used, and the permanent needs of the employer. The Labour Court noted that acceptable examples of such 'temporary needs' of the employer would include where a fixed-term contract was put in place to cover an employee on sick leave or maternity leave.

The Court referred to the CJEU's decision in *Kucuk v Land Nordrhein-Westfalen*,[23] which involved a claimant who was employed on 13 successive fixed-term contracts between 2 July 1996 and 31 December 2007 to replace other employees who were on leave. The fixed-term employment contracts were always entered into because of temporary leave granted to permanent court clerks. The CJEU stated that while covering leave can be an objective justification for fixed-term contracts, every case should be closely examined by the national court to ensure that the use of fixed-term contracts is justified on objective grounds and is not, in actual fact, fulfilling the permanent needs of the employer. Furthermore, the CJEU stated that general and abstract reasons cannot be utilised to objectively justify the use of fixed-term contracts.

---

22.   *Angelidaki & Ors v Organismos Nomarchiakis Autodioikisis Rethymnis* [2009] ECR 1–3071.
23.   *Kucuk v Land Nordrhein-Westfalen* [2012] IRLR 697.

The Court also considered its previous decision in *University College Dublin v A Worker*[24] where the work undertaken by the fixed-term employee had no relationship to the work that had been carried out by the two staff members that she was allegedly replacing. In that case, the Court determined that the employee was not employed on a fixed-term basis due to the temporary needs of the employer, but rather was fulfilling a permanent need of the employer that was separate to covering for employees on leave. The Court in that case held an employer could not simply name employees that were absent on maternity leave to discharge the requirement to objectively justify the fixed-term contracts, but rather the fixed-term worker must be a genuine replacement for absent employees.

In this case, the Court found that teaching of maths and science was a permanent fixed need of the respondent. It stated that the fact that one of the teachers on reduced hours could teach one of the complainant's subjects was an insufficient ground to justify renewal of successive fixed-term contracts. The Court accepted that keeping a position open for a permanent employee who has a right to return can be a legitimate objective which an employer is entitled to pursue. However, the employer must show that the absent person is actually returning to his/her duties. In this case, the respondent had not provided evidence that the employee on reduced hours would seek to resume full-time work.

The Court also referred to the decision of the High Court in *An Post v Monaghan & Ors*[25] where Hedigan J stated that the employer would have to ask whether continuing to employ an employee on a fixed-term basis was the minimum less favourable treatment necessary to enable the employer attain its objective. In this case, the Labour Court noted that there were arrangements in place by which teachers in the Gorey area who become surplus to requirements could be redeployed to other schools within a radius of 50 kilometres. The Court considered this to be an 'obvious alternative means of addressing the situation' that may arise, should the teacher on reduced hours seek to resume full-time work, resulting in the complainant becoming surplus to the respondent's requirements.

In relation to the other grounds relied on by the respondent to justify the renewal of a fixed-term contract (as set out above), the Court determined that the reasons provided by the respondent were of a general and abstract nature and did not relate to the precise and concrete circumstances of the work being performed, and therefore were not accepted as justifying the contravention of s 9(2) of the Act.

The Labour Court held that, in the absence of an objective ground justifying the renewal of the complainant's fixed-term contract, under s 9(3) of the Act, the complainant was entitled to a contract of indefinite duration as of the commencement of the school year 2011 to 2012.

[7.08] *Board of Management of St Joseph's School for Deaf Boys v Grehan*[26] *– Labour Court – appeal of decision of Rights Commissioner – Industrial Relations Act*

24.   *University College Dublin v A Worker* FTD1129.
25.   *An Post v Monaghan & Ors* [2013] IEHC 404. See *ACELY 2013* at 11.21.
26.   *Board of Management St Joseph's School for Deaf Boys v Grehan* FTD1416.

1946 to 2012 – Protection of Employee (Fixed-Term Work) Act 2003, ss 8, 9 and 15 –
written contract of employment – contract of indefinite duration – failure to give
written statement of objective grounds is more than a technical breach – objective
grounds – reinstatement

At the Rights Commissioner hearing, the complainant contended the respondent did not
recognise his entitlement to contract of indefinite duration under s 9(2) of the Protection
of Employees (Fixed-Term Work) Act 2003 (the Act). The complainant also claimed
that the respondent breached its obligations under s 8 of the Act by failing to provide
him with a written statement of the objective grounds justifying the renewal of his fixed-
term contract and the reasons for the failure to offer him a contract of indefinite
duration. The Rights Commissioner decided that there were objective grounds justifying
the renewal of his fixed-term contract and that the complaint under s 8 of the Act was
statute-barred. The complainant appealed to the Labour Court.

The Labour Court noted that the complainant commenced employment with the
respondent on 29 August 2007 on a fixed-term contract which was to expire on 28
August 2008. He was employed on five successive fixed-term contracts until 31 August
2012. Other than his first contract, the complainant did not receive a written contract of
employment stating the objective conditions determining the contract or the grounds
justifying the renewal of a fixed-term contract. In September 2010, the complainant
approached the principal of the respondent to ask whether he was entitled to a contract
of indefinite duration by virtue of his service in the school. The principal advised the
complainant that he had no such entitlement because he had 'subbed for different
teachers in the school', and his fixed-term contract was renewed on a further two
occasions up until August 2012.

During the course of the hearing, the respondent produced a letter from the
Department of Education and Skills dated 19 July 2010 which confirmed the approval
of the funding of a fully qualified teacher to replace a teacher who was on leave. The
letter stated 'funding of the replacement teacher's contract will cease on termination of
the secondment of [the teacher]' and instructed the Board of Management of the
respondent to 'include in the contract of the replacement teacher a statement to the
effect that he/she is being appointed to replace a teacher on secondment'. In addition,
the respondent produced a circular (Circular 0055/2008) issued by the Department
stating that 'a teacher engaged on a fixed-term contract shall receive written terms of
employment ... Each statement of terms of employment shall contain the objective
condition determining the fixed term contract.'

The respondent accepted it did not comply with the instructions set out in the letter
and the circular, and it did not dispute that it had failed to comply with s 8 of the Act;
however it gave evidence that there were objective grounds justifying the failure to
provide a contract of indefinite duration.

The respondent also relied upon the Primary Teacher Appointment Forms to
substantiate its position that the complainant was informed of the objective nature of his
fixed-term contract and that he was replacing a teacher who was out on special approved
leave.

In respect of the alleged breach of s 8 of the Act, the Court examined the Primary Teacher Appointment Forms for the academic years 2010/2011 and 2011/2012. The Court noted that the form for 2010/2011 did not contain a reference to the temporary nature of the contract and while the second form did refer to the teacher on leave, the complainant gave evidence that when he signed the form no reference to the teacher on leave was included and that the reference was subsequently included by the respondent. The Court also noted that this form was in reality for payroll purposes only and was reluctant to accept that this form constituted a written contract. The Court stated that s 8 placed a mandatory obligation on employers and that the respondent had failed to fulfil this obligation. The Court upheld the complainant's complaint under s 8 for the complainant's final fixed-term contract, but held that earlier claims of breaches of s 8 were statute barred.

In respect of the alleged breach of s 9(2), the Court stated that it must look 'no further than the objective grounds relied upon for the contract that prima facie contravenes s 9(2) of the Act'. The objective grounds put forward by the respondent in this case were that the complainant was filling in for a teacher on leave. However, no contractual information was ever provided to the complainant in this regard, nor was he provided with the letter from the Department dated 19 July 2011. Furthermore, the Primary Teacher Appointment Form provided to the complainant did not contain any reference to the temporary nature of the appointment or the objective grounds relied on for not furnishing the complainant with a contract of indefinite duration. The Court stated that on reading s 8 of the Act as a whole, it was clear that the purpose of s 8 is not just to ensure that a fixed-term employee is notified of why the fixed-term contract is being renewed, but also to ensure that the employer definitively commits itself, at the point at which the contract is being renewed, to the grounds upon which it will rely should the fixed-term employee bring a claim under s 9(4) of the Act. The Court concluded that failure to provide objective grounds in writing for renewal of a fixed-term contract infers that the objective grounds relied on were not the operative grounds for the impugned decision. It noted that it would be for the respondent to prove the contrary.

The Court accepted the complainant's argument that, by submitting the letter from the Department, the respondent was retrospectively seeking to justify its failure to offer the complainant a contract of indefinite duration on the basis that the post was suppressed by the Department. On the basis of decisions of the CJEU, it was held that this was insufficient to satisfy the objective justification test, namely that any justification should be strictly construed, should be on the basis of objective and transparent criteria and must be justified in the specific context in which it occurs as per the CJEU in *Lommers v Minister van Landbouw, Natuurbeheer en Visseri*.[27]

On the basis that no satisfactory, contemporaneous objective grounds justifying the renewal of the fixed-term contract had been put forward by the respondent, the Court held that the purported fixed-term contract dated 1 September 2010 gave rise to an entitlement to a contract of indefinite duration since it purported to extend the period of the complainant's fixed-term employment beyond four years.

---

27. *Lommers v Minister van Landbouw, Natuurbeheer en Visseri* (Case 476/99) [2002] IRLR 430.

The Labour Court overturned the decision of the Rights Commissioner, and made an order directing that the complainant be reinstated. The Court further directed the respondent to pay the complainant arrears of remuneration accruing to him since the date of his dismissal up to the date on which the reinstatement takes effect. The Court also ordered the respondent to pay €5,000 in compensation to the complainant for its breach of s 8 of the Act.

[7.09] *Dublin Institute of Technology v Scott[28] – Labour Court – appeal of decision of Rights Commissioner – Protection of Employees (Fixed Term Work) Act 2003 – complainant employee accepted further 'specified purpose contract' after he became entitled to contract of indefinite duration – employer cannot rely on its own errors to deny locus standi – contract of indefinite duration awarded following continuous of service after expiry of fixed-term contract – reinstatement ordered without loss of income from date of termination of employment*

A Rights Commissioner had determined that the complainant had acquired a contract of indefinite duration by operation of law in accordance with s 9(1) of the Act and had ordered the respondent to reinstate the complainant to his position with compensation for any financial loss he suffered in consequence of his dismissal. The respondent appealed this.

The complainant was initially employed on 6 February 2007 under a specified purpose/fixed-term contract of employment for the purpose of 'covering a staff members acting role'. The contract went on to state: 'When this acting post finishes your contract will cease.'

During the course of the hearing, it was established that the 'acting post' ceased sometime in mid-2008. At that point, the specific event terminating the contract had occurred and the contract was fulfilled. The complainant's employment was not terminated on the occurrence of that event, but rather he continued his employment with the respondent, carrying out the work that the respondent continued to assign to him. The respondent did not issue any further contract of employment to him. It was noted that s 2 of the Act defines a 'permanent worker' as an employee who is not a fixed-term employee, and as the complainant was not employed under a fixed-term contract of employment, the Court concluded that for the purposes of the Act the complainant was at that point a permanent employee of the respondent.

In January 2009, the respondent offered the complainant a further specified purpose contract which provided that, when the seconded staff member returned to his post, the complainant's contract would cease. The complainant signed the specified purpose contract. However, the Court noted that the contract did not purport to change or reduce the complainant's status as a permanent employee within the meaning of the Act. During the course of the hearing, the respondent had acknowledged that it was not clear what the complainant's employment status was subsequent to the expiry of the 2007 fixed-term contract. At no point during the complainant's employment did the respondent seek to diminish or alter the complainant's permanent status. The Court stated that it

---

28.   *Dublin Institute of Technology v Scott* FTD1417.

appeared that the respondent was at all times operating on the assumption that the complainant continued to be a fixed-term worker after the expiry of the 2007 contract and before it offered him a further fixed-term contract of employment in January 2009.

The complainant worked under that contract until 5 June 2013 when the respondent notified him that his employment would cease in July 2013 in accordance with the terms of his contract, and the respondent subsequently terminated the complainant's employment as notified.

As the respondent could offer no explanation for its decision not to offer the complainant a contract of indefinite duration in July 2008, the Court stated that it could not and did not seek to rely on s 9(4) of the Act to justify its decision. Accordingly the Court stated that it must conclude that the complainant acquired a contract of indefinite duration by operation of law in July 2008. The Court held that the fixed-term provisions of the contract issued to the complainant in January 2009 infringed s 9(2) of the Act and in accordance with s 9(3), the provisions relating to the fixed-term had no effect.

The respondent also sought to argue that, notwithstanding the fact that it had issued the complainant with a fixed-term contract, as the complainant had become entitled to a contract of indefinite duration as of 2008, he was a 'permanent employee' from that date, and therefore, as he was not a fixed-term worker within the meaning of the Act at the time he instituted his claim, he did not have *locus standi* to bring the claim under the Act. Accordingly, the respondent asserted that the complainant's claim should be dismissed.

The Court stated that the respondent could not seek to benefit from its own behaviour and deprive the complainant of the benefit of permanency by treating him as a fixed-term worker while simultaneously benefiting from his loss of *locus standi* under the Act. The Court held that this was particularly true where the respondent had never acknowledged either the complainant's permanency under the Act or clarified his status after the 2007 contract expired.

The Court therefore concluded that the complainant acquired a contract of indefinite duration with effect from July 2008. While the terms of that contract were not reduced to writing the Court found that they were identical to that under which the complainant was employed between February 2007 and July 2008 save for the fixed-term nature of that contract.

The Court made an order reinstating the complainant into the post he held before his employment was terminated in 2013, and ordered the respondent to pay back pay for the intervening period. The Court ordered that the complainant should receive an unspecified measure of compensation for the infringement of his rights under the Act.

[7.10] *University of Limerick v Arbuckle*[29] *– Labour Court – Protection of Employees (Fixed-Term Work) Act 2003 – Labour Court appeal and cross appeal of decision of Rights Commissioner – use of successive fixed-term contracts to meet specific temporary need – whether contract of indefinite duration should have been granted*

This was an appeal by the complainant against a Rights Commissioner's decision and a cross-appeal by the respondent against the part of the Rights Commissioner's decision

---

29.   *University of Limerick v Arbuckle* FTD1420.

that found it liable for having penalised the complainant contrary to s 13(1) of the Protection of Employees (Fixed-Term Work) Act 2003 (the Act).

The factual background to the case was not in dispute. The complainant was employed by the respondent on a number of fixed-term contracts for the purpose of undertaking research.

The complainant contended that his second contract contravened s 9(2) of the Act and that, by operation of s 9(3) of the Act, he became entitled to a contract of indefinite duration. He also contended that the work for which he was employed corresponded to a fixed and permanent need of the respondent and that, in these circumstances, the use of a fixed-term contract was inappropriate.

The respondent contended that the second contract was entered into to meet a purely temporary requirement for services required in connection with the FLASH project and that the conclusion of the contract was justified by objective grounds relating to the nature of the work being performed by the complainant. The respondent accepted that undertaking research, *per se*, is a continuing function of the university. However, it stated that individual projects are often dependent on external funding and are subject to temporal limitation.

The Labour Court held that it was well settled that the objective grounds relied upon as a justification for the extension of a fixed-term contract must be present and operating on the mind of the employer at the commencement of the contract. It stated that the grounds relied upon must also relate to the nature of the work and the Court referred to *Adeneler v Ellinikos Organismos Galaktos*[30] in this regard. The Court also referred to *Benson v National University of Ireland Maynooth*[31] in which the Labour Court stated that the source from which funding is derived for a post cannot constitute objective reasons justifying the use of a fixed-term contract. The Court stated that it is well settled that the fixed and permanent needs of an employer should normally be fulfilled by the use of a permanent employment contract.

However, the Court noted that it was also clear from the jurisprudence that the circumstances under which work that corresponds to an employer's fixed and permanent needs is to be performed can provide objective justification for the use of fixed-term contracts. The Court stated that there is no closed category of circumstances in which this can arise and that it could arise in circumstances where a regular workforce has to be augmented so as to meet some temporary requirement of the business. The Court pointed out that the Framework Agreement on Fixed-Term Work annexed to Directive 99/70/EC (upon which the Act is based) recognises that, while contracts of indefinite duration are to be regarded as the general form of employment relationships, fixed-term employment contracts are a feature of employment in certain sectors, occupations and activities. In addressing this, the Court said that it would normally look to see if the temporal nature of the post in issue is clearly discernible at the time the impugned contract is concluded.

The Court held that the object of the respondent employing the complainant was to conduct research on the specific project (the FLASH project). The Court acknowledged

---

30. *Adeneler v Ellinikos Organismos Galaktos* [2006] IRLR 716.

31. *Benson v National University of Ireland Maynooth* FTD1412 at **[7.06]**.

that the complainant had correctly pointed out that the reason for concluding the second contract for a fixed-term rather than for an indefinite duration was not set out with any level of clarity or particularly in the contract itself. The relevant provision in the contract merely recited the nature of the work to be performed and that it was subject to the continued availability of funding. However, the Court did state that it was clear from the contract itself, and from the circumstances surrounding its conclusion, that the complainant was recruited specifically to work on the FLASH project.

The Court stated that it was not disputed that, on completion of the FLASH project the respondent had no continuing requirement for the type of work in which the complainant had been employed in connection with the project. The Court was satisfied that this was anticipated by the respondent at the time the second contract was concluded and that this was the principal reason for limiting the complainant's tenure in employment to the duration of the task for which he was employed. The Court considered this to be a legitimate objective of the respondent.

In determining whether the means chosen to achieve the objective were proportionate and appropriate, the Court considered the High Court decision in *An Post v Monaghan & Others*[32] in which the High Court stated it should ask itself if the impugned measure (in this case employing the complainant for a fixed term) was the minimum unfavourable treatment necessary to enable the employer to obtain its objective. The Court held that it was satisfied that when the second contract was concluded the respondent knew with virtual certainty that its requirement for the work to which the contract related would not endure beyond the completion of the FLASH project and that the complainant would then become redundant. The Court considered this both proportionate and appropriate and was the minimum less favourable treatment necessary so as to attain the respondent's objective.

In these circumstances, the Court concluded that the respondent did not contravene s 9(2) of the Act.

The complainant also brought claims under ss 6, 8 and 13(1) of the 2003 Act. The Court held that as the complainant had withdrawn these claims before the Rights Commissioner, the Court now lacked jurisdiction to hear such complaints. Accordingly, the Court concluded that the respondent was entitled to succeed on its cross-appeal against that part of the Rights Commissioner's decision that found the respondent liable to the complainant for contravention of s 13(1) of the Act.

BREAKS BETWEEN FIXED-TERM CONTRACTS

[7.11] *Abbott v Department of Education & Skills*[33] *– Labour Court – appeal of decision of Rights Commissioner – Industrial Relations Acts 1946 to 2012 – Protection of Employees (Fixed-Term Work) Act 2003 – continuity of service where civil servant employed by one government department and then subsequently*

---

32.   *An Post v Monaghan* [2013] IEHC 404 see *ACELY 2013* at 11.21.

33.   *Abbott v Department of Education & Skills* FTD1331.

employed by another – break in service – resignation of position on request by employer

The complainant was employed by the Department of Finance as a temporary unestablished auditor in the ERDF Financial Control Unit from 20 March 2006. She resigned her post with effect from 23 May 2008, and was then employed by the Department of Enterprise, Trade and Employment (as it was then) from 16 June 2008, as a temporary non-established auditor in the European Social Fund Financial Control Unit (the ESFFCU) on a fixed-term contract of employment that ended on 15 June 2012. By Government order, the ESFFCU was transferred from the Department of Enterprise, Trade and Employment to the Department of Education and Skills, which became the complainant's employer.

The complainant's contract was not renewed after its expiry in June 2008, and her employment with the respondent terminated. She brought a claim under the Protection of Employees (Fixed-Term Work) Act 2003 (the Act) that she was entitled to a contract of indefinite duration by virtue of s 9(3) of the Act.

The Rights Commissioner determined that the complainant was not entitled to a contract of indefinite duration on the basis that, firstly, she had worked for two different government departments and that there was a break in her service between 23 May 2008 and 16 June 2008 from when she resigned from the Department of Finance to take up a position in the Department of Enterprise, Trade and Employment (which was later transferred to the respondent), and secondly, she was provided with objective grounds justifying the fixed-term contract.

The complainant appealed the determination to the Labour Court, asserting that:

(i)   she was employed on a series of fixed-term contracts of employment and became entitled by operation of law to a contract of indefinite duration with effect from 16 June 2008;

(ii)   she was treated less favourably than comparable permanent employees; and

(iii)   she did not receive the written terms of her employment.

The Court noted the definition of employee in the Act which provides that:

> ... for the purposes of this Act, a person holding office under, or in the service of, the State (including a civil servant within the meaning of the Civil Service Regulation Act 1956) shall be deemed to be an employee employed by the State or Government, as the case may be.

The Labour Court noted that it was common case that the complainant worked for the State whilst employed by two government departments. The Labour Court rejected the respondent's assertion that both governmental departments were separate employers and held that during both contracts of employment, the complainant was employed by the same employer (ie the State) at the relevant time for a period of four years and therefore the complainant fell squarely into the definition of employee as set out in the Act.

The respondent also contended that as the complainant resigned from her position at the Department of Finance to take up her position in the Department of Enterprise,

Trade and Employment, she voluntarily left employment and therefore could not rely on s 9(3) of the Act to obtain a contract of indefinite duration.

The Court rejected the contention that the complainant voluntarily left her employment. It accepted evidence from the complainant that the Department of Finance, in erroneously believing that it was a separate employer from the Department of Enterprise, Trade and Employment, informed the complainant that she was obliged to resign in order to take up her new position. The respondent could not seek to rely on the misinformation that it provided to the complainant to defeat her claim. The present case was distinguished from *Meath County Council v Reilly*,[34] where that complainant had decided to resign for personal reasons to improve his situation, whereas in this case, the complainant was advised that she had to resign by her employer.

The Labour Court also rejected the respondent's argument that, because there had been a break in the complainant's service between her former and new position, she did not have continuous service within the meaning of the Act. The Court held the complainant was instructed to resign her post and that the respondent could not rely on its own unlawful instruction to defeat the claim. To permit this would be grossly unfair to the complainant. In the circumstances, the Labour Court concluded that the break between the complainant's contracts with the Department of Finance and the Department of Enterprise, Trade and Employment should be considered a period of lay off, and the Court held therefore there was no break in her employment.

Having established that the complainant was continuously employed by the State for a period exceeding four years, the Labour Court assessed whether the respondent had put forward any objective grounds justifying it in issuing the complainant with a fixed-term contract in June 2008, rather than a contract of indefinite duration.

The Court stated that it was well established by the jurisprudence of the CJEU that derogations from the right to the entitlement to stability of employment enshrined in the Act must be construed strictly and that, since the derogations were a defence to a claim, the employer must establish every element of that defence.

It was held that the objective justifications proposed by the employer must be proportionate and must balance the detriment suffered by the worker with the benefit enjoyed by the employer. The Court cited the decision in *UCD v O'Mahony*[35] as setting out the Irish position in relation to objective justifications. This was that objective justifications could be permitted if they related to, for example, the specific nature of the tasks performed and the inherent characteristics of those tasks or the pursuit of a social policy objective of a Member State.

The respondent in this case argued that the objective grounds justifying the issue of a further fixed-term contract was that specific project, ie the provision of audit services of European Funds and, following the expiry of the complainant's contract, there would be no requirement for the services to be provided. The Labour Court found that the complainant was employed to audit funds, drawn down from the European Union. The funds are permanent, albeit, they are managed through operational programmes that run for set periods of time. However, it was noted that the State constantly makes

---

34. *Meath County Council v Reilly* FTD1230.
35. *University College Dublin v O'Mahony* FTD1234.

applications for funding under the EU programmes and that the audit of those funds remains a constant feature of administration in the State, and the auditing of ESF and ERDF funds continues to date.

The Court concluded that the respondent had not established that the objective grounds justifying dismissal in s 9(4) of the Act were for the purpose of achieving a legitimate objective and that such treatment was appropriate and necessary for that purpose. The Labour Court allowed the complainant's appeal on the basis of s 9(4). The Labour Court ordered the respondent to reinstate the complainant with effect from 16 June 2008.

The Court found that the complainant's claim of unfavourable treatment by not being promoted in 2009 was statute barred. The Court also rejected the complainant's claim that she had received less favourable treatment than comparable permanent employees with respect to pay.

[7.12] *Athlone Institute of Technology v McManus[36] – Labour Court – appeal of decision of Rights Commissioner by respondent employer – Protection of Employees (Fixed Term Work) Act 2003 – Industrial Relations Acts 1946 to 2012 – whether break between two fixed-term contracts of employment constituted period of layoff – whether employment of complainant on fixed-term contract appropriate and necessary to achieve legitimate objective of providing tuition for duration of career break*

The complainant was employed as a part-time assistant lecturer, initially under a fixed-term contract for the duration of the academic year 2007/2008. This contract expired on 3 July 2008. In June 2008, while still in employment, the complainant applied for a post as assistant lecturer in accountancy with the respondent, a vacancy that had been advertised nationally. The complainant was successful and was so informed by the respondent on 29 July 2008. The complainant commenced employment under this contract on 1 September 2008. This second contract stated that it was a fixed-purpose contract covering for the post-holder on career break. The contract stated that it would terminate when the post-holder returned to the position or left for any reason. At the time this contract was concluded, its duration was incapable of precise ascertainment, but it was anticipated that it could last for up to five years.

In any event, the complainant's employment did continue for five years and terminated on 31 August 2013. It should be noted that the post-holder was not named in the contract, but it was agreed that it was Ms S, who was also a teacher in accountancy and that the second contract's commencement date coincided with the departure of Ms S on her career break and its termination was to coincide with her anticipated return date, although it was noted by the Labour Court that Ms S did not return.

The complainant asserted that she was employed on two successive/continuous fixed-term contracts for an aggregate duration of six years, and in this regard the respondent contravened s 9(2) of the Act, as a consequence of which her fixed-term contract was transmuted to one of indefinite duration by operation of s 9(3) of the Act.

---

36.   *Athlone Institute of Technology v McManus* FTD1410.

The complainant asserted that in reality, she was not employed as a replacement for any lecturer; but that her employment was intended to meet the normal and fixed teaching needs of the respondent and that she never acted as a substitute for any teachers. The complainant also contended that her employment under the first and second contracts was continuous within the statutory meaning of that term and any break in her employment between the two should be properly classified as a layoff. The complainant contended that the work she engaged in was unrelated to the duties previously undertaken by Ms S and she provided evidence to show that her duties were the same as those she undertook during the currency of the first contract.

The respondent submitted that there was no continuity between the contracts and that the first contract terminated by dismissal on its expiry without renewal and the second contract was filled by open competition at which the complainant was successful. The respondent stated that neither it nor the complainant could have known with any probability that she would have been successful in that competition and thus the break between the employment could not be classified as a layoff within the statutory definition of that term. In so far as the Rights Commissioner construed the break as a layoff, the respondent asserted that the Rights Commissioner had erred. The respondent also contended that there were material differences in the job the complainant held under the first contract and the one she held under the second contract and thus the second contract could not be regarded as a renewal of the first. In the alternative, the respondent submitted that the continuance of the complainant's employment beyond four years was justified on objective grounds and was saved by s 9(4) of the Act.

The objective grounds relied upon were that the complainant was at all times employed as a replacement for a permanent post-holder who was on a career break and that her engagement on a fixed-term contract was both appropriate and necessary in order to facilitate the eventual return of the permanent post-holder. With regard to the contention that the duties she completed were different to that performed by Ms S, the respondent stated that the allocation of teaching duties was a matter for the head of the relevant department and could vary from year to year, but contended that both Ms S and the complainant were employed in a similar capacity. The respondent's case was simply that had Ms S not been on a career break, she would have undertaken the duties undertaken by the complainant.

In its determination, the Labour Court noted that in concluding that the break between contracts was a layoff, the Rights Commissioner had followed Labour Court decisions in the *Department of Foreign Affairs v A Group of Workers*[37] and in *Beary v Revenue Commissioners.*[38] The Labour Court considered the definition of layoff in s 11(1) of the Redundancy Payments Acts 1967 to 2014 and noted that under that section, a layoff arises only where notice to that effect is given. The Labour Court also noted the provisions of the Schedule 1 of the Minimum Notice and Terms of Employment Act 1973 to 2001, particularly reg 6, and the Labour Court noted the willingness of the Employment Appeals Tribunal to interpret the word 'immediate' in a liberal fashion. The Court also referenced the fact that the EAT has overlooked short

---

37. *Department of Foreign Affairs v A Group of Workers* [2007] ELR 332.
38. *Beary v Revenue Commissioners* [2011] 22 ELR 137.

breaks for the purpose of determining if an employee has one year's continuous service so as to come within the ambit of the Unfair Dismissals legislation. It should be noted that no claim under either piece of legislation was before the Labour Court.

The Labour Court concluded that reg 6 of Schedule 1 of the Minimum Notice and Terms of Employment Act 1973 to 2001 does provide scope for construing successive periods of employment as being continuous within the statutory meaning ascribed to that term. The Labour Court noted that in both the *Beary* case and the *Department of Foreign Affairs* case, the Labour Court had held that breaks in service of varying duration could be properly regarded as periods of layoff. However, the Court noted that in both cases the complainants were casual workers who were members of a panel from which they were provided with work as and when required and that on each occasion when their employment ended, they returned to the panel with the expectation of recall.

The Labour Court noted that this was not the position in this case where on the termination of the first contract in July 2008, the complainant had no entitlement to further work at that time. In the view of the Labour Court, the different factual matrix from the instant case diminished the precedent value of these cases. The Court concluded that it would be going too far on the facts to construe the period between the ending of the first contract and the commencement of the second contract as one of layoff. The Court further stated the ending of the first contract without its renewal had all the appearances of a dismissal. The complainant had applied for another vacancy that had arisen which was to be filled by open competition and the Court noted there was nothing in the evidence before it from which it could be reasonably inferred that the respondent knew or ought to have known that the complainant would be employed to the post.

The Court then went on to consider whether the ending of the first contract was followed by immediate re-employment by the respondent. It noted the dichotomy between the language of cl 5 of the Framework Agreement on Fixed-Term Work annexed to Directive 99/70/EC, which applies to the successive use of fixed-term contracts and the wording of s 9 of the Act, which applies to continuous fixed-term employment and the fact that this was considered in great detail by the Labour Court in both the *Beary* and the *Department of Foreign Affairs* cases.

The Labour Court held that the complainant was re-employed on or about 29 July and this was some 10 days (eight working days) after the termination of the first contract and thus the Court held that the expiry of the first contract amounted to a dismissal, but that the complainant was immediately re-employed on a second contract, thus preserving the continuity of her employment. This construction, in the view of the Court, ensured that the 2003 Act and the Directive 99/70/EC could be construed in harmony on the facts of the case.

The Labour Court then considered whether the complainant was doing the same job intermittently. The respondent suggested that the complainant was doing a different job and that she was an hourly paid part-time lecturer under the first contract, whereas she was a *pro rata* salaried lecturer under the second contract. The Court noted that there were frailties with this argument in light of the provisions of s 9(2) of the Act which applied to a situation where employees are employed on two more continuous fixed-term contracts *simpliciter*. The Labour Court noted that there was no requirement in the

Act that the contracts be for the same purpose; the only requirement is that the contract be for a fixed-term. Moreover, the Court noted that the complainant was employed as a college lecturer under both contracts and that there was nothing in statute by which it could be held that either the mode of payment or the complainant's status regarding part or full time is a material consideration. The Labour Court did not uphold the respondent's argument in this regard.

The Court concluded that the net issue for consideration was whether the second contract was in reality for the purposes of replacing Ms S during the currency of her career break. The Labour Court considered detailed submissions on this point and also noted its decisions in *University College Dublin v A Worker*[39] and *Dun Laoghaire VEC v White*[40] to review their precedential value in this case. In the latter case, the Labour Court stated that:

> Simply naming two people that are absent on maternity leave in the fixed-term contract is not sufficient in itself to discharge the burden of proof that lies with the respondent. It must also show that the work being undertaken by the person on that fixed-term contract of employment amounted to a genuine replacement of the two people on maternity leave. The Court takes the view that this might be either by way of a simple or direct assignment of the work of those on leave to the person who was contracted to replace them.

> Alternatively, it might be by way of a general reallocation of work within a group to match skillsets whilst the replaced personnel are on leave. However, whichever way is chosen the employer must demonstrate the reality of the replacement to the Court in order to rely on s 9(4) of the Act.

The Court noted that in this case the evidence established that there was a relationship between the work performed by the complainant and that performed by the absentee in that they were both lecturers in accountancy. The Court further accepted that the respondent did engage in a general reallocation of the work in the department in question. The Court accepted as a fact that there was a reallocation of teaching duties within the relevant department and also that there was a clearly discernible relationship between the work performed by the complainant and that performed by Ms S in that they both lectured in accountancy. The Court further considered its decision in *Dun Laoghaire VEC v White*[41] and noted the approach of the Court in that decision was to look at the content of the duties performed by the complainant and those performed by the person to whom she reputedly replaced. In that case, the Court found that the respondent had failed to explain the difference in the hours worked by the complainant relative to the teaching hours worked by the absentee. In this case, the Labour Court was satisfied on the evidence that the teaching hours assigned to the complainant arose because they had become available due to the absence of Ms S.

The Court then considered the legal principles in respect of objective justification and the findings of the CJEU. The Court concluded that in order to make out a plea of

---

39.   *University College Dublin v A Worker* FTD1129.
40.   *Dun Laoghaire VEC v White* FTD1329.
41.   *Dun Laoghaire VEC v White* FTD1329.

objective justification, the respondent must first establish the legitimate objective to which the impugned measure is referable and it must then show that the means chosen are appropriate and necessary means of achieving that objective. The Court noted that situations can and frequently do arise in which a worker is engaged on a fixed-term contract to perform work which corresponds to the fixed and permanent needs of the employer, but the primary purpose of that employment is to provide temporary cover for an absent employee. In those cases, it has been held that the conclusion of a fixed-term contract can be justified on objective grounds notwithstanding the work to which the contract relates forms part of the employer's fixed and permanent needs. The Labour Court gave the example of where this arises with most frequency such as cover for an employee's absence through illness, leave of absence or maternity leave. The Labour Court noted the judgments of the CJEU in *Kucuk v Land Nordhein-Westfalen*[42] and *Márquez Samohano v Universitat Pompeu Fabra*[43] and noted that these cases were relevant in so far as they demonstrated the circumstances that can exist in which it is objectively justifiable to use a fixed-term contract to fulfil what are essentially the fixed and permanent needs of the employers.

The Labour Court concluded that, where a worker is employed to cover the temporary absence of another, the use of a fixed-term contract for that purpose is inherently justified. What was necessary was to determine as fact whether the complainant was in reality employed to replace Ms S during her temporary absence, or was she not. The Court concluded that it was more probable than not that had Ms S not taken a career break, then there would have been no vacancy for the complainant to fill and moreover the Court was also satisfied that when the second contract came into being, it was objectively clear that the vacancy filled by complainant would subsist only during the currency of Ms S's absence. Under the terms of the career break, Ms S had a right of return to work on the termination of the career break and at the time the second contract was concluded, the respondent had no reason to believe that Ms S would not exercise that right.

The Court noted the decision of the High Court in *Russell v Mount Temple Comprehensive School,*[44] which confirmed that the existence of objective grounds justifying the renewal of fixed-term contract is to be ascertained by reference to the circumstances prevailing at the time the impugned contract is renewed. In that case, the judge pointed out that if a fixed-term contract is lawful at the time of the conclusion, it cannot be subsequently rendered unlawful by the occurrence of some unforeseen intervening event.

The Court, in applying this, found that the fact that Ms S had decided not to return to her former post could not affect the lawfulness of the renewal of the complainant's employment for a fixed-term if it was genuinely concluded for the purpose of filling what was expected to be a temporary absence. The Court noted that the provision of career breaks to staff is a desirable objective which can have important social benefits and that the respondent institute must still continue to provide tuition during the

---

42.   *KCK v Land Nordhein-Westfalen* Case ECLI: EU: 2012: 39, [2012] IRLR 697.

43.   *Samohano v Universitat Pompeu Fabra* (Case C–190/13). See **[7.01]**.

44.   *Russell v Mount Temple Comprehensive School* [2009] IEHC 533.

currency of the career break and must do so in a way that recognises the right of the person to leave or leave and return to his or her post at the end of the leave. The Court stated that if the respondent could not fill temporary vacancies created by an employee availing of a career break on a fixed-term contract; it is highly probable that this facility would not be made available to its employees.

The Court concluded that renewal of the complainant's fixed-term contract for a further fixed-term was saved by s 9(4) of the Act and thus the respondent was not in contravention of s 9. The Court allowed the appeal and set aside the decision of the Rights Commissioner.

[7.13] *HSE v Sallam[45] – High Court – Baker J – appeal of decision of Labour Court – Protection of Employees (Fixed-Term Work) Act 2003 – length of service – successive fixed-term contracts – whether employment continuous where two breaks in contracts of employment, one for 15 days and the other for 20 days – whether complainant has locus standi in circumstances where Labour Court found he was entitled to contract of indefinite duration*

The complainant was employed by the Health Service Executive (HSE) as a consultant obstetrician and gynaecologist on a series of fixed-term contracts between 3 June 2003 and 16 August 2011. In July 2007, the complainant commenced employment in the position of locum consultant in Sligo General Hospital. Dr M, for whom the complainant was acting as locum, retired in June 2010. The complainant was not informed of the doctor's retirement until October 2010. The HSE notified the complainant by letters in May and June 2011 that a successful candidate had been appointed to replace the retired doctor and that the complainant's contract would expire on the date that the successful candidate commenced employment. The replacement doctor commenced employment on 16 August 2011, on which date the complainant's contract was formally terminated.

The complainant contended that he was continuously employed by the HSE on a series of successive fixed-term contracts for a period of over eight years and, once Dr M retired, he was no longer acting as his locum but fulfilled the purpose of the contract through performance, such that his continued employment was under a contract of indefinite duration by operation of s 9 of the Act. The Rights Commissioner did not uphold these claims and an appeal was heard by the Labour Court in January 2013. The decision of the Labour Court formed the basis of this appeal to the High Court.

The High Court firstly considered whether the duration of the complainant's employment in the various hospitals was continuous.

Despite there being two breaks between the various contracts, the first being a period of 15 days and the second being 21 days, the Labour Court held that these periods could not 'provide a sufficient basis' to render the employment as not continuous. The Labour Court applied the decision of the CJEU in *Adneler v Ellinikos Organismos Galaktos[46]* in determining whether the complainant's contracts could be regarded as continuous. In

---

45. *HSE v Sallam* [2014] IEHC 298.

46. *Adneler v Ellinikos Organismos Galaktos* (Case C–212/04) [2006] IRLR 716.

that case, the CJEU held that contracts of employment separated by 20 days are to be regarded as 'successive' within the meaning of cl 5 of the Directive.[47] The High Court held that the Labour Court did not err in its approach by considering the jurisprudence of the CJEU.

The Labour Court noted the difference and apparent conflict between the language used in the Act (ie 'continuous' fixed-term contracts) and the Directive (ie 'successive' fixed-term contracts):

> While s. 9 of the Act is directed at preventing the unlimited use of continuous fixed-term contracts, the objective of the Directive is to combat the abuse of successive fixed-term contracts. While the concept of successive periods of employment can include those which follow on from each other even if separated by time, the notion of continuous employment connotes broken service.

The High Court recognised the possible interpretative difficulty that might arise as a result of the different words used in the 2003 Act and in the Directive. Baker J agreed with the Labour Court's conclusion that any conflict between 'continuous' and 'successive' could be resolved by 'ascribing a liberal and expansive meaning' to the term 'layoff'. The Labour Court resolved this conflict by interpreting the national law, as far as possible, in light of the wording and purpose of the Directive, so as to achieve the purpose and desired results of the Directive. Referring to *Eircom Ltd v Commission for Communications Regulation*,[48] Baker J noted that:

> A court in applying a domestic statute which incorporates an EU Directive into domestic law may, and indeed must, have regard to the jurisprudence of the CJEU in interpreting the legislative provision.

The second aspect of the appeal was whether the contract in Sligo General Hospital was broken up into two separate contracts, the first of which terminated on the retirement of doctor M, for whom the complainant was appointed as a locum, and the second of which arose by implication thereafter.

The complainant commenced employment in Sligo General Hospital on 1 July 2007 but received a written contract on the later date of 1 October 2007. The contract expressly identified the post as that of a locum consultant obstetrician and gynaecologist. Prior to the commencement of employment, the parties engaged in negotiations relating to terms of the contract. An email sent by the HSE in June 2007 stated:

> You are being offered a Specified Purpose Contract as Locum Consultant to fill the post as Dr. M's Locum. You are not being offered a post of indefinite duration as this post is vacant on a temporary basis and the duration of such a post will cease on the return of Dr. M or until alternative arrangements are put in place'.

The Labour Court noted that the words 'until alternative arrangements are put in place' did not appear in the written contract and ruled that, in the absence of clarity, the *contra*

---

47.   Council Directive 99/70/EC of 28 June 1999 concerning the framework agreement on fixed-term work.

48.   *Eircom Ltd v Commission for Communications Regulation* [2006] IEHC 138, [2007] 1 IR 1.

proferentem rule of construction should be applied to the wording of the email (ie any ambiguity in the terms proposed must be resolved in favour of the applicant). The High Court ruled that the Labour Court was incorrect as a matter of law in using this interpretative rule in relation to the email of 27 June 2007. Baker J noted that the written contract was perfectly clear and did not require any parol evidence.[49]

The judge noted that the email was not an attempt to add or vary the terms of the contract; it was rather a mere explanation of the locum contract offered. Baker J referred to *Analog Devices BV v Zurich Insurance Co*[50] in which the Supreme Court concluded that the *contra proferentem* rule applied only when a contractual provision was ambiguous or capable of more than one interpretation. In that regard, the High Court held that even if the contract was not perfectly clear, this rule of construction does not assist in the interpretation of the vague and uncertain term 'alternative arrangements'.

The Labour Court accepted that the fixed-purpose locum contract expired 'when its purpose was discharged on the retirement of the [named] doctor'. The Labour Court concluded that the purpose of the contract was for the complainant to act as the doctor's locum unless and until another doctor was appointed for that specific purpose. That purpose expired on the retirement of the doctor, at which point a second contract came into existence and the Labour Court ruled that this contract was a contract of indefinite duration which arose pursuant to s 9 of the 2003 Act. The High Court rejected the contention that this was a finding of fact by the Labour Court and not amenable to appeal. Baker J ruled that the Labour Court was correct in its view that the Sligo contract was divisible and that the first contract ended on the retirement of the doctor.

The High Court then examined the Labour Court's finding that the second Sligo contract gave rise to a contract of indefinite duration under s 9(3) of the Act.

Section 9(3) of the Act provides:

> Where any term of a fixed-term contract purports to contravene subsection (1) or (2) that term shall have no effect and the contract concerned shall be deemed to be a contract of indefinite duration.

The Labour Court identified no breach of s 9(1) or 9(2) of the Act, rather its finding was made on the basis of the continued performance of the contractual obligations by both parties. The High Court held that the Labour Court was wrong as a matter of law in ruling that s 9(3) of the Act applied in this instance as there had been no breach under s 9(1) or 9(2).

In relation to the question of whether the complainant had *locus standi*, the respondent claimed that, on the date of the complaint, the complainant was employed under a contract of indefinite duration and accordingly the Act did not apply to him. Some controversy arose as to whether this was exactly what the Labour Court found. Baker J referred to *Ahmed v Health Service Executive*[51] and *Minister for Finance v*

---

49. Note: the parol evidence rule states that if an agreement between two parties is made in writing, the parties may not present evidence in court of any oral or implied agreement that contradicts what is written down.

50. *Analog Devices BV v Zurich Insurance Co* [2005] IESC 12.

51. *Ahmed v Health Service Executive* [2006] IEHC 245.

McArdle.[52] The judge held that the complainant could not be denied standing because he was at the time by operation of law deemed to be employed under a contract of indefinite duration. The Court held that the complainant 'had a right to litigate the question of his current employment status under the Act and has standing to do so'.

The High Court also described the Labour Court's engagement in an analysis of the factual nexus to determine whether there was actually an objective justification for the renewal of the contract operating the mind of the respondent as 'unnecessary and incorrect'. Baker J referred to *Health Executive Service Dublin North East v Umar*[53] which held that the recruitment of a consultant pending the filing of a post by open competition was objectively justified under the 2003 Act. In this case, the Labour Court examined correspondence and concluded that no justifying reason existed for the creation of a fixed-term contract in regard to the second Sligo contract. The High Court acknowledged that this was a finding of fact with which the Court could not interfere. However, Baker J accepted the argument from the respondent that all of the evidence pointed to the fact that the HSE did intend to fill the doctor's position. In light of *Umar*, the creation of a further fixed-term contract in such circumstances could be objectively justified. The High Court found that the Labour Court did not deal with the question of justification correctly and concluded that the Labour Court's finding may have been made on a hypothetical basis and did not form part of its decision on the facts.

The High Court concluded that the finding of the Labour Court that a contract of indefinite duration existed was incorrect. The Court noted that the Labour Court was entitled to take the view that a second contract of employment came into existence after the doctor retired as a matter of implication from the conduct of the parties. However, the Court ruled that s 9(3) of the Act did not apply to such a contract as there had been no breach of s 9(1) or 9(2) of the Act.

LOCUS STANDI

[7.14] *Frobel College of Education v Raftery*[54] *– Labour Court – Protection of Employees (Fixed-Term Work) Act 2003 – appeal of Rights Commissioner decision – preliminary issue – whether complainant had locus standi to bring complaint under the 2003 Act against respondent to whom she was seconded from her employment as primary school teacher with her permanent employer*

The complainant, a primary school teacher, worked for a national school in Dublin and, in mid-2007, she availed of a career break from the school for the academic year of 2007/2008, during which time she worked on a sessional basis for the respondent as a substitute lecturer and was paid an hourly rate of pay. In 2008 the complainant applied for and was granted a secondment from the national school with effect from 1 February 2008 until 31 August 2008 and began working on a fulltime basis for the respondent on the same salary band she had previously been on. The complainant continued to be paid

---

52.   *Minister for Finance v McArdle* [2007] IEHC 98.
53.   *Health Executive Service Dublin North East v Umar* [2011] IEHC 146.
54.   *Frobel College of Education v Raftery* FTD 144.

by the Department of Education & Skills during this time and a letter was sent by the chairperson of the board of management of the school to the respondent's principal confirming that the board of management agreed to the secondment of the complainant to the respondent during the period in question. In March 2008 the position the complainant had been filling was advertised and she applied and was the successful candidate. In April 2008, she was offered the position on a fixed-term basis from 1 September 2008 to 31 August 2012. The salary offered to her originally was the respondent's assistant lecturer scale. However, as the complainant received a different rate of pay (by being successful in a competition for promotional position as assistant principal of the national school) she was paid on the same salary band as would have applied to her had she remained working in the primary school. Her pay continued to be paid by the Department and the respondent reimbursed the Department accordingly.

In February 2012, the complainant was advised that she would be offered a further fixed-term contract of employment with the respondent for a period of one year. However, on review of the contract, the complainant was unhappy with certain of the intellectual property provisions and she did not accordingly accept the renewal.

Before the Rights Commissioner, the complainant claimed that the respondent was her employer and it had failed to offer her a contract of indefinite duration and she further claimed that the respondent was in breach of s 6 of the Act in failing to afford her same terms and conditions of employment as comparable permanent employees and had failed to provide her with a written statement setting out the objective grounds justifying the renewal of a fixed term arrangements in breach of s 8 of the Act. The Rights Commissioner found that as the complainant had only one fixed-term contract, no breach of s 9 of the Act had occurred, that the claim under s 8 of the Act was out of time and her claim under s 6 of the Act was not well founded. The complainant appealed to the Labour Court.

The Labour Court determined that there was a preliminary issue as to the identification of the complainant's employer and as to whether the complainant had the necessary *locus standi* to maintain a claim under the Act. A hearing took place in relation to this preliminary issue and both parties made detailed submissions. The complainant submitted that it was not appropriate for the Court to look outside the relationship that existed between the complainant and the respondent. As an employee of the respondent, employed on a fixed-term basis, and in accordance with the definition of fixed-term worker as provided for in the Directive and the Act, the complainant was not a permanent employee of the respondent. The complainant stated that the fact that there existed a relationship of employer/employee between the complainant and the primary school was wholly irrelevant, and counsel noted that the complainant had not worked in the school for nearly a decade. Counsel for the complainant stated that she had integrated into the business of the respondent, was under the direct control of the respondent, and was no longer in employment of the school, and that her employment with the school was at least suspended. Counsel further stated that there was no change in her employment status with the respondent and that while the Department paid her teaching salary, this was recouped from the respondent and the respondent became the 'de facto pay master' and thereby responsible for every element of the complainant's employment under the fixed-term contract. Counsel for the complainant sought to rely on the Supreme Court decision in *O'Keeffe v Hickey*[55] and noted that the complainant was fully under the control and direction of the respondent as its employee and was fully integrated into the business. She had no ongoing responsibility towards the school and had no rights or entitlements arising from any contract of employment with the school, save only a potential right to return at some time in the future.

The respondent submitted that it was not the employer of the complainant and that she was and still is employed by the primary school. Counsel for the respondent noted that the complainant required the consent of her employer and the Department to the secondment arrangement in order to perform her duties with the respondent. Counsel for the respondent cited a number of Labour Court decisions[56] and stated that the reasoning in these decisions, that an employee cannot be both a fixed-term employee and a permanent employee with the same employer, should extend to a secondment arrangement, as the complainant was merely loaned out to the respondent and continued to be employed by her permanent employer. Reliance was placed by counsel for the respondent on *Denham v Midland Employers Mutual Assurance Ltd*[57] where the UK Court of Appeal held that an employee who was loaned to another employer remained employed by the original employer as it is only the use and benefit of the employee's services which had been transferred. Counsel for the respondent noted that the respondent could not dismiss the complainant as this was solely within the ambit of her employer, ie the board of management of the school, and that the rate of pay was linked to the permanent post. It was further contended by the respondent that the complainant at all times enjoyed the benefit of having her full public sector entitlements, including pension rights, security of tenure, promotional rights and that her period of secondment was recognised as being continuous service of an employee with assistant principal status.

In considering this matter, the Labour Court stated that it must decide whether or not the complainant was a fixed-term employee within the definition in s 2 of the 2003 Act. The Court relied on its decision in *Louth County Council v Kelly*[58] where it had held that a worker cannot be protected under the Act where that worker is already a permanent employee on secondment.

The Court made particular reference to the correspondence supplied by the respondent, including correspondence from the chairperson of the board of management of the school, which made it clear that the school was required each year to consent to the complainant's ongoing secondment with the respondent and also a letter from the president of the respondent to the Primary Payment Section, Department of Education & Science (as it then was), dated January 2008, stating that they wish to apply for the

---

55.   *O'Keeffe v Hickey* [2008] IESC 72.

56.   *Athlone Institute of Technology v Hannify* FTD 1117 and *University College Cork v Nieuwstraten* FTD 1122.

57.   *Denham v Midland Employers Mutual Assurance Ltd* [1955] 2 QB 437.

58.   *Louth County Council v Kelly* FTD 1320.

secondment of the above teacher to take up a lecturing administrative position and enclosing a board of management letter giving permission for the secondment.

The Labour Court noted further letters relating to the Department's approval of the complainant's secondment arrangement to the respondent, which confirmed it was in line with Circular 11/2002, and also relating to the arrangements for recouping the costs associated with the secondment and the details of her salary. The Labour Court also referenced the fact that there was a secondment agreement between the school and the respondent dated 2012 which the complainant was prepared to sign. However, due to an issue with a clause relating to intellectual property rights, she declined to do so and the Court noted that in this agreement, there was reference to an employing entity, ie the school, and the secondee entity, ie the respondent, and the statement as follows: 'to assist the secondee entity in the conduct of its business, the employing entity is prepared to provide the services of its employee, Ms Mary Raftery, to the secondee entity on the terms set out below'.

The Court stated that there was little doubt that the complainant was on a secondment arrangement each year from February 2008 until the end of the academic year and that all parties to the arrangement were clearly aware of and freely entered into such an arrangement in line with Department policy. The Labour Court noted that, while on secondment, the complainant had applied for a promotional post as assistant principal in the school and thus the salary attached to the role she was performing with the respondent was substantially increased to reflect her success in attaining this position and she continued to be paid her public sector salary by the Department. While the complainant was employed with the respondent on the secondment arrangement, her role as assistant principal was filled on an 'acting-up' basis and continued at the date of hearing. The complainant never resigned her position with the school and had a right of return to that role and, unlike the respondent's other employees who did not have reductions in their salaries, as a public sector employee the complainant was subject to reductions in accordance with the Financial Emergency Measures in the Public Interest Acts 2009 and 2010. The Court held that this demonstrated that, although employed to do the work of a private sector employee, the complainant retained her public sector status.

It was accepted by the parties that the complainant's employment continued to be reckonable for all public sector benefits during the entire secondment period and that also she was on the Public Sector Superannuation Scheme which cost the respondent an additional 25% of salary, whereas the respondent's other employees were on a PRSA contributed to by the respondent at a rate of 5%.

The Labour Court stated that, for these reasons, it was satisfied that the complainant was and remained a permanent employee of the school, and that her employment status was never at risk while on secondment with the respondent. In order to come within the ambit of the Act, a complainant must have the status of a fixed-term worker and, as it had found in the past, a complainant who can revert to the substantive grade and whose employment continues at the end of a fixed-term assignment, does not enjoy the protection of the Act and thus the complainant did not have the requisite *locus standi* to maintain her complaint.

COMPARATORS

[7.15] *A University v A Worker[59] – Labour Court – appeal of Rights Commissioner decision – Protection of Employees (Fixed-Term Work) Act 2003 – Industrial Relations Acts 1946 to 2012 – whether complainant treated less favourably than comparable permanent employees when she was not paid ex gratia redundancy payment over and above statutory redundancy terms – whether complainant could rely on s 5(1)(c) to identify comparable and permanent employees within higher educational sector when there appeared to be appropriate comparators within respondent*

The complainant was employed with the respondent in the higher education sector on fixed-term contracts from January 2008 until her employment was terminated by reason of redundancy in June 2012. The facts of the redundancy were not at issue.

She brought a complaint citing less favourable treatment than a comparable permanent employee in not being paid the same ex gratia payments as four identified comparators within the meaning of s 5 of the 2003 Act. She asserted she was entitled to the same ex gratia redundancy payment as were paid to permanent employees in St Catherine's College of Education for Home Economics, a permanent employee of the Royal College of Surgeons, permanent catering staff of NUI Maynooth and a permanent employee in Wexford VEC, all of whom, she asserted, received four weeks' pay per year of service in addition to statutory redundancy entitlements.

The complainant submitted that there were no proper internal comparators within s 5(1)(a) and (b) of the Act. She stated that the internal comparator cited by the respondent had been a person who had acquired a contract of indefinite duration and thus could not be held to be a permanent employee. She also sought to rely on the Labour Court determination in *University College Cork v Bushin*[60] where the Court held that the cited institutions and the respondent are in the higher educational sector and it was satisfied that the s 5(1)(c) of the Act was applicable.

The respondent, in denying the allegations, stated that the complainant was treated no less favourably in terms of the redundancy. Other permanent staff members were paid statutory redundancy and did not receive ex gratia redundancy terms. It was submitted by the respondent that they were the appropriate comparators under s 5(1)(a) and therefore the complainant's claim had no merit. The respondent disputed the complainant's reliance on the *UCC v Bushin* case or indeed staff in NUI Maynooth, contending that, by reason of s 5 of the Act, one must seek internal comparators in the employment in the first place and it is only where there are no such comparators that the complainant would be permitted to look for a comparator outside employment.

The Labour Court considered the relevant statutory provisions applicable in this case. The Court held that the combined effect of the statutory provisions is that a fixed-term employee is entitled to be treated no less favourably in respect of his or her conditions of employment than a comparable permanent employee, unless the difference

---

59.   *A University v A Worker* FTD 142.

60.   *University College Cork v Bushin* FTD1121.

in treatment is justified on objective grounds. The Court also noted that it had already been decided that ex gratia redundancy pay does constitute remuneration within the meaning of the Act. The Court concluded that s 5 of the Act provided that, in choosing a comparator, the complainant must under s 5(1)(a) first examine their own employer and any associated employer for a valid comparator. If unsuccessful, the complainant must proceed under s 5(1)(b) to examine any employees employed under a collective agreement, which agreement also affects them. If unsuccessful under s 5(1)(c) of the Act, the complainant may seek a comparator in the same industry or sector of employment with the proviso that the selected comparator must be engaged in the same or similar work or in work of equal or greater value. The Court stated that it was satisfied that s 5(1)(a) was applicable in this case as the respondent had correctly identified at least one internal comparator who was treated in the same manner as the complainant in that they were similarly made redundant with no ex gratia redundancy payment. The Court further noted that there was a collective agreement in place within the public sector regarding enhanced redundancy terms. However, the Court found that as s 5(1)(a) applied, there was no necessity to examine s 5(1)(b) or (c). Thus, the Court found that the complainant's claim was not well-founded and the appeal was rejected.

UNFAIR DISMISSALS CLAIM ARISING OUT OF A TERMINATION OF EMPLOYMENT AND FAILURE TO PROVIDE A CONTRACT OF INDEFINITE DURATION

[7.16] *Cunning v Dublin Institute of Technology*[61] *– Employment Appeals Tribunal – Unfair Dismissals Act 1977 to 2007 as amended – successive fixed-term and specified purpose contracts – failure to provide contract of indefinite duration pursuant to Protection of Employment (Fixed Term Work) Act 2003, s 9 – whether claimant unfairly dismissed*

The claimant was employed by the respondent as an assistant lecturer on a succession of fixed-term and specified-purpose contracts in a full-time capacity from 2006 until 2011 to cover for an employee, Dr C, who went on a career break and subsequently, to job share with Dr C on a part-time basis from 3 October 2011 until the cessation of her specified purpose contract on 31 August 2012.

In November 2011, Dr C tendered his resignation to the respondent, and the claimant was dismissed in on 1 December 2011, after the effective date of Dr C's resignation.

The claimant contended that her dismissal:

(i)   was outside of the remit of her contract, which did not specify that the resignation of the post holder was a reason to terminate her employment and contained a 'continuity of employment' clause; and

(ii)   caused a disruption to students, some of whom were left without a lecturer and other MSc thesis students were reallocated a supervisor two weeks before their submission deadline.

---

61.   *Cunning v Dublin Institute of Technology* UD1006/2012.

The claimant contended that she was dismissed to punish her for seeking a contract of indefinite duration and her employment was terminated in order to break her service, to deny her claim for a contract of indefinite duration and, ultimately, to impede her progression from assistant lecturer to lecturer.

The EAT noted that the claimant was initially employed on a fixed-term contract dated 11 November 2006, with an express termination date of 31 August 2007. The second contract was a specific purpose contract commencing on 1 September 2007 to cover a career break. The contract stated:

> This is a specific purpose contract, insofar as you are replacing Dr. C who has been granted a career break extension.

There was no termination date specified in this contract.

The EAT noted that the claimant received a letter dated 17 July 2008 from the respondent notifying her that her contract would cease on 31 August 2008. This letter provided that the claimant had been recommended for re-appointment, and that she would be employed on a specified purpose contract to cover Dr C's extended career break. A further letter was provided to the claimant on 22 July 2010, renewing her employment for the specific purpose of covering Dr C's leave. The EAT stated that it was noteworthy that the terms and conditions in relation to her remuneration changed.

The claimant's final contract was issued on 3 October 2011, but she did not sign the contract as she wrote to the HR manager on 3 October 2012 enquiring about her entitlement to a contract of indefinite duration. There is no written contract of employment between 31 August 2008 and 3 October 2011.

The respondent submitted that the claimant was employed on a specific purpose contract to cover for Dr C's career break for the entirety of her employment and that specific purpose ceased when he resigned. The EAT commented that if that was the case, it was difficult to comprehend why the letter of 17 July 2008 was issued at all and why a new contract would issue on 3 October 2011 in circumstances where the specific purpose remained consistent throughout that period.

The EAT did not accept the respondent's claim that the letter of 17 July 2008 was sent in error. It found that it was a very specific letter terminating the claimant's contract and it requested that she sign an acceptance letter should she wish to enter into another contract. The claimant duly signed this, and accepted the offer of a new contract, however the respondent failed to issue the contract, and the claimant worked on until October 2011 without a contract.

The EAT held that it had jurisdiction to hear the claim by reason of s 2(2)(b) of the Unfair Dismissals Act 1977 which is in the following terms:

> dismissal where the employment was under a contract of employment for a fixed term or for a specified purpose (being a purpose of such a kind that the duration of the contract was limited but was, at the time of its making, incapable of precise ascertainment) and the dismissal consisted only of the expiry of the term without its being renewed under the said contract or the cesser of the purpose and the contract is in writing, was signed by or on behalf of the employer and by the employee and provides that this Act shall not apply to a dismissal consisting only of the expiry or cesser aforesaid ...

The EAT noted that the claimant received two specific letters of termination from the respondent, one on 17 July 2008 and one on 21 July 2011, however, she had never actually ceased working for the respondent. The EAT found that the claimant had been working on successive fixed-term contracts with the full knowledge and consent of the respondent for a period exceeding four years, and therefore held that the respondent had failed to comply with its obligations under the s 9 of the Protection of Employment (Fixed Term Work) Act 2003 in failing to provide the claimant with a contract of indefinite duration.

Notwithstanding the respondent's assertion that the claimant was only ever employed on a specific purpose contract, the Tribunal held that the reality of the situation was that the claimant was given a series of contracts, some fixed, some deemed specific purpose and some implied.

The EAT upheld the claim of unfair dismissal and awarded the claimant compensation of €14,978.

NATIONAL EXCLUSIONS FROM THE STATUTORY ENTITLEMENTS

[7.17] *Fiamingo & Ors v Rete Ferroviaria Italiana SpA[62] – CJEU – maritime sector – successive fixed-term employment contracts – Framework Agreement on Fixed-Term work concluded by ETUC, UNICE and CEEP – clause 3(1) – concept of 'fixed-term employment contract' – clause 5(1) – measures to prevent abuse arising from use of fixed-term contracts – ferries crossing between two ports in same Member State*

This was a preliminary reference from the Italian *Corte de Cassation* (Italian Supreme Court) on the interpretation of cls 3 and 5 of the Framework Agreement on Fixed-term work.[63]

The appellants were seafarers, employed by Rete Ferroviaria Italiana SpA (RFI) from 2001 under successive fixed-term contracts concluded for one or several voyages and for a maximum of 78 days. The appellants worked for RFI for less than one year, with periods of less than 60 days elapsing in each gap between contracts.

Italian employment contracts of seafarers are governed by the Navigation Code. The Code specifies one year as the maximum duration of fixed-term contracts and requires specification of the start date and duration of the contract. The Code states every contract concluded for a period exceeding one year is a contract of indefinite duration. If several contracts are concluded for a fixed term, or for specified voyages, the employment is considered to be continuous where no more than 60 days elapse between contracts. Those employment relationships are thus not subject to the legislation which was adopted to specifically implement the Framework Agreement on fixed-term work.

The appellants claimed their employment relationship had been unlawfully terminated following their disembarkation. They wanted their fixed-term contracts

---

62. *Fiamingo & Ors v Rete Ferroviaria Italiana SpA* (Cases C–362/13, C–363/13, and C–407/13).
63. Council Directive 1999/70/EC of 28 June 1999 concerning the Framework Agreement on fixed-term work concluded by ETUC, UNICE and CEEP ([1999] OJ L 175/43).

declared void and converted into contracts of indefinite duration and sought reinstatement and compensation for loss suffered.

The Italian Court asked the CJEU whether the Framework Agreement applies to maritime labour and whether it permits national legislation as per the terms contained in the Navigation Code.

In summary the CJEU found that:

(i)   the Framework Agreement covers all 'fixed-term workers' and so was applicable to the seafarers' contracts;

(ii)   the Maritime Labour Convention of 2006 (MLC 2006), does not apply to seafarers employed on ships navigating exclusively in internal waters (as was the case here);

(iii)   it follows that all other provisions of EU law which are more specific or afford a higher degree of protection are applicable to seafarers. That is the case with the Framework Agreement;

(iv)   to prevent abuse of successive fixed-term contracts, the Framework Agreement obliges Member States to provide for objective reasons justifying the renewal of the contract, the maximum total duration of such contracts and the number of possible renewals of the contract. There is no requirement for conversion of fixed-term contracts into contracts of indefinite duration or specified conditions in which contracts of indefinite duration may be used, provided that national law – whatever measure is chosen – is effective in preventing the misuse of fixed-term employment contracts;

(v)   Italian legislation was proportionate since it provides for both a preventative measure (maximum duration of one year for successive fixed-term contracts) and a penalty in the event of abuse;

(vi)   when ruling on the use of successive fixed-term contracts, national courts must examine circumstances of the case, taking into account the number of successive contracts concluded with the same person or for the purposes of performing the same work;

(vii) a finding of abuse might be made if the maximum duration is calculated, not by reference to the number of calendar days covered by the contract, but by reference to the number of days' service actually completed by the employees; and

(viii) as the Framework Agreement contained no provisions regarding the formal particulars that must be included in fixed-term contracts, Italy was entitled under EU law, to provide in its legislation that only the duration of the contract (and not its termination date) has to be stated.

Chapter 8

FREEDOM OF INFORMATION

RELEVANT LEGISLATION

The Freedom of Information Act 2014

[8.01] The Freedom of Information Act 2014 was enacted on 14 October 2014. The reform rendered by this Act represents the most significant development in freedom of information (FOI) law in Ireland in over a decade. The Minister for Public Expenditure and Reform, Brendan Howlin, explained that the update to the law contained in the Act is intended to:

> restore the legislation and extend it to almost all public bodies, as well as consolidating and modernising it to improve the functioning of the Act and to improve the structure of the legislative framework.

[8.02] The Act represents a major overhaul of the current legislation, the Freedom of Information Act 1997, as amended by the Freedom of Information (Amendment) Act 2003 (together the previous Act), and the scope of FOI has been expanded to include almost all public bodies (including a number of high profile public bodies), as opposed to the specific schedule of prescribed bodies subject to the terms of the previous Act. Some of the key amendments introduced by the Act are discussed below.

What bodies are subject to FOI?

[8.03] The Act contains a broad definition of 'public body' which enables FOI to apply to all public bodies (an FOI body) unless specifically exempt. As new public bodies are established, they will automatically be subject to the terms of FOI, although provision is made for the Minister to make an order to specifically exclude certain bodies, in whole or in part, if required.

[8.04] The Act contains exemptions for some bodies so as not to affect the ability of these bodies to perform their core functions or in the interests of the security or financial position of the State. In this regard An Garda Síochána, the National Treasury Management Agency Group, the Central Bank of Ireland, the industrial relations bodies, the Insolvency Service of Ireland and the various Ombudsmen will all enjoy exemptions in part (of varying degrees and kinds). While the Act continues to exempt in full from FOI most commercial State bodies, records of those parties who provide services to a FOI body under a contract for services will be subject to the new Act (and this may include commercial State bodies to the extent that they provide services to a FOI body). Notably Irish Water and Eirgrid plc are excluded from the exempt agencies in the Act and accordingly they are FOI bodies.

Have the access rules changed?

[8.05] As before, the stated objective of the legislation is to ensure that official information is available to citizens to the greatest extent feasible, consistent with the public interest in safeguarding highly confidential and very sensitive information. In furtherance of this general principle, the Act introduces key principles to guide public bodies in the performance of their functions under the Act, regarding the need: (a) to achieve greater openness and promote transparency in Government and public affairs; and (b) to strengthen the accountability of public bodies and improve the quality of decision making.

[8.06] The Act provides that there is a general right of access to records and they should be released unless they are found to be exempt, and, in applying these exemptions, the right of access is only to be set aside where the exemptions very clearly support a refusal of access. The explanatory memorandum which accompanied the first version of the FOI Bill (published on 22 July 2013) explains that this amendment was considered necessary arising from the Supreme Court decision in *The Governors and Guardians of the Hospital for the Relief of Poor Lying-In Women v Information Commissioner*[1] (which found that in circumstances where a tension exists between a right of access under FOI and an exemption from disclosure under Pt III of the previous Act, the previous Act mandated a refusal of information).

[8.07] Exercise of the right to access records is dealt with in a similar fashion to the previous Act. However, in the interests of minimising the cost to the requester, and for administrative efficiency, an FOI body may advise a requester whether the records concerned may be accessed under: (a) the European Communities (Re-use of Public Sector Information) Regulations 2005 (SI 279/2005); or (b) the European Communities (Access to Information on the Environment) Regulations 2007 (SI 133/2011), instead of under FOI.

Does the Act take account of technological developments in record management?

[8.08] In advance of the commencement of the Act, the Minister commented that:

> the current legislation was essentially designed to deal primarily with paper records and the legislative framework for FOI needs to be updated to reflect the transformation that has taken place in ICT since that time. Many requesters use new technologies and seek records in electronic format and we must work with that and try to facilitate the provision of records in open format as much as possible in line with our Open Government objectives.

---

1. *The Governors and Guardians of the Hospital for the Relief of Poor Lying-In Women v Information Commissioner* [2011] IESC 26.

With this sentiment in mind, s 17 of the Act sets out the responsibility of FOI bodies in relation to requests for information contained in more than one record held electronically by the FOI body. Section 17(4) of the Act had been subject to revision during the legislative procedure. Departing from the position under the previous Act, FOI bodies are required to take reasonable steps to search for and extract such data, being steps that involve the use of any facility for electronic search or extraction that existed at the date of the request and was used by the FOI body in the ordinary course. Earlier drafts of the Bill had benchmarked the search of electronic files to that which would be considered reasonable with reference to an analogous search of a paper file. Section 17 of the Act also creates the potential for response to a request under the Act to require the creation of new records (although these records will not be relevant to the original request as per s 17(4)(b)).

[8.09] The provision relieving an FOI body of the obligation to take steps involving the creation of any program or code for the purpose of searching for or extracting the data (which existed in previous iterations of the FOI Bill) has been removed from the Act, as has the provision which relieved an FOI body of the obligation to carry out any manipulation, analysis, compilation or other processing of the data. In this sense, the search and retrieval obligations on an FOI body in relation to electronic searches could be said to be more extensive in the Act than in previous iterations of the Bill and, in any case, are more explicit than under the previous Act. The Act provides that where records are available in such form, they may be released in electronic and searchable format.

How does the Act address grounds for refusal of access to records?

[8.10] The Act considers refusal of access from a number of perspectives, most notably via administrative grounds, as well as through the operation of certain exemptions (Pt 4 of the Act).

Administrative ground for refusal

[8.11] The Act largely preserves the administrative grounds under s 10 of the previous Act but also adds some additional administrative grounds for refusal, such as: (a) if the FOI body intends to publish the record concerned within six weeks after receipt of the request; or (b) where the request relates to records already released to a requester. As under the previous Act, it remains permissible to refuse a request on administrative grounds if granting the request would cause substantial and unreasonable interference with or disruption of the work of the body concerned, although this provision is amended to provide that a refusal can be made on the basis of disruption to the work of a particular functional area, rather than only to the body as a whole.

Exempt records

[8.12] Certain of the exemptions are narrowed in application. For example the protection of records relating to meetings of the Government is restored to the position in s 19 of the Freedom of Information Act 1997, ie prior to the commencement of the Freedom of Information (Amendment) Act 2003. Records relating to the deliberative process may be refused, but only where disclosure would be contrary to the public interest, again substantially returning this provision to its position under the 1997 Act. The period during which records of Government are exempt from FOI is reduced from ten to five years (this had increased to 10 years under the 2003 Act). An anomaly is removed by allowing information obtained orally in confidence, and noted by a member of staff of a FOI body, to enjoy the same protections as information received in writing or electronic means.

[8.13] Where the disclosure of information could reasonably be expected to have serious adverse effects on the financial interests of the State or the ability of the Government to manage the economy, it continues to be open to exemption, with additional types of records being potentially added to the classes of records covered by this exemption including:

(i)   records relating to investment by or on behalf of the State or a FOI body;

(ii) records relating to liabilities of the State or a FOI body; and

(iii) records advising on or managing public infrastructure projects, including PPP arrangements.

Have the fees been reduced?

[8.14] The search and retrieval fees regime has been revised such that there are a number of factors to take into account when determining the fee to be charged to a requester. The upfront application fee of €15 per non-personal request has been abolished and the fee for internal review has been reduced from €75 to €30. The fee for an appeal to the Information Commissioner has also been reduced to €50 (from €150). Most notably, a search and retrieval fee will not be charged where the requester is requesting only those records pertaining to his or her personal information unless the request relates to a significant number of records and, in this respect, the means of the requester will be taken into account.

Does the Information Commissioner have any additional powers? Are there any penalties for non-compliance?

[8.15] The Act allows, for the first time, the Commissioner to apply for a Court order to oblige a covered body to comply with a binding decision of the Commissioner where that body has failed to do so. Furthermore it is an offence to wilfully and without lawful excuse either destroy or alter a record that is the subject of an FOI request (with a Class B fine on summary conviction, ie up to €4,000). These are welcome reforms as the enforcement powers of the Commissioner in the previous Act were widely regarded as unsatisfactory, as were the consequences for non-compliance with the requirements of the previous Act.

Can a decision of the Information Commissioner be appealed?

[8.16] The grounds for an appeal have been broadened to allow an appeal to the High Court on a finding of fact in a case where a person contends that the release of a record would contravene a requirement imposed by EU law. In addition, the timescale to initiate an appeal to the High Court is reduced from eight weeks to four weeks on the recommendation of the Commissioner, although where a request is granted only in part by the Commissioner, the time limit for a requester to make an appeal to the High Court remains at eight weeks.

When will these new rules take effect?

[8.17] Public bodies brought within the ambit of FOI for the first time were allowed a lead-in period of six months after the law was enacted to allow them to prepare for FOI. As it currently stands, this lead-in period expires on 14 April 2015. However, this period may be extended by the Minister by order under the Act, subject to a business case being made to the Minister. The Act applies retrospectively from 21 April 2008 in the case of an entity that, prior to enactment of the new law, was not a public body within the meaning of the previous Act.

Next steps for public bodies

[8.18] For those bodies previously subject to FOI, ss 15 and 16 of the previous Act, which required that a FOI body maintain manuals outlining its structures and functions, detailing the services it provides, etc, are replaced by a requirement that FOI bodies establish a 'publication scheme' to promote the proactive publication of information outside of FOI. This scheme is intended to specify the classes of information that the FOI body has published or intends to publish, the terms on which it will make this available and any fees. When preparing a publication scheme, FOI bodies must have regard for the public interest:

(i)   in allowing access to information;

(ii) in providing reasons for decisions; and

(iii) in publishing information on its functions and activities.

There are detailed provisions setting out the information all publication schemes must include.

It was foreseen that in parallel with the enactment of the Act, a Code of Practice for FOI would be introduced; however, this has not yet occurred. Furthermore, it was thought that the Minister may make available model publication schemes for FOI bodies or guidelines on publication schemes for FOI bodies. A draft Code of Practice for Freedom of Information for Public Bodies has been made available by the FOI Central Unit of the Department of Public Expenditure and Reform. However, neither a final version of this Code of Practice nor any model publication schemes have yet been published.

RELEVANT CASE LAW/INFORMATION COMMISSIONER CASE STUDIES

[8.19] *Minister for Health v The Information Commissioner & Ors[2] – High Court – O'Neill J – records of judicial inquiry cannot be disclosed by Department of Health*

On 9 May 2014, O'Neill J allowed an appeal from the decision of the Commissioner and determined that the Minister for Health was not entitled to grant access to documents which had been lodged for safe keeping with the Department of Health as part of an inquiry into practices at Our Lady of Lourdes Hospital, Drogheda. O'Neill J found that for a document to be 'held' within the meaning of the previous Act, it must be either lawfully created by the public body in question or lawfully provided to that public body or lawfully obtained by the public body, in connection with the functions or business of that public body. Furthermore, the document must not be subject to any prior legal prohibition affecting its disclosure. O'Neill J was satisfied that the Department was not the legal owner of the record, and nor was there any basis upon which it could legitimately assert any form of control over the record resulting in the record being 'held' by the Department for the purposes of the previous Act. The High Court took the view that the only party who could assert a proprietorial interest or any other form of legal control over the document was the person who lodged the record for sake keeping and accordingly made an order setting aside the decision of the Commissioner.

[8.20] *Westwood Club v Information Commissioner and Bray Town Council[3] – High Court – Cross J – judicial review – Ombudsman and Information Commissioner's decision on financial records disclosure overturned*

Westwood Club successfully challenged a decision of the Commissioner to affirm Bray Town Council's refusal to grant Westwood Club access to the financial records of a competitor, Bray Swimming Pool and Sports Leisure Centre Ltd (trading as 'Shoreline'). In 2007, Shoreline signed a contract for construction of a pool in Bray. The Shoreline Board comprised directors of nominating bodies approved by Bray Town Council as well as some members of Bray Town Council. The project was also partially funded by the Council and by the Department of Arts, Sport and Tourism. After making an FOI request, Westwood Club was informed by the Council's FOI officer that Shoreline was a private company and therefore not subject to the previous Act. On foot of an appeal by Westwood Club, the Commissioner upheld her investigator's preliminary view that the Council was not required to disclose the records, partly on the grounds that the Council did not control the day-to-day operation of Shoreline and Shoreline was in business of its own account. Cross J found that the Council controlled Shoreline and the Commissioner's conclusion to the contrary was an error of law.

---

2. *Minister for Health v The Information Commissioner & Ors* [2014] IEHC 231.
3. *Westwood Club v Information Commissioner and Bray Town Council* [2014] IEHC 375.

Courts Service publishes judges' names in relation to expenses

[8.21] On 16 October 2014, the Courts Service released a breakdown by name of judicial expense claims. This followed a decision in August 2014 by the current Commissioner, Peter Tyndall, that the Irish Courts Service was not justified in withholding the names of individual judges when releasing information relating to judges expenses.

Details of judges' expenses had previously been released by the Courts Service on an anonymised basis since the organisation came under the remit of the previous Act. The Courts Service and the Garda Commissioner raised concerns about the release of the names in the context of judges' personal security. The Commissioner dismissed the objections holding that concerns about judges' personal safety were 'speculative in nature'.

NEW INFORMATION COMMISSIONER

[8.22] In December 2013, the Government announced the appointment of Mr Peter Tyndall as Information Commissioner to succeed Ms Emily O'Reilly. He also serves as Commissioner for Environmental Information. Mr Tyndall previously served as Public Services Ombudsman for Wales.

Chapter 9

HEALTH AND SAFETY

PENALISATION

[9.01] ***Bus Éireann v Browne[1] – Labour Court – appeal of a Rights Commissioner decision – Industrial Relations Acts 1946 to 2012 – Safety, Health and Welfare at Work Act 2005, s 29(1) – penalisation for making complaint of bullying and harassment – consideration of circumstances constituting penalisation***

The complainant, a clerical officer, appealed a Rights Commissioner's finding that she had failed to demonstrate that the respondent had penalised her for making a complaint of bullying and harassment under the 2005 Act.

Following her complaint of bullying and harassment in April 2010, the complainant and the respondent entered into a mediation agreement. In April 2012, the complainant complained that her supervisor had breached the terms of the mediation agreement and that a further incident occurred on 3 May 2012 which resulted in the complainant's supervisor being required to publicly apologise to her.

Following this, the complainant went on sick leave. The respondent subsequently wrote to the complainant, asking if she wished to use the formal grievance procedure. She confirmed that she did and two internal investigators were appointed to look into the complaints. When the complainant returned from sick leave on 12 September 2012, she was transferred to a different section on 25 October 2012, where she no longer had flexitime arrangements. On 23 October 2012, the complainant's solicitors lodged a claim asserting that the change in her circumstances constituted penalisation of her for making a complaint of bullying and harassment in April 2010.

In this appeal, the Labour Court examined the detriment that the complainant alleged constituted penalisation by the respondent. Firstly, the complainant asserted that the respondent's delay in preparing the report into her grievances constituted an omission which operated to her detriment. The Labour Court found that, on numerous occasions, the investigators had attempted to obtain submissions from the complainant which she failed to provide in a timely manner. On that basis, the Labour Court held that the complainant contributed to the delay and could not claim that the employer acted to her detriment in this regard.

The complainant also contended that the respondent's decision to relocate her when she returned from sick leave, the removal of her flexitime arrangement and the failure to notify her of a temporary promotional position, were retaliatory measures in response to her bringing a bullying and harassment claim in April 2010. The Labour Court noted that all of the above complaints related to incidents which occurred after she made the complaint of penalisation under the 2005 Act and therefore the Labour Court had no jurisdiction to hear the claims in hearing the appeal from the Rights Commissioner.

---

1.   *Bus Éireann v Browne* HSD1317.

The complainant argued that the respondent would have made the decision to transfer her prior to her return to work, and therefore the complaints were within the Labour Court's jurisdiction. The Labour Court accepted evidence from the respondent that the complainant had actually requested not to be placed in the same department as her supervisor, and that it had been explained to her that her new role did not have flexitime as it was a public interface role.

The Labour Court referred to *O'Neill v Toni & Guy Blackrock*[2] which established that, in order to establish a complaint of penalisation, the complainant must demonstrate that the detriment endured was imposed for having committed a protected act. The detriment must be retaliation for the complainant making a claim.

In this instance, the Labour Court was satisfied that the complainant could not establish a causal link between the change in her circumstances and her complaints in April 2010. The Labour Court also noted that the respondent's explanations for the change in circumstances were 'fair and reasonable'.

The Labour Court therefore found that the complainant had not established a nexus between the detriments complained of and her bullying complaints and it rejected her appeal.

[9.02] *Stobart (Ireland) Driver Services Ltd v Carroll*[3] *– High Court – Kearns P – appeal of decision of Labour Court on point of law – s 27 of the Safety Health and Welfare at Work Act 2005 – whether dismissal of respondent from his employment with appellant constituted penalisation under s 27 of 2005 Act – principles governing appeal on point of law – role of specialist tribunal such as Labour Court*

The respondent was employed by the appellant company as a truck driver. The appellant terminated his employment on 14 October 2011 after the respondent had made a complaint of being tired and unable to fulfil his driving duties. On 12 October 2011, the respondent completed a driving shift involving a 15.5-hour return journey from Dublin to Ballinasloe, inclusive of breaks of 1.75 hours. Before departing on this journey, the respondent's manager advised him that his next shift would begin the next day on 13 October at 23.55. The respondent asked not to be rostered that day as he believed he had worked excessive (53) hours. The respondent's manager took the position that drivers could work up to 60 hours but said that he would look into it. The respondent was told to speak to another manager, which he did on his return to site on the morning of 13 October 2011. That manager told the respondent to go home and get some sleep before commencing the shift later that evening at 23.55. The respondent left the site at 10.30 and went home to bed. He was advised that if he had a grievance he could pursue it through the appellant's grievance procedure.

The respondent woke at approximately 16.40 to a number of missed calls from a member of management. On checking his voicemails the respondent had a message from the manager that, having checked records, the respondent had worked 47 hours and had not yet reached his maximum working hours. A voicemail message informed him that his shift was due to start at 23.45. The respondent telephoned to speak with the

---

2.   *O'Neill v Toni & Guy Blackrock* HSDO95.
3.   *Stobart [Ireland] Driver Services Ltd v Carroll* [2013] IEHC 581.

manager but he was off site so he spoke with another manager. A number of conversations ensued in which the respondent repeatedly stated that he was too tired to drive. In the course of the last of these conversations at 18.45, the respondent advised that he was too tired to drive. The respondent went back to bed after being informed that the run would be left open. The respondent was concerned that his job might be at risk so later that evening he called his work to take on the shift but was informed that alternative arrangements had been made. The next day, 14 October 2011, the respondent received a letter from the appellant dismissing him on grounds that his withdrawal of labour was deemed to be a refusal of a reasonable management request/instruction and, under the appellant's disciplinary procedure, was deemed to amount to gross misconduct.

The Rights Commissioner decided that the respondent's complaint was well-founded and required the appellant to reinstate the respondent on his previous terms and to compensate him for his loss of wages.

In its appeal to the Labour Court, the appellant employer asserted that the Rights Commissioner had erred, that the respondent had not made out a claim of penalisation under s 27 of the Safety Health and Welfare Work Act 2005, that the respondent had not shown he had suffered a detriment within the meaning of s 27 as a result of a protected activity and that the remedy of reinstatement fell outside the remit of the Rights Commissioner. The respondent asserted that he represented to his employer that he was too fatigued to perform the driving as requested by the appellant. He contended that his actions came within s 13(a) of the 2005 Act and that he was 'complying with the relevant statutory provisions as appropriate to take reasonable care to protect his or her safety, health, welfare and safety of any other person who may be effected by the employee's act or omissions at work'.

The Labour Court upheld the respondent's claim and found that the respondent's notification to management of his tiredness did come within the parameters of actively complying with the relevant statutory procedures provided for within s 27(3)(a) of the 2005 Act. The decision to dismiss the respondent followed immediately after the complaint took place concerning his request not to be scheduled for duty. The Labour Court noted that the dismissal was carried out in a very precipitous manner and did not follow the appellant's disciplinary procedures and was a departure from its normal practice. The Labour Court concluded that, in these circumstances, the proximity of the dismissal following the raising of a health and safety matter raised a causal connection between the detriment complained of and the invoking of the 2005 Act. In summary, the Labour Court was satisfied that, but for the representations made by the respondent about being too tired to work, he would not have been dismissed as these were the reasons for his refusal to work.

The High Court considered the relevant statutory provisions in ss 13(1)(a) and 27 of the 2005 Act as amended. It was submitted to the High Court by the appellant that the Labour Court fell into an error of law in its analysis of the evidence and application of the relevant law. It was further submitted to the High Court that the respondent's notification of tiredness to management cannot be deemed to fall within s 27 of the 2005 Act. The appellant also claimed that the remedy of reinstatement as awarded by the Labour Court was not an appropriate remedy in the circumstances. The respondent asserted that he was dismissed after he had made a health and safety claim to the appellant in contravention of s 27 of the 2005 Act.

The High Court noted that there was no requirement in the 2005 Act to report any complaint via a grievance procedure. The 2005 Act specifically states 'report as soon as is practicable' and thus the respondent could be deemed to have made his complaint when he reported that he was too tired to drive. The High Court found that there was no requirement that he be 'at work' in the strict sense of the term when he does so, so long as the work was 'likely to be carried on'.[4]

The High Court concluded that, to limit an employee's ability to report a complaint to working hours, would greatly inhibit the application of the 2005 Act. The High Court noted that the Labour Court had the benefit of oral evidence, documentary evidence and legal submissions from both parties and it comprehensively considered the applicable law. Kearns P noted that the principles governing an appeal on a point of law from the Labour Court were well settled by the Superior Courts.

There is significant deference extended to a specialist tribunal which has heard and assessed the evidence. Kearns P stated that the High Court may only interfere in a finding of an expert tribunal where there was no evidence whatsoever to support it. In this regard, the Court noted the judgment of the Supreme Court in *Mara (Inspector of Taxes) v Hummingbird Ltd*.[5] Kearns P held that it could not be said that, by not invoking the grievance procedure, the respondent cannot be considered to have made a complaint under s 13 of the 2005 Act, as to do so would require the respondent to make a formal complaint, to work the shift for which he was fatigued, and then afterwards the issue he raised could be addressed. Kearns P held that this made no sense and put in peril both the fatigued employee and those he may encounter while driving a heavy duty truck over a long distance.

The High Court concluded that the reasons given by the Labour Court for its decision, including the decision to reinstate the respondent were adequate. Kearns P noted that the issue of reinstatement was a controversial issue and that, in this particular case, it was a significant step to direct. Kearns P noted that in most cases reinstatement may be impractical or even unworkable because of the lost trust and broken relationships. However he ruled that these were of minimum importance here as the respondent spends a large amount of his working time on the road and has minimum interaction with his employers. The High Court noted that the remedies specified in s 28(3)(b) of the 2005 Act included 'requiring an employer to take the specific course of action' and this, in the High Court's view, could be interpreted to include reinstatement.

It was submitted by the appellant that relief should not be granted because the respondent only had 11 months and three weeks service and thus did not have the requisite service under the Unfair Dismissals Acts 1977 to 2007 as amended. Kearns P noted that the respondent alleged he was penalised under s 27 for a complaint made by him under s 13 of the Act of 2005. It may not be submitted that the respondent was unfairly dismissed but that he was penalised due to his complaint made under s 13 and this resulted in a penalisation by way of dismissal as per s 27. Kearns P noted that s 27

---

4.   Safety, Health and Welfare at Work Act 2005, s 13(1)(h).
5.   *Mara (Inspector of Taxes) v Hummingbird Ltd* [1982] 2 IRLM 421.

provides that penalisation can include 'suspension, lay-off or dismissal including a dismissal within the meaning of the Unfair Dismissals Acts 1977 to 2007 as amended or the threat of a suspension or dismissal'. The High Court held that penalisation includes a dismissal under the Unfair Dismissals Act but does not in any way limit it to dismissal under that Act.

The High Court noted that both the Rights Commissioner and the Labour Court, to which the High Court extends deference, concluded that the respondent was subject to penalisation as set out by s 27 of the 2005 Act for making his complaint under s 13 of the same Act. Kearns P stated it was notable that the ethos behind the 2005 Act was to ensure the health and safety of employees and those they may encounter in the course of their work. Kearns P stated there was no issue as to fair procedures as it was not a mandatory requirement that a grievance procedure be followed for a complaint to have been deemed to have been made.

The High Court held that the respondent had acted appropriately in reporting his fatigue and was subject to penalisation as described by s 27 of the Act of 2005. The High Court dismissed the appellant's appeal and upheld the determination of the Labour Court.

[9.03] *Stobart (Ireland) Driver Services Ltd v Carroll*[6] *– Labour Court – action remitted to Labour Court from High Court to reach determination on respondent's loss of income*

As a question concerning the loss of income arising from the respondent's termination of employment could not be resolved between the parties following the judgment of the High Court, it was referred to the High Court and in turn remitted to the Labour Court with guidance that a payment of €9,447 was to be offset against payments for loss of income.

The Labour Court noted that the original determination stated that loss of earnings should be calculated on the complainant's average weekly earnings between 1 January 2011 and October 2011, that is a period of 41 weeks. The Labour Court calculated the average weekly earnings on the basis of figures supplied and then multiplied this by 118 weeks (ie from the date of dismissal to the date of reinstatement). Therefore the gross wages for the period were €71,080.84 less €9,447 = €61,633.84. The Labour Court did not accept the appellant's contention that its liability should be reduced by the respondent's effort to support his family financially while awaiting the outcome of the appellant's appeal to the High Court. The appellant was ordered to pay the sum of €61,633.84 to the respondent within six weeks.

---

6.   *Stobart (Ireland) Driver Services Ltd v Carroll* HSD 145.

Chapter 10

HUMAN RIGHTS

RIGHT TO A FAIR HEARING/STATE IMMUNITY

[10.01] *Benkharbouche v Embassy of the Republic of Sudan; Janah v Libya[1] – Employment Appeal Tribunal of England and Wales – State immunity for State missions – diplomatic privileges – discrimination – right to fair hearing – Charter of Fundamental Rights of the European Union, art 47 – European Convention on Human Rights, arts 6, 14*

This was a joint appeal of claims brought by claimants formerly employed by the Sudanese and Libyan embassies in London. Ms Benkharbouche (a Moroccan cook) brought claims against the Sudanese embassy for unfair dismissal, non-payment of the national minimum wage, unpaid wages and holiday pay and for breach of the Working Time Regulations 1998. Ms Janah (a Moroccan member of domestic staff at the Libyan embassy) brought claims against Libya for unfair dismissal, arrears of pay, race discrimination and harassment, holiday pay and a failure to provide regular breaks in contravention of the Working Time Regulations 1998.[2] Both claims were separately dismissed by two Employment Tribunals on the basis that the respondents were immune from suit under the State Immunity Act 1978 (the 1978 Act).

Under the 1978 Act, the general immunity of States does not apply to employment contracts unless, at the time of the relevant contract, the individual was neither a national of the United Kingdom nor habitually resident there or was employed by an embassy in the United Kingdom.

In the appeals to the UK EAT, the claimants asserted that the 1978 Act denied them access to a fair hearing to enforce their employment rights on grounds related to their national origin, which breached the right to a fair trial under art 6 of the European Convention on Human Rights. In support of their claim, the claimants relied on the decisions of the European Court of Human Rights in *Cudak v Lithuania*[3] and *Sabeh El Leil v France.*[4]

The claimants argued that UK nationals, or those habitually resident in the UK, did not face such a barrier of state immunity, and this was discriminatory. They also argued the Human Rights Act 1998 guaranteed a right to a fair trial and that the Charter of Fundamental Rights of the European Union had direct effect in national law and on this basis, the provisions of the 1978 Act which breached art 47 of the Charter should be disapplied.

---

1. *Benkharbouche v Embassy of the Republic of Sudan; Janah v Libya* UKEAT/0401/12/GE and UKEAT/0070/13/GE.
2. (SI 1998/1833).
3. *Cudak v Lithuania* (Case C–152/84), [1986] IRLR 140.
4. *Sabeh El Leil v France* 34869/05, [2011] IRLR 781 (ECHR).

In allowing the claimants' appeal, the UK EAT determined that state immunity must be balanced against an individual's right of access to the courts. In this case, it was found that the denial of the claimants' right of access to the court was not objectively justified by the legitimate aim of state immunity, as, on the facts, any determination in the matter would not interfere with the public function of the state mission. It was therefore held that art 6 of the European Convention on Human Rights had been breached by both embassies.

However, the UK EAT did not accept the claimants' argument that the 1978 Act could not be interpreted to bar claims in all circumstances on the basis that it discriminated against potential complainants on grounds of nationality. The UK EAT found that the 1978 Act distinguished between individuals, not only on the basis of nationality, but also on the basis of their relationship to the diplomatic mission which was not discriminatory. The clear intention of the legislature was evident from the wording of the 1978 Act, and therefore, as there was no uncertainty, the UK EAT could not interpret the 1978 Act to extend the right to bring such claims to categories of individuals in a manner which was not contemplated by the legislature.

The UK EAT then considered the claimants' argument that the 1978 Act conflicted with art 47 of the Charter of Fundamental Rights of the European Union. It referred to *Kücükdeveci v Swedex GmbH & Co KG*,[5] where the CJEU held that general principles of EU law (and therefore fundamental rights under EU law) can have horizontal effect. It also referred to *Marshall v Southampton & South West Hampshire Area Health Authority (Teaching)*,[6] where the CJEU held that courts must disapply provisions of domestic law which conflict with a fundamental principle of EU law.

The UK EAT found that the Charter of Fundamental Rights of the European Union had been recognised as being applicable in the United Kingdom and that of art 47 of the Charter broadly mirrored those of art 6 of the European Convention on Human Rights. It found that, notwithstanding the fact that the Human Rights Act 1998 does not permit the courts to disapply any domestic statute that conflicts with the European Convention on Human Rights, the EAT was obliged to adhere to the European Convention on Human Rights and the general principles of EU law to protect fundamental rights, including right of access to courts. The UK EAT stated that provisions of the 1978 Act which conflicted with art 47 of the Charter of Fundamental Rights of the European Union should be disapplied in respect of the claims which were covered by EU Directives, ie discrimination, harassment and breaches of the Working Time Regulations.

The UK EAT held that where rights emanate from statutory provisions, rather than EU law, such as unfair dismissals and national minimum wage, domestic legislation will apply, which in this case meant the Human Rights Act 1998 would apply. The UK EAT noted that it did not have jurisdiction to make a declaration that the Human Rights Act 1998 was incompatible with EU law, which would require an application to a higher court.

---

5.   *Kücükdeveci v Swedex GmbH & Co KG* (Case C–555/07), [2010] IRLR 346 (CJEU).
6.   *Marshall v Southampton & South West Hampshire Area Health Authority (Teaching)* (Case C–152/84) [1986] IRLR 140 ECJ.

The UK EAT granted leave to appeal this decision, on the basis that it was important that it be reviewed by a higher appellate court.

RIGHT TO RELIGIOUS FREEDOM

[10.02] *Mba v Mayor and Burgesses of the London Borough of Merton[7] – Court of Appeal of England and Wales – requirement to work on Sundays – practising Christian who believed Sunday was a day of worship and not for work – whether grounds justifying constructive dismissal – whether indirect religious discrimination – whether legitimate for Employment Tribunal to consider belief that treating Sunday as a day of rest was a 'core component of the Christian faith' where right to freedom to manifest religion under European Convention of Human Rights, art 9 invoked.*

The claimant was employed as a care assistant at a children's home and was contractually obliged to work on Sundays according to a shift rota. She was a practising Christian who had a deep belief that Sunday was a day for worship and not for work. Her work rotas were arranged so that she was not required to work on Sundays. However, after nearly two years the respondent council began to roster her for Sunday working. She refused to do so and ultimately resigned and claimed constructive dismissal. She brought proceedings against her employer for unfair constructive dismissal and indirect religious discrimination under reg 3 of the Employment Equality (Religion or Belief) Regulations 2003.[8]

The Employment Tribunal identified the relevant 'provision, criterion or practice' (PCP) as the requirement that staff work Sunday shifts as rostered. The Employment Tribunal accepted that the respondent had a legitimate aim in the effective running of its business and it then turned to consider whether the means of achieving that aim was proportional. It considered whether the alternative proposals advanced by the claimant were in reality viable and practical but concluded that none of the claimant's suggestions could have been undertaken without significant disadvantage to the respondent in terms of costs, equality and efficiency of service delivery. In weighing up the discriminatory impact of the PCP upon the claimant, the Employment Tribunal accepted that the PCP impacted on the claimant's genuine and deeply held religious beliefs but noted that efforts had been made to accommodate her for two years. It also noted that the respondent was prepared to arrange shifts in a way that enabled the claimant to attend church for worship on Sunday and that the respondent was of the view that her belief that Sunday was a day of rest and worship upon which no paid employment was undertaken 'was not a core component of the Christian faith'.

Having weighed up all of these matters, the Employment Tribunal concluded that the imposition of the PCP was proportionate and the claim of indirect discrimination failed. The UK EAT heard and dismissed the claimant's appeal.

---

7.   *Mba v Mayor and Burgesses of the London Borough of Merton* [2013] EWCA Civ 1562, [2014] IRLR 145.
8.   SI 2003/1660.

The Court of Appeal concluded, on the facts, that the Sunday working requirement was justified in the particular circumstances of the case because there were no viable and practical alternatives.

However, the Court of Appeal went on to consider whether the Employment Tribunal was entitled to take into account the fact that the refusal to work on Sunday, although a deeply held belief of the claimant, was not 'a core component of the Christian faith'. The Court of Appeal concluded (for different reasons) that the Employment Tribunal ought not to have weighed this in the balance in support for the justification defence. The majority of the Court, led by Elias LJ, noted that the right to religious freedom under art 9 of the European Convention on Human Rights was engaged in this case because the respondent was a public body. Elias LJ noted that the protection of freedom of religion conferred by art 9 does not require a claimant to establish any group disadvantage. The question is whether the interference of that individual right by the employer is proportionate given the legitimate aims of the employer. He referred to the decision of the European Court of Human Rights in *Eweida v United Kingdom.*[9] In *Eweida* the European Court of Human Rights concluded that the refusal of British Airways to allow Ms Eweida to wear a visible cross while on duty amounted to an interference with her right to manifest her religious beliefs. Elias LJ noted that the *Eweida* decision has not and could not affect the reach of the statutory jurisdiction and therefore the claimant's art 9 right was incapable of direct enforcement in the Employment Tribunal.

However, domestic legislation must be read so as to be consistent with the Convention rights where possible in accordance with s 3 of the Human Rights Act 1998. Elias LJ concluded that it did not matter whether the claimant has been disadvantaged along with others or not and it could not in any way weaken her case with respect to justification that her beliefs are not more widely shared or do not constitute a core belief of any particular religion. He concluded that it was for this reason that the Employment Tribunal was wrong to make the reference to this factor as one assisting the employer. Elias LJ concluded, however, that this was a peripheral part of the proportionality analysis of the Employment Tribunal and did not materially affect its conclusion and thus, notwithstanding the error, he would not dismiss the appeal.

It is noteworthy that Elias LJ stated that if the case was considered as a domestic law indirect discrimination case, independent of art 9 considerations, then it would, in his view, be at least indirectly a legitimate factor for the Employment Tribunal to consider. This is because if the belief which results in the disadvantage is a core principle or belief of a particular religion, a PCP which interferes with the manifestation of that belief will impinge upon a greater number of potential adherents than would otherwise be the case; and in general the greater the impact, the harder it is to justify the provision.

Kay LJ dismissed the appeal, but on different grounds. He found that the Employment Tribunal, in describing the claimant's sabbatarian belief as not a core component of the Christian faith, had opened the door to a quantitative test which was far too wide.

---

9.   *Eweida v United Kingdom* [2013] IRLR 231, paras 79–85. See paras 1.79 and 13.01 of *ACELY 2013*.

The Court of Appeal ultimately concluded that, although the Employment Tribunal should not have weighed in the employer's favour the fact that the claimant's religious belief was not a core belief of her religion, that had been a peripheral part of the proportionality analysis undertaken by the Tribunal, which had not materially affected its conclusion. The Court of Appeal concluded that the Employment Tribunal's decision that the imposition of the PCP had been proportionate was plainly and unarguably right. The respondent had established that there was really no viable or practicable alternative way of running the children's home effectively and the claimant's appeal was dismissed on this basis.

FREEDOM OF EXPRESSION AND THE RIGHT TO IMPART INFORMATION

[10.03] *Matúz v Republic of Hungary[10] – European Court of Human Rights – judgment – 21 October 2014 – whether dismissal of applicant (a television journalist) for divulging confidential information and documents was a breach of right to freedom of expression and in particular right to impart information – Convention for the Protection of Human Rights and Fundamental Freedoms, art 34*

This was an application against the Republic of Hungary under art 34 of the Convention for the Protection of Human Rights and Fundamental Freedoms by a Hungarian national, Mr Gabor Matúz. The applicant alleged, under art 10, a breach of his right to freedom of expression, in particular the right to impart information, on account of his dismissal from the state television company for divulging confidential information and documents. The applicant, a television journalist, was employed by the state television company for an indeterminate period. At the material time he was chairman of the trade union of public service broadcasters active within the television company.

The applicant was in charge as editor and presenter of a periodical cultural programme called Night Shelter which involved interviews with various figures in cultural life. As part of his employment contract, the applicant was bound by professional confidentiality and was obliged not to reveal any information acquired in connection to its position, the disclosure of which would be prejudicial either to his employer or any other person. The contract provided for immediate termination of employment in the event that there was a breach of such obligation.

On the appointment of a new cultural director, the applicant contacted the television company's president as he was concerned about the new director's conduct in modifying and cutting certain contents of his programme, which he contended was censorship but he received no response to this complaint. In June 2003, the editor in chief of the programme addressed a letter to the board of the state television company stating, amongst other things, that the appointment of a new cultural director had led to censorship of the programme by his suggesting modification to and deletion of certain contents. On 19 June 2003 an article appeared in the online version of a Hungarian daily newspaper containing this letter from the editor in chief as well as a follow up statement

10. *Matúz v Republic of Hungary* 73571/10 [2014] ECHR 1112.

of the state television company inviting the board to end censorship in the television company.

In 2004, the applicant published a book which contained extracts from different interviews recorded in 2003 which had not been broadcast in the cultural programme on the basis of instructions from the cultural director in question. In the extracts, the applicant included numerous in-house written exchanges between the cultural director and the editor in chief concerning suggested changes in the programme.

Subsequently, in November 2004, the television company dismissed the applicant and the editor in chief with immediate effect. The reason for summary dismissal was that, by publishing the book in question, the applicant had breached the confidentiality clause contained in his employment contract.

The applicant challenged his dismissal in the Hungarian Courts on the basis that he had received the in-house correspondence in connection with his position as the chairman of the trade union in order for him to take steps against alleged censorship at the television company and that he had published the impugned book in that capacity. However the Budapest Labour Court, the Budapest Regional Court and the Supreme Court all found against the applicant. The Supreme Court held that the scope of the case did not extend to the examination of the applicant's breach of his labour obligations set out in his contract of employment.

In this case before the European Court of Human Rights, the applicant complained that his dismissal from the state television company on the grounds of publishing a book including internal documents of his employer, amounted to breach of his right to freedom of expression and in particular his right to impart information and ideas to third parties. He relied on art 10 of the Convention for the Protection of Human Rights and Freedoms which provides as follows:

> 1. Everyone has the right to freedom of expression. This right shall include freedom to hold opinions and to receive and impart information and ideas without interference by public authority and regardless of frontiers. This article shall not prevent States from requiring the licensing of broadcasting, television or cinema enterprises.
>
> 2. The exercise of these freedoms, since it carries with it duties and responsibilities, may be subject to such formalities, conditions, restrictions or penalties as are prescribed by law and are necessary in a democratic society, in the interests of national security, territorial integrity or public safety, for the prevention of disorder or crime, for the protection of health or morals, for the protection of the reputation or rights of others, for preventing the disclosure of information received in confidence, or for maintaining the authority and impartiality of the judiciary.

The European Court of Human Rights declared the complaint to be admissible. It also considered that the disciplinary measure imposed on the applicant for publishing a book containing confidential information about his employer constituted an interference of the exercise of the right protected by art 10. It was therefore necessary to determine whether such interference was 'prescribed by law', whether it pursued one or more of the legitimate aims set out, or whether it was necessary in a democratic society in order to achieve those aims.

The European Court of Human Rights concluded that the applicant's combined professional and trade union roles must be taken into consideration for the purposes of examining whether the interference complained of was necessary in a democratic society. It considered that, having regard to the role played by journalists in society and to their responsibility to contribute to and encourage public debate, discretion and confidentiality constraints cannot be said to apply with equal force to journalists, given that it is in the nature of their functions to impart information and ideas. The European Court of Human Rights considered that the domestic authorities should have paid particular attention to the public interest attached to the applicant's conduct. It further noted that, although the publication of the document in the impugned book was a breach of confidentiality, the substance in general had been already made accessible through an online publication and was known to a number of people. The European Court of Human Rights also regarded as significant that the applicant's decision to make the impugned information and documents public was based on the experience that neither his complaint to the president of the television company nor the editor-in-chief's letter to the board had prompted any response. Thus, the European Court of Human Rights was satisfied that the publication of the book took place only after the applicant had felt prevented from remedying the perceived interference with his journalistic work within the television company itself; that is for want of any effective alternative channel. The Court noted that a rather severe sanction was imposed on the applicant, namely summary dismissal. The Court ultimately concluded that there had been violation of art 10 of the Convention for the Protection of Human Rights and Freedoms.

In terms of damages, the applicant claimed €32,250 in pecuniary damage comprising compensation for lost income which would have been awarded to him in case of success in the domestic proceedings and also claimed €10,000 in respect of non-pecuniary damage. These were contested by the government of Hungary. The European Court of Human Rights considered that the applicant must have suffered some pecuniary and non-pecuniary damage as a result of his dismissal. It awarded him €5,000 under both heads combined. In terms of costs, the applicant had claimed €1,440 for the cost and expenses incurred before the domestic Courts and this amount was awarded in full.

Chapter 11

IMMIGRATION

CASE LAW

[11.01] *Hussein v Minister for Justice and Equality[1] – High Court – McDermott J – judicial review – Immigration Act 2004 – long-term residency scheme – ministerial discretion*

This judicial review application challenged the decision of the Minister for Justice and Equality to refuse an application for 'long term residence with exemption from work permit conditions', also referred to as a five-year 'Stamp 4 permission'. The applicant, a citizen of Bangladesh who at the time of the proceedings had been working in Ireland since February 2005, was legally permitted to work and reside in Ireland in accordance with the terms and conditions of a work permit which had been granted and renewed over a period of five years.

In March 2010, the applicant applied to the Irish Naturalisation and Immigration Service (INIS) for long-term residency/Stamp 4 permission. If granted, this permission would have enabled the applicant to reside and work in the State for a period of five years without being tied to a particular job or employer, and would have allowed the applicant greater flexibility in obtaining employment. While his application was being processed by INIS, the applicant submitted additional information in relation to a conviction for driving a car without insurance for which he received a fine of €300. The applicant provided details of the fine and confirmation that it had been paid. The applicant was subsequently informed by letter that, on reviewing his application for a long-term residency visa, a character check had been carried out by the Garda National Immigration Bureau and a report had been received stating that the applicant had come to the adverse attention of the gardaí, having been convicted of the offence of driving without insurance. The applicant's solicitors wrote to INIS following receipt of this letter confirming that the information concerning his conviction was correct and stating that the applicant had already submitted this information to INIS and confirmed that the fine in relation to the conviction had been paid. The applicant received a letter from INIS stating that the Minister had reviewed the issues involved but had not changed his previous decision.

The applicant was granted leave to apply for judicial review in March 2012, seeking orders of *certiorari* and *mandamus* against the respondent on the grounds that:

(i)   the respondent erred in law in failing to determine the application by reference to the applicant's particular situation and his circumstances at the time of application;

---

1.   *Hussein v Minister for Justice and Equality* [2014] IEHC 34.

(ii)   the respondent had unlawfully fettered his discretion and that of his servants or agents by adopting an unreasonable and fixed policy to refuse long term permission to reside on Stamp 4 conditions to eligible persons on the basis of convictions for relatively minor offences;

(iii)   the respondent's decisions were unreasonable and disproportionate, given the nature of the defence; and

(iv)   the respondent failed to comply with the principles of natural and constitutional justice and the basic fairness of administrative procedures.

The High Court considered the decision of Cooke J in *Saleem v Minister for Justice, Equality and Law Reform*[2] in which the long-term residency scheme was considered. In that decision it was noted that the term 'long term residency' is not one used in the Immigration Act 2004 (the 2004 Act), but it appears to have its origin in what the respondent described as an 'administrative scheme'. It was also noted that s 4 of the 2004 Act did not prescribe any conditions for the grant of such permission; however s 4(3) of the 2004 Act describes a series of circumstances in which an immigration officer, acting on behalf of the Minister, may refuse to give a permission. In effect, therefore, the Minister has a statutory discretion in granting permission to land or to be in the State, and the 'administrative scheme' thus amounts in practice to a statement as to the circumstances and conditions in which the Minister is prepared to entertain and consider applications for the grant of permission to remain on the basis of Stamp 4 permission.

The Court noted that the decision to be made on receipt of an application for long-term residency requires an assessment of the merits of certain aspects of the case, for example whether the applicant was of 'good character'. The Court also noted that as per the *Saleem* decision, the grant of permission under the scheme is a matter for the exercise of discretion by the respondent under s 4 of the 2004 Act. Section 4(3) provides the grounds upon which permission may be refused and states that permission may be refused if the immigration officer, acting on behalf of the Minister, is satisfied that the non-national has been convicted (whether in the State or elsewhere) of an offence that may be punished under law by imprisonment for a period of one year or by a more severe penalty. The Court noted that the road traffic offence of which the applicant had been convicted provided for a fine not exceeding €5,000 or, at the discretion of the Court, imprisonment for a term not exceeding six months, or to both such fine and imprisonment. The Court noted that the possible penalty fell short of the 12-month period of imprisonment provided under s 4(3) of the 2004 Act. The Court stated that s 4(3) indicates the extent to which the legislature intended previous convictions to be taken into account.

The Court noted that it had been made clear to the applicant that his application for long-term residency was refused as a result of his criminal conviction alone. The Court was satisfied that the respondent had unlawfully and unreasonably restricted his discretion by refusing the application on the sole ground of the applicant's conviction,

---

2.   *Saleem v Minister for Justice, Equality and Law Reform* [2011] IEHC 55.

contrary to the intention of the Oireachtas as set out in s 4(3) of the 2004 Act which precisely delineates the nature of a criminal conviction which may result in refusal. The Court held, accordingly, that the applicant was entitled to an order of *certiorari* quashing the respondent's original and subsequent decision on appeal, in respect of his application for long-term residency.

THE EMPLOYMENT PERMITS (AMENDMENT) ACT 2014

[11.02] The Employment Permits (Amendment) Act 2014 (the 2014 Act), commenced on 1 October 2014, and is intended to streamline and update the current employment permit regime.

Basic requirements

[11.03] For any employment permit (EP) to be granted the following basic requirements must be fulfilled:

(i) the employer must be trading in Ireland and registered with the Revenue Commissioners and the Companies Registration Office;

(ii) the applicant must be an employee of the company and must have the relevant qualifications, skills and/or experience for the job in question;

(iii) the role must not fall into a prescribed list of ineligible roles, eg clerical or administrative roles;

(iv) employers seeking to hire non-EEA nationals must demonstrate compliance with the 50:50 rule, ie that they maintain a workforce of at least 50% of EEA nationals. This will be strictly enforced in the new regime; however, there will be some relaxation in respect of start-up companies or non-Irish companies who are seeking to establish operations in Ireland. In these cases, the companies will have two years from the date they commence business in Ireland to comply with the 50:50 rule;

(v) both employers and the non-EEA employees must comply with the 'labour market needs test' in respect of applications for the General and Contract for Services EPs. Certain grounds of waiver will apply:

    (a) where employment is one of the specified shortage occupations, including occupations in healthcare, information technology and financial services,

    (b) where gross annual remuneration is €60,000 or over,

    (c) where the application has been recommended by an enterprise development agency, eg IDA or Enterprise Ireland,

    (d) in the case of a former permit holder who has been made redundant, and

    (e) where a General EP application is in respect of a carer with a proven history of caring for a particular sick person.

The Regulations[3] also update the 'highly skilled occupations list' and the 'list of ineligible occupations' as contained on the Department of Jobs, Enterprise and Innovation website.

General employment permits

[11.04] General EPs replaced the work permits under the previous scheme, and will be available for occupations with a salary of €30,000 or more and, in exceptional cases,[4] in the salary range below €30,000.

In order to reach the minimum remuneration threshold of a General EP, the following components are deemed to be remuneration:

(i) basic salary to achieve at least national minimum wage or a rate of pay fixed under any enactment, as the first component of the remuneration package; and

(ii) health insurance payments made to a health insurer registered with the Health Insurance Authority on its Register of Health Benefits Undertakings under s 14 of the Health Insurance Act 1994 or what the Minister is satisfied is the equivalent.

General EPs can be issued for an initial period of up to two years and can then be renewed for up to a further three years. Following the expiry of the five-year period, the employee will no longer require an EP to work in Ireland.

Critical skills employment permits

[11.05] Critical Skills Employment Permits replace Green Cards. Applications for Critical Skills EPs can be made on the following grounds:

(i) where the gross annual salary (excluding bonuses) is €60,000 or more, and the applicant holds a third level degree or equivalent experience for the relevant job, the Critical Skills EP is available for all occupations, other than those which are contrary to the public interest or listed on the 'ineligible categories of employment'; and

(ii) Critical Skills EPs are available in the gross annual salary range €30,000–€59,999 (excluding bonuses) for a restricted number of occupations specified

---

3. See **[11.13]**.
4. Consideration may be given on an exceptional basis to applicants with remuneration lower than €30,000 in respect of the following:
    (a) a Non-EEA student who has graduated in the last 12 months from an Irish third-level institution and has been offered a graduate position from the highly skilled occupations list;
    (b) a Non-EEA student who has graduated in the last 12 months from an overseas third-level institution and has been offered a graduate position as an ICT professional from the highly skilled occupations list; and
    (c) certain roles in specialist, technical or sales support with support from the Enterprise Development Agencies.

on the 'high skilled occupations list'. Applicants are required to hold a degree qualification or higher.

The same components for the General EP are also deemed remuneration for the purposes of the Critical Skills EP. Employees must be offered a position with the Irish entity for at least two years on an initial basis. Following the expiry of the two-year period, the employees will no longer require an EP and will be eligible to apply for a Stamp 4.

Intra-company transfer permits

[11.06] Intra-Company Transfer Permits (ICT permits) are retained under the 2014 Act. The ICT permits allow for the transfer of senior management, key personnel or trainees who are non-EEA nationals from an overseas branch of a multinational corporation to its Irish branch, subject to the following conditions:

(i)   minimum gross annual salary of €40,000;

(ii)   the employee/transferee in question must have been working for a minimum period of six months with the overseas company prior to the transfer;

(iii) the overseas branch of the organisation in question must be *bona fide* and engaged in substantive business operations in the non-EEA country in question;

(iv)   the Irish company must have a direct link with the overseas company by common ownership, eg either one company must own the other, or else both must be part of a group of companies controlled by the same parent company. Documentary evidence of this link may be required by the Department of Jobs, Enterprise and Innovation. The Irish company must also be trading and engaged in substantive business operations; and

(v)   the employee must fall into one of the categories of senior management, key personnel or trainee.

There are three parties involved in an Intra-Company Transfer EP: the overseas employer; the connected person (Irish entity); and the non-EEA employee. The application is made by the connected person.

In order to achieve the minimum annual remuneration threshold for an Intra-Company Transfer EP, the following components are deemed to be remuneration:

(i)   basic salary to achieve at least national minimum wage or a rate of pay fixed under any enactment, as the first component of the remuneration package; and

(ii)   in addition, the following components may be added to bring the proposed remuneration to the appropriate EP threshold of either €40,000 or €30,000:

   (a) a payment for board and accommodation, or either of them, or the monetary value of board and accommodation directly provided by the connected person or foreign employer;

   (b) health insurance payments.

The foreign employer is responsible for payment of salary to achieve national minimum wage or a rate of pay fixed under or pursuant to any enactment. This may involve a top-up payment to the employee's salary. The top up payment can be made by either the foreign employer or the Irish entity.

All amounts which make up the basic salary, including any top-up payments, must appear as payments on the employee's payslips. Following the expiry of five years, the employee cannot apply for another ICT permit.

Dependent partner/spouse employment permit

[11.07] The objective of this type of EP is primarily to support the attractiveness of Ireland as a location of employment for potential and current Critical Skills EP holders and researchers.

Eligible dependant unmarried children, recognised partners, civil partners and spouses (where recognised as such by Department of Jobs, Enterprise and Innovation), who have been admitted to Ireland as family members of holders of Green Cards/ Critical Skills EPs and researchers may apply.

The scheme includes dependants over 18 years of age who were already in Ireland as part of the family unit prior to their 18th birthday.

The duration of the EP is linked to that of the primary Critical Skills EP holder / researcher.

Remuneration may be less than €30,000 per annum but cannot be less than the hourly national minimum wage rate.

The applicant must work for a minimum of 10 hours per week.

Contract for Services employment permit

[11.08] This type of EP is designed to facilitate foreign contractors fulfilling a contract to provide services to an Irish company in Ireland. The foreign company must have a direct contract with the Irish entity to provide services, and cannot outsource the provision of services. There are three parties involved in a Contract for Services EP:

(i)   the foreign contractor entity;

(ii)   the relevant person (Irish entity);

(iii)   the non-EEA national employee.

Permission for individuals providing services to work in Ireland for less than 90 days may fall under the Atypical Working Scheme which is administered by the Department of Justice and Equality.

The application for a Contract for Services EP is made by the foreign contractor.

The employee in question must have been working for a minimum period of six months with the foreign contractor prior to the transfer to the relevant person. The duration of the transfer must be for a period of at least 90 days. Contract for Services

EPs can only be considered for the term of the contract of the employee. If the employee's contract expires while in Ireland he/she will not be permitted to continue working on the Contract for Service EP.

In order to apply for the Contract for Services EP, the employee must have an Irish law contract of employment.

The foreign contractor must be registered with the Revenue Commissioners and, where applicable, with the Companies Registration Office/Registry of Friendly Societies. Registration details must be provided on application. Contract for Services EPs may be issued for an initial period for up to two years and may be renewed for up to a further three years.

Exchange agreement employment permit

[11.09] This EP replaces the old exchange agreement work permit. Under the new system, exchange agreement EPs shall facilitate the employment in Ireland of non-EEA nationals under prescribed agreements to which Ireland is a party. An example would be the Fulbright Programme for Researchers and Academics.

Eligible exchanges will be prescribed in Regulations to the 2014 Act.

Sports and cultural employment permit

[11.10] The Sport and Cultural EP is designed to facilitate the employment in Ireland of non-EEA nationals for the development, operation and capacity of sporting and cultural activities. It can be summarised as follows:

(i)   the employee must have the relevant qualifications, skills, knowledge or experience;

(ii)   the EP section of the Department of Jobs, Enterprise and Innovation may consult with governing bodies, which can provide a supporting letter to submit with the application;

(iii)   the employee's salary must be equivalent to Ireland's national minimum wage or higher;

(iv)   the 50:50 rule will apply at application and renewal stage. However, this restriction may be waived in the case of clubs with only one employee;

(v)   the labour market needs test is not required;

(vi)   Sports and Cultural EPs can be issued seasonally or for up to two years depending on the contract;

(vii)   renewal applications may be considered for a period up to three years; and

(viii) permits issued for seasonal employment are non-renewable.

Internship employment permit

[11.11] Internship EPs facilitate the employment in Ireland of non-EEA nationals who are full-time students (including post-graduate students) enrolled in a third-level institutions outside Ireland and pursuing a degree course or higher. The conditions are as follows:

(i)   the Internship EP is designed for facilitating employees gaining work experience;

(ii)   there is no requirement for the employing entity to conduct a labour market needs test;

(iii)   the Irish entity must provide an offer of employment to the intern;

(iv)   the occupation to which the intern is temporarily assigned must be in the highly skilled occupations list;

(v)   the intern's salary must be equivalent to Ireland's national minimum wage or higher;

(vi)   the course of study of the intern must be wholly concerned with the skills shortages identified on the highly skilled occupations list, and completing the internship must be a requirement for the completion of their course of study in their third-level institutions; and

(vii)   at the end of the internship, the employee must leave the State and return to the third level institution abroad to complete their course of study.

Reactivation employment permits

[11.12] Reactivation Employment Permits enable non-EEA nationals who entered Ireland on a valid EP but remained working in Ireland without a valid EP through no fault of their own, or who have been badly treated or exploited in the workplace, to work again. The conditions are as follows:

(i)   the employee must have previously held an EP;

(ii)   the employee must hold a temporary Stamp 1 and have a 'Reactivation EP' letter from the Department of Justice and Equality;

(iii)   the employee's salary must be equivalent to Ireland's national minimum wage or higher;

(iv)   this type of EP applies to all occupations except occupations in a domestic setting, other than certain carers; and

(v)   the employee must possess the relevant qualifications, skills or experience required for the employment as specified on his/her application form.

STATUTORY INSTRUMENTS

Employment Permits Regulations 2014

[11.13] The Employment Permits Regulations 2014[5] update the highly skilled occupations list to list the relevant occupations by reference to the Standard Occupation Classification system (SOC 2010).

Employment Permits (Amendment) Regulations 2014

[11.14] Following consultation, these lists were further updated by the Employment Permits Act (Amendment) Regulations 2014.[6] Examples of highly skilled roles include: IT specialist managers (SOC 2133); engineering professionals (SOC 212) and health professionals (SOC 221). Examples of ineligible roles include: managers in hospitality and leisure services (SOC 122); and therapy professionals (SOC 222) such as physiotherapists (SOC 2221); occupational therapists (SOC 2222); and speech and language therapists (SOC 2223).

Reasonable steps defence

[11.15] In order to address the anomaly identified in *Hussein v The Labour Court and Younnis*,[7] employees can now rely on the defence that they took all reasonable steps to comply with the requirement of having an employment permit and therefore should be entitled to avail of the employee protections contained in Irish employment legislation.

Ministerial action

[11.16] Again, to address concerns following the *Hussein*[8] case, the Act provides that the Minister may take a civil action against an employer on behalf of a non-EEA national where it is alleged that the non-EEA national has not been afforded his/her rights under Irish employment legislation.

Additionally, the 2014 Act proposes that where an applicant for an employment permit has not sought a review of the decision to grant an employment permit, the Minister may nonetheless direct that the decision to refuse to grant an employment permit be reviewed, where compelling information or evidence in relation to the application is received within 28 days of the decision to refuse.

---

5. Employment Permits Regulations 2014 (SI 432/2014).
6. Employment Permits (Amendment) Regulations 2014 (SI 506/2014).
7. *Hussein v The Labour Court and Younnis* [2012] IEHC 599 and see *ACELY 2013* at paras 1.109, 19.06.
8. *Hussein v The Labour Court and Younnis* [2012] IEHC 599.

The Trusted Partner Registration Scheme

[11.17] The Trusted Partner Registration Scheme (the Scheme) is a new form of registration available to certain employers to streamline the employment permit application process. It is a pilot scheme between the IDA and the Department of Jobs, Enterprise and Innovation which is expected to be introduced in early 2015.

The Scheme facilitates a faster turnaround for 'Trusted Partners' when making employment permit applications. The Department intends that processing time for employment permits under the Scheme will be reduced to five business days. There will also be a reduction in the supporting documents required for applications from Trusted Partners.

Initially, the Scheme will only be available to existing clients of the IDA and new start-up organisations that have been nominated by the IDA or Enterprise Ireland, and will remain under review. In particular, if a company has committed an offence under the Employment Permits Acts 2003 to 2014, it will not be eligible to apply for the Scheme.

The application for Trusted Partner status must be accompanied by an IDA/ Enterprise Ireland letter of support and the requisite fee. If the application is successful, the employer will be granted a unique Trusted Partner reference number which will be valid for a two-year period, which may be renewed. As part of the application for Trusted Partner status, the employer will be required to make certain declarations. Once registered, the employer can continue to use an agent to submit employment permit applications for its employees.

BRITISH IRISH VISA SCHEME

[11.18] On 16 June 2014, the Minister for Justice and Equality announced a new 'British Irish Visa Scheme'.

The scheme allows for travel to and around the Common Travel Area (CTA) on a single 90-day visa to avoid the necessity of requiring separate Irish and UK visas for tourists and business visitors to the regions. The first international visitors to benefit will be travellers from China and it will extend to India, and the scheme will be extended to other visa-required countries from 2015 onwards.

The scheme was formally launched on 14 October 2014 by UK Home Secretary Teresa May and Minister Frances Fitzgerald following the signing of a memorandum of understanding. Minister Fitzgerald stated that:

> Our aim is to boost tourism and business travel to our countries and, together, we are sending a clear and powerful message that these islands are open for business.

CHANGES TO THE IMMIGRANT INVESTOR PROGRAMME

[11.19] In recognition of the number of foreign investors who make valuable contributions to the Irish economy, the Government launched the Immigrant Investor

Programme (the IIP) in 2012. In June 2014, the Department of Justice and Equality published new guidelines on the IIP that seek to further facilitate investment into the Irish economy by presenting additional investment opportunities. The Government has taken steps to broaden the appeal of the IIP, and its extension to include investment funds and real estate investment trusts are options which are intended to appeal to investors.

The IIP is available to non-EEA nationals and their immediate family members who wish to obtain Irish residency permissions in exchange for investing in specific approved investments.

Benefits of the scheme

[11.20] The investor and their nominated family members will be granted permission to remain for a specific duration under a Stamp 4, which allows the investor and their family to live, work, study and start up their own business in Ireland.

This permission is granted for an initial two-year period and may be renewed for a further period of three years provided that the conditions are still being met.

Unlike other schemes operated by other states, there is no limit to the number of investors that may be accepted into the IIP. Nor is there any requirement for demonstrable experience in management.

Family members

Education

[11.21] In order to facilitate the education of investors or their families in Irish universities or institutes of technology the Government allows investors to discount up to €50,000 from their investment contribution to offset higher education expenses. This way, investors, their spouse and/or children will have access to education institutions at reduced cost.

Work

[11.22] Investors and their family will be entitled to work and/or study without requiring an employment permit or business permission on the basis of their Stamp 4 permission.

Extension of Permission

[11.23] Following the expiry of five years under the IIP, there is no further requirement for the investor to maintain the investment funds. The Department of Justice and Equality will continue to renew residency permissions on a five-year basis subject to the investor and their family not becoming a financial burden on the State and remaining of good character.

As the objective of the IIP was to provide investors and their families with Irish residency rights, there is no mandatory residency condition – all that is required is for the investor and their family members to visit Ireland once every year.

However, applying for Irish citizenship does require a period of continued residence. Where the investor or their dependants wish to apply for Irish citizenship they must have been habitually resident in Ireland prior to making the application for citizenship. In particular, the person must be actually resident in Ireland for at least five years preceding their citizenship application.

What investments are allowed under the scheme?

[11.24]

Type of Investment	Terms and Conditions
Immigrant investor bond	€1 million invested in an immigrant investor bond for a five-year term
Enterprise investment	€500,000 invested in an Irish enterprise (business) for three years
Investment funds	€500,000 invested in an approved investment fund
Real Estate Investment Trusts	A minimum investment of €2 million in any Irish REIT that is listed on the Irish Stock Exchange. The €2 million investment may be spread across a number of different Irish REITs
Mixed investment	Investment in a residential property of minimum value of €450,000 and a straight investment of €500,000 into the immigrant investor bond
Endowment	€500,000 philanthropic donation by an individual, €400,000 each for group donations of five or more investors

Details of the approved investments are set out below.

Immigrant investor bond

[11.25] This requires a minimum investment of €1 million into a specially designated immigrant investor bond. This bond is issued by the Government through the National Treasury Management Agency. The bond has a term of five years and currently carries a 0% interest rate. The bond is a Government guaranteed investment.

Enterprise investment

[11.26] This involves an investment of at least €500,000 in either a single Irish enterprise or spread over a number of Irish enterprises. The investment must be held for a minimum of three years.

In order to qualify for investment under the IIP, an enterprise must be headquartered in Ireland, the bulk of its operations must be in Ireland and at least 60% of both its employees and its cost base must be located in Ireland. An enterprise can be a start-up company established by the investor or it can be an investment into an existing Irish business. Importantly, the investment must support the creation or maintenance of employment in Ireland and, therefore, any investment proposal which may potentially provide for moving jobs abroad or a reduction in Irish employment will not be eligible.

The investment must be made in the name of the investor who is seeking residence under the IIP. Investments made through companies or corporations, even where 100% owned by the investor, will not qualify. However where a number of investors group together to invest jointly (and directly) this can also qualify for the IIP if each of the investors meet the investment threshold.

The Department of Justice and Equality has indicated that certain investments involving purchase of a commercial property may qualify as an enterprise investment, eg purchase of a hotel with a proposal to develop the hotel and maintain employment. However, a purchase of a hotel with a proposal to change it into private residences would not qualify under the IIP.

Investment funds

[11.27] This involves a minimum investment of €500,000 in an approved investment fund. The Department of Justice and Equality intends to publish a list of the approved investment funds on its website.[9] The investment must be committed for a term of three years.

The funds must be invested in Ireland and, specifically, in Irish registered companies that are not quoted on any stock exchange. The funds and fund managers must be regulated by the Central Bank of Ireland.

Real Estate Investment Trusts (REITs)

[11.28] A REIT is a company used to hold rental investment properties in a tax efficient manner. The Department of Justice and Equality requires that a minimum of €2 million is invested into any single Irish REIT or a number of Irish REITs which are registered on the Irish Stock Exchange. The full REIT investment must be held for a period of three years from the date of purchase. There is provision for the investor to divest a portion of their shares after the initial three-year period has passed, and, after five years investors are free to divest all of their shares.

---

9. www.justice.ie.

Mixed investments

[11.29] This is a combination of a residential property purchase and an investment in the immigrant investor bond. It allows for a residential property purchase of at least €450,000 combined with a minimum of €500,000 investment in the immigrant investor bond. The property may only be used for residential purposes of the investor and their immediate family. The property and the investment bond must be held for at least five years.

Endowment

[11.30] This involves a once off donation of a minimum of €500,000 in a project of public benefit in either the arts, sports, health, cultural or education field. Investors will not receive a financial return from the investment or a return of their principal.

If a group of five or more investors wish to contribute to a philanthropic cause, a minimum of €400,000 per investor will be sufficient to meet the criteria for this investment.

Application process

[11.31] There are four stages to the application process:

(i)   the investor submits their application to the Evaluation Committee in the Department of Justice and Equality, setting out their preferred investment option and investment proposal;

(ii)   the Evaluation Committee will review the application and, if successful, approval is granted for the proposal;

(iii)   once approval is obtained, the investor will make his investment in accordance with the investment proposal; and

(iv)   once it is confirmed that the investment has been made, the Department of Justice and Equality will issue residency permissions to the investor and nominated family members.

The transfer of investment funds is not necessary until approval has been obtained for the investment proposal. A non-refundable fee of €750 will be charged by the Department for the application.

CHANGES TO THE START UP ENTREPRENEUR PROGRAMME (STEP)

[11.32] In March 2014, the Minister for Justice, Equality and Defence (as it then was) announced changes to the STEP. The changes are intended to refine STEP and improve its appeal to potential migrant entrepreneurs. The Minister said of STEP:

> When we launched the Start-up Entrepreneur Programme in April 2012, I deliberately avoided making any predictions on the level of interest in the scheme.

This is new territory for Ireland and it was not possible to predict the level of demand at that time. The approach was to allow the Programme to operate for a reasonable time and to review it to establish whether improvements could be made. This has now been done and while the level of interest so far has been encouraging, I believe that we can do more in this area to attract entrepreneurs to Ireland and to offer those people already here a real option to stay on as entrepreneurs. With this important objective in mind, the Cabinet has agreed to my proposal that a number of adjustments be made to the Programme.

The STEP facilitates residence in Ireland for non-EEA national entrepreneurs who have a viable proposal for a high potential start-up (HPSU) company. A HPSU is classified as a start-up venture that is:

(i) introducing a new or innovative product or service to international markets;

(ii) involved in manufacturing or internationally traded services;

(iii) capable of creating 10 jobs in Ireland and realising €1 million in sales within three to four years of starting up;

(iv) led by an experienced management team;

(v) headquartered and controlled in Ireland; and

(vi) less than six years old.

The conclusions of the review and the recommendations approved by the Government are as follows:

(i) the target group for the STEP should remain unchanged and the programme should continue to facilitate HPSU;

(ii) the required minimum investment will be reduced from €75,000 to €50,000. Where more than one principal is involved in establishing the business the minimum investment for second and subsequent entrepreneur will be €30,000 per principal;

(iii) a 12-month immigration permission will be made available for non-EEA national entrepreneurs attending incubators or innovation bootcamps in Ireland. The 12-month permission will allow these entrepreneurs to prepare an application to the STEP and thus provide an identifiable route for migrant entrepreneurs to move from the start-up to realisation phase of their projects. This 12-month period will also be made available to non-EEA students who graduate with advanced STEM (science, technology, engineering, mathematics) degrees in Ireland and who wish to work on preparing an application for the STEP;

(iv) unsuccessful applications for the STEP will be referred to the Business Permission Scheme, operated by INIS, for assessment. The terms of the Business Permission Scheme are being reviewed to better facilitate entrepreneurship at the more traditional end of the scale; and

(v)   more emphasis will be placed on the marketing and promotion of the scheme and on aligning the STEP with Ireland's strategy to be among the most entrepreneurial nations in the world and acknowledged as a world class environment in which to start and grow a business.

CHANGES TO INTERNATIONAL EDUCATION SECTOR AND STUDENT IMMIGRATION

[11.33] Following a series of closures of private language schools and well-publicised difficulties facing students who were affected by such closures, the Task Force on Students affected by the Closure of Private Colleges (the Task Force) was established. The Task Force's primary focus was to coordinate efforts to source reasonable, alternative study courses for affected students and ultimately to report back to the Minister for Justice and Equality and the Minister for Education and Skills.

Arising from the report of the Task Force, the Ministers announced a series of changes to the area of international education and student immigration to take effect from 1 January 2015. These reforms[10] include the following:

(i)   a much more restrictive list of education programmes will be eligible for student immigration purposes. Only programmes which are accredited by Irish awarding bodies in the English language and higher education sectors will be permitted to recruit international students, with a few specific exceptions. Institutions will be required to have a track record of educational quality and immigration compliance;

(ii)   an enhanced inspection and compliance regime will be introduced to monitor educational quality and immigration compliance; and

(iii)   changes will be made to the operation of the work concession, which allows non-EEA students to work. The working year for the concession will be standardised to clamp down on abuse and to make the situation clearer for students and employers alike.

---

10.   Policy Statement: *Regulatory Reform of the International Education Sector and the Student Immigration Regime.*

Chapter 12

INDUSTRIAL RELATIONS

TRADE UNION RECOGNITION

[12.01] *Waterford Co Co v A Group of Workers, PNA (Irish Fire & Emergency Services Association)[1] – Labour Court – Industrial Relations Acts 1946 to 2012 – Industrial Relations Act 1969, s 20(1) – whether Waterford County Council should recognise claim for recognition by Irish Fire & Emergency Services Association – branch of established trade union – obligation on employer to recognise trade union for collective bargaining in circumstances where employer already has established arrangements in place with authorised trade unions*

This case concerned a claim for recognition, brought against the respondent employer by the Irish Fire & Emergency Services Association (IFESA), which is a branch of the Psychiatric Nurses Association (PNA), for the purpose of collective bargaining negotiations on behalf of its members. It was submitted by the respondent that IFESA is not recognised within the local government sector for the negotiation of terms and conditions applicable to the grade of retained fire fighters. It was accepted that the PNA is an established trade union and holder of a negotiation licence. IFESA is affiliated as a branch of the PNA and, of the fire fighters employed by the respondent, 80% were members of the PNA. The respondent explained that it had 530 employees who were currently represented by five trade unions for negotiation purposes and submitted that a further fragmentation of the existing arrangements would not be to the benefit of the employees. The respondent argued that it was not obliged in law or statute to negotiate with a particular trade union and furthermore it was asserted that negotiation rights in respect of an individual local authority could not be considered on a stand-alone basis as it was a sectoral issue.

The Labour Court noted that the respondent had well-established arrangements for the conduct of collective bargaining with authorised trade unions. The Court noted that the applicants were in effect a break-away group who were seeking to establish negotiating rights through the convenience of another trade union that had no recognised involvement in negotiations in the local authority sector. The Labour Court noted that employees have a right to be members of whatever organisation they choose. However the Court noted that the exercise of that right cannot imply a concomitant obligation on the employer to negotiate with their chosen organisation. The Labour Court concluded that recognition of this group would have a highly undesirable and destabilising effect on the established negotiating arrangements currently in place and would also impair the orderly conduct of industrial relations within the local authority sector. The Court did not recommend concession of the claim.

---

1. *Waterford Co Co v A Group of Workers, PNA (Irish Fire & Emergency Services Association)* LCR20726.

303

[12.02] *Unilever Ireland v SIPTU[2] – Labour Court – Industrial Relations Act 1969, s 20(1) – refusal by management to engage with trade union notwithstanding 30 years of collective bargaining history between parties*

The employer did not attend the Labour Court hearing.

It was submitted by the trade union (SIPTU) that management had informed three field sales team members that they were to be made redundant. SIPTU submitted that no consultation whatsoever had taken place with management on this issue, which was totally against the norm as there had always been previous consultation. SIPTU wrote to management in April 2014 and received no response. Further correspondence was sent to management and the dispute was then referred to the Labour Relations Commission. Management responded to the Labour Relations Commission advising that they intended to deal with the workers directly.

It was submitted by SIPTU that for over 30 years it had engaged in collective bargaining on its members' terms and conditions of employment on a continuous basis. By custom and practice it had developed a healthy working relationship with the company and its most recent engagement with the company was in May 2014.

The Labour Court concluded that it could see no reason why the industrial relations relationship should not continue, particularly where there had been a history of stable industrial relations. The Court noted the submission of SIPTU that a substantial number of employees were members of the union across several grades, to include sales, administration and management. The Labour Court recommended that management should restore the working relationship with SIPTU and engage with it on issues relating to its members' terms and conditions as sought by the union.

[12.03] *Cavan and Monaghan Community Area Services v SIPTU[3] – Labour Court – Industrial Relations Act 1969, s 20(1) – refusal of employer to recognise trade union for industrial relations purposes – recommendation that respondent employer (who was supported by public funds) should enter into negotiations with union*

This case concerned the refusal of the respondent company to recognise the trade union for industrial relations purposes. SIPTU wrote to the respondent seeking a meeting and received a response from the respondent which sought the names of the union members. SIPTU repeatedly wrote to the respondent seeking meetings and, as no response was forthcoming, referred the case to the LRC. The respondent did not commit to attending the LRC and again requested the names of the union members. It was submitted that the union members were reluctant to give their names for fear they would be discriminated against in the workplace. A Labour Court hearing took place and the respondent did not attend.

The Labour Court noted that the respondent had declined to participate in the Court investigation of this dispute. It further noted that the respondent was community-based and was supported by public funds. The Labour Court stated it was disconcerting that the respondent had chosen not to cooperate with the dispute resolution machinery of the

2.   *Unilever Ireland v SIPTU* CD/14236, LCR20826.
3.   *Cavan and Monaghan Community Area Services v SIPTU* LCR20838.

State in those circumstances. The Court noted that the core issue of the dispute related to the refusal of the employer to recognise the trade union for industrial relations purposes.

The Court recommended that the respondent should enter into negotiations with SIPTU for the purpose of concluding a collective agreement covering terms and conditions of employment of its members and the procedural framework within which normal industrial relations could be conducted between the parties. It further recommended that the negotiations should commence immediately and should be concluded within a period not exceeding two months. The Court further recommended that, in the event of disagreement on the appropriate terms and conditions of employment, or any other aspect of a collective agreement governing the conditions, the industrial relations machinery of the State, to include the services of the Labour Court, should be fully utilised.

BIAS IN INTERNAL SELECTION PROCEDURES

[12.04] *A University and a Worker[4] – Labour Court – Industrial Relations Acts 1946 to 2012 – Industrial Relations Act 1969, s 13(9) – appeal of decision of Rights Commissioner – grievance resulting from internal selection process in university – allegations of bias*

This appeal of a decision of a Rights Commissioner by the respondent university followed an internal selection process within the university. The claimant was a senior lecturer and was interviewed for promotion but he was unsuccessful at interview and received one mark less than the successful candidate. He submitted a grievance in which he claimed he was not dealt with appropriately. It was submitted on behalf of the respondent that the post had become available as a result of a retirement and it was advertised nationally. Twelve applicants applied and five were shortlisted, including the successful candidate and the claimant. The Rights Commissioner concluded that the selection process outlined in the university's regulation on appointments to professional posts was adhered to and that no candidate was specifically disadvantaged by the process. With regard to the allegations of bias raised by the claimant, the Rights Commissioner found that if there was a perception of bias or prejudice that may have affected the process then it should have been raised at the commencement of the process or prior to a candidate being selected.

In circumstances where the Rights Commissioner found the claimant to be held in high esteem, he recommended that the claimant be provided with a sabbatical of up to a maximum of 12 months to enhance his career, and on his return he was to be provided with a post-doc researcher to carry out research and that this was to be accepted by the claimant in full and final settlement of these matters.

This recommendation was appealed by the claimant in accordance with s 13(9) of the Industrial Relations Act and a Labour Court hearing took place. It was asserted on behalf of the claimant on appeal that there were repeated inappropriate comments made by a member of the interview panel prior to the interview and that the extreme closeness

---

4.   *A University and a Worker* AD1411.

of the marks should have resulted in a second interview. It was further alleged that there was a failure of the governing body to interview independent witnesses and act on evidence of a colleague. It was submitted on behalf of the respondent that it had conducted a fair, transparent, robust process in which the claimant was not successful and that the respondent must appoint the best available candidate for the position. It was noted by the respondent that the claimant had taken 12 months to file the grievance and that, after investigation by a sub-committee, the respondent was found to have no case to answer.

The Labour Court noted that serious issues had been raised in relation to the manner in which the competition was conducted, to include an allegation of bias. However, the Labour Court noted that the claimant had submitted to the process in the knowledge of the matters on which he grounded his allegation of bias and the Court further noted that these matters should have been raised before the interviews were held. The Court noted that the process was subject to review and that no fault was found with the process. The Court did conclude that, in the circumstances of this case and given the closeness of the result it may have been advisable to have held a second interview. The Labour Court ultimately disallowed the appeal and affirmed the recommendation of the Rights Commissioner.

ABILITY OF THE LABOUR COURT TO INVESTIGATE POST RETIREMENT DISPUTES

[12.05] *Health Service Executive v A Worker[5] – Labour Court – Industrial Relations Act 1969, s 20(1) – whether claimant entitled to gratuity payment on retirement – whether Labour Court had jurisdiction to hear claim where claimant retired from employment and issue not referred to Labour Relations Commission or Labour Court prior to retirement – reliance on opinion of Attorney General provided to Labour Court*

This case concerned a claim for a gratuity payment on retirement. The claimant retired in November 2011. In January 2012 this claim was referred to a Rights Commissioner under the Industrial Relations Acts 1946 to 2012 and the employer objected to the hearing in February 2012. In January 2014, a s 20(1) of the Industrial Relations Act 1969 referral took place. The Labour Court considered whether it had jurisdiction to hear the case, given the claimant had retired from the workforce and where the issue was not referred to it or to the LRC prior to her retirement. The Court noted its decision in *Forfás v A Worker[6]* in 2001 where the Labour Court found that a person who has retired from the workforce cannot be regarded as a worker and that the Court has no jurisdiction to investigate a case brought by such a person unless the matter: (a) is one that is ongoing during the currency of the individual's employment; and (b) was referred to the Labour Relations Commission or the Labour Court prior to the retirement.

---

5.   *Health Service Executive v A Worker* LCR20771.

6.   *Forfás v A Worker* LCR16970.

The Labour Court noted that the advices from which this recommendation derived came from two opinions provided to the Court by the then Attorney General in 1974 and again in 2001. In the *Forfás* case, the Court noted its concern that a large number of people may have no redress in situations of dispute between themselves and their previous employer and made a recommendation that a mechanism be put in place to address situations such as this. The Labour Court held that this finding was again reiterated in three subsequent cases as recently as in 2011. However, the Labour Court noted that it could not act *ultra vires* its statutory powers and thus, acting on the advices received from the Attorney General on this point, it must decline jurisdiction, and it decided accordingly.

CONCEPT OF NORMAL ONGOING CHANGE

[12.06] *An Post v Civil Public and Services Union (CPSU)*[7] *– Labour Court – Industrial Relations Act 1990, s 26(1) – dispute between respondent employer and trade union in relation to proposed introduction of online attendance reporting system – whether proposed changes constitute 'normal ongoing change' as recognised by Labour Court*

This claim centred on a proposal by the respondent employer to introduce a new online attendance recording system in place of the flexitime system in place for approximately 350 members of the CPSU based in the GPO. The respondent submitted that the current flexitime/swipe system was outdated and required modernisation as it was not linked to IT systems. The respondent further contended that it required standardisation of attendance recording systems across all grades of employees and that the new system was already implemented for other employees based at the GPO. The CPSU rejected this and presented a number of claims to be met before agreement on the new system could be reached. As the dispute could not be resolved at a local level, it was the subject of a Labour Relations Commission conciliation conference, at which agreement was not reached.

At the Labour Court, the CPSU submitted that, in return for agreement to the new system, it was seeking an overhaul of the current flexitime system, to include the widening of flexitime attendance bands and increasing the number of flexi days that could be accumulated within the flexi period, access to the flexitime system for new recruits who are currently subject to a six-month probationary period and retention of the zonal clocking arrangement. The CPSU contended that the introduction of the new system was a cost-saving initiative for the respondent and that the claims it had presented to the employer were not cost increasing in nature.

The respondent submitted that there was a business requirement to introduce a standardised and modernised attendance recording system for all employees and that this system would offer an enhanced service both to the company and employees. The respondent stated it was unable to concede the claims of the CPSU.

---

7.   *An Post v Civil Public and Services Union* LCR20805.

The Labour Court said that the first point for consideration was whether the changes constituted normal ongoing change. If the changes could be so characterised, then the CPSU is committed to cooperating under its existing agreement with the respondent. The Court noted its previous recommendations that the concept of normal ongoing change should be understood as involving the use of new systems or methods in providing the same service or undertaking what is essentially the same task.

In this instance, various systems of time recording are applied by the respondent, to include recording by management. What is now at issue involves a new and uniformed system of time recording and in that sense the Court held that it clearly is a new system of undertaking the same task.

The Court was satisfied that the disputed proposal constituted normal ongoing change and thus the union should accept and cooperate with the new systems. The Court recommended that the system be introduced and that its operation be reviewed after a period of six months at which point any operational issues identified could be addressed between the parties. In the circumstances, the Court did not recommend concession of the CPSU's claims associated with the introduction of the new system.

[12.07] *An Post v Public Service Executive Union*[8] – *Labour Court – Industrial Relations Act 1990, s 26(1) – linked to previous claim*

In this claim, which is identical to the previous claim and also concerns the respondent's proposed introduction of an online recording system, the Public Service Executive Union (PSEU) also rejected the proposal and presented a claim for a 2% pay increase in return for agreement on the implementation of the new attendance management system.

At the Labour Court hearing it was submitted by the PSEU that this proposal was a major change that would impact a significant number of its members and it was seeking a 2% pay increase in recognition of the 30 to 45 additional minutes per week that it would potentially take employees to clock in and out under the new system. The respondent asserted that it was a business requirement to introduce a standardised and modernised attendance system for all of its employees. The Labour Court concluded that it could not recommend concession of the union's pay claim in consideration of the introduction of the new system.

UNILATERAL AMENDMENTS TO COLLECTIVE AGREEMENTS

[12.08] *Tesco Ireland Ltd v Mandate and the Services Industrial Professional Technical Union (SIPTU)*[9] – *Labour Court – Industrial Relations Acts 1946 to 2012 – Industrial Relations Act 1990, s 26(1) – whether employer acted unilaterally to alter terms of collective agreement governing workers' sick pay arrangements*

---

8.   *An Post v PSEU* LCR20806.
9.   *Tesco Ireland Ltd v Mandate and SIPTU* LCR20808.

This case concerned a dispute between the claimant trade union and the respondent employer regarding sick pay arrangements. The respondent had adopted a policy of applying a notional social welfare deduction in respect of an employee's sick pay on their fourth, fifth and sixth days of illness. The claimants argued that this breached the terms of a number of collective agreements between the respondent and the trade unions establishing sick pay schemes. The claimants asserted that under the terms of the relevant sick pay schemes, no social welfare deductions could be made until an employee's sixth day of illness. The issue was complicated by the fact that there were approximately 26 sick pay schemes in place in this employment.

The parties failed to resolve the dispute at a conciliation conference organised by the Labour Relations Commission, and the matter was referred to the Labour Court.

The Court found that the respondent had breached the terms of the sick pay schemes. However, the Court refrained from issuing a definitive recommendation on the issue, instead recommending that the parties 'engage with a view to reaching agreement', and allowed a period of 14 weeks for such engagement. Should the parties fail to reach agreement within this time, the Court stated that it would issue a definitive recommendation.

[12.09] *New Boliden Tara Mines v SIPTU[10] – Labour Court – Industrial Relations Acts 1946 to 2012 – Industrial Relations Acts 1969, s 13(9) – appeal from Rights Commissioner – whether employer entitled to unilaterally alter arrangement whereby worker paid extra for shifts*

The claimant had a long-standing arrangement with the respondent whereby the claimant was remunerated for a 10.5 hour shift, notwithstanding that he had only worked 9.5 hours. Following the respondent's decision to discontinue this arrangement, the claimant referred the matter to the Rights Commissioner, alleging that the respondent was not entitled to act unilaterally to bring this arrangement to an end, and that the arrangement should be 'red-circled' for the worker. The Rights Commissioner ruled against the claimant, finding that the complaint was not well founded.

The decision of the Rights Commissioner was appealed to the Labour Court. The respondent submitted that it reserved the right to manage its workers, and that the bringing to an end of a 'windfall benefit' enjoyed by the claimant did not merit compensation. The Labour Court accepted these arguments, and upheld the Rights Commissioner's decision.

[12.10] *Dublin Airport Authority plc v SIPTU and Ryanair Ltd v SIPTU[11] – High Court – Gilligan J – 12 March 2014 – applications for interlocutory injunctions to restrain the defendant (SIPTU) from embarking on industrial action in the form of a work stoppage at Dublin and Cork Airports – whether the secret ballot complied with s 14 of the Industrial Relations Act 1990 – whether there was a trade dispute between the parties*

10.　*New Boliden Tara Mines v SIPTU* AD1450.

11.　*Dublin Airport Authority plc v SIPTU and Ryanair Ltd v SIPTU* [2014] IEHC 644.

These separate applications for interlocutory relief were heard jointly by Gilligan J. A 14-day strike notice was issued by the defendant trade union on 27 February 2014 confirming its intention to conduct industrial action by way of a work stoppage on 14 March 2014 in both Dublin and Cork Airports.

Gilligan J set out the background to the dispute and noted that the proposed industrial action related to the Irish Airline (General Employees) Superannuation Scheme (IASS) pension dispute. Gilligan J noted that the IASS is a multi-employer scheme with members from the Dublin Airport Authority (DAA) (the plaintiff) and also from Aer Lingus and SR Technics, and involved approximately fifteen thousand members to include active current employees of the employer, deferred pensioners and pensioners. The Court noted the DAA's acceptance that there was a substantial deficit in the scheme and that extensive negotiations and discussions with SIPTU and other trade unions were ongoing and parallel discussions had also taken place with the IASS trustees. The Court noted that a substantial part of these discussions took place under the Labour Relations Commission. Gilligan J stated that he was satisfied that the subject matter of the ongoing dispute between members of the IASS Pension Scheme and the plaintiff and Aer Lingus was a complex and difficult matter.

The Court noted that in January 2014, the defendant conducted a ballot for industrial action in relation to a variety of matters. The ballot was confined to members of the defendant who were involved in the IASS and the ballot further included several hundred members of the union who were governed by either or both the Airport Police, Fire Service Agreements or the Dublin Airport Search Agreement, each of which agreements expressly prohibited the taking of any industrial action during the currency of the agreement unless certain steps were taken. The Court further noted the averment in the DAA's affidavit that several hundred other members of the defendant union, who were also employees of the DAA, were not permitted by the defendant union to participate in the ballot, not being members of the IASS.

In response to strike notice, the DAA wrote to the defendant and outlined the serious consequences that industrial action would have for its business and the travelling public. In response, the defendant stated that the situation was most unsatisfactory for SIPTU members who appreciated the seriousness of the situation but who felt frustrated and disappointed at the lack of real progress such that they had no other option but to take industrial action.

The DAA submitted that it was clear from the defendant's strike notice that all of its members in the plaintiff, to include non IASS members, would be taking part in the industrial action despite the fact that not all of the members had participated in the ballot. It was further submitted that many of the defendant's members worked side by side, some of whom were IASS members and others who were not part of the scheme. The plaintiff asserted that it was inconceivable that the defendant could have anticipated that non-members of the IASS could continue to work and not be called upon to support the industrial action. The DAA submitted that the threat to engage in a work stoppage at Dublin and Cork airports on Friday 14 March, one of the busiest days of the year for both airports, would cause irreparable loss and damage to the DAA and that the withdrawal of labour, in particular that of the Police and Fire Service, Security Services and essential airfield staff, was likely to lead to the closure of both airports. The DAA anticipated that some 10,000 passengers would be affected in Dublin and approximately 1,200 passengers in Cork and the knock-on effect would cause significant disruption for at least 24 hours thereafter. It was averred by the DAA that it would suffer irreparable loss and damage which would run to the order or millions of euros and that, if injunctive relief was not granted, the damages would not adequately compensate it for its loss. The DAA further asserted that the balance of convenience favoured the granting of the injunction in all the circumstances. Counsel for the DAA highlighted to the Court that no replying affidavit had been received for from the defendant to contradict in any way the averments made on the DAA's behalf.

Gilligan J noted that two significant issues had been raised by the DAA in respect of the defendant's compliance with s 14(2)(a) of the Industrials Relations Act 1990. The Court held that it was apparent that only those persons who were employees of the plaintiff, members of the defendant union and participants in the IASS scheme were called upon to participate in the secret ballot and that amongst such persons were members of the Airport Police, Fire Service and Airport Search Units. Gilligan J held that a serious situation arose for determination, as to whether or not such persons, having regard to the collective agreements to which they were subject, were entitled to be called upon by the defendant to vote at all. The Court noted that the agreements provided for a series of events to take place prior to such persons taking part in industrial action, and held that there was no indication on the defendant's behalf that such procedures were complied with.

The Court further noted that only those persons who were members of the IASS were called upon to ballot and the question arose whether or not the defendant should have included all of its member employees whom it was reasonable at the time of the ballot for the defendant to believe would be called upon to engage in the strike or other industrial action. The Court noted the uncontroverted averment by the plaintiff that members and non-members of the IASS, all being members of the defendant union, were working side by side. The Court further noted the averment that it was inconceivable that the defendant could have anticipated that the non-members of IASS could continue to work and not be called upon to support the industrial action.

Gilligan J stated that he also had to bear in mind the various ballot papers, and the nature and extent of the industrial action, to include picketing, as proposed by the defendant. Gilligan J stated that for these reasons the legal validity of the secret ballot was clearly an issue and in the particular circumstance of this application no evidence had been offered by the defendant of compliance with the secret ballot requirement or that the averments of the plaintiff were mistaken. The Court concluded that a serious issue to be tried had arisen. The Court was also satisfied that participation in the ballot of union members who were subject to various agreements prohibiting industrial action, unless a series of procedural steps had been complied with, raised a serious issue to be tried as to whether or not their participation in any industrial action was lawful. This further raised a serious issue as to the entitlement of the defendant to procure a breach of legally binding employment agreements.

Gilligan J held that the onus lay upon the defendant to show that a secret ballot in compliance with s 14 of the 1990 Act had been held and in this regard he found that no evidence had been adduced to assist the Court. Accordingly, Gilligan J held that the defendant was accordingly not entitled to rely on the restriction of the right to an injunction as provided to a trade union pursuant to s 19(2) of the Industrial Relations Act 1990 and he proceeded to consider the application in accordance with the principles laid down in *Campus Oil v Minister for Industry and Energy (No 2)*[12] as summarised by Laffoy J in *McCann v Morrissey*[13] namely:

(i) whether the applicant has established that there is a serious issue to be tried;

(ii) whether damages would be an adequate remedy for the DAA if it was successful at the trial and conversely whether if the DAA was not successful at the trial, the entitlement of the defendant to resort to the undertaking as to damages which was given to the Court by the DAA would be an adequate remedy for it; and

(iii) whether the balance of convenience lies in granting or refusing the interlocutory injunction.

The Court also considered the issue raised by the DAA as to whether there was a valid trade dispute between the parties within the meaning of s 8 of the Industrial Relations Act 1990. The Court concluded that the issue was whether the pensions issue is a dispute connected with the employment or non-employment of workers and concerned of the terms of conditions of the workers. The Court considered the current and previous statutory definition as to the meaning of the term trade dispute. Gilligan J stated that he did not have sufficient information before him in relation to the IASS scheme to make a determination as to whether a serious issue arose for determination as regards on whether this 'pension crisis' gave rise to a trade dispute. He held that this was a matter for determination by the High Court at a full hearing and was not a basis for the granting of any injunctive relief against SIPTU on this application.

In relation to whether damages would be an adequate remedy, the Court held that it was clear on the facts as presented that if injunctive relief was not granted, the damages would run in the order of millions of euros and the reality was that the defendant union would not be a mark in respect of same. The Court held that if the relief sought was not granted, damages would not be an adequate remedy to compensate the plaintiff for the loss it would undoubtedly suffer.

Having regard to the significant disruption that would be caused to passengers and airlines and to the economy if injunctive relief was not granted, Gilligan J held that he was satisfied that the balance of convenience favoured the DAA and the granting of the relief sought. Gilligan J held that in circumstances where he was acceding to the plaintiff's application, he did not consider it necessary to consider the application by Ryanair Ltd or to decide on any of the issues that had arisen between Ryanair Ltd and the defendant and he made no findings or order thereon.

---

12. *Campus Oil v Minister for Industry and Energy* [1983] 1 IR 88.
13. *McCann v Morrissey* [2013] IEHC 288.

Chapter 13

INJUNCTIONS

RESTRAIN A DISMISSAL

[13.01] *Hartnett v Advanced Tyre Co Ltd T/A Advanced Pitstop[1] – High Court – Ryan J – application for interlocutory injunction to set aside purported dismissal of plaintiff for serious misconduct – whether procedure of investigation breached plaintiff's constitutional right to fair procedures – failure of employer to present principal witness for cross-examination – failure of plaintiff to disclose receipt of alleged gratuity from witness until appeal stage – balance of convenience*

This application for interlocutory relief arose in circumstances where the plaintiff, who was employed by the defendant as head of fleet truck sales, was dismissed for serious misconduct. The plaintiff was accused of misconduct for allegedly accepting secret commission payments from a supplier of tyres and for giving confidential information about tyre prices. Central to this matter was an email received by the defendant's parent company which recorded information from a third party containing serious allegations against the plaintiff. On receipt of this email, the defendant decided to investigate the matter and suspended the plaintiff during this process. Ryan J concluded that the defendant was justified in taking the view that these were serious complaints warranting investigation and held it was a matter for the defendant as to whether the plaintiff needed to be suspended during that process. Ultimately, a hearing took place at which the plaintiff was accompanied by his legal representative and, in the course of this hearing, the plaintiff denied any wrongdoing. The plaintiff made complaints that the principal witness was not present and thus was not available to be cross-examined by his legal representatives. The defendant confirmed that the witness was available on the telephone and that the plaintiff's legal representative could phone him and have a conversation with him. Ryan J noted that he did not have to decide what facility regarding the witness might have satisfied the requirement of fair procedures. However, he noted that had a video link been arranged that this would have been satisfactory, although he did not want to make conclusions in this regard. He also noted that the legal representative did not take up the opportunity proffered to contact the witness.

The defendant concluded the investigation and the plaintiff was found guilty of the charges and was dismissed. In the course of a subsequent appeal, the plaintiff's legal representative submitted a detailed document in which it was revealed that the witness had provided the plaintiff with a gratuity for attending the meeting (from which the initial allegations came). This was a new issue, but subsequently, at the appeal hearing, the plaintiff and his legal representative, when asked to provide details of same, refused

---

1.   *Hartnett v Advanced Tyre Co Ltd T/A Advanced Pitstop* [2013] IEHC 615.

to divulge any further details and referred the appeal decision-maker to the relevant witness and the defendant. The witness subsequently denied this. Ryan J noted that in the grounding affidavit to this application that the plaintiff had alleged that the witness had given him an envelope containing €1,500 in cash.

The Court noted that the defendant had fallen into errors of procedure. Whilst entitled to suspend the plaintiff and engage in an investigation, there were procedural flaws. The Court concluded that the defendant ought to have arranged for the plaintiff to have an opportunity and some satisfactory mode of cross-examining the witness, as his evidence was crucial and it was the only evidence of the alleged misconduct. The Court concluded that the witness was saying that the plaintiff had sought corrupt unauthorised payments at their meeting and that was the set of allegations the plaintiff was facing: it was therefore down to the witness versus the plaintiff, and the Court stated that the witness could not avoid some form of cross-examination by the plaintiff's representative.

The Court concluded that the investigation conducted by the defendant was a manifestly unfair and unreasonable way for an enquiry to arrive at a conclusion and, 'when one appreciates that this could have meant and did in fact mean the dismissal of the plaintiff, the gravity of the error becomes even more apparent'. The Court concluded that the plaintiff had a strong case to say that his constitutional rights were infringed and, furthermore, he had a strong case that his dismissal was unlawful because it was arrived at following a flawed process in one crucial respect.

The Court then went on to consider the balance of convenience and noted that there had been a series of cases concerning employment injunctions where the High Court had held that it was inappropriate to enjoin a dismissal where the relationship between the parties had broken down with a loss of trust and other necessary features. The Court specifically referred the judgment of MacMenamin J in *Joyce v HSE*.[2]

The Court concluded that the critical question on the balance of convenience was the importance to be attached to the revelation by the plaintiff in the appeal that he had received a gratuity from the witness at their meeting, to his subsequent refusal to furnish details of the appeal, his later claims in the grounding affidavit that the envelope had contained €1,500 and his failure to disclose that to his employer. The Court concluded that if the plaintiff's account was true it was a breach of his duty to the defendant and contrary to its code of conduct to accept money and not to report it. On the other hand, if the story was untrue it undermined the plaintiff's credibility just as he thought it would do for the witness. The Court concluded that any residue of trust that might have existed between the parties could not be considered to be intact and thus the plaintiff had failed to satisfy the balance of convenience test and was not entitled to an injunction.

[13.02] *Bradshaw v Murphy & Ors*[3] *– High Court – Finlay Geoghegan J – application for interlocutory injunction – orders restraining defendants from terminating or purporting to terminate employment of plaintiff – injunctions*

---

2.   *Joyce v HSE* [2005] IEHC 174.
3.   *Bradshaw v Murphy & Ors* [2014] IEHC 146.

restraining defendants from terminating or purporting to terminate partnership between plaintiff and first defendant

The plaintiff, a chef and restaurateur, was employed by the fourth defendant. The plaintiff contended that he was in partnership with the first defendant and that the business of the partnership related to the fourth defendant. The second and third defendants were director and shareholder respectively.

This application for interlocutory relief arose following a meeting between the plaintiff and the first and second defendants on 11 December 2013. There was a significant dispute as to what was said by the defendants at this meeting. It was alleged in an affidavit sworn by the plaintiff that he understood he was being placed on leave for a month, during which time he would be paid, and whilst the first defendant allegedly stated that he did not wish to work with him any longer, his understanding was that everything would be looked at a month later. It was submitted by the first defendant that he told the plaintiff he was being dismissed and the company would pay him for four weeks on certain conditions. Subsequently, the plaintiff understood from further conversations and information that the defendants intended to effect a dismissal and a dissolution of the partnership and these proceedings followed. The defendants offered undertakings to the High Court pending the hearing and determination of the interlocutory application as follows. They undertook:

(i) not to interfere with the plaintiff's share in the partnership the subject matter of the proceedings, partnership assets and the business known as the Copper Bar and Grill, the plaintiff's assets or those of the company and the plaintiff's shareholding the subject matter of the proceedings in the company;

(ii) not to dismiss the plaintiff or take any step to effect the dismissal of the plaintiff; and

(iii) to resume payment on a weekly basis of wages and to make other payments to the plaintiff in specified amounts.

Finlay Geoghegan J noted that the defendants had proffered an open undertaking to the High Court at the outset of the interlocutory hearing, which was limited to an undertaking not to dismiss the plaintiff or cause the fourth defendant to dismiss the plaintiff on the ground of misconduct. The High Court noted that, for the avoidance of doubt, the defendants conceded, for the purpose of the giving of this undertaking only, that misconduct included the matters raised by the first defendant during the course of a meeting between him and the plaintiff that took place on 11 December 2013. The defendants and each of them further undertook not to communicate to any third party that the plaintiff's employment had been terminated on the grounds of misconduct or the matters raised by the first defendant during the course of a meeting between him and the plaintiff that took place on 11 December 2013. The Court noted that, notwithstanding the undertakings offered by the defendants, the plaintiff wished to continue to seek the following interlocutory injunctions:

(i) restraining the termination of his contract of employment with the company; and

(ii) restraining the defendants from terminating or purporting to terminate the partnership with the plaintiff and the first defendant.

Finlay Geoghegan J restated the law in relation to interlocutory injunctions as articulated in *Campus Oil Ltd v Minister for Energy (No 2)*,[4] namely that a plaintiff applicant has to demonstrate a serious issue to be tried, inadequacy of damages and that the balance of convenience lies in favour of granting the order. The Court further noted the obligations on an applicant who seeks a mandatory interlocutory injunction in light of the Supreme Court ruling in *Maha Lingham v Health Service Executive*.[5] Finlay Geoghegan J noted that in such cases it was necessary for the applicant to show at least that he has a strong case that he is likely to succeed at the hearing of the actions.

The Court concluded that the claim by the plaintiff in relation to the purported or potential dismissal from employment by the company was that, at the meetings on 11 December 2013 and in subsequent communications to third parties, it was indicated that the plaintiff was to be dismissed from his employment with the company by reason of alleged misconduct. Counsel for the plaintiff submitted that, having made such allegations of misconduct, any subsequent termination of the plaintiff's employment invoked a requirement for fair procedures. Counsel for the defendants did not dispute this. However, in light of the undertakings proffered by the defendants to the Court pending the final determination of the plaintiff's claim, counsel for the defendants submitted that these principles no longer applied in relation to the interlocutory application. It was submitted by counsel for the defendants that, between then and the trial of the action, the company and the defendants may only terminate the employment of the plaintiff in accordance with the contractual terms, including any implied term of reasonable notice. Counsel for the defendants further submitted that there was no claim made by the plaintiff that the fourth defendant was precluded from terminating his employment in accordance with the express or implied contractual terms of his contract. It was further submitted that there was no serious issue to be tried in relation to the company's entitlement at common law to terminate the employment of the plaintiff in accordance with its contractual terms.

Finlay Geoghegan J accepted this submission. She noted that, whilst the plaintiff may have raised a serious issue to be tried as to whether the fourth defendant was entitled to give effect to a dismissal indicated in the meetings of 11/12 December, it had not on the evidence shown a serious issue to be tried as to the company's entitlement at common law to terminate the employment of the plaintiff without cause in accordance with the relevant contractual provisions.

Finlay Geoghegan J further noted the defendants' undertaking to the Court not to dismiss the plaintiff by reason of the matters raised on 11 December 2013. She decided to refuse the plaintiff's application for an injunction to restrain the termination of his employment by the company by reason of the defendants' undertaking not to dismiss the plaintiff on grounds of misconduct.

---

4.   *Campus Oil Ltd v Minister for Industry and Energy* [1983] 1 IR 88.
5.   *Maha Lingham v Health Service Executive* [2005] IESC 89.

In relation to the other orders sought by the plaintiff with regard to the termination or purported termination of the partnership between the plaintiff and the first defendant, the Court noted that the orders sought were in broad terms. Finlay Geoghegan J noted the agreement between the parties that there was an agreement to form a partnership. She noted that it was common case that the agreement between the plaintiff and the first-named defendant included an agreement that a company be formed and that it was a company which was intended to carry out the proposed restaurant and bar business. She stated that she was not satisfied that the plaintiff on the facts had made out an arguable case that he and the first defendant would personally carry on a business with a view to profit. The plaintiff had made out an arguable case that he was to receive certain financial payments for his contribution to the organisation and establishment of the business to be carried out by the company. Finlay Geoghegan J stated that it was unnecessary to determine whether or not the agreement was arguably a partnership agreement having regard to the provisions of ss 1(2) and 2(A) of the Partnership Act 1890.

Finlay Geoghegan J concluded that, even if it were arguable that the alleged agreement between the parties constituted a partnership agreement, she was not satisfied that the plaintiff had established that damages would not be an adequate remedy for the alleged breaches or purported termination which he was seeking to restrain. The terms allegedly breached were terms relating to the financial reward due to the plaintiff for his contribution to the organisation and establishment of the business.

The Court held that if, at the full hearing of the action, the plaintiff succeeds in establishing that he had an agreement with the first defendant under which he was due to be paid certain sums over and above his salary as an employee, damages would be an adequate remedy. The Court concluded that the plaintiff had failed to establish that damages would not be an adequate remedy and thus the interlocutory injunction sought must be refused. The Court gave the parties liberty to apply in relation to the undertakings given by the defendants and gave directions for the exchange of pleadings for the purpose of effecting speedy determination of matters in dispute. The matter was remitted to the chancery list with liberty to apply for an early hearing date.

[13.03] *Hughes v Mongodb Ltd*[6] *– High Court – Keane J – application for injunction restraining dismissal – whether employer's right to rely on contractual notice provision dependent on reason for dismissal being 'good' – whether dismissal for 'poor performance' (rather than misconduct) gives rise to contractual entitlement of employee to be afforded fair procedures*

The plaintiff was offered employment with the defendant by way of letter of offer dated 3 July 2013 and began work as the defendant's technical director in September 2013. The letter of offer set out various terms of the employment relationship between the parties, including a provision permitting either party to terminate the employment relationship on the giving of one month's notice, with the defendant reserving the right to furnish pay in lieu of notice.

---

6.   *Hughes v Mongodb Ltd* [2014] IEHC 335.

On 8 May 2014, the defendant informed the plaintiff that his contract of employment was being terminated with immediate effect. The defendant acknowledged the plaintiff's contractual right to one month's notice in this regard, and informed the plaintiff that one month's salary would be paid in lieu.

On 9 May 2014, the plaintiff engaged a solicitor, who wrote to the defendant asserting that the termination breached the plaintiff's employment rights, in particular his right to fair procedures and a good name. The defendant replied, stating that the termination was undertaken in accordance with the terms of the plaintiff's employment. The defendant asserted that the termination was not due to any misconduct on the part of the plaintiff, but rather was owing to the fact that, in their opinion, the plaintiff was 'not a good fit' for the company. In subsequent correspondence the plaintiff disputed this, alleging that certain comments made to him by telephone on 8 May 2014 regarding 'performance-related issues' supported his contention that he was in fact dismissed for performance-related reasons not, as the defendant alleged, on a 'no fault' basis. In response, the defendant offered to assuage the plaintiff's fears by providing him with an undertaking that they would remind senior management that the termination was on a no fault basis.

The plaintiff issued proceedings on 14 May 2014, seeking:

(i)   a declaration that he remained employed with the defendant;

(ii) an injunction requiring the defendant to acknowledge and maintain his position; and

(iii) damages for breach of contract, breach of duty, breach of the plaintiff's constitutional right to fair procedures and intentional infliction of emotional suffering.

This judgment was given in relation to an application for an interlocutory injunction to restrain the dismissal. The Court reviewed the law relating to employment injunctions, and noted that the test to be satisfied is that set out by the Supreme Court in *Maha Lingham v Health Service Executive,*[7] namely that a plaintiff must show that he has a strong case and is likely to succeed at the hearing of the action.

The Court refused the plaintiff's request that the question be decided according to the lesser standard applied in *Wallace v Irish Aviation Authority*[8] on the basis that this case could be confined to its facts, and cannot be taken as 'diluting' the *Maha Lingham* test in any general sense. The Court also confirmed that the courts will, in general, be slow to grant interlocutory injunctions to enforce contracts of employment and that in general, 'according to the traditional law at any rate ... the employer was entitled to give notice so long as he complied with the contractual obligation of reasonable notice whether he had a good reason or bad for doing it'. For the purpose of determining whether the plaintiff had satisfied the *Maha Lingham* 'strong case/likely success' test for the grant of an employment injunction, Keane J proceeded to consider the strength of the plaintiff's case and its likelihood of success at trial.

---

7.   *Maha Lingham v Health Service Executive* [2006] 17 ELR 137.

8.   *Wallace v Irish Aviation Authority* [2012] IEHC 178.

To this end, Keane J noted that the plaintiff's claim consisted of three main contentions:

(i) that the traditional common law position has been reversed such that an employer is no longer entitled to terminate a contract of employment in accordance with the relevant notice provisions if his reason for termination can be established and can be shown to be bad;

(ii) that in fact the termination in this case was not 'no fault' as the defendant alleged, but rather was due to 'performance related issues'; and

(iii) that 'poor performance' was a bad reason for termination, and that an implied term must be read into the contract of employment that terminations for 'poor performance' must be undertaken only following a disciplinary process that applies all the relevant rules of natural and constitutional justice.

In relation to the first of the plaintiff's arguments, the Court stated that there was no authority for this proposition. Further, Keane J noted the decision of Finlay Geoghegan J in *Bradshaw v Murphy*[9] as authority to the contrary. In that case, the plaintiff's application for an interlocutory injunction was refused on the basis of the employer's prima facie contractual right to terminate for no reason by giving notice, notwithstanding the fact that proceedings were being taken alleging wrongful dismissal.

With regard to the plaintiff's second argument, the Court said that there was no evidence, notwithstanding the plaintiff's disputed evidence regarding matters discussed on the phone call of 8 May 2014, to back up that contention. In contrast, the Court noted that the defendant had repeatedly expressed its willingness to provide the plaintiff with excellent references, and to remind senior management of the 'no fault' nature of the dismissal. Referring with approval to the judgment of Clarke J in *Carroll v Bus Atha Cliath/Dublin Bus*[10] where it was held that an employer must afford an employee fair procedures if they dismiss them due to misconduct, but may dismiss for no reason just by giving notice, Keane J stated:

> I do not believe that there is any authority, and certainly none has been produced to me, for the proposition that a bad reason that informs, but which is not relied upon to justify, the termination of an employment contract in accordance with its terms, renders the dismissal wrong in law.

In relation to the plaintiff's third argument, the Court noted there was no such express provision contained in the plaintiff's contract of employment (ie the letter of offer). In such an instance, the plaintiff was asking the Court to read such a provision into the contract.

To this end, the plaintiff relied on the decision in *Naujoks v Institute of Bioresearch*[11] as authority for the proposition that dismissals for 'poor performance' attract the same requirement for disciplinary procedures as dismissals for misconduct. However, the

---

9. *Bradshaw v Murphy* [2014] IEHC 146 and *ACELY 2014*, para **[13.03]**.
10. *Carroll v Bus Atha Cliath/Dublin Bus* [2005] 4 IR 184.
11. *Naujoks v Institute of Bioresearch* [2007] ELR 25.

Court, examining the facts in *Naujoks*, stated that the decision in that case should be very much confined to its own facts, concerning as it did the interpretation of a contract that was drafted in such a way as to make 'failure to properly discharge duties' (or, arguably, 'poor performance') directly equivalent to dishonesty (ie 'misconduct'). Accordingly, Keane J stated that *Naujoks* cannot be taken as authority for a broad proposal that dismissal for performance is to be treated as equivalent to a dismissal on the grounds of misconduct in every case, thereby attracting an entitlement to fair procedures in either case that is to be implied into every contract of employment.

The Court concluded that the plaintiff had not established that he had a 'strong case' that was 'likely to succeed at trial', and thus had failed to meet the test for an employment injunction as set out in *Maha Lingham*. Accordingly, the injunction was refused, and the Court found it unnecessary to go on to consider the adequacy of damages or balance of convenience tests.

RESTRAIN SUSPENSION OF SICK PAY/DISCIPLINARY PROCEEDINGS

[13.04] *Elmes & Ors v Vedanta Lisheen Mining Ltd & Ors[12] – High Court – Ryan J – interlocutory injunction application – whether suspension of sick pay to plaintiffs was void and in breach of contract – whether any subsequent disciplinary proceedings should be injuncted – whether mandatory order should be granted to direct that proposed investigation be carried out by independent investigator*

The plaintiffs in an interlocutory application asserted that the suspension of their sick pay was void and in breach of contract and they further sought to prevent any disciplinary proceedings being taken. The plaintiffs also sought a mandatory order to direct that a proposed investigation would be carried out by an independent investigator.

The plaintiffs were members of the senior management team employed at Lisheen Mining, and, at the time of the hearing of this matter, each of them was on sick leave. Six weeks after the date on which each of the plaintiffs first certified themselves as unfit to work, their sick pay was suspended.

The Court noted that there was a history of 'suspicion and unease on the part of the plaintiffs' going back to the time when the defendant company took over Lisheen Mines in place of the previous employer and owner. The Court noted that a trigger for the current difficulties appears to have been a fatal workplace accident which occurred in April 2013. Subsequent to this tragic accident, two separate investigations were commenced – one by a senior employee of the defendant and the second by an expert in mining safety engaged by the defendant. In a video-link presentation to the executive committee of Vedanta Resources Worldwide, a slide was presented by the CEO of the defendant which referenced the fatality and the slide highlighted a number of 'specific remedial actions' to be taken, which included 'discipline of senior management at Lisheen for a failure of control/discipline'. It was the first time that Mr Elmes, one of the plaintiffs, and his colleagues had seen this particular slide and there had been no

---

12.   *Elmes & Ors v Vedanta Lisheen Mining Ltd & Ors* [2014] IEHC 73.

suggestion previously that disciplinary action was likely. Despite various assurances that were given after the fact that no decision had been taken with regard to any disciplinary action, the plaintiffs argued that 'the outcome of the internal and external investigation had been predetermined and that there had been no formal notification to any management with respect to any alleged failures'.

Ryan J reached some important conclusions on matters that occur frequently in these types of injunction applications. Firstly, he concluded that the plaintiffs were not entitled to an injunction to stop disciplinary action, if any. Ryan J noted the entitlement of an employer to subject workers to a disciplinary process and reaffirmed that:

> courts are reluctant to interfere in the internal affairs of a company in an area of legitimate corporate concern. The disciplinary process is governed by rules of law and contractual terms, express and implied, but until steps are taken, there is no basis or warrant for interference.

In the context of this case and the tragic fatal accident that had occurred, Ryan J noted as relevant that:

> it was proper for a company to be extremely concerned to establish all the relevant facts about a fatal accident and to want to look at how similar tragedies might be avoided in future. In that context, the people in charge of the location of the accident cannot expect to be immunised from criticism or sanction in advance by way of a court order.

With regard to the proposed investigation, Ryan J did not recognise any entitlement to an order that an independent investigation be carried out. He held that:

> how a company is managed is a matter for its own management and a court is not entitled, even if prima facie of opinion that an employee has a legitimate grievance or even a series of complaints, to dictate that there should be an independent or other sort of inquiry. Nor should the court supervise the process. If an employee exhausts the grievance procedure and is still dissatisfied, his options do not in my opinion include the right to demand an inquiry or specify its nature or have a court impose that.

Ryan J further restated the Court's unwillingness to nominate a person to hear certain grievances in this matter, but he did criticise the employer for 'insisting that the plaintiffs had to return to work before they could report the grievances'.

With regard to sick pay, there was an evidential conflict as to the past practice. The Court considered a SIPTU agreement which provided clearly for sick pay for six weeks. However, the plaintiffs argued that discretion had always been used to pay sick pay for longer periods. Ryan J stated that:

> the SIPTU agreement provides employees not with a maximum, but with a minimum entitlement of six weeks' pay, subject of course to proper certification. Custom and practice in the employer company are that this is not the only payment that is made during absence for illness. There are cases where only six weeks' pay was paid, but they are exceptional. That is what would be expected of a good employer in the modern world. The company has discretion which it exercises in the particular case to draw a line and cease the payment. That is what was missing

in these cases and which makes them inconsistent and in conflict with the reasonable and sensitive practice normally followed by the employer.

Ryan J then went on to consider what form of sick pay the employer should have continued and concluded that it should not be open-ended. He considered the seniority of the plaintiffs, their work records, the nature of their illnesses and the past discretionary practice of the company, and decided to fix a period of six months. He noted that the plaintiffs could apply for further additional sick pay but this would be a matter for the defendants to determine on the merits of the applications in light of the above information, the prognosis in each case, the views of the defendants' medical advisors, the plaintiffs' cooperation with medical examinations and other material examinations.

RESTRAIN A DISCIPLINARY PROCESS UNTIL THE DETERMINATION OF CRIMINAL PROCEEDINGS

[13.05] *Rogers v An Post[13] – High Court – Keane J – application for interlocutory injunction to restrain any further steps in disciplinary process relating to plaintiff until determination of criminal proceedings in Circuit Criminal Court – application refused where grant of interlocutory injunction not appropriate as means of maintaining status quo – effective contest between parties likely to be finally decided summarily in favour of plaintiff – defendant would be precluded from opportunity of having its rights determined at full trial*

The plaintiff was the acting branch manager at Roscommon Post Office and was suspended on full pay by the defendant pending the outcome of disciplinary proceedings against him. The investigation concerned whether the plaintiff had engaged in serious misconduct by allegedly tampering with an item of registered post containing a urine sample from another postal worker, which was en route from a member of An Garda Síochána in Roscommon to the Medical Bureau of Road Safety in Dublin for analysis in connection with a suspected drink-driving offence. The plaintiff was detained for questioning by An Garda Síochána and subsequently was charged with an offence of perverting the course of justice. A trial took place before judge and jury at Roscommon Circuit Criminal Court between 26 November 2013 and 5 December 2013. The jury could not agree upon a verdict and was discharged. A retrial was fixed, to commence in December 2014.

In September 2012, the defendant wrote to the plaintiff to advise him that he would be suspended on full pay pending the outcome of this process. He was advised that he would be afforded an opportunity to make representations and/or explanations to the defendant and would also be offered an oral hearing as an alternative to furnishing a written explanation. Following an exchange of correspondence between the plaintiff's and defendant's representatives, it was agreed that the process would be deferred pending the determination of the criminal charge against the plaintiff. The defendant

---

13.   *Rogers v An Post* [2014] IEHC 412.

agreed to permit the plaintiff to be represented at the proposed oral hearing by a solicitor and counsel even though that was not contemplated under its agreed disciplinary procedures.

After the outcome of the first criminal trial, the defendant wrote to the plaintiff to indicate its intention to restart the disciplinary process against him. The plaintiff objected to the resumption of the disciplinary process on the basis that it was proposed to conduct a retrial of the criminal charge against him. A plenary summons issued in April 2014 in which the plaintiff sought a single substantive relief, namely an injunction restraining the defendant from taking any further steps in the disciplinary process relating to the plaintiff until the determination of criminal proceedings then pending before Roscommon Circuit Criminal Court.

Keane J described the submissions of the plaintiff as follows: specifically that if the injunction was not granted he would suffer irremediable prejudice, either through being constrained or inhibited in his participation in the disciplinary process or, should he participate fully, by potentially losing (at least some of) the benefit of the privilege against self-incrimination in the criminal process, or the tactical advantage of not disclosing his line of defence in advance of trial or both. The plaintiff further submitted that there was a fair issue to be tried as to whether the due deference to those constitutional rights to a trial in due course of law and to a disciplinary process that accords with the requirements of natural and constitutional justice and fair procedures required that the disciplinary process should be suspended pending the determination of the criminal charge against him.

The High Court noted the Supreme Court decision in *O'Flynn v Mid Western Health Board*[14] in which the Supreme Court held that there is no immutable right that civil proceedings must remain at a standstill to await the outcome of a criminal investigation.

Keane J stated that the plaintiff must show more than that a criminal trial is pending arising out of the same events, as if this were enough then it seemed to him that there would be an immutable rule that disciplinary proceedings must remain suspended to await the outcome of a criminal prosecution in every case. The other arguments put forward by the plaintiff were that the defendant had not set out precisely what allegation was being levelled against the plaintiff, rendering it impossible for him to defend himself; no allegation could be fairly or properly established against him except through the evidence of witnesses and presumably such evidence to be given *viva voce* and subject to cross-examination and that the legal representation he was permitted to have at the proposed oral hearing conferred no benefit upon him unless the process was conducted in that way.

Keane J considered the decision of the High Court in *Carroll v Law Society of Ireland (No 2)*.[15] Keane J noted that one of the arguments put forward in that case was that the proposed hearing risked compromising the applicant's privilege against self-incrimination in the event of any subsequent criminal prosecution against him. Keane J noted that in that case, various declarations were sought by way of judicial review, to include a declaration that if the committee did have jurisdiction to hear and determine

---

14.   *O'Flynn v Mid Western Health Board* [1991] 2 IR 223.
15.   *Carroll v Law Society of Ireland (No 2)* [2003] 1 IR 284.

complaints against the applicant, it could not rely on hearsay evidence and must permit cross-examination of witnesses.

Keane J noted the finding of McGuinness J that:

> the committee's inquiry in this case was not a court of law, but ... it was crucial to the applicant's future professional career and it must act fairly in accordance with the principles of natural and constitutional justice. I would, however, accept the submission from counsel for the respondent that it is not the function of judicial review to direct procedure in advance.

McGuinness J, in that case, had regard to the *dictum* of Carroll J in *Philips v Medical Council*[16] and was not prepared to make the declaration sought by the applicant.[17] Keane J stated that there was some force to the argument that the same stricture must apply *mutatis mutandis* to any application for an injunction to restrain a proposed disciplinary process in an employment law context.

The Court noted the submission of the defendant that this process was still at a disciplinary inquiry stage aimed at establishing whether disciplinary proceedings against the plaintiff were warranted. In that context, the defendant submitted that it was still waiting for the plaintiff's explanation or representations which should be forthcoming and which it intended to consider at the proposed oral hearing which had been arranged at the plaintiff's own request. The Court noted the decision of McGuinness J in *Carroll* in respect of the privilege against self-incrimination and that, while this was a constitutionally-protected right, it was not an absolute one.

Keane J then considered the plaintiff's argument that the defendant had not set out precisely what allegation was being levelled against him and noted that this was an argument which was difficult to follow. The Court referred to correspondence sent by the defendant to the plaintiff indicating it was considering disciplinary action against him to include his dismissal and noted it contained very specific details of the misconduct at issue.

Finally, the Court considered the final argument of the plaintiff that a disciplinary process should be restrained on the further discrete ground that it was as yet unclear whether any telephone communications involving him or his detention in Roscommon Garda Station were unlawfully recorded or intercepted by An Garda Síochána. The Court noted that these were matters the subject of the Commission of Investigation on the operation of Garda Síochána Telephone Recording Systems established on 30 April 2014 by the Commission of Investigation (Certain Matters relative to An Garda Síochána and Other Persons) Order 2013. The High Court stated that it had not yet been made clear how any issues could be capable of affecting the disciplinary process concerning the plaintiff, particularly in circumstances where it was the plaintiff himself who wished to rely on the contents of the written caution statement that he made while in garda custody for the purpose of the proposed oral hearing that was to form part of the disciplinary process.

---

16.   *Philips v Medical Council* [1992] ILRM 469.
17.   Carroll J: 'Judicial review does not exist to direct procedure in advance, but to make sure bodies which have made decisions acceptable of review have carried out their duties in accordance with the law and in conformity with natural and constitutional justice.'

The Court considered the submissions made by the plaintiff in his contention that his application was governed by the *Campus Oil*[18] guidelines. Keane J stated that it was clear in this case that the grant of the interlocutory injunction would have the practical effect of determining the proceedings as a whole, because the plaintiff would have obtained in advance of trial the very relief that he is seeking at the trial of the action. Keane J noted the approach of Laffoy J in *Jacob v Irish Amateur Rowing Union Ltd*[19] where the plaintiff sought an order restraining the defendant from preventing him from competing at a rowing regatta which represented his final opportunity to compete for a place representing Ireland at the Single Schull Class at the 2008 Olympic Games. Keane J decided to approach the present application by reference to the principles identified by Laffoy J in that case and reached the following conclusions:

(a) That the grant of an interlocutory injunction is discretionary and it is intended to be temporary, maintaining the *status quo* until the rights and obligations of the parties can be properly determined at trial. Keane J had found it particularly telling that the temporal scope of the interlocutory injunction sought was that it should remain in force pending the determination of the criminal proceedings against the plaintiff, rather than pending the trial of the present action. He stated that the real significance of this particular wording was that it served to indicate an implied acceptance by the plaintiff that the interlocutory relief he sought would, if granted, determine the ultimate issue in the main action in his favour.

(b) This case is not one that is likely to go to trial at the instance of the plaintiff if he were granted the substantive relief that he sought in the action at the interlocutory stage. Keane J held that the grant of an interlocutory injunction is not appropriate in this case as a means of maintaining the *status quo* pending such a trial. Keane J said he was satisfied that this was a case in which if the injunction sought were granted, the effective contest between the parties is likely to have been finally decided summarily in favour of the plaintiff.

(c) It would be an injustice to grant the injunction now sought at an interlocutory stage as there was very great likelihood that this would effectively preclude the defendant from the opportunity of having its rights determined at a full trial.

(d) He was unable to conclude that this was an exceptional case in which the plaintiff's evidence was so strong that to refuse an injunction and to allow the case to go to trial would be an unnecessary waste of time and expense or that it would do an overwhelming injustice to the plaintiff. In this regard, he noted the judgment of May LJ in the Court of Appeal of England and Wales in *Cayne v Global Natural Resources plc*,[20] which was quoted by Laffoy J in *Jacobs*.

Keane J refused the application.

---

18. *Campus Oil Ltd v Minister for Industry and Energy* [1983] 1 IR 88.
19. *Jacob v Irish Amateur Rowing Union Ltd* [2008] 4 IR 731.
20. *Cayne v Global Natural Resources plc* [1984] 1 All ER 225.

RESTRAIN THE OPERATION OF THE PUBLIC SERVICE MANAGEMENT (SICK LEAVE) REGULATIONS 2014 TO MEMBERS OF AN GARDA SÍOCHÁNA PENDING THE OUTCOME OF JUDICIAL REVIEW PROCEEDINGS

[13.06] See *Garda Representative Association v Minister for Public Expenditure and Reform*: para **21.08**.

COSTS

[13.07] *Irish Bacon Slicers Ltd v Weidemark Fleischwaren GmbH & Co[21] – High Court – Rules of the Superior Courts, Ord 99 – whether plaintiff entitled to costs of motion seeking interlocutory injunction – delay on part of defendant in proffering undertaking*

The issue before the High Court was whether the plaintiff was entitled to the costs of its motion seeking an interlocutory injunction, in circumstances where the plaintiff had requested an undertaking from the defendant not to act on its threat of winding up the plaintiff company. However, no undertaking was received from the defendant until five weeks after the plaintiff's request at the High Court hearing.

The plaintiff claimed that costs should follow the event in accordance with Order 99 of the Rules of the Superior Courts; that event being the disposal of the plaintiff's motion by the giving of an undertaking by the defendant.

The defendant resisted the application for costs, submitting that the appropriate way to proceed was to give an undertaking and to then bring proceedings to recover the debt in the usual way when issues could be determined on oral evidence, ie that the costs of the injunction should await the outcome of the claim in relation to the debt. It submitted that no 'event' in the context of Ord 99 of the Rules of the Superior Courts had occurred in order for the award of costs to follow. It argued that the giving of an undertaking should not be seen as a capitulation or an acceptance that the plaintiff was not indebted to the defendant.

The High Court held that defendant's argument that no 'event' had taken place was incorrect. The Court stated that Ord 99 RSC supported this in that the new r 1(4A) contained no derogation from the general rule of discretion contained in r 1(1) of Ord 99 RSC. It stated that the Court is required simply to exercise its discretion and is not constrained by any rule that says that costs must follow the event.

The Court pointed out that as the defendant's undertaking had been accepted by the Court, it would constitute contempt of court if the defendant were to breach the undertaking. The Court held that the acceptance of the undertaking determined the application and that the Court was now required, by virtue of new r 1(4A) RSC to make an award of costs at its discretion.

---

21. *Irish Bacon Slicers Ltd v Weidemark Fleischwaren GmbH & Co* [2014] IEHC 293.

The Court exercised its discretion in favour of the plaintiff. It held that the plaintiff was entitled to take seriously the threat that a petition for winding up could be presented against the company. It stated that the plaintiff had acted reasonably in requesting an undertaking that the threat of winding up would not be followed through and that, where no response was obtained, an injunction be sought. The Court pointed out that almost five weeks had passed, during which the plaintiff had incurred significant additional costs in dealing with the motion and that it was only at the hearing that the defendant informed the Court of its willingness to give an undertaking to the Court in the terms of the plaintiff's motion. The Court pointed out that the undertaking did not emanate from any prior negotiations between the parties, but rather was an unsolicited act even though it had clearly been requested by the plaintiff some five weeks previously. In doing so, the Court stated that the reality was that it was only the defendant that prevented the matter being determined by the Court. It stated that the undertaking should have been given by the defendant five weeks previously when it was requested.

The Court acknowledged that it was of course desirable on policy grounds that parties should not needlessly pursue applications for injunctive interlocutory relief where it is possible to secure an agreed solution short of an injunction order, such as the giving of an undertaking. However given the facts of the case, the defendant would never have been justified in presenting a petition for the winding up of the plaintiff company as there would have been a real risk of abuse of process given the very early engagement of the plaintiff company in relation to the issue of liability for the debt claimed. Furthermore, it stated that it was the failure on the defendant's part to provide the undertaking sought that resulted in the granting of an interim injunction and the pursuit of an interlocutory injunction by the plaintiff.

The Court concluded that it was obvious in the circumstances that the costs should be awarded to the plaintiff. It accepted that each case depends on its own facts, but it said that the days are gone when the Court would, almost as a matter of convenience and routine, simply reserve the question of costs to the hearing. Furthermore, the Court stated that it should not have been necessary for the plaintiff to bring the motion and it would not have been brought if the defendant had simply given the undertaking to the plaintiff. The Court distinguished this case from *Callagy v Minister for Education & Ors*[22] in that the plaintiff in the latter case had unilaterally decided not to proceed with his case due to certain developments in the case.

---

22.   *Callagy v Minister for Education & Ors* (23 May 2003) SC.

Chapter 14

INSOLVENCY

EAT PROCEEDINGS AGAINST A RESPONDENT IN ADMINISTRATION

[14.01] *Tracey v Game Stores Group Ltd[1] – Employment Appeals Tribunal – Unfair Dismissals Acts 1977 to 2007 as amended – European Council Regulation (EC) No 1346/2000 – unfair dismissal – non-attendance by or on behalf of respondent – correspondence from UK administrators not accepted by Employment Appeals Tribunal*

In this case, the EAT considered an unfair dismissal claim brought against a respondent in UK administration.

The respondent did not attend the EAT, but the joint administrators of the respondent wrote to the EAT to advise the EAT of their appointment by the UK High Court. In their written submissions, the joint administrators asserted that in accordance with European Council Regulation (EC) No 1346/2000, the administration took precedence over any local legislation and that no legal proceedings could proceed without their consent, which was not forthcoming in this case.

The EAT stated that if the respondent wished to make a jurisdictional point, it should have appeared or instructed a representative to appear on its behalf with its submissions on jurisdiction. The EAT proceeded to hear the substantive case and upheld the claimant's claim.

See **CHAPTER 27** – Unfair Dismissals at **[27.23]**.

FALSE ASSURANCES BY LIQUIDATOR

[14.02] See *Phelan v REL Refrigeration Ltd[2]* in **[22.28]**.

---

1. *Tracey v Game Stores Group Ltd* UD1632/2011.
2. *Phelan v REL Refrigeration Group Ltd* RP411/2013.

Chapter 15

LEGISLATION

SELECTED ACTS
Irish Human Rights and Equality Commission Act 2014

[15.01] The Irish Human Rights and Equality Commission Act 2014 (the Act) provides for the dissolution of the Human Rights Commission and the Equality Authority and the transfer of their functions to a new body, the Irish Human Rights and Equality Commission. The Act also amends the Employment Equality Act 1998 and the Equal Status Act 2000.

The functions of the Commission are to protect and promote human rights and equality, to encourage the development of a culture of respect for human rights, equality, and inter-cultural understanding in the State, to promote understanding and awareness of the importance of human rights and equality in the State, to encourage good practice in inter-cultural relations, to promote tolerance and acceptance of diversity in the State, and to work towards the elimination of human rights abuses, discrimination and prohibited conduct, while respecting diversity and the freedom and dignity of each person.

Section 30(b) of the Act also provides that the Irish Human Rights and Equality Commission will have responsibility for providing information to the public and to keep under review the effectiveness of the Employment Equality Acts 1998 to 2011.

Section 12(1) of the Act provides that the Irish Human Rights and Equality Commission shall consist of not more than 15 and not less than 12 members, one of whom shall be the Chief Commissioner of the Commission. Section 12(2) prescribes gender balance in the composition of the Commission. Section 15(5) of the Act provides that members must have experience of any or all of the following issues; human rights matters or law; equality matters or law; public sector administration and reform; board management and corporate governance.

Section 32 of the Act states that the Commission may require an undertaking or group of undertakings to carry out an equality action plan or review. Section 33 of the Act makes provision for the Irish Human Rights and Equality Commission to issue substantive notices requiring information from a person or requiring a person or undertaking to take action in relation to equality reviews or equality action plans. Any substantive notices to be issued under this section must be notified to the person in writing in advance of being issued. The Act provides for a period of 42 days' notice. Previously the period of notice under the Employment Equality Act was 28 days.

Friendly Societies and Industrial and Provident Societies (Miscellaneous Provisions) Act 2014

[15.02] The Friendly Societies and Industrial and Provident Societies (Miscellaneous Provisions) Act 2014 has been introduced to reduce the regulatory burden on cooperative societies through the introduction of a number of reforms. The Act allows individual societies to set their own limit on individual shareholdings in the society; it extends the period of the preparation and submission of annual returns and accounts; and it makes it easier for cancelled societies to be restored to the Register of Friendly Societies. The Act permits cooperatives to avail of the examinership process and eases fundraising restrictions for non-agricultural societies.

Court of Appeal Act 2014

[15.03] The Court of Appeal Act 2014 provides for the establishment of the Court of Appeal. The Court of Appeal is the default court for hearing all appeals from decisions of the High Court and its decisions are final, save in certain limited circumstances. It is possible in exceptional circumstances to bypass the Court of Appeal and appeal a ruling of the High Court directly to the Supreme Court (a leapfrog appeal). Permission to bring a leapfrog appeal must first be obtained from the Supreme Court and is only granted if the Supreme Court is satisfied that (i) the High Court decision involves a matter of general public importance; and/or (ii) the interests of justice require that the appeal be heard by the Supreme Court. Parties wishing to appeal a decision of the High Court will need to carefully consider whether the decision is one which warrants a leapfrog appeal or whether the more appropriate route is to go directly to the Court of Appeal.

Decisions of the Court of Appeal are in the ordinary course final. However, permission to bring a further appeal may be sought from the Supreme Court. The Supreme Court will only grant such permission if it satisfied that: (i) the decision of the Court of Appeal involves a matter of general public importance; and/or (ii) the interests of justice require that the appeal be heard by the Supreme Court.

Social Welfare and Pensions Act 2014

[15.04] The Social Welfare and Pensions Act 2014[1] (the Act) was enacted to give further effect to Directive 2010/41/EU on the application of equal treatment between men and women engaged in self-employment. Section 16 of the Act provides that the spouse or civil partner of a self-employed worker can benefit from social protection. The amendments provided for in s 16 mean that liability for social insurance contributions is extended to spouses and civil partners of self-employed contributors who are not business partners or employees, where they perform the same or ancillary tasks.

Health Identifiers Act 2014

[15.05] The Health Identifiers Act 2014 provides for the assignment of a unique number to an individual to whom a health service is being, has been or may be provided; to provide for the assignment of a unique number to a person who provide a health service

---

1.   See **Ch 18**.

and the provision for the establishment and maintenance of registers in respect of these numbers.

Section 5(1) of the Act provides that the Minister for Health may assign a unique number, known as a 'health identification number', to an individual to whom a health service is being provided. This number of itself will contain no personal data. Section 6 of the Act provides for the establishment and maintenance of a National Register of Individual Health Identifiers. This register will contain the individual health identification number and such of the individual's other identification particulars that are known. This information is prescribed in s 2 of the Act and includes: name; date of birth; place of birth; sex; address; nationality; PPS number; date of death in the case of a deceased individual; signature; photograph (not being a photograph which falls within a class of photographs prescribed as a class of photographs to which this paragraph and does not apply); and any other particulars (excluding clinical information relating to the individual) prescribed for the purpose of this paragraph.

Section 13 of the Act provides that health service provider identifiers can be assigned to a health practitioner such as a general practitioner or dentist; a relevant body such as a hospital; and a relevant employee or agent of a health practitioner or relevant body. Section 14 provides for the establishment and maintenance of a National Register of Health Service Provider Identifiers.

Local Government Reform Act 2014

[15.06] The Local Government Reform Act 2014 was enacted on 27 January 2014. The Act gave legal effect to the reform programme set out in the Government's *A Guide to Putting People First – Action Programme for Effective Local Government* published in October 2012. The objective of the Act is to reform local government structures and strengthen governance and accountability in local government.

The main change to the local government structure was the dissolution of all 80 town councils and their replacement by municipal districts. Other structural reforms included the merger of city and county councils (in Limerick, Tipperary and Waterford), the establishment of Local Community Development Committees and provision for a vote for the establishment of an office of directly elected mayor for the Dublin Metropolitan area.

Staff from dissolved authorities (including town councils) transferred under the Act to the successor authorities on no less beneficial terms and conditions of service or on remuneration to which they were subject immediately before the transfer date, except in accordance with a collective agreement negotiated with a trade union or staff association. Any superannuation benefits awarded to such staff, and the terms and conditions relating to those benefits, must be no less favourable than those applicable immediately before the commencement of the Act.

The Act also provides for the replacement of the post of manager of local authorities with the post of chief executive. Every person who was a city or county manager of a local authority immediately before the establishment date shall continue in office and be referred to as the chief executive of the relevant authority. Elected members decide the appointment of the chief executive recommended by the Public Appointments Service on foot of the selection process for the post. The Act sets out the procedure for suspending or removing the chief executive for 'stated misbehaviour'. The chief executive holds employment until he/she dies, resigns or is removed from office, for a term specified by Ministerial order or until he/she attains an age specified by Ministerial order.

Employment Permits (Amendment) Act 2014

[15.07] See **[11.02]**.

Protected Disclosures Act 2014

[15.08] See CHAPTER 29.

Competition and Consumer Protection Act 2014

[15.09] The Competition and Consumer Protection Act 2014 provides for the establishment of a body, to be known as the Competition and Consumer Protection Commission, to provide certain statutory functions to include the promotion of competition, the promotion and protection of the interest and welfare of consumers, the carrying out of investigations into complaints made by any person into suspected breaches of statutory provisions, (arts 101 or 102 of the Treaty of the Functioning of the European Union, the Competition (Amendment) Act 1996 and the Competition Act 1991), to enforce the relevant statutory provision, to encourage compliance with the relevant statutory provisions and to set strategic objectives for the Competition and Consumer Protection Commission and to ensure appropriate systems and procedures are in place to achieve strategic objectives. The Competition and Consumer Protection Act 2014 also provides for the dissolution of the Competition Authority and the National Consumer Agency and amends the law in relation to medium mergers.

Industrial Development (Forfás Dissolution) Act 2014

[15.10] The Industrial Development (Forfás Dissolution) Act 2014 makes provision for the dissolution of Forfás and transfers certain functions of Forfás to the Minister for Jobs, Enterprise and Innovation, Enterprise Ireland, the Industrial Development Authority (IDA) and the Health and Safety Authority. The Act provides for the Irish National Accreditation Board as a committee of the Health and Safety Authority. The Act provides for the transfer of seconded staff to Enterprise Ireland, to the IDA, to Science Foundation Ireland, and to the National Standards Authority of Ireland immediately before the coming into operation of the Act in order to become a member of staff of each of those bodies.

Health (General Practitioners Service) Act 2014

[15.11] The Health (General Practitioners Service) Act 2014 (the Act) amends the Health Act 1970 to provide for the making available of a general practitioner medical and surgical service to persons who are ordinarily resident in the State and who have not attained the age of six years. It further amends the Nursing Home Support Scheme Act 2009 and the Opticians Act 1956.

National Treasury Management Agency (Amendment) Act 2014

[15.12] The National Treasury Management Agency (Amendment) Act 2014 (the Act) provides for the reconstitution of the National Treasury Management Agency (NTMA) and confers on the NTMA new functions in relation to State bodies, assets and proposals for investment and transfers certain functions of the National Development Finance Agency relating to infrastructure. The Act provides for the delegation to, and conferral on, the NTMA of functions in relation to the management of certain claims of a legal nature against or in favour of the State and certain related functions. The Act provides for the Ireland Strategic Investment Fund and the transfer to it of assets and liabilities of the National Pensions Reserve Fund and to provide for its management by NTMA. The Act further provides for the dissolution of the National Pensions Reserve Fund Commission, the National Development Finance Agency and certain committees.

Public Health (Sunbeds) Act 2014

[15.13] The Public Health (Sunbeds) Act 2014 (the Act) regulates the use and supply of sunbeds and prohibits persons under 18 from using a sunbed on a sunbed premises. The Act further prohibits the sale or hire of sunbeds to persons under 18 years. Section 14 of the Act provides that the Minister for Health shall prescribe training leading to a qualification in the use of sunbeds and further the Minister for Health may prescribe such qualifications to be held by persons who offer sunbeds for use, sale or hire.

The Act sets out the forms that prescribed training may take, and s 14(4) of the Act requires an owner or manager of a sunbed business to ensure that persons who supervise the operation of sunbeds in the course of their employment have satisfactorily completed the appropriate prescribed training and have been awarded the prescribed qualifications. Section 14(5) of the Act states that a person who has not completed prescribed training and does not hold a prescribed qualification in the use of sunbeds, shall not supervise the operation of, or sell or hire a sunbed in the course of his/her employment. Persons who contravene either subs (4) or subs (5) of s 14 of the Act will commit an offence.

SELECTED BILLS

Workplace Relations Bill 2014

[15.14] See CHAPTER 23.

Public Service Management (Transparency of Boards) Bill 2014

[15.15] This Bill would provide for the cessation of the practice of providing payment to persons who serve on the boards of public bodies or similar entities and would require that the employment or engagement of such persons by a public body be conditional upon their filing of a declaration with the Standards in Public Offices Commission. The Bill would further require that the payment of expenses to persons who serve on boards of public bodies be conditional upon the filing of a declaration with the Standards in Public Office Commission and to provide for related matters.

Education (Miscellaneous Provisions) Bill 2014

[15.16] This Bill would give effect to Government decisions to support the Government's internationalisation policies through provision for an authorisation to describe an education provider as a university for particular purposes outside the State, to amend the Student Support Act 2011 and to refuse access to certain information through amendment of the Education Act 1998.

Roads Bill 2014

[15.17] The Roads Bill 2014 provides for the dissolution of the Railway Procurement Agency (RPA) and the transfer of its functions and staff to the National Roads Authority (NRA). The Bill would provide that transferring staff will not have less favourable terms and conditions of service relating to remuneration than held in the RPA before its dissolution, and that a transferred person's superannuation arrangements will continue in accordance with the existing RPA pension schemes, as applied before the dissolution day. Section 14 of the Bill contains a technical provision to avoid a situation where RPA staff could inadvertently become members of the Single Pension Scheme, introduced by the Public Service Pensions (Single Scheme and Other Provisions) Act 2012, in addition to their existing RPA scheme.

The Bill would confer additional functions on the NRA including, a procurement function in relation to regional and local roads and an advice and services function with the ability to charge for services.

Provision would also be made for the CEO of the NRA to be accountable to the Public Accounts Committee and other committees established by the Houses of the Oireachtas.

Equality (Amendment) Bill 2014

[15.18] This Private Member's Bill would amend the Employment Equality Act 1998 and Equal Status Act 2000 by inserting a new protected ground under equality legislation as follows:

> That they have a particular social, economic, income or employment status including status as recipient of state financial assistance (in this Act referred to as the 'socio-economic ground').

Employment Equality (Abolition of Mandatory Retirement Age) Bill 2014

[15.19] This is a Private Member's Bill to amend the Employment Equality Act 1998, s 34. The substantive change is to abolish a mandatory retirement age for employees in An Garda Síochána and the Defence Forces, Fire Services and security related employment if an employee is capable of doing the job for which he or she is employed.

Immigration Reform for US Citizens Living in Ireland Bill 2014

[15.20] This Private Member's Bill would facilitate reciprocity in the making of available employment for citizens in the United States of America and would amend the Employment Permits Act 2006 and would also provide for related matters.

Immigration (Reform) (Regularisation of Residency Status) Bill 2014

[15.21] This Private Member's Bill would provide for the regularisation of the residency status of persons who have applied for refugee status and subsidiary protection of four years following the submission of such an application, which remains undetermined and to provide for related matters.

Intellectual Property (Miscellaneous Provisions) Bill 2014

[15.22] This Bill would provide for the amendments of the Patents Act 1992 to give effect to art 19(2) of the Singapore Treaty on the Law of Trade Marks and to amend the Trade Marks Acts 1996.

Defamation (Amendment) Bill 2014

[15.23] This Private Member's Bill would provide for the limitation of damages that certain public bodies may receive in defamation actions so as to protect public discourse from public bodies using resources of the State and the powers granted to them by the Defamation Act 2009 to influence comments by the press and the public.

Higher Education and Research (Consolidation and Improvement) Bill 2014

[15.24] This Private Member's Bill is intended to consolidate the Irish higher education research sector so as to ensure a more efficient, responsible and effective structure for delivering quality education, research and knowledge to the Irish people.

Adoption (Identity and Information Bill) 2014

[15.25] This Private Member's Bill would allow adopted persons to obtain a certificate of birth and to access information relating to their identity, origins and the circumstances of their birth subject to reasonable safeguards to address the position of the natural parents and the adoptive parents of such persons. This Bill would further allow a natural parent a right to access certain information, subject to the wishes of the adopted person, and to require certain bodies and persons to deliver records to the adoption authority.

State Boards (Appointments) Bill 2014

[15.26] This Private Member's Bill seeks to reform the method whereby persons are recruited and selected for appointment to State boards, and to ensure that persons of the highest quality are recruited and selected for such appointment.

Thirty-fourth Amendment of the Constitution (Right to Personal Autonomy and Bodily Integrity) Bill 2014

[15.27] This Private Member's Bill seeks to amend Art 40.3.3° of the Constitution to provide for the right of all citizens to personal autonomy and bodily integrity.

Industrial Relations (Amendment) Bill 2015

[15.28] On 16 December 2014, the Minister for Jobs, Enterprise and Innovation announced Cabinet approval for a proposal to amend the Industrial Relations (Amendment) Act 2001 (the 2001 Act) and the Industrial Relations (Miscellaneous Provisions) Act 2004 (the 2004 Act). The Bill is not yet available at the time of writing and publication is not expected until 2015.

The 2001 Act conferred on the Labour Court a special jurisdiction in cases where there were no collective bargaining arrangements in the employer in question. In summary, where a trade dispute exists, a trade union or an excepted body can make an application to the Labour Court under the 2001 Act seeking initially a non-binding recommendation, but ultimately a binding determination with regard to terms of employment but not collective bargaining arrangements, where certain conditions are met.

Those conditions, in summary, are:

(i) that it is not the practice of the employer to engage in collective bargaining negotiations in respect of workers who are party to the trade dispute and the internal dispute resolution procedures (if any) normally used by the parties concerned have failed to resolve the dispute;

(ii) either the employer has failed to observe a provision of the Code of Practice on Voluntary Dispute Resolution or, having been referred to the Labour Relations Commission under that Code of Practice, the Commission was unable to advance the resolution of the dispute;

(iii) the trade union or the excepted body or the employees have not acted in a manner that has frustrated the employer in observing a provision of the Code of Practice; and

(iv) the trade union or the excepted body or the employees have not had recourse to industrial action after the dispute in question was referred to the Labour Relations Commission under the Code of Practice.

The 2004 Act introduced mandatory time limits within which the Labour Court must deal with applications under the 2001 Act. It also prohibited victimisation of employees consequent on the invocation by a trade union or an excepted body of the jurisdiction of the Labour Court conferred by the 2001 Act.

The manner in which the Labour Court conducted a hearing under the 2001 Act was criticised by the Supreme Court in *Ryanair Ltd v Labour Court*[2] and the Supreme Court took a different approach to the meaning of the term 'collective bargaining'. After the Supreme Court's decision in *Ryanair,* the number of applications made under the 2001 Act dropped significantly.

It is contemplated that the Industrial Relations (Amendment) Bill, announced on 16 December 2014, will amend the existing regime, summarised above, as follows:

(i) the Bill would define the term 'collective bargaining' for the purpose of ascertaining whether the first of the conditions has been satisfied in any case. It is contemplated that collective bargaining would be defined as comprising of 'voluntary engagements or negotiations between any employer or employer's organisation on the one hand and a trade union of workers or excepted body on the other, with the object of reaching agreement regarding working conditions or terms of employment or non-employment of workers'. Furthermore, the term 'excepted body' (provided for in the Trade Union Act 1941), would be amended by providing that, in determining if a body is an excepted body for the 2001 and 2004 Acts, the Labour Court shall have regard to the extent to which the body is independent and not under the domination and control of the employer or Trade Union of Employers with which it engages or negotiates, in terms of its establishment, functioning and administration. In addressing this matter, the Labour Court would be obliged to take into account the manner of election of employees, the frequency of elections of employees, any financing or resourcing of the body beyond de minimus logistical support, the length of time the body has been in existence, and any prior collective bargaining between the employer and the body;

(ii) excepted bodies, that meet the enhanced definition, would no longer be entitled to institute proceedings under the 2001 Act because, by definition, they will be involved in collective bargaining and accordingly the first condition could not be met in circumstances where there is an excepted body for the workers concerned;

(iii) the Labour Court will be given jurisdiction to decline to conduct an investigation of a trade dispute under the 2001 Act where it is satisfied that, in the context of

---

2.   *Ryanair Ltd v Labour Court* [2007] 4 IR 1999.

the dispute, that the number of workers party to the dispute is insignificant. Furthermore, the Labour Court would not be permitted to admit an application by a group or grade or category of worker to which the trade dispute applies where the Court has made a recommendation or determination in relation to the same group or grade or category of worker in respect of the same employer in the previous 18 months;

(iv) for the purpose of initiating proceedings under the 2001 Act before the Labour Court, a statement made under the Statutory Declarations Act 1938 by the General Secretary or equivalent of the Trade Union applicant, setting out the number of its members and the period of membership in the group or grade or category to which the trade dispute refers and who are party to the trade dispute would be admissible in evidence without further proof. This removes any need for workers to be identified at the initiation of the proceedings;

(v) where an employer asserts to the Labour Court under the 2001 Act that it is the practice of the employer to engage in collective bargaining with an excepted body in respect of a grade or group or category of workers concerned, it would be for the employer to satisfy the Labour Court that that is the case;

(vi) the Labour Court, when examining terms and conditions of employment under the 2001 Act, would be obliged to take into account the totality of remuneration and of terms and conditions of employment and, in doing so look at comparators where available, which can comprise both unionised and non-unionised employers. Furthermore, in making any recommendation or determination under the 2001 Act, the Labour Court would be obliged to have regard to the sustainability of the employer's business in the long term;

(vii) the existing regime with reference to victimisation would be amended so as to prohibit the inducement of workers to relinquish trade union representation and thereby give effect to the decision of the European Court of Human Rights in *Wilson and Palmer v United Kingdom*.[3] Furthermore, the jurisdiction of the Circuit Court to grant interim relief pending the outcome of an unfair dismissals claim, created by the Protected Disclosures Act 2014, would be extended to cases in which it is contended that a dismissal was wholly or mainly occasioned by the claimant having had an involvement with a trade union or acting as a witness or comparator for the purpose of an application under the 2001 Act.

SELECTED STATUTORY INSTRUMENTS

Public Service Management (Sick Leave) Regulations 2014 (SI 124/ 2014)

[15.29] The Public Service Management (Sick Leave) Regulations 2014 (SI 124/2014) commenced with effect from 21 March 2014 for all public servants with the exception of teachers, special needs assistants, employees of a recognised school, employees of

---

3.   *Wilson and Palmer v United Kingdom* [2002] ECHR 552.

education or training boards and employees of universities, institutes of technology, or other higher education institutions, in respect of whom the Regulations became operative on 1 September 2014. The Regulations set out in detail the terms of a new sick leave scheme which applies across the public service.

The Regulations specify the sick leave remuneration limits in respect of illness or injury or critical illness or injury. The Regulations reduce the period during which paid sick leave will be available and cap the period during which temporary rehabilitation remuneration (formally pension rate of pay) may be paid. There is provision for extended paid sick leave on an exceptional basis where an individual becomes incapacitated as a result of a critical evidence injury.

The Regulations were the subject of a High Court application for interlocutory injunction and related judicial review proceedings by the Garda Representative Body. See **[21.08]** and **[21.09]**.

Employment Permits Regulations 2014 (SI 432/2014)

[15.30] See CHAPTER 11.

Employment Permits (Amendment) Regulations 2014 (SI 506/2014)

[15.31] See CHAPTER 11.

Education Act 1998 (Unregistered Persons) Regulations 2014 (SI 32/2013)

[15.32] The Education Act 1998 (Unregistered Persons) Regulations 2014 (SI 32/2013) provide for the employment and payment of unregistered teachers where the relevant employer has made all reasonable efforts to appoint a registered teacher to the position in question and a registered teacher is not available to take up said position.

Civil Partnership (Recognition of Registered Foreign Relationships) Order 2014 (SI 212/2014)

[15.33] The Civil Partnership (Recognition of Registered Foreign Relationships) Order 2014 (SI 212/2014) recognises certain legal relationships entered into by parties of the same sex in other jurisdictions to include the United Kingdom, Hawaii, and New Mexico.

Protected Disclosures Act 2014 (Section 7(2)) Order 2014 (SI 339/2014)

[15.34] The Protected Disclosures Act 2014 (s 7(2)) Order 2014 (SI 339/2014) sets out the list of prescribed persons as recipient of disclosures of relevant wrong doings in relation to certain organisations/sectors. See CHAPTER 29.

Protection of Young Persons (Employment) (Exclusion of Workers in the Fishing and Shipping Sectors) Regulations 2014 (SI 357/2014)

[15.35] The Protection of Young Persons (Employment) (Exclusion of Workers in the Fishing and Shipping Sectors) Regulations 2014 (SI 357/2014) recognise that young persons may be employed in the fishing and shipping sector on terms other than those specified in the Protection of Young Persons (Employment) Act 1996; however, where a young person is assigned work between the hours of 10pm on any one day and 6am on the following day, that employer has a statutory responsibility to ensure that the young person receives equivalent compensatory rest time.

Joint Labour Committee Orders

[15.36] On 28 January 2014, the Minister for Jobs and Enterprise and Innovation, signed a number of statutory orders to effect recommendations of the Labour Court Review on the Joint Labour Committee system. The following orders came into effect that day:

Contract Cleaning Joint Labour Committee Establishment (Amendment) Order 2014 (SI 25/2014);

Hairdressing Joint Labour Committee Establishment (Amendment) Order 2014 (SI 26/2014);

Hotels Joint Labour Committee (for the areas known until the 1st January 1994 as the County Borough of Dublin and the Borough of Dun Laoghaire) (Abolition) Order 2014 (SI 27/2014);

Hotels Joint Labour Committee Establishment (Amendment) Order 2014 (SI 28/2014);

Law Clerks Joint Labour Committee (Abolition) Order 2014 (SI 29/2014); and

Security Industry Joint Labour Committee Establishment (Amendment) Order 2014 (SI 30/2014).

Chapter 16

LITIGATION

WHETHER PROCEEDINGS SHOULD BE DISMISSED FOR WANT OF PROSECUTION

[16.01] *Vernon v AIBP Ltd[1] – High Court – Barrett J – whether proceedings should be dismissed for want of prosecution – whether delay inordinate and inexcusable – whether Court can have regard to socio-economic background of plaintiff when considering what is inexcusable delay*

This was an application to have the plaintiff's proceedings dismissed for want of prosecution. It was claimed that the plaintiff was injured in a factory accident in December 1999 following which proceedings were instituted against the defendant. Initial pleadings were exchanged. However, there was no substantive action in the case during the period between May 2004 and November 2012 when a second notice of intention to proceed was served on the defendant. Barrett J noted that, during this period of time, it appeared that the plaintiff had suffered from ill-health and a variety of personal and family misfortunes and had not been in contact with her solicitors. Barrett J said that the Court had to consider the extent to which it 'in determining what is inexcusable delay, can have regard to the socio-economic background of a plaintiff and perhaps apply a less rigorous standard of what is inexcusable than it would apply to those hailing from a more advantaged environment'. The defendant submitted that the delay in prosecuting the action was inordinate and inexcusable and the balance of justice lay against the case proceeding.

The Court noted the principles set out by the Supreme Court in *Primor plc v Stokes Kennedy Crowley.*[2] Barrett J then considered the judgments of McKechnie and Clarke JJ in *Comcast International Holdings Ltd & Ors v Minister for Public Enterprise & Ors*,[3] and noted the observations made by Clarke J as follows: 'The degree of expedition and compliance with time limits which could properly be expected of large corporations involved in commercial disputes cannot reasonably by required of poorly-resourced or otherwise disadvantaged litigants.'

Barrett J noted that, whilst the plaintiff's circumstances in this case were not so radically different as to render redundant the principles elaborated in *Comcast*, the plaintiff in this case was not as attentive to the progress of her case as one might have expected of a more advantaged person. He noted that there were no allegations against

---

1. *Vernon v AIBP Ltd* [2014] IEHC 98.
2. *Primor plc v Stokes Kennedy Crowley* [1996] 2 IR 459.
3. *Comcast International Holdings Ltd & Ors v Minister for Public Enterprise & Ors* [2012] IESC 50.

her solicitors as to grave delay and/or that they were the cause of the delay. Barrett J went on to paraphrase Clarke J in *Comcast*:

> the degree of expedition that would be required of a large corporation in her place cannot reasonably be required of Ms. Vernon. That is not an indulgence of Ms. Vernon or of delay generally; it is recognition of the harsh realities which some people endure may demand less stringency in the administrative and procedural standards that the courts might otherwise require to be observed.

Barrett J concluded that the delay was inordinate, as had been conceded by counsel on behalf of the plaintiff during the proceedings. However, he concluded that the delay was excusable in the circumstances applicable to the plaintiff and thus did not go on to consider where the balance of justice lay. Addressing concerns raised by the defendant that the passage of time in this case would mean that it would be prejudiced in its defence, the Court noted that while difficulties may arise for the defendant, as a going concern, it must have retained some relevant records and that the litigation, which, while not vigorously pursued, was extant and thus it was known to remain extant. Barrett J concluded that it did not appear to him, given all the circumstances, that the suggested difficulties arising or the total delay which occurred between the serving of the first and second notices of intention to proceed were such that a fair trial between the parties could not be had. The judge further noted that the defendant had not sought to bring any application to seek dismissal of the proceedings prior to receiving the second notice of intention to proceed and thus the proceedings were allowed to continue.

CAN A PARTY BE COMPELLED TO CONTINUE AN APPEAL THEY WISH TO WITHDRAW?

[16.02] *Tansey Transport Ltd v Sauter[4] – Labour Court – Organisation of Working Time Act 1997 – appeal of decision of Rights Commissioner – whether Labour Court could compel party to continue appeal they had withdrawn and no longer wished to pursue when other side had not availed of opportunity to put in appeal*

This was an appeal by the claimant of a decision of the Rights Commissioner under the Organisation of Working Time Act 1997 (the Act). The complaint initiated by the claimant concerned ss 11, 12, 13, 14, 15, 17, 19, 21 and 23 of the Act. However, at the commencement of the investigation by the Labour Court, the claimant withdrew his appeals in respect of the complaints (and decision) under ss 11, 12 and 15. It was argued by the respondent that the claimant had no entitlement to withdraw the appeal in respect of these subsections. The respondent submitted that the claimant had appealed against a Rights Commissioner decision and having done so he opened all of the complaints to investigation by the Labour Court.

The Labour Court considered ss 27 and 28 of the Act, which provided for the appeal. The Labour Court did not accept the arguments advanced by the respondent. It found that each complaint raised a possible contravention of the Act, which was independent

---

4.   *Tansey Transport Ltd v Sauter* DTW1417.

of the others and must be dealt with as such by a Rights Commissioner and by the Labour Court. The fact that a Rights Commissioner issued its decision on each of the complaints in one document does not alter the independent nature of each of the complaints. Accordingly, the Labour Court stated it was bound to consider only those complaints that had been appealed by either party and to hear evidence relating to each of them *de novo*. The Labour Court noted that it could not compel either side to enter or to continue an appeal under the Act.

The Labour Court noted that the respondent had had an opportunity to appeal against the Rights Commissioner decisions in respect of ss 11, 12 and 15 of the Act, but chose not to do so, but was now seeking to compel the claimant to continue with an appeal against his will. The Labour Court concluded that, to compel the claimant to continue with an appeal he clearly no longer wished to pursue would be contrary to public policy and a waste of court time. The Labour Court accepted that certain of the appeals were no longer before it as they had been withdrawn by the claimant and the Court went on to consider the remaining appeals before it.

JUDGMENT IN DEFAULT OF DEFENCE

[16.03] *Monaghan v United Drug plc[5] – High Court – Barrett J – whether party can seek to have judgment obtained in default of defence set aside where opponent complied with every rule of procedure and extended every professional courtesy*

The plaintiff claimed damages for personal injuries which allegedly occurred during his employment with the respondent employer. The plaintiff's solicitor sent the initiating letter in July 2010. Correspondence was sent in reply in October 2010 from the in-house solicitors of Royal & Sun Alliance, the defendant's insurers, denying liability. A notice for particulars and appearance were raised in August 2012 and a reply was received in November 2012. The plaintiff's solicitors sought the defendant's defence. Correspondence issued seeking the defence but was not replied to. A motion for judgment in default of defence was issued and served and ultimately on consent an order to strike out was made. The plaintiff was awarded the costs of the motion and the time for delivery of the defence was extended by three weeks. Barrett J noted that 'the greatest surprise in this case is even at this late stage Royal & Sun Alliance continue to dally'. Further correspondence was sent from the plaintiff's solicitor as no defence had yet been forthcoming and this correspondence was not replied to. A further motion for judgment in default of defence was issued and served. However, it appears to have been lost within the insurer and neither the motion nor the grounding affidavit were ever located. On the motion return date, the county registrar was satisfied that the motion had been properly served and ordered that judgment be given in the Circuit Court to the plaintiff in default of defence. The defendant appealed to the High Court and sought to have the judgment set aside.

---

5.   *Monaghan v United Drug plc* [2014] IEHC 183.

It was asserted by the insurer that the interests of justice require that the judgment in default of defence should be set aside and ordered that there might be a full hearing of the defence of these proceedings. Barrett J noted that the discretion of the Court to set aside a regular judgment obtained in default of defence appears to derive ultimately from the principle identified by Lord Atkins in *Evans v Bartlan*.[6] Barrett J also noted the need to do justice to the parties on particular facts of each case emphasised by Murray J in the decision of the Supreme Court in *McGuinn v The Commissioner of An Garda Síochána*.[7]

Barrett J noted that, in this case the insurer had indicated that at all times it wished to argue its defence. Barrett J suggested that it might be contended that the insurer had a curious way of achieving its objective in this regard, engaging in protracted delay, contravening the rules on the delivery of a defence, not observing a court order as to when a defence is to be delivered and ultimately losing documents that were duly served on it. Barrett J commented that it would be 'a most curious notion of justice that would require the court to conclude that when one party to proceedings appears to behave much as it wants while the other behaves exactly as is required, justice nonetheless favours the former over the latter'. Barrett J made reference to the decision of Peart J in *Allied Irish Banks plc v Lyons*[8] which concerned a case of mistake by a solicitor, rather than surprise. In that case, Peart J concluded that the interests of justice required that a summary judgment against the solicitor's client ought to be set aside, rather than leaving the client to a possible remedy against her solicitor in negligence. In this case, Barrett J stated that the Court had to consider whether the interests of justice might similarly require that the judgment in default of defence ought to be set aside on the basis that, the defendant should not suffer for its insurer's actions. However, he concluded that, in all the circumstances, this was a matter that fell to be resolved between the defendant and the insurer, two sophisticated commercial institutions that were capable of defending their respective interests. The interests of justice did not require that the consequences of the insurer's actions or inactions ought to be visited on the plaintiff, whose advisers at all times acted in compliance with the applicable rules of court and principles of professional courtesy. The High Court determined that the Circuit Court judgment in default of defence should not be set aside.

SHOULD CONSTRUCTIVE DISMISSAL PROCEEDINGS BE STAYED TO PERMIT HIGH COURT PERSONAL INJURY PROCEEDINGS TO RUN THEIR COURSE?

[16.04] See *Hickey v Bloomfield House Hotel and Bloomfield Hotel Co Ltd*[9] in **CHAPTER 27**, Unfair Dismissals, para **[27.11]**.

---

6.   *Evans v Bartlan* [1937] AC 473.
7.   *McGuinn v The Commissioner of An Garda Síochána* [2011] IESC 33.
8.   *Allied Irish Banks plc v Lyons* [2004] IEHC 129.
9.   *Hickey v Bloomfield House Hotel and Bloomfield Hotel Co Ltd* UD384/2012.

CAN EAT PROCEEDINGS BE RECORDED ON A MOBILE PHONE?

[16.05] *Przesmycki v Thomas Farrell & Sons (Garage) Ltd T/A Tramore Services Station[10] – Employment Appeals Tribunal – Unfair Dismissals Act 1977 to 2007 (as amended) – Minimum Notice and Terms of Employment Acts 1973 to 2005 – uncontested preliminary application by respondent to be allowed to record proceedings on mobile phone – whether legal requirement on EAT to permit such recording*

This was an uncontested preliminary application by the respondent to be allowed to record the proceedings on his iPhone, so he would have a verbatim account of the proceedings should this be required by him in the event of an appeal.

The EAT noted that there was no legal requirement on it to allow recording, nor was the EAT statutorily obliged to record proceedings electronically – indeed the EAT noted it had no technological facilities to record the proceedings. The EAT noted the inherent jurisdiction is a broad doctrine allowing certain legal bodies to control their own processes and procedures and that the EAT had a long-standing prerogative to decide whether or not to permit electronic recording of its proceedings. The EAT held that traditionally it had not exercised its discretion to allow electronic recording prompted by the desire to preserve the informality that is the hallmark of proceedings before the EAT and to ensure that an atmosphere of undue formality is eliminated. It was also considered undesirable to allow parties to record the proceedings for the following reasons:

(i) issues as to the security of any such recording, given in particular the potential for unauthorised or undesirable use of any such recording by someone other than the parties;

(ii) the lack of editorial control over any such recording;

(iii) the potential for witnesses to intimidated by the fact that they are being recorded by the respondent;

(iv) the potential for electronic recordings to be used later to coach later witnesses coming before the EAT; and

(v) the possibilities for data control breaches.

In stating the foregoing concerns, the EAT said it was not challenging the integrity of the would-be user of the recording equipment. However the EAT stated that it did not propose to depart from the current practice of not allowing such electronic recording. The EAT stated that its notes are the official record of the proceedings and that should the respondent wish to have a verbatim account of the proceedings then he would be permitted to use the services of an official stenographer. The EAT ultimately did not

---

10. *Przesmycki v Thomas Farrell & Sons (Garage) Ltd T/A Tramore Services Station* UD1066/2012 – MN688/2012.

accede to the request and further directed that neither of the parties to the proceedings nor anyone else may bring into the EAT hearing room any recording equipment or electronic device capable of recording sound.

See *Monnickendam v Limerick County Council* at **[27.42]**.[11] In that case, a preliminary application by the respondent to have his unfair dismissals case heard *in camera* was refused by the EAT.

COSTS

[16.06] *DTT Fuels Ltd T/A Econ Fuels v Cullen-Raleigh*[12] *– Employment Appeals Tribunal – appeal of recommendation of Rights Commissioner – Payment of Wages Act 1991 – Terms of Employment (Information) Acts 1994 to 2014 – failure of appeal for want of prosecution – award of costs by Tribunal to respondent employee*

The appellant employer did not attend this appeal hearing before the EAT. In its determination, the EAT noted that the appellant was properly notified of the hearing details and determined that the appeal failed for want of prosecution. The EAT accepted a submission made on behalf of the respondent employee that the appeal had been entered solely to delay and defeat the claim of the employee and that there was no meaningful appeal. The respondent employee argued his entitlement to a costs order. Unusually, the EAT decided to award costs to the employee in the amount of €1,250 exclusive of VAT.

FITNESS TO PARTICIPATE IN PROCEEDINGS

[16.07] *Riley v Crown Prosecution Service*[13] *– EW Court of Appeal – European Convention on Human Rights, art 6 – right to have matters dealt with justly and expeditiously without unreasonable expense – fitness to participate in litigation – decision to strike out claim where not possible for either party to have fair trial in foreseeable future and where appellant's prognosis not known*

The appellant was a senior crown prosecutor in the Crown Prosecution Service. On two occasions during her employment, in August 2006 and September 2008, she raised grievances against the respondent's employees, claiming that she had been bullied and harassed. Her grievances were not upheld and disciplinary action was initiated against her for making false allegations against her colleagues. The appellant had been on sick leave and an occupational health report found that she was unable to engage in the disciplinary process. In September 2009, the appellant initiated proceedings against her employer alleging race discrimination, alleged disability discrimination and victimisation.

---

11.   *Monnickendam v Limerick County Council* UD765/2012, MN569/2012.
12.   *DTT Fuels Ltd T/A Econ Fuels v Cullen Raleigh* PW44/2013, TE23/2013.
13.   *Riley v Crown Prosecution Service* [2013] EWCA Civ 951.

The Employment Tribunal struck out the appellant's claim as it was found that she was medically unfit to participate in the hearing of the matter, and she was unlikely to be in a position to do so in the near future. The Employment Tribunal found that it would not have been possible for either party to receive a fair trial where there was no prognosis of when, if ever, the appellant would be in position to partake in the proceedings. The UK EAT upheld the decision of the Employment Tribunal, finding that there was no error of law in the Employment Tribunal's decision to dismiss the claim.

The appellant was granted leave to appeal the decision. She submitted that the Employment Tribunal had been wrong to strike out her proceedings when she had not been in breach of any substantial order. She submitted that, as her medical condition had been as a result of bullying, intimidation and discrimination inflicted by the respondent's employees, it would be unfair for the respondent to be able to benefit from its own wrongdoing in stating that a fair trial was no longer possible.

The Court of Appeal upheld the UK EAT's finding and stated that, in light of the medical evidence, it was not possible for either party to have a fair trial in the foreseeable future. The Court of Appeal said that there was an overriding objective in civil cases to have matters dealt with justly and expeditiously without unreasonable expense and this was enshrined in art 6 of the European Convention on Human Rights. It was emphasised that this was an entitlement of both parties. The Court of Appeal said that this was indeed a 'chicken and egg' situation in that it could not assume that the respondent had in fact caused the appellant's medical condition without having had a hearing, however a hearing could not take place where the medical evidence suggested that the appellant would not be in position to engage in the process for at least two years.

The Court of Appeal concluded that neither party could receive a fair hearing considering the delays which resulted from the appellant's illness and dismissed the appellant's appeal.

PERSONAL INJURIES ASSESSMENT BOARD

[16.08] *PR v KC Legal Personal Representative of the Estate of MC Deceased[14] – High Court – Baker J – motion for judgment in default of defence – preliminary issue concerning prior authorisation as required by s 12(1) of the Personal Injuries Assessment Board Act 2003 – Civil Liability and Courts Act 2004 – whether the claim constituted a personal injuries action or a claim for damages for assault and trespass to the person – classes of action which are excluded from the 2003 Act – substance of the action must be examined*

Proceedings were originally commenced by the plaintiff on 8 June 2006 by way of plenary summons. Damages were claimed arising from alleged negligence, breach of statutory duty, assault, battery and breach of his constitutional right to bodily integrity. On 28 November 2007 a statement of claim was delivered which pleaded more narrow heads of claim including aggravated and exemplary damages for assault, battery,

---

14. *PR v KC Legal Personal Representative of the Estate of MC Deceased* [2014] IEHC 126.

trespass to the person, breach of the constitutional rights and the intentional infliction of emotional suffering and distress.

Baker J noted that it is the pleas in the statement of claim, as opposed to the plenary summons, that may properly be characterised as setting out the true nature and basis of a particular claim.

By motion dated 4 July 2013 judgment was sought against the defendant in default of defence. This judgment concerns a preliminary issue that arose to be determined prior to the hearing of the motion. The preliminary issue was whether the proceedings were barred by virtue of s 12(1) of the Personal Injuries Assessment Board Act 2003 (the 2003 Act) on foot of the fact that the plaintiff did not seek and obtain an authorisation pursuant to the 2003 Act prior to bringing the proceedings.

The question therefore arose as to whether the 2003 Act applied to the class of claim in the action. The defendant maintained that this was a civil action for personal injuries to which s 3(d) of the 2003 Act applied. The plaintiff argued that it was not a claim covered by the 2003 Act as it was one for damages for assault, as opposed to a personal injuries action. Accordingly the plaintiff maintained that prior authorisation from the Injuries Board (formerly PIAB) was not required in order to proceed with the claim.

The judge noted that s 4(1) of the 2003 Act excluded certain classes of action from its application. Two of these excluded classes of action were relevant in the present case, namely an action for which it is intended to claim damages or relief in respect of any other cause of action (in addition to relief for personal injury) and an action intended to be pursued in respect of an alleged breach of constitutional rights.

Section 12(1) of the 2003 Act is a jurisdictional provision which states that the courts do not have jurisdiction in a case to which the 2003 Act applies unless the procedures under the 2003 Act have been exhausted.

Baker J considered the principles laid down by various cases relating to the Injuries Board authorisation and stated that these were the principles which must be adhered to in determining the present case. Accordingly she was bound to decide the question of whether the civil action commenced by the plaintiff was a civil action for personal injuries by looking to the substance of the action itself, and not merely to the way in which it was pleaded. The question to be determined was essentially whether the action constituted an action for trespass to the person and assault or a civil action for personal injuries.

Baker J examined the nature of a claim for trespass to the person and assault and noted that such a claim is actionable per se, and no proof of actual damage is required for a plaintiff to succeed in recovering damages arising from the tort of trespass to the person or assault. She further considered that if a plaintiff claims, as his or her primary cause of action, damages for assault, trespass to the person or infringement to a person's constitutional rights to bodily integrity/protection of the person, the primary or substantive claim is a claim for damages arising out of these torts and is not a claim for damages for personal injuries. Having regard to this characterisation of an action for trespass to the person, the judge was of the view that the action in this case was not one for damages for personal injuries.

The judge considered the Civil Liability and Courts Act 2004 (the 2004 Act), which introduced a new procedural regime for the bringing of actions to recover damages for personal injuries. Actions which fall within the remit of the 2004 Act must be bought within two years of the cause of action. Expressly excluded from the definition of a 'personal injuries action' in the 2004 Act is an action where the damages claimed include damages for false imprisonment or trespass to the person. In addition, the 2004 Act does not require the use of a personal injuries summons in a claim arising from an assault. *Devlin v Roche*[15] is authority for the proposition that a claim for damages arising from trespass to the person did not constitute a personal injuries claim under the Statute of Limitations (Amendment) Act 1991 and that the relevant statutory time limit for such a claim was six years.

Baker J stated that it would be unrealistic to interpret the 2003 Act without regard to the 2004 Act, and vice-versa. She remarked that to ignore the definition of 'personal injuries action' in the 2004 Act when interpreting the 2003 Act could lead to an absurd result, namely that a plaintiff whose action for damages arising from alleged trespass to the person is rejected by the Injuries Board finds himself or herself in an entirely different procedural and other regime from that which would arise, were the action to be one for personal injuries. Baker J was of the view that the Oireachtas could not have intended this anomalous result. This view enforced her conclusion that a claim for trespass to the person was not one to which the 2003 Act applied.

The judge additionally noted that the 2003 Act expressly and unconditionally excluded from its operation, by virtue of s 4(1)(iii), any action intended to be pursued in respect of an alleged breach by a person of a provision of the Constitution.

Baker J concluded that the action commenced by the plaintiff was not a civil action for personal injuries. Rather, the plaintiff sought to vindicate his personal and constitutional right to bodily integrity and the person. Accordingly it was an action founded in tort which was actionable per se. In addition, Baker J confirmed that the claim was excluded from the operation of the 2003 Act by s 4(1)(iii), being an action for breach of the plaintiff's constitutional rights and not one ancillary to the claim for trespass to the person.

Baker J concluded that the claim was not one for which prior authorisation from the Injuries Board was required.

---

15. *Devlin v Roche* [2002] 2 IR 30.

Chapter 17

PART-TIME WORK

EQUAL PAY

[17.01] *University College Cork v Noonan[1] – Labour Court – Industrial Relations Acts 1946 to 2012, s 17(1) – Protection of Employees (Part Time Work) Act 2001 – appeal of decision of Rights Commissioner – whether complainant, a part-time library assistant, engaged in work of equal value with two full-time senior library assistants – whether complainant entitled to equal pay with these comparators – whether differences in pay are objectively justified by respondent's grading system, the terms of the Public Service Stability (Haddington Road) Agreement and the terms of the Financial Emergency Measures in the Public Interest (No 2) Act 2009 – whether cost capable of being objective ground justifying less favourable pay*

The complainant, a part-time library assistant, gave uncontroverted evidence that she was engaged in work of equal value or work that was identical in all material respects to that of two full-time senior library assistant colleagues and she claimed equal pay with these comparators. The Labour Court noted that the respondent had offered no evidence on this point, stating that it was precluded from conducting a job evaluation exercise and it was unable to say whether or not the complainant was carrying out like work with her comparators. The Court accepted the evidence given by the complainant that she was in fact performing like work to that of her comparators. The Court then went on to consider whether the respondent could rely on a defence of objective justification in accordance with s 9(1) of the 2001 Act. The Court noted that there was a wealth of authority in the jurisprudence of the CJEU and in the jurisprudence of the Superior Courts on how the concept of objective justification is to be implied.

The Labour Court made specific reference to *Del Cerro Alonso v Osakidetza-Servicio Vasco De Salud[2]* where the CJEU held that:

> … the concept must be understood as not permitting a difference in treatment between fixed-term workers and permanent workers to be justified on the basis that the difference is provided for by a general abstract national norm such as a lower collective agreement. On the contrary, that concept requires the unequal treatment at issue to be justified by the existence of precise and concrete factors, characterising the employment condition to which it relates, in the specific context in which it occurs and on the basis of objective and transparent criteria in order to ensure that the unequal treatment is in fact a response to a genuine need, is appropriate for achieving the objective pursued and is necessary for that purpose.

The Labour Court held that this principle was equally applicable in the case, involving part-time work. The Court determined that neither the Public Service Agreement nor the

---

1. *University College Cork v Noonan* PTD141.
2. *Del Cerro Alonso v Osakidetza-Servicio Vasco De Salud* [2008] 1 ICR 145 (Case C–307/05).

Financial Emergency Measures in the Public Interest (No 2) Act 2009 could be relied upon by the respondent in advancing the defence of objective justification. The Court noted that neither instrument purports to nor can have the effect of relieving the respondent from its obligation to apply the principle of equal treatment enshrined in the 2001 Act and the Directive from which it is derived.

The Labour Court then considered the respondent's reliance on grading as being an objective ground. The Court did not accept that grading of itself was capable of constituting an objective ground justifying less favourable treatment. The Court noted that grading was intended to provide an objective system of remunerating workers who are engaged in work having a different valuation. The Court noted that the uncontested evidence in this case was that the complainant and her comparators were engaged in work of equal value, notwithstanding that they were graded differently. In the circumstances, the Court found that the mere difference in grading between the complainant and her comparators could not be regarded as an objective justification within the statutory meaning of the term, in circumstances where the complainant and her comparators were engaged in the same work or work of equal value within the meaning of s 7 of the 2001 Act.

The Labour Court then turned to the final limb of the respondent's defence, namely the costs associated with remunerating the complainant, and stated that this could not be accepted as providing any defence to the claim. The Court noted the decision of the High Court in *Catholic University School v Dooley*[3] where Dunne J held that:

> there is an abundance of authority to which reference has already been made to the effect that the issue of cost cannot justify unequal treatment ... it seems to me very clear and obvious that the purpose of the Directive and the legislation transposing the Directive into Irish law would be defeated if cost alone was accepted as a defence because, as pointed out by the Labour Court, in every case in which it was necessary to implement principles of equality, there is a cost to the employer.

The Labour Court considered itself bound to follow the High Court in this case and thus held that cost considerations could not avail the respondent of a defence to this claim. The Labour Court held that the complainant was entitled to succeed and directed the respondent to adjust her pay and other conditions of employment so as to bring them in line with those of her comparators. The Court directed that this adjustment should be given effect from a date six months prior to the date on which her complaint was originally presented to the Labour Relations Commission Rights Commissioner Service. The appeal was allowed and the decision of the Rights Commissioner was set aside.

---

3.   *Catholic University School v Dooley* [2010] IEHC 496.

Chapter 18

PARTNERSHIP LAW

NON-DISCRIMINATION/EQUALITY/AGE DISCRIMINATION/ THE SELDON SAGA CONTINUES

[18.01] *Seldon v Clarkson Wright & Jakes (No 2)[1] – partnership – requirement to retire at 65 – age discrimination – Council Directive 2000/78/EC[2] – UK Employment Equality (Age) Regulations 2006[3]*

The claimant was a partner in the respondent law firm. He was required by the partnership agreement to retire when he reached the age of 65. The claimant brought a claim for unlawful age discrimination contrary to the UK Employment Equality (Age) Regulations 2006, which implemented Council Directive 2000/78/EC. The claimant instituted proceedings before a UK Employment Tribunal, alleging that his expulsion from the firm was an act of direct age discrimination and that the withdrawal of the offer of an ex gratia payment was an act of victimisation. The respondent had, from the beginning, set out three aims which were advanced by a mandatory retirement age of 65. Those aims were retention (ensuring that associates were given the opportunity of partnership after a reasonable period as an associate, thereby ensuring that associates do not leave the firm), workforce planning (facilitating the planning of the partnership and workforce across the individual departments by having a realistic long-term expectation as to when vacancies will arise) and congeniality/collegiality (limiting the need to expel partners by way of performance management and thereby contributing to the congenial and supportive culture within the firm). Ultimately, the respondent abandoned the congeniality/collegiality aim. The question before the Employment Tribunal was whether choosing to impose mandatory retirement on a partner's 65th birthday was appropriate and necessary having regard to the retention and workforce planning aims. The Employment Tribunal concluded that the mandatory retirement age was a proportionate means of achieving a congenial and supportive culture and encouraging professional staff to remain with the firm. Accordingly, the age discrimination claim failed. The victimisation claim succeeded.

The claimant appealed to the UK EAT,[4] which accepted that the aims of staff retention and workforce planning could be met by any fixed retirement age. However, it concluded that there was no evidential basis for the assumption that performance would drop off at around the age of 65 and thus for choosing that age in order to address performance management and promote collegiality. As the EAT could not be sure what

---

1. *Seldon v Clarkson Wright & Jakes (No 2)* [2014] IRLR 748, UK EAT.
2. Council Directive 2000/78/EC establishing a general framework for equal treatment in employment and education.
3. For the background see *ACELY 2013*, para 22.01 *et seq*.
4. *Seldon v Clarkson Wright & Jakes* [2009] All ER 435.

decision the Employment Tribunal would have reached had it assessed the justification by reference only to the other two objectives, the case was remitted to the Employment Tribunal to consider the question afresh.

The claimant appealed the decision of the UK EAT to the Court of Appeal. The Court of Appeal dismissed the appeal and affirmed the decision of the EAT.[5]

The claimant appealed to the Supreme Court.[6] The Supreme Court unanimously dismissed the appeal. The Supreme Court noted that, exceptionally, direct age discrimination (such as exists in the case of mandatory retirement age) is provided for at art 6(1) of Council Directive 2000/78/EC which provides that such discrimination might be justified because Member States may provide that differences of treatment on grounds of age shall not constitute discrimination if, within the context of national law, they are objectively and reasonably justified by a legitimate aim, including legitimate employment policy, labour market and vocational training objectives, and if the means of achieving that aim are appropriate and necessary. The Court noted that art 6 contemplates provision being made by the Member States within the context of national law but art 18 of Council Directive 2000/78/EC contemplates that, alternatively, Member States may entrust the social partners with the implementation of the Directive by way of collective agreements. Ultimately, the Supreme Court held that the question as to whether the mandatory retirement age of 65 was proportionate (in the case of being both appropriate and reasonably necessary to achieve the legitimate aims of the partnership) was a matter which should be considered by the Employment Tribunal on the basis that it had not been shown that the choice of age 65 (as distinct from any other age) was an appropriate means of achieving the aim of seeking to avoid the need to expel partners by way of performance management.

The claim was referred back to the Employment Tribunal which concluded in 2013 that the issue was whether the mandatory retirement age was proportionate in relation to staff retention and staff planning aims. The Tribunal ultimately concluded that, although the mandatory retirement age constituted age discrimination, it was justified. The Tribunal further concluded that the mandatory retirement age of 65 was proportionate, as well as being appropriate and reasonably necessary for the achievement of each of the aims. Accordingly the claim was dismissed. All of the foregoing was set out in considerable detail in the *Arthur Cox Employment Law Yearbook 2013*.

In 2014, the claimant's appeal against the Employment Tribunal decision, following the remittal of the case from the Supreme Court, was considered by the UK EAT and judgment was given on 13 May 2014 dismissing the claimant's appeal.[7]

The claimant advanced five grounds of appeal and each of them was considered by the EAT, as follows:

1.   It was contended that there was a principle that, where there is a provision which will achieve the legitimate aim with a less discriminatory impact than the measure relied on, the measure relied on cannot be justified. The claimant

5.   *Seldon v Clarkson Wright & Jakes* [2011] ICR 60, [2010] EWCA Civ 899.

6.   *Seldon v Clarkson Wright & Jakes* [2012] UKSC 16.

7.   *Seldon v Clarkson Wright & Jakes* [2014] IRLR 748.

contended that a mandatory retirement age of 68 or 70 would have served the aims just as well. It was noted by the EAT that this ground of appeal was considered and disposed of by the Court of Appeal. The mere fact that the firm might have chosen some other age to achieve the aims, cannot automatically lead to the conclusion that the mandatory retirement age of 65 is not justified. The selection of any age is going to be more discriminatory to people of that age. If the law were to be otherwise, it would be impossible to justify any retirement age introduced with those aims. Directive 2000/78/EC, at Recital 14, contemplates the legitimacy of a retirement age and it cannot be the law that it is impossible to justify one age because a different age would be less discriminatory to persons of the age chosen. The issue is whether the age chosen is a proportionate means of achieving those aims. Accordingly, if it is proportionate to fix 65 as the age, the fact that it might be less discriminatory to some to have chosen 66 cannot render a retirement at age 65 unlawful. The fact that the firm might have justified any age, does not mean that it is unable to choose an age. The EAT concluded that the Employment Tribunal was entitled to conclude that 65 was an appropriate age.

2. The claimant contended that the Employment Tribunal erred in law in finding for the respondent even though the partners, who bore the burden of proof, did not provide an explanation of why retirement at 65, as distinct from at any other age, was necessary. The EAT concluded that there was sufficient evidence to allow the Tribunal to come to the conclusion that it did.

3. The claimant argued that it was an error of law to take into account as relevant the consent of the claimant and others (in the partnership agreement deed) and the default retirement age. The EAT concluded that, having regard to the conclusions reached by the Supreme Court, the Employment Tribunal was entitled to have regard to those matters.

4. The claimant contended that the Employment Tribunal improperly took account of irrelevant factors, being the State pension age and the aim of collegiality. The EAT concluded that the Employment Tribunal had not done so.

5. The claimant contended that the Employment Tribunal should not have had regard to the congeniality/collegiality aim. The EAT concluded that the Employment Tribunal had made its decision by reference only to the workforce planning and retention aims.

The EAT held that the Employment Tribunal had been entitled to conclude that the aims of retention and workforce planning had objectively justified the retirement age of 65. The Employment Tribunal had not erred in law and the fact that it might have identified the different but similar age did not mean that there had been an error of law. The Employment Tribunal had been entitled to take into account factors such as the consent of the parties, the default retirement age, the State pension age and the aim of collegiality in helping it to conclude that the choice of a retirement age of 65 was justified.

WHISTLEBLOWING – IS A PARTNER A 'WORKER'?

[18.02] *Bates van Winkelhof v Clyde & Co LLP[8] – Supreme Court of the United Kingdom – limited liability partnership – whether partner a 'worker' entitled to statutory protection afforded to whistleblowers – Employment Rights Act 1996, as amended by Public Interest Disclosure Act 1998*

The claimant was an equity partner in the respondent law firm, which was a limited liability partnership. She reported alleged misconduct on the part of the managing partner of another law firm, with which the respondent had a joint venture, to the respondent's money laundering reporting officers. Shortly afterwards, she was expelled from the respondent firm. She brought a claim to an Employment Tribunal against the firm, and a senior partner in the firm, alleging that she had suffered detriment, contrary to the UK statutory whistleblowing protection provisions, and claiming that the firm had expelled her for having made protected disclosures. The respondents contended that, as a member of a limited liability partnership, she did not qualify as a 'worker' within the statutory provision and therefore did not have the statutory protection claimed by her. The Employment Tribunal concluded that she was not a worker and dismissed her claim. The UK EAT concluded that she was a worker and could prosecute the claim. The EW Court of Appeal allowed the appeal holding that a member of a limited liability partnership could not, by reason of that membership, be regarded as a worker for the purpose of the statutory provisions. The claimant appealed to the UK Supreme Court.

The statutory definition of a 'worker' is contained in s 230(3) of the Employment Rights Act 1996, as amended by the Public Interest Disclosure Act 1998. Section 230(3)(b) of the 1996 Act addresses the position of a claimant who is not an employee but who might nevertheless be a worker. An individual who has entered into or works under or worked under 'any other contract, whether express or implied and (if it is express), whether oral or in writing, whereby the individual undertakes to do or perform personally any work or services for another party to the contract whose status is not by virtue of the contract that of a client or customer of any profession or business undertaking carried on by the individual' is a worker.[9]

The Supreme Court, allowing the appeal, held that, as the claimant, as a member of a limited liability partnership, undertook to perform personally work or services for the firm and as her status was not that of a client or customer, she fell within the definition of worker in s 230(3)(b).

It was agreed by the parties that the claimant worked under a contract personally to perform any work or services and it was also agreed that she provided those services for a limited partnership which was not her client or customer.

---

8.   *Bates van Winkelhof v Clyde & Co LLP* [2014] ICR 703.

9.   The equivalent limb of the Irish definition of 'worker' is in s 3(1) of the Protected Disclosures Act 2014 and is as follows:

'worker' means an individual who – ... (b) entered into or works or worked under any other contract, whether express or implied and (if it is express) whether oral or in writing, whereby the individual undertook to do or perform (whether personally or otherwise) any work or services for another party to the contract for the purposes of that party's business ...

The decision of the Court of Appeal had been based on its conclusion that the statutory definition of worker had been implicitly modified by s 4(4) of the UK Limited Liability Partnerships Act 2000 which is in the following terms:

> A member of a limited liability partnership shall not be regarded for any purposes employed by the limited liability partnership unless, if he and the other members are partners in a partnership, he would be regarded for that purpose as employed by the partnership.

The Supreme Court concluded that the true construction to be given to s 4(4) of the 2000 Act was that, whatever the position would be were the limited liability partnership members to be partners in a traditional partnership, then that position is the same in a limited liability partnership. If Parliament had wished to exclude the possibility that partners or members of a limited liability partnership could be 'workers' it could be expected to have done so directly and expressly and it did not do so. The fact that the claimant was not in a subordinate relationship to any other person was not necessary in order to be a worker. A member of a limited liability partnership who undertook personally to work for that partnership fell within the statutory definition.[10]

---

10.   See also CH 29: Whistleblowing.

Chapter 19

PENSIONS

BUDGET 2015

[19.01] Budget 2015[1] was announced on 14 October 2014. The main pension-related change was that the 0.6% pension levy will be discontinued from 31 December 2014. The additional 0.15% pension levy introduced by the Social Welfare and Pensions (No 2) Act 2013 will continue until 31 December 2015. It is estimated that, in total, the levies will have generated €2.3 billion since their introduction in 2011. The ending of the pension levies is an opportunity for trustees and employers, who have not yet resolved who will bear the cost of the pension levies to reach a decision on the matter in the knowledge that no future levies are proposed for the time being.

It is proposed that the distribution rate applicable to Approved Retirement Funds (ARFs) and vested Personal Retirement Savings Accounts (PRSAs) be reduced to 4% in the Finance Bill 2015 for individuals aged between 60 and 70 years (for the whole of the relevant tax year) where the aggregate value of their ARF is €2 million or less. The 5% distribution rate would remain where the individual is over 70 (for the whole of the tax year) and the aggregate value of the ARF is €2 million or less. The 6% distribution rate for funds with a value in excess of €2 million would remain unchanged. It appears that the change is proposed in order to address a number of tax avoidance schemes which are linked to the use of ARFs.

From 1 January 2015, the higher rate of income tax will reduce from 41% to 40%. Consequently, for anyone considering withdrawing Additional Voluntary Contributions (AVCs) up to the 30% limit, there will be a slight advantage in making such withdrawals from 2015 onwards given the reduction in the higher rate of income tax which is applicable to such withdrawals. The rate of tax applicable to the chargeable excess over the standard fund threshold (SFT) and the personal fund threshold (PFT) is accordingly reduced.

LEGISLATIVE UPDATES – IRELAND
Social Welfare and Pensions Act 2014

[19.02] The Social Welfare and Pensions Act 2014 amends the Pensions Act 1990 to clarify provisions in relation to the notification to members of a defined benefit (DB) scheme regarding the restructure of scheme benefits as a result of a unilateral direction

---

1. Available at http://www.budget.gov.ie/Budgets/2015/2015.aspx.

of the Pensions Authority (renamed with effect from 7 March 2014 as the Pensions Authority or, in the Irish language, as An tÚdarás Pinsean) under s 50 or s 50B (wind-up) of the Pensions Act.

Section 24 inserts a new subs 50(2B) into the Pensions Act to require the trustees of a DB scheme to notify scheme members of the details of a unilateral direction issued by the Pensions Authority to the trustees of a scheme to restructure scheme benefits and of the right to appeal such a direction to the High Court. The trustees of the scheme will be required to submit a copy of the notification to the Pensions Authority within 10 days of the date of notification.

Occupational Pension Schemes (Sections 50 and 50B) Regulations 2014

[19.03] The Occupational Pension Schemes (Sections 50 and 50B) Regulations 2014 (SI 392/2014) set out the procedure to be followed when the Pensions Authority is making a direction under s 50 of the Pensions Act to restructure the benefits of a pension scheme or a direction under s 50B to wind up a pension scheme. The Regulations were signed into law on 2 September 2014. The Regulations set out the information and notification requirements to be carried out by scheme trustees before the Pensions Authority issues a direction under s 50 of the Pensions Act 1990.

The Regulations, combined with the changes introduced by the Social Welfare and Pensions Act 2014, represent a significant development for DB schemes that fail to meet the statutory minimum funding standard under the Pensions Act as, under ss 50 and 50B, the Pensions Authority has the power to direct trustees to wind up a scheme. The new Regulations are significant in light of an announcement by the Pensions Authority on 12 September 2014 that 'there are 61 defined benefit schemes which are non-compliant with the funding standard and the Authority will shortly begin to take action in respect of these schemes'.[2]

The Regulations put procedures in place for taking action against non-compliant schemes and involve the Pensions Authority proposing to make a direction, whilst giving the scheme an opportunity to respond. If a direction is proposed, the trustees must notify all scheme members, and any authorised trade unions, setting out the funding position of the scheme, the effect of the proposed Pensions Authority direction and the process whereby members and authorised trade unions can make written submissions to the Pensions Authority.

The Pensions Authority has the power to give trustees of a non-compliant scheme the choice of reducing benefits or the Pensions Authority directing that a scheme be wound up. The preferable option, if viable, would be for trustees to have the choice of reducing benefits as opposed to the application of the automatic rules imposed by the Pensions Authority which would apply in the event of a wind-up.

---

2.   Available at: http://www.pensionsauthority.ie/en/News_Press/News_Press_Archive/.

LEGISLATIVE UPDATES – EUROPE

EMIR (European Market Infrastructure Regulation)

[19.04] The EMIR (Regulation (EU) 648/2012)[3] was enacted on 16 August 2012. It is designed to ensure greater transparency in financial systems. In particular, it aims to regulate over-the-counter derivatives (OTCs) which are privately negotiated contracts.

Pension funds which use derivatives, eg to hedge against interest rates, inflation or currency risks, fall within the scope of EMIR, albeit with some exemptions from the full force of the Regulation. In practice the detail relating to any proposed investment is likely to be delegated to the investment manager dealing with the derivatives or a scheme's custodian. However, the trustees remain responsible for ensuring compliance with the Regulation.

Trustees of schemes using derivatives can expect to see EMIR reporting agreements from their custodian or derivative manager. These agreements are based on a template prepared by ISDA (the International Swaps and Derivatives Association). Unsurprisingly, not all of the terms of the agreements (which are targeted at financial trading institutions) are appropriate for pension scheme trustees and it may be appropriate to seek amendments to the standard documents.

EMIR divides market participants in derivatives into two categories:

(i)   Financial Counterparties (FCs); and

(ii)   Non-financial Counterparties (NFCs).

Pension schemes are included in the FC category. EMIR is targeted at financial institutions (banks, hedge funds, custodians) and pension funds are exempted from compliance with some aspects for a considerable period (see below).

From 12 February 2014, trustees of pension schemes or investment funds have to report any new OTC derivatives or exchange traded derivatives into which they enter to the Trade Repository (which collects and maintains the records of the derivatives) within one business day of entering the contract. In order to do this, trustees must acquire a Global Legal Entity Identifier (LEI). LEIs are essentially reference codes which identify parties who engage in financial transactions. Under the Regulation, trustees are entitled to delegate their duty to report to investment managers.

Any amendments to the terms of derivative transactions and any early terminations of derivative transactions must also be reported from 12 February 2014 onwards. Any derivative transactions that were entered into on or after 16 August 2012 and which remain outstanding on 12 February 2014 also have to be reported. Generally, both counterparties to a transaction are required to report on that transaction. However, one counterparty may report on behalf of the other if there is a prior agreement to do so.

All counterparties are also under an obligation to maintain a record of concluded or modified derivative transactions for at least five years after they have been concluded/modified. Pension schemes are exempt from the clearing requirements for certain

---

3.   http://eur-lex.europa.eu/LexUriServ/LexUriServ.do?uri=OJ:L:2012:201:0001:0059:EN:PDF.

derivative trades until 2015. The Central Bank has prepared FAQs on EMIR which are available on its website.[4]

Draft IORP II Directive

[19.05] The European Commission has published a proposed revision of the Institutions for Occupational Retirement Provision Directive (IORP Directive).[5] This does not make any changes to funding requirements for pension schemes following opposition from an alliance of five Member State governments, including Ireland, to the Commission's aspiration to bring the IORP Directive into line with Solvency II for insurance companies (Solvency II introduced a new harmonising EU-wide insurance regulatory regime replacing 13 existing EU insurance Directives). The revised directive focuses on governance and communication and prescribes a very detailed plan for a harmonised EU-wide format for member benefit statements. In addition, those who 'effectively run the scheme' are required to have professional qualifications. The current IORP Directive puts this obligation on those running the scheme or the scheme's advisers but the new draft now appears to envisage that trustees would be so qualified. The proposed IORP Directive, if it becomes law, for which the approval of the European Parliament and the European Council will be needed, is scheduled to be implemented by Member States by 31 December 2016.

It remains to be seen how a requirement for trustees to have professional qualifications would interact with the current requirement at Irish law for trustees to complete appropriate trustee training.

PENSIONS AUTHORITY, GUIDANCE AND MODEL DOCUMENTS

Statutory guidance ss 49 and 50 of the Pensions Act

[19.06] On 27 March 2014, the Pensions Authority issued revised statutory guidance, approved by the Minister for Social Protection, regarding applications to the Authority under ss 49 and 50 of the Pensions Act[6]. Section 49 of the Act relates to the funding proposals that trustees of underfunded pension schemes must prepare. Section 50 of the Act relates to the use of benefit reductions to resolve funding difficulties.

The updated guidance introduces a number of rules in relation to s 49, including a requirement that trustees who submit a funding proposal after the guidance comes into force must ensure their scheme will be at least 50% funded and expect it to be 70% funded by the commencement date of their 2017 annual scheme year. The 50% and 70% funding requirements include all funding standard liabilities under s 44 of the Act, apart from additional voluntary contribution benefits and wind-up expenses. Trustees who

---

4.   www.centralbank.ie/regulation/EMIR/Pages/FAQs.

5.   Directive 2003/41/EC.

6.   Available at http://www.pensionsauthority.ie/en/Regulation/Statutory_guidance/

submit funding proposals on or after 1 January 2017 must ensure their scheme is at least 70% funded. Funding proposals which are no longer on-track to meet the funding standard by their end date and which fall below 50% funding will not be permitted to use the 'two-year easement' facility. This is a flexibility option which gives schemes two additional years during which to recover.

The Pension Authority's guidance has been updated to reflect the fact that s 50 of the Act now permits pensions in payment to be reduced, subject to prescribed limits.

Statutory guidance in relation to transfer payments

[19.07] With effect from 1 June 2014, the Pensions Authority issued new statutory guidance regarding transfer payments under s 34 of the Pensions Act. The Pensions Authority's s 34 guidance sets out the assumptions which must be used when calculating a transfer payment on a standard basis. This guidance does not preclude the calculation of a transfer payment on an alternative basis.

Except where a scheme is in deficit on the statutory minimum funding standard basis, a transfer payment must not be less than the amount calculated using the assumptions set out in the guidance. The Occupational Pension Schemes (Preservation of Benefits) Regulations 2002 (SI 279/2002) (as amended) require that the transfer payment shall be calculated in accordance with the guidance issued by the Society of Actuaries in Ireland and guidance issued by the Pensions Authority. Therefore, the statutory guidance should be read in conjunction with the relevant professional guidance issued by the Society of Actuaries in Ireland which has recently been amended. Where there is any conflict between the two, the Pensions Authority guidance prevails.

Guidance notes in relation to family law acts

[19.08] In March 2014, the Pensions Authority issued Guidance Notes on the pension provisions of the Family Law Act 1995, the Family Law (Divorce) Act 1996 and the Certain Rights and Obligations of Cohabitants Act 2010. The Guidance Notes act as an aid to understanding pensions aspects of these Acts and provide information on the granting of pension adjustment orders, who can apply for such orders and the conditions for the granting of such orders.

Financial management guidelines for defined benefit schemes

[19.09] The Pensions Authority has indicated that since the early 2000s, a majority of defined benefit (DB) schemes have failed to meet the statutory minimum funding standard resulting in wind ups, reductions in benefits and membership freezes. As a result, the Pensions Authority has issued Guidelines for trustees which seek to ensure that schemes are managed effectively and which encourage trustees of schemes that are not meeting the statutory minimum funding standard to accelerate their efforts to find a solution to their funding deficit without Pensions Authority intervention.

The Guidelines examine four key areas:

1. *Scheme Data* – this sets out the minimum information the trustees of DB schemes should have available to them and what practices the Pensions Authority expects trustees to follow in order to understand and manage the funding and investments of their DB scheme.

2. *Governance* – this outlines governance practices relevant to the financial management of a scheme.

3. A list of *periodic tasks* to be undertaken by trustees to include:

    (a) review of investment strategy;

    (b) review of contribution and funding adequacy;

    (c) preparation and review of risk matrix by identifying and assessing risks, estimating their likely impact and deciding what steps to take to mitigate those risks;

    (d) discussions with employer about contributions and related issues;

    (e) review of investment management performance; and

    (f) review of scheme costs.

4. *Analysis by the trustees* – the purpose of which is to identify threats to the ability of a scheme to meet its liabilities and to consider what action is to be taken in response.

On 11 November 2014, the Pensions Authority published a synopsis of the submissions received in response to its consultation paper on financial management Guidelines for DB schemes.[7]

The Pensions Authority received a total of 19 written submissions. Suggestions were sought as to how the Pensions Authority could improve the proposed Guidelines. The following is a summary of the main suggestions:

(i) it was felt that greater emphasis should be placed on the need for trustees to have a full understanding of their powers, including clarity as to when they require employer consent in advance of appointing advisers;

(ii) it was generally accepted that trustees should have clear guidelines in determining contribution rates and their powers in this regard;

(iii) a minimum number of scheduled trustee meetings to be held should be specified in the guidelines;

(iv) statements of investment policy principles (SIPPs) should be improved as only the minimum amount of information is provided in these statements at present; and

---

7.   Available at: http://www.pensionsauthority.ie/en/News_Press/News_Press_Archive/
      Synopsis8_of_responses_to_the_Pensions_Authority%e2%80%99s_consultation_on_financial_
      management_guidelines_for_defined_benefit_schemes.pdf.

(v) expansion of the risk management section was suggested to include:

    (a) the ability of the sponsoring employer to meet its contribution obligations over the short and longer term,

    (b) the risk or likelihood that the sponsoring employer does not have the financial capacity to accommodate a future contribution increase,

    (c) the level of risk being taken on by different cohorts of member, eg by the remaining active members as members retire, and

    (d) inflation and currency risk;

(vi) internal control powers conferred on trustees such as appointment of chairperson/secretary should be set down in a governance document, and there was universal agreement among respondents that it would be useful to have sample risk matrices and case studies available as practical tools to assist trustees.

In addition, it was suggested that:

    (a) trustees should be required to carry out a formal assessment of the sponsoring employer covenant, to allow the trustees ascertain how willing and able the employer is to maintain/increase the contribution rate needed to pay the benefit, and to gauge the implications for the future financial risks in the scheme;

    (b) trustee boards should have a skilled chairperson, independent of the sponsoring employer, who could offer leadership and guidance based on experience, and who would ensure that meetings are focussed to cover all aspects of the administration of the scheme; and

    (c) the importance of trustee training should be emphasised.

Pensions Authority publishes model disclosure documents

[19.10] The Pensions Authority has published the first in a series of model documents[8] on disclosure of information requirements. The first model documents to be published are:

    (i) an annual benefit statement for a defined contribution scheme;

    (ii) a statement of reasonable projection (SRP);

    (iii) an annual benefit statement for a defined benefit scheme; and

    (iv) a leaving service options letter for a defined contribution scheme.

The publication of these documents is in response to submissions received to the Pensions Authority's defined contribution (DC) pension consultation paper published last year.

The Pension Authority proposes to issue further model disclosure documents over the coming months.

---

8.   http://www.pensionsauthority.ie/en/Publications/Model_disclosure_documents/.

Annual Report 2013

[19.11] The Pensions Board's Annual Report for 2013 (the Report)[9] was published in June 2014. It was the final annual report to be published under the old structures of the Pensions Board, prior to its renaming as the Pensions Authority with effect from 7 March 2014. The Report highlights that 2013 proved another challenging year for all aspects of pension provision in Ireland. The number of active members of occupational pension schemes fell by 12,249 with an overall decrease in defined benefit (DB) scheme membership of 20,627. Defined contribution (DC) schemes saw an increase in membership of 8,378. While the Report does not distinguish between public sector and private sector schemes, scheme membership statistics show that the great majority of DB schemes in the private sector have closed to new members.

The Report notes that 19 prosecution cases were concluded, with convictions secured in 13 cases. The other six, it should be noted, were struck out or withdrawn due to payment of arrears. Convictions in the 13 cases were as follows:

(a)   eight related to reduction and non-remittal of contributions; and

(b)   five related to failure to respond to a Pensions Board request for information.

DB schemes in deficit were each called upon to submit a funding proposal by 30 June 2013 and 122 proposals were received. Clarification is being sought in respect of 11 cases, one proposal was withdrawn and the remaining 18 were being processed at year end. In addition, 35 s 50 applications were received with 28 approved, one withdrawn and six being processed.

During 2013, the Board carried out 21 onsite investigations of Registered Administrators (RAs). The level of compliance was found to be good and indicated a marked improvement over the previous year. Fines totalling €36,000 were issued to RAs and remitted to the exchequer. The number of RAs reduced during the year as 19 opted not to renew their registration.

Previously unremitted employer and employee contributions were paid to the Construction Workers Pension Scheme (CWPS) totalling €700,948 bringing the total value of restored contributions since April 2008 to €7,982,205.

Pensions prosecutions 2014

[19.12] The Pensions Board continued to prosecute cases where employers failed to remit pension contributions. A sample of cases from 2014 is set out below:

In Wicklow Circuit Court on 31 July 2014, a two-year prison sentence was imposed on two directors of SM Morris Ltd for failing to remit employee pension contributions to the trustee of the CWPS within the statutory time limit. The directors pleaded guilty to a number of counts on indictment. Both sentences were suspended in their entirety upon each director entering into a bond. The case was originally taken by the Pensions

---

9.   Available at: http://www.pensionsauthority.ie/en/Publications/Annual_Report.

Board in the District Court but jurisdiction was refused due to the amount of arrears owing to the scheme.

In Navan District Court on 24 September 2014, a fine of €2,000 was imposed on a director of Acol Ltd for failing to remit pension contributions deducted from employees between January 2010 and December 2010 to the CWPS within the statutory time limit. Acol Ltd was also fined €1,000 and costs of €1,106.50 were awarded to the Pensions Board.

Pensions Ombudsman – Annual Report 2013

[19.13] According to his Annual Report for 2013[10], the emphasis for the Pensions Ombudsman in 2013 was on resolving older cases and shortening the duration of investigations. In 2013, the office of the Pensions Ombudsman closed 655 cases and reduced the number of cases on hand at end of year to 222 – a 40% reduction from 369 in 2012.

In April 2013 the Government announced its intention to amalgamate the Offices of the Pensions Ombudsman and the Financial Services Ombudsman. Following this, a steering committee chaired by an external expert from the World Bank conducted a review. The Pensions Ombudsman has indicated that preparatory work has commenced for the amalgamation.

LARGE CASES DIVISION OF THE REVENUE COMMISSIONERS

Updated Revenue Pensions Manual

[19.14] At the end of May, the Revenue Commissioners updated the Revenue Pensions Manual[11] (the Manual). The Manual sets out the basis of the Revenue's discretion to approve schemes and while not technically law, in practice it has the effect of law. The update to the Manual consolidates a number of ebriefs and circulars which have been issued by the Revenue since the last version of the Manual. In particular the following practices have been updated:

(i)   early withdrawal of additional voluntary contributions (AVCs) from occupational pension schemes;

(ii) the taxation of pension contributions, the application of the earnings limit and the regime in relation to lump sums on retirement;

(iii) the commutation of pensions and the payment of once-off pensions where the value of the pensions are considered 'trivial', which practices have now been extended to Retirement Annuity Contracts (RACs) and Personal Retirement Savings Accounts (PRSAs); and

---

10.   Available at http://pensionsombudsman.ie/cms/index.php?q=node/213.

11.   Available at http://www.revenue.ie/en/about/foi/s16/templates/pensions/.

(iv) the tax treatment of retirement benefits where members have private and public sector pensions.

CASE LAW – PENSIONS
Irish Case Law

[19.15] There have been some pension cases of note in Ireland in 2014.

Conduct of trustees – the Element Six case

[19.16] *Greene & Ors v Coady & Ors*[12] – *High Court – Charleton J – trustee standard of care*

The High Court judgment in *Greene & Ors v Coady & Ors* on 4 February 2014 provides confirmation under Irish law of the manner in which trustees of pension schemes should conduct themselves and the level of care that is required for trustees to be considered to have carried out their responsibilities effectively and in a manner that is in the interests of the beneficiaries of the scheme. The case confirms the state of the law on a number of issues such as: how trustees make decisions; whether it is appropriate for trustees to take into account external considerations (such as job security and contributions to other schemes for active members); and what constitutes 'wilful default' in considering whether there has been a breach of trust.

The plaintiffs were 124 members of the Element Six Ltd Pension Scheme (the Scheme) and they sued the Scheme trustees for breach of trust in accepting an offer from Element Six Ltd (the Principal Employer of the Scheme) of €37.1 million as a final employer contribution to the Scheme instead of demanding the entire minimum statutory funding standard (MFS) deficit of €129.2 million. Among the complaints of the members were that the trustees acted in 'wilful default' of their duties; that they were conflicted in their duties; and that they considered irrelevant factors in reaching their decision to accept the Principal Employer's offer. The members' claim failed on all grounds. The judge concluded that the trustees had conducted their duties in a manner that was honest and in the best interests of the members of the Scheme.

The case endorsed the familiar formula for trustee decision-making and confirmed that the Court will not apply its own judgment in relation to the facts. Instead the Court considered the trustees' position at the time of making the decision and the materials that were or ought to have been available to the trustees in reaching their decision. It then considered whether the trustees acted in good faith for the benefit of the members of the Scheme. Once a factor is relevant, it is a matter for trustees to decide how much weight to attach to it, even if a Court might consider the factor to be of greater or lesser importance. Therefore, unless the weight attached to a factor was outside the range of what a reasonable body of trustees would have given to it, the trustees' decision will stand.

---

12.   *Greene & Ors v Coady & Ors* [2014] IEHC 38.

Beneficiaries are entitled to expect that trustees pursue the trust's aims and objectives in an honest manner and in good faith. The judge noted that this cannot happen if a conflict of interest or duty is such as to 'paralyse any trustee so that he or she cannot rationally approach and decide upon a problem'. It was noted that sometimes in pension schemes there are unavoidable conflicts of interest because trustees often owe duties to their employer in respect of their contract of employment and duties to members in respect of the Scheme. This kind of conflict is often unavoidable but not sufficient to warrant the appointment of professional trustees. However, where a trustee assumes responsibilities or duties which are outside the normal contemplation of duties associated with the trust, and which conflict with the trustee's duties to the trust, that would be considered a breach of trust.

The High Court has inherent jurisdiction to assist trustees who find themselves in situations of conflict. The members argued that the trustees ought to have applied to the Court for assistance in considering the Principal Employer's offer. They argued that the trustees should have asked the Court whether they should demand greater contributions from the company or whether they should accept the Principal Employer's contention that, if the trustees were to pursue a higher level of contributions, jobs would be lost. Charleton J held that while the trustees did have discretion to ask the Court for assistance in making the decision, the mere fact that they did not choose to exercise this discretion did not invalidate their decision.

The members' claim that the trustees acted with wilful default by failing to make a contribution demand was considered and it was decided that in order for the trustees to be found liable for wilful default, it would be necessary for the members to show that the trustees' decision in refraining from making a contribution demand was made consciously and was known to be a purposeful breach of duty. It was held that if a failure to act is voluntary, then in order for liability to be found, it would be necessary to prove that the trustees acted in a manner that infringed the core duties of managing the trust honestly and in good faith. On the facts, it was found that there was no evidence of the trustees acting in a manner that could be described as dishonest or in bad faith and therefore no wilful default was found.

While not strictly at issue in the case, the Court expressed the view on the facts that the funding proposal amounted to a contract between the Principal Employer as funder and the trustees. As such, the Court considered that, on the particular facts of the case, the trustees had a right to sue the company in respect of the contributions due. However, the trustees had received legal advice that the funding proposal might not be interpreted as binding by the Courts. Relying on this legal opinion did not make their decision to refrain from issuing a contribution demand in respect of the outstanding sum irresponsible.

The Omega Pharma case

[19.17] *Holloway, Crowley & Vandenheede v Omega Teknika Ltd & Chefaro Ireland Ltd*[13] – *High Court – Moriarty J – trustees – contribution demand in excess of Minimum Funding Standard – engagement by employer*

The judgment of the High Court[14] and subsequent affirmation by the Court of Appeal in the case of *Holloway, Crowley & Vandenheede v Omega Teknika & Chefaro Ireland Ltd* is likely to be the catalyst for significant change to the defined benefit pension regime in Ireland.

The case was brought before the Irish courts by the trustees of the Omega Pharma Ireland Pension and Death Benefit Scheme against the overseas principal employer, Damianus BV, and Irish participating employers Omega Teknika Ltd and Chefaro Ireland Ltd. The case arose after the employers announced redundancies in September 2012 and the intention to wind up the scheme. Three months' notice of the employer's intention to terminate their liability to contribute to the scheme was issued to the trustees in accordance with the rules of the scheme.

Following the notice, the trustees consulted the principal employer with regard to it making a contribution in accordance with clause 8.1 of the scheme's 2004 trust deed. Clause 8.1 provided that the employers shall pay to the trustees 'the moneys which the trustees determine, after consulting the actuary and the principal employer, to be necessary to support and maintain the Fund in order to provide the benefits under the scheme'. The principal employer failed to respond to the trustees' correspondence and efforts to engage regarding the final contribution. In the absence of any engagement by the employers, the trustees served a contribution demand for €3.01 million (later reduced to €2.23 million because of two member transfers prior to the discontinuance date) on 7 December 2012.

There were two key issues in the case. The first issue necessitated technical interpretation as to when the employers' contribution liability terminated. The Court found as a matter of interpretation that there was a three-month notice period during which the trustees could make a final contribution demand.

The second issue looked at whether trustees are entitled to make a contribution demand in excess of the statutory minimum funding standard (MFS). It is important to note that the scheme was solvent on the statutory MFS basis. The trustees decided (having regard to professional advice) that funding at the MFS level was insufficient to provide the benefits under the scheme. They concluded that while MFS funding was insufficient, funding on an annuity buy-out basis alone would be 'excessive' (resulting in a deficit of €5.8 million). Accordingly, a funding combination of annuity buy-out (actuarially adjusted) and MFS was recommended by the scheme actuary – this was the basis of the amount inclusive of the contribution demand.

The employers argued that there was no justification for the demand given that the scheme was solvent on the statutory funding basis at the time. This argument was rejected in the High Court with Moriarty J concluding that the trustees had come to a reasonable decision in the absence of any response from the employer. The Court noted the trustees had 'moved away from an amount they believed would represent an excessive level of contribution from the employer. They sought to gauge responsibility

---

13.   *Holloway, Crowley & Vandenheede v Omega Teknika Ltd and Chefaro Ireland Ltd* [2014] IEHC 383. Note: no judgment published yet.

14.   *Holloway, Crowley & Vandenheede v Omega Teknika Ltd and Chefaro Ireland Ltd* [2014] IEHC 383.

effectively in a vacuum, where the employer gave no input.' Moriarty J further concluded that the demand did not appear to be one which no reasonable body of trustees would have made.

The High Court was critical of the lack of engagement on the part of the principal employer – the employers had ample opportunity to engage in discussions and to come to an agreement with the trustees. Moriarty J was of the opinion that it appeared 'that a deliberate decision was made by the employers to take this course of action and not to avail of these opportunities'. The High Court found in favour of the trustees, directing the employers to pay €2.23 million to the trustees.

The employers appealed the decision which was heard on 20 November 2014 in the Court of Appeal. The appeal was dismissed with Kelly J confirming the order of the High Court. An application for costs in respect of both hearings was sought, and granted on the relatively rare 'solicitor and own client' basis which provides the greatest degree of recovery of costs possible.

The decision is a positive one for trustees of pension schemes acting with the benefit of professional advice and reaffirms the position that a decision to overturn trustees' decisions will not be taken lightly. The Court of Appeal has heard an appeal and upheld the decision of the High Court and a reasoned judgment will be delivered in due course.

Until that decision is available, the interim conclusions are:

1. Contribution demands during notice periods are likely to be upheld where they are made in a manner consistent with the provisions of the trust deed and rules;

2. The statutory funding standard is a minimum contribution obligation which does not replace or supersede any greater obligations arising as a result of the provisions of the trust deed or from decisions of the actuary made in accordance with actuarial guidance;

3. Where the scheme provisions require consultation to take place, employers who ignore that requirement run the risk of being unable to raise their arguments later if the trustees take reasonable decisions in the meantime.

High Court clarifies rules for overseas transfer of PRSA funds

[19.18] *O'Sullivan v Canada Life Assurance (Ireland) Ltd*[15] *– High Court – Ryan J – Personal Retirement Savings Accounts (Overseas Transfer Payments) Regulations 2003 – transfer of PRSA funds overseas*

Under the Occupational Pension Schemes and Personal Retirement Savings Accounts (Overseas Transfer Payments) Regulations 2003 (SI 716/2003) (the Transfer Regulations), a Personal Retirement Savings Account (PRSA) contributor may transfer his fund to an overseas arrangement.

The plaintiff had a PRSA policy with Canada Life Assurance (Ireland) Ltd valued at €116,000. The plaintiff, who was neither resident nor employed in Malta, wished to transfer the policy to a Maltese pension scheme and instructed Canada Life to carry out

---

15.   *O'Sullivan v Canada Life Assurance (Ireland) Ltd* [2014] IEHC 217.

the transfer. Canada Life sought the approval of the Revenue Commissioners who felt that it was for Canada Life to determine whether it wished to carry out the transfer in light of the Transfer Regulations and the requirement that the transfer be for *bona fide* reasons. Canada Life subsequently declined the request as they did not believe that the transfer was being made for *bona fide* reasons, given that the plaintiff was neither resident nor employed in Malta. Consequently, the plaintiff issued proceedings seeking to compel Canada Life to make the transfer. Revenue were joined as an *amicus curiae* (friend of the court) to allow them to make submissions on the interpretation of the 2003 Regulations.

The Court found that there was no evidence of *mala fides* on the part of the plaintiff and that the Transfer Regulations did not require that he be resident in or employed in Malta in order to transfer his PRSA policy there. Ryan J noted that two conditions in the 2003 Regulations must be considered and satisfied when a transfer request is made, namely:

(i)   that the transfer is for *bona fides* purposes; and

(ii) that the overseas pension scheme administrator provides 'relevant benefits' as defined in s 770(1) of the Taxes Consolidation Act 1997 (the TCA).

On the issue of *bona fides*, the Court has to consider whether a pension scheme administrator has to perform an evaluation of the reasons for the requested transfer of the funds. The Court held that provided there is nothing in the facts of the case as presented to give rise to a suspicion as to the *bona fides* of the transfer, the pension scheme administrator is free to implement the wishes of the owner of the fund. However, the Court made it clear that it was not laying down a general rule and that each case would depend on its individual facts.

In the proceedings before the Court, the plaintiff had signed a transfer declaration form, in accordance with a requirement introduced by the Revenue in 2012, confirming that the transfer:

(i)   conformed with the requirements of the Transfer Regulations and Revenue pension rules;

(ii) was for *bona fide* purposes; and

(iii) was not primarily for the purpose of circumventing pension tax legislation or Revenue rules.

The Court held that, having regard to the facts before them, Canada Life was not obliged to conduct an independent examination and evaluation of the plaintiff's motives as he was transferring his PRSA from one EU Member State to another.

On the issue of 'relevant benefits', it was argued on behalf of the plaintiff that 'relevant benefits' are any pension, lump sum, gratuity or benefit paid on either death or retirement. As the benefits under the Maltese scheme were payable on either the death or retirement of the member, it was submitted that the scheme met the legislative requirement to provide 'relevant benefits'.

The Court stated that, while it made sense for there to be a proviso concerning an employment connection in the case of occupational pension schemes, the same did not apply in the case of PRSAs which can be opened regardless of employment status. The

Court noted that the clear intention of the 2003 Regulations was to facilitate the transfer of both occupational pensions and PRSAs to overseas pension scheme administrators. If the proviso as to 'relevant benefits' was interpreted to require an employment connection, the effect would be that PRSAs entered into by self-employed persons could not be transferred overseas.

The Court concluded that the 2003 Regulations did not require that the plaintiff be resident or employed in Malta in order to transfer his PRSA policy there.

UK CASE LAW

Employer's duty of good faith

[19.19] *IBM United Kingdom Holdings Ltd v Dalgleish*[16] *– High Court of England and Wales – employer duty of good faith – reasonable expectations of employees – 'Imperial' duty*

IBM UK sought declaratory relief concerning changes which it proposed to make to two of its DB pension schemes by closing them to new entrants and to future accrual, making future pay increases non-pensionable for DB purposes, opening an early retirement window for active members and ending enhanced early retirements. IBM proposed to close the schemes to future accrual by invoking an 'exclusion power' in the scheme rules permitting the principal employer to exclude 'any specified person or class of persons from membership' and claimed that these changes were required in order to address their lack of competitiveness and profitability. Members were invited to sign 'non-pensionability' agreements by which any future rises in pay would not increase the value of members' past service DB pension rights; the alternative being that the members would receive no pay rise. The changes were to be effected under 'Project Waltz' – the third set of benefit changes implemented by IBM since 2004. It is important to note that in 2004 and 2006 there had been an increase in contribution rates and members were given the option of either part of their pay increase being non-pensionable or migrating to a defined contribution (DC) scheme in respect of future benefits.

The defendants in the IBM case were the beneficiaries under the scheme and the sole trustee of the schemes. The trustee had two concerns about the proposed changes, namely whether IBM had breached its contractual duty of trust and confidence to employees and whether it had breached its implied duty of good faith.

There were a number of issues for determination by the High Court including:

(i) the relevance of the *Imperial* duty (summarised below);

(ii) the issue of members' reasonable expectations; and

(iii) IBM's consultation with members.

The *Imperial* duty may be summarised as follows: 'an employer should not without reasonable and proper cause conduct himself in a manner calculated or likely to destroy

---

16. *IBM United Kingdom Holdings Ltd v Dalgleish* [2014] EWHC 980 (Ch).

or seriously damage the relationship of trust and confidence between the employer and employee'.[17] (The *Imperial* duty was recognised in Irish law by the High Court in *Boliden Tara Mines Ltd v Cosgrove & Ors*).[18] The Court considered the *Imperial* duty relevant to the IBM proceedings in relation to the closure of the DB schemes to future accrual and the changes to the early retirement policy. The contractual duty was relevant in relation to (i) the failure to properly consult; and (ii) the non-pensionability agreements.

As a result of earlier pensions projects and communications from IBM, the Court found that members had a reasonable expectation about the future of the schemes, more particularly, an expectation that accrual and early retirement would continue until 2014 unless there was a relevant justification for a change in policy. Previous communications were examined closely by the Court with phrases such as 'a continuing commitment' to DB schemes and a 'commitment to underpin their sustainability' leading the Court to conclude that these statements were not merely vague expressions of intent, but communications upon which affected members made informed decisions in respect of their careers and retirement.

IBM argued that closure of the UK schemes was necessary in order to improve the financial standing of IBM and comply with directions from its parent company in the US, IBM Corporation. The Court noted that this argument was not strong enough to justify interference with the reasonable expectations of members, as the targets set by the parent company were given subsequent to statements by IBM which gave rise to members' reasonable expectations.

The Court found that no reasonable employer in IBM's position would have proposed such changes and this breached IBM's duty of good faith. The Court also found that the implied contractual duty of good faith was distinct from the *Imperial* duty, but that each derives from the same origin. On the facts of the case, IBM had breached both.

IBM's breach of contractual duty arose as a result of the way in which it consulted with members. The Court held that IBM did not consult in an 'open and transparent' manner. The members had been provided with misleading and incomplete information and the employers did not come to the consultation process with an open mind, given that they had already decided upon the course of action they were going to take. In light of UK legislative requirements to consult on pension issues, in addition to IBM's own 'business conduct guidelines' and its 'core values', the Court was unimpressed with the manner in which IBM had conducted the consultation process.

[19.20] *Briggs v Gleeds*[19] – *High Court of England and Wales – defect in executing deeds – trust law requirements*

The UK High Court in *Briggs v Gleeds* determined that a defect in executing deeds of amendment had the result of invalidating the changes contained in those deeds. The principal employer of the pension scheme in question was a partnership and as such the

---

17.   *Imperial Group Pension Trust Ltd v Imperial Tobacco Ltd* [1991] 1 WLR 589.
18.   *Boliden Tara Mines Ltd v Cosgrove & Ors* [2007] IEHC 60.
19.   *Briggs v Gleeds* [2014] EWHC 1178 (Ch).

UK Law of Property (Miscellaneous Provisions) Act 1989 applied to the manner in which it executed deeds. Instead of executing deeds as required by a partnership under the 1989 Act, it executed various deeds in relation to its defined benefit scheme as if it were a limited company. The result was that the signatures of the partners executing the various deeds were not witnessed. During the period in question (1991–2008 during which period some 30 deeds were executed), a number of significant changes were made to the scheme including: the benefits of the scheme were equalised to take into account the principle of equal pensions treatment; the benefit structure was amended (including a reduction in the accrual rate); two defined contribution sections were added; and the defined benefit section was closed to future accrual.

The principal employer claimed its consultants, who were advising on the scheme, impliedly represented that the deeds could be executed in the manner appropriate for a limited company and members were estopped from challenging the manner in which the deeds were executed. The judge disagreed and the consequences for the principal employer and the members are significant, especially those members who were in the defined benefit section and who, as a result of the judgment, continued to accrue benefit despite the attempted closure to future accrual. It is estimated that as a result of the judgment, the scheme's deficit increased by £45 million.

Decisions of the UK Pensions Ombudsman

[19.21] *Thompson[20] – UK Pensions Ombudsman – past practices not sufficient to give rise to reasonable expectations*

The UK Pensions Ombudsman, in August 2014, rejected a claim that an employer breached its duty of trust and confidence to scheme members in exercising its decision not to grant a discretionary annual pension increase after 20 years of annual increases. The decision was subsequent to the decision of the UK High Court in *IBM v Dalgleish* (see para **[19.19]**).

Mr Thompson was a member of the GE pension plan (the main plan) and an additional top-up arrangement. Mr Thompson brought a complaint before the Pensions Ombudsman arguing that the principal employer had breached its implied duty of good faith in discontinuing increases from 2010 onwards. Additionally, he asserted that members had been given assurances in 2002 that the discretionary practice would continue. Mr Thompson, relying on the decision in *IBM*,[21] argued that affected members had 'reasonable expectations' that the benefit would be continued into the future.

The Pensions Ombudsman rejected Mr Thompson's arguments, stating that the decision in *IBM* did not support the view that past practices alone are sufficient to give rise to reasonable expectations. Mr Thompson was unable to provide the Pensions Ombudsman with any evidence of the assurances given in 2002.

Mr Thompson further argued that the principal employer acted in a manner that was in contravention of the scheme rules as the principal employer made the first

---

20. *Thompson* (PO–1203).
21. *IBM United Kingdom Holdings Ltd v Dalgleish* [2014] EWHC 980 (Ch).

representation in advance of the trustees' decision. The rules provided for the award of discretionary increases by the trustees 'if the principal employer so agrees'. Additionally, the rules of the top-up arrangement provided that the principal employer could make increases 'if the Trustees so agree'. These arguments were rejected by the Pensions Ombudsman as, even if the trustees had agreed to the increase, agreement of the principal employer was required nonetheless. It was considered that the fact that the company made the first representation was of no significance.

It is important to note that, although the UK Pensions Ombudsman rejected the claim, the decision of the UK Pensions Ombudsman deviates from that of the Court in *IBM* with respect to the issue of past promises, guarantees and statements of intention. The UK Pensions Ombudsman held that 'there would need to be more than a statement of intention to give rise to a reasonable expectation'. In contrast, the Court in *IBM* indicated that a guarantee, promise or statement of intention could create a reasonable expectation.

Chapter 20

PROTECTIVE LEAVE

ENTITLEMENT TO MATERNITY OR ADOPTIVE LEAVE ON SURROGACY

[20.01] *Z v A Government Dept and the Board of Management of a Community School[1] and CD v ST[2] – CJEU – whether mothers who have had a baby through surrogacy arrangements should be entitled to maternity leave or its equivalent – Council Directive 92/85/EEC of 19 October 1992 – Council Directive 2006/54/EC of the European Parliament and of the Council of 5 July 2006 – whether refusal of paid leave equivalent to maternity leave or adoptive leave constitutes discrimination contrary to Pregnancy Workers Directive – whether refusal of paid leave constitutes discrimination on grounds of gender or disability – Council Directive 2000/78/EC*

Each of the female complainants in these cases (a hospital worker in the United Kingdom and a secondary school teacher in Ireland) used surrogacy in order to have a child.

The complainant CD entered into a surrogacy agreement in accordance with UK law and the child was conceived using her partner's sperm and a donor egg. CD and her partner were granted full and permanent parental responsibility for the child in accordance with UK legislation on surrogacy. CD commenced breastfeeding and caring for the relevant child one hour after birth and continued to breastfeed the child for three months. She sought paid leave under her employer's adoption policy and sought surrogacy leave.

In the Irish case, the complainant Ms Z, a teacher, had a rare condition which meant that, although she had healthy ovaries and was otherwise fertile, she had no uterus and therefore could not support her pregnancy. She and her husband had their child as a result of an agreement with a surrogate mother in California. Genetically, the child is the couple's and under Californian law, Z and her husband are considered the baby's parents. She sought leave from work equivalent to adoptive leave, but was refused on the grounds that she did not satisfy the requirements laid down by the existing maternity or adoptive leave scheme. She asserted that she had been subject to discriminatory treatment on grounds of gender, family status and disability, that her employer had failed to reasonably accommodate her as a person with a disability and that her employer had refused to provide her with paid leave equivalent to maternity or adoptive leave, although she had undergone IVF treatment. The Equality Tribunal decided to stay those proceedings and refer the questions to the CJEU for a preliminary ruling.

---

1.   *Z v A Government Dept and the Board of Management of a Community School* (Case C–363/12).
2.   *CD v ST* (Case C–167/12).

The CJEU delivered its judgment in both cases on 18 March 2014. The CJEU held that EU law does not provide for commissioning mothers to be entitled to paid leave equivalent to maternity leave and adoptive leave.

The CJEU in the *CD* case concluded that maternity leave was intended to protect a woman's biological condition during and after pregnancy and secondly to protect the special relationship between a woman and her child over the period which follows pregnancy and childbirth. The CJEU held that it followed from the objective of Directive 92/85/EEC[3] that the maternity leave provided for in art 8 of that Directive is to protect the health of the mother of the child in the especially vulnerable situation arising from her pregnancy. The CJEU stated that the grant of maternity leave under art 8 presupposes 'that the worker entitled to such leave has been pregnant and has given birth to a child'. The CJEU therefore held that 'a female worker who as a commissioning mother has had a baby through a surrogacy arrangement does not fall within the scope of art 8 of Directive 92/85, even in circumstances where she may breastfeed the baby following the birth or where she does breastfeed the baby. Consequently, Member States are not required to grant such a worker a right to maternity leave under that article'. The CJEU noted, however, that Member States were not precluded from applying or introducing laws, regulations or administrative provisions more favourable to the protection of the safety and health of commissioning mothers who have had babies through surrogacy arrangements by allowing them to take maternity leave as a result of the birth of the child.

In light of this decision, the CJEU held in the *Z* case that a refusal to provide paid leave equivalent to maternity leave to a woman who has had a baby through a surrogacy arrangement did not constitute discrimination. The CJEU further held that a commissioning father who has had a baby through a surrogacy arrangement is treated in the same way as a commissioning mother in a comparable situation in that he is not entitled to paid leave equivalent to maternity leave either and thus the refusal to grant maternity leave to a commissioning mother such as Ms Z does not constitute direct or indirect discrimination on grounds of gender. Further, the CJEU found that a commissioning mother who has had a baby through a surrogacy arrangement cannot by definition be subject to less favourable treatment in relation to her pregnancy given that she has not been pregnant with that baby.

In the *Z* case, the CJEU considered whether refusal to provide paid leave equivalent to adoptive leave to a commissioning mother such as Ms Z constituted discrimination on grounds of gender in the meaning of Directive 2006/54.[4] The CJEU said that it was clear from art 16 of Directive 2006/54, read in conjunction with recital 27 of the preamble to that Directive, that the Directive preserves the freedom of Member States to grant or not to grant adoptive leave and that the conditions for implementation of such leave, other

---

3.   Council Directive 92/85/EEC of the Council of 19 October 1992 on the introduction of measures to encourage improvements in the safety and health at work of pregnant workers and workers who have recently given birth or are breastfeeding.

4.   Directive 2006/54/EC of the European Parliament and of the Council of 5 July 2006 on the implementation of the principle of equal opportunities and equal treatment of men and women in matters of employment and occupation.

than dismissal and return to work, are in both of the Directives. Thus, the CJEU concluded that the situation of a commissioning mother as regards the grant of maternity leave or adoptive leave was not within the scope of Directive 2006/54/EC.

The CJEU also considered whether the refusal to provide paid leave equivalent to maternity or adoptive leave to Ms Z, who was unable to bear a child and who had availed of a surrogacy arrangement, constituted discrimination on grounds of disability. The CJEU noted Ms Z's condition and held with regard to the concept of disability, it is not disputed that such a condition (as presented by Ms Z) constitutes a limitation which results in a particular form of physical, mental or psychological impairment, or that it is of a long-term nature. In particular, it could not be disputed that a woman's inability to bear her own child may be a source of great suffering for her. However, the CJEU found that the concept of 'disability' within the meaning of Directive 2000/78/EC[5] presupposes that the limitation from which the person suffers in interaction with various barriers, may hinder that person's full and effective participation in professional life on an equal basis with other workers. The Court noted that in this case it was not 'apparent from the order for reference that Ms Z's condition by itself made it impossible for her to carry out her work or constituted a hindrance to the exercise of professional activity'. The CJEU ultimately concluded that her condition did not constitute a disability within the meaning of Directive 2000/78 and that the Directive was not applicable in the proceedings.

[20.02] *Ms Z v A Government Dept and the Board of Management of A Community School[6] – Equality Tribunal, 9 July 2014 – whether mothers who have had a baby through surrogacy agreements should be entitled to maternity leave or its equivalent – whether refusal of paid leave constitutes discrimination on grounds of gender or disability*

A preliminary hearing of this case took place in the Equality Tribunal in November 2010. Further submissions were exchanged before a further hearing took place in April 2012. This matter was referred to the CJEU for a preliminary reference in accordance with art 267 of the Treaty of the Functioning of the European Union in July 2012 and the judgment was delivered on 18 March 2014 – see above at **20.01**. A further hearing of the Equality Tribunal hearing took place in April 2014, at which closing arguments were heard and this decision of the Equality Tribunal issued on 9 July 2014.

The Equality Tribunal noted that surrogacy is an unregulated area in Ireland. The Equality Tribunal referred to its decision to refer this matter for a preliminary ruling under art 267.

Based on the judgment of the CJEU, the Equality Tribunal found that the respondents did not discriminate against the complainant by refusing to grant her maternity leave or adoptive leave following the birth of her daughter through a surrogacy arrangement.

---

5. Directive 2000/78/EC of the Council of 27 November 2000 establishing a general framework for equal treatment in employment and occupation.

6. *Ms Z v A Government Dept and the Board of Management of A Community School* DEC–E2014–050.

EXCLUSION OF WOMEN ON MATERNITY LEAVE FROM A TRAINING COURSE

[20.03] *Napoli v Ministero della Giustizia-Dipartimento dell 'Amministrazione Penitenziaria*[7] *– CJEU – reference for preliminary ruling – Directive 2006/54/EC – whether exclusion of complainant, who was on maternity leave, from training course required to acquire status of public official was discriminatory*

The complainant was successful in a competition for the appointment of Deputy Commissioner of the Prison Service Corps and was admitted on 5 December 2011 to the requisite training course scheduled to start later that month. On 7 December 2011, the complainant gave birth and was placed (in accordance with national legislation) on compulsory maternity leave for three months until 7 March 2012. She was informed by a document dated 4 January 2012 that under national legislation, once the first 30 days of maternity leave had elapsed, she would be excluded from the training course and that payment of her salary would be suspended. She was advised that she would be admitted as of right to the next course organised.

The Lazio Regional Administrative Court asked the CJEU whether Directive 2005/54/EC[8] precludes national legislation which excludes a woman, because she has taken compulsory maternity leave, from a vocational training course which forms an integral part of her employment and which she must attend in order to be appointed to a post as a civil servant and thereby benefit from an improvement to her employment conditions whilst nevertheless guaranteeing her the right to participate in a subsequent course organised at an unknown future date.

The CJEU noted that the complainant suffered harm as a result of going on maternity leave because she was placed in a less favourable position than her male colleagues who were successful in the same competition and were admitted to the initial training course. The CJEU noted that the complainant would lose the pay and the social contributions to which she would have been entitled had she been able to attend the initial course. The CJEU noted that it was common ground that the complainant 'is in an employment relationship and the course from which she was excluded as a result of her absence on maternity leave, is provided in the context of that employment relationship and is intended to prepare her for examination which, should she be successful in it, would allow her access to a higher grade'. The CJEU concluded that the course must be regarded as forming part of working conditions inherent to the complainant's post.

The CJEU noted that this question must be examined in light of art 15 of Directive 2006/54 and concluded that being excluded from the vocational training course as a result of having taken maternity leave has had a negative effect on the complainant's working conditions. The CJEU noted that the measure in question, which provides for automatic exclusion from a training course and 'rendered it impossible to sit the

7. *Napoli v Ministero della Giustizia-Dipartimento dell 'Amministrazione Penitenziaria* (Case C–595/12).
8. Directive 2006/54/EC of the European Parliament and of the Council of 5 July 2006 on the implementation of the principle of equal opportunities and equal treatment of men and women in matters of employment and occupation.

examination organised at the end of the course, without account being taken in particular either of the stage of the course at which the absence for maternity leave takes place or of the training already received and which merely grants the woman who has taken such leave the right to participate in a training course organised at a later but uncertain date, does not appear to comply with the principle of proportionality.'

The CJEU further noted that this was all the more blatant as there was uncertainty as to the start of the next training course because the competent authorities were under no obligation to organise such a course at specified intervals.

The CJEU concluded that art 15 of Directive 2006/54 must be interpreted as precluding the national legislation in question. The CJEU reached this conclusion as the national legislation excluded a woman on maternity leave from a vocational training course which formed an integral part of her employment while noting that the training course was compulsory in order to be able to be appointed definitively to a post as civil servant and to benefit from an improvement in her working conditions. The CJEU also noted that, although the woman was guaranteed the right to participate in the next training course, the date of same was uncertain. The Court further concluded that the provisions of arts 14(1)(c) and 15 of Directive 2006/54 were sufficiently clear, precise and unconditional to have direct effect.

ENTITLEMENTS OF AN EMPLOYEE DISMISSED WHILST ON PART-TIME PARENTAL LEAVE AND A REDUCED SALARY

[20.04] *Lyreco Belgium NV v Rogiers[9] – Directive 96/34/EC Framework Agreement on Parental Leave – CJEU, 27 February 2014 – whether contrary to Framework Agreement for fixed-term protective award payable to worker who is unilaterally dismissed whilst on part-time parental leave to be determined on basis of reduced salary earned at date of dismissal*

The complainant worked as a full-time employee of Lyreco under a contract of indefinite duration since 2005. She availed of maternity leave in January 2009 until 26 April 2009 and was due to resume work on 27 April 2009 on a part-time basis also availing of part-time parental leave which she had been granted for a period of four months. She received a letter dated 27 April 2009 terminating her employment with a notice period of five months, taking effect on 1 May 2009. Her employment ended on 31 August 2009.

She brought an action challenging her dismissal to the Dutch Labour Court. That Court ordered Lyreco to pay a fixed sum protective award equivalent to six months' salary because of the unilateral termination of the complainant's employment, without compelling or sufficient reason, during her parental leave. As part of the judgment, the amount of the award was calculated on the basis of the salary paid to her at her date of dismissal, ie the part-time salary. This was appealed by both parties; in terms of the decision regarding dismissal by the employer and also by the complainant in respect of the quantum of compensation awarded. In the appeal judgment, the Court confirmed

---

9. *Lyreco Belgium NV v Rogiers* (Case C–588/12).

that the complainant had been dismissed without compelling or sufficient reason during parental leave and that she was entitled to payment of a fixed sum of the equivalent to six months' salary.

The appeal court decided to refer this matter for a preliminary ruling to the CJEU, and the question was whether it was contrary to Directive 96/34[10] for the fixed sum protective award to be determined on the basis of a reduced salary earned by that worker at the date of dismissal.

The CJEU noted that, in order to ensure that workers can actually exercise their right to parental leave provided for by the Directive 96/34, Clause 2.4 thereof requires Member States and/or management and labour to take the necessary measures to protect workers against dismissal on the grounds of an application for or taking of parental leave in accordance with national law, collective agreements or practices. The CJEU noted that the national legislation provides that where an employer unilaterally terminates a worker's full-time contract of indefinite duration without compelling or sufficient reason, while the worker is on parental leave, the worker is to be awarded, in addition to compensation due for breach of contract, a fixed sum protective award equivalent to six months' salary and that this was classified as part of 'measures to protect workers against dismissal on grounds of the application or of taking up parental leave' within the meaning of Clause 2.4 of the Directive 96/34.

The CJEU noted that such a protective measure would lose a great part of its effectiveness if, in the situation where a worker employed on a full-time basis, like the complainant in this case, is unlawfully dismissed during part-time parental leave and the protective award to which she is entitled were to be determined, not on the basis of the salary earned under full-time employment contract, but on the basis of a reduced salary earned during part-time parental leave. Such a method of determining the amount of a fixed sum award would likely not have an effect sufficient to prevent the dismissal of part-time workers on parental leave.

The CJEU referenced its decision in *Meerts v Proost NV*[11] in which 'the court concluded that when a worker employed under a full-time contract of indefinite duration has been unlawfully dismissed as in the main proceedings during part-time parental leave, a fixed-term protective award such as that provided by the Belgian legislation must, in order to satisfy the requirements of the Framework Agreement be determined on the basis of the full-time salary of that worker.'

CAN AN EMPLOYER UNILATERALLY WITHDRAW PAID MATERNITY LEAVE?

[20.05] *Red Ribbon Project v A Worker*[12] *– Labour Court – Industrial Relations Act 1969, s 13(9) – whether employer entitled to unilaterally withdraw provision of paid maternity leave where employee had contractual right to same*

---

10.   Directive 96/34/EC of the Council of 3 June 1996 on framework agreement on parental leave.
11.   *Meerts v Proots NV* ECR 1–10063 (Case C–116/08).
12.   *Red Ribbon Project v A Worker* AD1420.

This was a Labour Court appeal by the respondent employer of a Rights Commissioner recommendation which upheld the original complaint. Due to a cut in its funding, the employer sought to reduce costs and from December 2011 sought to discontinue paid maternity leave benefits. However, it was asserted by the claimant that she had a clear contractual entitlement to paid maternity leave on foot of her terms and conditions of employment which were entered into in 1997. The Labour Court concluded that as the claimant had a longstanding contractual entitlement to the benefit, she should be entitled to retain it on a personal to holder basis. The appeal was rejected.

DO PERSONS UNABLE TO WORK BECAUSE OF PHYSICAL CONSTRAINTS IN THE LATE STAGES OF PREGNANCY RETAIN THE STATUS OF 'WORKER'?

[20.06] *Saint Prix v Secretary of State for Work and Pensions[13] – CJEU, 19 June 2014 – Directive 2004/38/EC – request for preliminary ruling from Supreme Court of United Kingdom – whether EU law and in particular Treaty on the Functioning of the European Union, art 42 and Council Directive 2004/38, art 7 to be interpreted as meaning that woman who gives up work or seeking work, because of physical constraints of late stages of pregnancy and aftermath of childbirth retains status of worker within meaning of those articles*

This request for a preliminary ruling was made in the context of proceedings between the complainant and the respondent concerning the respondent's refusal to grant income support to the complainant. Income support is a benefit in the United Kingdom which is granted to certain categories of people whose income does not exceed a defined amount. Women who are pregnant or have recently given birth may be eligible for that benefit, in particular during the period surrounding childbirth. However, persons from abroad, ie those who are not habitually resident in the United Kingdom are not entitled to income support unless they have acquired the status of worker within the meaning of Directive 2004/38/EC.[14]

The claimant was a French national who worked as a teaching assistant in the United Kingdom and she enrolled on a post graduate certificate educational course in London. She then took a number of agency positions working in nursery schools. However, when she was nearly six months pregnant she stopped that work on the grounds that the demands of caring for nursery school children had become too strenuous for her. Eleven weeks before her expected date of confinement, the claimant made a claim for income support which was refused. Three months after the premature birth of her child the claimant resumed work. The first tier tribunal upheld her appeal. The upper tribunal upheld the appeal brought by the respondent against that decision. The Court of Appeal confirmed the decision of the upper tribunal. The CJEU noted that neither art 45 of the

---

13.   *Saint Prix v Secretary of State for Work and Pensions* (Case C–507/12).

14.   Directive 2004/38/EC of the European Parliament and of Council of 29 April 2004 on the right of the movement and residence of a European citizen.

TFEU[15] nor art 7 of the Directive 2004/38/EC defines 'worker'. The CJEU noted that art 7(3) of Directive 2004/38 provides that an EU citizen who is no longer a worker or self-employed person shall retain the status of worker or self-employed person in specific cases, namely where he is temporarily unable to work as a result of illness or accident, where in certain situations he is involuntarily unemployed, or where under specified conditions he embarks on vocational training. The CJEU noted that Directive 2004/38/EC did not expressly envisage the case of a woman who is in a particular situation because of the physical constraints of the late stages of pregnancy and the aftermath of childbirth.

The CJEU noted its previous decision that pregnancy must be clearly distinguished from illness and stated that it followed that a woman in the situation of the claimant who temporarily gives up work because of the late stages of her pregnancy and the aftermath of childbirth could not be regarded as a person temporarily unable to work as a result of illness in accordance with art 7(3)(a) of Directive 2004/38.

The CJEU concluded that the claimant was employed in the territory of the United Kingdom before giving up work less than three months before the birth of her child because of the physical constraints of the late stages of pregnancy and the immediate aftermath of childbirth. She returned to work three months after the birth of her child, without having left the territory of that Member State during the period of interruption of her professional activity. The fact that such constraints require a woman to give up work during the period needed for recovery does not in principle deprive her of the status of worker within the meaning of art 45 TFEU. The fact that she was not actually available on the employment market of the host Member State for a few months did not mean that she ceased to belong to that market during that period, provided she returned to work or found another job within a reasonable period after confinement.

The CJEU stated that the approach adopted in its judgment is consistent with the objective pursued by art 45 TFEU of enabling a worker to move freely within the territory of other Member States and to stay there for the period for the purpose of employment. An EU citizen would be deterred from exercising her right to freedom of movement if in the event that she was pregnant in the host state and gave up work as a result, even if, only for a short period, she risked losing her status as a worker in that state. The CJEU pointed out that EU law guaranteed special protection for women in connection with maternity.

The CJEU concluded that art 45 TFEU must be interpreted as meaning that a woman who gives up work or seeking work, because of the physical constraints of the late stages of pregnancy and the aftermath of childbirth, retains the status of worker within the meaning of that article, provided she returns to work or finds another job within a reasonable period after the birth of her child. In order to determine whether the period that has elapsed between childbirth and starting work again may be regarded as reasonable, the national court concerned shall take account of all of the specific circumstances of the case in the main proceedings and the applicable national rules on the duration of maternity leave.

---

15.   Treaty on the Functioning of the European Union.

FAILURE TO OFFER SUITABLE ALTERNATIVE EMPLOYMENT ON A RETURN FROM MATERNITY LEAVE

[20.07] *Cahill v Focus Suites Ireland Ltd (In Liquidation) T/A Focus Suites*[16] – *Employment Appeals Tribunal – Unfair Dismissals Acts 1977 to 2007 (as amended) – Redundancy Payments Acts 1967 to 2014 – Maternity Protection Act 1994 (as amended) – failure to offer claimant suitable alternative employment upon return from maternity leave*

The claimant had worked for the respondent on a continuous basis from March 1998 to the date of her dismissal in November 2012. On 2 November 2009, the claimant commenced work with an associated company of the respondent that was registered in Northern Ireland. However the claimant was at all times based in an office in Dublin and was paid a salary of €50,000 per annum.

The claimant commenced unpaid maternity leave in November 2011. When she sought to return to work, following her maternity leave, on 30 October 2012, she was informed by a director of the respondent company that her employer company was in financial difficulty and that her previous role was no longer available to her. She was informed that she would be offered an alternative role in the employer company with a significantly reduced salary. Having notified the claimant of the proposed role, the respondent failed to provide any additional information to the claimant in respect of the changes to her terms and conditions of her employment, the proposed liquidation of her employer, the payment of a redundancy payment to her or her suggestion that she could work four days per week. The claimant was informed on 2 November 2012 that the employer company would be put into liquidation and that her role would be made redundant. The company did not, however, enter liquidation until 3 July 2013.

The EAT concluded that the claimant was unfairly dismissed as she was not offered suitable alternative employment and the respondent company had failed to comply with s 27 of the Maternity Protection Act 1994 (as amended). The EAT was also critical of the respondent's failure to consult with the claimant. The EAT found that the claimant's claim under the Unfair Dismissals Acts 1977 to 2007 (as amended) should succeed and awarded the claimant compensation of €26,992.84. The EAT dismissed the appeal under the Redundancy Payment Acts 1967 to 2014.

---

16. *Cahill v Focus Suites Ireland Ltd (In Liquidation) T/A Focus Suites* UD723/2013.

Chapter 21

PUBLIC SERVANTS

PUBLIC SERVICE STABILITY AGREEMENT 2013 TO 2016 – THE 'HADDINGTON ROAD AGREEMENT'

[21.01] *Health Service Executive v Irish Medical Organisation[1] – Labour Court – Industrial Relations Acts 1946 to 2012 – Industrial Relations Act 1990, s 26(1) – Haddington Road Agreement – whether a proposed reduction in working time was a cost-increasing measure – application of established rates of pay for job or shift rates*

Following an unsuccessful LRC conciliation conference, this matter was referred to the Labour Court for a recommendation. The Irish Medical Organisation (IMO) represented non-consultant hospital doctors who sought to have their working hours reduced to a 48-hour week, in line with the Organisation of Working Time Act 1997 and the EU Working Time Directive.[2] The Health Service Executive (the respondent) argued that it was prohibited from reducing the working hours of non-consultant hospital doctors as this would necessarily result in an increase in cost, which was prohibited under s 1(9) and 1(10) of the Haddington Road Agreement and s 1(27) of the Public Service Agreement.

The IMO argued that the proposed reduction in working time was not a cost-increasing measure as the non-consultant hospital doctors were simply seeking to align their pay with other health service staff who worked night shifts and that the new roster would allow a net reduction in hours which would reduce the individual employees' salaries and reduce cost to the respondent.

The respondent argued that although the non-consultant hospital doctors did not receive the standard night-duty pay, they were compensated by a one-hour paid meal break and annual study leave.

The Labour Court found that, as the non-consultant hospital doctors were on call during their meal-break, they were entitled to be paid for these breaks. Further, as the non-consultant hospital doctors were on training contracts, study leave was intrinsic to that programme, and this was not an extra benefit afforded to the non-consultant hospital doctors. The Labour Court concluded that these benefits did not offset the shift pay paid to other workers in the health service.

The Labour Court distinguished between claims for pay increases and claims in which workers were seeking the application of the established rates of pay for the job shift rates. This case was found to be in the latter category and therefore the Labour Court recommended that the doctors receive payment for night work in line with normal practice for night shift workers in the Health Service Executive.

---

1. *Health Service Executive v Irish Medical Organisation* LCR20671.
2. Directive 2003/88/EC of the European Parliament and of the Council of 4 November 2003 concerning certain aspects of the organisation of working time.

[21.02] *South Dublin Co Co v Services Industrial Professional Technical Union (SIPTU)* [3] *– Labour Court – Industrial Relations Acts 1946 to 2012 – Industrial Relations Act 1990, s 26(1) – entitlement to 'working in the rain' allowance – whether cessation of allowance was breach of Haddington Road Agreement*

This dispute concerned a proposal to cease payment of a 'working in the rain' allowance which was paid to approximately 27 workers employed in the Public Realm Division of South Dublin County Council. The respondent council proposed to eliminate the allowance on the grounds that the claimants were now part of a larger group of 140 workers, all of whom were required to work in inclement weather as part of their normal duties when safe to do so. It was submitted by SIPTU that the workers were entitled to retain the allowance under the Haddington Road Agreement. The dispute was the subject of an LRC conciliation conference and, as agreement was not reached, the dispute was referred to the Labour Court.

SIPTU claimed that the allowances were paid in respect of the conditions under which the workers performed. It was further asserted that, as the allowance was pensionable, it had the status of 'an allowance in the nature of pay' and therefore any cessation of the allowance would be a breach of the Haddington Road Agreement. It was asserted by the respondent council that payment of the allowance was no longer justified and would be inequitable in circumstances where the claimants formed part of a larger group of employees carrying out similar tasks as part of their normal duties. It was further submitted that the payment of the allowance was outdated in circumstances where the workers had been provided with protective clothing and essential equipment to aid them to carry out their duties. The Court concluded that the allowance was a category 1 allowance within the meaning of the *Guidelines for Addressing Allowances – Local Government Sector* of 13 November 2013 and thus the claimants were entitled to retain the allowance on a personal to holder basis.

OUTSOURCING

[21.03] *Personal Injuries Assessment Board v Public Services Executive Union & Ors* [4] *– Labour Court – Industrial Relations Act 1990, s 26(1) – whether outsourcing of preparation of files for statutory assessors is breach of Haddington Road Agreement – circumstances when Employment Control Framework applied*

This dispute concerned a decision by the Personal Injuries Assessment Board (PIAB) to outsource the preparation of files for statutory assessors. It had been asserted by the unions that, in so doing, management did not comply with the procedures contained in the Public Service Agreement. As the dispute was not resolved at local level, or in LRC conciliation conferences, it was referred to the Labour Court.

---

3.   *South Dublin Co Co v SIPTU* LCR20713.

4.   *Personal Injuries Assessment Board v Public Services Executive Union & Ors* LCR20820.

The unions argued that staff had been accommodating and cooperative in relation to outsourcing of non-core work but that the outsourcing of core work was done without any consultation and without a benefit analysis. It was further argued that as PIAB, which is self-funding and not a burden on the exchequer, has effected savings of €1 billion in the last 10 years, this outsourced work could be undertaken by directly employed staff rather than by outsourcing.

It was submitted by PIAB that it was subject to the Moratorium on Recruitment, and as an employer it had an Employment Control Framework staff allocation number of 67. PIAB advised that if it received sanction to recruit additional staff in the future the work would be brought back in-house.

The Labour Court concluded that the allocation of the work to an outside agency constituted outsourcing for the purposes of the Haddington Road Agreement. The Labour Court further concluded that, in outsourcing this work, PIAB had not complied with the outsourcing provisions of the agreement and recommended that PIAB take necessary steps to comply with the provisions of the Haddington Road Agreement.

PUBLIC SERVICE AGREEMENT 2010 TO 2014 (CROKE PARK AGREEMENT)

[21.04] *Department of Education and Skills v SIPTU/IMPACT/TUI/IFUT/UNITE[5] – Labour Court – Industrial Relations Acts 1946 to 2012 – Industrial Relations Act 1990, s 26(1) – dispute in relation to proposals for harmonisation of annual leave arrangements – Public Service Agreement 2010 to 2014*

This dispute concerned proposals for the harmonisation of annual leave arrangements envisaged under the Public Service Agreement 2010 to 2014. In line with the harmonised terms and conditions of employment in the Public Service Agreement, an agreement was reached between the parties in December 2011 that there would be standardised annual and related leave arrangements. In drawing up a circular to cover non-academic staff in the education sector, a number of issues were not agreed and formed the basis of the referral to the Labour Court.

Three issues were identified and the Labour Court made the following recommendations:

(i) Equity of Application of Annual Leave:

The unions submitted that the proposal to incorporate a standardised allocation of four days for Christmas and 1.5 days for Easter into annual leave allowances would have a detrimental effect on non-academic grades when compared to academic staff and sought the introduction of a more flexible arrangement instead.

Management submitted that the proposed standardised leave arrangements would be in line with similar and analogous grades common across the public service.

---

5.   *Department of Education and Skills v SIPTU/IMPACT/TUI/IFUT/UNITE* LCR10679.

The Labour Court noted that the methodology used to decide on the number of days to take into account of in respect of Christmas and Easter was devised on the basis of the average over a period of 21 years and accordingly should in general be reflective of the norm. The Labour Court was satisfied that the proposed arrangements were in line with those which applied to similar and analogous grades across the public service. The Labour Court recommended in favour of the proposals as outlined in the draft Circular which it stated should be accepted by the unions.

(i)   List of Grades Excluded:

The unions submitted that they required a list of grades to be excluded from the new Circular as they maintained that there were a number of grey areas.

Management gave details of the grades which would be impacted by the Circular and stated that, due to the number of institutions which would be covered by the Circular, it would be difficult to prepare such a list.

The Labour Court recommended that the list of excluded categories from the Circular should be devised by management at local level and the trade unions concerned should be supplied with the list.

(ii)   Impact of the Public Service Stability (Haddington Road) Agreement:

The unions submitted that the impact of the Public Service Stability Agreement, under which certain members of staff may decide to opt for a reduction in annual leave instead of a pay reduction, will have the effect of reducing discretionary annual leave for some employees to an unacceptably low level.

Management submitted that omitting non-discretionary closure days in the annual leave allowances would lead to wide disparities among similar grades, contrary to the objective of the standardisation agreement.

The Labour Court stated that the application of reduced annual leave under the Public Service Stability Agreement applies across all grades to those who opt for this arrangement. The Labour Court stated that it did not recommend in favour of special arrangements in this case, and therefore recommended in favour of the proposals as outlined in the draft Circular.

[21.05] *National University of Ireland Galway v Irish Federation of University Teachers[6] – Labour Court – Industrial Relations Act 1990, s 26(1) – whether decision to make claimant, a researcher, redundant following termination of research grant was breach of Croke Park Agreement*

This case arose from the respondent employer's decision to make an employee redundant following the termination of a research grant. There was an LRC conciliation conference, but as agreement was not reached, the dispute was referred to the Labour Court under s 26(1) of the Industrial Relations Act 1990. It was asserted by the union,

---

6.   *National University of Ireland Galway v Irish Federation of University Teachers* LCR20742.

for and on behalf of the employee, that there had been a breach of the Public Service Agreement 2010–2014 (Croke Park Agreement) (cls 1.15 and 1.6) by the respondent. The respondent university asserted that cls 1.15 and 1.6 were not applicable.

The respondent asserted that all staff employed as researchers in the university came within the Public Service Agreement 2010–2014, which states that a public servant may be made redundant only where existing exit provisions apply.

The Labour Court made a number of noteworthy findings in relation to this matter, as follows:

(1) the employment protection measures set out in s 1.6 of the Public Service Agreement 2010–2014, as amended by the Haddington Road Agreement, apply to all public servants;

(2) the employment protection measures are not absolute and, in order to avail of them, a public servant must cooperate with the redeployment or relocation measures set out in the Agreement. Otherwise, they may be made redundant where the work they perform is no longer required; and

(3) a public servant may be made redundant where existing exit provisions apply.

The Labour Court stated that any party seeking to derogate from the general employment protection provisions of s 1.5 of the Agreement must prove that there are existing exit provisions in place in the employment that apply in all respects to the worker concerned. It cannot rely on a general statement that an entire category of employees does not enjoy the job protection guarantees unless expressly identified in the Public Service Agreement 2010–2014 as amended. The Labour Court found that the respondent had not presented sufficient evidence to the Court to meet that requirement and noted that, while the contract offered to the employee in question made reference to funding extending to July 2009, there was no reference to his employment being contingent on the availability of funding and the Court further noted that the employee continued in employment beyond the July 2009 date.

The Labour Court found that the employee came within the employment protection measures set out in the Croke Park Agreement and therefore as long as he cooperated with the redeployment or relocation terms of the agreement, he was entitled to job security and to the protection of his terms and conditions of employment, save as amended by the terms of the Public Service Agreement and Haddington Road Agreement. The Court recommended that the respondent reinstate, with full retrospection, the employee's salary and the terms and conditions of employment under which he was employed prior to his dismissal.

[21.06] *National University of Ireland Galway v Irish Federation of University Teachers*[7] *– Labour Court – Industrial Relations Act 1990, s 26(1) – claim for ex gratia redundancy payment to worker – whether payment of statutory redundancy amounted to existing exit provision within meaning of Public Service Agreement 2010 to 2014, para 1.6*

---

7.   *National University of Ireland Galway v Irish Federation of University Teachers* LCR20772.

The claimant employee was employed under a contract of indefinite duration and it was accepted that her role was redundant and she was paid a statutory redundancy payment in August 2013. Her union submitted that she was entitled to an ex gratia redundancy payment reflective of the education sector in general or as agreed under the terms of the Public Service Agreement 2010–2014, ie three weeks' pay per year of service in addition to statutory redundancy entitlements.

The respondent confirmed that the claimant was notified of the fact that funding would expire on the conclusion of her assignment and she was made redundant. Each year a number of research posts are made redundant as a matter of practice, with payments limited to statutory redundancy and those redundancies are covered by the existing exit provisions within the meaning of para 1.6 of the Public Service Agreement 2010–2014.

The Labour Court noted para 1.6 of the Agreement which provided that compulsory redundancy will not apply within the public service except where existing exit provisions apply and noted that the respondent was covered by the terms of the Agreement. The Labour Court noted correspondence dated February 2012 from the Public Service Agreement Implementation Body to the Education Sector Implementation Group specifically dealing with para 1.6 and the issue of existing exit provisions. The Labour Court noted the contents of the letter which stated: 'There are established practices for making public servants redundant in appropriate circumstances, on the expiry of employment contracts or where redundancy terms had been agreed or generally applied.' The Labour Court noted that this same provision was included in the Enhanced Redundancy Agreement agreed between the Department of Education & Skills and the Public Services Committee of ICTU on 10 July 2012, which provided enhanced redundancy terms over and above statutory of no more than three weeks' pay per year of service.

The Labour Court concluded that in circumstances where a redundancy was not in dispute, the enhanced redundancy payment terms set out in the Agreement must apply. The Court stated that the references to existing exit provisions or where redundancy terms have been agreed or generally applied refer to the right to make people redundant and not to the enhanced redundancy payments as set out in that Agreement. The Court recommended that, in accordance with the terms of the Public Service Agreement, the claimant should be paid three weeks' pay per year of service in addition to her statutory redundancy payment.

MORATORIUM ON RECRUITMENT AND PROMOTIONS IN THE PUBLIC SECTOR

[21.07] *Teagasc v A Worker[8] – Labour Court – Industrial Relations Acts 1946 to 2012 – Industrial Relations Acts 1969, s 13(9) – whether claimant entitled to remain in permanent part-time job share role – whether effect of moratorium on recruitment*

---

8.   *Teagasc v A Worker* AD13102.

and promotions in the public sector was to change or revoke local employment agreement with claimant

The claimant brought a claim under the Industrial Relations Acts 1946 to 2012 in circumstances where she was not permitted to remain on a permanent part-time job share following her career break and she was not in a position to return to full-time employment. The claimant sought to rely on a local agreement with her employer which provided that where a staff member was on a job sharing programme beyond four years, the staff member would be regarded as having a permanent part-time job share, and the other half of their post would be filled on a permanent basis.

The claimant was employed on a job sharing basis from 15 October 2007 to 26 October 2012, and her contract specified that she would be on job-sharing to cover the period that another named employee was on part-time. Following the expiry of this arrangement, the respondent requested that the claimant return to work on a full time basis. It argued that the agreement with the claimant became redundant when the moratorium on recruitment and promotions in the public sector was introduced one month after the agreement had completed, and therefore the respondent was prohibited from recruiting another employee to fill the other half of the claimant's post.

The Labour Court found that while there was merit in the claimant's claim, the Court was constrained by the terms of the moratorium from allowing the claim. As the claimant was not in a position to resume full time work, the Labour Court recommended that a redundancy payment, inclusive of the public sector ex gratia terms, should be paid to the claimant.

PUBLIC SERVICE MANAGEMENT (SICK LEAVE) REGULATIONS 2014

[21.08] *Garda Representative Association v Minister for Public Expenditure and Reform[9] – High Court – Peart J – 7 May 2014 – judicial review – application for interlocutory injunction to restrain Minister from applying Public Service Management (Sick Leave) Regulations 2014 to members of An Garda Síochána pending determination of judicial review proceedings*

This was an application for an interlocutory injunction to restrain the respondent Minister from operating the Public Service Management (Sick Leave) Regulations 2014[10] (the Regulations) which came into operation on 31 March 2014, in respect of members of An Garda Síochána, pending the determination of judicial review proceedings.

The applicant association was granted leave by the High Court to challenge the lawfulness of the Regulations on the grounds that they were *ultra vires* the respondent Minister. The applicant contended that the Regulations were brought into effect in

---

9. *Garda Representative Association v Minister for Public Expenditure and Reform* [2014] IEHC 237.

10. Public Service Management (Sick Leave) Regulations 2014 (SI 124/2014).

breach of fair procedures and/or the legitimate expectation of the members of the applicant. The High Court noted that the Regulations introduced a sick leave scheme for all public servants which is radically different from those previously operating, particularly in respect of An Garda Síochána, whose sick leave arrangements were particularly favourable historically. Peart J noted that the Minister's proposal to reform sick leave in the public service was the subject of a consultation process between the applicant association and the Minister for Justice and Equality and the respondent during 2012 and 2013. Part of the process involved a working group which presented its recommendations to the respondent Minister in November 2013. An Garda Síochána had indicated its view that there should be a derogation for members of the Gardaí in any new sick leave regime for public servants.

The applicant association stated that it was assured that any changes to pay and conditions for its members would be negotiated through the conciliation and arbitration committee. However, no such derogation was provided for by the Oireachtas in the Public Service Management (Recruitment and Appointments (Amendment)) Act 2013. Further, the applicant stated that it was given an assurance by email that its members would not be included in the proposed new Regulations in the first instance. The respondent stated that immediately thereafter, it was announced that the Regulations would include An Garda Síochána, but those new Regulations would be deferred until the end of March 2014. It was further submitted on behalf of the respondent that the applicant association and its members were aware of this and in addition, this was made clear in speeches to the Oireachtas in December 2013. It was submitted by the respondent that sufficient time and opportunity for consultation and discussion was provided to the applicant and its members and, whilst their views were considered, they were ultimately rejected.

Peart J noted that the applicant was not making the case that the Minister did not have the power to make the Regulations without a derogation for its members. Rather, the applicant's argument was that it was given an assurance, amounting to a legitimate expectation, that the Minister would not do so prior to the conclusion of the conciliation and arbitration process and/or that he would not so act prior to the conclusion of the Haddington Road Agreement negotiations which commenced in September 2013 and were due to conclude in June 2014.

Peart J noted that the first issue to address was the issue of *locus standi* of the applicant. It was accepted by the respondent that the applicant had the necessary standing to bring a challenge to the new Regulations on the basis of its legitimate expectation and on the basis that it would be consulted as alleged. However, the respondent did not accept that such standing could extend to an entitlement to seek an injunction on behalf of all of its members to suspend the operation of the Regulations pending the determination of that challenge and insofar as the applicant seeks an injunction, it did so only on the basis of a *ius tertii*.[11]

The respondent submitted that only an individual member who stands to be personally affected by the new Regulations could have an entitlement to seek such an injunction, since only in such case could the Court realistically consider matters such as

---

11.   A right of a third party.

the adequacy of damages, the balance of convenience and the worth of any undertaking as to damages which may be available. Reference was made by the respondent to the judgment of McCracken J in *Construction Industry Federation v Dublin City Council.*[12]

Peart J stated that to grant an injunction as sought would be to do so on a hypothetical basis and on an assumption that in all cases which might arise, damages would not be an adequate remedy for any individual member on sick leave. He noted the line of jurisprudence that had developed in employment cases where an employee may be granted a mandatory injunction requiring his or her salary to be paid pending the determination of a claim that his/her dismissal is unlawful, but the Court distinguished this as being a discrete area of law. The Court noted that it was perfectly possible for a garda, if sufficiently adversely affected by the new Regulations, to seek to be joined in the present proceedings for the purposes of seeking an interlocutory injunction to enable him/her to receive sick pay under the old regime, but it would be dependent on the actual facts and circumstance of his/her particular case. Peart J stated that it was inescapable that the Court must reach conclusions in relation to any such injunction restraining the operation on the 2014 Regulations by reference to a particular case and particular facts in circumstances affecting a particular garda. Peart J stated that he was not satisfied that the applicant had standing to seek injunctive relief and on that basis alone, he refused the application.

Peart J then went on to find that the balance of convenience did not lie in favour of granting the injunction. He noted the judgment of Finlay CJ in *Pesca Valentia Ltd v Minister for Fishery, Forestry & Ors*[13] where Finlay CJ was satisfied that there was no impediment to the Court granting an injunction pending the determination of a claim with regard to the constitutionality of a statute, even where a consequence was to postpone or suspend the trial of an offence under the impugned legislation. Peart J noted that that case involved penal legislation which was not the situation in this case. Peart J further referred to the judgment of Clarke J in *D v Ireland & Ors*[14] and noted that whilst a jurisdiction clearly existed it was nevertheless one that ought to be exercised most sparingly.

Peart J noted that the new Regulations had been introduced in order to reduce the very significant cost to the taxpayer of the sick leave arrangements for public servants, to include An Garda Síochána and this was a pressing need of national interest. Peart J stated that it must weigh heavily in the balance when the Court comes to consider the balance of convenience. He further noted that the applicant would not suffer any direct loss as a result of the new Regulations coming into operation. He stated that if one was to overlook that issue and consider the question of an injunction from the standpoint of an individual member of An Garda Síochána, the question of the adequacy of damages would loom large and that if the member was to seek to challenge the new Regulations, the Court would have to consider whether that individual is likely to suffer loss pending the determination of the proceedings which could not be compensated in damages. Peart J concluded that adequacy of damages would be sufficient in his view to disentitle such

---

12. *Construction Industry Federation v Dublin City Council* [2005] 2 IR 496.
13. *Pesca Valentia Ltd v Minister for Fishery, Forestry & Ors* [1985] IR 193.
14. *D v Ireland & Ors* [2009] IEHC 206.

an individual member to an interlocutory injunction barring some exceptional circumstances which any particular individual member may be able to demonstrate.

He concluded that if the Court got as far as having to consider the balance of convenience that he had no doubt, barring some truly exceptional circumstances in an individual and exceptional case, the balance of convenience must lie against prohibiting the operation of measures which are prima facie lawful pending a determination of the issues arising.

Finally, Peart J noted the judgment of Clarke J in *Okunade v Minister for Justice, Equality and Law Reform*[15] in relation to the role that can be played by the assessment of the strength of the plaintiff's case in judicial review proceedings, where the risk of injustice may be evenly balanced. Peart J stated that in the present case he did not consider the question of the greater injustice to be evenly or finally balanced but, had he done so, he would have considered that the applicant's case as argued had weaknesses even though the low threshold required at *ex parte* leave stage was considered to be surpassed.

[21.09] *Garda Representative Association and Bourke v Minister for Public Expenditure and Reform*[16] – High Court – judicial review – Kearns P – whether provisions of Public Service Management (Sick Leave) Regulations 2014 should apply to members of An Garda Síochána

The applicants sought a declaration that the Public Service Management (Sick Leave) Regulations 2014[17] should not apply to members of An Garda Síochána. They contended that the inclusion, without differentiation, of An Garda Síochána in the Regulations was in breach of fair procedures, the duty to consult and the legitimate expectations of the applicants that certain procedural steps would be concluded before any question of including An Garda Síochána in the range of public service employees affected by the Regulations would occur.

It was further submitted that the respondent, in bringing forward the Regulations, considered irrelevant information and failed to have regard to relevant information when arriving at his decision to include An Garda Síochána in the Regulations. It was further submitted by the applicants that the Regulations are legally incoherent. It was noted that the Garda Representative Association was not permitted to join any umbrella organisation such as ICTU and therefore was not party to any negotiations that ICTU conduct on behalf of members in relation to salary or sick leave. In May 2012, a briefing was held at the Department of Justice & Equality with representatives of the applicants, the respondent and other garda staff associations. This was part of a consultative process with all staff associations in the public service in relation to proposals to change sick leave arrangements in the public sector. It was submitted that an officer of the Department stated at the meeting that it was simply the start of the negotiation process with the garda organisations and the matter would likely be dealt with through the

---

15. *Okunade v Minister for Justice, Equality and Law Reform* [2012] 3 IR 153.
16. *Garda Representative Association and Bourke v Minister for Public Expenditure and Reform* [2014] IEHC 457.
17. Public Service Management (Sick Leave) Regulations 2014 (SI 124/2014).

conciliation and arbitration scheme. This is a formal non-statutory scheme for the determination of claims and proposals relating to the conditions of service of members of all ranks of An Garda Síochána. The principal officer of the respondent stated in her replying affidavit that it was clearly stated at this meeting that any derogation for a particular sector would have to be justified by objective reasons and was ultimately a decision for the respondent Minister.

In support of their contentions, the applicants argued that a process of consultation was established and was in progress under which they were led to believe that either they would receive a derogation from the Regulations or they would receive differentiated treatment from other public servants or at least that the consultation process would continue to a conclusion before the Regulations were applied to the applicants. By email of 2 December 2013, the applicants asserted that they had been informed by officials in the Department that the respondent Minister would defer inclusion of An Garda Síochána and the new sick pay scheme. However, nonetheless on 4 December, in circumstances that were far from clear, the Minister decided to reverse that decision and include An Garda Síochána.

It was argued by the respondent that any case based on legitimate expectation was unsustainable. Counsel for the respondent stated that any attempt to rely on the doctrine of legitimate expectation ran into the immediate difficulty that the doctrine could not be invoked to fetter the powers of the Minister. Counsel for the respondent further argued that, even if the applicant was entitled to have or hold an expectation as to the manner in which he would be consulted, any such expectation could be disappointed in the public interest in view of the economic circumstances of the State.

Kearns P concluded that it was clear that the first question to be addressed is whether or not a promise or representation had been made by a public authority, in this case the Minister, such as would warrant the granting of procedural relief. He did not accept any of the contentions made by the applicants and noted that they were informed as far back as May 2012 of the respondent's intention to adopt a sick pay scheme across the public sector, which would include members of An Garda Síochána. He noted that the applicants were unable to point to any documentation or meeting where a particular form of consultation was promised by the respondent, nor could they point to any detriment suffered by them or any action taken by them on foot of a supposed representation. Kearns P stated that, even if he was mistaken, any expectation harboured by the applicants was liable to be disappointed in the public interest in the context of the financial circumstances of the State, a backdrop against which all of these negotiations were taking place. He concluded that the applicants' claim of legitimate expectation must fail.

Kearns P noted that, as this case progressed, the applicants' claim morphed entirely into a claim based on fair procedures – essentially that there was a failure on the part of the respondent to adequately consult with the applicants prior to the introduction of the Regulations. It was contended that the duty to consult arose from the lengthy process of consultation and resolution which was still in progress when the Minister 'guillotined' the process by his decision of 4 December 2013. It was further asserted that this decision was arrived at in a highly inappropriate way, The applicants allege that, having decided that it was appropriate to consult with An Garda Síochána (and other sectors within the public service) prior to making any changes to the sick scheme, the Minister nonetheless changed his mind without affording the applicants the opportunity to address the putative reasons for the *volte face* and thereby converted a fair and meaningful consultation process into one which was unfair and spurious.

It was asserted by the respondent that the applicants enjoyed no right to consultation such as would fetter the power of the executive to legislate and certainly the applicants enjoyed no right to consultation in any particular forum. It was further asserted that the applicants had been afforded a more than fair opportunity of making their case and noted that a working group had sent in its report and same was considered by the Minister before any decision was arrived at.

Kearns P engaged in a lengthy analysis of the general principles regarding the control by courts over legislative decisions. He noted in particular in *Gorman v Minister for the Environment*.[18] Kearns P noted that Carney J's finding that while there was a constitutionally protected right provided for in Article 40.3 to fair procedures in decision-making, it did not apply with equal force in every situation. Carney J held in that case:

> A public body is entitled to resile from its previous practice and representation where there actually exists in the particular case objective reasons which justify this change of position. A person or groups of persons who have benefitted from a previous policy can legitimately make representations as to why the policy should not be changed. They cannot, however, legitimately expect to fetter the body's statutory discretion to adopt a new policy in the public interest, as it is the public interest and not the private rights incidentally created that the public body must ultimately seek to vindicate.

Kearns P stated that this legal position had withstood the test of time and remains the law in this jurisdiction. Kearns P noted that the case being advanced before him had shifted and it was now a contention that once there was a process in being, as undoubtedly was the situation in this case, the applicants were entitled to expect that the process would be continued to a conclusion, presumably one satisfactory to their members, before the Minister was free to introduce the Regulations in question. Kearns P stated that he could not accept this proposition when the views of the applicants had been articulated through various mediation and conciliation mechanisms and when the report of the working group dealing with the issue had been submitted to the respondent at the end of November 2013. Kearns P noted that the report in itself was a means of consultation and communication and the evidence before the Court was that the Minister was briefed on its contents. Kearns P stated that, if the applicants' submissions were correct, a process of consultation which might have had the effect of unravelling the process across the entire public service should have continued until the demands of the applicants, either to be together excluded from the process or to receive special differentiated treatment, was realised. Kearns P stated that such a fetter on the power of the Minister in a particular context and circumstances cannot in the view of the Court be justified.

---

18.   *Gorman v Minister for the Environment* [2001] IR 414.

Kearns P noted the further argument that the applicants are entitled to relief because the respondent took irrelevant considerations into account on the one hand and failed to have regard to relevant considerations on the other. Specifically referenced was an intervention by the general secretary of another union, which the applicants described as highly inappropriate. It was submitted that the utterance of a threat by that person that he would seek to ballot union members on industrial action if the applicants received special treatment was 'reprehensible and highly inappropriate and not a consideration to which the Minister should have had regard'. It emerged from the email discovery that that person had also asserted that the whole process of negotiating the sick pay scheme across the public sector would unravel if An Garda Síochána were treated as a special case.

The Court noted that the respondent had not denied that that person did communicate these points of view and did not seek to challenge the historical narrative conveyed by the discovered emails. Kearns P stated that even if he took the applicants' case at its strongest, he was satisfied that the facts emerging from a study of those emails fails to have the implication suggested by the applicants. The Court stated its satisfaction that in any democracy, it is to be expected that persons charged with obligations to represent the interests of their members will communicate their concerns at a political level and the respondent is certainly entitled to take them into account, particularly if one consequence of treating An Garda Síochána differently would have been to unravel the entire process.

It was further alleged that the Minister failed to take into account relevant considerations such as the fact that An Garda Síochána are engaged in shift work, had no occupational injury scheme and of the health concerns of those employed in An Garda Síochána. The Court did not uphold any of these arguments. Kearns P concluded that there was no failure to have regard to the need to protect the health of members of An Garda Síochána as public servants, as the discretion conferred upon the Minister is a particularly broad one. In essence, the Regulations themselves evidence the protection of the health of public servants. Nothing in the legislation requires the Minister to provide that protection to a level demanded or asserted by An Garda Síochána. The Court said it was clear that the respondent did not consider that there was an objective justification to warrant permitting more favourable treatment for members of An Garda Síochána than other public workers. Insofar as shift work is concerned, the chief medical officer pointed out in December 2013 that shift work was not unique to the gardaí and indeed was common within the Health Service Executive and within the civil service.

Kearns P noted the final argument of the applicants that regs 9 and 10 are legally incoherent, entirely inconsistent and incapable of rational explanation. Kearns P noted the position of the respondent that the Regulations were not legally incoherent as they do achieve their aim of reducing eligibility to absence due to sickness on full pay to a period of three months followed by a further period of three months on half pay. It was submitted that the Regulations clearly provide for a sick pay regime as set out in the explanatory note to the Regulations.

Kearns P held that the contentions of the respondent were correct and that their interpretation of the Regulations is the correct one.

Kearns P said the Court must ask exactly what was it hoped that these proceedings would achieve. He stated that, at most, the applicants' case was for a limited form of procedural relief, which would defer the application of the Regulations to one specific public service sector, namely An Garda Síochána, until a consultation process proceeded to a conclusion. He stated that this, in reality, could only be taken as meaning that the applicants believe that the Minister's power to introduce the Regulations clearly mandated by statute can be fettered indefinitely by the prolongation of a consultation process designed solely to achieve an outcome satisfactory to the applicants.

Kearns P held that this basic proposition was untenable and would be tantamount to the imposition of a serious limitation on the power to legislate. He refused the declarations sought.

FINANCIAL EMERGENCY MEASURES IN THE PUBLIC INTEREST (NO 2) ACT 2009/REDUCTIONS IN PAY

[21.10] *Nic Bhradaigh v Mount Anville School – Employment Appeals Tribunal – Payment of Wages Act 1991 – appeal of decision of Rights Commissioner – consideration of pay reduction in accordance with Financial Emergency Measures in the Public Interest (No 2) Act 2009 (FEMPI) – whether employees of privately funded schools fall within definition of public servants for purposes of FEMPI*

The appellant was employed as the secretary of the respondent, a private fee paying school. A Rights Commissioner held that the reduction in pay of the secretary was a lawful deduction as per s 5(1) of the Payment of Wages Act 1991.

The Department of Education and Skills (the Department) had deemed the respondent to be a 'recognised school' for the purposes of circular 70/2010 (the circular) which outlined the reductions in pay in accordance with FEMPI. The circular instructed the respondent to make the appropriate reductions to the remaining staff not paid by the Department. It also specified that staff working in a 'recognised school' came within the definition of public servant 'regardless of the source of the money used to fund their salary ... and irrespective of whether or not they are eligible for ... a public service pension scheme'.

The appellant argued that she was not a public servant and that the reduction in pay was a reduction as opposed to a statutory deduction as allowed under the 1991 Act. She argued that, as her salary was paid by the respondent using private funds, there was no benefit to the exchequer in ordering the reduction in salary.

The appellant also wrote to the Minister for Finance and the Minister for Education and Skills, each of whom confirmed that FEMPI applied to all staff of recognised schools and that because the appellant worked for a recognised school, she was deemed to be a public servant.

This case is unusual in that it contains a lengthy and detailed dissenting opinion, with little detail provided in the majority decision.

The dissenting opinion of the EAT[19] stated that the appellant was a private employee who had none of the benefit of the terms and conditions inherent in an employment contract enjoyed by public servants. Furthermore, it stated that s 1 of FEMPI centres the definition of 'public servants' and 'public servant body' on the fact as to whether or not a public service pension exists. The preamble to FEMPI highlighted that this legislation was introduced during a time of economic turmoil and, *inter alia*, to save the State revenue to ensure that there were funds available to discharge the public service pensions into the future. The appellant could not be deemed to be a public servant as she did not enjoy the benefits of a public service pension and due to the fact that any reduction/deduction in her salary could not in any way result in a saving to the State. The dissenting decision found that FEMPI clearly stated that there had to be a public element in the pay received which hinged on the actual existence or application of a public pension. The dissenting decision concluded by saying that any deduction from the pay paid to the appellant did not achieve the objective of FEMPI and therefore, the appellant fell outside the remit of FEMPI.

The majority decision rejected the appeal and held that the deduction from the appellant's pay was lawful under s 5 of the 1991 Act.

JUDICIAL REVIEW

[21.11] *Gormley & Scott v Minister for Agriculture, Food and Marine (No 2)[20] – High Court – Hogan J – judicial review proceedings – challenge to Minister's decision to exclude applicants from certain internal competitions – test of bona fides, factual sustainability and showing that decision made was not unreasonable[21] – adequacy of reasons provided for refusing applications – equivalency of qualifications – Public Service Management (Recruitment and Appointment) Act 2004, s 29(9)*

The applicants were technical agricultural officers in the Department of Agriculture and Food and each held a BSc in Rural Development. One of the applicants also had a Masters qualification in rural environmental conservation and management. The applicants had been formally advised that their posts as technical agricultural officers were surplus to requirements in March 2011 and were not subsequently redeployed under the Public Service Agreement 2010–2014, which provides a mechanism for redeployment of surplus staff within the civil service. The applicants sought to challenge the Minister's decision to exclude them from certain internal competitions for the post of assistant agricultural inspector (AAI).

In 2012, seven AAI positions became available in the Department through open competition. The applicants' applications were rejected on the ground that they did not satisfy 'the essential requirements' for the post. The application criteria included an honours degree in agricultural science or its equivalent and, furthermore, all applicants had to possess 'a broad scientific knowledge of the sectors'. The applicants maintained

---

19. The identity of the dissenting member of the Tribunal is not known.
20. *Gormley & Scott v Minister for Agriculture, Food and Marine (No 2)* [2013] IEHC 459.
21. *Mallak v Minister for Justice* [2012] IESC 59, [2013] 1 ILRM 73 at 91 *per* Fennelly J.

that their degree qualifications should be regarded as equivalent to a degree in agricultural science for the purpose of the application process. The applicants' trade union engaged with the Department and was informed that an internal competition would be held for the posts.

In April 2013, an internal competition for the positions was advertised. The specifications regarding skills and qualifications were the same as that of the open competition, but in this instance it was the Department, rather than the Public Appointments Service, which considered the applications. The applicants applied for the posts and were informed by letter in June 2014 that they 'did not meet the educational requirements as set out in the competition circular'. The applicants claimed that their exclusion from the internal competition was unfair and arbitrary. Furthermore, they contended that the reasons stated by the Department were inadequate.

Critical to the claims advanced by the applicants was that two individuals previously appointed to the post of AAI held qualifications identical to theirs. The Department considered these two appointments as incorrect decisions but noted that the Public Appointments Service made the appointments, and the Department was restricted in raising an objection. The Department noted that there were 19 candidates for the AAI posts in total who were deemed not to have equivalent qualifications by reference to the application criteria. The Department gave evidence of the differences between the two degrees. The degree in rural development is a three-year, part-time distance learning course covering subjects such as rural development, rural organisation, rural economy, rural environment and integrated rural community planning. In contrast, the degree in agricultural science is a full-time, four-year course. Students are required to take courses in the core science subjects (ie chemistry, biology, animal and plant biology) in their freshman years before taking more specialist subjects (eg genetics, animal husbandry or crop husbandry) in their final years.

In considering whether the decision to exclude the applicants was unreasonable or arbitrary, the High Court noted that the internal competition did not exclude applicants *ex ante* simply for not possessing an honours degree in agricultural science. The job advertisement stipulated that applicants could possess a relevant qualification 'which is acceptable to the Department of Agriculture, Food and the Marine as equivalent'. The High Court noted that the Department expressly envisaged that other candidates might apply and the Department in fact did deem two such candidates as possessing *'equivalent qualifications'*. The High Court noted that it was critical that such candidates possessed a scientific degree, with a focus on either agriculture or animal science.

The High Court noted that, in deciding whether the applicants' degree in rural development could be regarded in this context as equivalent to a degree in agricultural science, Department officials were required to abide to the three prong test of *bona fides*, factual sustainability and a showing that the decision was not unreasonable.[22] As the *bona fides* of the Department officials had not been challenged in the pleadings, the Court refused to entertain any such argument and instead focused on determining whether the decision to reject the degree in rural development as not meeting the

---

22.   *Mallak v Minister for Justice* [2012] IESC 59, [2013] 1 ILRM 73 at 91 *per* Fennelly J.

equivalence requirements was factually sustainable and reasonable. In that regard, the High Court noted the differences between the degrees in terms of entry level requirements, the duration and nature of the courses and the fact that the agricultural science degree is science-based. The High Court further noted that a broad scientific knowledge of the food and agricultural sectors was an essential requirement of all applicants. Hogan J referred to s 29(9) of the Public Service Management (Recruitment and Appointment) Act 2004 which provides that a candidate shall not be appointed to a post 'unless he or she is fully competent … to undertake and be fully capable of undertaking the duties attached to that position having regard to the conditions under which those duties are, or may be required to be, performed'. The High Court held that the Department's conclusion that the applicants' qualifications were not equivalent to that of a degree in agricultural science was factually sustainable and not unreasonable.

Hogan J also considered whether adequate reasons had been provided to the applicants. He noted that the duty to give reasons will often be somewhat attenuated in a competitive forum such as the present case. Hogan J noted that such cases are distinct from instances where administrative decisions are made which are 'unique and personal' to the applicant, such as a decision to refuse to grant citizenship.[23] The judge referred to the decision of the Supreme Court in *Orange Communications Ltd v Office of Director of Communication Regulation (No 2)*,[24] in which Geoghegan J had stated: 'the simple statement that the appellant was not the winner of the competition was the most substantive reason one could expect to get.'

In light of these comments, the judge held that the reasons given in the present case were not inadequate. It was necessarily implicit in the Department's reasons that the applicants' qualifications were not regarded as equivalent to that of a degree in agricultural science. Hogan J further noted that, even if the Court was incorrect in ruling that the reasons given were not inadequate, he did not consider the applicants to have suffered any real prejudice as a result. Hogan J noted that he was personally sympathetic to the position of the applicants but denied the application for judicial review.

---

23.   *Mallak v Minister for Justice, Equality and Law Reform* [2012] IESC 59.
24.   *Orange Communications Ltd v Office of Director of Communication Regulation (No 2)* [2000] 4 IR 159.

Chapter 22

REDUNDANCY

CHANGING THE PLACE OF WORK MOBILITY CLAUSES

[22.01] *Murphy & Ors v Orbit Security Ltd[1] – Employment Appeals Tribunal – Redundancy Payments Acts 1967 to 2014 – entitlement to redundancy payment – alternatives to redundancy – mobility clause – whether alternative location proposed was too far due to distance and travel*

Due to the closure and demolition of the site, security was no longer required and the security contract under which the claimants were employed ceased. Alternative temporary positions at other locations were offered to the claimants in the Donegal region but it was intended that when contracts became available in the Mayo region (where the claimants were based) the claimants could return to the Mayo area.

The EAT held that although the contracts of employment of the claimants included a mobility clause, it was unreasonable to expect the claimants to re-locate to the proposed alternative location due to the distance and travel which would have to be undertaken. The claimants were entitled to receive statutory redundancy payments.

[22.02] *Fitzpatrick v Greenberry Ltd[2] – Employment Appeals Tribunal – Unfair Dismissals Acts 1977 to 2007 as amended – Redundancy Payments Acts 1967 to 2014 – whether claimant entitled to redundancy payment in respect of proposal to move her place of employment from Carlow to Waterford – mobility clauses – requirement on employers to act reasonably and responsibly*

This was a claim for unfair dismissal and also for a redundancy payment. The claim of unfair dismissal was withdrawn by the claimant at hearing.

This claim arose from a decision by the respondent to close its office in Carlow and to require the claimant to relocate to Waterford and do her job from there. The claimant's contract of employment stated her position to be 'Area Manager Carlow' and contained a mobility clause which provided for the right of the employer to relocate or establish operations and to transfer the claimant to another department or place of work.

Importantly the contract provided as follows 'before implementing any changes we will consult with you and consider any reasonable objection which you may have to the proposed changes'. The claimant gave evidence that she was located exclusively in Carlow and that the terms of employment offered to her with regard to the proposed relocation were less favourable in so far as she was no longer to be paid overtime. She asserted that in those circumstances it was reasonable for her not to relocate and she

---

1.   *Murphy & Ors v Orbit Security Ltd* RP597/2012, RP598/2012, RP599/2012.
2.   *Fitzpatrick v Greenberry Ltd* UD893/2012, RP703/2012.

sought a redundancy payment. The respondent submitted that the claimant's role was not redundant, but that she was required to move to Waterford where her job would continue. Reference was made to the fact that the claimant's contract provided for a change to a place of work.

The EAT considered the exercise of the mobility clause by the employer and noted that the respondent company was required to 'act reasonably and responsibly'. The EAT concluded that the respondent had not so acted in circumstances where it was seeking to relocate the claimant without consultation, without considering her reasonable objections and where any such move was to be on terms that were fundamentally different to those already enjoyed by the claimant. The EAT concluded that it was reasonable for the claimant not to relocate and thus the claimant was entitled to a redundancy payment based on her service.

[22.03] *Heavey v Casey Doors Ltd[3] – Redundancy Payments Acts 1967 to 2014 – Minimum Notice and Terms of Employment Acts 1973 to 2005 – relocation of business premises – whether decision of claimant not to move location from Baldoyle to Balbriggan reasonable in all circumstances – whether claimant disentitled to redundancy payment as result?*

The claimant was employed in the respondent's door manufacturing business and was based in the Baldoyle office, working three days a week. Following a management buyout during 2013, a new premises was needed and an alternative premises was identified in Balbriggan. The respondent's staff were notified of the takeover and relocation at a staff meeting in September 2013. As the claimant was not present, the managing director contacted her by telephone to inform her of the changes. The claimant expressed a concern that the new location might not be suitable for her.

The respondent did not accept that a redundancy situation had arisen as the managing director was endeavouring to retain everyone, including the claimant, as she was a valuable member of staff with 14 years experience. The respondent's position was that Balbriggan was not too far away. The journey was 30 minutes as per the travel route planner and as stated by other employees. All employees subsequently transferred to the new location, with the exception of the claimant.

The claimant's contract of employment did contain a clause regarding site location but there was no signed copy available. Written correspondence had been exchanged between the parties, in the course of which the claimant was asked to try the new location for a period of two months but she was unwilling to do so.

The parties disagreed as to how often the claimant had driven to work when the company was based in Baldoyle. The claimant asserted that she had driven to work only 50% of the time and that as she only lived 10 minutes away, she often walked to work or obtained a lift when her husband required the car for work. The managing director submitted that the claimant drove to work 90% of the time. The claimant stated that if

---

3.   *Heavey v Casey Doors Ltd* RP1040/2013–759/2013.

she travelled to Balbriggan by public transport it would entail her getting three trains or two buses and could take a considerable length of time. Due to family circumstances, the claimant would have incurred child minding costs as a result and, even having the use of a car, she felt the distance would be too much. She did not accept the journey time was 30 minutes and stated that it was in fact 50 minutes.

The respondent submitted that the new location was accessible as it was based along the M1 motorway in the opposite direction to the bulk of traffic. Had the claimant raised the issue of additional cost of travelling time with the managing director, he would have considered flexibility if possible. The respondent did not employ someone to replace the claimant but rather shared the role among three members of staff, to include the wife of the managing director. The EAT noted that the claimant had subsequently gained new employment in the Baldoyle area.

The EAT noted that the new location in Balbriggan was 28.6 kilometres from the old premises. It further noted that access to the new location required one of three options: bus, train or car. As the claimant did not have access to a car daily, driving was not a reasonable option for her. The EAT considered s 15(1) of the Redundancy Payments Acts 1967 to 2014. The EAT stated that the legal test to be applied is a subjective one. It is not what the employer finds reasonable; it is only the employee's subjective view that the EAT has to consider. The EAT, by majority decision, found that in all the circumstances it was reasonable for the claimant to turn down the proposal to move to the new location. The claimant's claim for a statutory redundancy payment succeeded.

CONSULTATION REQUIREMENTS IN A COLLECTIVE REDUNDANCY

[22.04] *Tangney and 27 others v Dell Products Limerick[4] – High Court – Birmingham J – European Communities (Protection of Employment) Regulations 2000 (SI 488/2000) – Protection of Employment Act 1977 – obligation to consult with employees and employee representatives when collective redundancies contemplated – whether appeal of decision of Employment Appeals Tribunal dismissing complaints under Protection of Employment Act 1977, s 9 valid – whether any points of law validly raised by appellant*

This case arose from the announcement in 2009 by Dell that it was ceasing its manufacturing operation in Limerick. On 8 January 2009, the appellants and other employees received a written communication from the respondent furnishing information as to the respondent's plans and a staff meeting was held on the same day at which employees were briefed by senior management. It was submitted by the appellants that what occurred on 8 January 2009 was effectively a notice of dismissal and thus any discussions taking place thereafter could not constitute consultation.

The appellants brought claims to a Rights Commissioner that the respondent was in breach of s 9(1) of the Protection of Employment Act 1977, that is, the obligation to

---

4. *Tangney and 27 others v Dell Products Limerick* [2013] IEHC 622.

consult with employee representatives when collective redundancies are contemplated. The Rights Commissioner concluded that there had been a breach of s 9 of the 1977 Act. However, this was overturned on appeal by the EAT.

The appellants appealed to the High Court under s 8(4)(b) of the Terms of Employment (Information) Act 1994, which makes provision for an appeal to the High Court on a point of law.

The respondent submitted that the appeal did not raise any valid point of law arising from the adjudication of the EAT and submitted that the appellants were effectively seeking a further appeal on the facts, which was not permissible. Birmingham J set out the applicable Irish and European legislation at issue. He concluded that the question before him was whether the consultation process required by the 1977 Act commenced on 8 January 2009, or whether a breach of s 9 of the 1977 Act occurred by reason of the fact that the respondent had already made a decision to terminate employment prior to 8 January 2009, ie whether the respondent had merely communicated a decision already taken in absence of consultation.

Birmingham J summarised the key decisions of the CJEU and those of the Courts of England and Wales as to when the obligation to consult arises.[5] He concluded the approach taken by the CJEU in *Fujitsu Siemens*[6] was relevant, as that was what the EAT was seeking to apply when it reached the conclusions that it did. Reference was also made to the Court of Appeal of England and Wales decision in *United States of America v Nolan,*[7] who concluded that the interpretation of the CJEU decision in *Fujitsu Siemens* was not straightforward. In light of this, Birmingham J said that he was required to give 'serious consideration to the question of whether a reference is necessary'. He also noted that under the Terms of Employment (Information) Act 1994, there was no appeal from his decision.

Birmingham J concluded that the EAT had determined as a matter of fact that the Dell communication in January 2009 did not constitute a notice of dismissal and that the employer had commenced its consultation process at an appropriate stage. He made reference to the finding of the EAT that:

> the entitlement of the employer to make a strategic decision in the concluding paragraph of the determination must mean that the EAT was taking the view that the employer had, as it was obliged to do, embarked on consultation when a strategic or commercial decision compelling it to contemplate or plan for collective redundancies had been taken.

Birmingham J then reviewed what occurred subsequent to 8 January 2009 and made specific reference to the fact that certain matters of substance had changed between that date and the date of the end of consultation on 27 March. Reference was made to the redeployment of a number of employees, the extension of actual leaving dates and also a significant improvement in the severance pay package that was available to employees. Birmingham J also noted the text of the letter of 8 January 2009 which made reference

---

5.   *Junk v Kuhnel* (Case C–188/03) [2005] ECR1–855.

6.   *Akavan v Fujitsu Siemens Computers OY* (Case C–44/08) [2009] ECR I–8163.

7.   *United States of America v Nolan* [2010] EWCA Civ 1223.

to the fact that the content was for information purposes only and did not constitute contractual terms or conditions. The letter also contained estimated ranges of leaving dates associated with individual production lines, and made several references to estimated severance figures. The judge acknowledged the level of detail in the letter and stated it did not suggest the employer had an open mind, but also held that a communication 'couched in generalities would be of little assistance to employees and would not be well received'. Ultimately, the Court concluded that a point of law had not been identified which would provide a basis for overturning the decision of the EAT and that that decision was one of fact and thus the appeal was dismissed.

ENTITLEMENT TO CONSULTATION AND REPRESENTATION IN AN INDIVIDUAL REDUNDANCY

[22.05] *Nigrell v Graham[8] – Employment Appeals Tribunal – appeal of decision of Rights Commissioner by respondent employer – Unfair Dismissals Acts 1977 to 2007 as amended – redundancy – genuine honest redundancy – lack of representation or consultation does not render genuine redundancy to be unfair dismissal – no automatic right of appeal – dismissal by reason of redundancy*

The claimant was a pharmacy programme manager of the respondent's weight watch product. Her role was to visit the pharmacies who sell the product to provide training to the pharmacists. The role of training the pharmacists diminished in 2009 and 2010 as the pharmacists selling the products had been sufficiently trained. It was becoming difficult to fill the employee's work day. There was another role within the respondent, to meet and discuss the product with GPs, however the employee did not have the appropriate qualifications to speak to GPs about the product. The respondent made the decision to make the claimant redundant.

The claimant accepted that there was a valid redundancy situation. The complaint related to a lack of fair procedures. The claimant gave evidence that she was shocked to hear that she had been made redundant. She submitted that she should have been given a trial period of working with GPs with supervision or set up appointments or anything to give the respondent an opportunity to find something suitable for her in the company.

The EAT determined that there was a genuine redundancy due to the changing nature of the business and the consequent change in the required skill sets and qualifications for the role of programme manager. The EAT concluded that while it may be good and prudent practice to facilitate an employee by having a representative present or by having the employee's view on the proposed redundancy fairly and impartially considered. However these procedures are not mandatory or legally required. The EAT held that a failure to provide these procedures does not result in a genuine redundancy being considered an unfair dismissal. The EAT also held that a failure to allow for an

---

8.   *Nigrell v Graham* UD690/2013.

appeal of a decision to make an employee redundant does not result in a redundancy being considered an unfair dismissal. The EAT disagreed with the findings of the Rights Commissioner and determined that the claimant was fairly dismissed by reason of redundancy.

[22.06] *Murtagh v Galmere Freshfoods Ltd[9] – Employment Appeals Tribunal – Unfair Dismissals Acts 1977 to 2007 as amended – whether claimant fairly selected for redundancy – failure to consider alternatives to redundancy – lack of meaningful engagement or consultation with claimant*

The respondent supplied and distributed major fresh food brands to supermarkets and multiples. In late 2012, the respondent lost a large contract and as a consequence was required by its bank to produce a survival plan. A decision was made to make a number of employees redundant, to include the claimant.

Evidence was given to the EAT as to the financial position of the respondent and particularly the loss of the key contract, which triggered the financial difficulties. The survival plan was presented to the bank, which included a multitude of changes, to include redundancies. The managing director made the decision to make the claimant redundant while taking on the operations manager role himself. It was submitted that the employees were consulted in the course of a number of meetings. The claimant asserted that his performance had never been an issue and that he had managed to secure new contracts with large companies. Although he had not met his bonus target in the first year, he was complimented for his work and could see some turnaround and was confident he would achieve the targets in the second year. The claimant submitted that, while meetings did take place, no alternatives or options of a pay cut were considered or offered.

The EAT concluded that no meaningful engagement or consultation process took place. The respondent failed to provide evidence that it gave adequate consideration to alternatives and the respondent never gave the claimant the opportunity to come up with suggestions on saving his role. It appeared from the evidence, which was not refuted by the respondent, that a pre-prepared signed letter was given to the claimant at the final meeting advising him of his redundancy. The EAT concluded that the claimant was unfairly dismissed and awarded him compensation of €25,000.

[22.07] *Murray v Ridgeway International Ltd (in Receivership) T/A Toughers Restaurant[10] – Employment Appeals Tribunal – Unfair Dismissals Acts 1977 to 2007 as amended – dismissal on grounds of redundancy – clear reasons as to why redundancy was not fair and reasonable*

The respondent entered into receivership prior to the hearing of this matter and whilst both named receivers were notified at the hearing, they did not attend. Thus, the case proceeded by way of uncontested evidence on the part of the claimant.

---

9.   *Murtagh v Galmere Freshfoods Ltd* UD493/2013

10.   *Murray v Ridgeway International Ltd (in Receivership) T/A Toughers Restaurant* UD1321/2012.

The claimant gave evidence as to the circumstances which led him to being informed that his employment would terminate by reason of redundancy. He worked out his notice period and said that no alternatives were considered and nor was a reduction in salary put forward. He did receive a statutory redundancy payment and a further payment of €5,000 for extra hours worked for holidays and public holidays.

The EAT found that the respondent did have a need to effect redundancies in an effort to reduce costs, but found that the redundancy of the claimant was not effected in a fair and reasonable manner for the following reasons:

(i) the respondent failed to adhere to any fair procedures;

(ii) there was no discussion whatsoever with the claimant in advance of the decision to make him redundant – the claimant was simply told that he was being made redundant and that there was no point in discussing the matter;

(iii) there were no discussions as to the possibility of alternatives to redundancies;

(iv) the claimant was not offered a right to appeal the decision to make him redundant.

The EAT upheld the claim of unfair dismissal and awarded the claimant compensation of €9,800 over and above the statutory lump sum and other payments already paid to him.

CROSS BORDER EMPLOYMENT

[22.08] *Meehan v College Freight Ltd T/A Target Express[11] – Employment Appeals Tribunal – claim under Redundancy Payments Acts 1967 to 2014, s 25(3) – whether eligibility for redundancy payment could include period of continuous employment in Northern Ireland*

This was a claim for a redundancy payment by the claimant who had worked for his employer in their Northern Irish branch for 11 years. Because of his disability, he was then moved to the employer's branch in Clones in County Monaghan, and was then made redundant 11 months later. He asserted an entitlement to a redundancy payment based on his 12 continuous years of service. The EAT examined the eligibility criteria for redundancy in this jurisdiction, and concluded that the claimant satisfied the criteria and was entitled to redundancy. The EAT noted s 25(3) which provides that, in computing a period of continuous service employment, 'any period of service in the employment of the employer concerned while the employee was outside the State shall be deemed to have been in service of the employment of that employer within the State'.

---

11. *Meehan v College Freight Ltd T/A Target Express* RP347/2013.

ENTITLEMENT TO A REDUNDANCY PAYMENT ON CESSATION OF PARTICIPATION IN A COMMUNITY EMPLOYMENT SCHEME

[22.09] *Donohoe v The Dunboyne Area Community Employment Co Ltd[12] – Employment Appeals Tribunal – Redundancy Payments Acts 1967 to 2014 – whether claimant entitled to redundancy payment on cessation of his contract under community employment scheme*

The claimant sought a redundancy payment in circumstances where he was employed by a Community Employment Scheme for three consecutive years and received a social welfare payment plus a weekly top-up. The scheme operated by way of yearly contracts for the purpose of providing training and work experience which were renewed in the claimant's case on two separate occasions. The contract was not subsequently renewed as there was a waiting list for the scheme and it is required that as many applicants as possible be given an opportunity to avail of the scheme. The rules of the scheme stated that under 55s may participate for a maximum of three years on the scheme. The claimant did not pay a social insurance stamp but instead received a credit as if on social welfare and was paid through the scheme which was funded by the Department of Social Protection.

The EAT determined that the claimant's employment on the community employment scheme was not insured under the Social Welfare Acts for the purpose of redundancy payment and therefore his claim for a statutory redundancy payment failed.

UNFAIR SELECTION

[22.10] *Barrett v GEA Farm Technologies (Ireland) Ltd[13] – Employment Appeals Tribunal – Redundancy Payments Acts 1967 to 2014 – Unfair Dismissals Acts 1977 to 2007 as amended – Minimum Notice and Terms of Employment Act 1973 to 2005[14] – unfair selection for redundancy – compensation of €45,000 awarded*

The claimant was appointed as office manager of the respondent's Irish operation in 2009. The Group provides equipment and servicing in the field of milk production. The claimant was responsible for the running of the Irish business and, whilst her initial duties included the setting up of an Irish office and presence in Ireland, she then project managed the setting up of an office warehouse, and, ultimately, interviewed staff and the Irish employees reported to her. The claimant reported to a director in the UK, who was nominated as Irish director. Before leaving employment, he had appointed the claimant

---

12. *Donohoe v The Dunboyne Area Community Employment Co Ltd* RP1006/2012.

13. *Barrett v GEA Farm Technologies (Ireland) Ltd* UD106/2012, RP75/2012, MN 55/2012, WT 26/2012.

14. At the outset of this hearing the claims under the Redundancy Payment Acts and the Minimum Notice of Terms of Employment Acts were withdrawn.

as branch manager. After he had departed, the claimant reported directly to individuals in the UK.

The claimant had expressed the wish that she would be considered for the role of Irish director if one was to be appointed but in November 2010 a new Irish director was appointed from the UK. The claimant raised certain informal grievances regarding her job title and it was ultimately accepted by the respondent that the claimant had been appointed as branch manager by the previous Irish director. She had also requested that her job role be defined and sought clarification of her reporting line but this was not done.

Evidence was given by both sides that there were concerns in 2010 about the operation of the Irish business and that the lack of technical support on the ground was a contributory factor. Evidence was given by the respondent that the Irish business was suffering from a reduction in turnover and accrued losses and, because of its debt, the group's bankers concluded that the increase in turnover in 2011 could not sustain the overheads of the business. The directors had received a mandate to develop the Irish market and thus needed to increase sales. They looked at the cost of the business in Ireland and decided that two synergies could be implemented, both of which would result in the branch manager's role being put at risk and that they could employ a low level administration person and a sales person in place of the branch manager.

A consultation process commenced with the claimant on 4 November. She was advised that her position was at risk and she was asked for her proposals to avoid redundancy. Evidence was given by the respondent that the proposals put forward by the claimant, such as reduced days or a self-employed contract, were considered but that there would be an additional cost of €15,000 borne by the respondent to hire a sales person. The claimant had suggested that the alternatives proposed by her were not considered and she was not offered the sales position and training for the position that they intended to fill. Two further meetings were held with regard to the proposed redundancy. All proposals put forward by the claimant were decided against and the decision to make the claimant redundant with immediate effect was made after a short recess on the same day. She was given an opportunity to appeal but she did not.

The EAT allowed the claim under the Organisation of Working Time Act 1997 and awarded the claimant €1,003.85 (in respect of six days' outstanding pay) for Sunday work.

The EAT accepted that the respondent was in an economic decline which needed some sort of restructuring and that there was a justified anticipation of redundancy. The EAT however concluded that the claimant had been unfairly selected. While noting the consultation process, the EAT was satisfied that the decision to make the position of branch manager redundant had been decided prior to the commencement of the consultation process with the claimant. Options put forward by her regarding various roles she could perform were not adequately considered during the process, and as a consequence, she was unfairly selected. The EAT criticised the respondent's speed of decision making at the last meeting in that the decision to confirm the redundancy was both immediate in its communication and effect. The claimant was awarded compensation of €45,000 in addition to the redundancy payments already received.

[22.11] *Andreucetti v Spark Glade Ltd[15] – Employment Appeals Tribunal – Unfair Dismissals Acts 1977 to 2007 as amended – whether claimant unfairly selected for redundancy, and thus unfairly dismissed – employer did not appear to realise that what was being proposed was collective redundancy with certain obligations to engage in consultation process and notification process – compensation of €32,000 awarded*

The EAT noted that the respondent operated a number of franchised retail outlets and the claimant was a manager within one of the stores which was not at the time in question operating with a comfortable profit level. In 2011, the respondent employer was anxious to try and enhance the company's financial position and thus considered the possibility of making redundancies. A decision was taken that it would be preferable to make redundancies and reduce the annual wage bill by €120,000 than to cut the hourly rate of pay for all staff. The respondent decided that the only way of achieving this target was by making at least five persons redundant. The EAT noted that the respondent did not appear to have realised that it had proposed the dismissal of the critical number for the application of the collective redundancy rules.

On 18 July 2011, staff were informed that redundancies would be made. No mention was made to staff that there were obligations to notify the Minister and/or to engage in a consultation process. It was noted by the EAT that subsequently the Minister was notified on or about 19 July on advice from IBEC. On 19 July the claimant was called to a meeting where she was told her position was on the line and that she would be in all likelihood made redundant. The EAT noted that the scenario flew in the face of the respondent's obligations surrounding the making of a collective redundancy and in particular it noted that there was no 30-day consultation period. The claimant received a letter on 21 July notifying her that her position had been made redundant. There was a subsequent attempt to recognise the need for consultation period by letter of 12 August, but the EAT stated that this could not be effective given the fact that the claimant was clearly targeted for redundancy from the start.

The EAT accepted that the claimant was never informed how her position came to be selected for redundancy and that, even in the course of the evidence before it, the criteria for making the selection was never clearly articulated. The claimant was therefore never allowed the opportunity to make her case and given the fact the claimant was told that she was being made redundant one day after the general announcement was made, the EAT accepted that the claimant was fighting a 'rear-guard action'. The EAT noted that, by way of a fall-back, the respondent attempted to rely on its entitlement to make the claimant statutorily redundant by reason of the fact that she was being replaced by an immediate family member. However, the EAT was not persuaded by this argument where the respondent was a limited liability company. The EAT concluded that the claimant had been unfairly selected for redundancy and was unfairly dismissed. The EAT stated it could never know whether or not the claimant would have been made redundant at the conclusion of a lawful consultation process which afforded her a reasonable and fair opportunity to make her own representations. It awarded her

15.   *Andreucetti v Spark Glade Ltd* UD29/2012.

compensation in the sum of €32,000 and held that any redundancy payment made would be offset against the award.

[22.12] *Duffy v National University of Ireland Galway*[16] *– Employment Appeals Tribunal – Unfair Dismissals Acts 1977 to 2007 as amended – unfairly selected for redundancy – no proper consultation or discussion with claimant – failure to justify reasons for redundancy – €30,000 in compensation awarded*

The claimant was employed under a contract of indefinite duration as 'GMP Facility Manager' from January 2005. The respondent gave evidence that in order to progress the facility, the university needed to hire an operations manager. This had implications for the claimant as it was claimed that her role was subsumed by the new position. The respondent gave evidence that the heads of all the university departments were contacted to ascertain if any vacancies existed within their departments. Ultimately, no suitable alternative employment was found for the claimant. The EAT heard evidence that the claimant applied for a number of positions within the university but was unsuccessful in those applications and subsequently the claimant was made redundant on 31 May 2012.

The claimant gave evidence that she had been placed on temporary lay-off for the month of January 2012. She was never given a reason for this. The claimant gave evidence that she had been made to feel ostracised in her work place and was not invited to two social functions in August 2011.

When the claimant was informed of her redundancy, she wrote to human resources raising a number of grievances. In the letter she stated that she had been unfairly selected for redundancy as the work that comprised her role was still ongoing and continued to exist. She received a reply in June 2012 but submitted that it did not explain the reasons for her selection for redundancy and that it did not address the grievances raised. She submitted that the reasons for her redundancy were never discussed and no consultation ever occurred in relation to her redundancy.

The EAT found that the claimant was unfairly selected for redundancy. The respondent acted unreasonably in that there was no proper consultation or discussion with the claimant. The claimant's letter, in response to the redundancy offer, was not addressed and no investigation of the grievances raised was conducted. The facility where she worked continued to operate and the work which comprised her role continued to exist. Personnel who possessed shorter service, and personnel who were employed after the claimant's dismissal, were retained. The respondent failed to justify why the claimant was selected for redundancy.

The EAT upheld the claim and awarded €30,000 in compensation.

[22.13] *Brady v Home Lee Beddings (1975) Ltd*[17] *– Employment Appeals Tribunal – Unfair Dismissals Acts 1977 to 2007 as amended – redundancy – unfair selection process – compensation of €32,000 awarded*

---

16. *Duffy v National University of Ireland Galway* UCD1387/2012.
17. *Brady v Home Lee Beddings* (1975) Ltd UD941/2012.

The EAT was satisfied that all parties were on notice of the hearing but there was no appearance on behalf of the respondent.

The claimant commenced employment with the respondent company in September 1978 as a general operative and later became a supervisor. The claimant gave evidence that his many years of experience working in the business meant he could take on any task, including the sewing of products. Over the course of the claimant's employment he was at one stage the trainer of all new employees in the sewing area of the factory. On 27 October 2011 the claimant was informed of a rationalisation plan within the respondent and was informed of his dismissal. No alternatives were offered to him and his employment ended on 22 December 2011.

The claimant maintained that previous redundancies within the respondent were selected on the basis of the last in first out (LIFO). However, in his case LIFO was not applied.

The EAT determined that the selection process applied to the claimant in this case was unfair as the respondent had previously used the LIFO selection process but deviated from that process in this case. The claimant was not offered any alternatives, nor was he given an option to suggest an alternative to redundancy. The EAT noted that the claimant had worked for the business for over 30 years. The EAT found that the claimant was unfairly dismissed and, having taken the statutory redundancy payment he received into account, awarded him compensation of €32,000.

[22.14] *Anderson & Ors v Ascension Lifts Ltd*[18]*– Employment Appeals Tribunal – Unfair Dismissals Acts 1977 to 2007 as amended – genuine redundancy – unfair selection process*

The second claimant (EB) did not attend the hearing and accordingly his claim was dismissed for want of prosecution. The two other claimants were present at the hearing. The claimants' employment, as lift engineers, was terminated on 22 March 2013 by reason of redundancy. The claimants contended that the dismissal was unfair, as they were given a choice of either accepting inferior pay and conditions of employment or accepting redundancy.

The managing director of the respondent gave evidence to the effect that the respondent was in severe financial difficulties and contended that the redundancies were made due to the financial situation of the respondent.

The first 'at risk' meeting was held on 21 January 2013 with all five lift engineers. The employees were informed that the respondent was in financial difficulty and that their roles were at risk. The managing director suggested options such as week on/week off, voluntary redundancy or compulsory redundancy on a last in first out (LIFO) basis. He also sought suggestions from the employees, but only a suggestion of three weeks on/one week off was made, which was not a viable option for the respondent. Only two employees were amenable to working week on/week off. At the end of the meeting, each of the employees was given a letter advising them that their positions were at risk. The letter advised the employees that, in the event that cost saving measures did not resolve

---

18.   *Anderson & Ors v Ascension Lifts Ltd* UD570/2013, UD569/2013, UD568/2013.

the respondent's financial issues, the respondent anticipated making two positions redundant on LIFO selection criteria.

Individual meetings were held with the claimants and their trade union representative on 28 January 2013 to discuss cost cutting proposals in order to avoid possible redundancies. The trade union representative indicated that if redundancies were being discussed, a package of four weeks' pay per year of service plus statutory redundancy was what he wished for his members on a LIFO basis and indicated that his members would not accept voluntary redundancy if only statutory was being offered. They were the terms of an earlier Labour Court recommendation that the trade union had obtained. The respondent did not accept that it was party to any Labour Court recommendation on pay for lift engineers and offered statutory redundancy only. The respondent agreed to look at the LIFO principle if redundancies arose. The trade union representative indicated that he would be unhappy if the respondent retained non-union employees over unionised ones. The respondent indicated that this would not be taken into account. The two remaining employees whose positions were at risk were not up to date with their trade union dues and so were not represented by the trade union. Evidence was given that the respondent decided to restructure by way of three of the manager/directors assuming engineering roles as they were all qualified engineers. The claimants were informed of this at meetings on 1 February 2013 and that the number of possible redundancies was two or three. The remaining positions would be field engineers, junior to their current positions on an hourly rate of €22.50.

The meetings scheduled for 7 February 2013 did not proceed as the claimants wished to have a group meeting, which the respondent objected to, as it believed it was best to discuss the situation individually. Individual meetings were arranged for 12 February 2013. The three unionised employees arrived together and insisted on a group meeting. As they would not agree to individual meetings, the meeting finished early. Ultimately a group meeting with the three unionised employees was held on 21 February 2013. At the meeting the employees were informed that the respondent's restructure was going ahead. The claimants' trade union representative indicated that the claimants were unwilling to accept the new posts on offer due to the reduced pay and conditions. The trade union representative was seeking to have engagement through the LRC to discuss redundancy terms but the respondent refused to do this. The claimants indicated that they were not interested in the positions available. The claimants were given until 4pm the following day to decide if they wanted the positions on offer and were advised that if no response was received the positions would be offered to the other engineers on a LIFO basis.

A further meeting with the claimants was held on 22 February 2013. They advised the respondent that they did not intend to accept the new positions offered or statutory redundancy. The managing director advised them that if they did not accept the new positions, redundancy would have to take place. The three claimants' positions were made redundant. An appeal heard by an independent consultant on 11 March 2013 found that the selection process was fair and that the roles had been made redundant due to company restructuring. Subsequent to the redundancies, one extra junior engineer was hired to fill the field engineer position. The two other engineers accepted the new roles on offer. FA, one of the claimants, and CD2 one of the other engineers at risk, were the last two in and would have been made redundant under the LIFO principle. As the other two claimants refused the new roles, CD2 remained in employment.

The first and second claimants gave evidence that they believed that they were dismissed because they would not accept the new terms and conditions and that they were unaware of the extent of the respondent's financial difficulties.

The EAT accepted that due to the economic downturn a genuine redundancy situation arose and two redundancies were required. It was deemed appropriate by all parties that the LIFO selection criteria should apply. However, the respondent decided not to proceed on the foregoing basis and decided on a complete restructure which resulted in three redundancies being implemented. In order to effect the restructure the respondent unilaterally proposed a new job title, pay rate and some altered conditions of employment. These proposals were unacceptable to the claimants and, due to their refusal, their employment was terminated. In the circumstances the EAT found that the claimants were unfairly selected for redundancy and unfairly dismissed.

Accordingly, the EAT awarded compensation of €8,000 to the first claimant (FA) and €10,000 to the third claimant.

[22.15] *Kennedy v Edmar Golf Ltd[19] – Employment Appeals Tribunal – Unfair Dismissals Acts 1977 to 2007 as amended – unfair selection for redundancy – no selection matrix – no consideration of alternative roles – no cost analysis carried out – €10,000 compensation awarded*

The claimant contended that he was unfairly selected for redundancy. The commercial director of the respondent company gave evidence. The respondent provides management and maintenance services for golf courses and maintenance represents 50% of the cost of running a golf course. The respondent gave evidence that it reduces this cost through centralised management and procurement.

The claimant was employed from 1996 as general manager of a large golf and sports complex in Dublin which went into receivership in 2010. The respondent took on a caretaking role for three months in 2010 and after a complicated bidding process the respondent took on the lease of the premises in April 2012. A number of meetings were held with staff in respect of voluntary redundancies and cost saving measures that may need to be implemented. Individual meeting were held with all staff who requested same but the claimant did not do so. There was a discrepancy between the respondent's notes of the meetings and the claimant's notes and initially there was no specific warning given to the claimant that he was attending an at risk meeting.

Subsequently the respondent's commercial director had one to one meetings with the claimant and the claimant brought his father to one of these. There was a suggestion of an alternative role for the claimant for which the claimant's wages would be reduced by circa €40,000. This was not explored between the parties as the claimant was not happy with this option.

The commercial director gave evidence that, although he consulted with other directors in the respondent, it was his decision to make the claimant's role redundant as

---

19.   *Kennedy v Edmar Golf Ltd* UD1102/2012.

it did not fit into the respondent's operating model. In making this decision he did not carry out any cost analysis to determine the cost of retaining the role versus losing it; no matrix was created and there was no consideration of alternative roles in the respondent or within the controlling company.

The EAT found that the respondent did not discharge the onus to show that the decision to make the claimant redundant was impersonal and based on objective criteria, entirely divorced from the individual employee, and the respondent had failed to show that it explored alternatives to redundancy. The EAT noted that it was unfortunate that there was no clarity as to the decision-making process and the basis of the decision provided by the respondent. The EAT, however, was not satisfied that the claimant made anything approaching a full attempt to mitigate his loss (he had not sought alternative employment as he was setting up his own business and had now succeeded in doing so). In light of all the circumstances, the EAT awarded the claimant compensation of €10,000.

[22.16] *Merity v Dolan and Garvey practising as DCA Accountants*[20] – *Employment Appeals Tribunal – Unfair Dismissals Acts 1977 to 2007 as amended – whether claimant unfairly selected for redundancy – whether purported redundancy of claimant fair where neither impersonal nor objective and where claimant appeared to have been replaced by another colleague on departure*

The claimant was employed as an office bureau manager within the respondent's chartered accountancy business. Evidence was given that at all times the bookkeeping department, of which the claimant was manager, had no more than five staff and that that number fluctuated according to business requirements. Due to the claimant's pregnancy and subsequent maternity leave, the respondent hired another person in early 2012 on a fixed-term contract for that section. Evidence was given that that individual was hired to replace the claimant during her period of absence. He was taken on as an accounts technician at a lower remuneration than the claimant. Between January and April 2012 before the claimant went on maternity leave, she worked alongside him assisting and guiding him on several tasks. The claimant was due to return to work from maternity leave in December 2012. As there was communication between the claimant and one of the partners relating to work issues, the respondent sought a meeting with her to discuss everything. This meeting took place in November 2012 in a coffee shop. At the meeting the claimant was asked to move to a technician role, which entailed a significant drop in her overall remuneration, but she refused. Evidence was given that the other option put to her was a proposal to work three days a week but no actual specifics on that proposal were discussed. Redundancy was also mentioned as an option. It was acknowledged by the respondent that the claimant was not notified of the agenda prior to the meeting.

The claimant gave evidence that she was surprised at the content of the November meeting and was not asked at that meeting to put forward alternatives and there was no mention of a three-day week. She felt she had no choice in the options presented to her

20. *Merity v Dolan and Garvey practising as DCA Accountants* UD814/2013.

and thus accepted and received a statutory redundancy payment in December 2012 and her employment ceased one week later. As a consequence, the respondent extended the contract of the fixed-term employee.

The EAT noted that when considering and deciding on redundancy, an employer is obliged to focus on the job and role concerned as distinct from the person holding that job and role. The EAT accepted that, in 2012, the respondent was experiencing financial difficulties pertaining to its bookkeeping department and that this decline in revenue coincided with the claimant's maternity and other leave. The EAT found that meeting the claimant while she was still on leave, and in such an informal way, was not the ideal way to impart important business information to her. The EAT decided that at the very least the proposed nature and subject of the meeting should have been relayed to her prior to the encounter or upon her return to work. The EAT was not satisfied that the role or functions performed by the claimant as manager were not undertaken by another colleague subsequent to her permanent departure in December 2012. This rendered the redundancy unfair as it was neither impersonal nor objective. The EAT found that the claimant had been unfairly dismissed and awarded her a gross amount of €43,941.67, less the statutory redundancy payment already received.

[22.17] *McCarey v Hugh Lennon and Associates Ltd[21] – Employment Appeals Tribunal – Unfair Dismissals Acts 1977 to 2007 as amended – unfair selection for redundancy – absence of selection criteria*

The claimant was employed in the respondent's secretarial department, where she did all of the company secretarial work, annual returns, changing directorships and also, during quiet periods, wrote up accounts, VAT returns, cash receipt expenses and payroll. Evidence was given that business in the area where the claimant worked had decreased significantly during 2009 and 2010. In November 2010 the claimant was given a choice of taking a redundancy package or working a three-day week and she opted for a three-day week but protested saying that her job was being done by others. The claimant returned from maternity leave on 5 December 2011 and, as her work had been taken over by other employees, she was advised of a decision to make her redundant. At a meeting on the claimant's final day at work, the claimant expressed her unhappiness at the situation and refused to sign a waiver presented to her.

The claimant asserted that on her return from maternity leave it was evident that the respondent's daughter was using her computer for emails and company returns. The claimant was told she could leave that day and that there was no need to work her notice period. No selection criteria were gone through, nor was anything put in writing. She was called to the office and asked to sign an RP50 but the date on it was incorrect and she again protested that other people were doing her job. In the course of evidence before the EAT the respondent had agreed that no other person in the practice had their days of work reduced and it was accepted that the managing director's daughter had been hired before the claimant went on maternity leave.

The EAT was not satisfied that the respondent had acted fairly and reasonably when addressing the need to reduce the number of employees or if indeed that there was a

---

21.   *McCarey v Hugh Lennon and Associates Ltd* UD909/2012. See **[27.12]**.

genuine redundancy at all. It found that where an employer is making an employee's position redundant, while retaining other employees, the selection criteria used should be objectively applied in a fair manner. While there are no hard and fast rules as to what constitutes the criteria to be used, the criteria adopted will come under close scrutiny if an employee claims that he or she was unfairly selected for redundancy.

The EAT held that the employer must follow agreed procedures when making a selection for redundancy and when there are no agreed procedures, as in this case, then the employer must act fairly and reasonably. The EAT concluded that the respondent had not acted fairly and reasonably. The claimant had not been considered for another position in the firm, even though she had longer service than another employee. At the meeting on her final day at work, the claimant advised the employer that the situation was, in her view, all wrong and she refused to sign a waiver presented to her. The claimant was told of the redundancy on the day she returned from maternity leave and no previous engagement with her took place and no selection criteria was discussed with her.

The EAT concluded that the claimant had been unfairly selected for redundancy. The EAT noted that the selection criteria, which should be impersonal and objective, were not discussed with the claimant and neither was there any meaningful discussion on alternative positions in the respondent. She was just told that her position was gone. The EAT upheld the claim of unfair dismissal and awarded the claimant compensation of €25,000 in addition to the amount of €7,800 that she had already been paid under the Redundancy Payments Acts 1967 to 2014.

[22.18] *McCann v CIL Precision Ltd*[22] *– Employment Appeals Tribunal – Terms of Employment (Information) Act 1994 and 2014*[23] *– Unfair Dismissals Acts 1977 to 2007 as amended – appeal of decision of Rights Commissioner by claimant – unfair selection for redundancy where 'last in first out' not considered*

The claimant was employed as one of four engineers working in the engineering department of the respondent's metal fabrication business. Each engineer worked with specific customers. One third of the claimant's time was spent on a contract with company A and there was interchangeability with engineers.

In June 2009, the respondent lost a major contract with company A and an announcement was made to all staff about the loss of this important contract which resulted in 35% of the respondent's business being lost. It was hoped that the respondent could avoid redundancies and measures to secure alternative business were outlined to staff. In February 2010, staff were informed that a number of redundancies would be made due to the imminent loss of business from company A as this was a huge percentage of the respondent's turnover and the business was now in difficulty. The respondent selected a number of positions for redundancy. In terms of selection, 'last in first out' (LIFO) was not considered. The claimant was informed that his position would be made redundant as there were no alternatives and eight other redundancies were also

---

22. *McCann v CIL Precision Ltd* UD1619/2012, TE259/2012.
23. At the hearing, the appeal under the Terms of Employment (Information) Acts 1994 and 2014 was withdrawn.

being effected in the company. The claimant queried the redundancy process and the proposed redundancy payment and enquired whether any alternatives had been considered. Subsequent to this, a job-sharing arrangement commenced with the claimant and another colleague for the period August to December 2010. In early January 2011, it was apparent the respondent had not sourced new business and the claimant had commenced a period of lay-off until March 2011, after which he was made redundant. It was noted that the claimant had subsequently secured consultancy work with another employer and had secured a small amount of work as a sub-contractor with the respondent. The claimant submitted that, notwithstanding the lost contract, redundancies in the engineering department were not merited in his view. He had suggested alternatives such as reduced hours and reduced pay, but was informed that all options had been explored and nothing could be done.

The EAT concluded that the reduction in workload and income entitled the respondent to effect redundancies. The EAT noted that work in the engineering section had not decreased as a result of the loss of contract A and therefore the claimant's role still remained, albeit that the respondent was entitled to decide that the work in the engineering department should be carried out by three engineers, rather than four, to effect savings.

The EAT concluded from the evidence that the roles of the four engineers were interchangeable and that there was no discernible differences in their skillset and, in those circumstances, selection for redundancy in order to be fair and reasonable should have been effected on the basis of LIFO. Had the respondent done so, the claimant would not have been selected for redundancy. The EAT was critical of the respondent for failing to consider voluntary redundancies and failing to consider alternatives to the redundancy of the claimant, such as a pay cut across the board, reduced hours or other cost-cutting measures. The alternative of job sharing did not come from the respondent, albeit that the respondent agreed to it, but was put forward by two other engineers and could be discontinued and in fact was discontinued by the other engineers. The respondent had failed to act reasonably and fairly when it failed to consider or offer the claimant a three-month rolling contract being worked by another colleague and for an alternative position in the engineering department and/or for the position of planner, which became available some time later, even though the respondent had undertaken to the claimant that it would do so.

The EAT found there was an unfair dismissal by reason of unfair selection for redundancy. The EAT awarded the claimant compensation in the amount of €30,000 over and above the statutory redundancy lump sum already received by him. In calculating the award, the EAT took into account that the claimant was unavailable for work for six months during the relevant period and the evidence of his mitigation of loss, which the EAT held fell short of the standards expected.

[22.19] *Ryan v Signature Flight Support Shannon Ltd T/A Signature Flight Support*[24] *– Employment Appeals Tribunal – Unfair Dismissals Acts 1977 to 2007 as amended –*

---

24.   *Ryan v Signature Flight Support Shannon Ltd T/A Signature Flight Support* (UD1638/2012).

restructuring – redundancy selection process – unfair selection for redundancy – case under appeal the Circuit Court

The claimant, the operations manager of the respondent, claimed that he had been unfairly selected for redundancy and that this amounted to a constructive dismissal. The respondent's position was that there had been a restructuring under which two management positions (one held by the claimant) were to become one position, but that the claimant had opted not to apply for the new position, with the result that the other manager applied for and was appointed to the new position.

The claimant alleged that the other manager, having married a senior manager in the respondent group, was facilitated in that there had been a camouflaged plan to give the claimant's position to the other manager. The claimant contended that the proposed interview process was a sham and the odds of him succeeding were stacked against him. The claimant submitted that he had considerably longer service than the other manager and believed that a 'last in first out' (LIFO) selection procedure should have been used by the respondent. This was not accepted by the respondent.

The EAT accepted that the respondent was entitled to restructure its workplace and to identify the claimant's role for redundancy. This process involved creation of a new position of station manager which encompassed elements and functions of the two managers' previous roles. The EAT was satisfied that the procedures adopted by the respondent in inviting the two candidates (the claimant and the other manager) for an interview process to select one of them for the newly created position of Station Manager Ireland were not unfair.

The claimant gave evidence that he refused to engage in the interview process as he believed the outcome was pre-ordained in favour of the other manager. He did not however raise these concerns with the respondent in his correspondence prior to the proposed interview process. In his correspondence with the respondent, the claimant stated that the only process that should apply was LIFO. The EAT did not accept that LIFO is the only criteria that should apply.

The EAT held that the refusal of the claimant to engage in the interview process was not a reasonable course of action. The claim was dismissed accordingly. Note this case is under appeal to the Circuit Court.

THE USE OF SELECTION MATRICES

[22.20] *Goodison v Rigney Dolphin*[25] *– Employment Appeals Tribunal – Unfair Dismissals Acts 1977 to 2007 as amended – whether dismissal of claimant for redundancy reasons fair in circumstances where employer failed to explain the redundancy process and criteria for selection adequately to claimant – scoring matrix not made available to employee – incomplete records kept by employer in relation to redundancy process – no right of appeal provided to claimant – no alternatives to redundancy considered*

---

25. *Goodison v Rigney Dolphin* UD1475/2012.

The claimant was one of three operations managers who was informed of a need to restructure following the loss of a large contract, which would reduce the number of operations managers' roles from three to two. Each of the three operations managers, including the claimant, was required to complete a personality profile, to make a presentation and to attend an interview. Following the claimant's presentation and interview, a matrix was devised by the respondent. The next day the claimant was advised that she was unsuccessful and that her role was being made redundant. The EAT noted that no minutes of this meeting were available. The claimant immediately went on garden leave and was not afforded a right of appeal. The claimant gave evidence to the effect that no alternatives to redundancy were discussed with her and her request for a copy of the selection process was not agreed to. The claimant's first sight of the selection matrix was at the EAT hearing.

In its determination, the EAT noted that the respondent's witness who gave evidence was not involved in the actual process of terminating the claimant's employment and thus could only give evidence by reference to the respondent's paper files. The EAT concluded that the respondent did not meet the onus on it to show the dismissal was fair. The EAT's findings were that:

(i)   neither the redundancy process nor the selection criteria were explained to the claimant;

(ii)   the role and weighting of the various presentations, interviews and personality profiles were not disclosed to the claimant nor was the respondent's witness able to explain how these criteria were applied or weighted;

(iii)   the scoring matrix was seen by the claimant for the first time at the EAT hearing, notwithstanding that she had sought a copy on previous occasions;

(iv)   the respondent was unable to explain the purpose of the personality profile, because while it was an element of the process, it did not feature in the scoring matrix;

(v)   the EAT was not satisfied that the process of selection was objective and fairly applied and was not satisfied that extraneous matters were not a factor in the decisions.

The EAT accepted the claimant's evidence that the reason for her selection was not explained to her or discussed with her and that she was not afforded the opportunity to make representations. The EAT noted that the claimant was not allowed to work her notice and that the decision confirming redundancy was communicated to the claimant, the day after her presentation and interview and that no explanation for the 'undue haste' was forthcoming. The claimant had not been given a right of appeal and there was no evidence to indicate that alternatives to redundancy were considered. The EAT noted a complete absence of any meaningful record of a process on the respondent's file and found that this gave credence to the claimant's evidence.

The EAT concluded that the claimant had been unfairly dismissed. On the issue of loss, the EAT noted that the claimant had secured alternative employment and that she had provided detailed information in relation to her current terms and remuneration. The

EAT awarded the claimant the sum €40,000 by way of compensation in addition to the monies already received in respect of her redundancy.

[22.21] *Mulqueen v Prometric Ireland Ltd T/A Prometric*[26] *– Employment Appeals Tribunal – Unfair Dismissals Acts 1977 to 2007 as amended – whether decision to terminate claimant's employment by reason of redundancy fair in all circumstances – use of selection matrix – flawed procedures used by respondent*

The respondent is a worldwide test administration company and the claimant was employed as a mobile driver tester in the Cork region. Evidence was given by the respondent that the volume of its work and revenues in Ireland had decreased by over 40% from 2010 to 2012. This triggered a need to control costs, and, over a three-month review period from February 2012, the respondent looked at changing its cost structure. It was submitted that all employees were kept informed of this process through an employee forum meeting in March 2012, although it was not clear that the claimant was so informed. It was submitted by the respondent that an employee forum meeting took place (the minutes of which were circulated to all employees) at which employees were informed that the respondent had to look at its operation with a view to operating more efficiently. Following this review period, a decision was made to reduce staffing levels in Sligo and Cork, with two positions in Cork and one in Sligo identified as being at risk of redundancy.

The respondent used a selection criteria matrix with five headings which had been previously used in the UK and the claimant and other employees were not consulted in relation to its design. The selection criteria were based on performance, adaptability and flexibility, disciplinary, attendance and knowledge, skills and experience. On 17 May, the four Cork employees were met and the matrix scoring system was completed on that date. Later on the same day, the respondent met with each individual and they were informed of the outcome. As the claimant had scored the least amount of points, he was notified that his position was to be made redundant. The claimant gave evidence that he had no advance warning of the meeting, he had not received any communication from the aforementioned employee forum and was only informed of the redundancy process at the meeting with no prior knowledge of the criteria used for selection for redundancy. The claimant objected to certain headings in the matrix when it was shown to him, but they remained in place. The claimant was invited back to the meeting after a short break and was advised that he was being made redundant with immediate effect. He had no representation at these meetings. He subsequently contacted a trade union representative and appealed the decisions.

An appeal hearing took place and the original decision to make him redundant was upheld. The claimant was paid in lieu of notice.

The EAT concluded that the procedures used by the respondent were flawed. The EAT was critical of the respondent for having produced the matrix only when informing the claimant and his colleagues they were to be made redundant. The EAT noted that the claimant had no previous knowledge of the content of the matrix, its significance or its

---

26.   *Mulqueen v Prometric Ireland Ltd T/A Prometric* UD1259/2012.

implications for his continuing employment. The claimant was given no opportunity to examine, query or object to the matrix. The unfair dismissal claim was upheld and compensation of €25,000 was awarded, in addition to the redundancy payment already made.

[22.22] *DLRS Group Security Concepts v SIPTU*[27] *– Labour Court – Industrial Relations Act 1990, s 26(1) as amended – what selection criteria should be used in redundancy in case of five compulsory redundancies*

This matter came before the Labour Court on foot of an unsuccessful LRC conciliation conference and a failure to agree at local level. The dispute concerned the issue of selection criteria to be used in the case of five compulsory redundancies in the respondent company.

The union submitted that it was totally opposed to any form of selection matrix and requested that the redundancies be on a last in first out basis. The union went on to set out a number of submissions as regards the groups to be considered for redundancy. It was submitted by the respondent that the operational skills that were required now and into the future were totally different to those that had pertained in the past and thus the retention of key skills was essential for its future. The respondent submitted that it had no choice but to look at discrete selection criteria for the five redundancies concerned. It submitted reasons why each of the categories of employees' roles was redundant in the circumstances.

Initially, the Labour Court advised the parties to engage with each other, with the assistance of an independent facilitator, to reach agreement on the outstanding issues. The Court noted that whilst progress was made during that process they failed to reach agreement. The Court noted the report from the facilitator on the progress made.

When the matter came before the Labour Court again, the Court recommended that the parties adapt the respondent's selection matrix with two new headings to include service as a selection factor with the weighting of 10% of the total marks, and attendance record to be included as a selection factor with the weighting of 10% of the total marks. The Court recommended that the pass mark for appointment to the available position to be set at 60%. The Court finally recommended that what the jobs investigator agreed with the facilitator together with the recommended pass mark and the extended matrices be accepted by both sides in full and final settlement of the dispute.

SHORT TIME OR REDUNDANCY?

[22.23] *Nolan v Nolan T/A Tivoli Dry Cleaners*[28] *– Redundancy Payments Acts 1967 to 2014 – Employment Appeals Tribunal – whether reduction of hours constituted short time – whether claimant in redundancy situation*

---

27.   *DLRS Group Security Concepts v SIPTU* LCR20819.
28.   *Nolan v Nolan T/A Tivoli Dry Cleaners* RP523/2013.

The respondent operated a dry cleaning business from two sites and the claimant worked for the business since 1973. The hours worked by the claimant changed over time – originally from a five-day week, to a three-day week in 2006 and then to a two-day week in and around 2010. The claimant regularly sought a return to five days a week or any additional hours. In 2011, the respondent offered the claimant a full time position in another premises which the claimant turned down. The claimant worked flexible hours to facilitate the respondent and would receive text messages when he was required to work. From 19 March 2013, the claimant worked one day a week. Around this time the claimant sent the respondent a RP9 form which was returned unsigned. When the respondent received the RP9 form from the claimant, the claimant was offered to return to a three day week but refused on the basis that a three day week was not sufficient and he wanted to return to five days a week.

The first issue to be determined by the EAT was the claimant's normal working week as of 26 March 2006. The EAT found that the claimant had agreed to changes to his working hours and terms since 2006 on a permanent basis. The EAT found that, notwithstanding the fact that the claimant requested to return to a five-day week in 2013, the claimant never envisaged actually returning to the 40-hour week worked in 2006 and it was not understood or agreed that he would do so. The EAT also found that the claimant had rejected the offer to work a five-day week between two different premises as the income that the claimant would receive was not worth his while in light of the social welfare benefits that he was receiving. The EAT was of the view that the claimant's normal working week was the two day week worked by the claimant in 2010. The EAT found that the reduction in working hours from a two-day week to a one-day week did not constitute short time for the purposes of the Redundancy Payments Acts 1967 to 2014 as the claimant's normal working week was not reduced by more than 50% nor was the claimant's remuneration so reduced.

The second issue to be determined by the EAT was whether the claimant was in a redundancy situation. The EAT found that, as the claimant had not been placed on short time, he was not entitled to trigger a redundancy by serving a RP9 form on the respondent. Accordingly, the EAT determined that the respondent employer sought to be reasonable in offering the claimant additional hours which the claimant rejected and since the claimant terminated his own employment he had no right to a redundancy payment.

ENTITLEMENT TO A COOLING OFF PERIOD

[22.24] *McFarland v Stanley Security Ltd[29] – Employment Appeals Tribunal – Unfair Dismissals Acts 1977 to 2007 as amended – Payment of Wages Act 1991 – appeal of a decision of Rights Commissioner – whether claimant unfairly dismissed when he accepted his redundancy – where immediate and unfair pressure placed on claimant to accept redundancy – failure to afford 'cooling off' period*

---

29. *McFarland v Stanley Security Ltd* UD2323/2011, PW519/2011.

The claimant was originally employed to manage and maintain the respondent's security account held with AIB. Due to the economic downturn, the claimant was required to adapt and take up other duties and functions. He was advised in June 2010 that he would have to move from a fixed pay scheme to an incentivised pay scheme, which the claimant asserted would have led to a reduction in his guaranteed salary from €62,000 to €42,000 and with an effective cap on commission of €8,000 from €12,000. The claimant was extremely unhappy about this proposed change, given it followed an 8.5% reduction in basic salary in the preceding year. A process of dialogue took place between the claimant and the respondent. The claimant had stated he could not continue providing the appropriate services to AIB, continue to manage the engineers and deliver €1.2million worth of sales from new clients per annum. It appears that over a number of weeks, correspondence and meetings exchanged and took place between the claimant and the respondent. The matters were left open. The claimant wrote to the respondent and stated that he was not prepared to take a proposed cut in salary and further he asked for a colleague to accompany him to the next scheduled meeting. On 13 August, some three days later, the respondent notified its staff that there was a need to implement redundancies. The EAT noted that the figures submitted by the respondent seemed to suggest a catastrophic falloff in business to the tune of 90%. However, the EAT noted that on evidence, it emerged that the figures were not as drastic and that the financial institutions were still turning a healthy profit, albeit reduced.

The EAT noted that there was no doubt that staff numbers were being reduced at the time and that the workplace was in the process of being reduced. At no time between 13 August and 30 August was the claimant advised that the notification regarding the proposed pay structure terminated. In fact, on 30 August, the claimant was called in and advised that his position was now being made redundant and was given one day, and on request two days, to consider his position. The EAT accepted that the claimant was shocked by the fact that he had been selected for redundancy and noted that the claimant's view that there was a definite link between his refusal to take the significant diminution in salary and the sudden decision to make him redundant. The EAT found that the respondent applied immediate and unfair pressure on the claimant to make a decision which could only be made, therefore, with haste and in anger. The EAT noted the long recognised need in employment situations for a 'cooling off' period where rash decisions have clearly been made. The EAT stated that there was no doubt that the claimant had made a wrong decision in not looking to see what alternative positions might be available or what salary might be offered in respect of the proposed amalgam job being opened up to the redundant account managers.

The EAT concluded that the respondent had acted in an unfair way and that it knew as of 6 September that the claimant was aggrieved, even as he took his redundancy cheque. The EAT concluded that the claimant had been unfairly dismissed and awarded him €32,500 compensation over and above any payments already made to him in relation to the termination of his employment. The appeal in respect of the Rights Commissioner decision under the Payment of Wages Act 1991 failed for want of prosecution.

ENHANCED EX GRATIA REDUNDANCY PAYMENTS

[22.25] *Alzheimer's Society of Ireland v Four Workers[30] – Labour Court – Industrial Relations Act 1969, s 20(1) as amended – whether workers entitled to ex gratia redundancy payment of four weeks per year of service in circumstances where respondent is a not-for-profit organisation substantially funded by Health Service Executive*

The background to this case is that in May 2014 the four workers were issued with a notice of redundancy and were offered statutory redundancy terms. As the workers were made compulsorily redundant and were not offered an alternative role they sought an enhanced redundancy package. The respondent employer did not attend the Labour Court hearing. The Labour Court noted that the respondent was a not-for-profit organisation substantially funded by the HSE. The Court recommended that, in line with the provisions of the Public Service Agreement 2010–2014 regarding enhanced redundancy payments for public servants, the workers should receive an ex gratia payment of three weeks' pay per year of service, in excess of the statutory redundancy payment already paid, with the total statutory redundancy and ex gratia payment not exceeding either two years pay or one half of the salary payable to preserved pension age, whichever was less.

KNOWLEDGE OF THE RIGHT OF APPEAL

[22.26] *Brody v Bradley & Doyle practising under the style and title of Malcomson Law[31] – Employment Appeals Tribunal – Unfair Dismissals Acts 1977 to 2007 as amended – unfair selection for redundancy – right of appeal – whether claimant, a solicitor, ought to have known of right of appeal in circumstances where she was legally represented during process*

In June 2012, the respondent employed an independent consultant to assess the financial efficiency of each department within the law firm. During the course of the expert's investigation he met with the claimant and the issue of voluntary redundancy was discussed. The claimant stated that she would 'grab it with both hands'. Following this discussion however the claimant changed her mind.

Paragraph 4.4 of the expert's report stated:

> The firm is over staffed in the litigation area with work for one solicitor and the appropriate support staff.

At the time there were only two solicitors in the litigation department, the claimant and a partner. The respondent selected the claimant for redundancy. The respondent submitted that he offered the claimant a position in the Dublin office but she declined for personal reasons. Furthermore the issue of part-time work was discussed, but the claimant stated

---

30. *Alzheimer's Society of Ireland v Four Workers* LCR20827.
31. *Brody v Bradley & Doyle practising under the style and title of Malcomson Law* UD1703/2012.

that part-time work would not suit her financial situation. The respondent informed the claimant of the redundancy by letters dated 22 June and 4 July 2012. There were several meetings prior to that.

The claimant submitted that she had not been informed at the time of her redundancy that she had a right of appeal. The EAT was of the opinion that the claimant, a solicitor practising in the area of employment law, ought to have known that there was a right of appeal. It was set out in her contract. In any event, the EAT also noted that prior to being made redundant the claimant had employed legal counsel who would have been in a position to advise her of her right to appeal.

The EAT was satisfied that the respondent had fulfilled all of its legal obligations in relation to the redundancy process. The process was fair, independent and objective. All alternative possibilities were exhausted. The claim failed.

ATTEMPTS TO BREAK AN EMPLOYEE'S CONTINUOUS SERVICE

[22.27] *Moloney v Keg Securities Tralee Ltd[32] – Employment Appeals Tribunal – Unfair Dismissals Acts 1977 to 2007 as amended – redundancy – attempt by employer to break employee's continuous service*

It was the claimant's evidence that he commenced his employment with the respondent as a security officer on 24 February 2008. A contract of employment was provided to him at that time. The employment appears to have been uneventful until late 2011 when the director said to the claimant that it had come to his attention that the claimant was not registered with the Private Security Authority. This was an oversight on the part of the claimant; however he rectified this and the Private Security Authority re-registered him retrospectively to March 2011 when he should have renewed his registration. The claimant informed the director that he had rectified the matter. At the hearing the claimant provided a letter from the Private Security Authority which stated that he was registered from 13 March 2009 to 12 March 2011 and from 12 March 2011 to 12 March 2013.

On 16 January 2012 the director told the claimant that his position was terminated but that if he agreed to sign a letter stating that he had requested a P45 then he would be re-employed as a new employee. The claimant thought the situation might be linked to the issue of his registration with the Private Security Authority but by then he had assured the director that he was registered. The claimant was not given time to take advice on the situation and he signed and dated the letter put before him under duress. The claimant gave evidence that he signed the letter as he felt he had no option but to do so as due to his personal circumstances at the time he needed to continue working. The claimant was then provided with a P45 and a new contract, which he signed. The contract appeared to have identical terms and conditions but stated a date of commencement of 21 January 2012.

---

32.   *Moloney v Keg Securities Tralee Ltd* UD870/2012.

The claimant was subsequently informed by the respondent on 23 April 2012 that his position was redundant. He acknowledged that there was a mention of reduced hours in either November or December 2011. The claimant was informed that the selection was carried out on the basis of being last in, first out. It was the claimant's case that that this was based on the contract and P45 issued to him in January 2012 when in fact he had a continuous period of employment from 2008. In or around April 2012 three relatives of the manager began employment in the company.

Following the termination of his employment, the claimant received a telephone call from the respondent offering him a shift to help him out. The claimant was employed after April 2012 on a temporary basis, working whatever shifts were available, until June 2013 when the respondent company lost the contract with the shopping centre. The claimant was subsequently employed by a new company in June 2013 under a new contract of employment and on a full-time basis. The claimant gave evidence of loss.

Based on the claimant's uncontested evidence, the EAT determined that the respondent attempted to break the claimant's service in January 2012, the impact of which was the selection of the claimant's position for redundancy in April 2012 on the basis of the last in, first out selection process. The EAT found that the dismissal of the claimant was unfair and awarded the claimant compensation in the sum of €20,592 under the Unfair Dismissals Acts 1977 to 2007 as amended.

TIME LIMITS

[22.28] *Phelan v REL Refrigeration Group Ltd[33] – Employment Appeals Tribunal – Redundancy Payments Acts 1967 to 2014 – extension of time limit for lodging claim on basis of false assurances made by liquidator*

This case concerned an application for an extension of the time limit for lodging a claim under the Redundancy Payments Acts 1967 to 2014 on the basis of the assurances made by the liquidator of the respondent.

The claimant was employed by the respondent since June 2007 and was dismissed by reason of redundancy in January 2012. An appeal was lodged with the EAT in April 2013. The liquidator had initially assured the claimant that the claim would be paid but subsequently (more than one year after she had been made redundant) informed her that the claim would not be paid. This evidence was not contested.

The EAT found that there was a reasonable cause for the delay and extended the time limit to two years under s 24 of the Redundancy Payments Acts, thus accepting jurisdiction to hear the appeal. The EAT awarded a lump sum redundancy payment under the Redundancy Payments Acts 1967 to 2014. In relation to quantum, the EAT noted that the claimant's salary was reduced one year prior to redundancy (ie from €80,000 to €40,000) due to a pay cut and reduction in hours. For the purposes of calculating redundancy payment, the EAT based gross pay on the higher figure (ie €80,000).

---

33. *Phelan v REL Refrigeration Group Ltd* RP411/2013.

VALIDITY OF A SETTLEMENT/COMPROMISE AGREEMENT

[22.29] *Healy and Healy v Bia Ganbreise Teoranta[34] – Employment Appeals Tribunal – Redundancy Payment Acts 1967 to 2014 – whether EAT had jurisdiction to hear claims in light of settlement agreements signed by parties – failure to specify full extent of waiver of claims – matters not contemplated by employee at time of settlement*

The claimants made an application to the EAT to receive statutory redundancy entitlements from their employer, the respondent, who had refused to make the payments on the basis that:

(i) the claimants had signed a waiver of claims against the respondent, which included claims for redundancy payments; and

(ii) the claimants' break in service with the respondent meant that they did not have the requisite 104 weeks' service to qualify for statutory redundancy payments.

By way of background, the claimants sold their company, Company A, to Company F, and took up fixed-term employment with Company F from 8 July 2008 to 7 July 2011. The claimants instituted Circuit Court proceedings against Company F for unpaid wages. However, prior to the claim being heard, Company A (a wholly owned subsidiary of Company F) was sold to Company X (the respondent in this case).

In July 2011, the claimants were informed by the accountant of Company F and, separately, two directors of Company X that their fixed-term contracts would be renewed as of 16 July 2011 but that they would be required to accept a reduced salary. The claimants accepted the reduced salary and signed a compromise agreement with Company X under which they received their unpaid wages (in the amount of €31,750) in full and final settlement of any claims they had against Company F and Company A.

The relevant sections of the settlement agreement were set out in the decision of the EAT:

> Clause 7: The Employee agrees that the terms of the Agreement provide a full and final settlement of the proceedings and all or any claims that he/she has or may have against the company and/or the employer and/or any of their respective group of companies, officers and/or employees agents and shareholders, howsoever arising, including, without limitation, arising out of or in connection with the employment of the Employee of the company and/or the employer and /or any of their respective Group companies, and the employee hereby fully and finally releases all such entities from all or and any such claims, whether in statute or common law in tort, in equity or otherwise howsoever arising.
>
> Clause 13: This Agreement shall enure to the benefit of and be binding upon the respective parties hereto and their respective personal representatives and successors.

On or around 7 February 2012, the respondent placed the claimants on temporary lay-off, and on 21 March 2012, the respondent advised the claimants that their positions

---

34.   *Healy and Healy v Bia Ganbreise Teoranta* RP493/2012.

were being made redundant, however the respondent did not pay the claimants any statutory redundancy payments.

In July 2012, the claimants lodged claims with the EAT seeking a statutory redundancy lump sum. The respondent contended that the EAT had no jurisdiction to hear the claims because the claimants had previously waived all claims against the respondent in the settlement agreement. The respondent also contended that due to the break in service between the expiry of their fixed-term contract (7 July 2011) and the renewal of the contract (16 July 2011), the claimants did not have the requisite 104 weeks' service to bring a claim under the Acts.

In response to the preliminary issue, the EAT stated that the rule against contracting out of statutory protections (such as the entitlement to receive statutory redundancy payments) does not preclude severance agreements or claims being compromised. The EAT found that claimants were legally represented in the negotiations leading up to the settlement, and on that basis concluded that the claimants gave informed consent to the settlement.

The EAT then examined the specific provisions of the settlement agreement (as set out above). It noted that the waiver did not list the specific employment legislation under which the appellants might have waived their statutory entitlement to bring claims, nor did it make clear that the appellants had been notified of the specific claims that they were waiving. Based on *Sunday Newspapers Ltd v Kinsella and Brady*[35] and *Minister for Labour v O'Connor and Anor*,[36] the EAT stated that it was necessary to consider what the parties actually discussed at the settlement meeting to determine whether it was envisaged that the claimants' entitlement to bring claims under the Acts had in fact been waived.

The uncontested evidence was that the only issue discussed between the parties was the settlement of wages dispute, which was corroborated by the fact that the settlement figure of €31,750 was the precise amount of the unpaid wages owing to the claimants. The claimants were issued with payslips dated 30 July 2011 for €31,750 less payroll tax and the respondent had written to the Revenue Commissioners on 23 September 2011 confirming that that the payment was in respect of a number of weeks worked by the appellants between 2009 and 2011. The respondent argued that the claimants must have considered that they were waiving claims under the Acts due to the fact that their fixed-term contracts were due to expire. The EAT rejected this argument on the basis that, in May or June 2011, Company F's accountant and the two directors of Company X informed the claimants that their employment was being continued.

The EAT also concluded that, as the claimants had been informed that their contract was being renewed, there was no break in the claimants' service between 7 July 2011 and 16 July 2011, and rejected the respondent's argument that the claimants did not have the requisite service to bring a claim under the Acts.

The EAT awarded the claimants statutory redundancy payments, minus the period of lay-off between 7 February 2012 and 22 March 2012.

---

35. *Sunday Newspapers Ltd v Kinsella and Brady* [2008] ELR 53.

36. *Minister for Labour v O'Connor and Anor* (6 March 1973) HC.

ENTITLEMENT TO A REDUNDANCY PAYMENT FOLLOWING A BUSINESS TRANSFER WHERE TUPE NOT APPLIED

[22.30] *Striuogaitiene v Noonan Services Group Ltd[37] – Employment Appeals Tribunal – Redundancy Payments Acts 1967 to 2014 – whether claimant entitled to redundancy payment in circumstances where contract under which claimant worked brought in-house by respondent's client and claimant's employment did not transfer under TUPE or otherwise – EC (Protection of Employees on Transfer of Undertakings) Regulations 2003*

The claimant's employment transferred to the respondent company in 2008 and she was employed as a contract cleaner and was based on one client's site. Subsequently, the respondent's client decided to bring the contract in-house and insisted that the TUPE regulations did not apply. The client was unwilling to accept the respondent's employees who worked on the contract. Notwithstanding that, the respondent company did dispute this with its client. The client maintained its position that TUPE did not apply.

The claimant asserted that she had an entitlement to a redundancy payment as her employment had not transferred to the respondent's client. The respondent's position was that had the claimant transferred to the client then some of the client's staff with shorter service may have been selected for redundancy. The EAT noted that further submissions and case law were submitted to it on these issues.

The EAT held that in the circumstances of this case the client ceased the contract with the respondent and this business did not transfer to any other entity, it was merely brought in-house. The EAT noted the statement of Morrison J in *ECM v Cox*:[38]

> The Directive does not aim to protect employees from the chill wind of redundancies, it does seek to protect them when the business to which they were dedicated has been transferred and a new employer has come on the scene.

The EAT noted that this case was differentiated from the *ECM* case by virtue of the fact that no new employer was within the case before the EAT and thus the EAT found that the claimant was entitled to a redundancy payment on that basis.

CAN A REFUSAL OF PART-TIME WORK CONSTITUTE A REDUNDANCY?

[22.31] *Tuczynski v Students Union Áras Na Mac Leinn[39] – Employment Appeals Tribunal – Redundancy Payments Acts 1967 to 2014 – refusal of part-time work for student who returned to university following full-time position*

---

37.   *Striuogaitiene v Noonan Services Group Ltd* RP747/2013.
38.   *ECM v Cox* [1998] IRLR 416.
39.   *Tuczynski v Students Union Áras Na Mac Leinn* RP1257/2012.

The claimant had been employed on a full-time basis by the respondent as a shop assistant. The claimant subsequently went back to college and asked the respondent if he could work on a part-time basis. This was refused and the claimant sought a redundancy payment.

The EAT heard conflicting evidence from both parties regarding the claimant's availability. The claimant never provided the respondent with his college timetable when he was asked for this and a witness for the respondent said that the claimant was never sure of his availability. The claimant gave evidence that he was available for work every evening from 6pm and on Sundays.

Upon receiving a letter from the claimant asking for part-time work, the respondent issued the claimant with a P45. The claimant's position was then filled by another person who continued to work in the position on a full-time basis and on the same hours as the claimant had previously worked.

The EAT held that the letter sent by the claimant to the respondent indicated to the respondent that the claimant would not be available to work on a full-time basis. The EAT held that there was no real and genuine redundancy in the circumstances and found against the claimant.

Chapter 23

REFORMS

WORKPLACE RELATIONS BILL 2014

Introductory Note

[23.01] The Workplace Relations Bill 2014 was presented to the Oireachtas by the Minister for Jobs, Enterprise and Innovation on 28 July 2014 as part of a broader reform programme within the Department of Jobs, Enterprise and Innovation.

As at 1 January 2015, the Bill was before Dáil Éireann at the Final Report Stages. The Bill will move to Seanad Éireann where it may be subject to further amendments, before being enacted into law. For that reason, we have set out below a summary of the core principles of the Bill as at 1 January 2015, but which we do not expect will change substantially before its enactment.

Aims of the Bill

[23.02] The aim of the Bill is to deliver a modern, world-class workplace relations service which is simple to use, effective, independent, cost-effective and provides for a workable means of redress and enforcement within a reasonable period of time. The Bill proposes to consolidate the various adjudicating employment fora; place an increased emphasis on informal resolution of employment disputes, such as mediation; provide for greater use of standardised electronic forms for filing complaints; introduce a standardised procedure and time-frames for instituting employment claims; and introduce a more cost efficient method of enforcing compensation awarded.

The Bill proposes to replace the current five employment fora with two bodies:

(i) Adjudication Officers appointed by the Workplace Relations Commission (the WRC) to hear all claims at first instance; and

(ii) the Labour Court to hear appeals.

It is envisaged that the EAT will continue to operate to dispose of all legacy first instance complaints and appeals referred to it prior to the commencement of the new Act. The WRC will deal with all employment complaints at first instance; subsuming the responsibilities of the Labour Relations Commission (Rights Commissioners), the EAT, the Equality Tribunal, the Labour Court and the National Employment Rights Authority including conciliation, dispute resolution, workplace mediation, inspection, advisory services and research into matters pertaining to workplace relations. The Labour Court will be the sole appellate body for decisions of the Adjudication Officers. Appeals may be brought to the High Court on a point of law only.

Redress procedure

[23.03] All complaints will be referred to the Director General of the WRC utilising a standard referral procedure for all employment legislation. The Bill introduces standardised limitation periods of six months extendable to 12 months where the claimant can show reasonable cause.

The Bill provides for two avenues of alternative dispute resolution: (i) early resolution; and (ii) mediation. The aim of these initiatives is to facilitate resolution at the earliest possible opportunity so as to reduce waiting times for cases which proceed to adjudication and subsequently to an appeal before the Labour Court. Where the Director General is of the opinion that a complaint or dispute is capable of being resolved by either early resolution or by mediation, the Director General may refer the matter to a case resolution officer or a mediator (as appropriate), with the consent of the parties. The case resolution officer or mediator concerned may employ such means as he or she considers appropriate for the purpose of resolving disputes. Any resolution of claims under the resolution procedures will be binding on all parties thereto. Unless resolved by agreement through the early resolution service or mediation, complaints will be heard by Adjudication Officers. All existing Rights Commissioners and Equality Officers will become Adjudication Officers. Additional Adjudication Officers are being appointed.

Adjudication Officer hearings will be held in private. Every decision of an Adjudication Officer will be published on the WRC website on an anonymous basis.

If the decision of the Adjudication Officer in favour of the complainant is not appealed by either party but remains unimplemented after a period of 56 days, the complainant concerned, a trade union or body acting on behalf of the complainant, or the WRC in certain circumstances, may apply to the District Court for an order directing the employer to carry out the decision in accordance with its terms.

Appeals to the Labour Court

[23.04] All appeals from decisions of Adjudication Officers will lie to the Labour Court.

The Labour Court will act as a court of final appeal, subject to the right of either party to bring a further appeal from a determination of the Labour Court to the High Court on a point of law only. Appeals to the Labour Court will be *de novo* hearings held in public (other than where the complaint is one that raises confidential or sensitive issues, in relation to disability or sexual orientation, for example). Decisions of the Labour Court will be published on the WRC website. All appeals must be instituted within 42 days of the date the WRC decision issues.

If the decision of the Labour Court in favour of the complainant is not appealed by either party, but remains unimplemented after the period of 42 days, the complainant concerned, a trade union or excepted body acting on behalf of the complainant, or the WRC in certain circumstances, may apply to the District Court for an order directing the employer to carry out the decision in accordance with its terms.

Appeals to the High Court

[23.05] A party to proceedings before the Labour Court may appeal a decision of the Labour Court to the High Court on a point of law and the decision of the High Court will be final and conclusive.

Advisory and information functions of the WRC

[23.06] In addition to hearing complaints, the WRC will replace the National Employment Rights Authority by discharging advisory and information functions. The WRC will be tasked with taking proactive steps such as providing advice, information and the findings of research conducted by the WRC to joint labour committees and joint industrial councils, and advising and appraising the Minister in relation to the application of, and compliance with, relevant enactments in order to encourage compliance with employment legislation and relevant codes of practice, and shall have a role as a mediator in the conduct of industrial relations.

Powers of inspection and enforcement

[23.07] The Bill provides for the appointment of WRC inspectors who will have similar functions and responsibilities to the current National Employment Rights Authority inspectors. WRC inspectors may enter employer's premises for the purposes of inspecting employment documents. Written reports of WRC inspectors may be used in employment law hearings by employees who have instituted claims against the relevant employer and may form evidence in any subsequent prosecution of employers.

The Bill also provides for the imposition of sanctions such as compliance notices and fixed payment notices (up to a maximum €2,000) by the WRC, where, following inspection of an employer's employment records by WRC Inspectors, it is established that an employer has contravened a provision set out in the Bill in relation to any of his or her employees or has committed an offence under employment legislation. Sanctions of the WRC pursuant to compliance notices can be appealed to the Labour Court.

Fees and costs

[23.08] Unlike in the UK where fees for the submission of claims to Employment Tribunals were introduced in 2013, the Bill does not introduce charges for access to the WRC or Labour Court. The current position, that each party bears its own costs in prosecuting/defending a claim, is set to prevail and there is no provision in the Bill as currently drafted for costs to 'follow the event' (meaning that the unsuccessful party pays both sides' costs) as is the custom in the civil courts. However, the Bill is proposing to introduce a fee of €300 where a party who failed to appear at a first instance hearing of the WRC without good cause and subsequently wishes to appeal the decision to the Labour Court. If the Labour Court determines that the party in question had good cause for failing to attend the first instance hearing, the fee will be refunded.

Annual leave

[23.09] An amendment has been made at the report stage to the Bill to propose that s 19 of the Organisation of Working Time Act 1997 be amended to provide that employees may accrue annual leave while on certified sick leave.[1]

Conclusion

[23.10] The Bill provides for extensive reform to the existing system, and the streamlining of the employment fora is to be welcomed. However, it remains to be seen whether the WRC will experience the same backlogs and delays in progressing to adjudication hearings as is currently being experienced before the EAT and Equality Tribunal in respect of their functions at first instance. It is possible that the new focus on early resolution of claims and mediation may ameliorate this to some extent.

---

1.   See CH 30.

Chapter 24

TAXATION RELATING TO EMPLOYMENT

FOREIGN EARNINGS DEDUCTION

[24.01] Section 16 of the Finance Act 2014 amends s 823A of the Taxes Consolidation Act 1997 (TCA) which provides for the foreign earnings deduction (FED). The relief, which applies only for the tax years 2012–2017 inclusive, provides for relief from taxation on certain emoluments of certain individuals who are tax resident in Ireland but who spend a significant amount of time working in qualified countries. It is designed to support companies seeking to expand into any of these countries. The maximum relief available in any tax year is €35,000.

Changes made by Finance Act 2014 include:

(i) from 1 January 2015, an expansion of the number of countries where FED will apply, with the addition of Japan, Singapore, South Korea, Saudi Arabia, the United Arab Emirates, Qatar, Bahrain, Indonesia, Vietnam, Thailand, Chile, Oman, Kuwait, Mexico, and Malaysia;

(ii) time spent travelling to a relevant state, or from a relevant state to Ireland or to another relevant state will be deemed to be time spent in a relevant state;

(iii) the number of whole days of continuous presence requirement in a relevant state will be reduced from four to three; and

(iv) the number of qualifying days requirement in a continuous period of 12 months will be reduced from 60 to 40.

SPECIAL ASSIGNEE RELIEF PROGRAMME

[24.02] The Special Assignee Relief Programme was introduced in Ireland, with effect from 1 January 2012, as an incentive to encourage companies to locate high value employees in Ireland. Section 15 of the Finance Act 2014 amended s 825C TCA by providing for:

(i) an extension of the programme to 2017;

(ii) the removal from 1 January 2015 of the upper ceiling of income eligible for relief (previously €500,000); and

(iii) a reduction in the amount of time an employee needs to be employed to qualify for relief (reduction from 12 to six months).

The operation of the relief will remain unchanged and applies against an income tax (but not USC or PRSI) charge using the following formula:

$$\text{Relief} = (A - B) * 30\%$$

Where:

A   is the total remuneration of the employee (subject to a limit of €500,000 for the year 2012–2014); and

B   is €75,000.

RELEVANT CONTRACTS TAX

[24.03] Section 17 of the Finance Act 2014 amended s 530F of the TCA, which states the penalties applicable for the non-operation of relevant contracts tax by the principal contractor. From 1 January 2015 the old hybrid fixed penalty/outstanding tax regime will be replaced with a penalty based on the percentage of outstanding tax. The percentage will vary between 3% and 35% dependant on tax compliance status of the person to whom the relevant payment was made.

EMPLOYMENT INCENTIVE AND INVESTMENT SCHEME

[24.04] Changes are proposed to the Employment Incentive and Investment Scheme which aims to provide alternative sources of financing to SMEs by providing investors who subscribe for shares in these qualifying SMEs with income tax relief. Section 27 of the Finance Act 2014 amended Part 16 of the TCA and, subject to EU approval and ministerial commencement, changes include:

(i)   increasing the minimum holding period from three to four years;

(ii)   expanding the scheme to include medium-sized enterprises in non-assisted areas and companies engaged in internationally traded financial services;

(iii)   raising the amount of capital that can be raised annually (from €2.5 to €5 million) and over its lifetime (from €10 to €15 million); and

(iv)   restricting relief claims to investment in companies which qualify for a tax clearance certificate.

INCOME TAX

[24.05] Section 3 of the Finance act 2014 amended s 15 of the TCA by increasing the band threshold and reducing the marginal tax rate for the tax year 2015. The threshold for paying income tax at the marginal rate will be increased by €1,000 (to €33,800) for a single person and €2,000 (to €67,600) for a double income household. The marginal rate itself will be reduced from 41% to 40%.

UNIVERSAL SOCIAL CHARGE

[24.06] Section 2 of the Finance Act 2014 proposes to amend Part 18D of the TCA by setting out revised band thresholds and tax rates, and introducing a new band of tax for the tax year 2015. The changes are proposed with the intention of reducing the tax burden on employees earning less than €70,000 annually, but negating the income tax rate reduction for those who earn above €70,000.

USC Thresholds

2014	Rate	2015	Rate
Income up to €10,036.00	2%	Income up to €12,012.00	1.5%
Income from €10,036.01 to €16,016.00	4%	Income from €12,012.01 to €17,576.00	3.5%
Income above €16,016.00	7%	Income from €17,576.01 to €70,044.00	7%
		Income above €70,044.00	8%

DOMICILE LEVY

[24.07] *eBrief* 72/14 published a Revenue update regarding the Domicile Levy and the process of calculating the amount of Irish income tax paid by an individual in a tax year to be allowed as a credit against the Levy.[1] Revenue, in this ebriefing, reminded practitioners and taxpayers that the Income Levy, Universal Social Charge, Pay Related Social Insurance and Health Levy are not allowable as a credit against the Domicile Levy for any year as they are not income tax.

HIGHER EARNERS RESTRICTION

[24.08] *eBrief* 75/14 published an amendment to the method of calculating how much relief against the restriction can be claimed under a double taxation agreement.[2] In granting double taxation relief in situations where the restriction applies, the effective rate which should be used when foreign income is being re-grossed is calculated as tax (after application of the high earners restriction) over adjusted income. Before this amendment, the effective rate was calculated as tax (before application of high earners restriction) over total income. This change will grant additional relief in some cases and was necessary to ensure that full effect was given to relief provided by double taxation treaties.

This change is retrospective and applies to claims to relief contained in tax returns submitted on or after 1 January 2008. A taxpayer who is entitled to a greater tax credit for double taxation under this provision than under the pre Finance (No 2) Act 2013 provisions, may make a claim for repayment of tax. For 2012 and previous years of assessment, ROS will not calculate the correct double tax relief. Therefore, so that Revenue can assess if any such claim is a valid claim (under s 865 TCA), each claim should be supported by calculations showing how the revised claim to double taxation relief was arrived at.

---

1.   http://www.revenue.ie/en/practitioner/ebrief/2014/no-722014.html.

2.   http://www.revenue.ie/en/practitioner/ebrief/2014/no-752014.html.

RESEARCH AND DEVELOPMENT TAX CREDITS

Key employees engaged in research and development activities

[24.09] The Revenue Income Tax, Capital Gains Tax and Corporation Tax Manual has been updated as of May 2014 to reflect Finance (No 2) Act 2013 changes regarding relief for key employees engaged in research and development activities.[3] In particular, the Manual outlines an obligation on an employer to pay all tax due under the Pay As You Earn (PAYE) system before employee emoluments can be reduced and an obligation on employees to file a tax return for all years in which credit has been claimed.

LOCAL PROPERTY TAX

Deduction at source from wages, salary or an occupational pension

[24.10] *eBrief* 43/14 (June 2014) updated the position regarding employers and pension providers who are required by the Revenue to deduct Local Property Tax (LPT) and Household Charge (HHC) arrears at source from wages, salary or an occupational pension. The update requires deductions to be commenced by the employer/pension provider as soon as possible on receipt of the Tax Credit Certificate and spread evenly over the pay periods occurring up to the end of December 2014.[4]

    The employer/pension provider must also account for and remit the deducted LPT/ HHC to Revenue on Forms P30 and P35, and to employees on payslips, P60s and P45s as appropriate.

Filing and payment of LPT by employers in respect of employees

[24.11] Where an employer/pension provider does not make mandatory deductions as instructed by Revenue, they will become liable for the amount due. Non-operation of the instruction may result in interest charges, penalties, the refusal of a tax clearance certificate as well as increasing the chance of a tax audit. *eBrief* 45/14 (June 2014) indicated that these instructions are continuing to issue in relation to LPT and arrears of HHC.[5]

COMPLIANCE CODE FOR PAYE TAXPAYERS

[24.12] *eBrief 07/14* (January 2014) published the Compliance Code for PAYE taxpayers which sets out the Revenue's approach to PAYE compliance interventions and advises PAYE taxpayers as to how they can regularise their tax affairs where an error is discovered.[6]

---

3.   http://www.revenue.ie/en/practitioner/ebrief/2014/no-322014.html.
4.   http://www.revenue.ie/en/practitioner/ebrief/2014/no-432014.html.
5.   http://www.revenue.ie/en/practitioner/ebrief/2014/no-452014.html.
6.   http://www.revenue.ie/en/practitioner/ebrief/2014/no-072014.html.

The Compliance Code is in effect from 18 November 2013 and all PAYE compliance interventions undertaken by Revenue from that date will be made under the terms of the Code.

PAYE (EMPLOYER) COMPLIANCE MANUAL

[24.13] Revenue published *Tax Briefing Issue No 5* (June 2014) updating the PAYE (Employer) Compliance manual as regards an employer's obligation to register as an employer for PAYE purposes and to send notification to Revenue of details of new employees and the obligation on employers to keep and maintain a Register of Employees.[7] The Tax Briefing lists what must be maintained on the register, who must retain it and the penalties that can apply if a register is not maintained or provided to Revenue on request. Section 903(5) TCA provides that the employer shall be liable to a penalty of €4,000 for failure to comply with a requirement of an authorised officer to produce records required for the purposes of an enquiry.

TERMINATION PAYMENTS

[24.14] In March 2014, the European Commission officially asked Ireland to amend its tax treatment of termination payments which, according to the Commission, discriminated against the allowable 'time of service' for an employee working with a group company in EU/EEA Member States other than Ireland.

The Revenue Income Tax, Capital Gains Tax and Corporation Tax Manual has been updated as of April 2014 to consolidate all previously published materials relating to termination payments under s 123 TCA and sets out changes to the exemptions and reliefs, as amended by Finance Act 2013 and Finance (No 2) Act 2013.[8] Revenue clarified that when counting the number of years of a person's service, periods of foreign service are included where an individual was employed by one employer or served in different member companies in the same group.

Other changes expanded upon in the Tax Manual included a restriction of Top Slicing Relief for the year of assessment 2013 and an abolition of the same relief with effect from 1 January 2014.

TAXABLE ILLNESS/INJURY BENEFIT VIA ROS

[24.15] The Revenue Income Tax, Capital Gains Tax and Corporation Tax Manual has been updated as of June 2014 to reflect Finance (No 2) Act 2013 which restricts relief where an employer pays a medical or dental insurance premium to the insurer net of the tax relief due in respect of the director or employee on whose behalf the policy is paid.[9] The Revenue recovers that reduced premium benefit obtained, by imposing on the

---

7.   http://www.revenue.ie/en/practitioner/ebrief/2014/no-422014.html.
8.   http://www.revenue.ie/en/practitioner/ebrief/2014/no-282014.html.
9.   http://www.revenue.ie/en/practitioner/ebrief/2014/no-472014.html.

employer a charge to income tax, (in accordance with s 112A(3) TCA), equal to the relievable amount at the standard rate of tax. The tax paid is allowable as a deduction in charging the employer's profits to tax and must be taken into account when calculating the preliminary tax and corporation tax payable as normal.[10]

USC – SPLIT YEAR RESIDENCE, PAYMENT OF ARREARS AND BONUSES

[24.16] The Revenue Income Tax, Capital Gains Tax and Corporation Tax Manual has been updated as of July 2014 to clarify that where an individual is deemed not to be resident as a consequence of the Split Year Relief scheme (s 822 TCA) and they receive income, such as arrears or bonuses, arising from employment while he/she was resident in Ireland but which is paid after he/she has left Ireland, then the income is emoluments to which the PAYE system applies and is liable to USC in the year in which it is paid to the individual.[11]

EXPENSES OF TRAVEL – NON-EXECUTIVE DIRECTORS ATTENDING BOARD MEETINGS

[24.17] The Revenue Income Tax, Capital Gains Tax and Corporation Tax Manual has been updated as of July 2014 setting out the position regarding the tax treatment of expenses of travel incurred by non-executive directors in attending board meetings. It states that where such expenses are met by a company on a director's behalf or are reimbursed to him, PAYE/USC must be deducted at source.[12]

Pursuant to s 114 TCA, directors are entitled to make a claim in respect of expenses of travelling in the performance of the duties of the office of director which he or she is necessarily obliged to incur, as well as in respect of other expenses wholly, exclusively and necessarily incurred in the performance of those duties. Notably, the case law highlighted by the Revenue suggests that the rule is subject to a very narrow interpretation so as to exclude personal circumstances from affecting expenses, and so generally speaking the cost of travel by a non-executive director from home to board meetings will not qualify for a deduction.[13]

PAYE BALANCING STATEMENT/END OF YEAR REVIEWS

[24.18] Revenue has issued an explanatory note for employees claiming income tax refunds following PAYE balancing statement/end of year reviews. However, it is

---

10.   Part 1501–14 of the Income Tax, Corporation Tax and Capital Gains Tax Manual.
11.   http://www.revenue.ie/en/practitioner/ebrief/2014/no-522014.html and Part 18d–04–06 of the Income Tax, Corporation Tax and Capital Gains Tax Manual.
12.   http://www.revenue.ie/en/practitioner/ebrief/2014/no-612014.html.
13.   Part 05–02–19 of the Income Tax, Corporation Tax and Capital Gains Tax Manual.

suggested that it is simpler to claim refunds from the employer during the course of the tax year rather than contacting Revenue at the end of the year.[14]

START YOUR OWN BUSINESS RELIEF

[24.19] *eBrief* 03/14 (January 2014) published the Start Your Own Business Relief Revenue Guidance Note following the introduction of a new income tax relief for long term unemployed by the Finance (No 2) Act 2013.[15] This scheme provides an exemption from income tax up to a maximum of €40,000 per annum for a period of two years to individuals who set up a qualifying business; having been unemployed for a period of at least 12 months prior to starting the business.

UK DECISIONS

[24.20] *HMRC v Apollo Fuels Ltd & Ors and Edwards & Ors v HMRC*[16]

The Upper Tribunal held that where cars were made available to an employee by an employer and were available for private use, this does not constitute a lease with proprietary rights nor produce a taxable employment benefit. Therefore, it falls outside of the scope of s 114 of the Income Tax (Earnings and Pensions) Act 2003 (ITEPA 2003) whose benefit rules concern the transfer of property. Tax should only arise under the benefit rules if there is actually a benefit to the employee. The Tribunal ruled that employees were not subject to tax or National Insurance Contributions on cars leased to them on arm's length terms by their employer. However, this section is repealed from April 2014.

[24.21] *Essack v HMRC*[17]

The appellant submitted tax returns on the basis that a payment received for the surrender of his right to receive shares on termination of employment for 'compensation for loss of employment and loss of all and any entitlements to shares in the [c]ompany' was a capital sum. The First-tier Tribunal held that the unenforceable promise to receive shares did not constitute an asset or right for the purposes of capital gains tax. Furthermore, income tax was given priority under s 401 ITEPA 2003 and the compensation payment therefore fell to be treated as an income payment on termination of employment.

---

14.   http://www.revenue.ie/en/personal/end-year-reviews.html.

15.   http://www.revenue.ie/en/practitioner/ebrief/2014/no-032014.html.

16.   *HMRC v Apollo Fuels Ltd & Ors and Edwards & Ors v HMRC* [2014] UKUT 0095 (TCC).

17.   *Essack v HMRC* [2014] UKFTT 159 (TC).

Chapter 25

TEMPORARY AGENCY WORK

SELECTED LABOUR COURT DECISIONS

[25.01] *O'Reilly Recruitment Ltd v Zaremba & Ors[1] – Labour Court – appeal of decision of Rights Commissioner – Protection of Employees (Temporary Agency Work) Act 2012, s 25(2) – whether complainants' rates of pay infringed s 6(1) of the 2012 Act where directly employed workers doing same or similar work received higher hourly rate*

The complainants were agency workers employed by the respondent recruitment agency and were assigned to work in AQF Ltd (the hirer) doing the same or similar work as the hirer's directly employed workers. The complainants were paid €8.65 per hour and directly employed workers were paid €10.08 per hour. It was submitted by the complainants that their basic working and employment conditions were less favourable than those of directly employed workers and this was an infringement of s 6(1) of the 2012 Act. Whilst acknowledging that the complainants performed the same work as directly employed workers, the respondent submitted that the hirer's directly employed workers had longer service. It was further submitted by the respondent that the hirer would have paid new recruits €8.65 per hour and not, what it claimed, was a historic rate of €10.08 per hour. In support of its position, the respondent submitted to the Labour Court a letter sent to it by the hirer confirming that it would apply the rate of pay of €8.65 per hour for direct workers employed from 5 December 2011, the effective date of the 2012 Act. The Labour Court noted that the complainants were assigned to the hirer on or before 5 December 2011 and were thus deemed to have commenced their assignment on that date.

The Labour Court noted that all but one of the workers directly employed by the hirer was paid a rate of €10.08 per hour. The single exception came to the hirer under a transfer of undertakings arrangement and was paid the rate of €8.65 per hour which rate was subsequently increased by the first phase of the relevant national agreement then in force. The Court distinguished this worker from the rates that generally applied within the hirer. The Labour Court held that s 6(1) of the 2012 Act must be read together with s 2 of the Act and the Directive which stated 'basic working and employment working conditions' means terms or conditions required to be included in the contract for employment by virtue of any enactment or collective agreement or any agreement arrangement that generally applies in respect of employees or any class or employees of a hirer. The Court noted that art 2(1) of the Directive[2] stated 'the basic working and employment conditions of a temporary agency worker shall be for the duration of their

---

1.   *O'Reilly Recruitment Ltd v Zaremba & Ors* AWD 141.
2.   Directive 2008/104/EC.

assignment at a user undertaking at least those that would apply if they had been recruited directly by that undertaking to occupy the same jobs.'

The Labour Court held that the test set out in s 2 of the 2012 Act is an objective one. It must determine if there is a legitimate provision, collective agreement or general arrangement in place that sets the general working and employment conditions, including the basic rate of pay, of directly employed workers. Where such an arrangement that applies generally to directly employed worker is in place, the Court must, in order to apply the principle of equal treatment set out in the Directive and transposed into Irish Law by the 2012 Act, apply that rate to agency workers assigned to the hirer.

The Labour Court noted that it could not substitute a hypothetical rate posited by the hirer for the actual rate of pay that in fact applied to directly employed workers doing the same work as assigned agency workers. The Court noted that were it to do so it would defeat the purposes of the Directive and the 2012 Act and could not be lawful. The Court determined that the complaint was well founded. In terms of redress, the Court directed the respondent to adjust the complainants' rates of pay to €10.08 per hour with effect from the 5th December 2011. The decision of the Rights Commissioner was set aside.

[25.02] *MK Human Resources Ltd T/A Temple Recruitment v Jacek & Ors[3] – Labour Court – appeal of Rights Commissioner decision – Protection of Employees (Temporary Agency Work) Act 2012 – same basic working and employment conditions for agency workers and directly employed workers – definition of pay*

This was an appeal by the complainant employees against the decision of a Rights Commissioner in a complaint under the Protection of Employees (Temporary Agency Work) Act 2012. The respondent, an employment agency, supplied agency workers to Ryanair Ltd (the hirer). The complainants, employees of the respondent, were assigned to work for the hirer at Dublin Airport as ground handling agents. The complainants brought a claim under s 6 of the 2012 Act claiming that they were remunerated at a lower rate of pay than that which applied to direct employees of the hirer. The Rights Commissioner found that the claim was not well-founded. The complainants appealed to the Labour Court.

The complainants alleged that the respondent breached s 6 of the 2012 Act by paying the complainants an hourly rate of pay of €10.20 per hour, whereas direct employees of the hirer performing identical duties were being paid at a higher hourly rate. The complainants submitted payslips and written terms of employment of the direct employees of the hirer as evidence of this allegation. A copy of a contract of employment issued by the hirer to a new starter employee was submitted which stated that the annual salary would be: basic pay: €15,708; shift premium: €3,476, and attendance payment: €1,651. Four payslips issued to four direct employees of the hirer in 'Ground Operations "Pier A"' dated 28 June 2013 were also submitted which indicated that the basic rate varied from €10.65 to €13.52 per hour. On this basis, the

---

3.　　*MK Human Resources Ltd T/A Temple Recruitment v Messrs Jacek & Ors* AWD148.

complainants sought the application of an hourly rate of €13.52 per hour to their remuneration. The complainants also submitted that the written terms of employment issued to direct employees of the hirer provided for salary reviews in April of each year whereas the salaries of the complainants remained stagnant at €10.20 per hour.

The respondent contended that the allegation that the complainants were paid less than direct employees of the hirer was factually incorrect. The respondent stated that in accordance with s 15 of the 2012 Act, the respondent had provided details of the applicable rates of pay paid to direct employees of the hirer carrying out the same work as the complainants. This demonstrated that a rate of €10.02 per hour was paid to the direct employees as confirmed by the hirer. The respondent confirmed that the annual salary comprising of basic, shift and attendance payments in the sample contract of employment submitted were correct, and accordingly the hourly rate of pay paid to direct employees of the hirer was below the hourly rate paid to the complainants.

The respondent objected to the submission of the payslips furnished by the complainants on the basis that names had been redacted and accordingly they could potentially relate to non-comparable direct employees of the hirer, as there are nine different positions which are categorised under the 'Ground Operations "Pier A"' designation on the hirer's payslips; these positions ranged from management and supervisory positions to entry level positions.

The Court considered ss 2 and 6 of the 2012 Act and noted that the purpose of the Agency Workers Directive and the 2012 Act is to ensure that agency workers and directly employed workers occupying the same job enjoy the same basic working and employment conditions including, among other things, pay rates: where the basic working and employment conditions of directly employed workers are established by law or by collective agreement, agency workers come within the scope of the legislation or collective agreement; where no collective agreement or legislation applies, agency workers are entitled to 'any arrangement that applies generally' in respect of directly employed workers occupying the same job. The Court noted that no collective agreement or legislation applied in this case, and accordingly that regard must be had to any arrangement that applies generally in determining whether the respondent was in compliance with the 2012 Act.

The Labour Court also noted that there is a requirement on the complainants to prove the primary fact upon which they rely, and the Court was not satisfied that the anonymised payslips submitted were probative of the contentions made by the complainants as the names of the employees had been redacted. The complainants submitted that one of them could give evidence as to the origin of the payslips and that they were reflective of directly employed workers performing the same work as that performed by the agency workers. The Court concluded that the redacted payslips could not be relied upon by the complainants as any such evidence on the origins of the payslips would be inadmissible hearsay evidence, as the person to whom the payslip was attributed to was not available to give evidence.

The Court examined the information supplied relating to the sample contract of employment for direct employees of the hirer which both parties accepted as representing the basic pay and conditions of employment for comparable employees of the hirer. The Court noted that directly employed workers of the hirer are paid an annual salary made up of the following elements: basic pay: €15,708; shift premium: €3,476 and attendance payment: €1,651.

The Court noted that by comparison, the complainants' pay comprised of the following annual payments: basic pay: €17,992; shift premium: €1580.80, and attendance payment: €1,651.

The Court observed parity in attendance payments and noted that these were contingent payments, paid depending on the employees' attendance pattern. The Court then examined the remaining elements of pay, noting that it was accepted by both sides that the liability to work shift, weekends and Sundays was identical for both sets of employees, and in such circumstances, the pay elements must be combined to arrive at its decision. The Court concluded that in accordance with the definition of 'pay' as contained in the 2012 Act, and when the pay elements were aggregated, the complainants are paid the sum of €21,223.80 per annum whereas the direct employees of the hirer are paid €20,835 per annum. Since the pay of the complainants is greater than that of the direct employees for performing the same work, the decision of the Rights Commissioner was upheld and the appeal failed.

The meaning of temporary in the UK Agency Work Regulations 2010

[25.03] *Moran & Ors v Ideal Cleaning Services Ltd and Anor*[4] *– UK Employment Appeal Tribunal – whether claimants who had been placed with second respondent for up to 25 years could be regarded as agency workers – meaning of 'temporary' in the Agency Workers Regulations 2010 – intended effect of Directive on Temporary Agency Work*[5]

The claimants were employed as cleaners by the first respondent and were placed with the second respondent for periods of many years (in one case for 25 years) until they were made redundant. They asserted that they were agency workers within the meaning of the UK Agency Workers Regulations 2010 (SI 2010/93) which defines in reg 3 that an 'agency worker' is an 'individual who so far as material was supplied by a temporary work agency to work temporarily for and under the supervision and direction of a hirer'.

In a preliminary ruling, Judge Swann in the Employment Tribunal considered the meaning of the concept 'temporary' in the 2010 Regulations and made reference to the dictionary definitions of temporary being 'not permanent' and 'lasting only a short time'. Swann J concluded that the claimants were not agency workers as defined in the 2010 Regulations as they were not supplied by the first respondent to the second respondent to work temporarily. This preliminary ruling was appealed by the claimants on the basis that the judge had erred in interpreting 'temporary' to mean 'short term'. The claimants further argued that all agency workers would fall within the scope of the 2010 Regulations provided they met the 12-week qualification period and this was

---

4.   *Moran & Ors v Ideal Cleaning Services Ltd and Anor* UKEAT/0274/13/DM.

5.   Directive 2008/104/EC.

necessary to give effect to the purpose of the Directive on Temporary Agency Work, which the 2010 Regulations were intended to implement.

The UK EAT dismissed the appeal, and found that the concept of 'temporary' in the 2010 Regulations and the Directive meant 'non-permanent'.

The word 'temporary' can mean something not permanent or it can mean something fleeting, short term. The two are not necessarily the same and the UK EAT gave the example of a contract of employment of a fixed duration of many months or years, which can be regarded as temporary as it is not permanent, but would not ordinarily be regarded as being short-term. To use the word permanent does not mean forever, as every contract is terminable on proper notice being given but what is meant is that it is indefinite, ie open ended in duration, whereas a temporary contract will be terminable upon some other condition being satisfied, for example the expiry of a term or satisfaction of a purpose.

To hold that all agency workers come within the 2010 Regulations and Directive would give no meaning to the word 'temporary' at all and would fail to give true effect to the underlying purpose of the 2010 Regulations and the Directive. The UK EAT noted that the draft Directive was amended to introduce the concept of 'temporary', suggesting that the introduction of that word was intended to have legal significance and should be given effect.

The UK EAT found that the Employment Tribunal had found that the arrangements under which the claimants worked were indefinite in duration and therefore permanent and not temporary and it had not erred in concluding that the claimants were outside the scope of the 2010 Regulations.

Chapter 26

TRANSFER OF UNDERTAKINGS

CHANGE IN SECURITY/CLEANING CONTRACTORS

[26.01] *An Employee v An Employer and An Employer[1] – Employment Appeals Tribunal – Redundancy Payments Acts 1967 to 2014 – Minimum Notice and Terms of Employment Acts 1973 to 2005 – European Communities (Protection of Employees on Transfer of Undertakings) Regulations 2003 (SI 131/2003) – whether transfer of undertaking had taken place – retention of identity of economic entity*

This case concerned a change in the provision of security services. At the initial hearing of the case, the claimant's representative disputed that a transfer of an undertaking had taken place and the EAT considered the matter. Subsequently, the EAT directed that the Form T1A be amended to include the second respondent so that they could be a party to the proceedings to assist the EAT in establishing if a transfer of an undertaking took place.

The second respondent gave evidence that the contractor had not provided it with information regarding a transfer of undertaking and they had had no contact with the first respondent before they took over the contract on site. The second respondent argued that it conducted the security service in a different manner from the way it had been conducted by the first respondent.

The EAT referred to the decision of the CJEU in *Ayse Süzen v Zehnacker Gebäudereinigung GmbH Krankenhausservice[2]* where it was held that Directive 2001/23/EC does not apply to a situation where there is no concomitant transfer from one undertaking to the other of significant tangible or intangible assets or the taking over by the new employer of a major part of the workforce. The EAT noted that the second respondent did take over most of the existing workforce, but it was also clear that there was no transfer of assets. The EAT noted from *Ayse Süzen* that an entity cannot be reduced to the activity entrusted to it. The EAT held that there was clearly no asset transfer, nor could it be said that the business retained its identity, and therefore, following *Ayse Süzen*, it did not amount to a 'transfer' within the meaning of the Directive.

---

1.   *An Employee v An Employer and An Employer* RP2097/2010, MN1500/2010, WT660/2010.
2.   *Ayse Süzen v Zehnacker Gebäudereinigung GmbH Krankenhausservice* (Case C–13/95).

INTERACTION OF THE DIRECTIVE WITH MEMBER STATES LAWS TO LIKE EFFECT

[26.02] *Amatori v Telecom Italia SpA[3] – CJEU – Council Directive 2001/23/EC[4] – request for preliminary ruling – whether Directive precluded national legislation which on transfer of part of undertaking permits transferee to take over employment relationship from transferor if that part of undertaking does not constitute functionally autonomous economic entity existing before transfer – whether Directive precluded national legislation which enables transferee to take over employment relationship, if after transfer of part of undertaking concerned, transferor exercises extensive and overriding powers over transferee*

This was a request for preliminary ruling referred by an Italian Court following on from an internal re-organisation by Telecom Italia SPA (Telecom Italia).

Telecom Italia's technology and operations division was divided up into pieces, which included the IT operations section. The employees in that section continued to collaborate with employees from another of the newly formed sections. Mr Amatori and the other 74 applicants were assigned to the IT operations section. In April 2010, Telecom Italia transferred that section to its subsidiary, Telecom Italia Information Technology SRL (TIIT) in the form of a contribution in kind to TIIT's capital. The applicants continued, without their consent, their employment relationship with the transferee in accordance with Italian law.

The applicants brought proceedings to an employment tribunal seeking a declaration that their employment relationship with Telecom Italia had continued. They argued that the transfer had not been a transfer of an undertaking, as, before the transfer, the IT operations section had not constituted a functionally autonomous subdivision within the structure of Telecom Italia and moreover the section had not existed before the transfer; the transferor exercised overriding power over the transferee and the transferee continued to carry out the greater part of activities for Telecom Italia.

The relevant sections of the Italian Civil Code were art 2112, paragraph sub-s 1 and art 2112 sub-s 5. Art 2112(5) provided:

> the provisions of this Article shall also apply to the transfer of part of an undertaking, understood as a functionally autonomous part of an organised economic activity within the meaning of this paragraph, existing as such before the transfer and retaining its own identity during the transfer.

The applicants took the view that the legal transfer could not be classified as a transfer of an undertaking within the meaning of the Italian Civil Code. The applicants argued that, before the contribution of the IT operations section to the capital of TIIT, that section had not constituted a functionally autonomous subdivision within the structure of Telecom Italia and moreover that section had not existed.

---

3.   *Amatori & Ors v Telecom Italia SpA and Anor* (Case C–458/12).
4.   Council Directive 2001/23/EC on the approximation of the laws of the Member States relating to the safeguarding of employee's rights in the event of transfers of undertakings, businesses or parts of undertakings or businesses.

The CJEU noted that the Directive is applicable wherever, in the context of contractual relations, there is a change in the natural or legal person responsible for carrying out the business who incurs the obligations of an employer towards employees of the undertaking.[5]

The CJEU made reference to the settled case law when determining whether there is a transfer of the undertaking within the meaning of art 11 of the Directive. The decisive criterion is whether the entity in question maintains its identity after being taken over by the new employer. The Court stated that the transfer must relate to a stable economic entity whose activity is not limited to performing one specific works contract. Any organised grouping of persons and/or assets enabling the exercise of an economic activity pursuing a specific objective and which is sufficiently structured and autonomous, constitutes such an entity. The CJEU stated that the economic entity concerned must have a sufficient degree of functional autonomy.

The concept of autonomy refers to the powers granted to those in charge of the group of workers concerned, to organise, relatively freely and independently, the work within that group and more particularly to give instructions and allocate tasks to subordinates within the group without direct intervention from other organisational structures of the employer. The CJEU held that if it should prove that the entity transferred did not before the transfer have sufficient functional autonomy, which is for the national court to ascertain, that transfer would not be covered by the Directive. In such circumstances there would be no obligation arising under the Directive to safeguard the rights of the workers transferred.

However, the CJEU found that the Directive is not to be read as prohibiting a Member State from providing for the safeguarding of employee rights in the situation described in the preceding paragraph of the judgment. The Court therefore held that the mere lack of functional autonomy of the entity transferred cannot in itself prevent a Member State from providing in its national law for the safeguarding of employee rights after the change of employer. The Court stated that this was supported by art 8 of the Directive which provided that the Directive does not affect the right of Member States to apply or introduce laws regulations or administrative provisions which are more favourable to employees.

The CJEU confirmed that the Directive intended to achieve only partial harmonisation of the area in question. It is not intended to establish a uniform level of protection throughout the European Union on the basis of common criteria, but to ensure that the employee is protected in his relations with the transferee to the same extent as he was in his relations with the transferor under the legal rules of the Member State concerned. The CJEU, in answer to the first question, held that the Directive must be interpreted as not precluding national legislation such as that at issue in this case which, on the transfer of part of the undertaking, permits the transferee to take over the employment relationship from the transferor if that part of the undertaking does not constitute a functionally autonomous economic entity existing before the transfer.

---

5.   *CLECE SA v Valour and Anor* (Case C–463/09).

In a second question, the national court asked whether the Directive must be interpreted as precluding national legislation, which allows the transferee to take over the employment relationships from the transferor if, after the transfer of part of the undertaking concerned, the transferor then exercises extensive overriding powers over the transferee. The CJEU stated that it did not appear from any provision of the Directive that the European Union legislature contemplated that application of the Directive would be conditional on the autonomy of the transferee regarding the transferor. The Court noted that it had been previously held that the Directive was intended to cover any legal change in the person of the employer if the other conditions it lays down are also met and that it can therefore apply to the transfer between two subsidiary companies in the same group which are distinct legal persons each with specific employment relationships with their employees. The fact that the companies in question not only have the same ownership, but also the same management and the same premises and that they are engaged in the same work makes no difference in this regard. An outcome, which would exclude transfers between companies in the same group from the scope of the Directive, would be precisely contrary to the Directive's aim which is, according to the Court, to ensure, insofar as possible, that the rights of employees are safeguarded in the event of change of an employer by allowing them to remain in employment with a new employer on terms and conditions agreed with the transferor.[6]

The CJEU found that in a situation such as in the main proceedings where the transferor undertaking exercises extensive overriding powers over the transferee, which manifests itself through a tight commercial bond and the comingling of business risk, this cannot of itself prevent the application of Directive. The Court stated that a different interpretation would enable the objective of the Directive (to ensure continuity of the employment relationships existing within an economic entity irrespective of any change of ownership) to be circumvented with ease. Thus the Court concluded that the answer to the second question is that the Directive must be interpreted as not precluding national legislation which enables the transferee to take over the employment relationship, if after the transfer of part of the undertaking concerned, the transferor exercises extensive and overriding powers over the transferee.

CHANGE IN WAREHOUSE AND DISTRIBUTION CONTRACTOR

[26.03] *Bligh & Ors v Stobart Ireland Driver Services Ltd[7] – Employment Appeals Tribunal – appeal of decision of Rights Commissioner – European Communities (Protection of Employees on Transfer of Undertakings) Regulations 2003 (SI 131/ 2003) – whether transfer of undertakings occurred when contract for operation of chilled and frozen foods warehouse and national distribution centre transferred from company K to respondent*

---

6.   *Allen v Amalgamated Construction Co Ltd* (Case C–234/98).

7.   *Bligh & Ors v Stobart Ireland Driver Services Ltd* TU 29/2011–TU46/2011.

This was an appeal by the named employees against a Rights Commissioner decision. At the second day of resumed hearing, the EAT was informed that the respondent was no longer defending the appeals.

The appellants were employed by company K, which was contracted to a large supermarket chain to operate a chilled and frozen foods warehousing and national distribution centre. Company K operated the facility from its site in Ballymun. On or about September 2010, company K was notified that the contract was being awarded to the respondent. Subsequently, on 22 October 2010, the contract for the transport section of the business transferred to the respondent. The appellants asserted that a transfer of undertaking occurred, but this was denied by the respondent.

The EAT heard evidence that the contract was for the logistics and transportation of chilled and frozen products from the retailer's Ballymun depot. The transfer function was separate from the warehousing function at the time the appellants contended the transfer occurred. At the time of the alleged transfer, there were a total of 147 company K employees allocated to the transport contract, to include 126 drivers, with the remaining employees working in transport, management and administration. Evidence was given that the drivers represented by the trade union were a distinct bargaining unit and had their own separate agreement with company K to govern pay and terms and conditions of employment and other procedural matters. The use of contractors was minimal and only for a short period in the month prior to the alleged transfer date. At the point of transfer, there were 63 tractor units, 131 trailers, eight rigid trucks, as well as a number of tug-masters and double-deckers. All of this equipment was taken over by the respondent on 22 October 2010. Between February and April 2011, the tractor units and trailers were gradually replaced by units owned by the respondent. The other three vehicle categories owned by the retailer were still used by the respondent. At the point of the alleged transfer, there were a number of support facilities in the retailer's depot owned by the retailer and utilised for the purpose of servicing the transport contract. These facilities included a transport office, parking facilities, refuelling facilities, and truck wash vehicle maintenance operated by a contractor. The facilities were taken over by the respondent from 22 October 2010 and the respondent continued to use the facilities, with the exception of the vehicle maintenance facility, which was later taken on directly by the respondent at the end of 2011.

Evidence was given that there were negotiations between the respondent and company K prior to the transfer with regard to staff either being made redundant or transferring employment to the respondent on existing pay and benefits. However, no consultation took place with the affected employees.

It was asserted by the appellants that a transfer of undertakings had occurred within the meaning of the 2003 Regulations. It was noted that a number of employees did not transfer, but accepted a redundancy payment and a number of other employees had accepted a redundancy payment, but had re-commenced new employment with the respondent under different terms and conditions. The day after the respondent took over, 18 of the appellants started work with the respondent without any break in employment and without being offered either a redundancy payment or new employment. They transferred to the respondent's terms and conditions and their statutory entitlements were preserved in agreement with the respondent. However, due to the refusal of the respondent to acknowledge the transfer of undertaking, the trade union was reluctant to enter into an agreement with the respondent without prejudice to the rights of the members to pursue claims under the 2003 Regulations for their full rights and entitlements and without prejudice to the driver's collective agreements. It was asserted by the appellants that the parties were in breach of reg 4 of the 2003 Regulations in so far as it provides that the transferor's rights and obligations arising from a contract of employment existing at the date of transfer shall, by reason of such transfer, be transferred to the transferee.

It was noted by the EAT that, prior to the transfer of employment, company K confirmed in writing the terms and conditions of those employees whose employment was transferring to the respondent and the letter which issued to the employees was signed by company K's HR manager and was reflective of the conditions in the collective agreement. It was submitted by the appellants that the respondent had not honoured certain aspects of the contract of employment with reference to rostering, a Christmas bonus and also paid release for local meetings.

It was further asserted by the appellants that the respondent had failed to honour certain aspects of the collective agreement with company K, such as the requirement to consult and agree changes to terms and conditions of employment, provisions in relation to employee representation, procedure and consultation, a clause in relation to disputes, grievance and disciplinary procedures and also with regard to the collective agreement. It was also alleged that the respondent was in breach of reg 7 of the 2003 Regulations as, post-transfer, the status and function of the employees' representatives was greatly reduced by the respondent to the extent that the number of employee representatives had been unilaterally reduced from three to one and that the facilities for the now sole driver representative to carry out his role and function had been greatly reduced, with meetings not scheduled in a timely manner or cancelled with short notice.

It was asserted by the appellants that the respondent did not comply with any part of reg 8 of the 2003 Regulations which requires the transferor and transferee to provide the employees with the information in good time prior to the transfer relating to the legal implications of the transfer and a summary of any relevant economic and social implications of the transfer for them. It was alleged that this was not complied with in any way as the application of the 2003 Regulations to the transfer was disputed and no consultation took place. It was asserted that those drivers who transferred from company K to the respondent, to include the appellants, were constrained to enter into a voluntary agreement. However, the terms of that agreement were considerably less favourable than those provided for in the collective agreement and thus the voluntary agreement constituted a breach of reg 9 of the 2003 Regulations. Finally, it was submitted that the respondent had also failed in its obligations under reg 5 of the 2003 Regulations.

The EAT noted that the information that had been given to the Rights Commissioner regarding the transfer which took place had differed significantly from that given to the EAT and specifically it was noted that the Rights Commissioner had been informed that no tangible assets were transferred between company K and the respondent. However, the EAT was informed by the appellants that all the trucks and other equipment which transferred from company K to the respondent were used as and from that date by the respondent. The EAT noted that, while it appeared that only a small proportion of staff were claiming a transfer of undertaking took place, a very large proportion of staff actually ceased to work with company K on 21 October 2010 and commenced with the respondent the next day. The EAT observed that if the Directive applied, those staff who took or received redundancy at the time could not have been dismissed and, if no dismissal took place (as no dismissal is allowed to take place where the Directive applies) then there could be no redundancy as a matter of law because there must be dismissal in order for there to be a redundancy.

The EAT reviewed the case law and noted as follows:

1. the major criterion in establishing if a transfer took place is whether the undertaking retains its identity after the transfer in that the operation must be the same or similar to that which existed prior to the transfer (*Rask and Christensen v ISS Kantinesservice A/S*);[8]

2. the transfer must relate to an undertaking which is a stable economic entity. This does not mean that the undertaking must be profitable or profit-making. There is no such requirement and the undertaking can be a charity or a public body. The main requirement is that it can be identified as that which operated before the transfer;

3. the transfer must go from one natural or legal person to another natural or legal person who is or who are responsible for operating the entity and who take on the function of an employer with regard to the employees of the undertaking;

4. the EAT must consider whether tangible assets such as trucks, trailers, building equipment or other tangible assets used by the undertaking prior to the transfer have been transferred (*Ayse Süzen v Zehnacker*);[9]

5. intangible assets, such as the knowledge of the workforce, procedures for working, goodwill and customer base was transferred. The value of the intangible assets to the undertaking at the time of the transfer must be also considered;

6. the extent to which the undertaking after transfer resembles the undertaking before transfer. Consideration of the name of the undertaking prior and following the transfer is not of great significance;

7. if the workforce after the transfer is identical or similar to that which existed prior to the transfer, and if the locations of the workforce before and after the transfer are identical or similar, that suggests that a transfer took place;

8. the type of undertaking transferred is also a factor that must be given consideration;

9. there is no need for a direct contractual relationship to exist between the transferor and transferee. The transfer may take place through a third party such as the proprietor of the tangible assets or the person who awards the contract; and

---

8. *Rask and Christensen v ISS Kantinesservice A/S* (Case C–209/91).

9. *Ayse Süzen v Zehnacker Gebaüdereinigung GmbH Krankenhausservice (*Case C–13/95).

10.   whether there was a period of suspension of the activity and, if so, the length of that suspension.

The EAT held that the contract was the transportation and distribution of the retailer's goods in this country and this was the contract that was taken away from company K and given to the respondent on 22 October 2010.

It was noted that the only change that took place was the overall management of the contract and that the passing of the contract between the parties necessitated the transfer of staff vehicles and the use of premises from one party to another. The EAT concluded that this was an easily identifiable undertaking or part of an undertaking. The EAT noted that the question of the undertaking being a stable economic entity did not need much consideration because the facts spoke for themselves. The EAT noted that trucks, trailers, equipment and premises were transferred to the respondent by the retailer. Where such assets are not owned by either the transferor or the transferee, but owned by a third party, such as a retailer, and used by the transferor or transferee during the course of the contract, it is settled law that the Directive would apply. There is no requirement for a direct link between the transferor and the transferee.

The EAT noted that tangible assets did transfer from company K to the respondent and indeed on the facts the respondent had replaced some of the assets subsequent to the transfer which must have been a requirement of the contract between the retailer and the transferee. The EAT noted that an identifiable workforce in almost its entirety also transferred and the expertise and knowledge of the various itineraries used by the workforce in delivering the goods of the retailer must have been a factor in consideration of the retailer when awarding the contract. The EAT noted that the experience of the workforce must be considered an intangible asset of some value to the respondent. In retaining this workforce, they were in a position to provide a continuation of the transportation of the goods to the retailer following the transfer. The EAT noted that the undertaking on 22 October 2010 was almost identical in terms of vehicles, premises, staff, customers, routes to that which existed prior to that date. The only aspect of the undertaking that had changed was the name of the company discharging the duties under the contract.

It was noted that the retailer's contract held by company K prior to 21 October 2010 was not the sole work of company K and the company still traded on this other work subsequent to the passing of the contract. Company K continued to trade without the identifiable element of their workforce which had been working for the retailer contract subsequent to 22 October 2010.

The EAT noted that the type of undertaking in this case encapsulated all of the elements that would be necessary to comprise an undertaking (economic entity) for the purposes of the Directive. It was a stable economic unit containing tangible assets of considerable value along with a stable workforce working to a contract that had an identifiable customer base of the retailer's outlets all over the country.

The EAT considered whether the lack of a contractual relationship between the transferor and transferee would impact on the application of the 2003 Regulations, or whether the question of ownership of the assets transferred would have an effect. The EAT noted that there was no requirement for the transferor or transferee to own the undertaking and no need for a contractual link between the transferor and the transferee.

The EAT noted the provisions of art 11(a) of the Directive, which provided that it shall apply to any transfer of an undertaking or business to another employer as a result of a legal transfer or merger and noted that this made no mention of a requirement for the transferor or transferee to have ownership of such an undertaking or business and therefore there may be no need for the undertaking to be owned by the transferor or transferee.

The EAT noted that there was no gap or period of suspension of the activity of the undertaking as that activity appears to have been continuous. As such the EAT did not need to give consideration to that factor.

The EAT concluded that the passing of the contract from company K to the respondent was a transfer of an undertaking and set aside the decision of the Rights Commissioner. The EAT concluded that the complaints of the appellants that the respondent was in breach of regs 4(2), 7(1) and 8(1), (2) and (3) of the 2003 Regulations were well-founded. The EAT directed the respondent to honour all of the conditions of employment and the terms of the agreement made between the transferor and the representatives of the appellant prior to the transfer and compensate each of the appellants for all and any financial loss suffered by them by reason of the non-adherence of the respondent to the terms and conditions of their employment from the date of the transfer of 22 October 2010 to the date of the determination.

POST SHARE ACQUISITION DE FACTO MERGER

[26.04] *Jackson Lloyd Ltd and Mears Group v Smith*[10] *– UK Employment Appeal Tribunal – Transfer of Undertakings (Protection of Employment) Regulations 2006 (SI 2006/246) – whether claimants transferred under TUPE after transferee purchased all shares of transferor*

This was an appeal of a determination of an Employment Tribunal which found that a TUPE transfer did take place. Jackson Lloyd Ltd (JL) was engaged in the repair and maintenance of social housing and in so doing employed 400 to 450 people. In September 2010 it was in severe financial difficulty and on 1 October 2010, Mears Ltd, (ML) a subsidiary company of Mears Group plc (MG), purchased 100% of the shares of JL. On acquisition, the original board of JL resigned with immediate effect and were replaced by MG Nominees and it was announced by MG, the parent company of ML, to JL's workforce that MG had acquired JL and it was now embarking on a programme of integration. Employees were informed that there would be no changes to their terms and conditions of employment.

The process of the integration began immediately and a team of integration managers and support staff arrived at JL sites to assess working methods and its current situation and to see the integration of JL business and methods into those of MG. Prior to the share purchase the CEO of MG appointed an integrated consultant to manage the integration of JL into MG. The Employment Tribunal noted that this consultant was ultimately pursuing policies and strategies given to him by the CEO of MG and neither

---

10. *Jackson Lloyd Ltd and Mears Group v Smith & Ors* UKEAT/0127/13/LA.

his initial appointment or any instruction given to him emanated from the Board of JL. He was the servant of MG. It was further noted that the CEO and contract director of JL were both removed from office at the date of acquisition without any resolution of the JL.

The UK EAT noted that the Employment Tribunal had established as a matter of fact that, from the date of acquisition by its subsidiary, MG imposed major changes on JL through its integration team and in the absence of any meetings of the JL Board. The Employment Tribunal further noted that control was found to be exercised by MG not by JL or ML and the changes affected every aspect of JL's organisation. However it was noted that, for commercial reasons and to preserve JL's contracts and to avoid the risk that a re-tendering process would be triggered, the outward appearance was given that JL was autonomous, separate and in competition with MG. The UK EAT found however that in reality JL was not an autonomous independent company but from 1 October 2010, JL was nothing other than trading name. From that date on JL's directors and human resources team had no say and no involvement in the dismissal of staff by redundancy or otherwise. These matters were dealt with and decided upon by MG.

Ultimately the Employment Tribunal had to consider whether the claimants had transferred and whether they could bring a claim for a protective award. The Employment Tribunal ruled that a transfer had incurred and that the share purchase by MG's subsidiary provided the context within which MG began to operate JL's business so as to trigger TUPE.

The UK EAT dismissed the respondent's appeal. The EAT found that no error of law was disclosed in the Employment Tribunal's legal directions or in their analysis of facts and conclusions which the UK EAT found to be sufficiently reasoned given their clear findings of fact on the evidence they heard.

LOSS OF A SERVICE CONTRACT

[26.05] *Cavan Industrial Cleaning Services Ltd v Germanaviciene & Ors[11] – Employment Appeals Tribunal – European Communities (Protection of Employees on Transfer of Undertakings) Regulations 2003 (SI 131/2003) – appeal of decision of Rights Commissioner on whether transfer of undertaking in circumstances where loss of a service contract – whether any assets, tangible or intangible, transferred*

This case was heard simultaneously with three other linked cases to determine the correct employer of the respondents and who was liable for outstanding entitlements. The appellant employer denied that any transfer of undertakings took place and stated that everyone was made fully aware that it was not taking on existing staff. The appellant contended that no assets had transferred and relied on the *Ayse Süzen[12]* case. It was submitted by the appellant that the CJEU emphasised in that case that the mere loss of a service contract to a competitor cannot by itself disclose the existence of a transfer within the meaning of the TUPE Directive. In those circumstances, the service

---

11.   *Cavan Industrial Cleaning Services Ltd v Germanaviciene & Ors* TU29–TU36/2013.

12.   *Ayse Süzen v Zehnacker Gebaüdereinigung GmbH Krankenhausservice* (Case C–13/95).

undertaking previously entrusted with this contract did not, on losing a customer, thereby cease to fully exist and it could not be considered that a business or part of a business belonging to it has been transferred to the new awardee of the contract, the appellant.

The EAT noted that in the present circumstances the respondent employees argued that tangible assets had transferred, ie the central vacuum system and the washing machines. However the EAT noted evidence to the effect that the vacuum system and the washing machines belonged to a third party and thus were not assets that could be transferred. Furthermore, the EAT noted that the central vacuum system was inoperative and that the washing machines were, in the opinion of the appellant, not suitable for washing material that contained cleaning chemicals and thus were not used.

The EAT concluded that no assets, tangible or intangible, transferred to the appellant and that the service undertaking previously entrusted with the contract did not, on losing the contract, cease to fully exist and that it could not be considered that the business or part of the business belonging to it had been transferred to the appellant. The EAT was satisfied that a transfer of undertakings within the meaning of art 11 of the 2003 Regulations did not occur. The EAT thus allowed the appeal and overturned the recommendation of the Rights Commissioner in this case.

Chapter 27

UNFAIR DISMISSALS

PRELIMINARY ISSUES

Time limits

Settlement negotiations

[27.01] *O'Connor v McInerney Holdings plc[1] – Employment Appeals Tribunal – Unfair Dismissals Acts 1977 to 2007 as amended – constructive dismissal – preliminary issue – whether exceptional circumstances to extend time period for bringing complaint under s 8(2) of Unfair Dismissal Acts 1997 and 2007 as amended – ongoing settlement negotiations between parties*

This was a constructive dismissal claim arising out of the cessation of the claimant's employment with the respondent company. A preliminary issue arose as to whether the Form T1-A was submitted in accordance with s 8(2) of the Acts and 2007, that is within six months beginning on the date of the relevant dismissal.

The evidence and submissions from the claimant were that his employment had been brought to an end on 16 April 2010. The T1-A was initially received on 25 February 2011 and subsequently returned and completed and received on 14 March 2011, outside the six-month time limited allowed by statute.

It was submitted by the claimant that he did not bring his claim within six months as he had been unaware of the timeframe, and had been in continuous negotiations with the respondent in an attempt to agree a settlement under which the subsequent claim would be avoided.

The EAT noted that the claimant had been managing director of a substantial company and had been in employment since March 1988 with the respondent and held that the situation could not be deemed 'an exceptional circumstance'. The EAT stated that an exceptional circumstance need not be a rare or unprecedented situation, but it cannot be a fact that is commonly, regularly and routinely encountered. The EAT noted that it was not unusual for parties to enter into negotiations after the termination of employment and such negotiations do not prevent or preclude the parallel making of a claim for redress to the EAT or other avenues available. On that basis, the EAT declined jurisdiction to hear the substantive claim.

Medical grounds

[27.02] *Hayes v Cork Education Support Centre[2] – Employment Appeals Tribunal – Unfair Dismissals Acts 1977 to 2007 as amended – preliminary issue whether exceptional circumstances to extend time limit – where claimant's medical report did*

---

1.   *O'Connor v McInerney Holdings plc* UD688/2011.
2.   *Hayes v Cork Education Support Centre* UD254/2014.

not state that her medical issues had prevented her from lodging claim within prescribed time period

The EAT heard detailed submissions from both parties in relation to the circumstances surrounding the initiation of the claimant's claim. It was submitted by the claimant that she was prevented from lodging her claim during the prescribed six-month timeframe due to illness but the respondent did not accept this. The EAT noted that the claimant had presented with a very substantial number of medical issues as outlined in the medical report provided to the EAT. However, the EAT noted that the medical report did not state that the claimant's medical issues had prevented her from lodging her claim form with the EAT. On that basis, the EAT was bound by strict rules laid down by statute and was only allowed to extend the period of six months to twelve months in the event of exceptional circumstances being presented. The EAT noted that it did not have discretion in the absence of exceptional circumstances. The EAT concluded that it had no jurisdiction to hear the claim as it was not satisfied that in this case exceptional circumstances existed.

[27.03] *Keenan v The Governor and the Company of the Bank of Ireland[3] – Employment Appeals Tribunal – Unfair Dismissals Acts 1977 to 2007 as amended – preliminary issue – whether exceptional circumstances justified claim being brought outside of six-month period – medical diagnosis of depression*

The claimant commenced employment with the respondent in January 2001 and her employment ended on 21 October 2011. The claimant lodged a workplace relations complaint form on 19 October 2012, 11 months and 29 days after her employment ended. The claimant and her husband gave evidence in respect of the exceptional circumstances preventing her from lodging her application within the six-month time limit required under the Act. In 2006 she gave birth to her first child and was absent on certified medical leave for depression. She explained to the EAT that she had suffered postnatal depression. In 2010 her second child was born and again she was diagnosed with postnatal depression. She attended her doctor and was certified unfit for work and prescribed antidepressant medication. A letter from the respondent dated 21 October 2011 informed the claimant that due to the lack of submission of further medical evidence and her failure to return to work they were treating her as having resigned and her employment had terminated.

The claimant told the EAT that when she received this letter she was shocked. She continued under medical supervision and was prescribed medication due to her depression which, she stated, was so severe as to prevent her from lodging her application before the six-month time limit elapsed. The claimant gave evidence that she was not even able to attend to everyday tasks, including caring for her children alone or carrying out household tasks. The claimant's husband gave evidence to that effect also. Medical certificates were produced to the EAT up to July 2012 stating the claimant was unfit for work due to depression. These certificates were furnished to the Department of Social Welfare in respect of invalidity benefit.

---

3.   *Keenan v The Governor and the Company of the Bank of Ireland* UD1574/2012.

In August 2012, the claimant began to feel slightly better and in mid-October 2012 she felt strong enough to lodge her application to claim unfair dismissal to the EAT. On cross-examination she stated that she had not lodged her application within the six-month time limit due to her depression but had known when she eventually lodged the claim that there was a 12-month time limit.

The EAT found the claimant to be a credible and cogent witness and took into account the medical certificates submitted up to and including July 2012 stating the claimant was unfit for work due to depression. These certificates corroborated her evidence and the evidence given by her spouse. The EAT noted that it was clear that the claimant was medically diagnosed with depression and was under treatment for same, for at least six months after the date of dismissal. Depression has been recognised as a disability under the Employment Equality Acts 1998 to 2011. The EAT accepted the claimant's evidence as to the debilitating and disabling effects of the illness upon her, and that it prevented her from submitting her claim within the time limited for same.

The EAT therefore found that there were exceptional circumstances preventing the claimant submitting her claim for unfair dismissal within the six month time limit and extended the time to submit the claim for a further six months. Accordingly, the EAT found in favour of the claimant regarding the preliminary issue and determined that it would hear evidence regarding the substantive issue in due course.

Taking up new employment

[27.04] *O'Dwyer v Blackstar Ltd[4] – Employment Appeals Tribunal – Unfair Dismissals Acts 1977 to 2007 as amended – statutory time limits for bringing claim – exceptional circumstances – whether act of taking up new employment constituted acceptance of dismissal*

The claimant lodged her unfair dismissed claim outside of the prescribed six-month time limit. The claimant was dismissed by letter dated 26 July 2011, which stated that the termination date was 10 August 2011. She appealed the decision under the respondent employer's disciplinary procedure. The T1A form was lodged on 13 June 2012, more than 10 months after the specified date of dismissal. The claimant was unaware of any time limits and it was her understanding that her employment status was not finalised until the conclusion of the internal appeal process. In any case, the decision to dismiss was upheld on appeal in December 2011, also outside of the prescribed six-month time limit for filing a complaint.

The EAT heard evidence that the claimant was represented by her union throughout the disciplinary process but represented herself at the appeal stage. After the claimant received the letter of dismissal in July 2011, she took up new employment in nursing from August 2011 until 30 October 2011. Following the appeal hearing the following month, the claimant cared for her terminally ill father and did not seek legal advice until June 2012.

The EAT was satisfied that by taking up new employment in August 2011, the claimant had accepted her dismissal as per the letter dated 26 July 2011. Furthermore,

---

4.   *O'Dwyer v Blackstar Ltd* UD952/2012.

the EAT found the fact that the claimant was capable of taking up new employment demonstrated that there were no exceptional circumstances preventing the bringing of a claim, that would enable it to extend the time for making a claim under the Unfair Dismissals Acts 1977 to 2007 as amended from six months to 12 months. The claim was rejected.

Insufficiency of legal advice

[27.05] *Higgins v Superquinn Ltd T/A Musgrave Operating Partners Ltd[5] – Unfair Dismissals Acts 1977 to 2007 as amended – Employment Appeals Tribunal – appeal of Rights Commissioner recommendation –whether exceptional circumstances to extend time limit for bringing claim on grounds of insufficiency of legal advice*

The claimant gave evidence that he had worked for the respondent's supermarket chain as a retail assistant for more than 30 years. The respondent issued a letter of dismissal in March 2012 and an appeal hearing took place in April 2012 and the dismissal was upheld. The claimant lodged his appeal on 9 October 2012. The claimant asserted that he was unsure as to his legal rights and tried to contact his trade union and later contacted the Glin Centre for advice. He dealt with an officer who told him that he would be able to help him and to leave matters with him. The situation dragged on for five months, at the end of which the officer told him he could not do anything to help. The officer told him to try his local law centre and the claimant went to the law centre in August 2012, where he met a solicitor. The solicitor told him that he would call in 10 to 14 days, but when he contacted him he told him that there was no funding to pursue the matter.

The claimant was referred to another law centre when he rang the centre he did not receive a call back. Ultimately the claimant sought separate advice from a solicitor and the claim was filed with the LRC. The claimant acknowledged that he was a member of a trade union and that his trade union representative had attended the disciplinary meeting and appeal meetings. The respondent had asserted that the claimant had not been prevented from taking a claim within the six-month time limit and indicated that no exceptional circumstances existed in this instance.

The EAT noted that the claimant had submitted that exceptional circumstances warranting an extension of the statutory time limits existed on ground of insufficiency of legal advice. The EAT noted that the claimant's employment was terminated on grounds of misconduct, during which process he was represented by a trade union. The finding of the Rights Commissioner was that there were no exceptional circumstances such as to extend the time limit. The EAT concluded that the claimant was aware of the entitlement to further redress and failed to appropriately adequately or actively pursue the entitlement. The EAT was not satisfied that the claimant was sufficiently proactive in seeking advice and assistance in respect of further redress, particularly from his trade union official, who was in the best position to advise the claimant in respect of initiating a claim. The EAT noted that the claimant had not produced any evidence of a medical condition preventing the initiation of a claim and further the EAT noted that the claimant

---

5.   *Higgins v Superquinn Ltd T/A Musgrave Operating Partners Ltd* UD498/2013.

was in a position to secure alternative employment within three weeks of the termination of his employment. The EAT concluded that the failure on the part of the claimant to obtain further advice and representation following dismissal was solely due to a lack of proactivity on his own part and therefore there were no exceptional circumstances to extend the time limits.

Does a P45 terminate employment?

[27.06] *Vasilveca v Maybin Sports Services (Ireland) Ltd trading as Momentum Support[6] – Employment Appeals Tribunal – appeal of Rights Commissioner decision – Unfair Dismissals Acts 1977 to 2007 as amended – Minimum Notice and Terms of Employment Acts 1973 to 2005 – Redundancy Payments Acts 1967 to 2014 – preliminary issue as to when employment ended – whether sending of P45 definitive*

An preliminary issue arose as to when the employment of the claimant had ended. The respondent submitted that the employment ended in 2009. It was the claimant's case that her employment ended in 2012. The EAT noted that the claimant worked in a number of different offices as a contract cleaner. Her hours began to reduce and one of the respondent's clients engaged her directly in May 2009, which the respondent did not appear to have any issue with. She was offered alternative work in a different part of Dublin, however these offers were not acceptable to her and were refused.

Evidence was heard from the claimant's former manager to the effect that she met her from time to time in various buildings and she had offered work to the claimant which was always refused. The manager gave evidence that she was not aware that the respondent had sought to terminate employment in 2009. The respondent submitted that a P45 together with a payslip in respect of outstanding holiday pay was sent to the claimant in November 2009. The claimant accepted that she received the payslip but insisted she had never received a P45. The respondent adduced no evidence as to when the P45 was initially sent to her. The claimant sent an email in October 2010 advising of a change of address. No reply was received and in October 2011 she wrote to the respondent seeking clarification of her status.

The EAT considered whether the claimant had been advised of a dismissal. The EAT concluded that the claimant had not been notified of any dismissal in 2009 and whilst she had not worked for the respondent since July 2009 the EAT stated that it was satisfied that she remained in employment. It noted that on the occasions she had met her manager subsequent to this date in 2009 she had been offered work.

The EAT found that 'in order to be dismissed an employee must in general be told in clear and unequivocal terms that the employment has come to an end. What these terms might be will depend on the facts of any given case'. In this particular case the EAT did not make a finding in respect of whether the sending of a P45 was sufficient to constitute a clear and unequivocal ending of employment however it did conclude in favour of the claimant and overturned the original decision of the Rights Commissioner in that the substantive claim was not validly brought in time.

---

6. *Vasilveca v Maybin Sports Services (Ireland) Ltd T/A Momentum Support* UD1655/2012, RP421/1012, MN436/2012.

Where a claim is filed before the alleged date of dismissal

[27.07] *Brady v Employment Appeals Tribunal and Bohemians Football Club (Notice Party)*[7] *– High Court – Barrett J – application for judicial review – whether unfair dismissals claim validly filed with Employment Appeals Tribunal when filed before alleged date of dismissal*

The applicant was employed as a bar manager by the respondent for three years when he was dismissed from his employment by reason of redundancy on 16 December 2011. He queried when his dismissal was effective and was informed '*now*'. However, no written notice of dismissal was ever provided to him, nor did he receive a P45 form. A T1A claim form was completed on the applicant's behalf, dated 22 December 2011 and lodged in the EAT on 23 December 2011. The date of redundancy was stated to be 16 December 2011. The High Court noted that no jurisdiction issue was raised by the respondent in its T2 form, which was filed on 12 March 2012. At the hearing of this matter before the EAT, the respondent raised the issue that the unfair dismissals claim was out of time as it was received by the EAT before the dismissal took effect when the alleged two-week redundancy period was taken into account. The EAT subsequently held that it had no jurisdiction to hear this matter as the claim had been filed before the actual date of dismissal.

This claim was an application for judicial review seeking an order of *certiorari* quashing the decision of the EAT that it did not have jurisdiction to hear the claim and a further *mandamus* order compelling a different division of the EAT to hear the appeal and further or in the alternative a declaration that the EAT did have jurisdiction to hear the substantive claim and further or in the alternative a declaration that the employer was estopped from relying on the jurisdictional point having regard to its actions.

Barrett J considered the law of estoppel as enunciated by Charleton J in *National Asset Loan Management Ltd v McMahon & Ors, National Asset Management Ltd v Downes*.[8] The High Court noted that the employer in this case gave the clearest indication to the applicant that the termination of his employment had immediate effect from the moment it was advised to him. This express oral representation by a representative of the employer was so clear and unequivocal that reasonably construed it would be unfair and inequitable to allow the employer to subsequently rely on the contention that in fact the date of dismissal occurred some two weeks later. Barrett J concluded that the employer was estopped by its actions from raising the contention, but noted that this did not have the effect that the EAT was wrong in denying jurisdiction to hear the claim. Barrett J then went on to consider the time limits set out in s 8(2) of the 1977 Act (as amended) and noted that there was provision in the Act for a limited extension of the time period, but this was not relevant here. The Court noted that prescribed time periods are typically intended to thwart the tardy and not to punish the prompt. The Court also noted the longstanding principle of equity that 'equity aids the

---

7.   *Brady v Employment Appeals Tribunal and Bohemians Football Club (Notice Party)* [2014] IEHC 302.

8.   *National Asset Loan Management Ltd v McMahon & Ors, National Asset Management Ltd v Downes* [2014] IEHC 71.

vigilant, not the indolent'. The third issue identified by the Court was whether the EAT could be said not to have received notice within a prescribed period, if it had notice immediately prior to, at the commencement of, and throughout that period.

Barrett J stated that it would be absurd to hold that, where the EAT had notice of the claim at the commencement of and throughout the six-month period, the applicant should be denied the opportunity to bring his claim because the EAT, through no fault of the applicant, may have also have had notice of the claim immediately prior to the applicable six-month period. Barrett J stated that, in reaching this conclusion, no violence was done to the language of the Act. Section 8(2) required that notice be given within the period of six months from the date of dismissal. The Court noted a decision of the EAT in *Matthews v Sandisk International Ltd*[9] where the EAT found that leaving the T1A with the secretariat to the EAT prior to the commencement of the statutory period, where the form was with the secretariat at the commencement of the statutory period and throughout that period, meant that the claimant had given notice within the statutory period as well as for an additional period.

By way of conclusion, Barrett J stated that the purpose of the law, the principles of equity, the practical reality and the previous case law of the EAT all led to the same conclusion, which was that the EAT does and did have jurisdiction to hear the applicant's claims. The Court ordered that the decision that the EAT did not have jurisdiction be quashed and that a different division of the EAT be constituted to hear the applicant's claim. The Court further declared that, having regard to the unequivocal representation of the employer that the applicant's determination of employment was of immediate effect, the employer was now and in the circumstances of this case thereafter estopped from relying on the contention that in fact the date of dismissal occurred some two weeks later.

[27.08] *Barry v Newbridge Silverware Ltd*[10] *– Employment Appeals Tribunal – Unfair Dismissals Acts 1977 to 2007 as amended – preliminary issue – whether in terminating employment for gross misconduct, employer intended notice payment to be made – whether claimant submitted her T1A too early and prior to expiry of her notice period – whether EAT can have jurisdiction in such circumstances*

The EAT considered a preliminary issue arising from a decision of the respondent to terminate the claimant's employment for gross misconduct. In a letter dated 10 September 2012, the respondent stated 'the company views your actions as gross misconduct and therefore has taken the decision to terminate your employment with immediate effect'. The letter then stated: 'I have instructed the payroll department to pay eight weeks' basic salary from Monday 10 September'.

Evidence was given to the EAT to confirm that the claimant was entitled to eight weeks' notice under statute, based on her length of service, and this was paid through payroll on 13 September, accompanying the claimant's P45. The claimant submitted a T1A challenging the termination of her employment on 4 October 2012. The respondent

---

9.   *Matthews v Sandisk International Ltd* UD331/2010.

10.   *Barry v Newbridge Silverware Ltd* UD1517/2012.

claimed that this T1A claim was pre-emptive and did not take into account the eight-week notice period, which would have run from 10 September 2012. It was submitted by the respondent that the actual date of termination must have been the date of the expiry of the notice period for which the claimant was paid in lieu, which was 12 November 2012. The claimant referred to the fact that this was a summary dismissal for gross misconduct and referenced the reference to 'immediate effect' in the letter received by her. She asserted that the sum of money paid by the respondent was intended as a 'goodwill gesture' as opposed to notice pay.

The EAT noted that the date of dismissal is prescriptively imposed by legislation as being the date on which notice expires, whether notice is imposed by contract or statute. The EAT noted that it had been asked by the claimant to resolve any ambiguity in her favour. However, the EAT stated that it was of the view that 'where such an ambiguity exists, the first thing the Tribunal should do is imply that notice is always intended to be given and such an implication is in the employee's favour'. The EAT concluded that it could not accept that the instruction to payroll to pay eight weeks of basic pay from a particular date could be interpreted as meaning anything other than an intention to dispose of the respondent's notice obligations. The EAT concluded that the date of termination of employment was 12 November 2012, being the expiry of the notice period and thus the claimant's T1A was received too early and in the course of her ongoing employment. The EAT thus declined jurisdiction to hear the substantive unfair dismissal claim.

Locus standi

[27.09] *O'Farrell v County Dublin VEC[11] – Employment Appeals Tribunal – Minimum Notice and Terms of Employment Acts 1973 to 2005 – Unfair Dismissals Acts 1977 to 2007 as amended – Redundancy Payments Acts 1967 to 2014 – Organisation of Working Time Act 1997 – preliminary application – locus standi – whether claimant was office holder of VEC and therefore excluded from protection afforded by Unfair Dismissals Acts 1977 to 2007 in reliance on Vocational Education Act 1930, s 23 – whether employee employed as permanent part-time hourly paid tutor or fixed-term employee as at date of termination*

The claimant was employed since October 2008 as a part-time tutor of Food, Catering and Nutrition placed in The Priory Youth Reach Centre, teaching students who were early school leavers. The claimant initially worked 12 hours per week on the basis of a four-day week. On commencing employment, the claimant was given a contract of employment for the period from 28 October 2008 to 30 January 2009. This contract expressly stated that the employment was temporary and that the Unfair Dismissals Act would not apply to a dismissal on expiry of the term. It was accepted by the parties that this document was not signed by either party and no further contract issued when it expired. The claimant was laid off for August 2009 due to academic holidays and was re-engaged on a temporary specific purpose basis from 2009, pending the filling of a fixed-term post through an open recruitment competition, which was advertised in

---

11.   *O'Farrell v County Dublin VEC* UD114/2012, MN60/2012, RP87/2012, WT29/2012.

March 2010. The claimant applied for the position in open competition, which was stated to be fixed-term/part-time class contact hours, and took up the position on 29 June 2010. The claimant alleged that she was without a contract of employment or renewal of same for a period from February 2009 to September 2010 and it was argued on her behalf that the provision of a purported fixed-term contract to her in September 2010 could not disentitle her to the status of permanent part-time hourly paid employee.

The claimant was placed on a period of layoff during August 2011, as was standard, and she resumed her duties as normal in early September 2011. However, without any warning, at the end of her first week in September 2011 she was advised that her contract would not be renewed. It was submitted on the claimant's behalf that there was no mention of redundancy and that the reason she had her employment terminated was due to her perceived temporary and fixed-term status, which was not a fair reason for dismissal.

The respondent conceded that the claimant was an officer of the VEC and accordingly excluded from protection under the Acts.

It was submitted by the claimant that s 23 of the 1930 Act was repealed in its entirety by the Vocational Education (Amendment) Act 2001 effective from 20 July 2001. Whilst there was a very limited saving provision contained in the 2001 Act, which applies to officers appointed prior to the date of repeal, this had no application to the claimant. Since the repeal of this legislation, the powers of VECs to appoint employees emanate entirely from s 20 of the Vocational Education (Amendment) Act 2001, which is a section under which the claimant would have been appointed. This section refers to the powers of VECs to appoint persons to be members of staff as it may from time to time determine. The claimant submitted that there was no longer a power of VECs to appoint any officers, save as to a chief executive officer.

The reference to members of staff in s 20 clearly meant that the claimant was not an officer of the respondent and could not lawfully be treated as such, given the repeal of s 23 of the 1930 Act.

The EAT noted the submission made by the respondent that the claimant was an office holder of the VEC and was therefore precluded from the protection afforded by the Unfair Dismissals Act under s 2(1)(j). The EAT stated that it preferred the claimant's legal submissions and it was mindful of the fact that s 23 of the Vocational Education Act of 1930 had been repealed since 2001. This fact undermined the respondent's definition of the claimant as an office holder as the 2001 Act now afforded such appointees the description 'members of staff'.

Application for a postponement pending the outcome of High Court proceedings

[27.10] *O'Doherty v Independent Newspapers (Ireland) Ltd[12] – Employment Appeals Tribunal – Unfair Dismissals Acts 1977 to 2007 as amended – preliminary issue – application for adjournment pending outcome of High Court defamation case and on*

---

12. *O'Doherty v Independent Newspapers (Ireland) Ltd* UD234/2014.

basis that claimant's application to EAT for expedited hearing date was made ex parte
– application for expeditious hearing dismissed

The EAT was asked to determine two preliminary issues in respect of the claimant's unfair dismissal claim. Firstly, whether the claimant's claim ought to be adjourned to the date it would have normally been allocated had the claimant not applied *ex parte* for an expedited hearing and secondly, whether the hearing of the claim should be adjourned pending the outcome of the claimant's High Court defamation proceedings.

The claimant was a journalist with the respondent newspaper since 1995. Her position was made redundant in August 2013. The claimant challenged this redundancy, arguing that the redundancy was a sham and that it was retribution for her work on a particular story. The respondent denied any retribution and contended that the claimant's employment ceased by reason of genuine redundancy.

On 7 February 2014, the claimant instituted High Court defamation proceedings against the respondent and, on 8 February 2014, the claimant lodged her appeal of the rights commissioner decision with the EAT. During the preliminary hearing before the EAT, it was also noted that there was evidence to suggest that the claimant might also institute personal injuries proceedings against the respondent. On 15 April 2014, the claimant made an *ex parte* application to the EAT to have her unfair dismissals case expedited. The sitting EAT acceded to the application; however, it was noted in this decision that it was unclear why the EAT permitted the claimant's case to be expedited.

The respondent argued that the EAT should not have permitted the claimant's case to be advanced for an expedited hearing. The respondent submitted that, having regard to the existence of the defamation and possible personal injury proceedings, the unfair dismissals case should not have been afforded priority over other cases. Counsel for the respondent noted that the EAT had the power to adjourn the proceedings where it deemed it appropriate to do so.

The respondent argued that as the defamation case would be heard by a jury, whatever would be said at the EAT would be likely to have a prejudicial effect on the jury. Counsel for the respondent referred to a number of cases where the EAT had adjourned cases where the case before it was inextricably interlinked with ongoing High Court proceedings in the same matter. The respondent argued that to permit the unfair dismissals case to proceed would result in an obvious unfairness to the respondent.

The claimant argued that there was no reason why the claimant's unfair dismissals case should not be dealt with expeditiously. It was submitted that pursuing an unfair dismissal case was intended to be an inexpensive remedy for financial loss suffered by the claimant as a result of the unlawful actions of the employer. It was further submitted that if the unfair dismissal case were adjourned pending other proceedings, it would cause hardship to any employee bringing other claims, resulting in the loss of the opportunity to be compensated for wrongful/unlawful actions by the employer. Counsel for the claimant submitted that if a personal injuries action and/or defamation action arose out of the same set of facts, the employee should not have to choose between the remedies available to them.

The EAT examined the statement of claim in the defamation proceedings to ascertain if there was an overlap or an inextricable link between the defamation and unfair dismissal action. The EAT noted that in her statement of claim, the claimant did not make a claim for compensation for loss of earnings other than by referring to 'loss'. The EAT was satisfied that in the claim before it, a 'demarcation line' could be drawn between the case before the High Court and the unfair dismissals claim.

The EAT also referred to the fact that in the unfair dismissals claim the onus of proof was on the respondent to satisfy the EAT that the dismissal was fair having regard to all the circumstances. In contrast, in the High Court proceedings, the onus of proof would rest with the claimant to satisfy the jury that the respondent/defendant defamed her. In reaching this conclusion the EAT accepted that the alleged defamation conduct arose directly from the plaintiff/claimant's employment, however, it was not 'intimately interlinked' with the unfair dismissals claim. The EAT accepted the claimant's submission that it would be unfair for employees to be deprived of the right to a speedy hearing in unfair dismissals cases on the basis that the employee had other claims against their employer.

The EAT dismissed the application for adjournment.[13]

[27.11] *Hickey v Bloomfield House Hotel and Bloomfield Hotel Co Ltd[14] – Unfair Dismissals Acts 1977 to 2007 as amended – claim of constructive dismissal arising out of claimant's employment with respondent hotel – preliminary application to postpone EAT hearing to allow High Court personal injury proceedings to proceed*

The respondent made an application for the postponement of these proceedings on the second day of hearing, in circumstances where the claimant was still under oath having given a half day's evidence to the EAT.

The respondent sought a postponement of the proceedings for at least an 18-month period to allow High Court personal injury proceedings to run their course. The claimant had initiated these proceedings one year after the alleged dismissal. The personal injury summons had been opened to the EAT and the claim was one for personal injury arising out of the respondent's purported treatment of the claimant in the workplace.

The respondent contended that the pleadings outlined in the personal injury summons were exactly the same as the evidence given by the claimant in the oral hearing on the first date of hearing before the EAT in October 2013 and that at some point in the future the High Court would be asked to hear the exact same evidence and the facts to which the EAT will have already heard. The respondent had expressed concerns the prejudicial nature of any findings of fact and in particular where the EAT makes findings of facts adverse to the respondent.

Reference was made to the principle in *Henderson v Henderson*[15] which supported the proposition that there should be finality in litigation and that a party should not be twice vexed in the same matter. Hedigan J accepted this in *Cunningham v Intel Ireland*[16]

---

13.   It should be noted that this EAT claim was settled between the parties in December 2014.

14.   *Hickey v Bloomfield House Hotel and Bloomfield Hotel Co Ltd* UD384/2012.

15.   *Henderson v Henderson* [1843] 3 Hare 100.

16.   *Cunningham v Intel Ireland* [2013] IEHC 207.

when he said 'all matters and issues arising from the same set of facts or circumstances must be litigated in the one set of proceedings save for special circumstances'.

The EAT stated it must be absolutely mindful of the desirability of not duplicating proceedings but must balance this with the honest exercise of its own limited statutory function and jurisdiction. The EAT noted that it had been asked by the claimant to make a finding that she had terminated her contract of employment in circumstances where her employer's conduct had made it reasonable for her to do so. If successful, the claimant would be entitled to redress for financial loss which could be attributed to her dismissal.

The EAT held that such a financial loss is in practice limited to loss of income as experienced by a claimant who has been found to be unfairly dismissed and where such financial loss is attributable to that dismissal (up to the value of 104 weeks). The EAT noted the decision of MacMenamin J in *Stephens v Archaeological Development Services Ltd*[17] which had followed the observations of Lavin J in *Quigley v Complex Tooling and Moulding Ltd.*[18] The EAT noted that these cases created a line of authority for the proposition that where an employee has acquired a common law cause of action against an employer prior to his dismissal, the cause of action in tort might proceed in the High Court and may exist independently of the infringement of the statutory right not to be dismissed unfairly.

The EAT noted that it was established practice that redress can only be made in respect of periods of time where a claimant is available for work and making active efforts to find such employment. Thus where a claimant is found to be unavailable for work by reason of ill health, the EAT is not in a position to compensate for those periods of time.

The EAT therefore recognised that the question of avoiding double recovery should be guarded against at all times. The claimant acknowledged that there could be no question of double recovery and the High Court would not be asked to award damages for periods of time post-dismissal where the plaintiff suffered financial loss attributable to the fact of dismissal.

The EAT held that there was a very real demarcation line between the consequential financial loss suffered by the employee who was being unfairly dismissed and the general damages awarded to the plaintiff who has suffered personal injury as a result of how she was purportedly treated at the hands of a defendant employer. The EAT could not make any assessment in relation to personal injury issues as that is a preserve of the civil courts. The EAT could however assess financial loss which is directly attributable to the unfair dismissal.

With reference to *Cunningham v Intel Ireland Ltd*[19] the EAT found that a clear distinction can be drawn between that case and the line of authority set up by Lavin and MacMenamin JJ in so far as the Equality Tribunal and the Labour Court on appeal can assess compensation in the manner comparable to the way in which the civil courts might be expected to assess general damages for personal injury. The EAT noted the

---

17.   *Stephens v Archaeological Development Services Ltd* [2010] IEHC 540.

18.   *Quigley v Complex Tooling and Moulding Ltd* [2005] IEHC 71.

19.   *Cunningham v Intel Ireland Ltd* [2013] IEHC 207.

Labour Court's approach in *Notoko v City Bank*[20] where the Labour Court observed it would not be inappropriate for it to consider the plaintiff's medical reports in assessing the compensation to be awarded. The EAT stated that this could certainly give rise to the possibility of double recovery which is to be avoided.

In evidence before the EAT the claimant stated that she was anxious to have her EAT case proceed as expeditiously as possible and the EAT stated its sympathy for the claimant in this regard. The EAT noted that this case had stated in October 2013 and the claimant had given comprehensive evidence in relation to workplace relationships. The EAT noted that, to date, not much evidence had been given on any health issues which may have arisen and the thrust of the evidence already heard was in connection with the claimant's need to establish that she had acted reasonably in opting to resign her position. The EAT took into consideration the fact that the time for making such an adjournment application was in October 2013 before it had engaged with the process of hearing this case. The EAT concluded that it would be unfair to the claimant if she were now asked to put these proceedings on hold for an indefinite and notable length of time. The EAT noted that the respondent was vague about when the personal injury proceedings might be expected to come on and no effort was made to come to an agreement about pushing the civil action on as quickly as possible. The EAT concluded that there were special circumstances which allowed it in the interest of justice and expediency, to refuse the application for the postponement.

Parallel claims

[27.12] *McCarey v Hugh Lennon & Associates Ltd*[21] *– Employment Appeals Tribunal – Unfair Dismissals Acts 1977 to 2007 as amended – Employment Equality Acts 1998 and 2011, s 101(2) – preliminary issue – parallel claims of discriminatory dismissal and unfair dismissal – whether or not EAT should decline jurisdiction – whether Director of the Equality Tribunal had commenced an investigation*

The respondent contended that, as the claimant had lodged claims relating to her dismissal under both the Unfair Dismissals Acts and the Employment Equality Acts, the EAT did not have jurisdiction to hear the appeal unless or until the Director of the Equality Tribunal directed otherwise. Reference was made to s 101(2) of the Employment Equality Acts 1998–2011, which provides that if an individual has referred a case to the Director of the Equality Tribunal and either a settlement has been reached by mediation or the Director has begun an investigation, the individual shall not be entitled to recover damages at common law in respect of that failure. The question in this case was when it can be said that the Director has begun an investigation.

The EAT concluded that s 101(2) did not prevent a claimant from pursuing an unfair dismissal action and a claim for discriminatory treatment under the Employment Equality Acts and recover under both, provided that the discriminatory treatment element is entirely distinguishable and unconnected with the unfair dismissals claim.

---

20.   *Notoko v City Bank* [2014] ELR 116.

21.   *McCarey v Hugh Lennon & Associates Ltd* UD909/2012.

The facts of the case as set out in the appeal to the EAT and the claim to the Equality Tribunal were examined and the EAT noted that these were largely similar and therefore not distinguishable. The EAT referred to the EAT decision in *Cullen v Connaught Gold Ltd*[22] where it was accepted that the requirements of s 101(2) were met when a claim is delegated by the Director of the Equality Tribunal to an Equality Officer and not until then can a Director be said to have begun an investigation. In this case, the Director of the Equality Tribunal had not yet delegated such an investigation and therefore the EAT had jurisdiction to hear the appeal.

See **[22.17]** for EAT decision.

Whether there has been a dismissal

[27.13] *Cullen v Argos Distributors (Ireland) Ltd*[23] *– Employment Appeals Tribunal – Unfair Dismissals Acts 1977 to 2007 as amended – preliminary issue – whether or not employee in fact dismissed – claim under the Unfair Dismissals Acts 1977 to 2007 as amended cannot be made before dismissal takes place*

The claimant was employed by the respondent in its Wexford branch and instituted a claim for unfair dismissal on 10 December 2012. At the hearing of the case the EAT heard evidence on a preliminary issue only – whether or not the claimant had in fact been dismissed.

The respondent argued that when the claimant lodged her claim with the EAT, she was still an employee of the respondent and therefore the EAT had no jurisdiction to hear the claim.

The claimant had not worked for the respondent since 18 June 2012. The claimant gave evidence that on this date an incident happened at which her supervisor and another colleague were present. When the incident complained of took place, the claimant told her supervisor that she could not 'do this anymore' and that she was 'going' and announced her intention to clear her locker. As this evidence was not contested by the respondent, the EAT accepted it, but was not satisfied that it constituted clear and unambiguous words of resignation.

In August 2012, the claimant sent an email to the respondent's HR department in which she sought to explain the circumstances surrounding her absence from work rather as being other than a resignation. In the email the claimant made a claim of bullying and harassment. The claimant subsequently attended a grievance meeting at which there was some discussion in respect of her return to work in another store.

In addition, the claimant submitted medical certificates to the respondent until March 2014. The claimant gave evidence that, as she was claiming a social welfare disability benefit, she thought that she had to continue submitting certificates to her former employer. The EAT noted that, whether or not that was the case, by continuing to submit medical certificates the claimant clearly created the impression for the respondent that she considered herself in employment.

---

22.   *Cullen v Connaught Gold Ltd* UD787/2006.

23.   *Cullen v Argos Distributors (Ireland) Ltd* UD23/2013.

The EAT was satisfied that at no time did the claimant resign from her employment in clear and unambiguous terms and that her actions during her absence from work, namely the submission of medical certificates, submission of a grievance, discussions regarding an alternative place of work and the fact that she made no reference to her resignation in the submission of her grievance but rather referred to her absence from work, were all actions that the claimant would not likely have done if she had in fact resigned.

The EAT determined that it did not have jurisdiction to hear the claim as an unfair dismissal claim could not be made before a dismissal, within the meaning of the Acts, had in fact taken place.

Where an employee continues in employment

[27.14] *Schonfeld v Centre for Effective Services Ltd[24] – Unfair Dismissals Acts 1977 to 2007 as amended – preliminary issue – whether Employment Appeals Tribunal had jurisdiction to hear claim where claimant continued in employment of respondent on same terms and conditions of employment, but in different position after claim form submitted to EAT*

The EAT considered whether it had jurisdiction to hear the complaint of unfair dismissal in circumstances where the claimant continued in employment with the respondent on the same terms and conditions, albeit in a different position, for a number of months after he submitted his claim form to the EAT. The T1A was received by the EAT on 9 January 2013, but the date of termination was agreed as being 12 April 2013. In circumstances where the claim for unfair dismissal was lodged months before the claimant's employment terminated, the EAT declined jurisdiction on the basis that it is fundamental if one claims to have been unfairly dismissed that one must already have been dismissed.

Admissibility of evidence

[27.15] *White v Dawn Meats Group T/A Dawn Meats[25] – Unfair Dismissals Acts 1977 to 2007 as amended – Employment Appeals Tribunal – two preliminary issues – whether collection of photos should be before EAT at outset of hearing – admissibility of certain witness evidence*

This was a claim of unfair dismissal where the EAT was asked to rule on two preliminary issues raised by the claimant. The first issue referenced a collection of photographs which the respondent sought to put before the EAT at the hearing. The EAT determined that only those photographs shown to the claimant during the course of the investigation and disciplinary processes will be admitted when introduced in evidence in the normal way. The EAT further found that should the claimant dispute that any of the photographs were shown to him; this dispute shall be a matter for cross-examination and

---

24. *Schonfeld v Centre for Effective Services Ltd* UD233/2013.
25. *White v Dawn Meats Group T/A Dawn Meats* UD852/2012.

submission. The EAT did reserve the right to admit any other photograph of the workplace, electrical installations or otherwise, that it considered would be of assistance to it in understanding evidence given, provided however that no such photograph would be viewed if the EAT is of the opinion that to do so could prejudice the claimant.

The second preliminary issue concerned an objection by the claimant to the EAT hearing evidence from four witnesses on the basis that none of the individuals had any part in the investigative or disciplinary processes and that no evidence or statement from any of the purported witnesses was put to the claimant during the investigative and disciplinary processes such that he was denied the opportunity to challenge them. It was asserted that to allow such witnesses to give evidence to the EAT could be tantamount to the EAT holding a rehearing of the complaint against the claimant with new evidence introduced that was not given during the course of the investigation/disciplinary procedures.

In considering this request, the EAT examined the agreed minutes of the disciplinary meeting and of the appeal as part of the preliminary application for the exclusion of witnesses. The respondent's representative was asked to give a brief indication to the EAT of the purpose for which she wished to call each of the disputed witnesses.

The EAT stated that it would not prevent the respondent from calling evidence that may have a probative value in the issues before the EAT on the basis of the assertion by the claimant that some of the evidence might be prejudicial. The EAT stated that it was a matter to be explored on cross-examination as to whether, as alleged, insufficient information and inadequate specifics were given to the claimant to enable him to challenge and respond to allegations made against him. The determination of this issue will ultimately be a matter for the EAT. The EAT concluded that as one of the issues in this case is the fairness of the procedures adopted by the respondent, the EAT was of the view that this is an issue that can be determined only on a full hearing of the substantive case. The EAT will not be re-running the respondent's case against the claimant. However, the EAT is entitled to hear the evidence relied upon by the respondent in reaching its decision. In summary, the EAT decided to hear evidence from three of the four witnesses but, in respect of one witness, it concluded that it was not necessary to hear their evidence as the parties were in agreement as to the factual matters concerning that witness.

Where a recommendation has already issued under s 13 of the Industrial Relations Acts 1946 to 2012

[27.16] *McGuire v Sleedagh Farms Ltd*[26] *– Employment Appeals Tribunal – Unfair Dismissals Acts 1977 to 2007 as amended – preliminary issue – whether EAT had jurisdiction to hear claim for unfair dismissal where claimant had already received recommendation from Rights Commissioner in claim under Industrial Relations Acts, s 13 – whether dismissal of claimant by reason of redundancy fair – failure to effect redundancy in fair and reasonable manner*

---

26.   *McGuire v Sleedagh Farms Ltd* UD1320/2012.

The respondent raised a preliminary issue that the EAT had no jurisdiction to hear the unfair dismissals claim brought by the claimant because of a recommendation received by him from a Rights Commissioner under the Industrial Relations Acts. The respondent relied on s 8(10)(b) of the Unfair Dismissals Act 1977 as amended which provides as follows:

> Where, in relation to a dismissal, a recommendation has been made by a Rights Commissioner, or a hearing by the Labour Court under the said Acts has commenced, the employee concerned shall not be entitled to redress under this Act in respect of the dismissal.

The EAT noted that the claim brought by the claimant under the Industrial Relations Acts 1946 to 2012 and in respect of which he received a recommendation, was not a recommendation in relation to the dismissal *per se*, but was a recommendation in respect of a claim regarding his contractual entitlement to an enhanced redundancy sum. The EAT noted that in his evidence to the Rights Commissioner, the claimant had not put his dismissal at issue, but merely sought a determination regarding his entitlement to an enhanced redundancy payment. The EAT, in determining the preliminary issue, noted that a claim in respect of an entitlement to an enhanced redundancy sum may be brought under s 13 of the Industrial Relations Act 1946 even where there is no dismissal and similarly, a claim in respect of a contractual entitlement is a claim that can never be brought to the EAT under the Unfair Dismissals Acts. The EAT concluded that it was not prohibited by s 8(10)(b) as amended, from hearing and determining the claim for unfair dismissal in the circumstances. The EAT further determined that the award made to the claimant by the Rights Commissioner in respect of an enhanced redundancy sum falls to be dealt with in the same way as an award of statutory redundancy lump sum received by a claimant who pursues a claim for unfair dismissal.

Fixed-term contracts

[27.17] *Walshe v Department of Arts, Heritage and Gaeltacht*[27] *– Employment Appeals Tribunal – Unfair Dismissals Acts 1977 to 2007 as amended – Minimum Notice and Terms of Employment Acts 1973 to 2005 – whether EAT had jurisdiction to hear claim where claimant employed under series of fixed-term contracts from 2002 to 2011 – gap of four months between each contract, every year*

The claimant was employed as a visitor guide on a series of fixed-term contracts from 2002 to 2011. Each contract commenced at the end of February and expired at the end of October with a four-month gap between each contract every year. Following the completion of three consecutive seasons of employment, visitor guides could be awarded an exempt status from the open recruitment process for the following season. The claimant received this exemption status for a number of seasons, but following an unsatisfactory performance during the 2011 season, she was required to undergo the normal recruitment and selection process for the 2012 season. She was invited to apply

---

27. *Walshe v Department of Arts, Heritage and Gaeltacht* UD569/2012, MN430/2012.

for the position by way of letter in 2012, but she did not apply for the position and claimed unfair dismissal instead.

The respondent contended that the EAT had no jurisdiction to hear this claim by reason of the fact that the series of contracts under which the claimant was employed were fixed-term contracts for a specified duration and for a specific purpose and were not renewed within a three-month time period as required by s 2(2)(B) of the Unfair Dismissals Act 1977. The respondent claimed that there was no dismissal in circumstances where the fixed-term contract simply expired and the essence of the claimant's case is that her contract was not renewed. The respondent claimed that the claimant could have gone through the selection process and reapplied for the position the following year, but she failed to do this.

The claimant asserted that she was dismissed by reason of the fact that she was required to go through a selection process in circumstances where, for the preceding seven years, she had not been required to go through such process, having acquired during these years an annual exemption. She argued that she had an expectation that her contract would be renewed for the following year. Secondly, the claimant argued that the four-month period that elapsed between the expiry of one contract and next year's contract was a period of layoff.

The EAT noted the provisions of s 2(2A) of the Unfair Dismissals Act 1977. [28] The EAT restated s 2(2B) of the 1977 Act as to what is meant by 'antecedent contract'. The EAT noted that it was common case that the claimant was not re-employed under the contract the subject matter of this claim, or any previous contract within three months of the expiry of her preceding contract. Therefore, the definition of antecedent contract to comply with s 2(2A) was not complied with. It would be open to the claimant to invoke the jurisdiction of the EAT through s 2(2A) of the 1977 Act only if a claimant complied with the four criteria set out therein and on complying with all of these criteria, then the

---

28.　　Section 2(2A) as inserted by s 25 of the Protection of Employment (Exceptional Collective Redundancies and Related Matters) Act 2007: Where, following dismissal consisting only of the expiry of the term of a contract of employment of a kind mentioned in subsection (2) ('the prior contract') without the term being renewed under the contract or the cesser of the purpose of the contract –

(a) the employee concerned is re-employed by the employer concerned within three months of the dismissal under a contract of employment of that kind made by the employer and employee (the subsequent contract) and the nature of the employment is the same as or similar to that of the employment under the prior contract;

(b) the employee is dismissed from the employment;

(c) the dismissal consisted only of the expiry of the term of the subsequent contract without the term being renewed under the contract or the cesser of the purpose of the contract; and

(d) in the opinion of the Rights Commissioner, the Tribunal or Circuit Court, as the case may be, the entry by the employer into the subsequent contract was wholly or partly for or was connected with the purpose of the avoidance of liability under this Act, then

(1) this Act shall, subject to its other provisions, apply to the dismissal and

(2) the term of the prior contract and of any antecedent contracts shall be added to the subsequent contract for the purpose of ascertainment under the Act of the period of service of the employee with the employer and the period so ascertained shall be deemed for those purposes to be one of continuous service.

contracts combined can be regarded by the EAT for computing continuous service so as to qualify under the Unfair Dismissals legislation and to invoke the jurisdiction of the EAT.

The EAT then looked at the contract itself. The EAT rejected the argument that the four-month period between each successive contract was a period of layoff and noted that layoff itself and the circumstances in which it arises quite clearly dealt with in the terms of the written contract. The EAT also rejected the argument that it could disregard the three-month time period under s 2(2B) and consider solely whether under s 2(2A)(d) the purpose of entering into a subsequent contract was for the avoidance of liability under the 1977 Act. The EAT was satisfied that the gap between each annual contract was too long (being over three months) and therefore the claimant failed to satisfy this first hurdle. In the EAT's view, the claimant's argument that she was dismissed for poor performance disentitling her to an exemption from the selection process for a subsequent contract was misconceived as she could only make a claim for her contract being one for a fixed term having complied with s 2(2A) of the 1977 Act as amended. The EAT thus declined jurisdiction in this matter and the claim under the Minimum Notice and Terms of Employment Act failed and was dismissed.

[27.18] *Kemmy v Amgen Technology (Ireland)[29] – Employment Appeals Tribunal – preliminary application – non-application of Unfair Dismissals Acts 1977 to 2007 as amended on expiry of fixed-term contract – Unfair Dismissals Acts, s 2(2)(b) – validity of unfair dismissals exclusion clause*

The respondent employed the claimant on a fixed-term basis from March 2010 to May 2013. On 30 November 2011 his second fixed-term contract lapsed and he did not enter into a third fixed-term contract until May 2012. This contract had a retrospective commencement date of 1 December 2011 and expired on 16 May 2013. The claimant's fixed-term employment was not renewed on the expiry of the third fixed-term contract and the claimant brought an unfair dismissal claim against the respondent. The respondent raised a preliminary issue that the EAT did not have jurisdiction to hear the claim as it was precluded by virtue of s 2(2)(b) of the Unfair Dismissals Acts. Specifically, the respondent asserted that as the claimant's last fixed-term contract was in writing, signed by the claimant and the respondent, and expressly stated that the Unfair Dismissals Acts 1977 and 2007 as amended would not apply on the expiry and non-renewal of the fixed-term contract, the claimant could not proceed with his claim.

The EAT accepted that the respondent had raised a valid preliminary objection to the claimant's proceeding with his claim and determined that it did not have jurisdiction to hear the claimant's claim under the Unfair Dismissals Acts.

Notice entitlement and continuous service

[27.19] *Viel v Mongodb Ltd[30] – Employment Appeals Tribunal – Unfair Dismissals Acts 1977 to 2007 as amended – preliminary point on jurisdiction – claimant accrued*

---

29.   *Kemmy v Amgen Technology (Ireland)* UD1079/2013, MN563/2013, WT187/2013.

30.   *Viel v Mongodb Ltd* UD1772/2012.

11 months service and had entitlement to one month's pay in lieu of notice on termination – whether this could be aggregated to bring claimant within scope of legislation

The respondent contended that the claimant's employment commenced on 7 November 2011 and ended on 19 October 2012 and accordingly constituted less than one years' service as is required under the Unfair Dismissal Act 1977 in order to bring a claim. The respondent also contended that cl 13 of the contract of employment entered into between the parties permitted the respondent to summarily terminate, without notice.

The EAT noted that there was conflict between cl 13 (which permitted summary termination without notice) and cl 3 (which permitted termination and payment in lieu of notice). In effect cl 13 could render cl 3 of the contract redundant. Therefore the EAT placed particular importance on the letter of 19 October 2012 from the respondent to the claimant wherein the respondent stated:

> The Company will pay your contractual entitlements to one month's salary in lieu of notice and for the all outstanding holiday entitlements and or commission that may be due to you as of the 19th October 2012.

The EAT found that it was clear that, as of 19 October 2012, the respondent was affording the claimant one month's notice in line with cl 3 and consequently the EAT was satisfied that the notice period ran from the date of the letter 19 October 2012. Consequently the EAT determined that it had jurisdiction to hear the substantive matter.

Validity of a release

[27.20] *Browne v AA Ireland Ltd*[31] *– Employment Appeals Tribunal – Unfair Dismissals Acts 1977 to 2007 – preliminary point on jurisdiction – waiver/disclaimer in respect of future claims*

In this case a preliminary issue was raised as to whether the EAT had jurisdiction to hear the case as the claimant had been paid an ex gratia payment on top of statutory redundancy and had signed a release in respect of any potential claims against the respondent.

Evidence was given on behalf of the respondent that there had been previous redundancies within the company and ex gratia payments were also made in those cases. During consultations in respect of the ex gratia payments, the claimant was represented by her trade union and the claimant was afforded time to consider the package and disclaimer before signing it. The claimant was also given the option of alternative employment within the respondent. The claimant was informed that she could seek legal advice in relation to the disclaimer if she so wished. Accordingly, it was the respondent's position that the EAT had no jurisdiction to hear this claim as the claimant had signed a

---

31.   *Browne v AA Ireland Ltd* UD191/2013.

disclaimer of her own volition having, been properly advised by her union representative.

The claimant contended that in June 2012 she was already dismissed by way of redundancy (and was paid statutory redundancy) before she later accepted the ex gratia payment and signed the disclaimer. Initially the claimant understood that the ex gratia payment was not dependent on her signing the disclaimer; however, this was not the case. The claimant claimed that she believed that she ultimately had no choice but to sign the release and accept the ex gratia payment. She did not believe that her union representative told her that there was a possibility of alternative employment available nor did her union representative explain the terms of the release to her fully. The claimant acknowledged that she chose not to seek legal advice on the matter before signing the release in July 2012.

The EAT examined the correspondence issued to the claimant in relation to the redundancy, the release, the ex gratia payment, and in particular the letter dated 12 July 2012 attaching the release. The terms of the release essentially discharged any future claim that might arise against the respondent in relation to the claimant's employment, provided for an enhanced redundancy package, set out the legislation under which a possible claim could arise, and advised the claimant to take independent legal advice in relation to the matter.

The EAT noted that the terms of the release were clear and were set out in plain English. Furthermore, the claimant told the EAT that she was aware that it said she could take independent advice but she chose not to (albeit because she indicated that she could not afford a solicitor). The EAT noted that the claimant had an adequate opportunity to consider the terms of the release and adequately inform herself of the consequences of accepting it. The EAT determined that it had no jurisdiction due to the release signed by the claimant discharging any future claim that might arise against the respondent. Accordingly the claim under the Unfair Dismissals Acts 1977 to 2007 failed.

Failure to return from a career break

[27.21] *McDonagh v Enterprise Ireland[32] – Employment Appeals Tribunal – Unfair Dismissals Acts 1977 to 2007 as amended – Redundancy Payments Acts 1977 to 2014 – Minimum Notice and Terms of Employment Acts 1973 to 2005 – career break – failure of claimant to return to position following extended career break – refusal of claimant to accept alternative role – date of termination*

The claimant took a two-year career break on 28 September 2004 which was extended by a further three years to 27 September 2009. The respondent's career break policy provided:

> In the event that the individual does not resume duty on the re-entry date, employment will be deemed to have terminated from the commencement [of] the career break.

---

32. *McDonagh v Enterprise Ireland* UD2179/2011, RP2789/2011, MN2214/2011.

The relevant terms of the career break contract were as follows:

> ... should you wish to be re-employed by [the respondent]. [The respondent] will endeavour to re-employ you as soon as a suitable vacancy arises after the due date of return and no later than 12 months after the end of your Career Break (subject to the policy which is in operation at the time).
>
> There is no guarantee that you will be returned to your original geographic location.
>
> In the event of being unable to resume duty on a designated date you will be deemed to have terminated your own employment.

On 23 March 2009, six months prior to the expiry of the extended career break, the claimant wrote to the respondent indicating that she wished to return to work and she met with the human resources manager to discuss her return. The claimant stated that she wished to return to a research role in Cork. Following this meeting, the respondent commenced the process of looking for a suitable position for the claimant and identified the position of regional development executive for the south west or south east region which would be located in Cork. This option was presented to the claimant at another meeting on 6 August 2010. A profile of the role was sent to her the day before. The claimant sought time to consider this role. She maintained that she had been informed that she would not receive training in the role and that following the meeting the salary scale and grade for the proposed position was not forthcoming. The respondent maintained that the claimant had been informed that she would receive mentoring and that her salary and grade would remain unchanged. The respondent no longer engaged in primary research so there was no such role available to the claimant.

The claimant rejected the proposed role by letter on 23 August 2010. The respondent continued to seek a suitable position for the claimant but failed to identify any other position carrying her salary and grade. By letter dated 10 June 2011, the respondent again offered the claimant the position of regional development executive. A job description was enclosed with the letter and the respondent sought a response within seven days.

The respondent on 22 July 2011 wrote to the claimant outlining its position and again offering her the position of regional development executive. The claimant was asked to communicate her decision by 2 August 2011 and was further informed:

> Should you decide not to return to [the respondent] to commence in this post, in line with the organisation's policy, your employment will be deemed to have been terminated from the commencement of your career break.

No further communication was received from the claimant and thus she received a letter dated 20 September 2011 terminating her employment.

The respondent argued that as per the career break policy, the termination of the claimant's employment was brought about on 28 September 2004 and therefore the claim for unfair dismissal was statute barred and the EAT no longer had jurisdiction. The EAT stated that the date of dismissal is a statutory construct which cannot be changed by agreement between the parties. The de facto termination of the employment was brought about by communications between the parties on some date subsequent to the respondent's letter dated 22 July 2011 or at the latest on receipt of the respondent's letter dated 20 September 2011. Regardless, the termination was within the six-month period for bringing a claim under the Act.

The EAT was not satisfied that the respondent had acted unreasonably. The respondent was no longer engaged in laboratory research and endeavoured to re-employ the claimant in a suitable position carrying the same salary scale and grade. The EAT accepted the respondent's evidence that the claimant had been made aware that her grade and salary would remain unchanged and that she would receive training and mentoring in her new position. The claimant's evidence was that she was aware of the consequences of her failure to respond to the respondent's letter of 22 July 2011.

The EAT found that there was no dismissal and therefore the claim failed.

Where the respondent company is a dissolved entity

[27.22] Devine v GE Grainger Enterprises Ltd T/A Stephen Grainger[33] – Employment Appeals Tribunal – Redundancy Payments Acts 1967 to 2014 – Minimum Notice and Terms of Employment Acts 1973 to 2005 – whether in circumstances where respondent company was dissolved at date of hearing, a decision could be made against an entity that no longer existed

This case concerned a redundancy claim payment brought against an employer which, at the date of hearing, had been dissolved. A preliminary question arose as to whether a decision could be made against an entity that no longer existed. The EAT noted that while the former employer would carry primary liability for an EAT award, there was a secondary liability on the Social Insurance Fund under the Redundancy Payment Acts and therefore the EAT was empowered to make a decision. The EAT determined that to rule otherwise would require the redundant employee to apply to the High Court for an order restoring the dissolved company to the register for the purposes of the proceedings after the liquidation was complete and the EAT stated its view that such a process would be totally uneconomic, apart from all the complications involved. The EAT further noted that such a process would also be unreal as the effect of liability in this case would be the secondary liability on the social insurance fund.

Thus the EAT found that the claim succeeded and awarded the claimant a redundancy lump sum with the caveat that any award made from the Social Insurance Fund was subject to the claimant being in insurable employment during the period.

Does the EAT have jurisdiction where employer is in UK administration?

[27.23] Tracey v Game Stores Group Ltd[34] – Employment Appeals Tribunal – Unfair Dismissals Acts 1977 to 2007 as amended – European Council Regulation (EC) No 1346/2000 – proceedings against respondent in UK administration – requirement of

---

33. *Devine v GE Grainger Enterprises Ltd T/A Stephen Grainger* RP265/2013, MN185/2013.

34. *Tracey v Game Stores Group Ltd* UD1632/2011.

respondent to attend EAT in order to submit its case that EAT did not have jurisdiction to hear case

The claimant sought to bring an unfair dismissal claim against the respondent. The respondent was not represented at the EAT, but the joint administrators of the respondent wrote to the EAT to notify it of the following:

(i)   the appointment of the joint administrators by the English High Court;

(ii) the administration was a UK insolvency procedure; and

(iii) 'In accordance with European Council Regulation (EC) No 1346/2000 (the Regulation), the administration takes precedence over any local legislation. Administration provides that no legal process can be brought or continued against the company without the consent of the administrators or the permission of the court. At this stage, and in the interest of all creditors, the administrators do not consent to the commencement or continuance of any proceedings against the company'.

The EAT stated that if the respondent (and/or the administrators) wished to make a jurisdictional point they should have appeared or instructed a representative to appear on their behalf with their submissions as to why the EAT did not have jurisdiction to hear the claim by virtue of the European Council Regulation.

The EAT examined art 4(1) of the Regulation, which states:

> Save as otherwise provided in this regulation, the law applicable to insolvency proceedings shall be that of the member state within the territory of which such proceedings are opened, hereafter referred to as the State of the opening of proceedings.

The EAT then referred to art 10 of the Regulation, which provides that the effects of insolvency proceedings on employment contracts and relationships will be governed solely by the law of the Member State, governing the employment.

In the present case, the EAT noted that, although the claimant did not have a written contract of employment, it was satisfied that he worked under an implied contract of employment in Ireland and his contractual relationship with the respondent was subject to, and governed by, Irish law. As a consequence, the EAT found that notwithstanding that the insolvency proceedings commenced in England, it had jurisdiction to hear the claim and awarded the claimant compensation of €30,000.

DISMISSALS ON GROUNDS OF CONDUCT

Fair procedures

Obligations on an employer when dismissing for misconduct

[27.24] *Bentley v Tesco Ireland Ltd[35] – Employment Appeals Tribunal – Unfair Dismissals Acts 1977 to 2007 as amended – whether decision to dismiss claimant for*

---

35.   *Bentley v Tesco Ireland Ltd* UD818/2012.

gross misconduct was fair and reasonable – respondent had overpaid claimant for a number of months – discovered by claimant's wife but not revealed to him by her – proportionality of sanction – obligations on employer when dismissing for misconduct[36]

The claimant was employed as a stock control manager in one of the respondent's largest stores and he reported to the duty manager. A number of months after he had started working in Ireland, he was asked to attend a meeting as it was discovered that a double payment was being made to the claimant. It transpired that the UK hub store, where the claimant had previously worked, had continued to pay him in addition to his Irish salary.

An initial fact-finding investigation meeting took place with the claimant who was shocked when the issue was put to him. His first explanation was that his wife dealt with all his finances and that he had no knowledge of any such payment in his UK bank account. After a short break he returned to the meeting and confirmed that, having spoken to his wife, she had been aware of the payments to the UK account but that the money had been spent. A further investigation meeting took place during which the claimant accepted that the money should not have been spent but he insisted he knew nothing of the payments and he claimed his household was under financial strain. The claimant offered to repay the respondent following the sale of his UK home and after his UK debts were cleared. However the claimant showed no remorse and continued to blame his wife for spending the money and asserted that the UK company was in error in continuing to pay him. The claimant was suspended on pay on the grounds of a breach of the respondent's honesty policy; however the suspension was not confirmed in writing.

At a further meeting the claimant supplied the decision maker with the letter from his wife in which she took full responsibility, stating the claimant had no knowledge of the payments. A question arose as to whether the claimant had accessed online pay slips which was denied by him. The claimant stated his wife must have accessed them as she had access to all his codes. The respondent concluded that this explanation was not credible.

In her evidence, the claimant's wife confirmed that she took responsibility for all of the family finances and that at the time the family finances were poor as they were renting accommodation in Ireland and also had private school fees. She realised that the payments were wage payments but decided not to tell the claimant and hoped it would go unnoticed. She admitted spending money on clothes and home furnishings and stated that she was embarrassed by her actions. At the time, she offered to meet with management of the respondent company but that offer was not acceptable to the respondent. The claimant attended a disciplinary meeting. He was not advised in advance that the meeting was disciplinary in nature. In his evidence the claimant said that, had he known, he would have picked a different representative to attend with him. At the final meeting, which was conducted by the same person who conducted the

---

36. There was a preliminary issue in this case as to whether the claimant's period of continuous service with the respondent included his previous service with the company in the UK. The EAT held that it did have jurisdiction to hear the case and noted that the previous service in the UK was recognised by the Irish company and had transferred to the Irish company.

investigative and disciplinary meetings, the claimant was advised that he was being dismissed based on the honesty policy of the respondent. The decision was upheld on appeal.

The EAT noted that some of the dates and numbers of meetings were disputed. It was further disputed whether the bank statements were provided in the course of the investigation. On cross-examination, the store manager described the claimant's reaction when he was informed of the double payments 'as I genuinely believe he was shocked'. The EAT noted that the respondent's policy documents were not furnished to the claimant until after the dismissal. The claimant had attended a meeting which in fact was a disciplinary meeting but he was not informed that it was a disciplinary meeting. The respondent's policy at the relevant time was that the same person should conduct the investigative and disciplinary processes. The exact sum of money due and owing to the respondent was in dispute and the double payment incident was due to an error on the part of the respondent.

The EAT found that the respondent had not discharged the onus of proof required and that the claimant was unfairly dismissed. The EAT accepted the claimant's version of events even though the EAT noted that he was somewhat easy-going and casual with regard to his family finances. The EAT found that the procedures adopted by the respondent were inadequate, given the serious accusations made against the claimant and the equally serious consequences emanating accordingly.

The EAT held that in cases such as these, where serious allegations are made attracting serious consequences to one's reputation, career and general prospects and were allegations bordering on or amounting to criminal liability, it is essential that the procedures adopted in the investigative and disciplinary procedures be carried out with the utmost vigilance, care, fairness and especially when the onus of proof lies on the party making such allegations.

The EAT noted that the claimant had an unblemished record and that his integrity had never previously been impugned in any way. The EAT was further critical that at the appeal hearing no proper account was taken of his previous record, nor was his personnel file available at that hearing. He did not receive a letter informing him of his suspension and was not advised that a meeting was a disciplinary meeting. He did not receive a copy of the honesty policy which he was accused of breaching. The EAT noted 'with some trepidation' that, during the whole process both investigatory and disciplinary, certain personnel were active and involved in both roles.

The EAT noted the peculiar circumstances of this case including an error on the part of the respondent which meant that a double payment was paid to the claimant's account and the involvement and culpability of a third party namely the claimant's wife. The EAT held it was inconceivable that the respondent had refused to meet with the claimant's wife and to engage with her on this matter on the grounds of a blanket policy, especially when the offer to meet was made at an early stage. The EAT queried whether such a policy should be allowed to operate on a universal basis and stated that, in certain exceptional cases such as this, exceptions should be made or allowed by appropriate personnel. The EAT noted that if this had been done at an early stage, there would have been less confusion over the exact money due and that an appropriate payment plan for any money due to the respondent could have possibly been implemented.

It was noted that the claimant's wife had provided a written document to the respondent. The EAT concluded that a document cannot be a substitute for a one-to-one interview or meaningful personal engagement and discussion that could have taken place with a view to a possible resolution of the issues or potential issues involved.

The EAT referred to a number of its previous decisions but particularly had regard to the judgment of Flood J in *Frizell v New Ross Credit Union Ltd*.[37] The judge stated a number of factors which must be established to support the decision to terminate employment for misconduct as follows:

(i)   the complaint must be a bona fide complaint unrelated to any other agenda of the complainant;

(ii)   where the complainant is a person or body of intermediate authority it should state the complaint factually clearly and fairly without any innuendo hidden inference or conclusion;

(iii)   the employee should be interviewed or his or her version noted and furnished to a deciding authority contemporaneously with the complaint and again without comment;

(iv)   the decision of the deciding authority should be based on the balance of probabilities flowing from the factual evidence and in light of the explanation offered;

(v)   the actual decision as to whether a dismissal should follow should be a decision proportionate to the gravity of the complaint and of the gravity and effect of the dismissal on the employee.

Flood J summarised that: '[p]ut very simply, principles of natural justice must be unequivocally applied'.

The EAT concluded that in this case those principles were not applied or sufficiently applied. The EAT concluded, having regard to all of the prevailing circumstances, that the appropriate award of compensation to the claimant was €70,000.

Suspension without pay

[27.25] *Morrissey v Central Garage Clonmel Ltd*[38] *– Unfair Dismissals Acts 1977 to 2007 as amended – Employment Appeals Tribunal – dismissal of employee for gross misconduct – suspension of employee without pay before establishing employee's account of what occurred – dismissal of employee without giving adequate time to consider allegations put to employee*

The respondent company operates a car dealership and over the period of the claimant's employment also operated a repairs and services business. The respondent employed the claimant for over 40 years as a mechanic. The claimant's dismissal arose from an incident involving a vehicle that was booked in for repair. The claimant checked the vehicle but could not identify the exact fault. There was a dispute between the claimant and the service manager as to what parts were required in order to fix the vehicle. The

---

37.   *Frizell v New Ross Credit Union Ltd* [1997] IEHC 137.

38.   *Morrissey v Central Garage Clonmel Ltd* UD1039/2012.

service manager ordered a timing belt for the vehicle and when the claimant discovered this he indicated that a camshaft sensor should also have been ordered. The service manager interpreted this as the claimant attempting to put obstacles in the way of repairing the vehicle and reported this to the managing director, who took the decision to pass the repair job to another garage in order to avoid delays in having the repair work done. Following the report by the service manager of the claimant's behaviour, the managing director said that it appeared to him from the claimant's behaviour that the claimant did not want to do the job. The managing director suspended the claimant without pay by letter dated 14 March 2012 without first having heard the claimant's account of the incident. At an investigation meeting the claimant challenged the allegations against him. There was a clear conflict between the facts given by the service manager and the claimant. The managing director dismissed the claimant for gross misconduct.

The claimant was of the belief that his representative had sought to appeal the dismissal on his behalf. The respondent denied ever having receiving any communication from the claimant or his representative appealing against the dismissal.

The EAT found that the respondent had suspended the claimant without first establishing the claimant's account of what occurred and the respondent had dismissed the claimant without first giving him time to consider the allegations put to him, and affording the claimant the opportunity or the time to give his account of the incident. The EAT found that the claimant was not guilty of gross misconduct and could not accept the contention that there was any intention by the claimant to obstruct the respondent in carrying out repair on the vehicle. The EAT upheld the claimant's claim for unfair dismissal and awarded the claimant compensation of €29,000.

Failure to comply with reasonable procedures

[27.26] *Reilly v O'Reilly Ledwith Consultants Ltd T/A O'Reilly Ledwith Consultants Ltd*[39] *– Unfair Dismissals Acts 1977 to 2007 as amended – Minimum Notice and Terms of Employment Act 1973 to 2005 – Employment Appeals Tribunal – unfair dismissal – failure by respondent to comply with reasonable procedures leading to dismissal – failure by claimant to engage in appeals process – Employment Appeals Tribunal did not exercise its discretion under Unfair Dismissals Act 1997, s 7 as amended by Unfair Dismissals Act 1993, s 6(a) and therefore made no award in this case*

The claimant was employed by the respondent company and was promoted from account manager to team leader in January 2011. The claimant returned to work from maternity leave in May 2012. There was a dispute between the parties as to the work carried out by the claimant on her return from work. The claimant gave evidence that, before she went on maternity leave, her role had been customer service related but on her return the focus of the business was on sales. The claimant said that her workload increased considerably on her return to work. The managing director of the respondent

---

39.   *Reilly v O'Reilly Ledwith Consultants Ltd T/A O'Reilly Ledwith Consultants Ltd* UD347/2013, MN189/2013.

company in evidence denied that the claimant's work had increased after her maternity leave or that the claimant had returned to a changed working environment. The managing director gave evidence that the only change to the claimant's work was to the claimant's line of reporting.

On 14 June 2012 the claimant told her sales manager that she could not keep up with her workload and that she was being belittled by certain of her colleagues. One of the claimant's colleagues told her that she must work harder as a team leader and rang a customer to check on the claimant's performance. There was no process of performance review within the respondent. The sales manager told the claimant only to deal with him for the future but the claimant gave evidence that her working environment did not change. The claimant gave evidence that an issue arose in May 2012 when the claimant noticed customers that had been incorrectly set up on base rates and were not getting lower rate entitlements on phone accounts. The sales manager told the claimant to 'leave it' and that new customers would be looked after.

A grievance meeting took place on 20 August 2012 which the claimant attended with a colleague. The managing director did not attend this meeting as he was one of the named persons involved in the accusations made by the claimant. The claimant gave evidence that she could not get an answer at this meeting as to how her grievance was being dealt with but she was informed that the staff members in question had been spoken to.

The claimant went on sick leave in August 2012. The claimant attended a welfare meeting with the managing director on 23 October 2012 at which she agreed to attend an occupational therapist. An appointment was arranged by the respondent company for the claimant to attend an occupational therapist, but the claimant claimed that she did not receive notice of the appointment until the day of same and therefore missed the appointment. The managing director assumed that the letter notifying the claimant of the appointment had been posted to the claimant. The claimant claimed that she requested another appointment but the respondent never sent her one.

The managing director claimed that he had informed the claimant that her complaints were unfounded after investigation and that the claimant had refused to attend any meetings regarding an investigation.

The claimant received a letter from the managing director on 8 January 2013 terminating her employment on the grounds of ill health. The letter gave the claimant an opportunity to appeal the dismissal within five days but no appeal was initiated by the claimant. The claimant claimed that she did not appeal the termination of her employment as she felt that her grievance was never attended to by the company and she felt that the appeal would not address the issues. The claimant had been told that she would receive a copy of the grievance report but she never received same.

The EAT found that the claimant was unfairly dismissed on the basis that the respondent had failed to comply with reasonable procedures leading up to the dismissal. The EAT determined that at no stage was the claimant informed by the respondent that her job was at risk or the disciplinary procedure invoked if she failed to provide a date upon which she would return to work from sick leave.

The EAT noted that the claimant was on disability benefit from August 2012 and was not available for work. Furthermore, the claimant admitted to engaging in child minding for payment. The EAT also criticised the claimant for failing to engage at some level in the appeals process offered by the respondent. In the circumstances, the EAT did not exercise its discretion under s 7 of the Unfair Dismissals Act 1997 (as amended by s 6(a) of the Unfair Dismissals Act 1993) and therefore made no award of compensation to the claimant.

Defective disciplinary procedures

[27.27] *Fox v National Gallery of Ireland[40] – Employment Appeals Tribunal – Unfair Dismissals Acts 1977 to 2007 as amended – breach of procedures – disclosure of sensitive security information – defective disciplinary procedures – investigator making conclusions of misconduct at fact-finding stage – investigator's conclusions followed by decision maker – contribution to dismissal*

The claimant was a former security guard in the National Gallery of Ireland. He was dismissed for gross misconduct for assisting a former colleague in preparation for a Rights Commissioner investigation of the colleague's unfair dismissals claim. The respondent submitted that the sending of emails containing the security sensitive information by the claimant to the agency worker through an unsecure email network breached security procedures by disclosing sensitive security information to an outside party. The respondent submitted that the disclosure of this information could present a significant risk to the respondent's security. The respondent also submitted that the submission to the Rights Commissioner and the accompanying emails contained derogatory references to employees of the respondent. The respondent submitted that, given the claimant's experience and seniority, his role in the preparation of the submission was a breach of trust and confidence, making his continued employment with the respondent untenable.

The claimant stated that he felt obliged to assist the agency worker with his unfair dismissal claim, as the claimant was a trade union activist. However, the claimant submitted that his assistance in preparing the submission to the Rights Commissioner was limited to correcting grammar and structuring the submission, as English was not the first language of the agency worker. The claimant also claimed that the Rights Commissioner submission did not contain any sensitive security information. The EAT noted that the claimant had been employed by the respondent for 22 years, and had not previously received any disciplinary sanction.

The EAT heard that the respondent's disciplinary procedure consisted of a fact-finding investigation and a four-day disciplinary hearing. The investigation was conducted by the librarian in the respondent gallery, and the EAT heard that this was her first time conducting an investigation of this nature. The claimant had objected to the librarian conducting the investigation, on the basis that he claimed that she did not have the requisite understanding of security arrangements of the gallery and that she was not the appropriate person to conduct the investigation, as the respondent's disciplinary policy stated that an investigation should be conducted by the accused employee's line manager. The claimant also objected to the appointment of an external investigator.

---

40.   *Fox v National Gallery of Ireland* UD950/2012.

The EAT determined that the procedures implemented by the respondent in dismissing the claimant were defective. The EAT found that the investigator had made conclusions in respect of the claimant's guilt at the fact-finding stage of the disciplinary process, and that the investigator's conclusions were acted upon by the decision maker in the disciplinary hearing, which resulted in the claimant's dismissal. The EAT did not award re-instatement, as sought by the claimant, but awarded €25,000 by way of compensation. This award reflected the fact that the EAT held the claimant contributed significantly to his dismissal.

[27.28] *Farnan v KM Healthcare Enterprises Ltd T/A Castleross[41] – Unfair Dismissals Acts 1977 to 2007 as amended – Employment Appeals Tribunal – dismissal for gross misconduct on foot of complaints of abusive behaviour and verbal altercations – unfair procedures – lack of impartiality of decision-maker – failure to consider other sanctions*

The claimant, a carer, was dismissed for gross misconduct, namely for being abusive to a staff member and exhibiting aggressive or abusive behaviour towards a staff member in the presence of residents.

Evidence was given for the respondent by its director of care, who stated that four complaints were received from co-workers of the claimant, ranging from her not carrying her fair share of work and taking excessive breaks to aggressive behaviour and verbal altercations. The director of care conducted the investigation, in the course of which the claimant denied these allegations. The recommendation on foot of the investigation process was that the claimant be found guilty of gross misconduct and the matter was forwarded for disciplinary action to a human resources advisor to the respondent. As part of the evidence given before the EAT, the director of care did acknowledge that she had encountered the claimant in previous employment at another location and had suggested that the claimant had failed her probationary period in that employment mainly due to communication skills and loud behaviour. The claimant was dismissed and an appeal upheld the decision to dismiss.

Evidence was given by a former work colleague, that the claimant's previous employment did not come to an end as had been described, but that she was dismissed because she had had an issue with another colleague and, when it was brought to the director of care, she was called to the office and returned to duty crying and was subsequently dismissed. Evidence was given by the claimant that she was not an aggressive person and that she was a very good worker. The claimant asserted that all of the complaints made about her were untrue. She asserted that the director of care was biased and an inappropriate person to do the investigation because of her involvement in and awareness of previous issues with the complainant in past employment. It should be noted that in the course of the investigation conducted by the respondent, the director of care interviewed all the persons on the team. She gave the complainant a copy of the statements made by her co-workers and asked that she sign a confidentiality agreement stating that any breach of same would lead to summary dismissal. The claimant, in her

---

41. *Farnan v KM Healthcare Enterprises Ltd T/A Castleross* UD847/2012.

evidence, suggested that because of the confidentiality agreement, everybody knew what was going on except her.

The EAT concluded that the respondent did not utilise fair procedures in dismissing the claimant from her position, which she had held for three-and-a-half years. The procedural flaws highlighted by the EAT were the fact that a confidentiality clause inhibited the claimant from conducting her defence and the person conducting the investigation had, in a previous employment, dismissed the claimant. The EAT noted that this alone made the procedure biased. The EAT noted that the investigation report concluded that the incidents reported indicated gross misconduct. The EAT stated that the investigation was a fact-finding mission and should not have reached any conclusions. The EAT noted that no other sanctions, such as suspension without pay, were ever considered. The EAT noted that what was meant by 'aggressive behaviour' was never questioned by the respondent and there did not appear to be any clear management structure regarding the delegation of work. The EAT determined that it was appropriate to award the claimant €30,000.

[27.29] *Maher v Allied Irish Banks plc[42] – Employment Appeals Tribunal – Unfair Dismissals Acts 1997 to 2007 as amended – whether disciplinary process flawed where decision to dismiss based on 'final' investigatory report of uncertain authorship – whether independent appeals process not based on this report could render decision to dismiss fair*

The claimant commenced working for the respondent bank in 1982, and at the time of his dismissal in 2011 was employed as a branch manager. In 2009, the respondent commenced an investigation into a number of possible irregularities and conflicts of interest involving the claimant. The investigation was conducted by the manager of the special investigations unit (Mr G), who was charged with gathering information and facts and delivering a formal report to the general manager of the bank.

The investigation centred around three allegations of irregular or inappropriate behaviour made against the claimant. First, it was alleged that a letter written by the claimant as branch manager and addressed to a partnership of which the claimant was a member, was inappropriate, in breach of the claimant's authority and represented a clear conflict of interest. The letter, dated 21 April 2005, was described as a 'letter of sanction in principle' (ie a conditional approval) of a loan of €60m to the partnership. At the time of writing of the letter, the claimant's authority to grant a loan application was limited to €160,000. The letter, for which the claimant had not sought or obtained internal approval, stated:

> I refer to your recent application, on behalf of (the) Partnership-Consortium 1, to borrow $60m ... I can confirm we are agreeable in principle to advance these funds to your group, subject to the following ...

Further issues examined by Mr G during the investigation involved a complaint from a customer about possible conflicts of interest in relation to the purchase and letting of a

---

42.   *Maher v Allied Irish Banks plc* UD2189/2011.

local hotel by the claimant, and three other complaints made by customers of the bank regarding the claimant.

The report issued by Mr G, referred to as the initial report, concluded that if the aforementioned letter was considered a 'letter of sanction in principle' there could be no doubt that the claimant breached the lending authority granted to him by the respondent. However, as the initial report was conducted on the understanding that it was a preliminary fact-finding assignment only, it made no findings that the claimant should be subject to a disciplinary process.

Following the conclusion of the initial investigation process, another member of the respondent's personnel was asked to examine the case and reach to a conclusion on the matter. In this regard he relied upon documentary evidence only, being a 'final report' (which was ascribed to Mr G, but which came to significantly different conclusions than the initial report and the authorship of which was denied by him), a copy of a letter from the respondent to the claimant detailing the various allegations against him, and a detailed letter/submission from the claimant dated 19 July 2010. The general manager did not meet with the claimant prior to reaching his conclusion. Following the conclusion of his investigation, the general manager found that the letter amounted to a 'letter of sanction in principle' and that in issuing same, the claimant had breached his duty and irreparably damaged the relationship of trust and fidelity between himself and the respondent. On the basis of this and of the consequential exposure of the respondent to reputational damage and potential financial loss, he concluded that the claimant should be dismissed with immediate effect subject to the payment of 12 week's salary in lieu of his contractual notice entitlement.

The claimant appealed this decision in accordance with the respondent's internal appeals mechanism. The appeal was conducted by a third party, and was by way of *de novo* hearing at which the onus was on the respondent to prove that dismissal was the appropriate sanction. Both parties were represented by solicitors and counsel. The findings arising from the appeal, upheld the decision to dismiss on the basis that the letter of April 2005 was a 'letter of sanction in principle' and a total conflict of interest by the claimant. The appeal concluded that the claimant, in using his position to advance his personal interests, had exposed the respondent to a risk of damage and totally and irrevocably undermined the trust and confidence which was the cornerstone of his employment relationship.

The claimant alleged that this decision to dismiss was in breach of his right to fair procedures. During the hearing, the EAT heard evidence from a number of witnesses for the respondent, all of whom accepted that the letter amounted to a 'letter of sanction in principle'. One witness, the head of credit sanctioning who had been employed by the respondent since 1982, gave evidence that the claimant's role as author of the letter, in circumstances where he was also part owner of the partnership, amounted to clear conflict of interest of which he should have made the respondent aware. The witness expressed his opinion that it was inappropriate for the claimant to have considered the loan application in these circumstances, and he should have absented himself from the matter.

In response, the claimant submitted that he had dedicated a large part of his life to developing his career with the respondent, and that his dismissal had been both financially and psychologically devastating for him. With regard to the letter, the claimant submitted that it was not a 'letter of sanction in principle', rather was an expression of interest in a business deal. As such, the letter did not require prior approval and was not a breach of the claimant's authorised lending limit. The claimant gave evidence that he did not keep the deal secret, in contrast he called and reported it to the respondent's branch in America, believing that it represented a genuine opportunity for the respondent. The claimant also questioned the fairness of the appeals process, alleging that insufficient evidence had been heard.

The EAT concluded that the respondent's disciplinary process was flawed, being based on evidence (namely the final report) whose origin was not confirmed. The non-disclosure of the initial report and the presentation of the final report as the report of Mr G (in circumstances where it was not his report) tainted the entire disciplinary process and the appeals thereafter, notwithstanding the fact that the appeal did not rely on the final report and was by way of full de novo hearing. The EAT found that the issue of the letter of sanction by the claimant was entirely inappropriate and warranted a significant disciplinary sanction. However, the EAT stated its opinion that an appropriate sanction would have been to demote the claimant, not to dismiss him. Accordingly, it was found that the claimant was unfairly dismissed.

In determining the sum to be granted in respect of compensation, the EAT stated its opinion that the conduct of the claimant 'was so egregious and of such a contributing factor' that it warranted a significant reduction in the level to be awarded, and the EAT awarded €25,000.

Dismissals for a breach of policy/procedure

Breach of mark-down sales policy

[27.30] *Bermingham v Marks & Spencer (Ireland) Ltd [43] – Employment Appeals Tribunal – Unfair Dismissals Acts 1977 to 2007 as amended – Minimum Notice and Terms of Employment Act 1973–2005 – dismissal for breaches of company policy – fairness of procedures – whether sanction imposed proportionate – bias and procedural flaws – re-engagement*

The respondent had a strict policy in respect of mark-down sales. Mark-down sales consist of selling stock at below cost price in order to clear stock. It is strictly against store policy for staff to purchase stock before the opening hours of the store. Customers and employees are given an equal opportunity to buy the stock. The claimant was the duty manager on duty on the day of the incident and she had started work at 6.30am in order to mark-down the items and oversee the work of that morning. The claimant purchased a number of items approximately 30 minutes before the opening of the store, as well as allowing other employees to make purchases. She had also confirmed to another employee that making the purchase was permitted. The respondent became

---

43. *Bermingham v Marks & Spencer (Ireland) Ltd* UD601/2011,MN639/2011.

aware of these actions and considered same to be gross misconduct, for which it had a zero-tolerance policy.

At a disciplinary meeting with her line manager, the claimant did not believe that she had breached company policy as she had heard it happened in a different store. She claimed that she did not do it maliciously. The claimant was dismissed on two breaches of reservation of sale policy, breach of till procedures and engaging in shopping on company time. It was submitted to the EAT that another employee who engaged in similar misconduct only received a final written warning. The respondent justified this, by explaining that as the claimant was the duty manager, she had overall responsibility. At the EAT hearing, the investigator confirmed that he did not interview any of the other employees whom the claimant had allowed to purchase stock. In relation to claims of different practices pertaining in the other stores, the investigator checked with a colleague in a Dublin store and found that this was not the case. The human resource manager who had conducted the appeal hearing also gave evidence and confirmed that she upheld the decision to dismiss the claimant. However, she confirmed that she did not interview anyone other than the claimant as part of the appeals process as she did not deem it necessary to do so. She further did not check CCTV footage.

The EAT noted its duty was to decide firstly the reason for dismissal, and secondly whether this reason was fair or unfair. The EAT was satisfied that it had established the reason for the claimant's dismissal as being the breach of company policy. In relation to the fairness of the dismissal, the EAT stated that it was clear from the evidence furnished that the investigation process was flawed in the following aspects:

(i) the claimant only received one hour's notice of the investigation meeting and was not informed fully of the agenda for this meeting;

(ii) the disciplinary hearing was not objective as it was overseen by a person with whom the claimant had a past history/past dealings;

(iii) the appeal was heard by a person who did not carry out an independent and objective review of the matter.

Accordingly, the EAT found that the dismissal was unfair. However, the EAT found that the claimant contributed to her own dismissal by her actions, particularly in light of the position held by her in the respondent. The EAT directed the claimant to be re-engaged by the respondent from the date of receipt of this determination and no monetary payment was made.

Breach of policy on reserving sales items

[27.31] *McCrann v Marks & Spencer Ireland Ltd*[44] *– Employment Appeals Tribunal – Unfair Dismissals Acts 1977 to 2007 as amended – appeal of decision of Rights Commissioner – whether summary dismissal of claimant for gross breach of*

---

44. *McCrann v Marks & Spencer (Ireland) Ltd* UD3/2013.

regulations in breach of respondent's policy on reserving sale items was fair and reasonable – proportionality of sanction

The claimant was employed in one of the respondent's clothing outlets. The respondent operates a policy that sale items may not be reserved by customers or staff. This case followed an investigation by the respondent into a suspicion that the claimant had placed sale items behind non-sale items on the shop floor so as to reduce the chances of these items being bought by customers. CCTV footage showed the claimant returning to these items once he finished work and purchasing them. The claimant was invited to a disciplinary hearing at which it was decided to dismiss him and a subsequent dismissal hearing upheld the original decision to dismiss him.

The respondent submitted that the claimant was fully aware of the policy and had wilfully breached it. The claimant did not accept that his actions had breached the policy by placing items back on the shop floor, albeit at an inappropriate rail. He noted the original policy did stipulate that a breach was gross misconduct. However, it had been superseded by a more recent policy that stated that failure to comply with these procedures may lead to serious action being taken. The claimant submitted that the sanction of dismissal was too severe in the circumstances.

The EAT agreed and stated that the respondent had acted unreasonably in deciding to dismiss the claimant. The EAT noted that it was open to the respondent to consider sanctions other than dismissal. However, no such other sanction was considered. The EAT concluded that the sanction of dismissal was disproportionate to the alleged action of the claimant and was contrary to fairness and natural justice and the EAT overturned the determination of the Rights Commissioner and awarded the claimant €13,000 compensation.

Breach of sales and refunds procedure

[27.32] *O'Callaghan v Dunnes Stores*[45] – *Employment Appeals Tribunal – Unfair Dismissals Acts 1977 to 2007 as amended – Minimum Notice and Terms of Employment Acts 1973 to 2005 – Organisation of Working Time Act 1997 – whether respondent justified in dismissing claimant store manager following breaches by him of respondent's sales and refunds procedure – whether his following instructions to junior staff to carry out false sales and refund transactions was gross misconduct – whether having same person conduct investigation and decision making role breach of fair procedures – whether claimant had by his actions destroyed relationship of trust and confidence between claimant and respondent*

The claimant joined the respondent's employment whilst still in school and, having completed a business course in college, he went into management with the respondent in a number of different roles, culminating in being appointed store manager, a position he held at the time his employment came to an end.

The facts were common case: the claimant's store (store M) was located on the same street as the respondent's flagship store (store F) and store M was carrying a high level

---

45.   *O'Callaghan v Dunnes Stores* UD54/2012, MN25/2012, WT14/2012.

of refunds. Under the respondent's exchange policy, goods bearing tags and labels could be returned to any store on the production of a valid receipt and it was submitted in evidence by the claimant that, as store M was in close proximity to store F, it was taking back the majority of the returns for store F. It was accepted that the respondent had been directed by senior management to control the level of refunds as these were detrimental to the claimant's sales figures.

This case arose from a decision by the claimant to open the store 30 minutes early on a Sunday, during which time there was a high level of refunds, thus cancelling out the sales made at the same period. Later that afternoon, the claimant decided to seek refunds from store F on some of the items that had been returned to store M and he instructed the customer service till operator to process a number of returned items as sales and on further instructions from the claimant, three employees returned those items to store F for refunds. Ultimately, a security manager from store F noticed unusual transactions being engaged in by store M's staff and this was brought to the attention of senior management. An investigation took place at which the claimant acknowledged that he had opened the store early to generate sales and further admitted to the transactions being carried out on his instructions by the three employees. It was asserted by the claimant, who had apologised fully for the events, that the respondent's characterisation of the transactions as fraudulent was 'harsh'. He explained his actions by way of being under pressure to reach certain sales targets.

A senior manager of the respondent conducted both the investigation and the subsequent disciplinary meeting. This manager concluded that the claimant, as custodian of the company's policies and procedures, had a responsibility to achieve sales targets and delivery of Key Performance Indicators (KPIs) within the policies and procedures and his breach had distorted the store's KPIs and he had compromised the position of the three staff members by instructing them to carry out the false sales and refund transactions. The claimant was advised that his behaviour amounted to gross misconduct. It was submitted by the respondent that the claimant as manager had devised a plan to breach the procedures and had instructed three members of the team to breach them which was grave and serious misconduct. It was asserted by the respondent that trust was an important element of the employment relationship and having manipulated sales by way of fraudulent transactions, the claimant could not be trusted in the future. An appeal took place to a regional grocery manager who, having heard the claimant's grounds of appeal, upheld the decision to dismiss.

It was contended to the EAT that having the same manager conduct both the investigation and disciplinary process was an unfair procedure. The EAT did not accept this. In particular, the EAT noted that the claimant had made an immediate and full admission to the wrongdoing at the investigation meeting and that the facts of the alleged wrongdoing were not in dispute.

The EAT found that trust and confidence are 'essential elements in the employment relationship and a particularly high level of trust and confidence is reposed in a manager'. The EAT concluded that breaching sales and refunds procedures is a serious/ gross misconduct, but instructing subordinates to engage in fraudulent transactions and compromise their trustworthiness is even more serious. The EAT concluded, that in the circumstances, a sanction of dismissal was fair and thus the claim failed.

Breach of staff purchasing policy

[27.33] *O'Brien v Dunnes Stores[46] – Employment Appeals Tribunal – Unfair Dismissals Acts 1977 to 2007 as amended – dismissal of claimant who took and wore tie whilst working and later brought it home – breach of staff purchasing policy – procedural flaws rendered dismissal unfair – failure to consider options other than dismissal*

This case arose from the dismissal of the claimant, a section manager in one of the respondent's stores. On the day in question, he arrived at work without a necktie. The respondent required that he wear a tie while on duty. Before he started his shift, he removed a twin pack of ties from the shop floor and wore one and later went home still wearing it. A manager thereafter asked the claimant if he knew anything about the remaining tie of the twin pack, which was left on the desk in his office, and the claimant denied any knowledge of this.

At an investigation meeting with the store manager and a HR manager, the claimant acknowledged that he had taken the tie with the intention of wearing it for the day and returning it to the packet for sale. He further stated that he had never intended to buy the tie but was borrowing it for the shift.

A decision was taken by the store manager to dismiss the claimant for a breach of the staff purchasing policy. The decision was subsequently considered in an appeal. However, the appeal decision maker did not meet with the claimant. It was noted that the claimant had returned the tie during the investigation but had never offered to pay for it. It was submitted by the appeal decision maker that staff were not allowed to borrow goods, use them and return them. It was submitted by the claimant that the decision to dismiss him was disproportionate to the incident as his intention was only to borrow the tie. He submitted that there was an accepted practice of staff borrowing items while at work and gave an example of staff in another branch borrowing an umbrella to go to the bank and returning it to stock afterwards.

The EAT concluded that the claimant was unfairly dismissed by the respondent and stated its concern that the claimant was not given access to an oral appeal hearing, as was the case with other employees. The EAT also determined the procedure to be flawed in that the person who conducted the investigation also made the decision to dismiss the claimant. The EAT noted that the evidence from both the initial decision maker and appeal decision maker was to the effect that the respondent staff purchasing policy was so rigid that any breach of it would inevitably lead to dismissal and that they had no alternative but to dismiss. The EAT however noted that both had given evidence to the effect that had the claimant offered to pay for the tie at a much later stage, he may not have been dismissed. The EAT concluded that in itself suggested that there other options apart from dismissal. The EAT awarded the claimant €25,000 compensation.

[27.34] *McNally v Olhausens limited (in receivership)[47] – Employments Appeal Tribunal – Unfair Dismissals Acts 1977 to 2007 as amended – appeal against decision*

---

46.   *O'Brien v Dunnes Stores* UD1133/2012.

47.   *McNally v Olhausens Ltd (in receivership)* UD701/2013.

of Rights Commissioner – dismissal for breaches of staff purchasing procedure – reliance on CCTV footage – willingness of EAT to award compensation in respect of loss of potential redundancy payment under heading of 'financial loss'

The claimant, a delivery truck driver, worked in the respondent's meat processing and distribution plant from November 2006 until his dismissal on 5 June 2012. The claimant was observed on CCTV selecting and loading goods into his truck while on duty in the late evening or early hours of the morning on four separate occasions and there was no record of these items being paid for. This footage was of concern to the respondent as normally orders are filled and loaded to the trucks by warehouse staff other than drivers, with some exceptions.

A preliminary investigation took place with the claimant and the relevant manager to look for an explanation as to why he was loading the stocks. The claimant explained he was loading the stock for staff orders and that he had forgotten to pay for them. He then offered to pay for the items but he was informed by the manager that it was too late as the investigation had already started. There was a procedure in place for staff purchase of goods and the claimant was aware of the system. Evidence was given by the warehouse manager that the claimant would normally write down what stock he had taken on a piece of paper and later give this to the warehouse manager who would then write it up on a docket and enter it on the system as per procedures. Sometimes the claimant would be chased for late payment up to two weeks later. The matter was then referred to an independent third party for further investigation, in the course of which the claimant admitted he had removed the stock and had not paid for it at the time. A disciplinary process was convened and the claimant was informed of his right to have a union representative present but he declined same. He was presented with a copy of the investigation report, and a further meeting was scheduled to allow him time to respond to the report. At the resumed hearing the claimant said he had nothing to add and a letter of dismissal was handed to him at that hearing.

At the internal appeal hearing in which the claimant was represented, the claimant put forward the fact that he was on medication as a possible reason why he had forgotten to pay for the items he had taken. The claimant's evidence was that he was going through a personally difficult time and was suffering from depression. The appeal board took this into account when making a decision and found that this could be a further breach of trust by the claimant as the medication may have affected his ability to drive and he ought to have informed the respondent at the time. The appeal board upheld the original decision to dismiss.

The EAT noted that there had been a change of procedures implemented by the employer in the purchasing of stock by staff. The EAT also noted that the warehouse manager had previously had to chase the claimant for payment of his purchases from the stock of the company. The EAT noted that when the CCTV footage was put to the claimant, he offered to pay for what was taken and was at all times aware that what he was taking was recorded on CCTV. The EAT noted that the claimant's practice was to record his purchases on a piece of paper and in this case he was able to produce the paper to support his contentions. It is acknowledged by the respondent that this was an *ad hoc* arrangement which they had taken into consideration at the time of their decision. The respondent did not admit the paper in the investigation.

The EAT further noted that, at the appeal, the question of the taking of medication by the claimant was considered as another factor in deciding to dismiss the claimant without informing him of this fact or without obtaining medical evidence to make such a finding.

It was also noted that the letter of dismissal was written prior to the meeting at which they were to make a decision on his employment, which indicated that they had decided the issue prior to the meeting. The EAT concluded that the claimant had been unfairly dismissed in all of the circumstances.

The EAT noted that the claimant was unfit to work after his dismissal and therefore had no loss of earnings. However in October 2012 the entire workforce was made redundant. The EAT in considering the award took cognisance of s 7(3) of the Unfair Dismissals Act 1997 as amended which provides that 'financial loss' includes any actual loss and any estimated prospective loss of income attributable to the dismissal, and the value of any loss attributable to the dismissal, of the rights of the employee under the Redundancy Payments Act 1967 to 2014 or in relation to superannuation.

The EAT decided to overturn the decision of the Rights Commissioner and awarded the claimant compensation of €18,175.30.

Dismissal for alleged misrepresentation, forgery and fraud

[27.35] *Preston v Dunnes Stores*[48] *– Employment Appeals Tribunal – Unfair Dismissals Acts 1977 to 2007 as amended – Redundancy Payments Acts 1967 to 2014*[49] *– Minimum Notice and Terms of Employment Act 1973 to 2005 – employee in retail management position dismissed for misrepresentation, forgery and fraud – mitigating personal circumstances – disproportionate sanction*

The claimant was employed as a department manager for a large supermarket chain. The supermarket allowed various community groups and charities to carry out bag packing to raise funds. The procedure for this was that the group must write to the respondent requesting a bag pack and then the claimant, as department manager, would put all of the request letters in a diary and then was responsible for scheduling the bag packs, limiting them to two a month. A letter of complaint was received by the store manager from a local community group which asserted that the claimant had opened an account in their name at a cash and carry store and had used the community group's letterhead to open the account.

A meeting was held with the claimant at which she admitted that she had taken the community group's letter requesting a bag pack and had doctored it for the purposes of opening an account with a cash and carry store as she was in financial difficulty and earned extra money from selling the cash and carry goods. The meeting adjourned and then reconvened later on that day as a disciplinary meeting. The claimant was offered, but declined, representation. The claimant again admitted using the letter to open an account, but denied selling the goods to respondent staff. She then admitted to selling goods purchased on a different cash and carry account to staff of the respondent. The

---

48.   *Preston v Dunnes Stores* UD517/2012, RP385/2012, MN396/2012.

49.   The claim under the Redundancy Payments Acts was withdrawn at the outset of this hearing.

claimant was suspended and warned that the outcome of the process could be dismissal. At a subsequent disciplinary meeting, the store manager outlined the allegations as constituting misrepresentation, forgery and fraud. The claimant put forward mitigating personal circumstances to explain her actions. Ultimately, the claimant was dismissed for conduct, including conduct unbecoming of an employee of the company, or contrary to its best interest, and which could bring the company into disrepute.

The store manager gave evidence to the effect that he had thought long and hard over the weekend and so delivered his decision to dismiss the claimant when the meeting reconvened after a 15-minute break. The claimant was advised that she was being dismissed for gross misconduct as the trust between her and the respondent had been irrevocably broken. The letter of dismissal issued to the claimant on the same day and she was advised of her right of appeal. The appeal proceeded by way of a review of the disciplinary meeting notes and all relevant documentation. No appeal meeting took place. The appeal decision-maker upheld the decision to dismiss.

The claimant gave evidence to the effect that she had admitted the offence, that it was a serious error of judgment made during a period of great turmoil in her personal life and she asserted that the decision to dismiss had been taken at the first meeting and that her good record with the respondent was not taken into consideration.

The EAT concluded that the sanction of dismissal was disproportionate in circumstances where this was the claimant's first offence and was committed in a time of great personal difficulty, which the respondent was aware of. The EAT upheld the claim under the Unfair Dismissals Act and awarded the claimant €14,000 in compensation. The claimant's minimum notice claim also succeeded.

Selling alcohol to a minor during a test purchase conducted on behalf of An Garda Síochána

[27.36] *Fitzpatrick v Dunnes Stores[50] – Employment Appeals Tribunal – Unfair Dismissals Acts 1977 to 2007 as amended – Minimum Notice and Terms of Employment Act 1973 to 2005 – whether dismissal of claimant for gross misconduct for selling alcohol to minor acting on behalf of gardaí as a test purchaser – whether dismissal for gross misconduct reasonable in circumstances*

The claimant was employed as a cashier in a convenience supermarket operated by the respondent, with 28 employees. Evidence was given that the claimant had been trained in the sale of alcohol, tobacco and paracetamol products on a one-to-one basis with the respondent's personnel officer for approximately 20 minutes on a biannual basis. It was accepted by the claimant that she had sold alcohol to a minor, but she had not done it knowingly. The minor was participating in a test purchase for An Garda Síochána. It was submitted by the claimant that she had been having a conversation with the assistant manager during the sale and that the assistant manager could have intervened to stop the sale. The claimant submitted she had not been shown the CCTV footage during the process, but received stills of the CCTV footage through a data protection request. Evidence was given confirming that the assistant manager was present in the store on

---

50.   *Fitzpatrick v Dunnes Stores* UD196/2012, MN150/2012.

the evening in question. A garda present had identified himself to the assistant manager following the sale and warned that the shop could be prosecuted.

The store manager and the security manager met with the claimant the following day. The assistant manager and another till operator were interviewed as part of the investigation, but were found not to have been involved in the transaction. The CCTV footage demonstrated that, while the assistant manager was in the vicinity of the customer service till, she did not have a clear view and was not visible on the CCTV. The other till operator had her back to the person making the purchase. The claimant explained to the store manager that she was not thinking; she was worrying about her sick child at home, and had end of shift jobs to do.

The claimant was suspended on 12 December 2011 and was dismissed on 15 December 2011. Two meetings were held on 15 December and an appeal to a different store manager was offered. The witness considered other sanctions, but considered the breach to have been so serious as to warrant dismissal, notwithstanding that the claimant had 12 years' service and no previous disciplinary issues. The EAT noted that the claimant had accepted that she sold alcohol to a minor without adhering to the correct procedures of the respondent relating to the sale of alcohol and that issue was not in dispute. The EAT further noted that this action of serving alcohol to any person under the legal age is deemed an example of serious misconduct and was a breach of the policies and procedures of the respondent. The EAT noted that in such cases, the respondent may dismiss an employee without giving full notice entitlements, but only after there is (as outlined in the respondent's policies and procedures) 'a thorough investigation of all the relevant circumstances and also where the employee is informed of the action being considered and given a full opportunity with accompanying work colleague to present his or her case'. The EAT held that an employee must be given fair procedures at all stages of the disciplinary process. In this case, the EAT concluded that the dismissal was unfair as fair procedures were not given to the claimant.

In terms of the procedural failings, the claimant was not offered the right to bring a witness or to be accompanied at the first meeting as this was just for information gathering. At the subsequent meeting she was afforded an opportunity to bring a witness. The store manager confirmed that he presided over both the investigation and the disciplinary process and he alone decided the sanction. The claimant's trade union representative had written on her behalf to seek an appeal, setting out the grounds of appeal, but the respondent had requested that the claimant make her own request for an appeal. She then applied for an appeal, setting out the same reasons for the appeal and understood that there would be an appeal meeting, but then received a letter informing her that her appeal had failed. She was advised that appeals are always conducted in writing in the respondent and the claimant should have been aware of that.

The EAT concluded that there was a lack of proportionality with the decision to dismiss. The EAT was not satisfied that there was an assessment or consideration of other sanctions given the claimant's background of long service. The EAT noted that there was no evidence given to it as to the appeal process undertaken against the decision to dismiss. The manager who undertook the appeal of the disciplinary procedure was not called in evidence, and whilst the respondent's policy set out that any appeal 'will be heard by an appropriate member of management', in this case there was no oral hearing offered to the claimant. It was presented that this was usual practice for there not to be an actual appeal hearing. The EAT upheld the claim and noted that the claimant was seeking reinstatement to her previous employment. The EAT concluded that in the circumstances, this would be impractical. The EAT decided to award the claimant compensation of €13,500 and also notice on the basis of her 12 years' service in the amount of €1,623.60.

Breach of staff purchasing procedure

[27.37] *Meade v Adelphi Carlton Ltd T/A Cineworld[51] – Employment Appeals Tribunal – Unfair Dismissals Acts 1977 to 2007 as amended – breach of company policy on staff purchasing from cinema shop – automatic determination of 'gross misconduct' – failure of respondent to take into account employee's innocent mistake – proportionality of sanction*

The claimant was employed as a multi-functional operator in a cinema operated by the respondent. The claimant was dismissed for gross misconduct after the respondent found that he had breached its policy regarding the purchase of food items in the cinema shop.

Following a review of its CCTV footage and an investigation, the respondent discovered that nine employees, including the claimant, had received goods at the sales desks without paying the correct price for the items.

The respondent operated a staff discount policy which provided staff with a discount card with which they could get a 40% discount on items bought in the cinema shop. At the shop, staff would be provided with a receipt in respect of their items, which they were required to check to ensure that the goods received matched the items on the receipt. They were then required to sign a copy of the receipt to verify the items and return the receipt to the till operator. The policy provided that failure to adhere to the policy constituted gross misconduct, for which the sanction could be dismissal.

On the CCTV footage reviewed, the respondent observed the claimant receiving one large hotdog and a packet of wine gums. The receipt signed by the claimant stated that he received a regular hot dog and a packet of maltesers, each of which was less expensive than the items actually purchased by the claimant. The total difference in price between the items was approximately €1 (taking into account the 40% discount).

On foot of the CCTV footage, the claimant was requested to attend a disciplinary hearing. During the course of the disciplinary hearing, the claimant admitted that he had inadvertently breached the policy by failing to read the receipt to ensure it correctly itemised his purchases. The claimant stated that he was unaware of the serious implications for breaching the policy and stated that he had never received a copy of the policy. The respondent found that the claimant had breached the policy and dismissed him. The claimant unsuccessfully appealed the decision.

During the EAT hearing, the respondent gave evidence that it had discussed the policy with staff at a meeting in November 2011, and a copy of the policy was made

---

51. *Meade v Adelphi Carlton Ltd T/A Cineworld* UD892/2012.

available to all staff. The EAT concluded that the dismissal was unfair. The EAT noted the evidence of the decision makers who stated that the mere fact that there was a breach of the policy meant that an act of gross misconduct had occurred and that dismissal was the appropriate sanction. The EAT noted that whether or not this meant the breach could have been the result of an innocent mistake could have no impact on the outcome of the disciplinary process.

The EAT was not satisfied the respondent reached a reasonable conclusion that it was an act of gross misconduct and awarded the claimant compensation of €20,000.

Dismissal for tampering with stock

[27.38] *Boyne v Keelings Logistics Solutions and Moran v Keelings Logistics Solutions[52] – Employment Appeals Tribunal – Unfair Dismissals Acts 1977 to 2007 as amended – appeal of Rights Commissioner's determination – dismissal arising out of breach of policy – stock tampering – disciplinary process fair and objective – sanction proportionate and reasonable*

The claimants, who were employed as warehouse operatives, were videoed engaging in misconduct on several occasions on the shop floor.

The respondent discovered that two jam tarts were missing from a packet in a box situated in a cage in lane 52. The claimants were observed at a cage in lane 52. Neither claimant had been assigned to lane 52 at the time. The claimants stated that they were not eating the jam tarts but were sharing a bar of chocolate. The matter was investigated and it was determined that there was a high probability that the claimants had tampered with stock in the warehouse. Both claimants claimed that they returned again to lane 52 to view a video on the first claimant's mobile phone. It was determined that the claimants had no reason to be in the vicinity of lane 52 and there was a high probability they had interfered with the stock.

The matter was recommended for disciplinary action. The claimants' explanations for the CCTV footage were found not to be credible. At no stage during the viewing of the footage did it become clear that the claimants were eating mars bars or viewing footage on a mobile phone. It was decided that the claimants had tampered with stock. This amounted to gross misconduct and the claimants were dismissed.

The claimants were offered a right of appeal. On the balance of probabilities it was decided that the claimants had tampered with stock. The claimants were dismissed on 19 May 2012.

The respondent stated that its function is to accept deliveries, process them and dispatch it to a third party's stores. The third party is their only client. There is a high level of trust between the respondent and the third party that must be maintained at all times. This is why there is a zero tolerance policy on staff tampering with stock.

The EAT found that the claimants' evidence was not credible and on the balance of probability found that they did in fact tamper with the stock. The EAT was of the

---

52.   *Boyne v Keelings Logistics Solutions* and *Moran v Keelings Logistics Solutions* UD829/2013, UD828/2013.

opinion that the investigation, disciplinary meetings and appeal were thorough, fair and objective.

The EAT accepted that the respondent's zero tolerance policy was reasonable in the circumstance and that the dismissal was arising out of breach of the policy was fair and proportionate. The EAT upheld the decision of the Rights Commissioner that the dismissal was fair.

Dismissal for removal of money and stock and the use of 'IOUs'

[27.39] *Murphy v Cara Pharmacy[53] – Employment Appeals Tribunal – Unfair Dismissals Acts 1977 to 2007 as amended – unfair dismissal – acknowledgement by claimant that she had removed money and stock without authorisation and had utilised IOUs until money and items were refunded or replaced – dissenting determination of the EAT – claimant's contribution to her dismissal*

The claimant worked in one of the respondent's pharmacy stores and was employed as a sales assistant. The claimant worked four days a week and took extra responsibilities when the manager of the store went on sick leave. The claimant looked after wages, the rota and trained in two employees on the tills. CN was joint director of the respondent since 2002 and regional manager and CB was the operations manager for the past 11 years.

In January 2012 it was brought to CN's attention that there was an IOU in the lodgement bag in the store. CN and CM called to the store and questioned staff about the IOU. The employees were not asked to furnish written statements. The employees were aware that the claimant was placing IOUs in the lodgement bag and that the claimant was removing money from the till on occasions. The claimant was not present in the store that day.

CN and CM met the claimant on 19 January 2012. Prior to this meeting, the claimant was unaware of the allegations against her. The claimant admitted that she had removed money from the lodgement without authorisation up to the value of €200 to pay her bills but that this was always replaced some days later, that she had removed stock from the store without authorisation, that she had removed money from the tills and given to her son but had always refunded the money, that staff were unaware of this and that she had come into the store after hours to catch up on work. The meeting ended amicably. The claimant was suspended with pay for two weeks pending an investigation into the matters.

The claimant gave evidence that because of the additional duties she was required to carry out, she had returned to the store some evenings to 'catch up' on her work.

The claimant gave evidence that IOUs were common in the store since the commencement of her employment and everyone knew about them. The claimant stated that when she needed to borrow money from the till she wrote an IOU with her name on it. On one occasion she borrowed €20 for a school jumper for her son, wrote an IOU and the money was subsequently repaid. At that time she made her co-worker A aware

---

53.   *Murphy v Cara Pharmacy* UD871/2012.

of the IOU. She never felt guilty about writing an IOU. As a result of the IOUs in the till the store's lodgement was carried out the following day. The money was always repaid. Neither CM nor CN was ever made aware of the IOUs during the course of the claimant's tenure.

A disciplinary meeting took place on 31 January 2012. The claimant and her solicitor attended this meeting. There was no issue surrounding the claimant's performance. All the issues were discussed again. By letter dated 6 February 2012 the claimant was dismissed from her employment for gross misconduct. The respondent gave evidence to the effect that they had lost trust in the claimant and they did not consider any other sanction. The claimant chose not to appeal her dismissal to RN director as RN was related to CN and the claimant felt she would not get a fair hearing. The claimant did not secure alternative employment until September 2012.

The EAT noted that while the initial investigation meeting was not best practice, nonetheless the claimant was offered a full disciplinary hearing. The EAT, by majority, accepted the evidence of the claimant that the practice of IOUs had been in place when she started employment and continued on during the course of her employment. The EAT found that the use of IOUs to be both irregular and extremely poor practice and the claimant should have realised this. The EAT accepted that at all times any monies removed by the claimant from the till were returned and were documented by IOUs.

The EAT by majority held that while the claimant contributed substantially to her dismissal the decision to dismiss was unfair in the circumstances. Taking the claimant's contribution to her dismissal into account, together with evidence of loss, and mitigation, the EAT considered compensation to be the appropriate remedy and awarded the claimant the sum of €4,000.

Breach of health and safety rule – use of mobile phones

[27.40] *Burczy v Tesco Ireland Ltd – Employment Appeals Tribunal*[54] *– Unfair Dismissals Acts 1977 to 2007 as amended – whether dismissal of claimant for breaching health and safety rule in using his mobile phone whilst operating mechanical handling equipment vehicle was fair – proportionality of sanction*

The claimant, a warehouse operative, was observed using a mobile phone while operating a mechanical handling vehicle in the warehouse. It was believed the claimant was reading a text message and then laughing, whilst continuing to drive the vehicle. The claimant was fully trained on the safe handling of vehicles and was aware the use of mobile phones was prohibited while operating a vehicle. Evidence was given to the EAT by the section manager that staff had been briefed recently on the use of mobile phones while operating a vehicle. An investigation took place in which the claimant explained that he was looking at his phone to check the time. In the course of the investigation the claimant had apologised for his behaviour. He was suspended with immediate effect and

---

54.   *Burczy v Tesco Ireland Ltd* UD618/2012.

with pay, pending the outcome of the investigation and was made aware of the possible consequences of his actions.

A disciplinary meeting took place where the claimant disputed nothing other than that he had checked the time on his phone and was not reading a text message. The claimant again apologised and stated he would not repeat the action.

The operations manager gave evidence to the effect that the purpose of using the mobile was not relevant at all as holding or checking a mobile phone was not permitted while operating the vehicle. On this basis, a decision was taken to dismiss the claimant. The EAT noted that the operations manager did not interview or meet with the depot manager, who had witnessed the breach prior to dismissing the claimant, and no CCTV footage covered the area where the breach occurred. An appeal upheld the original decision to dismiss.

The claimant said that he was shocked to learn of his dismissal as he was aware of other employees who had breached the policy and had received final written warnings and that there was no consistency in approach on the part of the respondent. The EAT noted that this case was about the proportionality of the sanction as the claimant had accepted he should not have used his mobile phone. It was noted by the EAT that the respondent's case was that, following other incidents, it had decided to impose a heavier sanction on the employees observed using mobile phones and at a weekly team meeting it was said that they communicated the severity of the sanctions should an employee be observed using or holding a mobile phone. The EAT noted that evidence had been heard that other employees had received final written warnings for using mobile phones, once whilst operating the vehicle, the other whilst having stopped operating. The EAT noted that the respondent relied heavily on the assertion that using a mobile phone when in control of an mechanical handing vehicle will lead to lead to disciplinary action being taken which could lead to a sanction up to and including dismissal and seemed to believe that this allowed it to impose a zero tolerance policy. However, the EAT noted that the briefing did allow for a lesser sanction and in the view of the EAT there were a number of lesser sanctions that the respondent could have imposed on the claimant.

The EAT concluded that the claimant had been unfairly dismissed from his employment. However, he had contributed significantly to his dismissal by his conduct, in circumstances where he had received extensive training in health and safety and where it was repeated consistently that he should not use his mobile phone while operating the vehicle. The EAT awarded compensation of €20,000.

Dismissal following findings of harassment and sexual harassment

[27.41] *Sheridan v Ampleforth Ltd T/A The Fitzwilliam Hotel[55] – Employment Appeals Tribunal – Unfair Dismissals Acts 1977 to 2007 as amended – dismissal on grounds of gross misconduct arising from allegations of harassment and sexual harassment – predetermination of decision-maker – failure by decision-maker to*

---

55. *Sheridan v Ampleforth Ltd T/A The Fitzwilliam Hotel* UD273/2010.

exercise judgment – lack of evidence against employee – reinstatement where compensation is inadequate

The claimant, a former deputy general manager of the respondent hotel, was dismissed on the grounds of gross misconduct for allegedly sexually harassing a female worker who was an employee of a cleaning company which provided services to the hotel. The claimant argued that he was unfairly dismissed on the basis that the respondent had failed to investigate the allegations properly, had reached a conclusion that did not reflect the evidence and had imposed a disproportionate sanction.

In a written statement dated 12 July 2009, the female employee of the cleaning company (the complainant) made allegations of harassment, including sexual harassment, against the claimant. Subsequently, on 15 July 2009, the claimant was suspended pending an investigation. Interviews were conducted with nine members of staff. On 6 October 2009 the human resources manager of the respondent wrote to the complainant advising her that her sexual harassment complaint had been upheld against the claimant, prior the disciplinary hearing taking place. The EAT determined that, on the evidence of this letter alone, the respondent had predetermined the outcome of the disciplinary hearing and accordingly the dismissal of the claimant by the respondent was procedurally unfair.

The EAT went on to consider other elements of the investigation/disciplinary procedure.

A general manager at the respondent carried out this investigation. In the body of the investigation report, the manager upheld the complaint of sexual harassment. The EAT found that this statement and the generality of the evidence in the case clearly predetermined the outcome of the disciplinary hearing such that the dismissal was procedurally unfair.

Following the issue of the investigation report, the respondent held a disciplinary hearing. The EAT noted that at numerous stages in the disciplinary hearing, the decision-maker made reference to the conclusion of the investigator that the allegation of sexual harassment had been upheld. By letter dated 21 October 2009, the decision-maker wrote to the claimant confirming that the charge of sexual harassment was upheld and the claimant was dismissed.

The claimant appealed the decision to managing director of the company that manages the respondent hotel. The managing director responded to the claimant, stating the outcome of the appeal and confirming the dismissal of the claimant. The appeal decision contained a reference to the decision-maker having regard for the conclusions of the investigator.

The EAT concluded that both decision-makers had treated the investigation report as a fixed conclusion that the claimant was guilty of sexual harassment, and had failed to exercise any judgment themselves. The EAT concluded that this was a breach of fair procedures, which rendered the dismissal unfair.

Other evidence of predetermination of the issue was produced to the EAT at the hearing. The claimant gave an account of a meeting with his manager at which his manager claimed that he was in serious trouble and that the best thing that the claimant could do was take 'walk money' and go, notwithstanding that the particular manager was of the view that the allegations against the claimant were false. The EAT noted that the respondent's solicitor attempted to assert that these conversations were on a without prejudice basis and should not be in evidence. The EAT admitted them into evidence on the basis that such conversations were not covered by a form of privilege known to law.

The EAT stated that it must be cognisant that employers are cynically terminating the employment of employees even where the complaint is on the balance of probabilities untrue, in order to avoid being found vicariously liable for the misconduct of its employees in costly personal injuries actions. In this regard, the EAT found that the fact that the manager did not believe the complaints, but yet still advised the claimant to 'take walk money' was evidence of an employer acting in bad faith in dealing with the disciplinary allegations against the claimant.

The EAT also referred to the fact that the decision maker in the appeal met with the claimant's manager, in the absence of the claimant or his representative, after the appeal hearing, and by taking into consideration evidence so obtained from the manager in reaching the decisions, had breached the principle of *audi alteram partem*.

The EAT also found that the respondent had not applied fair procedures to the claimant by failing to take into account his explanation of why the complainant had made such allegations against him. The claimant asserted that the complainant made the allegations as some kind of pre-emptive strike against him, to damage and to discredit him, because he had obtained information implicating her in the illegal sale of false passports. The EAT found on the evidence that the claimant's assertion was credible, and should have been taken into account by the respondent.

It was also noted that neither the complainant nor any corroborating witness attended the disciplinary hearing or any subsequent appeal hearing. The EAT found that the respondent reached the conclusion that the claimant had sexually harassed the complainant without hearing any substantiating evidence, and failed to consider the evidence of the claimant that he was not guilty. In this regard, the EAT concluded that the decision-maker failed to satisfy himself of the truthfulness of facts in dispute by hearing the evidence directly from the relevant witnesses, but rather relied on the conclusions of an investigation report.

The EAT rejected the contention that the complainant did not attend either the disciplinary hearing or the EAT hearing as she was intimidated by the claimant, as the respondent could have facilitated her giving evidence in such a way that no intimidation would have taken place.

The EAT concluded that the respondent had insufficient evidence to conclude that the claimant had sexually harassed the complainant and that the procedures which ultimately led to the claimant's dismissal were unfair.

The EAT upheld the unfair dismissals claim and ordered that the claimant be reinstated (against the stated wishes of both parties) with an award of arrears of payment of €922.50 gross per week. It stated that in the circumstances, compensation would have been an inadequate remedy both from the point of view of quantum and reputation. The EAT found that the award of compensation, being limited to a maximum of two years' remuneration would be an insufficient amount to recoup the claimant's financial loss.

[27.42] *Monnickendam v Limerick County Council[56] – Unfair Dismissals Acts 1977 to 2007 as amended – Minimum Notice and Terms of Employment Acts 1973 to 2005 – preliminary application to have case heard in camera – whether claimant unfairly dismissed for gross misconduct following investigation which upheld complaints of harassment and sexual harassment against him*

The EAT refused a preliminary application by the respondent to have this case heard '*in camera*'.

The claimant worked as a supervisor in the Fire Safety Emergency Control Room in the respondent county council. He was dismissed for gross misconduct, following an investigation into and the upholding of a complaint of harassment and sexual harassment against him. In the course of the hearing before the EAT, there was significant witness evidence, including that of the complainant and a number of respondent witnesses, who had been part of the investigation. Evidence was given that on foot of the allegations which were set out in detail for the EAT, the respondent engaged an independent company to conduct the investigation. The lead investigator gave extensive evidence to the EAT on the process and procedure used by her in carrying out the investigation. It was noted by the EAT that there was no allegation of bullying made by the complainant but, as it forms part of the respondent's policy, any possible bullying was also investigated as well as possible harassment and sexual harassment. The findings were that the claimant engaged in repeated inappropriate behaviour both directly and indirectly.

In his evidence the claimant had confirmed that, prior to the complaint, things had become difficult between him and the complainant because of work performance issues. He did not have a recollection of the complainant asking him to stop his behaviour towards her or her drawing any issues to his attention as had been claimed in evidence by her. The claimant submitted that there was a culture of sexual banter in the respondent which was established before the claimant took up employment and that name calling was normal behaviour and that all respondent staff were engaging in inappropriate behaviour. The claimant did not accept that he was bullying, harassing or sexual harassing the complainant.

In its determination the EAT considered the evidence adduced and based its decision on the evidence, the investigation report and all of the witnesses provided. The EAT concluded that the claimant was informed of the allegations against him. The respondent engaged independent consultants to investigate and evaluate in a forensic manner the allegations of bullying, harassment and sexual harassment made against the claimant. Thirteen allegations were investigated and in respect of four, adverse findings were made against the claimant. Both the claimant and the complainant were interviewed extensively in the investigation process. The results were notified to the claimant and an opportunity was given to him to comment on and made submissions on same. The EAT stated that they did not believe that the investigator had commented on the status of the complaint to any of the witnesses as was alleged by the claimant. The EAT noted that the claimant was offered and declined the right to appeal the decision to dismiss him and, in

---

56. *Monnickendam v Limerick County Council* UD765/2012, MN569/2012.

both the decision to dismiss and the appeal, recourse was had to the investigation report. The EAT held that the claimant's unfair dismissal claim failed.

Reliance on CCTV

[27.43] *Deegan v Dunnes Stores[57] – Employment Appeals Tribunal – Unfair Dismissals Acts 1977 to 2007 as amended – Minimum Notice and Terms of Employment Acts 1973 to 2005 – whether dismissal of claimant for having consumed food without payment was fair – use of and reliance on covert CCTV footage as part of disciplinary process – extent to which claimant contributed to her own dismissal by her conduct*

The claimant was employed as a deli assistant. Unknown to her and other staff, there were two CCTV cameras installed in the retail area and in the food preparation area in September 2011 in response to a request from the store manager. On 7 October 2011, the claimant was called to attend a meeting with the store manager and the human resources manager, for which she received no advance notification. She was asked questions in relation to purchasing and consuming food on the premises and confirmed she understood the employee purchases policy. She was then shown CCTV footage from her workplace area and admitted to consuming chicken wings and goujons without payment. She was suspended without pay and was asked to report to a further meeting the next day, in the course of which she admitted she had done wrong. She was subsequently informed that her employment was being terminated with immediate effect.

The respondent gave evidence that employees who purchased food on the premises were required to get their receipt signed by a store manager, but there had been serious breaches of company policy in the deli area of the store in relation to the employee purchases policy. The respondent had issues with other employees, to include the claimant, and they were all treated in the same manner. The EAT considered all of the evidence and noted that there was an issue with the consumption of food by staff. The EAT acknowledged the seriousness of the issue for the respondent and the fact that the claimant had admitted the conduct. However, the EAT stated that the investigation and disciplinary process invoked by the respondent fell short of acceptable practice. The EAT found that the claimant was unfairly dismissed, but stated that she had contributed by two-thirds to her dismissal and awarded her compensation of €8,800. She was also awarded notice.

[27.44] *Circuit Court – appeal of decision of Employment Appeals Tribunal – Judge Linnane*

The respondent employer appealed the decision of the EAT to the Circuit Court. The claimant was dismissed having admitted she had eaten food from the deli counter without paying for it. The EAT found that, while she had contributed substantially to the loss of her job, she had been unfairly dismissed. However Judge Linnane in the Circuit

---

57.   *Deegan v Dunnes Stores* UD202/2012, MN152/2012.

Court found that there were substantial grounds justifying the respondent's decision to dismiss the respondent employee, along with seven other members of staff. She overturned the EAT's finding and dismissed the claim by the claimant who, in a cross-appeal, had asked the Circuit Court to increase her compensation award.

Judge Linnane awarded costs against the claimant and stated that there was not only a breach of company policy of which she was aware, but there was a breach of trust. Judge Linnane also noted that seven members of staff were similarly dismissed for similar breaches.

[27.45] *Hayes v Kinsella T/A Kinsellas of Rocklands*[58] *– Employment Appeals Tribunal – appeal of decision of Right Commissioner – Terms of Employment (Information) Act 1994 – Unfair Dismissals Acts 1977 to 2007 as amended – dismissal of employee in retail sector in reliance on CCTV footage – dismissal for theft*

The claimant worked in one of the respondent's premises for a number of years and was promoted to senior supervisor. In 2011, she was moved to work at another premises. Evidence was given that a member of management reviewed CCTV footage in September 2011 due to an issue that had arisen in relation to missing mass card money. In the course of viewing this footage, it was found that the claimant was carrying out her duties contrary to policy and using her mobile phone while working. The claimant was observed on CCTV taking items from the shop and not paying for them.

The claimant was asked to attend a meeting the following day. She stated that she was asked at this meeting about missing mass card money and using her phone at work. She stated she was not informed she could bring representation to the meeting. She subsequently was on sick leave from October to the following January when her sick leave expired and she was then asked to attend a meeting at which she would be shown CCTV and that she could bring a representative. It was disputed that the claimant was informed that it was a disciplinary meeting. At the meeting, the claimant was shown the CCTV footage of her in the shop on the phone and not carrying out tasks and it was put to her that on a number of dates and times she had taken items from the shop and had not paid for them. Management had reviewed CCTV footage for a period of 10 days in light of what footage from September 2011 had shown. Evidence was given by the respondent that the claimant was advised that the matter was serious and could lead to dismissal and that she had offered to pay if there was anything she had not paid for.

A further disciplinary hearing took place at which the claimant was shown more footage and was told not only did the footage show her on the phone in front of customers, but also for every day of footage there were items she had not paid for. The claimant stated she could provide receipts for these and the meeting concluded. As the CCTV footage could not be downloaded and given to the claimant, she was invited to review it again at any stage and was suspended without pay. A final meeting was held in February 2012 and the claimant was informed that she was being dismissed for theft, which came under the heading of 'gross misconduct'. A letter of dismissal issued in February 2012 advising the claimant that her employment was ending. Evidence was

---

58.   *Hayes v Kinsella T/A Kinsellas of Rocklands* UD690/2012, WT211/2012, TE80/2013.

given in the course of the hearing that the CCTV footage was examined for 23 September 2011 and it was found that the claimant did not pay for items taken. The claimant stated that she had receipts as proof of payment, but ultimately only three receipts were produced that were relevant. There were 20 to 30 items not paid for over 10 days of footage. It was agreed that the CCTV footage was not independently assessed which would have been costly for the respondent, but that it was open to the claimant to view as many days of footage as she wished. Anything that was noted on CCTV was checked against the corresponding till read, but the till reads were not provided to the claimant. The claimant stated the words 'theft' and 'stolen' were not used at the meetings. The claimant stated that management would have known that she would have taken goods and paid later as most employees did.

The EAT noted that it was not a matter of deciding the issue of guilt or innocence, but the question for the EAT was whether, following a fair and transparent investigation and disciplinary process, the respondent's decision to dismiss was one that a reasonable employer might have made.

The EAT noted the dismissal was for theft and this is clear from the dismissal letter. However, at no time did the claimant accept that she had stolen goods from the shop or had purposely failed to pay for items. She conceded that she might have overlooked paying for some items but suggested that the procedures for payment were not followed and that she often paid at the end of the day or occasionally on the following morning. The EAT stated that it was important to recognise that investigative and disciplinary procedures that might be sufficient in one instance may not be in another, particularly where a criminal act is at issue. Where there is a possibility of a finding being made by an employer that an employee has stolen goods, particular care must be taken. The EAT stated a significant concern was that the decision to dismiss appeared to have been made principally on a subjective analysis of a vast amount of CCTV footage.

The EAT noted the view of the claimant that there was an agenda to get rid of her and stated that, while this may or may not have been the case, it was clear that the claimant may have been surplus to needs and the objectivity of management in reviewing the footage had to be considered. The EAT said it could not discount evidence that had been given in the Rights Commissioner case to the effect that the claimant would have been made redundant if she had not moved to this site and stated that the evidence before it was suggestive of an employer looking to find fault on the part of the claimant. While fault may well have been found, the objectivity of the respondent's witnesses had to be questionable.

The EAT, having considered the totality of the evidence, was of the view that the investigative and disciplinary procedures undertaken fell short of the appropriate standards where an employee faces potential dismissal for alleged criminal behaviour and noted the following concerns:

(i) the claimant should have received in writing details of the precise charges against her and the basis for those charges;

(ii) there was no clear delineation between the investigation and the disciplinary processes, with both conducted by the same individuals and considerable overlap between the two processes;

(iii) no evidence was forthcoming at the EAT from the decision-maker so the EAT could not be satisfied that the latter's deliberations were independent and without influence from those who investigated and conducted the disciplinary process; and

(iv) the claimant was not provided with all of the evidence against her, nor given an appropriate opportunity to consider an allowed adequate time to prepare her response.

It was noted that the CCTV footage had come from an older system that could not be copied onto a DVD or a memory stick. No expert evidence was produced and the till record that was used as part of the investigative process was not produced, either to the claimant in any investigative or disciplinary processes, or to the EAT. The EAT stated that every effort to place this information in an accessible manner before the claimant should have been made. The EAT stated that it was not satisfied that the respondent had discharged the onus upon it by inviting the claimant to attend in person at her workplace, whilst suspended, to view long hours of CCTV footage or to attend at the management's house to go through till records. The EAT concluded that the information should have been independently analysed and presented to the claimant in a format that could be properly considered by her. The EAT stated there was an issue around the opportunity given to the claimant to test the evidence against her – she was not offered the option of having her own expert view on the information. Other concerns noted by the EAT were that there was no clear agenda set out for the meetings between the parties, the minutes of the meeting were not agreed and signed by the claimant and in addition her request for copies of the minutes was ignored. The EAT stated that the minutes should have been circulated after each meeting. Notwithstanding the terms of her contract of employment, the claimant was given no right of appeal against the decision to dismiss her.

The EAT stated it would have expected not only the CCTV footage, but also the corresponding till receipts and stock figures, to be put to the claimant. The EAT found that there is an inherent danger in relying on a subjective review of CCTV footage, where evidence that the respondent claims to be available is not presented to a claimant, nor indeed put before the EAT. The EAT concluded that the investigative and disciplinary processes did not meet the standard that could be expected where an employee is accused of being a thief and for that reason the claimant was unfairly dismissed and was awarded a compensation of €11,000. The claim under the Organisation of Working Time Act 1997 was dismissed.

[27.46] *Graham v Newlands Cross Hotel T/A Bewley's Hotel Dublin Airport*[59] – *Employment Appeals Tribunal – Unfair Dismissals Acts 1977 to 2007 as amended – Minimum Notice and Terms of Employment Acts 1973 to 2005 – dismissal following confrontation between staff at respondent's Christmas party – lack of engagement by claimant in disciplinary process – reliance on CCTV footage*

The claimant, an employee of the respondent hotel, attended the staff Christmas party, in the course of which a confrontation occurred between the claimant and another

---

59.   *Graham v Newlands Cross Hotel T/A Bewley's Hotel Dublin Airport* UD886/2012, MN625/2012.

employee, resulting in the dismissal of the claimant. The other party to the confrontation was not disciplined.

The general manager sought advice from the group human resources manager as to how to proceed. They immediately reviewed the CCTV footage of the incident and then contacted the claimant's manager for his knowledge of what had happened. After a meeting with the financial director, a letter of suspension was sent to the claimant advising him that a disciplinary meeting would take place to discuss the incident. He was advised that witness statements would be provided to him in advance of the disciplinary meeting and the group human resources manager was responsible for carrying out the investigation. In a subsequent letter, the claimant was asked to attend a disciplinary meeting to discuss incidents regarding his conduct at the annual staff Christmas party. It informed the claimant that he was entitled to be accompanied by a work colleague and enclosed certain witness statements.

The EAT noted that neither the suspension letter nor the disciplinary invitation letter gave the claimant notice of the possible disciplinary action that could be taken against him. Evidence was given that the claimant was unprepared and unwilling to engage in the process and the disciplinary meeting and the meeting was adjourned. The claimant denied all wrongdoing and the meeting was reconvened, but then adjourned and the claimant was asked to be prepared for the next disciplinary meeting. He was offered the opportunity to view CCTV footage, but replied: 'What's the point?'

At a subsequent meeting, the claimant refused the offer of representation and the group human resources manager provided a work colleague to attend with him. The claimant was warned that his failure to cooperate in the process could be deemed reason for a dismissal. The respondent was unable to obtain a statement from the claimant as to his version of events.

Subsequent correspondence was sent to the claimant stating that:

(i) he was alleged to have engaged in physical violence and violent and threatening behaviour; and

(ii) he had failed to cooperate with the investigation to date.

He was again asked to provide a statement in advance of the meeting and was offered the right to bring a representative. At the final meeting, the CCTV footage was viewed by everybody present, including the claimant, who acknowledged that it was a serious incident. A decision was taken to summarily dismiss the claimant for engaging in deliberate acts of violence and threatening behaviour towards fellow employees. The claimant was afforded the opportunity to appeal, but did not avail of it.

In the course of the EAT hearing, the CCTV footage referred to by the respondent was shown. In his evidence to the EAT, the claimant outlined the circumstances which had led to the confrontation with his colleague. The EAT considered all of the evidence, to include the CCTV footage, which it noted was not completely conclusive and did not provide the EAT with any clear or accurate evidence of what occurred on the night in question. The EAT noted the acceptance by the claimant that a confrontation had occurred, followed by an altercation, and that he was not proud of his behaviour. The respondent had accepted that the investigation procedure that followed the incident leading to the claimant's dismissal for gross misconduct was not perfect. The EAT stated that it did not condone violence in the workplace. However it noted that the claimant was the only employee disciplined following the incident at the staff Christmas party which was organised by the respondent. The EAT held that the claimant had contributed to his own dismissal by his behaviour on the night. The EAT concluded the dismissal was unfair and awarded the claimant €25,000.

[27.47] *Murtagh v TLC Health Service Ltd[60] – Employment Appeals Tribunal – Minimum Notice and Terms of Employment Acts 1973 to 2005 – Unfair Dismissals Acts 1977 to 2007 as amended – whether dismissal of claimant as a result of his conduct in respondent nursing home fair – procedural failings – reliance on CCTV footage by respondent which was not shown to claimant during process – reliance on witness statements by parties who were not present when conduct of concern took place – failure to have regard to witness statements that exonerated claimant – failure to verify legitimacy of allegations*

The claimant had received a number of written warnings, to include two final written warnings prior to the decision to dismiss him. An investigation was carried out with respect to a complaint by two colleagues in relation to his conduct on a particular weekend. In the course of the investigation, statements were taken from all staff members on duty over that weekend and also from a member of staff who was not on duty, but whom it was believed had something to contribute to the investigation.

It was submitted by the respondent that the investigation disregarded the majority of statements (approximately 14) as they did not add to the investigation as these people did not witness any of the alleged behaviour/incidents and thus these statements were not given to the claimant during the investigation process. It was submitted by the claimant that the decision to dismiss him was based on three statements from colleagues, one of whom was not present on the weekend on which the incidents were alleged to have incurred, and two allegations made by the claimant's ex-girlfriend and her friend. The claimant submitted that these matters were not considered relevant at any stage of the process.

It was acknowledge by the respondent that CCTV footage was viewed by the investigator, but was not shown to the claimant during the investigation as it was deemed by the investigator to be of no consequence. The disciplinary decision-maker provided copies of the statements from staff who said they witnessed the claimant's behaviour/incident and permitted the claimant to ask them questions. However the claimant did not avail of this opportunity. The claimant was also provided with copies of the statements provided from other employees and these were forwarded by email to him the evening before the rescheduled disciplinary date. The claimant did not attend the meeting and the disciplinary process concluded with the decision to dismiss the claimant. The claimant's appeal was not upheld. The claimant asserted that the process leading to his dismissal was flawed and unfair in that he only received the witness statements on the evening before the final disciplinary meeting. The claimant noted that these statements

---

60.   *Murtagh v TLC Health Service Ltd* UD1425/2012, MN821/2012.

were from people who were present on the weekend in question but saw or heard nothing to corroborate what his accusers alleged happened.

The EAT held that, whilst it appeared at first glance the respondent had a very comprehensive disciplinary process, on careful analysis the flaws became obvious. The EAT noted that four separate allegations had been made against the claimant. The EAT noted that in respect of the first allegation the complainant was the ex-girlfriend of the claimant and no investigation was pursued or questions asked to verify the legitimacy of those allegations. The EAT noted that witness statements had been taken by everyone who was in the vicinity of the dining room. However the respondent completely disregarded those statements which exonerated the claimant on the basis that they had 'heard nothing' and therefore had nothing to add to the investigation.

The EAT noted that the fact that those statements supported the claimant's defence did not seem to dawn on the respondent. The EAT held that, to disregard the statements exonerating the claimant and to rely only on those that accused him, was a fundamental breach of the claimant's right to fair procedures. The EAT stated it was all the more alarming that the respondent placed no importance on the fact that two of the statements relied upon by its accused were by individuals who were not present at all. The EAT held that this too was a fundamental breach of the claimant's right to fair procedures.

A number of the allegations related to the giving of food to residents. However, the EAT noted that, following its enquiries at the hearing of this matter, the claimant was not responsible for giving food to the residents and that serving of meals to residents was something outside of the claimant's control. The EAT stated it was noted that one of the staff serving the meals was the claimant's ex-girlfriend, one of the complainants in the process.

In relation to the CCTV footage, the EAT noted the claimant had been denied access to the footage until close to the end of the process on the grounds that it 'showed nothing'. The EAT held that the very fact that it showed nothing could have been used by the claimant in his defence, and his rights to fair procedures in this regard were breached. The EAT held that in every disciplinary process, the claimant is entitled to have sight of each and every piece of evidence the respondent has, regardless of the respondent's view of its evidential value. The claimant is entitled to have sight of it and to use it in his defence however he sees fit. The vital pieces of information were withheld from the claimant at various stages of the process and that was fundamentally unfair and potentially prejudicial.

The EAT upheld the claim of unfair dismissal and awarded the claimant compensation of €30,000.

Criminal convictions

[27.48] *Moore v Tesco Ireland Ltd*[61] *– Unfair Dismissals Acts 1977 to 2007 as amended – Employment Appeals Tribunal – dismissal of employee because employee convicted of criminal offence relating to supply of drugs with intent to sell – whether conviction brought respondent company into disrepute and constituted serious*

---

61.   *Moore v Tesco Ireland Ltd* UD2423/2011.

misconduct – whether dismissal unfair – procedures for considering appeal inadequate and procedurally unfair

The claimant was employed by the respondent company since 1996 and was working as a charge hand in one of the respondent's stores. His role involved working in the back store and handling deliveries of a variety of goods. Other than the issue for which he was dismissed, the claimant had a clean disciplinary record with the respondent. In 2009, when the claimant was charged with a criminal offence in relation to a supply of drugs with intent to sell, he informed the then store manager of this fact and continued in his employment thereafter. In July 2011, the claimant received an eight month suspended sentence. The store manager held a meeting on the 2 August 2011 at which the claimant confirmed that he had received a conviction. The store manager explained to the claimant that this fact could have repercussions for his employment, up to and including dismissal. The claimant was placed on suspension with pay pending further investigation.

A series of investigation meetings were held with the claimant in the presence of a union representative. One issue that was raised during the investigation meetings was whether or not the claimant's conviction had or would bring the respondent company into disrepute. The union representative enquired as to how the respondent company's name was in disrepute given that the conviction was not reported by the newspapers. The store manager outlined that the concern was that the conviction could bring the respondent company into disrepute.

Having concluded the investigation, the store manager made a decision to invoke the disciplinary procedure and held a disciplinary meeting on 20 September 2011 and a subsequent meeting on 26 September 2011 at which the claimant was informed that he was dismissed. The letter of dismissal stated the claimant was dismissed on grounds of serious misconduct under the following headings of the respondent's disciplinary policy:

(i)   conviction by a court of law for any serious criminal offence considered damaging to the company or its employees; and

(ii)   conduct which brings the company's good name into disrepute.

The claimant's representative wrote a letter detailing his grounds of appeal. The appeal decision-maker was the manager of another store of the respondent and was appointed by the group personnel manager to hear the appeal but he was not provided with the claimant's letter setting out the grounds of appeal. At the appeal meeting the appeal decision-maker listened as the claimant set out each point of appeal. The appeal decision-maker travelled to the store where the claimant worked to review his personnel file but did not speak to the store manager, the personnel manager or anyone else working at that store in relation to the matter. The appeal decision-maker considered the fact that:

(a)   the claimant had kept the respondent appraised;

(b)   the claimant was provided with a character reference from the personnel manager for court; and

(c)   the conviction was not in the public domain.

The appeal decision-maker utilised the notes from the meetings held with the claimant when considering the appeal. Given the grounds of appeal, the appeal decision-maker did not deem it necessary to speak to anyone other than the claimant. The appeal decision-maker upheld the decision to dismiss as he found that the claimant's conviction could easily bring the respondent into disrepute. During cross-examination at the EAT, the appeal decision-maker confirmed that he did not find evidence that customers or members of the public were aware of the claimant's conviction but he considered how it would be viewed if it came into public domain.

The EAT found that the dismissal was unfair. The respondent's process (particularly in relation to the appeal) was insufficient by failing to consider sanctions other than dismissal in light of the claimant's previous good record and given the claimant's efforts to keep the respondent appraised of the situation. Although it was the right of the respondent to consider dismissal as a remedy open to it under its procedures, the respondent did not demonstrate that it genuinely considered the alternative sanctions that could have been applied. In considering all of the circumstances of the case the EAT awarded compensation of €11,500.

Prising opening a locker

[27.49] *Occipital Ltd v Wojtun*[62] *– Employment Appeals Tribunal – appeal of decision of Rights Commissioner – Unfair Dismissals Acts 1977 to 2007 as amended – Terms of Employment (Information) Acts 1994 and 2014 – whether dismissal of claimant for gross misconduct for forcing open a locker (in the company of the locker owner) proportionate sanction*

The claimant was employed as a contract cleaner and worked as a supervisor at a distribution centre in Donabate where the respondent company had a contract. The EAT noted that the issue of security was extremely important on the site and that the majority of personnel had very limited access throughout the premises. The claimant was unusual in that he had access to all areas and could move freely throughout the premises in carrying out his duties. The EAT also heard evidence to the effect that all personnel on site were required to keep their personal items in assigned lockers for the duration of the working day and security around the locker rooms was significant.

An incident arose when the claimant, along with an employee of the distribution centre operator, were found in the locker room attempting to prise open a locker. It was subsequently discovered that the locker belonged to the centre operator employee and that the two men had impulsively and without thought set about the task of prising open the locker as the centre operator employee wanted to return or give something therein to the claimant. The EAT noted that the claimant, to his credit, had never resiled from the fact that he and the centre operator employee were in the act of forcing open the locker when they were spotted by a centre operator manager. The EAT noted that there was no question of theft as the contents of the locker were owned by the centre operator employee who was present and the centre operator employee was complicit in the act. When the centre operator management notified the respondent management, the

---

62. *Occipital Ltd v Wojtun* UD283/2013 TE44/2013.

claimant was immediately suspended on full pay pending the outcome of an investigation.

In its decision, the EAT expressed sympathy with the respondent and noted that its position was difficult as a much trusted and valued employee had been caught in the act of wilfully damaging property belonging to its client. The EAT noted that in the commercial world, contracts of this sort are highly prized and the respondent company had to protect its own commercial position when an employee turns 'rogue', as in this case.

However, notwithstanding the circumstances, the EAT stated that it did not allow for abandonment of the tenets of fair procedure and rationality and even-handedness. The EAT noted that no malice emanated from the claimant and that the decision to try and force open a locker was rash and lacked foresight and certainly was never, in the claimant's mind, an act which could lead to his dismissal. The EAT further criticised the respondent for the flaws in the investigation process. The EAT noted that the procedures allowed for a two-person investigation. However, only one investigator conducted the investigation. Furthermore, reliance was placed on a statement that was never shown to the claimant. The EAT also noted, as being more important, the fact that the claimant seemed to have no idea that the matter was moving in the direction of a summary dismissal and he was thus disadvantaged by the fact that he did not obtain representation and was ignorant as to the seriousness of the situation. The EAT further noted that the claimant was not invited to make a plea of mitigation and it was not persuaded as to the proportionality of the sanction imposed.

The EAT accepted that to have to return the claimant to the site may have been sensitive for the respondent. The EAT did not accept, however, that dismissal was the only alternative. The EAT held that any lesser sanction would have been sufficient and thereafter there was nothing to prevent the respondent from making a *bona fide* attempt to place the claimant in an alternative position when another arises, albeit stripped of the supervisor status. The EAT issued the caveat that it did not know if this was possible, but noted that no attempt was made and the sanction of being dismissed in response to the claimant's impulsive action was too great. In assessing compensation, the EAT took account of the claimant's contributory conduct and also the fact that he had made no concerted effort to mitigate his loss and awarded him compensation of €20,000.

Selling illegal cigarettes in workplace

[27.50] *Maslova v Golden Mushrooms Ltd[63] – Unfair Dismissals Acts 1977 to 2007 as amended – Employment Appeals Tribunal – appeal of Rights Commissioner decision – whether dismissal of claimant for gross misconduct reasonable – selling of illegal cigarettes in workplace during working hours – investigation by Revenue Commissioners – harassment of co-workers and failing to follow instruction to cease harassment of co-workers*

---

63.   *Maslova v Golden Mushrooms Ltd* UD18/2012.

The claimant was employed as a mushroom picker and was promoted to supervisor some three years later. Evidence was given by the respondent that there were issues with the manner in which the claimant spoke to and referred to other employees and also with her apparent lack of respect for the claimant's manager. These issues were addressed with her and she was subsequently issued with a first written warning. Two months later, while at work, the claimant was observed selling illegal cigarettes in the workplace. Initially, no action was taken, but she was observed on two further occasions selling cigarettes to work colleagues. A director of the respondent informed the local office of the Revenue Commissioners who commenced an investigation. The Revenue officer asked the respondent not to take any further action and/or alert the claimant. Subsequently, the respondent became aware that the Revenue officers had investigated the matter, but no prosecution had resulted. The claimant was then called to an investigation meeting and a list of allegations were put to her, to include selling of illegal cigarettes in the workplace during work hours, harassment of co-workers and failing to follow an instruction to cease harassing employees. The claimant was suspended on full pay, pending the outcome of the process, and was given statements of three employees who admitted to having purchased cigarettes from her. She was sent the respondent's code of practice and a letter of suspension.

A disciplinary meeting was held where the claimant admitted selling cigarettes and she offered an apology. The respondent decided to dismiss the claimant for gross misconduct and she was offered a right of appeal, but did not appeal this dismissal.

At the EAT, the claimant stated that she wished to keep her job, but had not realised the seriousness of selling cigarettes until she was contacted by the Revenue officers. She further asserted that the director of the respondent was fully aware of a culture of selling illegal cigarettes in the organisation and this had not been condemned by him.

In its determination, the EAT did not accept the claimant's evidence that she did not realise the seriousness of her illegal activity until such time as the Revenue officers had spoken to her. The EAT concluded that the respondent's decision to dismiss the claimant on grounds that her conduct constituted gross misconduct was reasonable in all of the circumstances. The appeal failed and the decision of the Rights Commissioner was set aside.

Being untruthful

[27.51] *Lynott Thomas v Atlantic Homecare Ltd[64] – Employment Appeals Tribunal – Unfair Dismissals Acts 1977 to 2007 as amended – whether summary dismissal of claimant for gross misconduct fair where she was found to have told a lie to her line manager whilst taking day of sick leave when not genuinely sick and had previously unsuccessfully sought the day as annual leave – whether telling of lie by employee breach of bond of trust which must exist between employer and employee rendering dismissal fair*

---

64. *Lynott Thomas v Atlantic Homecare Ltd* UD1671/2012.

The claimant was employed as a qualified horticulturist working in the respondent's garden centre. In the summer months, the days Thursday through Sunday were particularly busy. The claimant worked four days one week and six days the next, thus ensuring that she had one weekend off in every two. The claimant requested Friday 1 July 2011 off as an annual leave day. She had already been rostered off the weekend of 2 and 3 July meaning that she would get three days off. The parties disagreed as to whether the claimant's request for the day off was approved and it was denied by her line manager that she was ever informed that she could have the day off. The claimant then learnt that her driving test was scheduled for Thursday 30 June, which she was anxious to sit. The claimant was told by her line manager that she could not have four days off and was expected at work on Friday 1 July. The claimant made a counter proposal whereby she would work late on the Wednesday and come in on the Sunday. However, there was no agreement on this and the claimant, in evidence, fully accepted that she knew that she was expected to work on Friday 1 July.

The claimant decided to ring in and pretend she was sick on Friday 1 July when she was not sick. The EAT noted that the line manager who took the call did not believe or accept that the claimant was genuinely sick. The EAT found that her line manager was well aware that the claimant wanted a day of annual leave on the Friday. The claimant's employment was subsequently terminated.

The EAT noted that the respondent did not pay sick pay, so there was no financial loss to the respondent. The EAT noted the evidence that there was a demand for a horticulturalist on the premises, but noted the counter argument that, when the claimant is absent every second weekend, other sales staff had to fill in for her. The EAT found there was an unreasonableness to the decision not to allow a day of leave to be given that Friday. However, the EAT stated it was unable to overlook or condone the blatant lie told by the claimant to her line manager on 1 July, which was compounded by repetition. The EAT stated it could not accept the normality and/or acceptability of ringing in sick, which was suggested in evidence by the claimant as some sort of justification. There were procedural aspects to the investigation and the disciplinary process which were not satisfactory. In this regard, the EAT particularly noted that the commencement of an investigation without proper notice was most unsatisfactory, and the fact that the claimant was not adequately advised as to what was happening and the significance of this. However, on balance, the EAT found that the decision by the claimant to actively tell a lie could not be anything other than a breach of the bond of trust which must exist between employer and employee and in the circumstances the EAT held that the dismissal was not unfair. The claim therefore failed.

Call centres and customer service dismissal

[27.52] *McCaffrey v Telefonica Ireland Ltd[65] – Employment Appeals Tribunal – Organisation of Working Time Act 1997 – Minimum Notice and Terms of Employment Acts 1973 to 2005 – Unfair Dismissals Acts 1977 to 2007 as amended – customer service agent disciplined as result of frequency and duration of her line*

---

65. *McCaffrey v Telefonica Ireland Ltd* UD1668/2011, MN1725/2011, WT662/2011.

hanging and voicemail manipulation activities – obligations on employer in gross misconduct cases – disproportionate sanction

The claimant was employed as a customer service agent for the respondent, which traded as O2 in Ireland. Her role was to contact customers whose contracts were close to expiring, to persuade them to renew those contracts. Certain concerns arose regarding practices called 'line hanging' and 'voicemail manipulations', which involved sales agents behaving in a certain way whilst undertaking and receiving calls from customers. The customer service department and its agents were subject to targets which were regularly audited. As a result of an audit, the claimant's call report between June 2010 and February 2011 was reviewed because the respondent considered the frequency and duration of her line hanging and voicemail manipulation records for that period. The time spent by her on those activities was labelled as unproductive time and she was ultimately subjected to a disciplinary hearing, and a decision was taken to dismiss her.

The decision-maker gave evidence to the EAT that the decision was taken following consultations with other entities, but that consideration was given to the fact that the claimant had suffered a recent bereavement and other personal factors. The decision-maker acknowledged that the claimant was a great employee, who was well-liked and said she was surprised to have seen the claimant's name on a list linked to reported abuse of line hanging and voicemail manipulation. The conclusion reached by the respondent was that the claimant was avoiding work and not doing her job and that her actions had exposed the company to breaches of data protection legislation. However, it was acknowledged that no actual breaches had taken place.

It was noted by the EAT that gross misconduct was mentioned twice in the dismissal letter and evidence was given by the decision-maker that, in breaching certain procedures, the claimant had behaved in a dishonest way and thus the trust and confidence that the respondent had in her had been undermined by her conduct. The appeal decision-maker, who acknowledged that the claimant had been a model employee, gave evidence that her avoidance of work and the broken trust that it entailed were decisive factors in her decision to uphold the original sanctions. The claimant gave evidence to the effect that she loved her job and found it easy to reach her targets. She acknowledged that it had become more difficult to retain and incentivise customers and that, along with a serious family illness and subsequent bereavement, had combined to deflate and demotivate her at work. She stated that she was surprised and shocked to learn that she was to be subjected to an investigation relating to line hanging and voicemail manipulation. She stated that the call list between June 2010 and February 2011 represented a tiny proportion of the calls involved in that period. She understood line hanging was unacceptable, but she did not accept it was wrong and stated that this was common practice amongst her colleagues. With reference to voicemail manipulation, she stated that this gave the appearance that she was still on the phone, but in reality was working taking notes and updating information.

The EAT concluded that, where an employer dismisses an employee on the grounds of gross misconduct, it needs to be able to defend and justify that sanction. In this case, the EAT found that the respondent was unable to do this and the EAT upheld the claim of unfair dismissal. The EAT noted that, while the claimant may have been remiss at times, she certainly was not deviant or dishonest as an employee of the respondent and, on the contrary, her work rate and contribution to her employer was well regarded and constructive. The EAT found that the respondent had overreacted to her alleged shortcomings and was far too fast to subject her to a disciplinary process. The EAT further found that the sanction of dismissal was highly disproportionate, undeserved and unreasonable. The claimant was awarded compensation of €35,000.

[27.53] *Mooney v Oxigen Environmental[66] – Employment Appeals Tribunal – Unfair Dismissals Acts 1977 to 2007 as amended – Minimum Notice and Terms of Employment Acts 1973 to 2005 – dismissal for gross misconduct for inappropriate language used in telephone conversations and for poor handling of customer phone call – flawed procedures – disproportionate sanction*

The claimant was employed as a customer service representative from March 2007 until her dismissal for gross misconduct in April 2012. She worked in an open plan call centre environment. The reason given by the respondent for taking the decision to dismiss the claimant was her inappropriate language and telephone conversations. It was alleged that she used bad language during telephone conversations with colleagues and that she kept one customer on hold for five minutes while talking to a colleague, which was deemed unacceptable. Up until the termination of her employment, the claimant had not been the recipient of any reprimands or sanctions from her employer. The claimant gave evidence to the effect that she was given less than 48 hours' notice to attend a formal meeting with some management. No details were given to her about this meeting and she was not offered the right to have a representative accompany her. During the meeting, an audio recording of some of her telephone conversations was played back to her and the respondent stated that the claimant was unapologetic for the potential damage and the unacceptable language used. The respondent concluded that the only option was to dismiss the claimant. The claimant stated that the meeting was adjourned for approximately an hour and when she returned, she was shocked to be informed of the respondent's decision to dismiss her. She did not recall receiving a dismissal letter and a letter initiating an appeal was not responded to. The evidence given by the respondent was that it was never received. The claimant accepted in evidence that on occasions her language and choice of words to colleagues were of a colourful nature.

The EAT concluded that there was no doubt that the claimant, in verbally expressing herself at work, used expletives and offensive language, which was unacceptable to some of her listeners and that this scenario could not be condoned. However, the EAT noted the obligation of an employer to apply fair procedures and act reasonably when sanctioning an employee for any misdemeanour. The EAT noted that the claimant had an unblemished record and that there was no evidence of any investigation or suspension in this matter. The EAT viewed the notice for and nature of the meeting that took place on 18 July 2012 as being too short and brief. In the view of the EAT, a clear warning would have sufficed for this first offence and the sanction of dismissal was disproportionate. The claimant's claim for unfair dismissal succeeded and she was awarded compensation of €12,500.

---

66.   *Mooney v Oxigen Environmental* UD1525/2012, MN866/2012.

Childcare workers

[27.54] *Burke v Egan T/A Little Sunflowers Crèche & Montessori[67] – Employment Appeals Tribunal – Unfair Dismissals Acts 1977 to 2007 as amended – dismissal of crèche worker for misconduct – fair procedures*

On 18 January 2012, the manager of the crèche noticed that the claimant and another member of staff were acting 'out of character'. The member of staff stated that she had witnessed the claimant slap a child's hand in order to separate two children. She provided a written statement to that effect. The manager checked the respondent's disciplinary procedure and concluded that the claimant's action could potentially amount to gross misconduct.

Prior to this event, the manager had occasion to talk to the claimant about not handling children by the wrist/arms and the need for gentle treatment and had witnessed similar behaviour by the claimant on the day of the incident.

That evening, the manager brought the claimant into the office and explained the allegation. The claimant was suspended on pay for alleged gross misconduct and pending a full investigation. The claimant was given a letter confirming the above along with a copy of her colleague's written statement and was invited to a disciplinary meeting on 20 January. The following day, the director of the crèche interviewed the manager and the member of staff who had witnessed the event and did a walk-through of the incident. On the advice of the HSE Child Protection worker, the parents of the child involved were informed. Both the director and the manager attended the meeting of 20 January. The claimant was accompanied to the meeting. At the meeting the claimant denied she had slapped a child but had picked up the child to separate two children. She stated that she had been working for the respondent for six years and no complaint had been made against her previously. The manager reminded her that she had been warned not to catch the children by the wrist and arms and that she had engaged in this behaviour on the day of the incident. The director concluded that the claimant's actions amounted to gross misconduct and warranted a dismissal. At a meeting on 25 January, the director informed the claimant of his decision to dismiss her and of her right to appeal the decision. The business partner of the director's accountant heard the appeal, and the dismissal was upheld.

In her evidence to the EAT, the claimant accepted that she had been warned about her treatment of the children, but she did not agree that her actions could be characterised as rough.

The HSE pre-school service officer carried out an investigation and concluded that the respondent had taken the appropriate measures.

The EAT took cognisance of the nature of the respondent's business and the respondent's disciplinary policy which formed part of the claimant's contract of employment, and which provided that slapping, shaking or treating children roughly under a carer's supervision constitutes gross misconduct.

---

67. *Burke v Egan T/A Little Sunflowers Crèche & Montessori* UD902/2012.

The EAT noted that the standard to be applied in determining the fairness or otherwise of a dismissal is that of the reasonable employer. This test is satisfied if the employer had a genuine belief based on reasonable grounds arising from a fair investigation that the employee is guilty of the alleged misconduct and if the sanction is dismissal, it must not be disproportionate.

The EAT noted that, while the meeting of 20 January 2012 had been labelled a disciplinary meeting, it was in reality an investigation meeting at which the claimant had the opportunity to put forward her version of events and to answer the allegations made against her. She was informed of her right to bring a fellow employee or other appropriate representative to the meeting. The EAT accepted that there was a conflict of evidence but the EAT concluded that the director had reasonable grounds for believing the allegations.

The EAT stated that, while the respondent's procedures were flawed, they were not so flawed as to render the dismissal unfair. The EAT held that the dismissal was not disproportionate and the claim for unfair dismissal failed.

[27.55] *Fox v Clevercloggs Full Day Care Nursery Ltd*[68] – *Employment Appeals Tribunal – Unfair Dismissals Acts 1977 to 2007 as amended – dismissal of crèche worker for misconduct was unfair – failure of respondent to ensure adequate door closing mechanisms in place – disproportionate sanction in circumstances where parents of children were not informed*

The claimant, an employee since 2007, brought a claim for unfair dismissal arising out of the termination of her employment. The claimant did not deny that a number of incidents occurred, but argued that they were a result of the crèche's staffing issues on the day in question.

On 11 March 2011, the manager observed a child crying and lying beside a radiator, and the claimant was holding another child. The manager felt that the claimant should have comforted the upset child and told the claimant so. The following Monday, the manager was also informed of a number of other incidents that had occurred that day. She was told that a child left the room unaccompanied to go to the toilet area and was playing in a toilet bowl. The same child again left the room unaccompanied on at least two occasions and later evening another child was left alone and a parent complained.

The claimant stated that, on the morning in question, she was informed that the other staff member was off work. She expressed her dissatisfaction with the situation. A replacement was brought in who was not familiar with the children and this put the claimant under a lot of pressure. The incident involving the toilets occurred while the replacement worker was on her break. She accepted that the incident should not have occurred but stated that she should not have been left in a room on her own with the children and doors had to be left open so that she could keep an eye on the babies when she was changing nappies.

An investigation meeting took place, at which the claimant was advised of the allegations made. Statements were taken and the claimant was suspended on full pay

---

68.   *Fox v Clevercloggs Full Day Care Nursery Ltd* UD49/2012.

pending a full investigation. The claimant did not challenge the allegation, but outlined her version of events in a letter. The claimant accepted that she had signed the minutes of the meetings but stated that she was unaware that she could challenge the statements made against her.

A disciplinary meeting took place on 5 April 2011. The claimant was advised to bring a representative but did not do so. She did not deny that the incidents had occurred but stated that it had been a stressful day and the incidents could have been avoided if somebody else had been working with her. A decision was taken to dismiss the claimant.

The appeal was held on 29 June 2011, and the original decision was upheld. The appeals decision-maker was of the opinion that too many incidents had occurred on the same day. The appeals decision-maker checked the ratio of staff to children for that day and the figures did not add up. In her evidence to the EAT, the appeals decision-maker stated that she did not recall the claimant expressing unease about the lack of staff that day. She agreed that the claimant was given no opportunity to challenge the people who made the allegations against her.

The EAT determined that the dismissal of the claimant was unfair. The respondent had failed to provide any adequate child proof door closing mechanism to ensure that children could not leave rooms unattended. Also, while the managers stated that they viewed the incidents as serious, the EAT noted that they were not brought to the attention of the parents. The EAT determined that although she had contributed to her dismissal to a moderate degree, the claimant's part in each of the incidents recorded on that day did not individually or collectively amount to misconduct. The claimant was awarded €15,000 in compensation.

[27.56] *McNulty v Ballyheane Community Sports Club Ltd[69] – Employment Appeals Tribunal – Unfair Dismissals Acts 1977 to 2007 as amended – whether decision to dismiss claimant from her position as childcare worker unreasonable in circumstances where she had been accused of mistreatment of children – whether respondent's failure to offer claimant an oral appeal hearing, as opposed to an appeal by way of review, rendered the respondent's decision to dismiss unfair*

The claimant was employed as a childcare worker in the respondent's community childcare facility. Following the receipt of complaints from other employees regarding the claimant's treatment of children in her care, the respondent conducted an investigation. The claimant was met by a representative of the respondent's voluntary management committee, who put the complaints to her and gave her an opportunity to respond. Following this, a disciplinary hearing was held which returned a finding of gross misconduct, and it was decided to dismiss the claimant summarily.

This finding and decision to dismiss was appealed by the claimant, and the appeal was conducted by a board member who had been uninvolved with the original investigation and decision to dismiss. The claimant failed to engage with either the disciplinary process or the appeals process, failed to deny the allegations levied at her,

---

69.   *McNulty v Ballyheane Community Sports Club Ltd* UD26/2012.

and did not offer any alternative explanation in response to the allegations of misconduct made against her. The decision of the disciplinary committee was upheld.

The claimant's unfair dismissal claim was grounded on two related contentions: that the respondent's decision to dismiss was unreasonable given the circumstances of the case; and that the failure of the respondent to offer the claimant an oral appeal hearing rather than an appeal by way of review was unfair.

The EAT affirmed that it is not its function to consider whether, on the facts of the case, they would have reached the same decision to dismiss as the respondent did. Rather, it is for the EAT to consider whether the decision reached by the respondent, in light of the facts of the case, could be considered a reasonable one. With this in mind, and having regard to the facts of the case and the nature, extent and outcome of the inquiry conducted, the EAT found that the respondent's decision to dismiss the claimant was reasonable.

With regards the fairness or otherwise of the procedures followed by the respondent during the appeal process, the EAT found that they were not unfair. In particular, the failure of the respondent to offer the claimant an oral appeal as opposed to an appeal by way of review, whilst not in accordance with best practice, in and of itself did not render the dismissal unfair. The EAT assessed the fairness of the process in light of the nature of the respondent organisation, the claimant's actions and the high quality of the procedures adopted by the respondent in the context of the disciplinary process up until the time of appeal. Accordingly the EAT found that the claimant was not unfairly dismissed.

Refusal to engage with grievance or disciplinary procedure

[27.57] *Finegan v PhoneWatch Ltd[70] – Employment Appeals Tribunal – Unfair Dismissals Acts 1977 to 2007 as amended – introduction of new working rota – failure of claimant to attend work and consequent disciplinary process – dismissal for refusal of claimant to engage in grievance or disciplinary procedure and failure to comply with reasonable requests – case under appeal to the Circuit Court*

The respondent is a provider of alarm services. The claimant was employed in its customer support team as a customer support representative. He had previously been employed as a driver but was facilitated in the customer support role following a long-term sickness absence.

The respondent stated that the standard contract of employment on which the claimant was employed was negotiated with the recognised trade union. It was noted that the claimant was not a member of the union. This contract allowed for a working week of Monday to Saturday. However, at the time of negotiating the contract, the normal working week was Monday to Friday.

Subsequently, in December 2009 and January 2010, it was decided by the respondent that, due to an increase in customer demand, there would be a change in relation to the rota to introduce Saturday working. The trade union was consulted and had no issue with the change to the rota. It was proposed that each employee would have to work one

---

70.   *Finegan v PhoneWatch Ltd* UD749/2012.

Saturday in every nine to 10 weeks. The majority of the customer support team agreed to this change.

The claimant raised his objection with his line manager and failed to attend for work on the first Saturday for which he was rostered. Subsequently, a meeting took place between the claimant and his line manager at which the claimant maintained that his contract of employment did not require him to work on Saturdays. The line manager confirmed that the respondent's standard contract of employment specified that the employees could be rostered to work between Monday to Saturday and he asked the claimant to produce his contract for review if he felt it contained something different. A further meeting took place between the line manager and the claimant, together with the human resources manager. Arising from this meeting it appeared that a signed copy of the claimant's contract was not on his personnel file.

Following these meetings, the claimant continued his failure to attend work on Saturdays and he did not produce a copy of his contract of employment which he claimed did not provide for Saturday working. A disciplinary process ensued and a verbal warning issued for the claimant's failure to attend for scheduled duty in April 2010. In June 2010, the claimant again failed to attend a second Saturday work shift and a further disciplinary meeting was held. Thereafter, the claimant was issued with a written warning for misconduct. Subsequently in August 2010, the claimant failed to attend for work on Saturday in accordance with the roster and at this point a further written warning for gross misconduct was issued.

The claimant continued his pattern of not attending work on his scheduled Saturdays. At the same time, the claimant also attempted to invoke the respondent's grievance procedure. The respondent granted him a two-week grace period to progress his grievances. However, the claimant did not follow through with his grievance and instead served the respondent with a High Court plenary summons claiming injunctive relief against the disciplinary process. No further action was taken by the respondent to progress the proceedings or to make an interlocutory application.

Further disciplinary meetings were scheduled with the claimant in February and March 2011. However, the claimant failed to attend these meetings. The claimant was invited to a further meeting on 29 April 2011. On the morning of this meeting, the claimant gave the respondent's chief operations manager an envelope which contained an amended contract of employment with the claimant's handwritten manuscripts. It was the respondent's contention that this is the first time that they had seen the amended contract. In light of this new information, the chief operations manager called the claimant and urged him to attend the meeting as there were points of clarification required but the claimant refused to attend. Subsequently, a final written warning for gross misconduct was issued. At this point, the claimant was informed that dismissal was a possibility and that a further meeting was scheduled with the chief operations manager. The claimant attended this meeting and the chief operations manager queried whether he had anything to suggest that the amended contract had been received and accepted by the respondent. The claimant was given a period of two weeks to locate the documents. However, the claimant did not provide any further documents to support his case and neither the claimant's manager nor the human resources team had any recollection of receiving the amended contract. Subsequently, the decision was taken by the chief operations manager to dismiss the claimant as he consistently refused to engage with them and would not comply with reasonable requests.

The claimant exercised his right of appeal to the CEO who postponed the date of dismissal for the purposes of his own investigation. Ultimately, however, the decision to dismiss was upheld and this was confirmed to the claimant on 27 October 2011.

The EAT found that the dismissal was not unfair in light of the respondent's attempts to avoid dismissal and the process followed was fair. The claimant's claim was dismissed.[71]

Dismissal for refusal to engage in disciplinary process

[27.58] *Healy v United Cinemas International Ltd T/A Castletroy Cinemas[72] – Employment Appeals Tribunal – Unfair Dismissals Acts 1977 to 2007 as amended – Redundancy Payments Acts 1967 to 2014 – Minimum Notice and Terms of Employment Acts 1973 to 2005 – whether respondent's decision to dismiss claimant following claimant's refusal to engage with disciplinary process unfair when failure to engage was attributable to stress*

The claimant commenced employment with the respondent in 2005, occupying the position of general manager. The claimant was placed on suspension following a routine inspection of his workplace, which found it to be unclean, and the raising of concerns regarding his clocking-in practice. The following day, the claimant provided the respondent with a medical certificate, which stated that he was suffering from 'severe occupational anxiety and stress'. There followed an exchange of correspondence between the parties, in which the respondent attempted to schedule investigatory meetings with the claimant, who replied with a further medical certificate and a letter from his doctor expressing the opinion that the claimant was not in fact well enough to attend any such meeting. At the respondent's suggestion, the claimant also attended an occupational health physician, who expressed a contrary opinion, namely that the claimant, although unfit for work, was well enough to attend investigatory hearings.

The respondent continued to attempt to convene such a meeting with the claimant, but their attempts went unanswered. Accordingly, a disciplinary hearing was held in the claimant's absence, and the decision to dismiss was reached on the basis of the claimant's failure to comply with company policy regarding absence reporting and continuing unauthorised absence. The claimant requested and was granted a hearing to appeal this decision. However, upon arriving to the hearing with his solicitor, the claimant was informed that he was not permitted legal representation, and the hearing did not proceed.

The EAT concluded that, although the failure of the claimant to engage in any way in the investigatory and disciplinary procedures of the respondent was conduct that would generally justify an employee's dismissal, dismissal in this case was not in fact justified, because the claimant's behaviour in this case was attributable to his severe and

---

71.   This case is under appeal to the Circuit Court.
72.   *Healy v United Cinemas International Ltd T/A Castletroy Cinemas* UD1256/2011, RP1655/2011, MN1354/2011.

debilitating stress and anxiety. In reaching this conclusion, the EAT placed much weight on the claimant's demeanour and believability when giving his evidence at the hearing. Accordingly, the decision to dismiss was unfair.

Further, the EAT found that the decision to dismiss had its genesis in the original decision to suspend, which action it found to be disproportionate and excessive. The decision in *Shortt v Royal Liver Insurance*[73] which the respondent had sought to rely on, was distinguished on the basis that the proposition for which it is authority, ie that one can assume that employee can withstand a certain level of stress, only applies 'in the absence of evidence to the contrary'. In this case, the EAT noted; there was plenty of evidence to the contrary. In these circumstances, the respondent should have made more of an attempt to accommodate the claimant. The EAT suggested that the claimant should have been permitted legal representation at the appeal hearing, and the respondent should have sought the opinion of medical specialist before taking the decision to dismiss.

Internet usage at work

[27.59] *Adeagbo v Mitie Facilities Management Ltd*[74] – *Employment Appeals Tribunal* – *Unfair Dismissals Acts 1977 to 2007 as amended* – *appeal of determination of Rights Commissioner by employee* – *dismissal for time spent on internet and for falsification of documents* – *neglect of fundamental duties and attempt to cover-up incident was gross misconduct*

The claimant, a security guard, was responsible for looking after a site which included a car park, shops, apartments and private tenants. An incident occurred where a number of people gained access to the car park at 1am whilst the claimant was on duty, which resulted in damage to a car. It was alleged and admitted by the claimant that he was looking at a number of websites on the respondent's computer at the time and did not notice that the car park was broken into.

The claimant did not dispute that he was on the internet and admitted the conduct complained of. A decision was taken to dismiss the claimant due to the fact that he had spent time on the internet when he should have been undertaking his duties and as he had falsified documents which indicated that all checks had been done when this was not the case. The decision was upheld on appeal.

The EAT noted that the person who had dismissed the claimant was not in a position to attend the EAT as he was sitting exams. Evidence was given that the claimant had received full training and he was aware of what constituted gross misconduct. The claimant had not carried out a patrol of the car park. The appeal decision-maker gave evidence that it was a simple exercise to locate the incident on CCTV as a culprit had attempted to open the car door. Whilst it was accepted that it was not possible to look at every camera, diligence and discipline were paramount in undertaking the claimant's duties. It was noted that the incident in the car park took place over a nine-minute period. On cross-examination, it was confirmed that there was no obligation on the

---

73. *Shortt v Royal Liver Insurance* [2008] IEHC 332.
74. *Adeagbo v Mitie Facilities Management Ltd* UD692/2013.

appellant to undertake a physical patrol, but what he had done was a serious breach of trust and procedures.

The claimant did not give evidence to the EAT due to ill-health, but his representative outlined to the EAT the efforts he had made to mitigate the loss. The EAT found that the prolonged neglect of his fundamental duty on the night in question and the falsification of documents to cover up for such neglect of this incident was gross misconduct. Thus, the decision to dismiss him for these admitted acts was fair and reasonable in the circumstances.

Falsification of manufacturing records

[27.60] *Haughey v Becton Dickinson Penel Ltd[75] – Employment Appeals Tribunal – Unfair Dismissals Acts 1977 to 2007 as amended – alleged gross misconduct for falsification of records – re-instatement following breach of procedural fairness requirements*

The claimant was employed for 31 years as a maintenance engineer with the respondent, a medical devices manufacturer. The claimant recorded the temperatures of top and bottom dies which were used for sealing sterile syringes that were packed in blister packs.

The claimant was dismissed following a disciplinary process after he recorded the temperature of one of the dies incorrectly, which resulted in the disposal of a sizeable quantity of the product. The Friday before the incident, the fire brigade had attended the respondent premises and the bottom die was turned off by an unknown individual after the respondent building was evacuated. The claimant also asserted that it appeared to him one of his screens had been replaced in the process.

The claimant was summoned to a disciplinary meeting by his team leader when he was walking down a corridor. He was told to meet at 11am that day and that he might want to bring a representative. When the claimant asked if there was a reason for the meeting, he was told that it might be disciplinary. The claimant said he would not attend a meeting without representation.

The claimant was subsequently suspended on full pay and was told to leave the premises for the duration of his shift in order for the respondent to conduct the investigation into the matter.

The claimant asserted that there were far more questions asked than were documented at the disciplinary meeting and that some of the questions and answers noted were selective. At the end of the meeting, he was not told that the outcome of the meeting could result in his dismissal. The claimant was not given statements or evidence that were being used against him. He voiced his surprise that, after 31 years of service in the same job, the respondent suddenly could not trust him. The claimant maintained that if the respondent had listened to him earlier, when he had reported problems with the machine, it would not have sustained the substantial loss that it did on the product.

The respondent submitted that initially the claimant was definite in saying that he had checked the screen and had made all checks he was required to do in order to record

---

75.   *Haughey v Becton Dickinson Penel Ltd* UD65/2012.

the temperature reading. It was not until later that the claimant admitted that he may have made a mistake and not read the screen. The respondent stated that the claimant was given every opportunity to challenge any point made to him. The respondent stated that it did not wish to employ someone who it could not trust. The claimant appealed the severity of the respondent's decision to dismiss him. However, the decision was upheld.

The EAT concluded that the dismissal was unfair and that there had been a breach of procedural fairness in the decision to dismiss the claimant. The EAT stated that 'constitutional and natural justice should be inherent within any decision made by an employer and particularly where the employee had been in employment of the respondent for upwards of thirty years'. The EAT stated that the claimant should have been given copies of the statements and evidence that was being used against him so that he could assess and question same. In the circumstances, the EAT concluded that the claimant should be re-instated in his previous employment from the date of dismissal.

Disruptive and unacceptable conduct

[27.61] *Myers v Direct Fuels Ltd*[76] *– Employment Appeals Tribunal – Unfair Dismissals Acts 1977 to 2007 as amended – Minimum Notice and Terms of Employment Acts 1973 to 2005 – dismissal where claimant's conduct disruptive and unacceptable – decision to dismiss reasonable in all circumstances*

The claimant was an account manager engaged in telesales for the respondent's promotion and sale of fuel cards business.

In September 2007 the claimant was issued a verbal warning on account of disruptive behaviour. In June 2011, a second verbal warning was issued to the claimant in relation to his making personal calls from the respondent's phone during working hours. The claimant admitted his mistake and paid for the calls. This second warning encompassed the claimant's unacceptable attitude in challenging every decision made, his general negative attitude, his incorrect insistence that his supervisor (who was also a sales manager) was on a 'power trip', his disruptive behaviour, his negative attitude to canvassing, his defiance, objection, opinion and constant conflict and his lack of interaction with his fellow team members.

In July 2011 the sales manager/supervisor was promoted and became the claimant's line manager. The claimant was unhappy with this and said in a fleeting comment that he was bullied. The sales manager had a good relationship with the claimant prior to her promotion.

On 8 September 2011 the supervisor/sales manager sent an email to the claimant asking him why he had not made calls related to the new sales campaign. The claimant did not respond to this email and opted to meet the supervisor in person the next day 9 September 2011. The supervisor and claimant went to a back room to talk and an altercation arose. The claimant was agitated and shouted and swore at the sales manager and challenged her position. The supervisor was upset that the claimant was loud and aggressive towards her. The claimant then made a bullying complaint against his supervisor. The managing director investigated the complaint and obtained written

---

76. *Myers v Direct Fuels Ltd* UD2412/2011, MN2423/2011.

statements from all staff present in the vicinity at the time of the incident. However, no member of staff appeared to have directly witnessed the event and merely heard raised voices. Following the investigation, the claimant was suspended on full pay on 9 September 2011.

The managing director informed the claimant of the disciplinary hearing by letter on 12 September 2011 and enclosed statements of the other staff in relation to the incident. The claimant was advised that he could bring a work colleague or trade union representative to the meeting. However, the claimant did not avail of this. No written complaint was received from the claimant until after the disciplinary process had started.

The hearing took place and addressed the claimant's failure to follow reasonable management instruction, insubordination towards his manager and use of aggressive and abusive behaviour towards his manager. One witness stated that the claimant could be challenging but could do the job. Another stated that the claimant could be very difficult to deal with and that you would know when he came in the door what kind of day you would have. They also stated that he was argumentative and confrontational.

The claimant was informed by letter that he was summarily dismissed and he was notified of his right to appeal. The credit director who heard the appeal requested the claimant to send her information on his appeal to enable her to consider the information prior to the meeting. However, this information was never received. The claimant contended that he had not been given enough notice of the disciplinary hearing. However, he did not ask for a postponement. The claimant asked for re-instatement.

The EAT concluded that the respondent had acted reasonably in dismissing the claimant as it had given the claimant every opportunity to improve and had given him more than sufficient notice that his behaviour was unacceptable. The EAT stated that, following the first verbal notice in September 2007, the claimant was on clear notice that his behaviour was disruptive. The respondent afforded the claimant opportunities to defend his position and to bring witnesses and evidence to support his claim, both at the disciplinary hearing and the appeal hearing.

The EAT concluded that the claimant's behaviour warranted dismissal and the claim failed.

[27.62] *Feery v Oxigen Environmental T/A Oxigen[77] – Employment Appeals Tribunal – Unfair Dismissals Acts 1977 to 2007, as amended – unacceptable conduct of claimant on telephone call with management – claimant's expectation of paid sick leave – appeal – no regard for previous record or current circumstances – €6,500 compensation awarded*

In April or May 2012 the claimant suffered a back injury at work for which he was put on two days paid sick leave. The back injury did not improve and towards the end of June the claimant went on sick leave for a week, having been prescribed pain-killing injections. The claimant believed, based on his past experience, that he would be paid

---

77.   *Feery v Oxigen Environmental T/A Oxigen* UD184/2013.

during his certified sick leave, but payment for illness was at the discretion of management.

On 5 July 2012, the claimant noted that he had missed a week of pay. Having taken up the issue with his line manager, the claimant was given the impression that this was due to a general disbelief that the back injury had ever occurred. He phoned the payroll manager who advised him that the accident report form which was needed to sanction sick pay had never been prepared or filed. This led to an outburst by the claimant which resulted in his dismissal.

The EAT was in no doubt that the claimant overreacted and noted that the tone and content of the phone call was clearly unacceptable. The phone call was intercepted by the human resources manager who also confirmed to the claimant that there was no evidence of an accident. The claimant did not temper his tone when speaking to the human resources manager and the conversation ended abruptly when the claimant heatedly hung up. The claimant was dismissed for unacceptable conduct.

The EAT noted that the onus rested with the respondent to demonstrate that it acted reasonably in all the circumstances. The EAT accepted that the claimant lost his temper and behaved in a way that was unacceptable vis-à-vis his work colleagues. However the EAT noted that the claimant had an expectation that he would be paid while on sick leave. He was never informed that he would not be paid or why he would not be paid. Furthermore two months later the respondent represented to him that they were of the belief that the accident never actually occurred.

The EAT concluded that both the operations director, and the managing director on appeal, made their decision to dismiss based on the claimant's unacceptable telephone outburst, without having any regard to the claimant's disciplinary record, or financial circumstances and in ignorance of the respondent's modus operandi.

The EAT found that the claimant was unfairly dismissed. The EAT took into account the claimant's contribution to his own dismissal, as well as the fact that the claimant was unavailable for work by reason of a disability from February 2013. The claimant was awarded €6,500 compensation.

Must an employer accept the decision of an internal appeal panel which had overturned the decision to dismiss

[27.63] *Kisoka v Ratnpinyotip T/A Rydevale Day Nursery[78] – UK Employment Appeal Tribunal – appeal of decision of Employment Tribunal – summary dismissal for gross misconduct in circumstances of suspected involvement in arson – claim of unfair dismissal – reasonableness of dismissal – whether employer must follow decision of internal appeal panel which had overturned initial decision to dismiss*

It was alleged that the appellant was involved in arson and she was suspended to allow time to investigate the incident. The appellant was invited to a disciplinary hearing. The decision was taken by the respondent to dismiss the appellant without notice for gross misconduct based on the fact that CCTV evidence had established the appellant to be the

---

78.   *Kisoka v Rydevale Day Nursery* UKEAT/0311/13/LA.

only person who could have been in the vicinity of the potential fire. The appellant was advised that she was entitled to appeal the decision and an independent body heard her appeal.

The appeal panel met with the appellant and their decision overturned the respondent's decision to dismiss due to procedural defects. The respondent was unhappy with the outcome of the appeal and wrote to the panel asking for further information to be taken into account and inviting them to reconsider the decision. The panel refused to reconsider. Subsequently, the respondent decided not to implement the appeal panel's decision. The appellant alleged that, by failing to implement the decision of the appeals panel, she was effectively denied the right of appeal. The Employment Judge stated that the test was whether the respondent's conduct was reasonable in all the circumstances. The Employment Judge observed that the respondent had given consideration to the appeal panel's views, but felt they could not be adopted. The Employment Tribunal found that the respondent's decision not to follow the appeal panel's decision was reasonable in the circumstances and therefore the Employment Tribunal upheld the appellant's dismissal as fair.

The appellant appealed on the basis that the Employment Tribunal erred in concluding that the respondent was not bound by the decision of the appeal panel. The appellant submitted that, as a matter of principle, a reasonable employer would not depart from an appeal panel decision without a very good reason, amounting to an exceptional circumstance. As there is no such exception in this case, it was submitted that the appellant's dismissal was therefore unfair. Furthermore, the appellant claimed that if the respondent was entitled to depart from the decision of the appeal panel, the Employment Tribunal erred in law because in such circumstances, the appellant would not be afforded an effective appeal hearing.

The UK EAT found that the fact that an appeal to which an employee is contractually entitled (which is not the case in the current proceedings) has been denied to the employee does not by itself render a dismissal unfair. The question is whether, by depriving an employee of a contractual right to an appeal, an employer has thereby denied to the employee the opportunity of showing that, in all of the circumstances, the employer's real reason for dismissing him cannot reasonably be treated as sufficient. The EAT considered that all the circumstances have to be considered. In particular, the EAT quoted from the decision of the Privy Council in *Calvin v Carr,*[79] which stated:

> what is required is an examination of the hearing process, original and appeal as a whole, and a decision on the question of whether after it has been gone through the complainant has had a fair deal of the kind that he bargained for.

The EAT upheld the decision of the Employment Tribunal and found in particular that it was entitled to take into account the fact that the respondent is responsible for the welfare of children and the respondent's concern not to re-employ a member of staff in circumstances where it still considered that there were reasonable grounds that the appellant was involved in the fire. The EAT upheld the entitlement of the Employment

---

79.   *Calvin v Carr* [1980] AC 574.

Judge to take into account the advice given in the ACAS Code of Practice and particularly where it states that it may not always be practicable for all employers to take all of the steps set out in the Code. The EAT found that the respondent did attempt in good faith to involve an independent appeal panel. The appeal was dismissed.

Dishonesty

[27.64] *Vesey v MBNA Ltd*[80]*– Employment Appeals Tribunal – Unfair Dismissals Acts 1977 to 2007 as amended – disciplinary procedure – adequacy of training – whether respondent went beyond allegations put to claimant in disciplinary process by accusing claimant of 'dishonesty'*

The claimant in this case had been employed as a customer specialist in the collections department for a period of eight years when he was dismissed from his employment. It was acknowledged by the respondent that the claimant was a very experienced employee with an exceptional performance record. The dismissal in this case derived from an allegation that the claimant had submitted incorrect action codes and incorrectly notated customers' accounts, thereby exposing the respondent credit card company to regulatory and compliance risks.

The claimant's manager initially discovered the issue and met with the claimant on to discuss it. The claimant was suspended pending an investigation into the allegations and subsequently invited to attend a disciplinary meeting. The claimant faced allegations of that he submitted incorrect action codes, potentially inflating monthly incentives and breaching trust and integrity. In a meeting that lasted for five hours, the claimant maintained that no malice was intended. The respondent did not find his explanations satisfactory and he was dismissed by letter.

At the appeal hearing, the claimant noted that he had only been employed in a new role for a number of months and had only received approximately 20 minutes of training. The claimant also maintained that his monthly incentives had not been inflated. Management concluded that the claimant had in fact received significant training on an ongoing basis and acted dishonestly in an attempt to maintain a level of performance. The dismissal was upheld on appeal.

The EAT noted that the claimant had not been in the position for a significant period and was experiencing 'teething problems'. The EAT found that the finding of dishonesty by the respondent was unreasonable and not supported by evidence. Such a finding went beyond the allegations which were put to the claimant in the context of the disciplinary process (ie the submission of incorrect action codes). The EAT held that the decision to dismiss the claimant was unfair and disproportionate.

The claimant gave evidence that he had secured employment approximately five months after the date of his dismissal. The majority of the EAT found that the claimant's actions did not contribute to his dismissal and awarded the claimant compensation of €25,000.

---

80. *Vesey v MBNA Ltd* UD953/2012.

Disclosure of Sensitive/Confidential Information

[27.65] *Jessup v Power Home Products Ltd[81] – Employment Appeals Tribunal – Unfair Dismissals Acts 1977 to 2007 as amended – whether dismissal of claimant for sharing sensitive confidential information by email in alleged breach of confidentiality fair in all circumstances*

The claimant was employed in credit control in the respondent company. In September 2012 she was called to a meeting, together with a colleague who was to be a witness to her suspension. The claimant gave evidence to the EAT that she was lost for words when the administrative director told her that she could not tell her the reason for her suspension. The claimant asked for and was given a copy of her contract of employment, together with a suspension letter, and was told to gather her belongings and leave. It was two days later when the claimant was informed of the allegations against her and she was not given a copy of the disciplinary procedure.

In evidence to the EAT, the managing director of the respondent company stated that he came across two emails sent by the claimant to her husband, giving details of supplier information and stock information belonging to the respondent, which would be valuable information to competitors. Accordingly the claimant was suspended with pay pending investigations.

In evidence the claimant stated she had done nothing wrong and she stated that her husband was known to the three directors of the respondent company and had no reason to be interested in the information sent. The first email from the managing director to the claimant and other employees had caused frustration to the claimant and that was why she sent it on to her husband. The claimant asserted that she required her husband's help with a formula for a spreadsheet calculation and this was the purpose of sending him the second email containing the spreadsheet. An investigation meeting took place, following which the claimant was invited to attend a disciplinary meeting. An outside human resources specialist, who was married to an employee of the respondent company, was invited to conduct the investigation.

The claimant accepted that the emails had been sent but did not accept that sending the emails was wrong and stated that if the managing director, or other directors had an issue with the emails, they should have first raised the issue with her informally. The sales director conducted the disciplinary hearing and, in evidence before the EAT, he stated that the emails sent by the claimant to her husband were 'dynamite' because they contained a list of suppliers and potential suppliers to the business. This subsequent email contained a complete stock list with a valuation and margins that could be used to undermine the business. In his view the information was highly confidential.

It was accepted that the respondent's business had not suffered any loss as a result of the emails. In cross-examination, the sales director acknowledged that he did discuss the claimant and her actions in an exchange of emails with his sister and her husband in

---

81.   *Jessup v Power Home Products Ltd* UD346/2013.

Australia before the disciplinary hearing. The claimant was dismissed and the internal appeal of same upheld the original decision.

The EAT stated that the claimant was dismissed because she sent two emails to her husband containing information that was in the respondent's view confidential and commercially sensitive. This was despite the respondent's director being acquainted with the claimant's husband and knowing that neither he nor his employer were likely to benefit from the information. Further, the EAT noted that the emails had been sent several months before the respondent had raised them as an issue and the respondent had accepted that it had suffered no loss as a result.

The EAT held that there were flaws with the process used to dismiss the claimant. It was noted that when she was suspended, the claimant did not receive details of the allegations made against her and neither did she receive a copy of the procedure to be used. The EAT noted that the claimant had no previous disciplinary record and had 12 years' service. Yet when the issue of the emails arose, the managing director spoke to his fellow directors, a salesman and the salesman's wife, but did not mention the matter to the claimant. It was noted by the EAT that the sales director also did not speak to the claimant about the emails but he had spoken to his sister and her husband regarding the matter, two persons who were not involved in the respondent company. The EAT considered this to be a similar type of breach of confidentiality to the one of which the claimant was accused. The EAT concluded that the dismissal of the claimant was unfair, and that her claim for unfair dismissal should succeed. She was awarded compensation in the amount of €19,000.

Unauthorised absence

[27.66] *Rutkowski v Café Nestors Ltd T/A Abrakebabra Ennis and Goodblend Catering Ltd T/A Abrakebabra Ennis*[82] *– Employment Appeals Tribunal – Unfair Dismissals Acts 1977 to 2007 as amended – Minimum Notice and Terms of Employment Act 1973 to 2005 – Organisation of Working Time Act 1997 – refusal of request to take holidays during Christmas period – whether dismissal of claimant for failing to attend work over Christmas period reasonable in all circumstances*

The respondent gave evidence that Christmas was the busiest time of the year for its fast food restaurant and, as a result, employees were not permitted to take any annual leave during the Christmas period. The claimant was aware of the practice and had never taken annual leave at this time in his previous eight years of employment. In July 2012 the claimant requested and was refused holidays for the Christmas period by his manager and the same request was also refused by the respondent's owner. However the claimant gave evidence that, while his initial request for holidays was refused, when he reiterated the request in September 2012 he was given permission to take holidays and he booked his flights subsequently in November 2012. The respondent owner was informed by other staff members that the claimant intended to go on holidays on 17 December 2012.

---

82. *Rutkowski v Café Nestors Ltd T/A Abrakebabra Ennis and Goodblend Catering Ltd T/A Abrakebabra Ennis* UD285/2013, MN146/2013,WT30/2013.

The respondent sent a letter to the claimant on 13 December 2012 confirming that his numerous holiday requests for the Christmas period were refused and stating:

> [Y]ou will be rostered as normal over the Christmas period. If you fail to turn up over the Christmas period we will be accepting this as your resignation.

The claimant received this letter with his wages, which was the normal method of communication within the respondent company. The claimant did not attend after 16 December 2012. The respondent took his absence to mean that he had left employment and there was no further contact between the parties.

The EAT noted there was a clear conflict of evidence between the claimant and the respondent as to whether or not the claimant was told he had permission to take holidays at Christmas. The EAT stated it was difficult for it to resolve this conflict. However the EAT was of the view that the respondent did not behave reasonably in giving the claimant the letter. The EAT regarded this as a deficit of procedures and noted that the claimant had no contract of employment which would have outlined the mutual obligations of both parties. The EAT concluded the dismissal was effected in a curt and unfair matter and awarded the claimant compensation of €5,000.

[27.67] *Jordan v Mainway North Road Ltd[83] – Employment Appeals Tribunal – Unfair Dismissals Acts 1977 to 2007 as amended – dismissal for unauthorised absence and alleged failure to adhere to respondent's sick leave procedures – failure to exhaust internal disciplinary procedure not fatal to unfair dismissal claim – obligation on employer to take into account circumstances of employee's absence – €25,000 awarded*

The claimant was employed as a car valet in the respondent's motor business. The claimant was dismissed due to his unauthorised absence from work and his failure to notify the respondent of his absence, as required by the respondent's sick leave procedures. Prior to his dismissal, the claimant had a number of unauthorised absences, and had been given a final written warning for his involvement in a fight with a colleague in the staff canteen.

The claimant gave evidence that his three-day absence, which led to his dismissal, was due to his 18-month old daughter being ill. On discovering his daughter was ill on the morning of 18 October 2011, he telephoned the reception of the respondent on two occasions in order to inform his line manager that he would not be attending work. He was informed by the receptionist that she would request the claimant's line manager to telephone the claimant when he was available. The claimant's line manager did not return the claimant's call. The claimant produced his mobile phone records to the EAT, which showed that there were two calls placed to the respondent at 8.33am and 8.56am on 18 October 2011 from the claimant's telephone. The claimant informed the EAT that his colleague delivered a medical certificate to the respondent on his behalf on 20 October 2011 which stated that the claimant's daughter was ill and certified the claimant to be absent from work from 18 to 20 October 2011. The respondent gave evidence that

---

83.   *Jordan v Mainway North Road Ltd* UD1741/2012.

the claimant had been provided with a copy of the employee handbook and was aware of company procedures regarding notification of absences from work. It stated that it was not satisfied that there was an emergency situation at home to warrant the unauthorised absence of the claimant.

By letter dated 19 October 2011, the respondent notified the claimant that he was considered to be on an unauthorised absence, which may result in his dismissal. He was invited to a disciplinary hearing which took place on 25 October 2011. At the disciplinary hearing, the claimant explained the circumstances of his absence and advised that there was no one available to mind his daughter when she was ill. He also explained how he had contacted reception in the respondent on two occasions on the first day of his absence. The respondent did not accept the claimant's explanation and he was dismissed on 26 October 2011. The EAT noted that the claimant did not exercise his right to appeal the decision to dismiss him in accordance with the respondent's disciplinary procedure.

The EAT determined that the claimant had produced sufficient evidence that he had notified the respondent of his absence and that the reason for the claimant's absence should have been considered by the respondent. Notwithstanding that the claimant did not exhaust the respondent's internal procedures, the respondent did not act reasonably in terminating the claimant's employment in the circumstances. The EAT overturned the Right Commissioner's decision and awarded compensation of €25,000.

Refusal to return to previous working hours

[27.68] *Hooper v Philpot & Malone T/A Kudos Hairdressing*[84] *– Unfair Dismissals Acts 1977 to 2007 as amended – Employment Appeals Tribunal – dismissal of hairdresser for refusal to return to previous working arrangements as per her employment contract – claimant compromised her own position by such refusal*

The claimant was an experienced and qualified hairdresser who commenced working on a full-time basis in the respondent's salon in March 2005. It was accepted by the parties that the claimant was an excellent and valued employee. Initially the claimant worked on a full-time basis, five days a week. After the claimant had started a family, she and the respondent agreed that she would work on a part-time basis and the claimant commenced working three days a week. It was noted that the claimant did not always have a contract of employment and that the workplace was the subject of an NERA inspection at a date unknown but before 24 June 2008. On foot of that inspection, the claimant was issued with and signed a contract of employment which confirmed her permanent three days a week status with the respondent.

In 2011 the claimant's father became ill and the claimant's mother was no longer as available to mind the claimant's children. The claimant and the respondent agreed that, for the duration of the illness, the claimant could reduce her hours to one and a half days per week. This arrangement lasted for well over a year but, at the end of 2012, the respondent employer asked the claimant about returning to her contracted three-day week. At this time the business was going through a tough time economically and the

---

84. *Hooper v Philpot & Malone T/A Kudos Hairdressing* UD834/2013.

respondent had to make some difficult financial decisions to ensure the business would survive the downturn (such as letting go a recent full time recruit whose salary could no longer be sustained by the business) and, as a consequence the respondent needed her two longer serving members of staff to take up some of the additional work created and to work extra days. The EAT accepted that the claimant was very reluctant to change her working hours and that, at this time, the issue of not being able to afford and/or not wanting to pay for childcare was the primary reason why the claimant did not return to the three-day working week.

On 2 January 2013, the respondent business formally notified the claimant of the need to return to a three-day week and the claimant was due to commence same on or about 21 January 2013. The claimant gave no evidence of trying to secure child-minding help at this time. In March 2013, some six weeks after the claimant had been asked to return to her contracted three-day week, the claimant notified the employer in writing that she would not be in a position to work three days due to childcare costs. At this time a combination of doctor's notes and holidays due kept the claimant from the workplace for a number of weeks. Then, on 20 March 2013, the respondent wrote to the claimant terminating the contract of employment stating 'we now really needed you to return to work for the three days as agreed in your contract'.

On balance, the EAT found that there was nothing unfair about the termination of the claimant's employment. The respondent behaved reasonably at every juncture and the claimant knew or ought reasonably to have known that her actions (or, in this case, inaction) would give rise to the termination of her employment. The EAT found that in so acting the claimant compromised her own position and therefore her claim for unfair dismissal failed.

DISMISSALS ON GROUNDS OF INCAPACITY

[27.69] *London Central Bus Co Ltd v Manning[85] – UK Employment Appeal Tribunal – appeal of decision of Employment Tribunal – claim that dismissal on grounds of ill-health capability was unfair – reasonableness of dismissal – whether withholding of information at appeal stage converted dismissal into unfair dismissal*

The appellant was a long-serving employee of the respondent who was dismissed on ill-health / capability grounds in 2011. Medical enquiries by the respondent had showed that there was no indication as to when the appellant would be able to return to driving duties and it was decided that he should be dismissed, with pay in lieu of notice. The Employment Tribunal found that the appellant's dismissal was unfair on the basis that the respondent had made no effort to find alternative work for the appellant after he was certified fit for light duties and further that a list of alternative vacancies were not produced at the appeal hearing (although none were suitable for the appellant). Subsequently, the first reason was dropped at the Employment Tribunal and therefore the only unfairness was the failure to show the appellant a list of unsuitable vacancies at the appeal hearing. The Employment Tribunal found that the initial dismissal was fair at

---

85.   *London Central Bus Co Ltd v Manning* UKEAT/0103/13/DM.

the point of dismissal as there was no failure to consider alternative employment for the appellant. However, it was held by the Tribunal that the subsequent failure to show the list of unsuitable vacancies to the appellant at the appeal stage must render his dismissal unfair.

The UK EAT was unable to accept this reasoning and noted that, while the conduct of an internal appeals process is relevant to the overall question of fairness, the main question is whether the procedural defect denied the employee the opportunity to show that the employer's reason for dismissal was an insufficient reason. The UK EAT found that the appellant was not denied any such opportunity as to show him a list of unsuitable vacancies at the appeal hearing would have been a futile exercise. Accordingly, the procedural failing could not displace the fairness of the original dismissal. The appeal of the Employment Tribunal was allowed and the award of £10,000 set aside.

[27.70] BS v Dundee City Council[86] – Scottish Court of Session – Employment Rights Act 1996 – unfair dismissal – termination of employment for long-term sickness absence – factors to be considered when dismissing on grounds of incapacity

The Court of Session restated the relevant test for employers considering the termination of employment of workers on long-term sickness absence.

The claimant was employed by Dundee City Council's contract services department for 35 years. In September 2008, the claimant was signed off work due to depression and anxiety. The respondent arranged for the claimant to attend a number of occupational health appointments and received a series of reports stating that the claimant was unfit for work. In August 2009, the respondent met with the claimant and informed him that, if he remained unfit to work after 14 September 2009, his employment would be at risk of termination. On 11 September 2009, the respondent received a further occupational health report stating that, although the claimant's health was improving, he would not be fit to return work for a period of one to three months but that he would be 'happy for him to return to work when his GP issues a final certificate'. The claimant did not return to work on the scheduled return date of 14 September 2009, and was certified as being unfit for work for a further four weeks.

The respondent met with the claimant on 23 September 2009, and again advised him that consideration was being given to terminating his employment. During the course of the meeting, the claimant informed the respondent that he was feeling no better and did not think that he could return any time soon. Following this meeting, the respondent dismissed the claimant, with effect from 23 September 2009, on the basis that he was unlikely to return to work in the foreseeable future.

The claimant instituted unfair dismissal proceedings in the Employment Tribunal. The Employment Tribunal confirmed that, although it was permissible to dismiss an employee on grounds of capacity, the dismissal would be subject to the 'reasonableness' test. In this instance, the Employment Tribunal held that no employer would have dismissed the claimant nine days after receiving a medical report stating that the

---

86.   *BS v Dundee City Council* [2013] CSIH 91.

claimant may be in a position to return to work within one to three months and there was no medical evidence to contradict this report.

On appeal, the EAT held that because the Employment Tribunal did not specify how long the respondent should be required to wait for the claimant to return to work, it had made an error of law. The case was remitted to a freshly constituted Employment Tribunal to make a finding on whether the respondent could reasonably have been expected to refrain from dismissing the claimant for a longer period.

The claimant appealed this decision to the Court of Session. The Court of Session agreed with the finding of the EAT that the Employment Tribunal had failed to directly address the question of whether any reasonable employer would have waited longer before dismissing the claimant in the circumstances.

In reaching its conclusions, the Court of Session set out three factors which must considered in respect of dismissals arising from incapability due to ill health. Firstly where an employee is absent for a significant period, the essential question is whether any reasonable employer would have waited longer before dismissing the employee. Secondly, the employer must consult with the employee and take his or her views into account. It was noted that this obligation may operate for and against dismissal. For example, if an employee expresses the view that he or she will not be in position to return to work in the foreseeable future, the employer can take this into account in determining whether or not to dismiss the employee. Thirdly, employers must take steps to find out about the employee's medical condition and his or her likely prognosis, but it was stated that this merely requires the obtaining of proper medical advice and does not require the employer to pursue a detailed medical examination.

The Court of Session stated that while length of service will be relevant in misconduct cases, its relevance is not so clear in cases of ill health. The Court of Session held that an employee's conduct and attendance record would be relevant in determining whether it is likely that the employee will return to work.

In the present case, the Court of Session stated that the Employment Tribunal had failed to adequately address the above factors. In deciding the reasonableness of the respondent in the circumstances, the Employment Tribunal had referenced factors to be considered by an employer in determining whether to dismiss an employee on grounds of ill health, such as payment of salary and the availability of temporary staff, it should have considered the unsatisfactory situation where an employee was on long term sick leave. In such circumstances, the Court of Session held that it was open to the respondent to dismiss the claimant on grounds of incapacity.

Furthermore, the Court of Session held that the Employment Tribunal did not give adequate consideration to the claimant's contention that he would not be in a position to return to work in the near future.

In relation to the third factor, the Court of Session referred to the fact that the Employment Tribunal placed significant weight on the medical report which stated that the claimant would be in a position to return to work within one to three months. However, this medical report was contradicted by the claimant's own assertion that he would not be able to return to work. In circumstances where the claimant's own view was that he could not return to work, additional medical evidence was unlikely to resolve the issue. It was against this set of facts that the Employment Tribunal should have addressed whether the decision to dismiss the claimant was in the range of responses a reasonable employer would take. The Court of Session was also critical of the Employment Tribunal's finding that length of service was automatically relevant in respect of dismissals on grounds of ill health.

The Court of Session remitted the claim back to the Employment Tribunal to be reheard.

[27.71] *Farrell v Kepak Group (Meat Division) T/A Kepak Longford*[87] *– Employment Appeals Tribunal – Unfair Dismissals Acts 1977 to 2007 as amended – workplace injury – return to work to lighter duties – subsequent decision to appoint investigator to conduct covert surveillance on claimant on two dates – dismissal for inconsistent statements in relation to injury – disproportionate sanction*

The claimant was employed as a night cleaner supervisor at the respondent's meat processing plant. On 2 July 2012 the claimant was involved in a workplace accident when his arm got stuck in a blocked drain he was clearing. The fire brigade and a doctor were called and it took three to four hours to free his arm and he was hospitalised for three days. The claimant sustained heavy bruising to his arm and was absent from work for three weeks following the incident on medical grounds. He did not receive any sick pay during his absence from work.

The cleaning contract had been outsourced by the respondent around the time the accident took place. When the claimant returned to work, he was assigned lighter duties. He injured his back while he was carrying out these duties and asked to be moved from this task for a day or so. He was then moved to the by-products table which consisted of filling and lifting 25 kilo boxes. He remained in this post until the termination of his employment.

Following his return to work, the claimant contacted his solicitor who wrote to the respondent on numerous occasions on the claimant's behalf. The claimant brought a claim to the Rights Commissioner in respect of wages and working overtime. The claimant also pursued a personal injuries action against the respondent, which the respondent asked him to drop and he subsequently did.

In August 2012, the claimant's solicitor wrote to the respondent raising a number of grievances in respect of his treatment following his return from work. On 10 September 2012 the claimant's solicitor wrote to the respondent, claiming that the claimant was forced to engage in heavy cleaning duties without any assistance which exacerbated his injuries. Following this correspondence, the head of human resources was appointed to conduct an investigation into the claimant's grievances.

At the EAT hearing, the claimant demonstrated that he could not raise his arm above elbow height. The EAT also heard evidence that the respondent had engaged investigation specialists to monitor the activities of the claimant outside the workplace. The claimant was placed under surveillance on two separate dates and was observed carrying out gardening activities.

---

87.   *Farrell v Kepak Group (Meat Division) T/A Kepak Longford* UD1202/2013.

On 22 October 2012, the head of human resources wrote to the claimant and stated that the complaint in relation to sick pay was before the Rights Commissioner and therefore, she did not comment on it. In relation to the complaint about being given heavy duties in light of the claimant's injuries, and on foot of the discrepancies between the claimant's account and the surveillance investigators' report, the manager recommended that the matter proceed to a disciplinary investigation and the claimant was suspended on full basic pay from 22 October 2012.

A disciplinary investigation meeting and a further follow-on meeting were held in early December 2012. The claimant challenged the points made by the manager in the letter dated 22 October 2012. It was decided that the matter should progress to a disciplinary hearing.

The respondent sent a letter to the claimant setting out the allegations against the claimant which consisted of the claimant taking annual leave without having been granted leave and the inconsistent statements given by the claimant in relation to his fitness to work and in relation to his ongoing physical injuries.

A disciplinary hearing was held on 8 January 2013. In respect of the holiday leave taken, a witness stated that the request had not been granted as the claimant did not have the required level of leave to take. The hearing reconvened on 21 January 2013 and evidence was given that the claimant had given different accounts in relation to the duration and extent of his injuries. The disciplinary hearing upheld the allegations against the claimant. It found that the claimant's statements in relation to his injuries were misleading and untrue. It stated that misrepresenting his ability to work amounted to serious misconduct. It found that the relationship of trust and confidence between the claimant and the respondent had been irreparably damaged and therefore, it decided to dismiss the claimant.

The claimant appealed the decision but the decision to dismiss him was upheld.

At the EAT hearing, the claimant accepted that he had been given light duties on his return to work. However, he denied that the work in the by-products area were light duties. He stated that he was happy to carry out his duties. The claimant stated that he was unaware that his solicitor had been writing letters on his behalf to the respondent and he stated that he did not instruct his solicitor to bring a personal injuries claim.

In addressing the allegations of inconsistency in his statements of events, the claimant explained that in one of the meetings he had actually been talking about an injury he sustained while he was living in England which had nothing to do with the workplace incident. He also denied that he said he would be in agony if he did not wear a wrist support at work. He also stated that he had no issues or difficulties in working in the by-products area and that his shoulder was not hurting him.

The claimant accepted that he carried out gardening activities during the weekends. He said that he did not see a problem with carrying out these duties in his own time. In relation to the holiday request, he stated that he had left a form on his supervisor's desk, that it was granted four days later and that he had never spoken to his supervisor about the request.

The claimant had been unemployed since his dismissal and sought re-instatement to his former position.

The EAT concluded that the sanction imposed by the respondent was disproportionate, unfair and unreasonable in the circumstances. The EAT awarded the claimant compensation of €25,000.

DISMISSALS ON GROUNDS OF INCOMPETENCE/PERFORMANCE

[27.72] *Citti v Apple Distribution International T/A Apple Computer[88] – Employment Appeals Tribunal – Unfair Dismissals Acts 1977 to 2007 as amended – dismissal of claimant for his unwillingness to accept change in work practice and his failure to work to new sales model – performance management process – failure of claimant to engage with reasonable request – fair procedures used by employer*

The claimant was a sales executive in the inside sales teams. They dealt with transaction selling and business solutions and were concerned with three markets: Spain, Portugal and Italy. In 2012, the respondent changed its sales model from the fulfilment role to customer needs and complete solutions role involving a change in the interaction required with the customer. All of the employees, including the claimant, received extensive training from a dedicated training team within the respondent, which was mandatory and consisted of eight modules. In the course of the claimant's annual review, it was explained to him that he had done a good job when using the old sales model, but that he would have to move forward and adapt to the new model as the rest of the sales team had moved on to the new model and the overall sales had improved with the changes in work practice.

Evidence was given that along with the changes in work model, there was a change in payment system such that staff who had formerly been paid salaries plus commission on their sales changed to an increased salary and team bonus. The bonus was not just based on sales, but on customer satisfaction criteria also. A meeting was held with the claimant about his performance, but there was a lack of improvement and a lack of engagement from him. Evidence was given that the claimant appeared to have lost interest and appeared unwilling or unable to move to the new work model. A performance improvement plan was established for the claimant, but the claimant refused to sign it. It was put in place and implemented, but the claimant refused to engage with it at all. A disciplinary process was then instigated. However, the claimant did not wish to go through the process and sent a number of emails which were referenced by the EAT. Evidence was given that during the disciplinary process, the respondent was looking for a gesture from the claimant to say that he would try and improve and engage with the new system, but that never happened. Further evidence was given from the respondent's managers that it was clear, from speaking with the claimant, that he was not going to change or engage with the system the respondent was using. The claimant had expressed a wish to move on and the respondent had wished to negotiate a settlement. Ultimately, the respondent invoked the disciplinary process, leading to the claimant's dismissal and this was not appealed internally by the claimant.

---

88.   *Citti v Apple Distribution International T/A Apple Computer* UD994/2013.

Before the EAT, the claimant explained he was a dedicated and successful salesperson and at all times had done his job to the best of his ability. He explained he always wished to act in an ethical way with his customers, who trusted him, and he felt the revised system that the respondent wished to implement lacked integrity. He felt the customers were being sold unnecessary ancillary applications and insurance and he considered that he had been doing the fundamental job of selling the respondent's products well, but he was not comfortable with the changes that were being proposed. He acknowledged the contents of the emails that he had sent and that he would have indicated to his employer his desire to leave the respondent.

The EAT in its determination concluded that the claimant was an individual who made a career as a successful salesperson and who had strong beliefs in relation to ethical selling. The EAT noted his failure to engage with a reasonable request from his employers to adapt to a new system of working. The EAT concluded that the demands made on the claimant were not unreasonable and the claimant was given every opportunity over a period of months to act as in accordance with his employer's wishes. The EAT was unable to find fault with the disciplinary process adopted by the respondent and consequently was unable to make a finding of unfair dismissal in the case.

[27.73] *Berthold v Google Ireland Ltd[89] – Employment Appeals Tribunal – Unfair Dismissals Acts 1977 to 2007 as amended – Minimum Notice and Terms of Employment Acts 1973 to 2005 – whether dismissal of claimant for competency reasons following performance management process was fair in all circumstances*

The claimant was employed as a level 6 manager by the respondent and appears to have had no performance issues until the last quarter of 2009. Following an unsatisfactory performance review in the fourth quarter of 2009, the claimant was awarded performance rating of 2.9, which was below expectations and the evidence was that such a rating was unusual for a level 6 manager. The significance of this rating meant that the claimant did not receive a full bonus. The respondent deferred a performance improvement procedure with the claimant in the spring of 2010 because she was travelling on business and was then absent on bereavement leave. At the end of July 2010 the respondent began a short-term performance expectation plan (PEP) to assist the claimant in improving her performance. This plan detailed specific areas where her performance had come up short and set out what was required to demonstrate the necessary improvements. This PEP extended to September 2010, during which time meetings were held between the claimant and her manager by way of weekly review and feedback to provide her with coaching.

In September 2010 a decision to extend the review period was taken as the required improvement and performance was not demonstrated by the claimant. As the improvement targets set in July 2010 were not achieved, a disciplinary hearing was held in early November 2010 following which the claimant was issued with a first written warning in respect of her performance. In December 2010 a more detailed and longer

---

89.   *Berthold v Google Ireland Ltd* UD2147/2011, MN 2174/2011.

term performance improvement plan (PIP) was put in place. In January 2011 a mid PIP review conducted and, as the claimant had not achieved several objectives, a disciplinary hearing was held and she was issued with a final writing warning. This was upheld on appeal in February 2011.

In early March 2011 a meeting took place to assess the claimant's performance as against the PIP targets. The deadline for the achievement of the targets was extended to May 2011. An assessment took place on 18 May 2011 and, as the claimant had not succeeded in meeting the targets set for her, her employment was terminated on competency grounds. The claimant did not utilise the right of appeal.

The respondent submitted that it was entitled to terminate the claimant's employment and that the performance matters that had arisen had been dealt with by a thorough, transparent and fair process. The claimant submitted that she had no issues in work until 2010 when she was put on a PEP. Her manager had changed and a colleague with whom she worked closely subsequently died. On his death, she took over his team and had an increased number of reports at this point. In her evidence the claimant asserted that she had tried to achieve the deliverables set as part of the PEP and that while she thought she could meet the targets and had completed 95% of the plan, she was then put on a PIP. She stated she did not know why she was put on a PIP at this juncture and she did not feel she was fairly treated.

In relation to the respondent's method of performance assessment, the claimant gave evidence about her attendance at calibration meetings where she was asked to calibrate employees on the team and would have to rate employees and provide a score for everyone. She noted in her evidence that a manager who did not know an employee could suggest a lower performance rating score for an employee. The respondent operated a bell curve appraisal system so scores had to be reduced. At every meeting the claimant attended there had to be a performance score of 2.9 which was a negative rating which affected the bonus and salary of the relevant employee.

The EAT concluded that it had not been established to its satisfaction that the claimant had changed from being an employee with no disciplinary record to a less than competent employee within a short space of time. The EAT noted that the claimant had no performance issues until July 2010. The EAT did not accept the respondent's contention that this was a fair dismissal and it was linked to competency. The EAT noted that there was no evidence that the respondent had considered any option other than termination, eg demotion. The Tribunal was not satisfied that fair procedures were used and therefore concluded that the dismissal was procedurally unfair. The EAT held that the claim should succeed and awarded compensation of €110,000.

Use of mystery shopper as an assessment tool

[27.74] *Maxi Zoo Ireland Ltd v Caffrey*[90] *– Employment Appeals Tribunal – appeal of decision of Rights Commissioner – Unfair Dismissals Acts 1977 to 2007 as amended – dismissal of sales assistant for performance and conduct reasons – whether process of assessment by mystery shopper in accordance with fair procedures*

---

90.   *Maxi Zoo Ireland Ltd v Caffrey* UD83/2013.

The claimant was employed as a sales assistant in the claimant's retail unit. The respondent had high expectations of its employees and utilised the services of 'mystery shoppers' to call to stores on a monthly basis to check the knowledge, skill and demeanour of employees. Evidence was given by the claimant that the mystery shopper gave marks for sales and performance in an assessment which fed back to the respondent's sales team. In this case, the claimant scored 31% in a mystery shopper assessment, arising from which he was given a formal written warning, which remained on file for a period of nine months and not the stipulated six months. The EAT noted that this was how seriously the matter had been taken by management of the appellant. A subsequent assessment with a mystery shopper yielded an assessment mark of 70%, which was again below the standard required by the respondent. A subsequent disciplinary meeting was convened with the claimant, which, it was noted by the EAT, proceeded in the absence of the claimant's nominated representative who could not attend. Arising from this process, the claimant was given a final written warning, to remain on file for 12 months. The claimant was given an opportunity to appeal this decision, but did not do so.

Subsequently, management became aware that all of the staff and management in the particular retail unit had been failing to do on-shelf stock takes to ensure that out of date stock was not being left on the shelf. This was viewed as being an across the board failing on the part of the staff employed in this unit and all were subjected to a disciplinary process because this task was not being completed on a daily basis. It had particular consequences for the claimant, as he was on a final written warning, which meant that the respondent decided to terminate his employment.

The EAT determined that the claimant was treated most unfairly and noted that it was open to the respondent to have given him a further written warning. The EAT's determination contained criticism of the mystery shopper assessment. The EAT noted that 'there was no question of the employees not being hardworking' and queried whether the claimant should have in fact received a final written warning based on 'one-sided evidence of a mystery shopper about whose credentials the employer knew nothing'. The EAT concluded that the respondent's actions were heavy-handed and unfair and they decided to uphold the recommendation of the Rights Commissioner. The award was varied by the EAT and the claimant was awarded compensation of €10,000.

DISMISSALS ON OTHER SUBSTANTIVE GROUNDS

[27.75] *Veronko v James Kelly & Sons*[91] *– Unfair Dismissals Acts 1977 to 2007 as amended*[92] *– Employment Appeals Tribunal – dismissal of employee for failure to work hours required by employer – employer's actions objectively justified in light of needs of business and provided for in contract of employment – dismissal justified on other substantive grounds*

---

91.   *Veronko v James Kelly & Sons (Wexford) Ltd* UD624/2012, RP460/2012, MN475/2012.

92.   Claims under the Redundancy Payments Acts 1967 and 2014 and the Minimum Notice and Terms of Employment Acts 1973 and 2005 were withdrawn during the hearing.

The claimant worked night shifts at the respondent's bakery and was employed in the role of confectioner from February 2008. The respondent gave evidence that, due to a change in childcare arrangements, the claimant requested a change to day shifts effective from December 2011. The respondent agreed that, as long as the cake orders were not affected, it could facilitate the claimant with a day shift of 9.30am to 6pm. Although the respondent required the claimant to work until 6pm, the claimant's working hours were later amended to 8.30am to 5pm to allow the claimant some further time to put childcare arrangements in place. The claimant denied that she agreed to work these hours and stated that she had agreed with her supervisor to work from 8am to 4.30pm.

The respondent's management gave evidence as to how the claimant's working hours affected the business, namely instances where cake orders were not completed on the evening that they were received as the claimant had left work early. The caused delivery delays, resulting in the cake orders being carried over until the next morning which required other employees to start work early in order to complete same. The claimant in her evidence stated that she had always fulfilled orders received. The respondent made attempts to facilitate the claimant and her partner (who also worked at the respondent's bakery) by suggesting alternative working hours in order to assist the claimant's childcare arrangements. When matters did not improve the production manager met with the claimant to enquire if she had put childcare arrangements in place but the impression the claimant gave was that she did not intend to make any such arrangements. As a result, the claimant was issued with a verbal warning on 15 February 2012 which was confirmed in writing. It stated:

> ... I give you formal notice that you have received a verbal warning with regard to leaving work before your agreed time.

A director of the company gave evidence that she wrote an amendment to the claimant's contract stating the amended hours of work as 8.30am to 5pm. The amendment was provided to the claimant with the verbal warning. The claimant did not sign her acceptance to the amendment. Having issued the claimant with a verbal warning, the production manager then made further attempts to facilitate the claimant's situation. The claimant's partner worked the bread night shift and the production manager told him to facilitate the claimant's partner with a later start time. Despite these attempts, there was no improvement in the claimant's time keeping. He again met with the claimant on 20 February 2012 and she told him she could not work until 5pm. The production manager issued the claimant with a dismissal notice on 20 February 2012 which stated:

> ... whereby you are unable to comply with the new hours advised to you in December commencing at 08.30 and finishing at 17.00, and you are unable to go back on the previous nightshift which you worked up to December 2011, it is with regret that we must give you two weeks' notice.

In the week that followed the issuing of the dismissal notice, managers examined the possibility of changing the start time of the bread shift to 6.30pm and also allowing the claimant to finish at 4.30pm, thus allowing for a two-hour gap between the claimant's attendance at work and her partner's. However, in order to facilitate this, the production manager also had to ask the company's most important client if they would agree to an earlier cut-off time for cake orders. The production manager asked the claimant to consider this proposal. He later heard she had requested a P45. When he approached the claimant about the proposal, she said it did not matter as she was leaving the employment. The claimant acknowledged in her evidence that during her notice period there were discussions regarding her remaining in the employment but she did not consider this to be possible due to the earlier 'conflict'. In any event the claimant gave evidence that she did not receive anything further in writing following the letter of termination.

Having considered the evidence of the parties and the legal submissions, the EAT found that the claimant was dismissed by the respondent by letter of 20 February 2012. The reason for the dismissal was that the claimant was unable, for family reasons, to work the hours required by the respondent. The EAT found that this requirement was objectively justified in light of the needs of the business and the claimant's contract of employment allowed for it. Accordingly, the dismissal was justified under other substantial grounds.

The EAT accepted the submission of the legal representative for the claimant that the dismissal was other than in accordance with fair procedures and with the respondent's own disciplinary procedure. However, the EAT found that the dismissal was revoked in or about a week after the 20 February 2012. Taking into account this fact, and the very significant efforts made by the respondent to accommodate the claimant's requested hours of work, the EAT found that any procedural defects were cured. The EAT considered whether the claimant's reasons for refusing to accept the revocation of the dismissal constituted grounds for a constructive dismissal. The EAT found that the claimant should have at least tried to work the new hours suggested by the respondent, rather than deciding in advance that it would not work. The EAT did not accept that any conflict caused over the hours of work issue was insurmountable but rather the claimant wanted hours from 8am to 4pm and nothing else and despite the best efforts of the respondent this was not possible because of the nature of the respondent's business. The EAT found that the unfair dismissal claim failed.

DISMISSAL IN COMMUNITY EMPLOYMENT SCHEMES

[27.76] *Goold v Cashel Heritage and Development Trust Co Ltd*[93] – *Employment Appeals Tribunal – Unfair Dismissals Acts 1977 to 2007 as amended – participation on community employment scheme – whether operation of 10% discretionary retention option was reasonable in all circumstances – requirements on publicly funded body or employer to exercise discretion – failure to afford claimant opportunity to make case for her retention in employment in circumstances where she was not aware of retention option and criteria for its exercise*

---

93.   *Goold v Cashel Heritage and Development Trust Co Ltd* UD1031/2011.

The claimant was employed on a community employment scheme for 10 years. The majority of the time was spent working at a reception of a heritage and tourist centre. The scheme operated on a yearly basis and the participants were employed from October to the following October. The scheme was funded by FÁS, who also determined the eligibility criteria to participate in the scheme. The objective of the scheme is that participants will progress on to full-time employment or return to education. To become a participant in the scheme, a person must be unemployed for a period of at least 52 weeks. The time allowed on the scheme depends on the age bracket of the participant and whether or not the person is in receipt of disability benefits.

The claimant was eligible for seven years on the scheme (six years because of her age and a further year because she had a disability entitlement). Evidence was given that, in addition, a 10% retention allowance applied, which meant that a sponsoring employer could retain 10% of the total number of participants on the scheme from among those who had exceeded the eligibility criteria. The application of this 10% retention option was discretionary and usually applied to participants with special circumstances or key skills. The evidence to the EAT confirmed that the claimant's eligibility ended around the end of 2007. However, the respondent's evidence was that there was a high degree of flexibility regarding the retention option, which changed at the end of 2009 because of increased unemployment figures. There was an instruction by FÁS that participants should only be retained for one extra year under the 10% retention option and thus a large number of people exited the schemes in April 2010. Evidence was given to the EAT that the FÁS instruction came into effect in November 2009 and in February 2010, a list of participants whose eligibility had expired was considered as to whether they could be retained, to include the claimant.

As the respondent employed 15 participants on the scheme, this allowed for the retention of 1.5 people for one year or two people for 0.75 of the year. The supervisor opted to retain two participants and selected the two who were to be retained. The EAT considered the list of participants in the scheme, five of whom had exceeded the eligibility criteria. The claimant was not retained. Evidence was given that the claimant was advised of the instruction from FÁS and the fact that she was 120 weeks over the eligibility threshold. The claimant was not informed that the other participants were being retained. The claimant gave evidence to the effect that she was told in public by her supervisor that her employment was being terminated some three weeks before termination.

When querying the reason for her termination, she was advised that FÁS had given an instruction that older people were to be removed from the schemes to facilitate younger people who wanted to avail of them. The claimant had raised the possibility of a concession being made for her. However, this was viewed negatively and it was presumed by the claimant that concessions were not being made. Evidence was given by the claimant that some time after her dismissal, she observed two of her colleagues, entering the heritage centre dressed in their uniforms and they subsequently confirmed to her that they had been given special concessions to remain in employment. The claimant gave evidence that she was unaware throughout her employment of the 10% retention application process. She noted that when on one occasion her employment was to come to an end she had made representations to the FÁS office and was subsequently reinstated and that was the only time she had previously applied to be retained. Her supervisor had never mentioned anything to her in relation to a 10% retention option when she signed her contract. The EAT noted that the evidence from the respondent was that the operation of the 10% retention option was discretionary based on criteria, special circumstances and key skills of the participant. The EAT held that the exercise of a discretion of a publicly funded body or employer is not unfettered and must be exercised in a reasonable way such that those who may be affected by or who may benefit from its exercise know the grounds/criteria on which they might be affected so as to enable them to make a case so the discretion may be exercised in their favour.

The EAT concluded that the discretion vested in the respondent was not exercised in an open, transparent and reasonable way. Whilst aware that participants may be granted the concession of further years on the scheme and while she actively sought a concession herself, the EAT accepted that the claimant was unaware, not only of how the 10% retention option operated, but also of its existence. The EAT noted from the evidence before it that a number of participants, not just the claimant, had the discretion exercised in their favour on a number of occasions. The EAT stated it was clear that the claimant had a case to make, but not knowing about the option and the criteria for its exercise, she was deprived of that opportunity. The EAT noted that the respondent had cited the FÁS instruction to the claimant that participants only be retained for one extra year under the retention option as the reason for her dismissal. However, nonetheless, the respondent exercised its discretion in favour of two colleagues ignoring that same rule. The EAT awarded the claimant of €10,000 compensation.

PRE-EMPLOYMENT BACKGROUND CHECKS

[27.77] *Deegan v United Parcel Service of Ireland Ltd[94] – Employment Appeals Tribunal – Unfair Dismissals Acts 1977 to 2007 as amended – European Council Directive 185/2010 laying down detailed measures for implementation of common basic standards on aviation security – Pre-employment background checks – dismissal for failure to follow reasonable request*

The claimant commenced employment as a pre-loader with the respondent in October 2008. Pre-loading involves the security screening and sorting of packages into containers, which are subsequently loaded onto aircraft. The respondent company is regulated by the Irish Aviation Authority and is at all times subject to the audit of its compliance with industry regulations.

Under EU Directive 185/2010, it became necessary for all companies in the aviation industry to complete pre-employment checks on all prospective employees and existing employees. In July 2011, the human resources manager called a meeting to inform all staff of the legislative requirements and ongoing human resource audit. All employees were provided with a three-page set of audit guidelines, setting out the requirements in

---

94.   *Deegan v United Parcel Service of Ireland Ltd* UD894/2012.

detail. Requirements included: a five year reference history; proof of PPS number; proof of eligibility to work in Ireland; proof of address; and proof of identification. Employees were given over one year to complete the audit process.

The claimant was approached on numerous occasions regarding his employment history over the months following the staff meeting. By letter dated 17 January 2002 the respondent noted deficiencies in the claimant's responses, particularly in relation to the period from January 2007 until his employment commenced in October 2008. The respondent informed the claimant that failure to comply could result in disciplinary action, up to and including dismissal.

The claimant subsequently provided evidence of involvement in a FÁS training course in 2007 and 2008 but was unable to formally verify his employment history for the same period. He did provide correspondence from the Revenue Commissioners which evidenced employment with particular employer from January to October 2005. However, the claimant had previously asserted that he had worked with that particular employer in 2007.

The claimant was invited by letter to attend a disciplinary meeting on 6 February 2012. He declined the opportunity to be represented or accompanied to the meeting. At the meeting, the claimant gave further details of his employment in 2007 and 2008 but was unable to give references for both employments as he claimed that both posts had been on a cash-in-hand basis. The claimant sought the opportunity to swear an affidavit as provided for in the audit guidelines:

> Where the individual cannot provide an acceptable reference they must seek a
> signed affidavit from a solicitor to validate this period

The respondent refused and the claimant was given a week to provide further details about the gaps in his employment. The claimant was unable to do so and was formally dismissed by letter dated 24 February 2012 for failure to follow a reasonable request. The claimant was informed of a right to appeal to the country manager within five days. No request was made and a request made by the claimant's solicitor to extend the time in which to lodge the appeal was denied.

The EAT found that the claimant was not treated fairly by the respondent in relation to the denial of his request to provide an affidavit. The respondent argued that there was insufficient information on which to base the affidavit. However the EAT noted that the human resource audit guidelines provided for the production of affidavits in certain circumstances where the employee cannot provide an acceptable reference. Furthermore, the respondent had accepted affidavits from 17 other employees in respect of gaps in their employment. In those circumstances, the EAT could not be satisfied that the claimant had not been singled out and ruled that the dismissal was unfair.

Nonetheless, the EAT found the claimant's evidence to be unsatisfactory in relation to the gaps in his employment history and explanations offered. The EAT was not satisfied that the claimant had made any serious efforts to mitigate his loss. Taking these matters into account, the EAT awarded the claimant compensation of €2,000.

CONSTRUCTIVE DISMISSAL

Extreme working conditions and severe underpayment

[27.78] *Calderon & Ors v Nasser Rashed Lootah and Metad Alghubaisi*[95] – *Employment Appeals Tribunal – Unfair Dismissals Acts 1977 to 2007 – appeal against recommendations of Rights Commissioner – whether exceptional circumstances prevented the appellants from lodging their claims within six months – whether the EAT was barred from hearing the case on account of diplomatic or sovereign immunity – whether the appellants were constructively dismissed – extreme working conditions – excessive working hours – severe underpayment – verbal and physical abuse – whether the multiple breaches of the appellants' employment rights went to the root of their contracts of employment*

The respondents in this case were the Ambassador of the United Arab Emirates and his wife. The EAT noted that each of the appellants was employed by the respondents as domestic help in their private residence, initially in the United Arab Emirates and then in Ireland, without any interruption to their continuous service. As they were employed for a continuous period in excess of one year, the EAT accepted that the claims fell within the remit of the Acts.

There was no appearance by or on behalf of the respondents at the hearing. The EAT was, however, satisfied that the respondents had been properly served with notice of the hearing.

The appellants presented their claims to the Rights Commissioner on 5 October 2012 under the Acts and the Organisation of Working Time Act 1977. The claims were lodged more than six months after 12 January 2012, the date on which they left their employment. Section 8(2) of the Acts states that a complaint under the Acts must be presented within six months of the date of the relevant dismissal. However, s 8(2)(b) empowers the EAT to extend this time limit to twelve months if exceptional circumstances prevented the bringing of the claim within the first six months.

The EAT considered the circumstances in which the appellants, who worked as domestic help in the private residence of the respondents, were living and noted that they were less than ideal. During the course of their employment the appellants were subjected to extreme working conditions and were denied access to their employment, travel and identification documentation. The appellants commenced their duties daily at 6.30am and finished most days close to midnight and were not permitted to retire for the evening until the respondents had done so. They were only permitted to take a fifteen minute break in the morning and again in the evening and shared one bedroom with only two beds, forcing two of the appellants to share one bed. Their English was poor and they had very little money. Their employment terminated only when they were rescued from the respondents' residence in the middle of the night by the Migrant Rights Centre. The EAT concluded that these very exceptional circumstances prevented the appellants from lodging their claims within the six month time limit. On this basis the EAT

---

95.   *Calderon & Ors v Nasser Rashed Lootah and Metad Alghubaisi* UD1219/2013, UD1220/2013, UD1221/2013.

extended the time limit to twelve months, essentially granting itself jurisdiction to hear the appeal.

The EAT was notified of the fact that the respondents had relied on diplomatic immunity when this matter was heard before a Rights Commissioner. The EAT held that the onus was on the respondent to prove that the EAT lacked jurisdiction to hear the present case on the grounds of diplomatic or sovereign immunity. In the respondents' absence it was held that it would be both inappropriate and grossly unfair for the EAT to plead sovereign immunity on the respondents' behalf.

The EAT did however consider recent case law on sovereign immunity and held that the appellants' functions did not fall within the restricted form of state immunity as considered in *Government of Canada v Employment Appeals Tribunal*.[96] It was further held that their position did not involve them in the exercise of public powers, according to the test set out in *Mahamdia v Peoples' Democratic of Algeria*.[97]

The appellants alleged that they had been constructively dismissed from their employment with the respondents. The EAT noted that a high burden of proof rested on the appellants, who had to establish that their resignation was not voluntary. Firstly, the EAT had to consider whether a significant breach, going to the root of the employment contracts, had occurred. If this was not held to be the case, the EAT could examine the conduct of the parties, together with the circumstances surrounding the termination, in order to determine whether the termination was a reasonable one.

The EAT considered the working conditions to which the appellants had been subjected during the course of their employment and noted that they were forced to work fifteen hours per day, seven days per week in return for only €170 each in cash per month. One of the appellants gave evidence that she never received a payslip or any pay-related documentation. The appellants' evidence was that they were regularly subjected to physical and verbal abuse whilst performing their duties, which included caring for the respondents' children and a wide range of other domestic duties. The appellants felt scared and trapped, as they were not allowed to leave the residence and had no facilities to communicate with anyone outside of the residence.

The EAT concluded that there had been a complete lack of adherence to any of the appellants' employment rights. Every breach in the circumstances of the case went to the root of the contract. The breaches were numerous and varied, ranging from working hours far in excess of statutory limits to severe underpayment, little of no breaks, no annual leave, no bank holidays and being subjected to violent and degrading treatment.

Accordingly the EAT overturned the Rights Commissioner's recommendation and awarded each of the appellants compensation of €80,000 under the Acts.

Lack of engagement with employer

[27.79] *McDonnell v Dublin Airport Authority plc*[98] *– Employment Appeals Tribunal – Unfair Dismissals Acts 1977 to 2007 as amended – Redundancy Payments Acts 1967*

96. *Government of Canada v Employment Appeals Tribunal* [1992] 2 IR 484.
97. *Mahamdia v Peoples' Democratic of Algeria* (Case C–154/11).
98. *McDonnell v Dublin Airport Authority plc* UD1899/2011, RP2481/2011.

to 2014 – claim for constructive dismissal – sickness absence and subsequent resignation – lack of engagement with respondent – refusal to attend meetings without family member present – refusal to attend occupational health services

The respondent employed the claimant as a cleaner. In 2009, the claimant was diagnosed with a serious illness and thereafter accrued significant sick leave. Evidence was given that the claimant's GP had advised that the claimant was fit to return to work on a phased basis. However, attempts by human resources to obtain a return to work date from the claimant were not successful. The claimant also refused to attend occupational health services and thereafter submitted his resignation on 6 April 2011. The respondent had in correspondence asked the claimant to reconsider his position. However, the claimant did not engage and refused to cooperate.

The EAT noted that the core of the case was the refusal of the claimant to adhere to the norms of practice of the respondent and throughout industry, in particular in relation to accompaniment at meetings with management by a trade union representative or work colleague. The claimant's insistence that he would only attend meetings accompanied by his father created serious difficulties in this case. However, the EAT accepted that the respondent had tried everything possible to resolve the issues, including setting aside company policy and agreeing to the claimant's father's attendance. The EAT found that in essence, the claimant refused to engage with the respondent's procedures set out in its policy and noted that the claimant had developed a certain intransigence with regard to facilitating meetings towards a solution to the problem. In these circumstances, the EAT found that the claimant did not establish grounds for constructive dismissal and therefore the claim failed.

Delay on the part of an employer in dealing with a complaint

[27.80] *Shannon v Pat the Baker*[99] *– Employment Appeals Tribunal – Unfair Dismissals Acts 1977 to 2007 as amended – constructive dismissal – whether claimant's decision to resign her position was reasonable in all circumstances – whether delay on part of employer in progressing grievance/complaint procedure of such magnitude that reasonable for claimant to have no confidence in procedure itself*

The claim arose out of interpersonal difficulties between the claimant and her line manager. The claimant gave evidence that, following a change in her work patterns, her manager began to treat her differently from other employees. She asserted that he was aggressive towards her and corrected her constantly and she gave evidence that this upset her and led to her suffering panic attacks. Having raised this with the manager, the claimant subsequently went on leave and, on her return to work, she fainted in the workplace and was subsequently certified as being unfit to attend to work. The company doctor confirmed her unfitness to work and stated that she should not return to an environment which she perceived as hostile until mediation with satisfactory resolution

---

99.   *Shannon v Pat the Baker* UD1840/2011.

occurred. Evidence was subsequently given that the claimant remained on sick leave but began to improve and was subsequently advised to partake in a mediation process.

Correspondence was entered into with the respondent, part of which was a formal grievance raised by the claimant by way of letter to the general manager. A grievance meeting took place in June 2011. The claimant asserted that, following this meeting where she outlined her grievances, a number of letters were exchanged but ultimately there was no resolution to the matter.

On 8 September 2011, the claimant wrote to the general manager submitting her resignation and informed him of her intention to pursue a claim for constructive dismissal. Evidence by the general manager was that, following the meeting in June 2011, he undertook to investigate the matters raised by her. He decided to get an external consultant within two weeks of the meeting but then had an emergency operation and was on sick leave for over six weeks. He then wrote to the claimant in an attempt to clarify the nature of her claim, and he also identified the external consultant who was tasked with conducting the investigation. When he returned from sick leave, he discovered the resignation letter from the claimant. The respondent asked her to reconsider but there was no further engagement on the part of the claimant.

The EAT noted that the claimant was advised by letter of 27 July of the name of the consultant and, while an unfortunate series of events led to delay in the process, she chose to tender her resignation. The EAT was critical of the fact that the grievance/ complaint procedure did not set out an indicative timeframe for the process to be concluded. The EAT noted and accepted that there had been delay in the process. It stated that it was a matter for it to determine whether the conduct of the respondent was designed to or likely to undermine the claimant's confidence in the grievance/complaint procedure. Essentially, the EAT was forced to consider whether the delay was of such magnitude that the claimant ought reasonably to have no confidence in the procedure itself. The EAT concluded that it was satisfied that the respondent did not intentionally delay the appeal. It noted that the claimant did not exhaust the internal procedures. It noted that the general manager had an emergency operation and was absent for six weeks approximately but furthermore communicated with the claimant during this time. The EAT stated that it was not satisfied that the delay could be interpreted to be of such magnitude that it could undermine any reasonable employee's confidence in the grievance procedure and ground a claim for constructive dismissal. The reason for the delay, whilst unfortunate, was understandable in the circumstances. The claim was not upheld.

Resignation under duress

[27.81] *Canon v Black Bros Ltd*[100] *– Employment Appeals Tribunal – Unfair Dismissals Acts 1977 to 2007 as amended – constructive dismissal – resignation under duress – withdrawal of resignation – fair procedures in disciplinary process – obligation on employer to investigate alleged misconduct*

---

100. *Canon v Black Bros Ltd* UD2116/2011.

The claimant worked for the respondent's food distribution company as a warehouse worker and occasionally as a van delivery driver. The claimant was subsequently alleged to have committed an act of misconduct. This occurred in September 2011 when the claimant was accused of misappropriating certain items of the respondent's food stock and selling the stock for personal gain.

The claimant was informed that the respondent would institute an investigation and he was suspended pending the outcome of the investigation. A meeting was arranged away from the respondent's premises between the respondent's representative and the claimant. The claimant told the respondent how upset he was over the situation and explained exactly what happened in relation to his sale of company stock. The claimant was not, however, informed of the specifics of the complaints during this meeting.

The EAT heard evidence that the claimant repeatedly requested the name of the person who made the allegation against him, but the respondent's representative refused to give him this information. The respondent gave evidence that the claimant, following the initial meeting with its representative, informed the respondent's representative that he 'could not stand the pressure' and 'had bad thoughts', following which the respondent's representative agreed to meet the claimant on a further occasion. The respondent's representative gave evidence that the claimant confessed to the misconduct at the subsequent meeting, and was very upset. The respondent's representative gave evidence that at a further meeting the claimant asked him how much money he would receive if he resigned from the respondent, to which the respondent's representative responded that he 'could not say'. The respondent's representative stated that at a meeting on 29 September 2011, the claimant asked if the respondent's representative could assist him in typing a letter of resignation. The respondent's representative told the claimant that he could not be involved in accepting his resignation.

A further meeting took place between the claimant and the respondent's representative in a car park adjacent to a public house at a weekend. At this meeting, the respondent's representative gave a number of papers to the claimant, including the respondent's pre-prepared resignation letter. Contrary to the respondent's assertion, the claimant that he had not requested that the resignation letter be drafted. The claimant asserted was not provided with copies of any of the documents and gave evidence that he was highly stressed during this meeting and would have 'signed anything'. Following the claimant signing the letter of resignation, it was forwarded to the respondent the following Monday.

The EAT noted that it was difficult to conceive of a more broadly based criterion for dismissal than dismissal for 'conduct' as envisaged by s 6(4)(b) of the 1977 Act as no definition of 'conduct' is provided in the Act. The EAT stated that where an employee is dismissed by reason of conduct, the employer is required to engage in an investigation and the scope and requirements of the investigation will be determined by the facts of the case. The employer is required to demonstrate that the investigation was 'fair' in the sense of being open-minded and 'full' in the sense that no issue which might reasonably have a bearing on the decision was left unexplored. Failure to adhere to these requirements will generally render the procedure unfair.

The EAT highlighted a number of general conditions that should be part of an investigation. Specifically:

(i) the employee must be aware of all allegations and complaints that formed the basis of the proposed dismissal;

(ii) the employee must have an adequate opportunity to deny the allegations or explain the circumstances of the incident before the decision to dismiss is taken – this includes a right to be represented in appropriate circumstances;

(iii) the evidence of witnesses or other involved parties must be sought where the allegations were denied or the facts were in dispute;

(iv) all statements relevant to the investigation must be furnished to the employee; and

(v) the employee must have the right to be represented by a fellow employee or trade union official.

The EAT held that no such fair procedures had been complied with in this case.

The EAT held that, as part of his right to fair procedures, the employee is entitled to be furnished with any witness statements which may be necessary to determine the events which occurred. It also stated that witnesses' names may not be redacted from any such witness statement. In this case the respondent's failure to inform the claimant of the identity of the person who made the allegations against him was 'fundamentally unfair'.

In relation to the respondent's dismissal and the disciplinary procedure, the EAT stated that it would be concerned to see that the procedure is adhered to in all material respects, including any right of appeal therein. However it noted that failure of strict adherence to the procedures will not automatically make the dismissal unfair. In the context of a disciplinary hearing, it was noted that the employee must be made aware of the potential consequences of his alleged misconduct which may put him at risk of dismissal. It was noted that the respondent had failed to comply with any of its procedures and had not permitted the claimant to be represented by a colleague, as permitted by its disciplinary procedure. The respondent also failed to advise the claimant of the potential repercussions of his behaviour.

In determining the reasonableness of the conclusion reached by the respondent that the claimant was guilty of misconduct, the EAT stated that it was not its role to establish an objective standard but to ask whether the decision to dismiss came within the band of reasonable responses an employer might take having regard to the particular circumstances of the case. In considering whether the respondent's decision was in the 'band of reasonable responses of an employer', the EAT noted the respondent did not afford the claimant fair procedures, in the following ways:

(i) the respondent did not follow its own procedure;

(ii) the claimant was given a letter of resignation to sign in a car park, drafted by the respondent's representative;

(iii) the claimant was not given the opportunity to take independent legal advice;

(iv) the claimant was not given the statements taken from fellow employees/third parties;

(v) the claimant was not told to take independent legal advice; and

(vi) the claimant was not given a 'cooling off period' which would have allowed him reconsider his position.

The EAT referred to the Supreme Court decision in *Hurley v Royal Yacht Club.*[101] In *Hurley*, the Supreme Court held that there must be 'informed consent by the employee to contract out of his rights'. While the EAT accepted that the resignation letter did not amount to a severance agreement, it observed that the claimant, by signing the letter of resignation, effectively relinquished his employment rights, and therefore should have had informed consent to the consequences/repercussions of his actions.

The EAT also considered *Millett v Shinkwin,*[102] where the Labour Court held that where an employee resigns in circumstances where he is not fully informed because he is not in a position to fully evaluate his options, it would be unreasonable for an employer to deny an employee an opportunity to recant his resignation within a reasonable time once the true position becomes clear, and that refusing to allow an employee to retract his resignation in such circumstances could amount to a dismissal.

The EAT also referred to the High Court decision in *Sunday Newspapers Ltd v Kinsella and Bradley*[103] where the Court reinforced the notion that the employee should be advised in writing to seek appropriate advice as to his/her rights, but emphasised that there was no requirement on an employer to provide professional legal advice, rather the important aspect of the advice is that it be appropriate.

In the case at hand, the EAT found it was 'not remotely fair or reasonable' to arrange for an employee to sign a letter of resignation in the car park of a public house. Additionally it found that it was unfair of the respondent to fail to advise an employee in writing of the charges against him or that he could be represented; to fail to furnish him with statements which were taken in the course of the investigation; to fail to advise him that the allegations against him could lead to his dismissal, and to draft a letter of resignation and get him to sign it.

The EAT determined the claimant was dismissed and that his 'resignation' was a forced resignation in unacceptable circumstances. It awarded the claimant compensation of €30,000.

[27.82] *O'Farrell v Board of Management of St Brigid's School*[104] – *Employment Appeals Tribunal – Unfair Dismissals Acts 1977 to 2007 as amended – constructive dismissal – withdrawal of retirement – factors leading up to constructive dismissal – failure to raise grievance not fatal factor*

---

101.   *Hurley v Royal Yacht Club* [1997] ELR 225.
102.   *Millett v Shinkwin* [2004] 15 ELR 319.
103.   *Sunday Newspapers Ltd v Kinsella and Bradley* [2007] IEHC 324.
104.   *O'Farrell v Board of Management of St Brigid's School* UD2199/2011, MN2238/2011, WT905/2011.

The claimant was employed as the principal of the respondent school. In November 2005, following an inspection, concerns were raised in relation to the competence of a particular teacher. On 6 March 2009 the chairman of the respondent's board of management wrote to the Diocesan Bishop seeking approval to dismiss the teacher. On 21 December 2009 the Department of Education and Science wrote to the chairman advising that, as procedures in relation to the dismissal and suspension of teachers had changed, the respondent would have to restart the process.

Following the issue of the chairman's letter of 6 March 2009, the teacher lodged an appeal on the basis of failure to act with procedural fairness under the Maynooth Statute 264/2 (a mechanism involving canon law) to determine the issue. The appeal was upheld, and the respondent was denied permission to dismiss the teacher.

In the intervening period, the relationship between the claimant and the teacher deteriorated and, following the teacher's successful appeal of the decision to dismiss her, the claimant indicated an unwillingness to work with the teacher again. The claimant stated that the chairman informed her that when the teacher returned to the school she would be required to remain in the classroom to monitor the teacher's work. The claimant stated that this would adversely affect her role as principal in the respondent school. On 13 April 2011, the claimant wrote to the board of management advising that she would retire with effect from 31 August 2011. The resignation was accepted at a board meeting on 18 May 2011.

Concurrently, the board was attempting to find ways to appeal/challenge the decision under the Maynooth Statutes. On 28 June 2011, following a rejection of the proposal to seek judicial review of the decision under the Maynooth Statutes, the board of the respondent decided to resign. The parish priest, who was then the manager of the school in place of the board, attempted to convince the claimant to reconsider her decision to retire. The claimant retired from the school on 31 August 2011.

On 11 October 2011, the claimant's representatives wrote to the respondent contending that the claimant had been constructively dismissed from her position as principal, having been compelled to engage in extensive monitoring of the teacher, and that the claimant now wished to withdraw her retirement and resume her position as principal. The respondent did not reply to this letter.

In considering the proceedings, the EAT noted that the teacher whom the claimant was required to monitor, had been on administrative leave from 2009 when the respondent sought the patron's approval for her dismissal. It was the question of the return of the teacher to the school for the new school year beginning in September 2011 that caused an issue for the claimant.

The EAT found that, while that there were profound and fundamental problems in the school on an ongoing basis, the obligation to be imposed on the claimant to constantly supervise the teacher was irrational and it put the claimant in an impossible position and demonstrated the respondent's intention to undermine the employment relationship between the respondent and the claimant.

The EAT noted that the claimant had not raised a formal grievance with the respondent prior to her representative threatening proceedings. However, given the circumstances and based on the available evidence, the EAT was satisfied that the respondent was aware of the claimant's dissatisfaction with the proposals regarding her supervision of the teacher.

Furthermore, the EAT could not accept that the parish priest, who became the manager of the respondent following the resignation of the board, had no knowledge of the situation between the claimant and the teacher. The EAT also noted that the parish priest did not respond to the letter of 11 October 2011 or deny that the claimant would be required to engage in the supervision and mentoring of the teacher.

For all these reasons the EAT found that the claimant had been constructively dismissed and awarded compensation of €50,000.

Changes to sales territory and imposition of new sales targets

[27.83] *Beglan v Scanomat Ireland Ltd*[105] *– Employment Appeals Tribunal – Unfair Dismissals Acts 1977 to 2007 as amended – constructive dismissal claim – changes to claimant's sales territory and customer base – new sales targets unilaterally imposed on claimant*

The claimant was employed by the respondent from 1999. The respondent was engaged in the sale of coffee dispensing equipment and of coffee. In the course of his employment, the claimant was involved in various areas of the business, to include sales, working on new agreements at head office level, dealing with customers and managing van drivers. At the time his employment terminated, his role was a sales one only.

The claimant had reported to the managing director until his death in December 2010. It was the claimant's understanding up to 2011 that the respondent had been doing well and was very profitable. He was unaware that the respondent's new business sales were declining from 2009 to 2011. In January 2011, a replacement managing director took over the ownership and running of the business. Evidence was given that from this moment on, changes were initiated. As part of new changes, the claimant had to cover the South and South East territory for the first time and he was also given a list of specific customers. In January 2012, meetings were held with the claimant where it was clear that the replacement managing director was unhappy with the claimant's sales figures and the claimant was issued with a series of sales targets, which included a target for new business and a target for the existing territories. The claimant had never previously been issued with sales targets or territories, except in the first year of employment. He was not asked for input into the new business development target, nor the existing accounts target. The claimant gave evidence that he was upset and shocked when provided with targets, as he knew they were not achievable. The claimant then engaged in correspondence with the respondent, setting out his unhappiness with these changes. In February 2012 a meeting was held with the respondent, the claimant and his representative at which targets were discussed. The respondent acknowledged that the managing director first became aware of the claimant's grievances in the January letters. The claimant stated that the targets were unreasonable and that he believed that his performance was being criticised. The managing director gave evidence that performance needed to be maintained and grown, that the respondent had suffered

---

105. *Beglan v Scanomat Ireland Ltd* UD688/2012.

losses and that his family was putting money into the business to make it sustainable. He wanted two separate sales targets, but the claimant was not prepared to provide these.

The claimant requested that his grievance be referred to the Labour Relations Commission, but this was not accepted by the respondent, who felt it should be dealt with internally. The claimant acknowledged that he never thought of taking his own grievance to the LRC. The claimant wrote to the managing director stating that if he did not receive assurances in respect of his employment by no later than 12 March 2012, he would resign immediately. The managing director responded by writing on 12 March. In evidence, the managing director stated that he had only become aware that the claimant had suffered from work-related stress on two previous occasions in 2009. When the claimant tendered his resignation, the managing director wrote to him and asked him to reconsider his position and gave him seven days to do so as he was willing to discuss matters further with the claimant. Ultimately, the claimant's resignation was received and accepted by the respondent.

The EAT noted that the claimant had worked for the respondent for more than 12 years and had had a significant role under the previous managing director. The EAT concluded that the respondent had set unrealistic targets for the claimant, which by any standards would have been impossible to achieve. The EAT noted that the claimant's sales performance had been acceptable, given the trading conditions prior to discussions held in January 2012. The EAT, having considered the minutes of these meetings, noted that there was no real consultation with the claimant regarding the setting of realistic sales targets for him and that the targets appeared to have been increased by 69% (a figure agreed by both sides) at a time when sales had been reducing for a number of years. The EAT noted the request from the claimant to bring in outside mediation (the LRC) and noted the respondent's decision to ignore this request and to adhere to the original position. The EAT concluded that this approach was an effort to freeze the claimant out of his employment by setting such unrealistic targets to make his position untenable. The EAT noted that there was an onus on the claimant to pursue his grievances himself which he failed to do. The EAT upheld the claim of unfair dismissal and awarded compensation of €70,000.

Excessive disciplinary sanctions

[27.84] *McGinty v Gallagher T/A Hillcrest Nursing Home[106] – Employment Appeals Tribunal – Unfair Dismissals Acts 1977 to 2007 as amended – whether claimant was constructively dismissed following investigation of verbal altercation with colleague*

The claimant was employed as a healthcare assistant in the respondent's nursing home. The claimant and a colleague had a disagreement in the presence of an elderly resident of the nursing home and her daughter. The disagreement developed after the claimant and her colleague left the resident's room and resulted in both of them becoming very upset. It appears that both parties reported what had occurred to the nurse in charge and the respondent owner of the nursing home commenced an investigation. It was noted by the EAT that, from the first meeting of the respondent with the parties, no issue was

---

106. *McGinty v Gallagher T/A Hillcrest Nursing Home* UD501/2012.

taken with the information provided by the claimant's colleague, which was in stark contrast to the notes of the respondent's meeting with the claimant which referenced the claimant's version of events being inaccurate.

The EAT concluded that at this very early stage in dealing with the events, the respondent had demonstrated manifest prejudice against the claimant and the EAT further noted that, from reading notes of other witness meetings, they had both informed the respondent that the claimant had come to their office shouting and saying something about reporting an incident. In the course of a subsequent disciplinary hearing, the respondent sought to deny the claimant had gone to the nurse's office to complain about being abused by her colleague, despite it being in the notes of the respondent's meetings with the nurses. The claimant was written to and advised that she was suspended from duties to facilitate a full investigation and was required to present a statement of events. She was invited to a disciplinary meeting and was advised of her right to be accompanied and again it was noted that she had not supplied a statement in respect of the events.

The disciplinary hearing took place and, after a recess, the respondent informed the claimant that she was being dismissed for gross misconduct, namely fighting with another member of staff. The claimant was advised that the respondent would write to her setting out her decision and she was also advised of her right of appeal. Later that day, the claimant submitted her notice of appeal and shortly afterwards she received a letter entitled 'Outcome of Disciplinary Hearing', which made no mention of the fact that she had been told that she was to be dismissed. The letter stated that a very serious altercation had taken place, which was overheard by residents and relatives, and left a colleague in an extremely distressed state and in fear of leaving the nursing home after work. The claimant was advised she was being issued with a final written warning of 12 months' duration and was reminded again of her right of appeal. The claimant subsequently wrote to the respondent setting out her confusion over the versions between what she was told at the conclusion of the disciplinary hearing and the contents of the outcome letter. She made it clear she wished the appeal hearing to include an appeal against the outcome of the contents letter; in other words an appeal against the final written warning.

This appeal hearing took place and was conducted by the owner of another nursing home unconnected to the respondent. The appeal decision-maker was critical of the respondent and found that there was no dismissal in this case and that no letter of dismissal issued. There was no letter of final written warning. The letter that did issue was a letter stating an intention to issue a letter of warning and the appeal recommended that a return to work interview be arranged as soon as was practicable. Subsequent to this, the appeal decision-maker wrote to the claimant enclosing his findings and stated:

> You will note I will have recommended that you attend to a return to work meeting with management of the nursing home as soon as is possible. The matter of whether a warning is issued or not is still active and a matter for management at that stage.

The respondent subsequently wrote to the claimant and stated that the outcome was a final written warning and that she had a right of appeal. She was then invited to a return to work meeting. The claimant wrote to the respondent asserting that she felt the appeals process was now exhausted and that she should be able to return to work as the decision to dismiss her was incorrect and she was further of the opinion that the warning did not and should not arise. It appears that the return to work meeting never took place and the claimant resigned and claimed constructive dismissal.

The EAT noted that, despite having told the claimant she was to be dismissed at the end of the disciplinary meeting, when the respondent later wrote to her to say she was issuing a final written warning, no mention was made of the earlier decision to dismiss. Not only was the claimant told she was dismissed, she was told it was for fighting. The EAT was not aware of any evidence to support this finding. The EAT noted further the findings of the appeal decision maker that it was not clear if any investigation into allegations by the claimant against her colleague took place. The EAT concluded that no full and fair investigation into the events between the claimant and her colleague was ever carried out by the respondent. There was always a presumption on the part of the respondent that the claimant was the instigator. The EAT concluded that the conduct of the respondent was so unreasonable as to allow the claimant's claim of constructive dismissal to succeed. She was awarded compensation of €5,750.

Refusal to accept employer's solutions to grievance

[27.85] *Jarzab v OCS One Complete Solution Ltd*[107] *– Employment Appeals Tribunal – Unfair Dismissals Acts 1977 to 2007 as amended – claim of constructive dismissal – whether claimant unreasonable in her refusal to consider solutions offered by respondent to resolve difficult situation – whether her decision to resign was reasonable in all circumstances*

The claimant commenced employment as a cleaner with the respondent in February 2009 and resigned by notice in writing three years later. The stated reason for her resignation was that she could not continue to work with a colleague of whom she had complained to the respondent.

Evidence was given that there was personal animosity between the claimant and this colleague, which had 'spilled over' into the workplace. Evidence was given by the service manager of the respondent that she became aware of interpersonal difficulties between the claimant and other employees. A meeting took place between the service manager and the claimant and there was hope that matters would resolve themselves during the Christmas holidays. However, as the difficulties continued, the service manager met with both employees in early January 2012. A proposal that the employees would be rescheduled so they would not be in work at the same time and also mediation was offered. The claimant would not accept either option, although the other employee was willing to participate in mediation. The claimant believed that the proper solution would have been to transfer the claimant to another building and/or to dismiss the colleague. The respondent gave evidence to the effect that the claimant could not be reassigned to another site because the employees of the only other site in the locality worked full time and she was a part-time employee. The respondent stated that they had

---

107. *Jarzab v OCS One Complete Solution Ltd* UD1188/2012.

done everything they could do to resolve the situation and retain the claimant, but nothing they offered was acceptable to her and she subsequently resigned of her own volition.

The EAT found that the claimant had not been dismissed, constructively or otherwise, but that she had resigned of her own volition. The EAT held that the respondent had invoked fair procedures in dealing with the grievance raised by the claimant with regard to her colleague and had offered fair and reasonable solutions to a difficult situation, but the claimant was unreasonable in her approach. The claim failed.

Failure to investigate complaints

[27.86] *Hegarty v Clare Civil Engineering Co Ltd and Anor*[108] *– Employment Appeals Tribunal – Unfair Dismissals Acts 1977 to 2007 as amended – Organisation of Working Time Act 1997 – Redundancy Payments Acts 1967 to 2014 – Minimum Notice and Terms of Employment Acts 1973 to 2005*[109] *– claim of constructive dismissal – failure of respondent to deal with complaints made by complainant against colleague*

The claimant claimed that she was badly treated by a colleague for some time, as a result of which she complained to her manager, who was not often on site. Evidence was given to the effect that she told her manager that she felt bullied by the colleague to such a degree that she was afraid to come to work and that it was having an impact on her home life. The claimant asserted that she was told by the manager that it sounded like she was being bullied and that he would take advice and he would get back to her. The claimant's manager later informed her that he had spoken to her colleague. The claimant gave evidence that the behaviour of her colleague worsened after this and the manager never contacted the claimant again.

The claimant subsequently put her complaint in an email to the respondent, but got no response and subsequently went on sick leave and did not return to work again. She was certified by her doctor as suffering from severe stress and also attended a psychiatrist on a number of occasions. As she received no contact from her manager, she sought advice from the Citizens Information Centre who acted on her behalf and contacted the respondent on a number of occasions.

In response to this contact, the respondent acknowledged the claimant's complaint and sent her a copy of the employee handbook. The claimant responded positively to a suggestion that mediation be entered into. However, this was never arranged by the respondent. In evidence, the claimant's line manager suggested that she was unreasonable in refusing to engage in mediation and confirmed that, despite what was written in letter to her, she and her colleague were not expected to pay for this process, but that the respondent would pay. As she had not heard from the respondent, she again sought the assistance of the Citizens Information Centre, who engaged with the

---

108.   *Hegarty v Clare Civil Engineering Co Ltd and Anor* UD2093/2011, RP2672/2011, MN2115/2011, WT838/2011.

109.   The claims under the Redundancy Payments Acts 1967 to 2014 and the Organisation of Working Time Act 1997 were withdrawn by the claimant.

respondent on her behalf. Although informed that documents would be sent out, these were never received by the claimant who subsequently engaged a solicitor to write on her behalf. There was no response to any of the letters sent by the claimant's legal advisors and accordingly the claimant regarded herself as having been constructively dismissed. Evidence was given by the respondent that no reply was made to any of the claimant's solicitor's letters because the matter had been dealt with by the respective solicitors. The respondent submitted that its offer of re-engagement, which had been made by its solicitor to the claimant's solicitor, was a reasonable offer and one the claimant could have accepted.

The EAT considered the evidence and found that, on the basis of the complaints by the claimant and the consequential failure of the respondent to deal with the complaints in a reasonable manner and within a reasonable timeframe, the claimant was entitled to consider herself constructively dismissed. The EAT was satisfied that the claimant had engaged with the respondent's grievance procedure, but that the conduct of the respondent in dealing with her complaint fell well below what the EAT considered the behaviour of a reasonable employer. The EAT did not believe the offer to re-engage the claimant was a fair matter to be taken into account in light of the previous history and the fact that the complaints were still outstanding and had not been dealt with in any reasonable way by the respondent. The EAT stated it was clear that the relationship of trust and confidence had broken down. The EAT found that the claimant had been unfairly dismissed and awarded her compensation of €24,000. In respect of the claim for notice, the EAT found that as the claimant left her employment without giving notice to the respondent, there was no obligation on the respondent to pay her in respect of minimum notice.

[27.87] *O'Connor v Dairy Master[110] – Employment Appeals Tribunal – Unfair Dismissals Acts 1977 to 2007 as amended – whether claimant constructively dismissed in circumstances where claimant resigned due to alleged bullying and harassment on part of his supervisor – failure of employer to train employees in respect of its bullying and harassment policy – failure of management to take any action – unreasonable behaviour of respondent in failing to address claimant's complaints about supervisor's behaviour towards him*

The claimant was employed as a general operative in the respondent's manufacturing operation. The respondent manufactures machines and equipment for dairy farming and in particular for the milk industry and there were 300 employees on site. Evidence was given by the claimant that his difficulties in his employment commenced once one of his peers was promoted to the role of supervisor in 2003. From this moment on he was subjected to unwelcome and at times abusive language and behaviour on the part of the supervisor. His work and his work rate were criticised and insulted and offensive remarks about aspects of his private life were made by his supervisors. He also made certain complaints about the work that was assigned to him; specifically, that he was assigned particularly unpleasant and/or unfamiliar/complicated tasks.

---

110. *O'Connor v Dairy Master* UD351/2012.

The claimant gave evidence that he was somewhat reluctant to advise the managing director of the respondent of what was going on. However, when he did approach his superiors about the conduct of his supervisor, he gave evidence that he was told to get back to his job and forget about it. In September 2010, an anonymous letter was sent to the respondent criticising the supervisor and complaining about his treatment of some staff. Following receipt of this letter, the claimant and four others from the same section were called to individual meetings with members of management and interviewed about the letters. The claimant gave evidence that he was told that the gardaí would be involved and that his fingerprints and DNA would be taken. The claimant stated that he was asked whether he had problems with his supervisor, but when he tried to explain them, he was told to forget about the past and was not given a chance to explain. He confirmed that he had not written the anonymous letter and did not know who had. Evidence was given that the claimant was stressed, anxious and increasingly unwell and sick before going to work. He was put on medication in early August and was certified unfit to work up to December 2011.

Letters were sent by his solicitors citing bullying and the failure of the respondent to address same. In response the respondent's solicitors indicated that this was the first complaint that had been received about bullying and suggested that the claimant should contact the supervisor who would be happy to assist him. In December 2011, the claimant's solicitor advised the respondent that, because of the constant bullying and harassment to which he had been subjected, he was resigning and would claim constructive dismissal. The EAT also heard evidence from former colleagues of the claimant who corroborated his evidence with reference to aspects of the way he was treated by his supervisors.

The respondent gave evidence that management spoke to each employee at least once a week and they had plenty of opportunity to raise any issue, if they had any problems, and that on no occasion had the claimant ever mentioned anything about his supervisors. At the meeting regarding the anonymous letter, the claimant was given every opportunity to raise any issues of concern that he might have, but he did not do so. The managing director stated that he knew that the allegations about the supervisor were false because he had checked with many other employees. Evidence was given on behalf of the respondent by other members of management who confirmed that they had never received any complaints about the supervisor and had never witnessed any of the behaviour alleged. The supervisor himself gave evidence confirming that the work allocated to the claimant was repetitive in nature, but that he (the claimant) always had excuses for not doing the job properly. There were occasions that he had to reprimand the claimant about his poor work performance. The supervisor stated that the claimant was the most 'assisted employee on the factory floor and was never given tasks he was not trained or capable of doing'. He denied using any bad or offensive language towards the claimant and all of the other allegations made.

The EAT stated it was satisfied that the claimant was a vulnerable employee and a credible witness. It fully accepted the claimant's account of his difficulties at work and stated that it was satisfied that the behaviour complained of did constitute bullying in the workplace. The EAT accepted that the claimant had spoken to the supervisor about his conduct towards him to no avail and that he had attempted to raise the issue with senior management, but was rebuffed. The EAT noted that the respondent's bullying and harassment policy was not produced to the EAT until the third day of hearing of the case and the EAT noted that there was no evidence before it that the claimant had received any induction training in this policy. The EAT noted that such training would be necessary so that the employee could fully understand the policy and its requirements. The EAT concluded that management had adopted a closed mind and failed, not only to take any action, but in any way to entertain the possibility that there may have been some truth in the claimant's allegation. The EAT stated that it was difficult to accept the respondent's evidence that the supervisor's name was not mentioned by any party during the meetings relating to the anonymous letter when it was clear from the evidence that the respondent was seeking to establish the identity of the person who wrote the letters. The EAT concluded that the respondent had failed to address the claimant's complaint about the supervisor's behaviour towards him, had acted unreasonably, and that it was reasonable for the claimant in the circumstances to resign. His claim for constructive dismissal succeeded and he was awarded compensation of €25,000.

Resignation prior to outcome of bullying/harassment investigation

[27.88] *Zaino v SAP Service and Support Centre (Ireland) Ltd*[111] *– Unfair Dismissals Acts 1977 to 2007 as amended – Employment Appeals Tribunal – constructive dismissal – whether bullying/harassment policy made available to employees – whether employer had sufficient opportunity to resolve claimant's complaints prior to her resignation*

The claimant resigned in light of, *inter alia*, her dissatisfaction with the manner in which a complaint raised by her against her line manager had been handled by the respondent.

The claimant raised a complaint of bullying/harassment against her line manager, with whom she had a number of minor disagreements over a period of time. Her line manager ceased to be her manager a couple of months prior to her resignation and the claimant raised a bullying/harassment complaint against him a short time afterwards.

The claimant's line manager agreed to participate in a mediation process to resolve the interpersonal issues with the claimant. However she was not agreeable to such a process and instead insisted that a formal investigation take place. The investigation process commenced, but due to the annual leave of her line manager and the relevant human resources business partner, there was a delay in the progress of the investigation. The claimant resigned while the investigation process was postponed pending her line manager's return from annual leave.

In the course of the hearing, the claimant alleged that she had not been provided with a copy of the respondent's bullying/harassment policy at any time and further that no such policy was available on the staff intranet. The respondent insisted that the policy was available on the staff intranet and that it was readily accessible to all employees.

The EAT noted that there was a conflict of evidence between the claimant and her line manager as to how she had been treated by him. However, the EAT concluded that it was not necessary to resolve this conflict of evidence for the reason detailed below.

---

111. *Zaino v SAP Service and Support Centre (Ireland) Ltd* UD583/2011, MN621/2011.

The EAT noted that the test for constructive dismissal is a 'high one' and held that an employee with a grievance arising from his or her employment must, in the ordinary course, and unless special circumstances arise, inform his or her employer of the nature of the grievance and afford the employer an opportunity to resolve the matter.

In the present case, the EAT concluded that the respondent intended to investigate the claimant's complaints and found that, in circumstances where the claimant resigned while her line manager was on annual leave, the respondent did not have sufficient opportunity to investigate or resolve the claimant's issues prior to her resignation. The EAT held that as the claimant did not afford the respondent this opportunity prior to her resignation, she failed to meet the test for constructive dismissal. For that reason, the EAT ruled that it was not necessary to make any determination in relation to the merits or otherwise of the claimant's complaints against her line manager.

As regards the assertion made by the claimant to the effect that she could not find the respondents bullying/harassment policy on the staff intranet, the EAT stated that it was satisfied the policy was 'readily available' and that it was further satisfied that this had been explained to the claimant by personnel from the respondent's human resources department.

Excessive workload

[27.89] *Kelly v Charlie Shiels Ltd*[112] *– Employment Appeals Tribunal – Unfair Dismissals Acts 1977 to 2007 as amended – alleged constructive dismissal – alleged excessive workload on claimant – claimant's position within workplace not such that she had no alternative other than to tender her resignation*

The claimant worked as a permanent part-time accounts clerk with the respondent company which dealt with the wholesale supply and provision of electrical goods. The claimant had worked for the best part of 14 years with the respondent company, although there had been a break in service in and around 2005 when the claimant started her family.

The respondent's workforce of circa 38 had reduced to 13 by 2013. The claimant indicated that when she commenced her employment there were up to four people in the accounts office but from November 2011 the number had reduced to one; being the claimant who worked from 9.15am to 1pm five days a week. The claimant described how the accounts work could be divided into two sides; the creditor side and the debtor side. By November 2011, the claimant worked exclusively on the creditor side while her colleague worked on the debtor end full-time.

In November 2011, the claimant's colleague left the respondent and the claimant handled the accounts office on her own. The claimant continued in this role and gave evidence that she knew that there would be too much work for her but that the managing director simply said that, given the downturn in business, he hoped he could rely on everyone to 'muck in'. It was agreed between the parties at the hearing that the claimant had worked extremely hard and, whilst there was always a backlog, the claimant ran the accounts office as diligently and efficiently as she could.

---

112. *Kelly v Charlie Shiels Ltd* UD707/2013.

By April 2012, it became clear that certain aspects of the accounts side could not be covered by the claimant, and in particular debt collection was not being pursued. The claimant, in discussion with her line manager and the managing director asked for back up and was repeatedly asked if she would consider full-time work. The respondent's evidence was that management opted to get more involved in debt collection as being the task which needed attention and they did not perceive any particular difficulty with the claimant's handling of the accounts office.

The managing director gave evidence that he only ever expected the claimant to do whatever she could do in the 15 hours a week she was on the premises. The managing director relied on the claimant's skill and ability to prioritise what needed to be done and it was common case that the claimant was never ever criticised, nor was there ever any issue on how the accounts office was being operated. The employer was in fact delighted that the claimant's work ethic was such that she appeared to be largely covering the work of one and a half roles on a part-time basis.

By December 2012 the claimant consulted her GP, and went out for a number of weeks as a result of 'stress'. The employer was notified of the fact that she was out on stress, but the nature of the stress was only identified and made known to the respondent on 17 January 2013 at a meeting that the claimant looked for with her line manager and the managing director and a co-director, which took place in advance of the claimant's return to work.

It was made known to the respondent that the claimant was unhappy with her workload and that she was nervous and stressed and she had had a flare up of her eczema. A number of potential solutions were discussed and it is clear that the claimant was told that that she should not feel pressurised and that nobody expected her to do more than she could. The claimant was asked again if she could work full-time. The claimant was not happy with that solution and suggested instead that, as this really was a full-time position, she would happily train a new recruit and would take redundancy thereafter. The meeting closed with the managing director stating he would consider this option.

A further conversation was held between the claimant and her managers. At this time it was made known to the claimant that they did not want to make her redundant and were prepared instead to engage an assistant to work alongside her on a full-time basis. The claimant was advised that the financial controller, with whom the claimant had an excellent relationship, was going to recruit a new accounts person and the claimant understood that an advertisement was placed in Fás and that a number of CVs were received in response to this. Six weeks later the claimant resigned. In evidence the claimant said she did not feel the respondent was making real progress with sourcing assistance and that the pressure and stress she was under was not diminishing and she had no alternative but to resign.

On considering all the facts, the EAT determined that it could not make a finding that the claimant's position within the workplace was such that she had no alternative than to tender her resignation. The EAT found that a recruitment process had been entered into and that this was a perfectly reasonable response to the claimant's disclosure that the level of pressure she was putting herself under was damaging her wellbeing. The respondent noted that it was of significance that the respondent only knew of the diagnosed stress in January 2013 and that, prior to this, would not have known the claimant was under pressure and there was nothing to suggest she was not coping. The EAT found that as soon as the respondent knew there was a possibility that she was not coping, they agreed to get her assistance and it is noted that this assistance did in fact arrive two or three days before the claimant departed the workplace.

In conclusion, the EAT found that the claimant was not constructively dismissed.

[27.90] *Ronan v Wyse Transport Ltd[113] and Wyse Transport Ltd v Ronan[114] – Employment Appeals Tribunal – appeal of a Rights Commissioner decision – Unfair Dismissal Acts 1977 to 2007 as amended – Payment of Wages Act 1991 – Terms of Employment (Information) Acts 1994 and 2004 – constructive dismissal – reduction of wages – contract of employment – compensation*

This was an appeal by the claimant against a decision of a Rights Commissioner relating to an alleged unfair dismissal and an appeal by the respondent employer against the decision of the Rights Commissioner relating to the Payment of Wages Act 1991 and Terms of Employment (Information) Acts 1994 and 2014.

The claimant worked with the respondent as a truck driver since February 2007. He resigned from his position on 19 July 2011. The claimant contended that due to a number of incidents he felt he had no alternative but to resign.

On 10 January 2010, he met a colleague in a restaurant. This colleague swore at him and told him to go away. He pushed the claimant and the claimant fell down on his arm. He was taken to hospital and was absent from work for a time on certified sick leave. The claimant reported the incident to two of the respondent's directors. At the EAT, this colleague denied he had pushed the claimant but accepted that he had told him to go away as he did not want to speak to him. He stated that the claimant threatened to slit his throat. This incident was reported to the director.

In May 2011, the claimant left his car in the respondent's yard and when he returned the next day found that it was covered in grease and oil. He contacted a director who said he would check the CCTV footage, but nothing was found. On 29 July 2011, while loading a trailer the claimant was approached by a different colleague who asked why he had been given the 'easy' trailer. This colleague said that everyone knew the claimant was on drugs and also pushed him. The claimant contacted the director and told him that he could not take it any more. The director said he would look into the matter but never got back to him. The claimant gave evidence to the EAT that he was nervous of returning to work.

He contacted the director and later met him where he was asked to sign a form to receive a P45 and holiday money. The EAT stated that a claim for constructive dismissal requires that the claimant prove his situation had become so untenable that he had no choice but to leave his employment. The EAT found that the claimant had not established this.

---

113. *Ronan v Wyse Transport Ltd* UD1435/2012.
114. *Wyse Transport Ltd v Ronan* PW667/2012, TE217/2012, WT348/2012, UD1425/2012.

Change in working hours

[27.91] *Robinson v Johnston Logistics Ltd*[115] *– Employment Appeals Tribunal appeal of a decision of a Rights Commissioner – Unfair Dismissals Acts 1977 to 2007 as amended – constructive dismissal – whether change in working hours from morning to evening work rendered claimant working conditions untenable – whether claimant's failure to engage with respondent's proposed compromise unreasonable.*

The claimant had been employed by the respondent since 2005. Throughout his employment, the claimant's contract of employment was updated regularly to reflect legislative changes and updates in work practice. The claimant's most recent contract was issued to him in 3 August 2012. Amongst the changes that were incorporated into this contract was an obligation to carry out night work and the introduction of a reference to overtime pay, confirming that overtime would be paid at a flat rate (as opposed to a premium rate) as a cost-saving measure. Management had consulted with staff, and asked for volunteers to work a new late shift running from 2pm until 10pm. When no volunteers were forthcoming, the respondent was forced to select staff members to take on the shifts. The claimant was one of those selected.

The claimant was aggrieved at being selected to work for the late shift. The claimant worked a morning shift in the respondent, commencing at 7am and ending at 4pm. After work, the claimant took care of his granddaughter. The claimant alleged that the introduction of an obligation to carry out night work interfered with his working hours to such an extent that he believed he could no longer be expected to perform his duties.

The claimant initiated an internal grievance in response to his selection. However the respondent refused to alter its decision. The claimant appealed the decision internally, in accordance with company policy, to a more senior member of staff. By way of compromise, the respondent put forward a proposal under which the claimant would be returned to his usual day-time working hours by April 2013, once identified members of staff had received training to take over from him. The claimant did not accept this suggestion, and did not attend work for his first night shift. The claimant resigned from employment. He brought a constructive dismissal claim.

During the hearing, the respondent adduced largely uncontested evidence that it had suffered great financial hardship through the course of 2011 and 2012, losing many clients. Late shift workers were needed to accommodate changing customer demands, including the making of orders later in the day

The EAT reviewed the evidence and the history of the relationship between the parties. Finding no history of mala fides, it stated that there was no reason to believe that the respondent would not adhere to its promise to return the claimant to his original day-time shift by April 2013. In the circumstances, the EAT found that the claimant's blanket refusal to return to work and take up the new shift was unreasonable, and his claim for constructive dismissal failed.

---

115.   *Robinson v Johnston Logistics Ltd* UD821/2013.

[27.92] *Maher v Health Service Executive[116] – Employment Appeals Tribunal – Unfair Dismissals Acts 1977 to 2007 as amended – whether claimant constructively dismissed where reduction in her working hours – where claimant assigned to care for particular client under specified purpose contract*

The claimant worked for the respondent as a home help. She gave evidence that her working hours and conditions had changed over the years because her work was directly connected to certain clients who needed home help. One of the clients to whom she was assigned was a particularly difficult person and the claimant had asked to be removed from having to provide her with help, but this was not agreed to. Previously the claimant and other carers could cover for each other's hours if needed, for example if one had to go on leave or was sick. However, this practice was changed in May 2012 when the home help staff was told that they had to stick to their own contractual hours and could not cover other colleagues' hours.

Eventually, the claimant decided to leave employment in 2013 because she had not been getting enough hours and her hours had been significantly reduced without her agreement and because she was required to continue to work for a client who was extremely abusive and challenging, in circumstances where she felt her concerns were not adequately addressed by the respondent.

The EAT noted that the client had been assigned to the claimant under a specific purpose contract. The EAT noted that the nature of the duties of a home help can be extremely demanding and that the respondent faced a significant challenge of discharging its statutory duties while balancing the health and safety of requirements of its staff. The EAT noted that this was certainly an issue for the claimant. However, it was the EAT's view that, as her contract was a specific purpose contract for this named client and two others, any termination by her of this contract would not entitle her to maintain a claim of compensation.

The EAT concluded that the claimant's principal issue, which appeared to have led to her terminating her employment, was the significant reduction in her working hours. The EAT considered this issue at considerable length and noted that the contractual relationship between the parties was governed by a specific purpose contract, naming three specific clients. While the contract was not before the EAT, the claimant had accepted that she had signed the contract and that it was preceded by a similar arrangement as regards another client who subsequently went into care. The EAT further noted that those home helps on specific purpose contracts also received additional assignments for home help services when demand so dictated and where funding was available. In light of significant cutbacks, this additional work dried up with the reassessment of clients and significant adjustments in the services provided, and the claimant and her colleagues thereafter continued to discharge their duties under their specific purpose contracts. The EAT stated it was unable to ignore the financial constraints within which the respondent operates and the realities of the financial considerations that dictate its policies and provision of services.

---

116. *Maher v Health Service Executive* UD1185/2013.

The EAT held that the contractual relationship between the parties was governed by the claimant's specific purpose contract. The significance between the two streams of work is that the claimant was contractually bound to provide her services to three individual clients, named in her specific purpose contract. She was not, however, obliged to accept any additional clients unless she wished to do so and indeed was free to pursue private work, which she did. The arrangement as regards additional work lacked a certain mutuality of obligation in this regard. In the circumstances, the claimant's case had failed in that the respondent at all times complied with its contractual obligations to the claimant under her specific purpose contract.

Failure to facilitate a return to work

[27.93] *Carrick v Dublin Stevedores Ltd*[117] *– Employment Appeals Tribunal – Unfair Dismissals Acts 1977 to 2007 as amended – whether claimant constructively dismissed – dispute between original shareholders, including claimant's father – conduct of respondent towards claimant as consequence of dispute – failure of respondent to facilitate return to work for claimant after sick leave*

The claimant's father and another founder set up the respondent company which operated cargo handling. The claimant commenced employment in the role of assistant operations manager. He gave evidence to the EAT that the relationship between his father and the other founder deteriorated, resulting ultimately in his father leaving the respondent company and selling his shareholding. The claimant, however, continued to work in the respondent company. Court proceedings were initiated and the claimant was a witness for the defence. Before the court case the claimant had a good working relationship with his work colleagues. The claimant gave evidence that he had received a telephone call from the other founder concerning allegations about his father and afterwards he had been demoted, his health and safety role was removed without explanation and the respondent stopped paying his telephone bill and car insurance. The claimant was subsequently accused of viewing inappropriate material on a work computer, which he claimed was a computer also used by other work colleagues. He was never disciplined for this offence. Subsequently, the claimant was asked to come to head office and dismantle his father's desk and dump it, which he stated left him feeling humiliated. He asserted he was subjected to a tirade of bullying and harassment by the other founder and his family members and was repeatedly told to stay at home and go home.

The claimant alleged that his five-day working week was reduced to a three-day working week and further reduced to a two-day working week, notwithstanding that casual workers were being offered more work than he was. The claimant stated that he had started to eat lunch in his car as he was afraid of his colleagues. He enjoyed work and did not want to leave employment. The claimant asserted an issue had taken place in November 2012 when he had called to collect a pay cheque when there appears to have been a verbal altercation between the claimant and the other founder in front of a customer of the respondent, referencing the court case and the claimant's father.

---

117. *Carrick v Dublin Stevedores Ltd* UD831/2013.

The claimant suffered a work-related injury in December 2012 and was certified unfit for work for several weeks. He was fit to resume work in January and, notwithstanding attempts by his union representatives to agree a return-to-work date with the respondent, all efforts to obtain a return-to-work date proved unsuccessful. As the claimant could not obtain a return-to-work date from the respondent and had no income, he felt he had no alternative but to treat himself as having been dismissed. He never received a reference from the respondent and neither did he receive a P45, which was subsequently obtained from the Revenue Commissioners. Evidence was given by the claimant that he initially received social welfare payments, but up-skilled and secured a six-month contract which commenced in May 2014.

The respondent gave evidence that there had been issues with the claimant's punctuality, that inappropriate material had been witnessed on his work computer, and that he had been observed driving inappropriately in a customer's Mercedes car. No disciplinary action was taken at the time. A meeting did take place with the union representatives of the claimant regarding his return to work, which was attended by the respondent. The other founder was awaiting transcripts of the court trial before the claimant could return to work. The managing director admitted that since his verbal altercation with the claimant he had lost interest in the claimant and believed that the claimant had tried to blacken his name. He submitted that he had not dismissed the claimant. The claimant's solicitor wrote to the respondent seeking the P45, which was subsequently furnished.

The EAT's conclusion was that the claimant had been constructively dismissed. The EAT noted that, notwithstanding the dispute between the claimant's father and the other founder and the sale of the claimant's fathers shares in the mid-2000s, the claimant had remained working there, although there was clear animosity between the parties. The EAT noted that there had been a number of incidents in the course of the claimant's employment, but no action was taken against the claimant regarding these matters. The EAT noted that the claimant had been medically certified to return to work. However, the respondent required him to give an explanation about a comment he made (which he denied making). The claimant's return to work was contingent on giving an explanation. The EAT concluded that this was not relevant to his employment and it related to a personal issue unconnected with his employment. However, the respondent refused to engage and, despite numerous letters from the claimant's union, the respondent did not proffer a date for the claimant's return to work. The claimant therefore sought his P45, after four months without a response from his employers. The EAT upheld the claim for constructive dismissal and awarded the claimant compensation of €50,000.

Raising concerns about financial practices

[27.94] *Baldwin v Ace Compaction Systems Ltd (in liquidation)*[118] *– Employment Appeals Tribunal – Unfair Dismissals Acts 1977 to 2007 as amended – whether claimant constructively dismissed as consequence of raising concerns about financial practices in respondent company*

---

118.   *Baldwin v Ace Compaction Systems Ltd (in liq)* UD1314/2012.

The claimant, a qualified accountant, joined the respondent company (a waste compactor manufacturer) as financial controller. A company was set up to manufacture environmental compactor systems and this was a separately owned company. The claimant owned one share and the directors owned the other share. The second company bought machines from the respondent company and therefore the respondent was owed €150,000 for a period of time and this put a lot of pressure on the respondent company. The claimant suggested to the owners of the respondent that the second company be liquidated and assets sold for cash. Up until 2006, the respondent had grown and was profitable, but with the economic downturn the respondent had declined swiftly. The respondent suffered a loss of €261,000 in 2009. By March 2010, the claimant became aware of the year-end figures and the quarterly accounts for early 2010.

As a director of the respondent, the claimant was personally liable if the respondent was insolvent, and continued to trade recklessly. The respondent had run out of working capital and the claimant believed that the steps that were being taken to drain extra funds from the company. At this time, the claimant continued to hold one share in the second company and he suggested, to one of the directors, liquidating the second company. The other directors reverted to the claimant and told him that if he allowed them to take over the shares in the second company they would inject money into the second company which would pay money to the respondent. The claimant also held shares in the company. There was an arrangement in place that for every machine sold by a certain employee of the second company, commission of €3,000 was paid to the second company from the respondent and a decision was taken without a board meeting to double this amount. The claimant was informed of this change in December 2010 and raised this issue in an email. The claimant also noted there were advice notes missing and raised a query in relation to this, which was unresolved.

The claimant sent a further email where he raised the fact that a number of company cheques had bounced. He also raised concerns that invoices were sent to the bank where goods not yet been delivered, and no response was received. At a board meeting, the claimant submitted that it was time to put the respondent into liquidation and it was agreed to defer this matter until a shareholders' meeting. The shareholders meeting was held the same day and the minutes of this meeting were opened to the EAT. Again, the claimant reiterated its position that the company should be put into voluntary liquidation. When he was finished giving his report, a director asked if the discussion could be postponed for two days. The claimant was in in work the next day when he was informed that there was an emergency board meeting. The claimant was informed at the board meeting that he was being suspended for one month and was being removed as a director. The claimant was not informed of the reason of his suspension and he immediately contacted his solicitor and wrote a letter to the bank notifying it that he had been removed as a director. The claimant received a letter from the respondent stating he had been requested to step aside as financial controller and that 'he was aware that he had lost confidence in his ability to produce timely or accurate figures in respect of the company'. The claimant asserted that this issue had not previously been addressed with him.

The claimant returned to work after the period of suspension in August 2010, and a director told him he should not be there and suspended him again. He was advised that he was suspended pending the outcome of an external investigation that was ongoing, but not complete due to a lack of management accounts. The claimant responded to deny the contents of the respondent's letter and received no further contact regarding a return to work or regarding a dismissal. He subsequently received correspondence in October 2010 from the respondent's solicitor stating that if he resigned, the respondent was willing to endeavour to remove him from the guarantees. While the claimant was suspended, he could still access company bank accounts and was aware that there were no completed machines available for sale, yet an invoice in excess of €200,000 was submitted to a bank. The claimant still had personal guarantees at this stage so he wrote to the bank in February 2011 in light of a letter from the bank in 2010. He also wrote to the auditors by letter dated April 2011 asking them to investigate an issue in the course of their audit for year-end December 2010. In July 2011, the claimant received a letter from the respondent, stating that a board meeting would take place in July 2011 with the objective of holding an EGM of the respondent with a view to removing the claimant as a director. Once removed as a director, the claimant did not believe he would return to the respondent, but at no stage was the claimant informed that his employment as financial controller was terminated.

A minority shareholder of the respondent gave evidence to the EAT that there were no issues brought to his attention regarding the performance of the claimant as financial controller. He stated that there was no real conclusion to the shareholders meeting in July 2010. It was a concern to him that the respondent seemed to be failing so quickly.

In its determination, the EAT noted that on the second day of the hearing there was an attendance by the liquidator for the respondent who did not seek to oppose to claim, but to inform the EAT that he had given the directors of the respondent company permission to attend and give evidence on behalf of the company if they so wished. While two directors attended on the first day of the hearing, there was no attendance by the directors on the next date. The EAT found that the claimant was unfairly dismissed when he raised the issue of reckless trading and further sought to challenge certain questionable practices within the respondent. The EAT stated that, in attempting to ensure proper legal and financial compliance within the respondent, the claimant was ousted for not being a team player and under a completely fabricated and spurious charge that he had failed in his role as financial controller to the extent that he had placed the future of the respondent in jeopardy. The EAT upheld the claim of unfair dismissal and awarded the claimant compensation of €40,000.

Imposition of compulsory retirement age

[27.95] *Kane v Dublin Stevedores Ltd*[119] see **[2.16]**.

---

119.   *Kane v Dublin Stevedores Ltd* UD197/2012.

UNFAIR DISMISSALS CLAIM BROUGHT UNDER THE INDUSTRIAL RELATIONS ACT 1969

[27.96] *Kavanagh's Pharmacy v A Worker*[120]*– Labour Court – Industrial Relations Act 1969, s 20(1A) – whether worker unfairly dismissed – denial of fair procedures and natural justice*

It should be noted that the employer did not attend the hearing and made no submissions to the Labour Court on the matters before it. It was asserted by the claimant that he was given no prior indication that the employer was not satisfied with his performance and was given no valid reason for dismissal and furthermore was denied fair procedures and natural justice. The Labour Court found on the basis of uncontested submissions and statements of the claimant, that he was unfairly dismissed without justification or access to any procedures to determine any alleged efficiencies or misconduct on his part. The Court noted the claimant had suffered a considerable loss of income as a result of the unfair treatment and recommended that his former employer pay him compensation in the sum of €25,000.

---

120.   *Kavanagh's Pharmacy v A Worker* LCR20828.

Chapter 28

WAGES

TIME LIMITS

[28.01] *Moran v The Employment Appeals Tribunal and the Health Service Executive (as Notice Party)[1] – High Court – Keane J – Payment of Wages Act 1991, s 74B – Appeal of determination of Employment Appeals Tribunal – whether non-payment of pay increase because of Financial Emergency Measure in the Public Interest (No 2) Act 2009 constituted unlawful deduction contrary to Payment of Wages Act 1991, s 5 – time limits – interpretation of Payment of Wages Act 1991, s 6(4)*

This appeal arose from a complaint to a Rights Commissioner in respect of an alleged deduction of wages and subsequent EAT decision. The appellant identified the date of deduction as 'ongoing since 14/9/2007'. The appellant was employed by the notice party. The background to this claim was the acceptance by the Government of the recommendation of the Review Body on Higher Remunerations in the Public Sector which recommended a pay increase of 19.6% for relevant HSE managers with that increase to be implemented in three phases, commencing with an increase of 5% from 14 September 2007. In July 2008, the Government announced that all of the pending increases recommended by that report would not be implemented.

The relevant increase remained unimplemented up to the enactment of the Financial Emergency Measure in the Public Interest (No 2) Act 2009 (FEMPI2). FEMPI2 prohibited salary increases for public servants, subject to the power of the Minister for Finance to approve exceptions from that prohibition in exceptional circumstances. The Department of Finance subsequently confirmed, in correspondence to the CEO of the notice party, that the Minister had reviewed the matter and had decided not to grant an exemption in respect of the appellant's grade. It was asserted by the appellant that this industrial relations issue is also a breach of his employment law rights in that the non-implementation of the 5% increase that had been due to him with effect from 14 September 2007 was an unlawful deduction from wages properly payable to him with effect from that date, contrary to the provisions of s 5 of the 1991 Act.

As the Rights Commissioner hearing, it was noted that the notice party had raised a preliminary issue as to whether the appellant had complied with the time limits provided for in s 6(4) of the 1991 Act; however, this was not dealt with by the Rights Commissioner. The Rights Commissioner concluded that the appellant's claim was not well founded and concluded that the non-application of the salary increase was not 'a

---

1.   *Moran v The Employment Appeals Tribunal and the Health Service Executive (A Notice Party)* [2014] IEHC 154.

non-payment of the wages properly payable to the appellant'. This was appealed to the EAT.

The High Court noted that the EAT had stated reservations about its jurisdiction to hear the matter by reference to time limits set out in s 6(4) of the 1991 Act, in circumstances where the appellant did not present his complaint to the Rights Commissioner until 17 May 2010, more than 32 months after 14 September 2007. It was submitted by the appellant that the EAT should consider a complaint (or complaints) about the alleged deduction from the appellant's monthly wages in each of the six months immediately prior to 17 May 2010 of a sum representing the 5% increase to which the appellant claims he was entitled with effect from 14 September 2007 despite the enactment of FEMPI2. Keane J noted that the point of law which the appellant was seeking to raise in the High Court appeal was whether the EAT incorrectly applied s 6(4) of the Payment of Wages Act 1991 in respect of the time limits applicable to the bringing of the appellant's complaint under the Act and incorrectly ruled that the appellant's complaint was time-barred.

Keane J noted that the parties had exchanged extensive written legal submissions on the proper construction of s 6(4)(1) of the 1991 Act. It was put forward by the appellant that the reference to 'contravention' in s 6(4) of the 1991 should:

> ... be viewed as equivalent to or synonymous with the term deduction as defined through s 5(6) of the Act so that regardless of the date upon which any issue or controversy in relation to the amount of wages properly payable to an employee arises, the employee concerned can complain on any subsequent occasion on which he/she is paid wages (however long afterwards that may be) as long as that complaint is made within six months (or where special circumstances are found within 12 months) of each such payment.

It was submitted by the notice party that this construction would lead to an absurd result whereby the relevant section would function not as a time bar requiring complaints to be made within a reasonable time, but simply as a limitation of damages clause in respect of such complaints. The notice party contended that the provision must instead be accorded a construction that reflected the plain intention of the Oireachtas.

Keane J decided that it was not necessary or appropriate for him to address, much less resolve, the issue of statutory construction presented by the appellant in order to dispose of the appeal. He noted that the appellant did not as a matter of fact present a complaint to the Rights Commissioner in relation to a contravention of the 1991 Act alleged to have occurred on any specific date or dates within six months of 17 May 2012. Keane J noted that the issue of:

> how this Court should construe the provisions of s 6(4) of the 1991 Act for the purpose of applying it to a complaint that there has been an impermissible deduction from the wages of the appellant in each of the six months immediately prior to the presentation by him of that complaint (specifically a deduction in the form of a refusal to include in that payment an increase to which the complainant claims to have become entitled some years previously) is a hypothetical issue as far as the complaint actually presented by the appellant in this case is concerned.

Keane J noted Carroll J's confirmation in *MhicMhathuna v Ireland*[2] that the Court cannot take into account arguments based on assumptions or hypotheses outside of facts and circumstances of the action.

Keane J decided to dismiss the appeal and noted that if the appellant was correct in his contention concerning the proper construction of s 6(4) of the 1991 Act, then it was open to him to present a complaint to a Rights Commissioner relating to any alleged deduction in the wages paid to him on any specific date or dates within the period of six months beginning on the date of the first such payment. Keane J noted that it would be wrong for the Court to seek to anticipate the outcome of such a complaint before the Rights Commissioner or the EAT for the purpose of the present appeal just as it would be wrong for the Court to conduct the appeal as though the appellant had actually presented such a complaint to the Rights Commissioner or the EAT in this case.

[28.02] *Health Service Executive v McDermott*[3] *– High Court – Hogan J – appeal of decision of Employment Appeals Tribunal on point of law – Payment of Wages Act 1991, s 7(4)(b) – interpretation of s 6(4) of Act – time limits – meaning of 'date of the contravention to which the complaint relates'*

The respondent is a medical consultant in a hospital managed by the appellant. The respondent's contract of employment provided that he would receive certain additional payments on specified dates from 2007 onwards. Due to the financial crisis, the Minister for Health and Children declined to sanction the salary increases for public sector employees. On that basis, the appellant did not pay the contractual salary increases to the respondent. On 16 June 2011, the respondent made a complaint to the Rights Commissioner under the Payment of Wages Act 1991 in respect of the non-payment of the salary increases between 1 January 2011 and 30 June 2011.

At the hearing, the appellant argued that the complaint was time-barred because the respondent's cause of action emanated from the Minister's decision not to sanction the salary increases in either June 2009 or (at the very latest) August 2009. The Rights Commissioner rejected this argument, determining he had jurisdiction to hear the complaint insofar as the purported contraventions related to unlawful deduction in the six months prior to the date of the complaint.

The Rights Commissioner found against the appellant, who then appealed the determination to the EAT. The EAT considered the time-limit point as a preliminary issue and rejected the argument that a claimant must lodge the complaint within six months from the date of the first deduction or non-payment, holding that an employee has a new cause of action against his/her employer for unlawful deductions every six months from every such contravention.

Following this finding, the appellant appealed the decision of the EAT to the High Court on a point of law under s 7(4)(b) of the Payment of Wages Act 1991.

---

2.   *MhicMhathuna v Ireland* [1989] 1 IR 504, 510.
3.   *Health Service Executive v McDermott* [2014] IEHC 331.

In the High Court, Hogan J examined s 6(4) of the Payment of Wages Act 1991 which relates to time limits for bringing claims before the Rights Commissioner. Section 6(4) provides:

> A Rights Commissioner shall not entertain a complaint under this section unless it is presented to him within the period of 6 months beginning on the date of the contravention to which the complaint relates ...

In the first instance, Hogan J noted that no special meaning has been ascribed to the word 'contravention' by the Payment of Wages Act 1991, and therefore, the word must be given its ordinary, natural meaning.

Hogan J then assessed the phrase 'contravention to which the complaint relates'. He considered that this phrase meant that that every distinct and separate breach of the Payment of Wages Act 1991 amounts to a 'contravention' of the Payment of Wages Act 1991. He held that s 6(4) of the Payment of Wages Act 1991 provided, for the purposes of the Payment of Wages Act 1991, that the time for referring a claim runs not from the date of any particular contravention, or even the date of the first contravention, but rather from the date of the contravention 'to which the complaint relates'. Hogan J pointed out that had the Oireachtas intended that time was to run from the date of the first contravention, it could easily have so provided in the wording of s 6(4).

Hogan J stated that the manner in which the complaint was worded was relevant. For example, the complaint should only refer to alleged unlawful deductions which took place within the six months prior to the complaint being made to the Rights Commissioner. However, if the complaint is related to alleged unlawful deductions prior to this six months, such claims will be statute barred.

Hogan J rejected the appellant's argument that this interpretation would effectively mean there was no statutory time limit to bringing claims, which would lead to absurdity. Hogan J stated that it was clear from the wording of s 6(4) that only complaints which 'relate' to the last six months (or, if the Rights Commissioner is satisfied that there are 'exceptional circumstances' which prevented the bringing of the complaint within that time, 12 months) prior to a claimant making a complaint to the Rights Commissioner will not be time-barred.

Hogan J distinguished the case before him from Keane J's decision in *Moran v Employment Appeals Tribunal*.[4] In that case, the appellant had framed his claim in a way that related to alleged unlawful deductions in 2010, and therefore the claim was statute-barred. This was distinct from the respondent's claim which related solely to alleged unlawful deductions in the six months prior to instituting the claim under the Payment of Wages Act 1991. In this regard, Hogan J noted that Keane J clearly hinted that he would have arrived at a different conclusion had the complaint been formulated differently, so that it 'related' to a different time period which was not statute-barred.

Hogan J concluded that the EAT was correct in concluding that the respondent's complaint was not time-barred by reason of the operation of s 6(4) of the Payment of Wages Act 1991 as it related to a period of time which was presented to the Rights Commissioner within the six-month time limit as prescribed in the Payment of Wages

---

4.   *Moran v Employment Appeals Tribunal and the Health Service Executive* [2014] IEHC 154.

Act 1991. Hogan J dismissed the appellant's appeal on the preliminary timing issue and the matter was remitted to the EAT to determine the substantive issues in the respondent's complaint.

EXCEPTIONAL CIRCUMSTANCES

[28.03] *Cork Rape Crisis Centre Ltd v Knott & Ors[5] – Employment Appeals Tribunal – appeal of decision of Rights Commissioner – Payment of Wages Act 1991, s 6(4) – non-payment of increments – time limits – exceptional circumstances – dissenting determination*

The appellant is a registered charity that relies on funding from the Health Service Executive and private donations to operate its business. The staff pay scales are in line with the appropriate Health Service Executive's graded salary scale.

This case relates to the non-payment of increments due to the employee respondents. The Rights Commissioner found in favour of the appellant. All of the employees present at the hearing confirmed their start and finish dates and when they received their last increments.

Section 6(4) of the Payment of Wages Act 1991 states that:

> A Rights Commissioner shall not entertain a complaint under this section unless it is presented to him within the period of 6 months beginning on the date of the contravention to which the complaint relates or (in a case where the Rights Commissioner is satisfied that exceptional circumstances prevented the presentation of the complaint within the period aforesaid) such further period not exceeding 6 months as the Rights Commissioner considers reasonable.

Respondent two received her last increment in 2007 at point three of the scale, respondent three also received her last increment in October 2007 and respondents one, two and three made their complaints to the Rights Commissioner in May 2009. The case adjourned to 24 February 2014. The parties engaged in settlement talks. They were instructed to notify the EAT if they were successful. At a Tribunal hearing on 24 February 2014, the EAT was advised that the appeals were no longer being contested by respondents one and four.

Regarding s 6(4) of the Payment of Wages Act 1991, the respondents' representative submitted that there had been exceptional circumstances in that there had been negotiations and an LRC conciliation. It had been expected that all could be resolved. However, the matter was eventually referred to a Rights Commissioner. It was requested that the EAT use its discretion and extend the time limit.

The EAT determined by a majority that the circumstances outlined did not constitute exceptional circumstances such that they had the effect of preventing compliance with the Payment of Wages Act 1991 and therefore, the EAT determined by a majority that the employer's appeal under the Payment of Wages Act 1991 should succeed.

---

5.   *Cork Rape Crisis Centre Ltd v Knott & Ors* PW397/2011, PW398/2011, PW399/2011 and PW400/2011.

EMPLOYER ESTOPPED FROM REMOVING APPLICANTS FROM PAYROLL

[28.04] *Fuller & Ors v Minister for Agriculture, Food and Forestry[6] – Supreme Court – whether removal of applicants from payroll was unlawful – reliance on doctrine of estoppel to argue that Minister could not now seek to argue a different case than that previously pleaded*

These proceedings concerned the removal of a number of the applicants from the payroll of the Department of Agriculture. The same claims were also the subject matter of previous proceedings, *Fuller & Ors v The Minister for Agriculture and Food and The Minister for Finance (Fuller No 1)*.[7] In the instant case, the Supreme Court considered whether the Minister for Agriculture was estopped from pleading a particular argument, ie that the applicants were removed from payroll by reason of their strike action, in circumstances where the Minister had previously pleaded in *Fuller No 1* that the reason for the removal was solely due to the exercise by the Minister of its powers under s 16 of the Civil Service Regulation Act 1956. The applicants claimed that the Minister could not now submit a different reason for the officials' removal from payroll from what was previously pleaded and therefore it was too late for the Minister to seek to make a different case at this stage of the process.

The Supreme Court accepted the estoppel point and held that it was appropriate to set aside the order of the High Court and to grant a declaration that each applicant is entitled to be paid salary as if they had continued to work between the respective dates on which they were removed from payroll and the date on which they returned to work after the settlement of the underlying industrial dispute. The Supreme Court also made further orders that no pension entitlements would be lost by reference to the period when each applicant was not on the payroll.

ENTITLEMENT TO WAGES DURING A PERIOD OF LAY-OFF

[28.05] *McDonough v Shoreline Taverns Ltd T/A Daly's of Donore[8] – Employment Appeals Tribunal – appeal of decision of Rights Commissioner under Payment of Wages Act 1991 – whether claimant entitled to payment during period of lay-off – custom and practice in Ireland that employees not paid during lay-off*

This was an appeal by a former employee of a Rights Commissioner's decision. The appellant was employed as a bar and restaurant manager and was placed on lay-off on 6 February 2012, during which he did not receive any payment. The appellant accepted that there had been a downturn in the respondent's business from 2010 onwards. The appellant stated that he was never contacted by the respondent employer after February

---

6.   *Fuller & Ors v Minister for Agriculture, Food and Forestry* [2013] IESC 52.

7.   *Fuller & Ors v The Minister for Agriculture and Food and The Minister for Finance* [2003] IEHC 27.

8.   *McDonough v Shoreline Taverns Ltd T/A Daly's of Donore* PW674/2012.

2012 with an offer of work and, in May 2012, he sought his redundancy entitlement. It was alleged that a written contract of employment was never provided to him. The appellant argued that he was entitled to payment for the period of lay-off as he did not consent to a deduction in his wages. The respondent countered that the appellant was aware he would not be paid during his period of lay-off.

The EAT considered whether, by reason of the respondent having invoked the right to lay-off, the appellant's contractual and statutory right to pay during that period of lay-off was suspended. The EAT noted that, at common law, there is no general right to lay-off without pay. However, it has always been accepted that there are some limited circumstances wherein there will be such a right. The EAT further noted that it was a well-established practice that lay-off without pay is operable where an employer can demonstrate that it has been the custom and practice of the trade and/or workplace, and the custom must be reasonable, certain and notorious. Case law from the UK was cited which the EAT noted was helpful. However it was noted that the UK statutory position in relation to lay-off differed from the Irish position. No evidence was produced in relation to the custom and practice of the respondent in not paying during lay-off periods.

The EAT found that s 11 of the Redundancy Payments Acts 1967 to 2014 was validly invoked and that the respondent had satisfied s 11(1)(a) and (b). Accordingly, the EAT found that the contract of employment was temporarily suspended and there was no right to payment during this period. Furthermore, the EAT found that there is a notorious custom and practice in this jurisdiction that employees will not be paid during a period of lay-off.

[28.06] *Racyla v Sheridan*[9] *– Employment Appeals Tribunal – appeal of decision of Rights Commissioner – Payment of Wages Act 1991 – Redundancy Payments Acts 1967 to 2014 – right to be paid during periods of lay-off – notorious custom and practice in Ireland that employees not paid during period of lay-off*

The appellant was seeking to be paid for a period of lay-off amounting to five weeks. The appellant argued that as he did not have a written contract of employment, his contractual terms and conditions did not include a provision for not paying him in the event of lay-off. He argued that his non-payment amounted to an unlawful deduction under the Payment of Wages Act 1991. The respondent submitted that the lay-off was temporary. The EAT concluded that the respondent believed that the cessation of employment was not permanent and therefore s 11 of the Redundancy Payments Act 1967 to 2014 was satisfied in this case. The EAT then turned to consider whether by virtue of the employer having invoked s 11 of the Redundancy Payments Acts 1967 to 2014, the appellant's right to pay during that period of lay-off was suspended. It was noted by the EAT that no evidence was produced in relation to the custom and practice of the respondent in this case. However, the EAT referred to the fact that in Ireland, the custom and practice is that lay-off is without pay and noted this custom and practice had existed since the coming into force of the 1967 Act. The EAT concluded that s 11 had

---

9.   *Racyla v Sheridan* PW379/2012.

been validly invoked and furthermore that there was a 'notorious custom and practice in this jurisdiction that employees will not be paid during a period of lay-off'. The decision of the Rights Commissioner was upheld.

[28.07] *Strzelecki v Zahir Ltd (in liquidation)[10] – Employment Appeals Tribunal – appeal of decision of Rights Commissioner – Payment of Wages Act 1991 – Redundancy Payments Act 1967 to 2014 – whether claimant entitled to be paid during period of lay-off – belief of employer that lay-off period would not be permanent – custom and practice in Ireland*

This was an appeal by an employee of a decision of a Rights Commissioner under the 1991 Act. Conflicting evidence was given as to certain dates on which the appellant's employment came to an end. It was accepted by both parties that during his employment, the appellant was placed on lay-off and he had not been paid during these periods. It was contended by the appellant that the respondent had an obligation to pay him during the period of lay-off, that non-payment of wages during a lay-off period was a deduction which was not authorised by statute, was not a term of his contract, and was not consented to by him.

The respondent argued that an employer is entitled to lay-off an employee without pay if the lay-off at issue is temporary, and if there was a custom and practice which made the employer entitled to lay-off without pay and if notice was given that the lay-off was temporary. The respondent also relied on s 11(1) of the Redundancy Payments Acts 1967 to 2014. The EAT found that 'lay-off is a creature of statute' and reference was made to the provisions of s 11 of the 1967 Act. The EAT noted that the respondent believed that the cessation of employment would not be permanent, and notwithstanding a downturn in the market, they were still receiving same, albeit less work than before the recession. Work now available to the respondent was on a contract-to-contract basis. The EAT noted that in October 2011, both parties accepted that the appellant was placed on lay-off at that time. The EAT noted that from October to December 2011, the appellant did not serve an RP9 on his employer and therefore the EAT concluded that the appellant too was of the belief that his lay-off period would not be permanent and so the provisions of s 11(1)(a) and (b) were satisfied.

The EAT then considered whether, having invoked s 11 of the 1967 Act, the employee's contractual and statutory right to pay during the period of lay-off was suspended. The EAT noted that at common law there is no general right to lay-off without pay. The EAT considered a number of cases in this area and also the UK Employment Rights Act 1996. The EAT found, that generally in Ireland, the custom and practice is that lay-off will be without pay and that this is the custom and practice that has existed since the coming into force of the 1967 Act. The EAT concluded that where s 11 is invoked by an employer, then the contract of employment is temporarily suspended and there is no right to payment during that period. The EAT further found that there is a 'notorious custom and practice in this jurisdiction' that employees will not be paid during a period of lay-off.

---

10.   *Strzelecki v Zahir Ltd (in liq)* PW664/2012.

[28.08] *Stanisevskaja v Office and Industrial Cleaners Ltd[11]– Employment Appeals Tribunal – appeal of decision of Rights Commissioner – Payment of Wages 1991 – requirements of Redundancy Payments Acts 1967 to 2014, s 11 – entitlement to payment during lay-off*

This was an appeal of a Rights Commissioner decision which held that the respondent was not obliged to pay the appellant during lay-off. The appellant was employed as a cleaner to fulfil a contract to clean the Aviva stadium in preparation for its opening. The contract came to an end and the appellant and her colleagues were put on lay-off.

The appellant contended that she had not been properly informed of her lay-off as the respondent failed to notify her. She also submitted that she was entitled to be paid during the lay-off as the respondent did not comply with the Redundancy Payments Acts 1967 to 2014 by notifying the appellant that the lay-off would be temporary. It was common case that if the notification of lay-off was found to be effective, the appellant would not be entitled to payment during the lay-off period.

The appellant gave evidence that no one informed her of the lay-off. However, the respondent submitted that it had attempted to contact her by telephone and in writing to inform her of the lay-off, but she did not respond. It was noted that the relevant contract of employment allowed for non-payment during lay-off periods.

The EAT examined s 11 of the Redundancy Payments Act 1967, which states:

(i) it is reasonable in the circumstances for that employer to believe that the cessation of employment will not be permanent, and

(ii) the employer gives notice to that effect to the employee prior to the cessation,

(iii) that cessation of employment shall be regarded for the purposes of this Act as lay-off.

The EAT also considered the case law opened by the appellant. It referred to the decision in *Industrial Yarns Ltd v Greene and Manley*,[12] in which Costello J stated that: '[I]f there is no contractual power (express or implied) in the contract of employment to suspend the operation of the contract for a limited period then by ceasing to employ an employee and refusing to pay him wages the employer has been guilty of a serious breach of the contract amounting to a repudiation of it.'

The EAT noted that the corollary of this statement was that where there is such a provision, whether express or implied by statute or custom and practice, it is permissible to suspend the operation of the contract for a limited period.

In terms of notification of lay-off, the EAT accepted the respondent's evidence in finding that the appellant was informed of the lay-off. It was also accepted that there was a provision in the appellant's contract of employment which permitted unpaid lay-off.

The appellant argued that, notwithstanding the contractual provision, the statutory requirements for lay-off must be met or else she was required to be paid for this period.

---

11. *Stanisevskaja v Office and Industrial Cleaners Ltd* PW239/2011.

12. *Industrial Yarns Ltd v Greene and Manley* [1984] ILRM 15.

The EAT rejected this submission on the basis that the parties to an employment contract are allowed to agree the provisions of a lay-off such as in this case.

The EAT was not satisfied that there was a requirement to pay employees on lay-off under the statutory provisions, but it was not necessary to determine this point given the findings above. However, the EAT stated that it disagreed with the appellant's submission that the notice to be given to under s 11(1)(b) of the Redundancy Payments Act 1967 to 2014 is notice of the employer's reasonable belief that the cessation will not be permanent, ie notice of the provision of s 11(1)(a) of the 1967 Act.

The EAT held that s 11 only required the employer to give notice to the employee that it was unable to provide work for which the employee was employed, ie the principal requirement of s 11(1) of the Redundancy Payments Act 1967. The EAT stated that if the provision in relation to notice was to apply to s 11(1)(a), and to be notice of the employer's reasonable belief that the cessation will not be permanent, it would have been included in that subsection rather than put into a separate subsection. On that basis, the EAT concluded that the notice given to the appellant was more than sufficient to satisfy the requirements of the Redundancy Payments Act if there had been no contractual provision in relation to unpaid lay-off, in that it notified her that there was no work at the moment for her, but that it was hoped in the near future that there would be.

[28.09] *Matenko v Bocnara Ltd[13] – Employment Appeals Tribunal – appeal of decision of Rights Commissioner – Payment of Wages Act 1991 – entitlement to be paid during period of lay-off – no appearance by respondent – lay-off due to lack of work – recognised custom and practice*

This was an appeal of a Rights Commissioner decision which found that the appellant employee was not properly due wages during lay-off. There was no appearance on behalf of the respondent, a construction company, at the appeal hearing. The EAT considered whether the appellant was entitled to be paid during his period of lay-off. The appellant was notified in writing on 10 August 2009 that he was being temporarily laid off. The appellant sought remuneration for the period of lay-off from 26 October 2009 to 26 April 2010 under the Payment of Wages Act 1991.

The EAT referred to *Lawe v Irish Country Meats Ltd[14]* where the Circuit Court accepted that there is no inherent right to lay-off without pay at common law, though there are certain limited circumstances which give rise to the right to lay-off without pay. Those circumstances included where an employer can show that the entitlement arises out of well-established custom and practice. In *Lawe* a lay-off without pay was effected and whilst there was a recognised custom and practice which allowed for lay-off in certain circumstances, none of these circumstances applied, and the employer had in fact used the lay-off process as a preliminary step to redundancy. The lay-off in *Lawe* further lacked the reasonable belief that the cessation in work would not be permanent as is required under the definition of s 11 of the Redundancy Payments Acts 1967 to 2014.

---

13.   *Matenko v Bocnara Ltd* PW340/2011.
14.   *Lawe v Irish Country Meats Ltd* [1998] ELR 266.

The EAT was satisfied that the employment contract specifically allowed for and recognised the need to operate a scheme of lay-off. It noted that lay-offs allow the employer to buy time to secure contracts. The EAT also noted that *Pevkevicius v Goode Concrete Ltd (In Receivership)*[15] has affirmed the reasonableness of this approach. In light of the above, the appeal failed.

NON-PAYMENT OF INCREMENTS

[28.10] *Eucon Shipping and Transport Ltd v Hynes & Ors – Irish Ferries Ltd v Murtagh & Ors*[16] *– Employment Appeals Tribunal – appeal of decision of Rights Commissioner – Payment of Wages Act 1991 – non-payment of increments*

These appeals were heard simultaneously under the Payment of Wages Act 1991. These claims relate to the non-payment of increments by the appellant. Evidence was given that all clerical staff were paid an increment in January 2009 in addition to the first phase of the then National Pay Agreement. Subsequently, each employee was asked to waive the right to any further increase, and the 3.5% increase paid was revoked in May 2009. However, the increment remained at that time. In 2010, the appellant sought not to pay 2010 increments. After an intervention by the LRC, the parties reached an agreement that the 2010 increment would be paid. For 2011, two options were provided to staff, the first being an offer of a taxable lump sum in lieu of waiving the right to future increments with all other terms and conditions remaining the same. Option two was a transfer of employment to another company within the group with terms and conditions and salary backdated to January 2011. Certain staff accepted one or the other option, and those who did not accept either option lodged a claim with regards to the non-payment of the 2011 increment and further claims were then lodged in relation to the non-payment of the 2010 increment.

The appellant gave evidence that there was a deficit in the pension fund of over €90 million and that additional contributions, in excess of employer contributions, had been made by the appellant company. The appellant also gave evidence that its cost base was extremely high because of salaries and increased fuel costs. Evidence given by one employee on behalf of all of the respondents was that the individual contracts of employment provided for the incremental increases and that there had been no agreement regarding the non-payment of the increment in 2011/2012. The respondents alleged that s 1(a) of the 1991 Act, which provides that 'wage' means any sums payable to the employee, included increments and thus was a deduction under the 1991 Act. The appellant asserted that the non-payment of an increase did not fall within the definition of 'wages' in s 1(a) of the 1991 Act and therefore the EAT lacked jurisdiction to hear the claim.

The EAT, in its determination, referred to the decision of the High Court in *McKenzie*[17] and concluded that the 1991 Act 'had no application to reduction of

---

15. *Pevkevicius v Goode Concrete Ltd (In Receivership)* 2014 IEHC 66.
16. *Eucon Shipping and Transport Ltd v Hynes & Ors; Irish Ferries Ltd v Murtagh & Ors* PW222–PW225/2013.
17. *McKenzie and Anor v The Minister for Finance & Ors* [2010] IEHC 461.

increment as distinct from a deduction'. The EAT held that it was bound by the High Court in this case and overturned the decisions of the Rights Commissioner.

[28.11] *Byrne & Ors v Clare County Council*[18] *– Employment Appeals Tribunal – Payment of Wages Act 1991 – appeal of decision of Rights Commissioner – whether non-payment of increment a deduction within meaning of Payment of Wages Act 1991, s 5*

The appellants, as employees of Clare County Council, were bound by the civil service pay regulations. On appointment to their most recent positions, the appellants were placed on point 1 of the long service increment scale, and asserted that after three years they should have been entitled to move to the second point of the scale. The respondent asserted that the rules governing the scale dictated that a person must spend six years on the first point of the scale before moving to the second point, and further stated that the non-payment of an increment is not covered by the 1991 Act. The EAT noted the judgment in *McKenzie*[19] and noted that it was bound by the decision. The EAT concluded that the increment that may or may not be due to the appellants is not a deduction as prescribed in the Payment of Wages Act 1991 and thus the appeal should fail.

REDUCTIONS IN PAY/ALLOWANCES

[28.12] *Byrne and Kelly v Dublin 12 Congress Centre Ltd*[20] *– Employment Appeals Tribunal – appeal of Rights Commissioner decision – Payment of Wages Act 1991 – whether reduction in pay constituted unlawful deduction contrary to 1991 Act*

The appellants were employed as job initiative employees and became employees of the respondent by reason of a transfer of undertaking. It was argued on behalf of the appellants that the respondent had breached s 5 of the 1991 Act by unilaterally reducing wages without receiving their permission, conducting negotiations or engaging in a consultation process with them. The appellants' contracts stated that they would be paid subject to FÁS guidelines and while their contracts stated the rate of pay may be increased during the term of the contract, it was silent with regard to decreases. The respondent explained that the pay cut was imposed following an instruction from FÁS to the respondent's centre to reduce the rate of pay of the employees. The respondent did not have discretion in this regard.

In its determination, the EAT noted that reductions in wages were made across the board. The EAT deferred to the decision of the High Court in *McKenzie*[21] and concluded

---

18.   *Byrne & Ors v Clare Co Co* PW263/2012, PW264/2012, PW265/2012, PW266/2012, PW267/2012.

19.   *McKenzie and another v The Minister for Finance & Ors* [2010] IEHC 461.

20.   *Byrne and Kelly v Dublin 12 Congress Centre Ltd* PW257/2011, PW258/2011.

21.   *McKenzie and another v The Minister for Finance* [2010] IEHC 461.

that the 1991 Act has no application to reductions in wages as distinct from 'deductions'. The determination of the Rights Commissioner was upheld.

[28.13] *B&Q Ireland Ltd v Masters & Ors*[22] *and B&Q Ireland Ltd v Cleary*[23] *– Employment Appeals Tribunal – Payment of Wages Act 1991 – appeals of decisions of Rights Commissioner – removal of bonus and zone allowance – reduction in allowances payable as opposed to deduction from wages*

These joined cases came before the EAT by way of appeal by the appellant employer B&Q Ireland Ltd.

The EAT considered two issues, namely the cessation by the appellant of the summer/winter bonus and the cessation of the zone allowance.

The terms of the relevant contracts of employment differed in respect of the summer/winter bonus. One set of contracts stated:

> ... may amend or vary your terms of employment from time to time and these variations or amendments will be posted on their staff notice board if the change is minor or in writing if the change is more substantial.

The other set of contracts stated:

> [d]etails of the other terms and conditions of employment are given in the Employee Handbook. Any changes to the above details will be notified to you directly.

However, the EAT found that there was a clear, unequivocal statement in each set of contracts, namely that 'all bonus schemes are discretionary and are subject to scheme rules. They may be reviewed or withdrawn at any time' and such clause was incapable of any other interpretation.

On 1 April 2012, the respondent employees were notified that 'with effect from 1 April 2012, you will no longer receive the Summer/Winter Bonus traditionally paid in June and November of each year', and each employee was requested to sign a letter to confirm receipt of the notification of the amendment. The EAT found that it was clear from the letter that it was not a letter seeking consent to the amendment as contended by the appellant, but was seeking an acknowledgement of receipt of the amendment to the terms and conditions of employment.

The EAT found that if the respondents were not content with the appellant retaining the power to unilaterally withdraw the bonus, they should not have entered into a contract of employment which afforded the appellant the right to do so. Therefore, the EAT determined that withdrawal of the winter/summer bonus complied with s 5(1)(b) of the Payment of Wages Act 1991 and accordingly overturned the recommendation of the Rights Commissioner.

The evidence before the EAT was that the zone allowance only applied to employees working in the appellant's Dublin stores. The respondents contended that the zone allowance was payable as part of their basic salary, whereas the appellant argued that the

---

22. *B&Q Ireland Ltd v Masters & Ors* PW474/2013, PW475/2013 and PW476/2013.
23. *B&Q Ireland Ltd v Cleary* PW777/2012.

zone allowance did not form part of basic pay and that in any event the contract of employment allowed for variations in rates of pay dependent on company performance and market conditions.

The provisions of the contracts of employment also differed in respect of the zone allowance. The earlier contracts set out the zone allowance in the salary section of the contract: 'Your hourly rate will be €…with a 41 cent per hour zone allowance. This amount will increase to €…with a 41 cent allowance after your induction/training …'. The later contracts set out the zone allowance in the allowance section, a distinct and separate section to the salary section of the contract.

The EAT stated that it was noteworthy that the earlier contracts use the word 'with' a 41 cent allowance thus separating it from basic salary and the later contract set out the zone allowance in the allowance section, thus clearly separating it from the hourly rate. The EAT also noted that employees of the appellant doing like work both inside and outside the Dublin area were paid the same basic salary – the only difference being the fact that those working in the Dublin area got an allowance to compensate them for working there. The EAT found there was no doubt that the allowance paid was a separate and distinct payment from that of the salary and was for a separate and distinct purpose. The salary was paid for work done whereas the zone allowances were paid as a form of compensation for working in a particular area. The EAT found, therefore, that zone allowances came under the umbrella of s 1(1)(i) of the Payment of Wages Act 1991.

Furthermore, the EAT found that the removal of the zone allowance was done by the appellant in good faith and in an attempt to save the appellant which was insolvent. The EAT noted that this has no bearing on the company's contractual obligations to its employees but that: 'it is something the EAT can keep in mind'. The EAT applied the High Court decision *McKenzie*[24] and found that the removal of the zone allowance amounted to a 100% reduction in the zone allowance and as such was not a deduction from wages. Accordingly, the EAT also determined that the Payment of Wages Act 1991 had no application to the circumstances of the case and overturned the Rights Commissioner's decision.[25]

SUSPENSION WITH AND WITHOUT PAY

[28.14] *Hanuszewicz v Strand Security Ltd (In Liquidation)*[26] *– Employment Appeals Tribunal – appeal of decision of Rights Commissioner – Payment of Wages Act 1991 – whether suspension of appellant without pay was breach of 1991 Act – distinction between suspension with and without pay*

The appellant employee was suspended without pay in April 2012 but no disciplinary meeting was convened to investigate the alleged wrongdoing. The period of suspension continued until the respondent company ceased to trade in October 2012, a period of six

---

24. *McKenzie and another v The Minister for Finance & Ors* [2010] IEHC 461..

25. This case is now under appeal to the High Court.

26. *Hanuszewicz v Strand Security Ltd (In Liq)* PW317/2013.

months. The appellant's contract of employment was silent on the subject of whether suspension was to be paid or unpaid.

The EAT noted the distinction between suspension without pay, which is a disciplinary sanction following a disciplinary meeting, and suspension on full pay, pending a disciplinary hearing and for the purpose of conducting an investigation into allegations made against a particular employee. In this case, the EAT noted the appellant was suspended without pay pending an investigation and that there was no provision in his contract permitting this. The EAT noted that the Courts have made it clear that a suspension of an employee may only be for a finite time and indefinite suspension will not be tolerated.

The EAT determined that the appellant had been suspended for in excess of six months in a clear breach of fair procedures and the appellant's entitlement to natural justice. The EAT noted the decision of the Supreme Court in *Deegan v Minister for Finance*[27] that where a suspension constitutes a disciplinary sanction, the principles of natural justice should be considered before a decision is made to suspend an employee. However, when an employee is suspended pending an inquiry into whether disciplinary action should be taken, the principle of natural justice may not apply.

The EAT overturned the decision of the Rights Commissioner and awarded the appellant €8,575.

REQUIREMENTS OF S 7(2) OF THE PAYMENT OF WAGES ACT 1991 WHEN LODGING AN APPEAL

[28.15] *Ó Gógáin v Bord na Móna plc*[28] *– Employment Appeals Tribunal – appeal against recommendation of Rights Commissioner – Payment of Wages Act 1991– strict obligations on party who wishes to appeal decision of Rights Commissioner in accordance with 1991 Act, s 7(2)*

The EAT noted that there is an onerous obligation placed on a party who wished to appeal a decision of a Rights Commissioner under the Payment of Wages Act 1991.

Two acts must be completed in a six-week timeframe as per s 7(2) of the 1991 Act: firstly, the appealing party must issue a notice in writing to the EAT; and secondly, the appealing party must issue a copy of the notice in writing to the other party concerned, ie the respondent to the appeal.

The EAT reiterated the need for very strict compliance with s 7(2) and that the burden of proof rested with the appealing party to positively demonstrate that the EAT and the respondent have each been given the relevant notice within the six-week period.

In this case, the appellant submitted that he had placed the requisite notice in the internal post system in the respondent's premises. However, its intended recipient, the respondent's human resources manager, gave evidence that he had never received the notice and only became aware of the appeal after the six-week period and when contacted by the EAT. The appellant confirmed his awareness of the obligation on him

---

27. *Deegan v Minister for Finance* [2000] ELR 190.
28. *Ó Gógáin v Bord na Móna plc* PW234/2013.

to notify the relevant party but he saw no need to hand deliver, have witnesses, or register the delivery of the notice to his employer. The EAT stated that it could not be satisfied on the balance of probabilities that the respondent was given the appropriate notice in the six-week period and therefore it did not have jurisdiction to proceed and thus dismissed the appeal under the 1991 Act.

IMPLIED CONTRACTUAL ENTITLEMENT TO EQUAL ALLOWANCES ON THE BASIS OF LEGITIMATE EXPECTATION

[28.16] *Malanaphy v Minister of Transport, Tourism And Sport*[29] *– Employment Appeals Tribunal – appeal of decision of Rights Commissioner – Payment of Wages Act 1991 – legitimate expectation – whether term could be implied into appellant's contract of employment entitling him to equal allowances and benefits to those received by his predecessors*

The appellant was appointed to the position of costal unit sector manager with the respondent on 19 October 2009. Prior to his appointment, the appellant spoke to those who had previously carried out this role and to the respondent's director regarding the wages, allowances and increments paid as part of the employment package. He was satisfied that those carrying out the role at that time were paid a shift allowance, an on call allowance, a Sunday supplement and increments in addition to their wage. Upon his appointment, the appellant was not paid any of the abovementioned allowances.

On 24 August 2012, the appellant lodged a claim with the Rights Commissioner, alleging that the respondent, in failing to pay the allowances, was in breach of s 5(6) of the Payment of Wages Act 1991. The respondent denied this claim, maintaining that the appellant was not entitled to such allowances as his position was not graded, and his contract contained no provisions entitling him to the allowances. The Rights Commissioner accepted the respondent's arguments, and found no breach of the 1991 Act.

The appellant appealed the decision of the Rights Commissioner to the EAT. The EAT allowed the appellant's appeal, finding that the appellant had a legitimate expectation that the disputed payments would be made, and that such expectation was well founded, being based on information supplied by the respondent's director and the precedent set by payment of such allowances and benefits to his predecessors. In this regard, the EAT stated that the fact that the role carried out by the appellant had a different title to that performed by his predecessors was immaterial, as it would be 'fundamentally unfair to deny the appellant like payments for like work solely based on the premise that the newly named position was not yet graded'.

Accordingly, the EAT found that there had been a breach of an implied term of the appellant's contract of employment and a consequent breach of s 5(6) of the Payment of Wages Act.

---

29.   *Malanaphy v Minister of Transport, Tourism and Sport* PW655/2012.

Regarding the amount to be awarded, the EAT noted s 6(4) of the Payment of Wages Act 1991, the effect of which is to limit the EAT's jurisdiction to hear claims to those relating to a six-month period prior to the date of lodgment of the claim. Accordingly, the EAT was restricted to awarding the appellant the allowances he was owed for the six months preceding the claim date, while stating that as the Department is not bound by the effect of s 6(4), 'the increments when paid should be calculated in accordance with current custom and practice'.

PAYMENT OF WAGES DURING SICK LEAVE

[28.17] *Gallagher v Department of Arts, Heritage and the Gaeltacht[30] – Employment Appeals Tribunal – appeal of decision of Rights Commissioner – Payment of Wages Act 1991 – payment of wages during sick leave – requirement on employer to take circumstances of employee into account when withholding wages*

The claimant, a general operative at Glenveagh National Park, Co Donegal, was employed by the respondent from July 1978 until 13 January 2012. He made an application under the Payment of Wages Act 1991 in respect of the non-payment of wages for a period from 5 to 13 January 2012 during which he was on sick leave.

The claimant was on sick leave from 13 December 2011 as a result of back pain and he provided medical certificates certifying his absence until 13 January 2012. The claimant was due to retire on 13 January 2012. The respondent did not contest the fact that the claimant was unfit for work during this period, but withheld sick pay from the claimant on the basis that he did not comply with the Certified Sick Leave Policy for State Industrial Employees (the policy).

The respondent gave evidence that in accordance with the policy, an appointment was made for the claimant with the respondent's chief medical officer of the respondent in Dublin on 14 December 2011. The respondent confirmed that there was no actual written confirmation furnished to the claimant as to the date, time or location of this appointment.

The EAT heard that when contacted by the respondent to notify him of the appointment, the claimant stated that he would not attend the appointment as he had a difficulty travelling to Dublin. The respondent submitted that the claimant had claimed that he did not have the money to attend Dublin, whereas the claimant asserted that the reason for his non-attendance at the appointment was that the eight-hour round bus journey to Dublin would not be possible due to his back pain. The respondent attempted to make an appointment for a medical examination in Letterkenny, Co Donegal, but this was not possible in the circumstances.

As a result of his failure to attend the appointment, the respondent withdrew the claimant's sick pay.

The EAT, by majority, accepted that the respondent could remove the claimant from its sick pay scheme for non-compliance with the policy. The EAT noted that the policy stated that the 'employer reserves the right to have any employee medically examined at

---

30. *Gallagher v Department of Arts, Heritage and the Gaeltacht* PW32/2013.

any time'. It further held that the claimant ought to have furnished more complete medical certificates to the respondent which would have supported his contention that he would have had great difficulty in completing the eight-hour round-trip bus journey to Dublin for the medical appointment.

The claimant's appeal was dismissed.

UNLAWFUL DEDUCTION OF WAGES

[28.18] *Cleeve Link Ltd v Bryla[31] – UK Employment Appeal Tribunal – Employment Rights Act 1996 – deduction from wages provided in contract of employment – whether this had effect of penalty clause*

The appellant appealed the decision of the Employment Tribunal which had found that, by recouping certain costs from the respondent's final pay cheque, it was guilty of an unlawful deduction of wages, and this had the effect of a penalty clause.

The claimant was recruited from Poland as a live-in care worker. During the recruitment process, the appellant incurred certain costs in bringing the respondent to the UK, including transport, recruitment and training costs. The respondent's contract of employment contained a provision to the effect that if she resigned or was dismissed within six months of commencement of employment, the costs incurred by the appellant in her recruitment and training would be recoverable in full from her remuneration from the company. After a period of 12 weeks of work with the appellant, the respondent was summarily dismissed on grounds of gross misconduct. At the time of her dismissal, the respondent was entitled to approximately £1,200 by way of salary for that period of work. The appellant deducted the amount it had incurred in the respondent's recruitment from her wages, under the contract of employment, which resulted in the respondent not receiving any payment for her services for the 12-week period. The respondent claimed that she did not sign a contract of employment and therefore the deduction was unlawful.

The respondent successfully argued before the Employment Tribunal that the recruitment costs deducted from her final wages constituted unlawful deductions from wages. The Employment Tribunal held that the amounts deducted from the respondent's final wage was not a genuine pre-estimate of loss suffered by the appellant as a result of the respondent being dismissed within six months, and found that the arrangement overcompensated the appellant. On this basis, the effect of the contract of employment was deemed to be a 'penalty clause', and as such, was unenforceable.

The UK EAT found that the Employment Tribunal erred in finding that the effect of the clause was an unenforceable penalty and allowed the appeal. The UK EAT found that the Employment Tribunal had jurisdiction to determine whether a deduction in a contract of employment was a lawful deduction. The UK EAT stated that determining whether a deduction was lawful was a matter of construction and whether the main

---

31.   *Cleeve Link Ltd v Bryla* UK EAT/0440/12/BA.

purpose of the clause at the time the contract was entered into was to compensate the appellant for a breach, or to deter a breach.

The UK EAT stated that in determining whether the effect of the clause was to deter the respondent from breaching the terms of her contract, three factors should be considered:

(i) the Employment Tribunal should have regard to the prevailing circumstances at the time that the contract was entered in to;

(ii) the clause should be regarded on an objective rather than subjective basis, and the intentions of the parties should not be considered relevant; and

(iii) the difference between the fixed sum contained in the contract as the amount of the deduction and the amount that would be payable as damages in a breach of contract claim should be assessed. In this regard the UK EAT stated that if the difference between the two amounts is so great that it cannot be explained in any other way, the clause is likely to be considered a penalty clause and therefore unenforceable.

The UK EAT held that the Employment Tribunal had misdirected itself in failing to consider the position at the time the contract was entered into and focused only on the conditions at the time of breach. Furthermore, the Employment Tribunal did not address whether there was an extravagant or unconscionable gulf that existed between the maximum amounts that could be recovered in a common-law action for damages for breach of contract as opposed to the sum stipulated in the contract.

In addition, the UK EAT found that if the respondent had resigned the day after completing her training, then the sum that was recouped would have represented the loss to the appellant which demonstrated that the maximum loss was reflected by the amounts stated in the repayment clause of the agreement. On this basis, the UK EAT found that the Employment Tribunal should have concluded that the clause in issue was one for liquidated damages and that there was a reasonable relationship between the amount that could be recovered in a common law action for damages and the sum stipulated in the agreement. It followed that the deduction was a genuine pre-estimate of loss and was therefore lawful, both at common law and under the Employment Rights Act 1996.

CONTRACTUAL ENTITLEMENT TO A PAY INCREASE

[28.19] *Thorne & Ors v House of Commons Commission[32] – High Court of England and Wales – Supperstone J – whether claimants had contractual right to annual pay increases – express and implied terms – collective pay agreements*

The claimants were a representative sample of employees of the defendant, the House of Commons Commission, who were affected by the pay freeze announced by the UK Government during its Emergency Budget in 2010. The Government advised its

---

32.   *Thorne & Ors v House of Commons Commission* [2014] EWHC 93.

departments that progression payments in the civil service would be payable to staff where there was a contractual entitlement to them, but not otherwise.

The defendant is a statutory body established by the House of Commons (Administration) Act 1978 (the Act). The claimants were employed under various pay bands, ranging from A to E and claimed a contractual entitlement to annual pay increases until they reached the top of the pay scale for their respective pay bands. The claim was based on three alternative grounds:

(i)   an express contractual term;

(ii)   the continued application of the 2008–2010 Collective Pay Agreement; and

(iii) an implied term of custom and practice.

The Court rejected the claim on all three grounds.

The Court decided there was no express term in the claimants' contracts of employment giving rise to a contractual entitlement to annual pay increases. In accordance with the legal principles set out in *Investors Compensation Scheme Ltd v West Bromwich Building Society*[33] the Court examined the letters of appointment, staff handbook and collectively negotiated pay agreements which together formed the basis of the claimants' contracts of employment.

The Court held that the letters of appointment, which used the phrase 'progression through the pay band will be dependent on satisfactory performance,' were too vague to confer the right to annual pay increases because the financial value of the progression and its frequency was not specified.

The Court referred to para 9.3.2 of the staff handbook which provided for a mechanism to determine pay increases. The mechanism established limits within which increases could be considered following negotiations with trade unions, a ballot of their members and approval by the defendant. The 2008–2010 Collective Pay Agreement was made under para 9.3.2 of the handbook and provided for progression payments for those specific years. There was no pay agreement for 2011. The Court rejected the claimant's reliance on the decision of the UK EAT in *Bevan & Ors v Cabinet Office*[34] where a pay progression regime was guaranteed and intended to continue beyond the specified period of the agreement. The Court stated that each case depended on its own facts, and the *Bevan* decision turned on the wording of the final pay offer. The Court therefore rejected the claimant's second alternative argument that the collective pay agreement created a contractual entitlement to ongoing pay rises in subsequent years. To decide otherwise would undermine the procedure provided by para 9.3.2 and risk fettering the ability of the defendant to comply in those subsequent years with its statutory duty to remain 'broadly in line' with civil service pay under s 2 of the House of Commons (Administration) Act 1978.

The Court applied the legal principles summarised in *Park Cakes Ltd v Shumba*[35] and refused to imply a term into the contract which contradicted its express terms. The

---

33.   *Investors Compensation Scheme Ltd v West Bromwich Building Society* [1998] 1 WLR 896.

34.   *Bevan & Ors v Cabinet Office* 1501381/2012.

35.   *Park Cakes Ltd v Shumba* [2013] EWCA Civ 974.

2008–2010 Pay Agreement was evidence of the practice of following the mechanism under para 9.3.2 of the staff handbook, rather than evidence of the practice of providing annual pay increases.

The Court dismissed the claim as the claimants failed to establish a contractual entitlement, by way of express or implied term, to annual pay increases until they reached the top of the pay scale for their respective pay bands.

NATIONAL MINIMUM WAGE ACT 2000 AS AMENDED

Whether the monetary value of 'board' can be included in determining an hourly rate of pay

[28.20] *Skuja v Slieve Russell Hotel Property Ltd[36] – Labour Court – appeal of Rights Commissioner decision – National Minimum Wage Act 2000– inclusion of monetary value of 'board' in determining hourly rate of pay*

The claimant requested a statement of her average hourly rate of pay in accordance with s 23 of the National Minimum Wage Act 2000 to determine if it was in line with the national minimum wage, which at that time stood at €8.65 per hour.[37] The respondent replied in writing stating that the claimant was paid an hourly rate of pay of €9.09 per hour which included 'a meal allowance deduction' of €0.57 per hour. It stated that her rate of pay in the reference period of 8 February 2012 to 14 February 2012 was €8.52 per hour Monday to Saturday and €12.12 per hour on Sunday of that week together with an allowance of €0.57 per hour for board. The contract of employment and company handbook issued to the claimant contained no reference to deductions for meals provided to employees.

The claimant submitted a complaint to the Rights Commissioner under s 24 of the 2000 Act stating that her rate of pay was not compliant with the national minimum wage. She argued that the deduction made by the respondent in respect of board was not lawful as it was not declared for tax or social welfare purposes. The Rights Commissioner decided that the deduction made by the respondent was lawful and must be added to the hourly rate of pay which, taken together, brought her hourly rate of payment to at least €8.65 per hour and therefore in line with the national minimum wage in force at the time. The respondent appealed the Rights Commissioner's decision to the Labour Court under s 27 of the 2000 Act.

The Labour Court noted that under the Act, pay is defined as all amounts of payment, and any benefit-in-kind specified in Part 1 of the Schedule to the 2000 Act, made or allowed by an employer to an employee in respect of the employee's employment. Schedule 1 to the 2000 Act sets out what constitutes reckonable components of pay and includes 'the monetary value of board with lodgings or board

---

36.   *Skuja v Slieve Russell Hotel Property Ltd* MWD143.
37.   National Minimum Wage Act 2000 (National Minimum Hourly Rate of Pay) Order 2006 (SI 667/ 2006).

only or lodgings only, not exceeding the amount, if any, prescribed for the purposes of this item'.

The Labour Court noted that the claimant had advanced the argument that the deduction for 'full board' was not declared for tax purposes and, as a matter of public policy, could not therefore be taken into account for the purposes of determining the hourly rate of pay under the Act. The Labour Court found no support for that argument in the Act and noted that the issue of compliance with tax and social welfare obligations is dealt with in s 40 of the 2000 Act which states:

> (1) Where a term or condition of the contract of employment concerned contravenes the Taxes Consolidation Act, 1997, or the Social Welfare Acts, the employee concerned shall, notwithstanding the contravention, be entitled to redress under this Act for any under-payment of an amount of pay to which he or she would otherwise be entitled under this Act.
>
> (2) Where, in proceedings under this Act, it is shown that a term or condition of a contract of employment contravenes the Taxes Consolidation Act, 1997, or the Social Welfare Acts, the Rights Commissioner, the Labour Court, an inspector or the Circuit Court, as the case may be, shall notify the Revenue Commissioners or the Minister for Social, Community and Family Affairs, as may be appropriate, of the matter.

The Labour Court noted that the claimant's contract of employment states, 'PRSI, PAYE and USC are automatically deducted from your pay', and the pay slips submitted to the Labour Court showed the claimant's hourly rate of pay as €8.52 per hour. There was no reference to 'board'. The Court stated that if PAYE, PRSI or USC are due to the State in respect of the value of the board provided by the respondent to the claimant, the amount outstanding to the Revenue Commissioners and the Department of Social Protection is a matter that falls to be addressed by the employer and the relevant authorities.

The Court found that, taken together, the combined value of basic pay and the monetary value of board for the claimant exceeded € 8.65 per hour. The Court held that the complaint was not well founded and affirmed the decision of the Rights Commissioner.

Requirement of s 28 of National Minimum Wage Act 2000 to have requested a statement of average hourly rate of pay

[28.21] *Abcom Security Ltd v Ejaz*[38] *– Labour Court – National Minimum Wage Act 2000, s 27(1) – Industrial Relations Acts 1946 to 2012 – appeal of decision of Rights Commissioner – whether claimant received national minimum wage – requirement for claimant to request statement of average hourly rates of pay in accordance with 2000 Act, s 23*

The respondent did not appear at the hearing and was not represented.

---

38.   *Abcom Security Ltd v Ejaz* MWD1418.

The claimant worked as a security guard for the respondent for approximately three to four weeks, although the Labour Court noted that there was uncertainty as to the precise duration. The claimant asserted that he was paid a rate of €8.50 per hour rather than national minimum wage of €8.65 per hour. In the course of the hearing, it was confirmed that the claimant had not requested a statement of his average hourly rate for a pay reference period in accordance with s 23 of the National Minimum Wage Act 2000.

The Labour Court noted that of s 24(2)(a) of the 2000 Act provides that a dispute cannot be referred to a Rights Commissioner under the Act unless an employee has received a statement pursuant to s 23 or having requested such a statement the employer has failed to provide such a statement. The Labour Court noted that a request for a statement under s 23, is a condition precedent to the jurisdiction of a Rights Commissioner and consequently to the jurisdiction of the Labour Court. The Court noted that this matter was not considered by the Rights Commissioner.

In circumstances where the Labour Court concluded that the claim was not properly before a Rights Commissioner because the condition precedent for bringing a claim was not met by the claimant, the claim was not properly before the Labour Court and thus it held that it did not have jurisdiction to hear the appeal.

Chapter 29

WHISTLEBLOWING

PROTECTED DISCLOSURES ACT 2014

Enactment and Commencement

[29.01] The Protected Disclosures Act 2014[1] was enacted on 8 July 2014 and came into force on 15 July 2014. The Act has retrospective application to disclosures made prior to 15 July 2014 but the protections conferred by the Act apply only from 15 July 2014.

The Act applies to employers in all fields of activity, but does not replace, the 18 sectoral whistleblowing protection provisions enacted between 1998 and 2013 and which are listed in Sch 4 of the Act. See para **[29.26]** below.

Protected disclosure

[29.02] Where a worker makes a disclosure of relevant information about relevant wrongdoing through an appropriate disclosure channel, the disclosure will be a protected disclosure and will attract the protections provided for in the 2014 Act.

In general, the term 'protected disclosure' means a disclosure of 'relevant information' (whether made before or after the date of the passing of the Act), made by a 'worker', through one of the channels specified in ss 6, 7, 8, 9 or 10 of the 2014 Act.

Although the short title makes reference to disclosures made 'in the public interest', no other reference is made in the Act to the 'public interest' and there is no 'public interest' test or requirement.

'Worker' and 'employer'

[29.03] A 'worker' is defined as meaning an individual who:

(a)   is an employee;

(b)   entered into or worked or worked under other any other contract, whether express or implied and (if it is express) whether oral or in writing, whereby the individual undertook to do or perform (whether personally otherwise) any work or services for another party to the contract for the purpose of that party's business;

---

1.   The Irish Act is modelled on the UK Public Interest Disclosure Act 1998 and the Protected Disclosures Acts 2000 in both New Zealand and South Africa. See generally on the UK Act Bowers, Fodder, Lewis and Mitchell, *Whistleblowing Law and Practice* (2nd edn, 2012). See also the US Whistleblower Protection Act 1989. See also the Flowchart on the Irish Act at para **[29.29]**. The Act was commenced by SI 327/2014.

    (c)   works or worked for a person in circumstances in which –

        (i)   the individual was introduced or supplied to do the work by a third person, and

        (ii)   the terms on which the individual is engaged to do the work are or were in practice substantially determined not by the individual but by the person for whom the individual works or worked, by the third person or by both of them, or

    (d)   is or was provided with work experience pursuant to a training course or programme or with training for employment (or with both) otherwise than –

        (i)   under a contract of employment, or

        (ii)   by an educational establishment on a course provided by that establishment …

In addition, an individual who is or was a member of the Garda Síochána or a civil servant is deemed to be an employee and an individual who is or was a member of the Defence Forces or Reserve Defence Forces is deemed to be a worker and the employers are respectively the Garda Commissioner, the person designated as such under s 2A(2) of the Unfair Dismissals Act 1977[2] and the Minister for Defence.

The term 'employer', in the case of a worker who is an employee, means the person with whom the worker entered into or for whom the worker works or worked under a contract of employment. In the case of workers who fall within limb (b) of the definition of 'worker' above, the employer is deemed to be the person with whom the worker entered into, or works or worked, under the contract. In the case of individuals who are deemed to be workers by virtue of limb (c) of the definition (agency workers), the person for whom the worker works or worked and the person by whom the individual is or was introduced or supplied to do the work are each deemed to be the employer. This has obvious implications for the reporting channel which might be used by agency workers. See paras **[29.11]** and **[29.12]** below.

In the case of workers within limb (d) of the definition, the employer is deemed to be the person who provides or provided the work experience or training.

In summary, the term 'worker' means:

(i)   an employee,

(ii)   a non-employee who works under a contract whereby he or she undertakes to do or perform any work or services for the other party to the contract for the purpose of that party's business,

(iii)   an agency worker,

(iv)   a person undergoing work experience or training, and

(v)   a member of the Garda Síochána, a civil servant and a member of the Defence Forces or Reserve Defence Forces.

---

2.   The State, a Minister, a Department or a Scheduled Office.

Service Providers

[29.04] It is likely that limb (b) of the definition of worker will be the most troublesome in practice. Limb (b) echoes the definition contained in the UK Employment Rights Act 1996 (UK Act) at s 230(3)(b), namely an individual who has entered into or worked under:

> (b) any other contract, whether express or implied and (if it is express) whether oral or in writing, whereby the individual undertakes to do or perform personally any work or services for another party to the contract whose status is not by virtue of the contract that of a client or customer of any profession or business undertaking carried on by the individual.

There are, however, a number of key differences between limb (b) in the 2014 Irish Act and limb (b) in the UK Act. Firstly, the 2014 Irish Act specifically includes situations where the individual has not given a commitment to work 'personally'. Secondly, there is a carve-out in the UK limb (b) in respect of individuals whose contractual status is that of a 'client or customer of any profession or business undertaking carried on by the individual'. In effect, an individual who works in a professional services firm or a service business could not come under the UK limb (b) and be a worker in respect of a client or customer of the professional services firm or service provider business. There is no such exclusion under the Irish limb (b). Finally, the Irish limb (b) appears to exclude persons who, personally or otherwise, perform work or services for another party but not 'for the purpose of that party's business'. Accordingly, an individual (not an employee) who provides services at the home of or for the recreation of or for the non-business consumption of the recipient of the services cannot be a worker in respect of that recipient.

In order to satisfy the Irish limb (b) and be a worker on that basis:

(i) there must be an express or implied contract;

(ii) the contract must provide for the performance of work or services, personally or otherwise, by the worker, who must be a party to the contract or be working under the contract.

Non-executive directors are capable of satisfying limb (b) of the definition.

Partners in a partnership, and certainly those who are active partners in the sense that they perform work or services for a partnership of which they are a member, are capable of falling within limb (b) of the definition.[3] See **CHAPTER 18**.

Volunteers

[29.05] The requirement that there be a contractual relationship to which the worker is a party, or under which the worker works, suggests that where the person is truly a volunteer they will not enjoy the protection of the 2014 Act. If, however, it is found that the apparent volunteer has entered into a contract, express or implied, under which the

---

3. *Bates van Winkelhof v Clyde & Co* LLP [2014] ICR 703.

services are provided, the person would appear to be capable of falling within limb (b) of the definition. Likewise, the making of a payment to the volunteer could be sufficient to create an implied contract, whether of employment or otherwise.

'Information'

[29.06] If a disclosure is to be a protected disclosure it must be a disclosure of relevant information. The term 'information' is not defined in the 2014 Act. The 2014 Act does however distinguish between 'information' and any allegation contained in it. See ss 7(1)(b) and 10(1)(a). The question as to whether a disclosure contains 'information' has been considered in the United Kingdom where the Employment Rights Act 1996 (as amended by the Public Interest Disclosure Act 1998 and the Enterprise and Regulatory Reform Act 2013) includes similar provisions. In summary, it has been held in the United Kingdom[4] that:

(i)   a mere expression of concern and request for reassurance that there was no breach of a legal obligation did not involve any disclosure of information;

(ii)   there is a distinction between information (ie a statement of facts) and a bare allegation or a statement of a position; and

(iii)   the disclosure itself need not identify the particular relevant wrongdoing, if the wrongdoing can be inferred from it.

The fact that the disclosee is already aware of the information does not deprive the disclosure of protection. This is clear from the definition of 'disclosure' in s 3 of the 2014 Act, which provides that 'disclosure', in a case in which information disclosed is information of which the person receiving the information is already aware, means bringing to the person's attention.

'Relevant Information'

[29.07] Relevant information is information which satisfies two conditions, namely:

(i)   in the 'reasonable belief' of the worker, it 'tends to show'[5] one or more relevant wrongdoings; and

(ii)   it came to the attention of the worker 'in connection with the worker's employment'.

---

4.   *Everett Financial Management Ltd v Murrell* EAT 552/553/952/02, *Cavendish Munro Professional Risk Management Ltd v Geduld* [2010] ICR 325, *Maini v Department for Work and Pensions* ET, 2203978/01, *Goode v Marks & Spencer plc* [2010] All ER(D) 63, *Royal Cornwall Hospital NHS Trust v Watkinson* [2011] MED LR 636 and *Smith v London Metropolitan University* EAT/0364/10.

5.   The 'tends to show' test is not sufficient for two of the possible disclosure channels, namely disclosure to a prescribed person/regulator and disclosure through the 'other person' disclosure channels. See paras **[29.13]** and **[29.16]** below.

The position in the UK is identical and extensive consideration has been given to the 'reasonable belief' test by the UK EAT and the Court of Appeal.[6] The belief must be actually held by the person making the disclosure but it must also be reasonably held. Furthermore, the basis upon which the worker believed that the information tended to show a relevant wrongdoing must itself be reasonable. The reasonable belief test applies to both the facts and the existence of the relevant wrongdoing. The reasonable belief must be judged by reference to facts known to the person making the disclosure at the time that the disclosure was made and not the facts as ultimately found. Accordingly, the fact that the belief turns out to be wrong does not mean that it was not reasonable but is relevant to determining if it was a reasonable belief. What is reasonable depends on all of the circumstances from the worker's perspective at the time that the disclosure was made, including such matters as the worker's seniority, the circumstances in which the disclosure was made, the identity of the disclosee and the worker's direct knowledge or otherwise of the matters at issue. There may well be a higher test with regard to the basis for a reasonably held belief of a likely future event because it must be 'likely' to occur. See **[29.10]** below.

Motive

[29.08] The worker's motive for making the disclosure is specifically declared in s 5(7) of the 2014 Act to be irrelevant to whether or not the disclosure is a protected disclosure. Thus, for example, an employee's motivation for making a disclosure could be spite or financial gain. However, the motivation may be relevant in determining the amount of compensation awarded as a remedy to a worker who is dismissed, or penalised as a consequence of making a protected disclosure. See paras **[29.18]** and **[29.19]** below.

Furthermore, a disclosure which the worker knows to be false cannot be a protected disclosure and, if the worker's belief is not reasonably held, the disclosure will not be a protected disclosure.

The UK Act differs because motivation is relevant. Previously, there was a requirement in the UK that the disclosure be made in 'good faith' and, following the enactment of the Enterprise and Regulatory Reform Act 2013, the good faith requirement has been replaced by a 'public interest' requirement. Although 'public interest' is mentioned in the short title to the 2014 Act, it does not otherwise feature in the 2014 Act.

Onus of proof

[29.09] Section 5(8) of the 2014 Act creates a presumption in any litigation that a disclosure is a protected disclosure. Accordingly, the onus falls on the respondent/defendant in any litigation to demonstrate that a disclosure was not a protected disclosure.

---

6. The leading authority is the decision of the Court of Appeal in *Babula v Waltham Forrest College* [2007] ICR 1026. See also *Durnton v University of Surrey* [2003] ICR 615.

It can be expected, however, that the onus will be on the person making the disclosure to establish that he or she is a worker.

'Relevant wrongdoing'

[29.10] The term 'relevant wrongdoing' is defined in s 5(3) of the 2014 Act, which lists eight relevant wrongdoings. In each case, the relevant wrongdoing is one in respect of which the employee has some degree[7] of reasonable belief that the relevant wrongdoing has been, is being or is likely to be committed.

The relevant wrongdoings are as follows:

(i)   a criminal offence;

(ii)   a failure to comply with any legal obligation (other than one arising under the worker's contract of employment or other contract whereby the worker undertakes to do or perform personally[8] any work or services);

(iii)   a miscarriage of justice;

(iv)   an endangerment of the health or safety of any individual;

(v)   damage to the environment;

(vi)   an unlawful or otherwise improper use of funds or resources of a public body or other public money;

(vii)   an act or omission by or on behalf of a public body which is oppressive or discriminatory or grossly negligent or constitutes gross mismanagement; and

(viii) concealment or destruction of any information tending to show any of the foregoing items (i) to (vii).

Section 43B of the UK Employment Rights Act, on which s 5(3) of the 2014 Act is modelled, does not include items (vi) and (vii) above. Provisions similar to (vi) and (vii) feature in the New Zealand Act.

It is immaterial whether a relevant wrongdoing occurred, occurs or is likely to occur in the State or abroad, and whether the law applying to it is that of the State or of any other jurisdiction.[9]

A matter is not a relevant wrongdoing if it is a matter which it is the function of the worker, or of the worker's employer, to detect or investigate or prosecute and does not consist of or involve an act or omission on the part of the employer.[10] By way of

---

7.   Either that it 'tends to show' one or more relevant wrongdoings (disclosure to internally, to a Minister or to a legal advisor) or that the information and any allegation contained within it are 'substantially true' (disclosure to a prescribed person or another person). Contrast s 5(2) with ss 7(1)(b)(ii) and s 10(1)(a) of the 2014 Act.

8.   Note that limb (b) workers do not need to personally perform the work or services. This may be an oversight in the drafting process.

9.   Section 5(4) of the 2014 Act.

10.   Section 5(5) of the 2014 Act.

example, if the worker is a garda, the making of a disclosure about a criminal offence will be a protected disclosure only if the disclosure relates to some act or omission on the part of the gardaí but will not otherwise be a protected disclosure.

A disclosure of information in respect of which a claim to legal professional privilege could be maintained in legal proceedings is not a protected disclosure if it is made by the person to whom the information was disclosed in the course of obtaining legal advice.[11] In other words, a disclosure by a lawyer may not be protected disclosure, although, if the lawyer is acting as an agent for a worker, it may be a protected disclosure on the part of the worker. See also para **[29.15]** below.

There is no need for a connection between the worker's duties and the relevant information and there is no requirement that the relevant wrongdoing be material or serious.

The wrongdoing could be wrongdoing of the worker who makes the disclosure.

Disclosure channels

[29.11] The 2014 Act provides for five disclosure channels as follows:

(i) internal disclosure, namely disclosure to the employer or the employer's nominee or to a person who is reasonably believed by the person making the disclosure to be guilty of or responsible for the relevant wrongdoing (s 6 of the 2014 Act);

(ii) disclosure to a person prescribed by the Minister. The Minister has prescribed 72 regulators for that purpose[12] (s 7 of the 2014 Act) – see **[29.13]**;

(iii) disclosure to the relevant Minister in circumstances where the worker is or was employed in a public body and the relevant wrongdoing relates to the public body (s 8 of the 2014 Act);

(iv) disclosure to a legal advisor (a barrister or a solicitor or a trade union official) (s 9 of the 2014 Act);

(v) disclosure to other persons, but subject to specified conditions (s 10 of the 2014 Act).

Internal disclosures

[29.12] Section 6 of the 2014 Act, which is modelled on s 43C of the UK Act, and which is entitled 'Disclosure to employer or other responsible person', provides for a disclosure made by the worker to the worker's employer or, where the worker reasonably believes that any relevant wrongdoing which the disclosure tends to show relates solely or mainly to the conduct of a person other than the worker's employer or to something

---

11. Section 5(6) of the 2014 Act.
12. Protected Disclosures Act 2014 (Section 7(2)) Order 2014 (SI 339/2014).

for which a person other than the worker's employer has legal responsibility, then the disclosure can be made to that other person.

Additionally, a worker who, in accordance with a procedure provided by his or her employer, makes a disclosure to a person other than the employer (ie to a nominee of the employer) is treated as having made the disclosure to the employer.

Section 6 provides that a disclosure can be made internally either:

(a)   to the employer or to a person nominated by the employer in a disclosure/ whistleblowing procedure; or

(b)   to a third party whom the worker reasonably believes to have engaged in the wrongdoing or to be a person who has legal responsibility for the wrongdoing.

Employers are accordingly entitled to specify third parties to whom disclosures can be made and presumably some employers will take up that opportunity. It is of course open to the worker concerned to ignore any such nomination and to make the disclosure to the employer itself.

Likewise, it is open to a worker, under s 6, to decide not to make a disclosure to the employer or to the employer's nominee but instead, if a third party appears to be guilty of the relevant wrongdoing or to have legal responsibility for the relevant wrongdoing, to make the disclosure to that third party and not to the employer.

Issues may arise as to whether disclosures made to a colleague, perhaps in an informal way or in an informal or non-work setting, should be considered to be disclosures to the employer. If a disclosure is to fall within s 6, it must be disclosure to the employer in the capacity of employer. Furthermore, if the disclosure occurred in a private conversation between colleagues, we suggest that this would not be categorised as a disclosure to the employer.

An employee is not required to make the disclosure in the manner contemplated by the employer in any policy published by it for that purpose. Neither is it necessary that the disclosure be made in writing although it is preferable that should occur. Finally, it is open to the worker to make the disclosure at whatever level of the employer's management hierarchy the worker considers appropriate. It is of course the case that an employer should, by means of a policy, encourage disclosures to be made in writing and to one or more designated persons within or outside of the employer's business but such a policy/request will not be binding on the worker.

Prescribed persons/regulators

[29.13] Section 7 of the 2014 Act, which is modelled on s 43F of the UK Act, provides for a disclosure to be made to a prescribed person where the worker reasonably believes:

(i)   that the relevant wrongdoing falls within the description of matters in respect of which the person is prescribed; and

(ii)   that the information disclosed, and any allegation contained in it, are 'substantially true'.

The Minister for Public Expenditure and Reform has prescribed 72 persons for this purpose.[13] They are:

1.	CEO of the Adoption Authority of Ireland	25.	CEO of the Health & Safety Authority	49.	Director of Finance of the National Transport Authority
2.	CEO of SOLAS	26.	CEO of the Health & Social Care Professional Council	50.	CEO of the Nursing and Midwifery Board of Ireland
3.	Registrar of the Opticians Board	27.	CEO of the Health Information Quality Authority	51.	Director of Internal Audit in the Office of the Revenue Commissioners
4.	CEO of the Broadcasting Authority of Ireland	28.	CEO of the Health Insurance Authority	52.	An Coimisinéir Teanga in Oifig Choimisinéir na dTeangacha Oifigiúla
5.	CEO of Bord na gCon	29.	CEO of the Health Products Regulatory Authority	53.	Controller of Patents etc in the Patents office
6.	Persons designated as appropriate persons in s 37(1) of the Central Bank (Supervision and Enforcement) Act 2013	30.	CEO of the Higher Education Authority	54.	Pensions Regulator in the Pensions Authority
7.	Commissioners of Charitable Donations and Bequests for Ireland	31.	CEO of Horseracing Ireland	55.	Registrar in the Pharmaceutical Society of Ireland
8.	The Comptroller and Auditor General	32.	CEO of Inland Fisheries Ireland	56	Director of the Pre-Hospital Emergency Care Council
9.	HR Manager of Commissioners of Irish Lights	33.	Director/Official Assignee in Bankruptcy in the Insolvency Service of Ireland	57.	Secretary the National Standards Authority of Ireland
10.	Commissioner in the Commission for Aviation Regulation	34.	CEO of Irish Auditing and Accounting Supervisory Authority	58.	The Press Ombudsman of the Press Council
11.	Chairperson of ComReg	35.	Company Secretary of the Irish Aviation Authority	59.	Director of the Private Residential Tenancies Board
12.	Commissioner in the Commission for Energy Regulation	36.	CEO of the Irish Coursing Club	60.	CEO of the Private Security Authority

13.	Registrar of Companies	37.	Director of Film Classification in the Irish Film Classification Office	61.	CEO of the Property Services Regulatory Authority
14.	Chairperson/Member of the Competition Authority	38	Director General of the Irish Takeover Panel	62.	CEO of Quality and Qualifications Ireland
15.	Manager of Personnel in CIE	39.	CEO of the Irish Turf Club	63.	Company Secretary of the Railway Procurement Agency
16.	Data Protection Commissioner	40.	Director of Legal Metrology in the Legal Metrology Service	64.	Head of Administration in the Railway Safety Commission
17.	Registrar of the Dental Council	41.	Chief Executive of each Local Authority	65.	Registrar of the Registry of Friendly Societies
18.	Secretary General of the Department of Education & Skills	42.	CEO of the Marine Institute	66.	Director of Corporate Services in the Road Safety Authority
19.	Director of Corporate Enforcement	43.	CEO of the Medical Council	67.	Members of the Sea Fisheries Protection Authority
20.	CEO of Dublin Docklands Development Authority	44.	CEO of the Mental Health Commission	68.	Secretary to the Standards in Public Office Commission
21.	Director General of the Environmental Protection Agency	45.	Chairperson/Chief Executive of the National Consumer Agency	69	CEO of the State Examinations Commission
22.	CEO of Fáilte Ireland	46.	Deputy Director of the National Employment Rights Authority	70.	Director of the Teaching Council
23.	CEO of Food Safety Authority of Ireland	47.	CEO of the National Milk Agency	71.	Chief Executive of Waterways Ireland
24.	Members of the Garda Síochána Ombudsman Commission	48.	CEO of the National Roads Authority	72.	Registrar of the Veterinary Council of Ireland.

The standard of belief necessary if a disclosure made to a prescribed person is to be a protected disclosure is that the worker must reasonably believe that the information disclosed, and any allegations contained in it, are substantially true. This is a higher test

---

13.   Protected Disclosures Act 2014 (Section 7(2)) Order 2014 (SI 339/2014).

than the test applicable to internal disclosures, where the test is that there must be a reasonable belief that the information 'tends to show' one or more relevant wrongdoings.

Disclosure to a Minister

[29.14] Section 8 of the 2014 Act, which is modelled on s 43E of the UK Act, provides for a disclosure to be made by a worker, who is or was employed in a public body, to a Minister of the Government on whom any function relating to the public body is conferred or imposed by or under statute.

The term 'public body' is defined in s 3(1) of the 2014 Act as meaning:

(a)   a Department of State;

(b)   a local authority within the meaning of the Local Government Act 2001;

(c)   any other entity established by or under any enactment (other than the Companies Acts), statutory instrument or charter or any scheme administered by a Minister of the Government;

(d)   a company (within the meaning of the Companies Acts) a majority of the shares in which are held by or on behalf of a Minister of the Government;

(e)   a subsidiary (within the meaning of the Companies Acts) of such a company;

(f)   an entity established or appointed by the Government or a Minister of the Government;

(g)   any entity (other than one within paragraph (e)) that is directly or indirectly controlled by an entity within any of paragraphs (b) to (f);

(h)   an entity on which any functions are conferred by or under any enactment (other than the Companies Acts), statutory instrument or charter; or

(i)   an institution of higher education (within the meaning of the Higher Education Authority Act 1971) in receipt of public funding.

The relevant test with reference to the worker's belief in the relevant information is that the worker reasonably believes that the information 'tends to show' one or more relevant wrongdoings. The wrongdoing must be wrongdoing connected with the public body concerned.

Disclosure to a legal adviser

[29.15] Section 9 of the 2014 Act, which is modelled on s 43D of the UK Act (which does not extend to trade union officials), provides for a disclosure to be made by a worker in the course of obtaining legal advice (including advice relating to the operation of the 2014 Act) from a barrister, solicitor, trade union official or an official of an excepted body (staff association).

This disclosure channel is designed to ensure that a worker can obtain legal advice on the possible disclosure of relevant information through one of the other channels and, in the course of obtaining that legal advice, make the disclosure to the legal adviser concerned without thereby exposing the worker to jeopardy for having made a disclosure to his or her legal advisor. Perhaps uniquely in Irish law, a trade union official is specifically included in the category of legal adviser.

Also relevant in this context is s 5(6) of the 2014 Act which provides that a disclosure of information in respect of which a claim to legal professional privilege could be maintained in legal proceedings is not a protected disclosure if it is made by a person to whom the information was disclosed in the course of obtaining legal advice.

It follows from the foregoing that a disclosure made by a worker to a legal adviser can be a protected disclosure but a disclosure made in turn by the legal adviser will not be a protected disclosure. It would appear however that if a legal advisor makes a disclosure as an agent for the worker, possibly in the course of correspondence issued by the legal adviser to an appropriate recipient and through an appropriate channel, the worker will retain the protections.

Disclosure to other persons

[29.16] Section 10 of the 2014 Act, which is modelled on s 43G of the UK Act, entitled 'Disclosure in other cases', sets out the circumstances in which a disclosure of relevant information with regard to a relevant wrongdoing (made other than internally, to a prescribed person/regulator, to the Minister in the case of public body employees, and to a legal adviser) can be a protected disclosure. It strives to balance the competing interests of encouraging the reporting of wrongdoing on the one hand while at the same time seeking to respect the right of the employer to confidentiality and indeed to its good name. Accordingly, it is no surprise that the circumstances in which a disclosure can be made to other persons are heavily conditional and nuanced.

It is likely however that the presumption that a disclosure is a protected disclosure, and the consequential imposition on the respondent/defendant of the onus of proof, will create difficulties for an employer who seeks to contend that a disclosure made to another person is not a protected disclosure.

If a disclosure to another person is to be a protected disclosure, the following four primary conditions must be satisfied:

(i)   the worker must reasonably believe that the information disclosed and any allegation contained in it, are substantially true;

(ii)   the disclosure must not be made for personal gain but the term 'personal gain' excludes any reward payable under or by virtue of any enactment. Note also that 'personal gain' is a wider concept than 'financial gain';

(iii)   one of four conditions set out below must be satisfied;

(iv)   in all of the circumstances of the case, it must be reasonable for the worker to make the disclosure having regard to five matters in particular which are set out below.

The four conditions referred to above, one or more of which must be satisfied, are the following:

(a)   that at the time the worker made the disclosure, the worker reasonably believed that the worker would be subjected to penalisation by the worker's employer if the worker made the disclosure internally, to a prescribed person or to the relevant Minister;

(b)   in a case where there is no relevant prescribed person in relation to the relevant wrongdoing, the worker reasonably believed that it is likely that evidence relating to the relevant wrongdoing would be concealed or destroyed if the worker made the disclosure internally;

(c)   that the worker had previously made a disclosure of substantially the same information[14] either internally, to a prescribed person or to the relevant Minister; or

(d)   that the relevant wronging was of an exceptionally serious nature.

The five matters to be taken into account in determining whether it is reasonable for the worker to have made the disclosure to another person are the following:

(i)   the identity of the person to whom the disclosure is made;

(ii)   in a case falling within conditions (a), (b) or (c) above, the seriousness of the relevant wrongdoing;

(iii) in a case falling within conditions (a), (b) or (c) above, whether the relevant wrongdoing is continuing or likely to occur in the future;

(iv) in a case falling within condition (c) above, any action which the employer (or the person to whom the previous disclosure was made) has taken or might reasonably be expected to have taken as a result of the previous disclosure;

(v)   in a case where the worker previously made a disclosure of substantially the same information internally, whether, in making the disclosure to the employer, the worker complied with the employer's relevant and applicable procedure.

The use of s 10 by workers for the making of disclosures relating to law enforcement matters, and security, defence, international relations and intelligence matters, is severely restricted by ss 17 and 18 of the 2014 Act. See para **[29.27]** below.

Protections

[29.17] The six protections conferred by the 2014 Act in respect of a protected disclosure are as follows:

(i)   special unfair dismissal protection (s 11);

---

14.   A subsequent disclosure may be regarded as a disclosure of substantially the same information as that disclosed previously even though the subsequent disclosure extends to information about action taken or not taken by any person as a result of the previous disclosure, s 10(4) of the 2014 Act.

(ii)   protection against penalisation (s 12);

(iii)   civil liability protection from suffering detriment (s 13);

(iv)   civil liability immunity (s 14);

(v)   criminal law immunity (s 15); and

(vi)   protection of identity (s 16).

Two of the protections (special protection against unfair dismissal and penalisation) are available only to employees. The other protections (civil liability protection from suffering detriment, immunity from civil liability, immunity from criminal liability and protection of identity) are available to any 'person' who makes a protected disclosure, but if a disclosure is to be protected it must be made by a worker. One of the protections (civil liability protection from suffering detriment) is also available to third parties who suffer detriment because another person (a worker) makes a protected disclosure.

Special unfair dismissal protection

[29.18] Section 11 of the 2014 Act amends the Unfair Dismissals Act 1977 so as to create a special unfair dismissals regime for the benefit of employees who are dismissed wholly or mainly for having made a protected disclosure.

That special regime is as follows:

(i)   a dismissal which is found to have been occasioned wholly or mainly by the employee/claimant having made a protected disclosure is irrebuttably presumed to be an unfair dismissal;

(ii)   the normal exclusions of unfair dismissal protection in respect of dismissal during probation and training and dismissal during apprenticeship do not apply to dismissals wholly or mainly occasioned by the employee having made a protected disclosure;

(iii)   certain exclusions from protection against unfair dismissal will not apply to dismissals resulting wholly or mainly from the making of a protected disclosure by employees:

(a)   who have less than one year's service;

(b)   who have on the date of dismissal reached the normal retiring age for employees of the same employer in similar employment;

(c)   who have not on that date attained the age of 16;

(d)   who are employed by a family member in a private dwelling house or farm in which the employer and employee both reside;

(e)   who are members of the Garda Síochána;

(f)   who are SOLAS trainees and apprentices;

(g)   who are employed by or under the State who were dismissed by the Government; and

(h)   who are Local Authority Chief Executives or the Director General of the HSE.

(iv) where a dismissal of an employee results wholly or mainly from the employee having made a protected disclosure, the maximum compensation which may be awarded is increased from the usual cap of 104 weeks' remuneration to 260 weeks' (or five years) remuneration;

(v) where the dismissal of any employee results wholly or mainly from the employee having made a protected disclosure and where that it is found that the investigation of the relevant wrongdoing concerned was not the sole or main motivation for making the disclosure, the amount of compensation which would otherwise have been awarded may be reduced by up to 25%.

The special protections apply also to constructive dismissal cases and accordingly an employee who resigns by reason of the employee's failure to properly address a protected disclosure or who claims to have been penalised as a result, will benefit from the protections if the disclosure is a protected disclosure.

The special protections will not apply unless the dismissal results wholly or mainly from the making of the protected disclosure. A mere connection to the protected disclosure will not be sufficient. Accordingly, if an employee who makes a protected disclosure commits a related act of misconduct, it may well be that the misconduct could result in a dismissal to which the special protection does not apply.[15]

An entirely new interim relief regime is also introduced, such that a claimant who claims that he or she has been dismissed wholly or mainly for having made a protected disclosure may seek interim relief in the Circuit Court pending the hearing of the unfair dismissals claim. The application must be made within 21 days immediately following the date of dismissal, or such longer period as the Circuit Court may allow. The Circuit Court is obliged to determine the application for interim relief as soon as possible. The application must be made on notice to the employer. The entitlement of the Circuit Court to postpone the hearing of an application for interim relief is constrained and may not be exercised except where the Court is satisfied that special circumstances exist which justify it in doing so.

If, on hearing the employee's application, it appears to the Court that it is likely that there are substantial grounds for contending that the dismissal resulted wholly or mainly from the employee having made a protected disclosure, the Court must announce its findings and explain to both parties the powers that the Court may exercise and the circumstances in which it will exercise them. The Court is then obliged to ask the employer whether the employer is willing, pending the determination or settlement of the claim, to reinstate the employee or to reengage the employee in another position on terms and conditions not less favourable to the employee than those applicable to him or her prior to the dismissal and this includes matters such as seniority and pension and similar rights and the right to continuous service. If the employer is willing to reinstate the employee, the Court will make an order to that effect. If the employer is willing to reengage the employee in another position and specifies the terms and conditions on which it is willing to do so, the Court must ask the employee whether he or she is willing to accept the position on those terms and conditions. If the employee is willing to accept

---

15.   See *Bolton School v Evans* [2007] IRLR 140.

reengagement on those terms and conditions, the Court will make an order to that effect. If the employee is not willing to accept the offer of reengagement on those terms and conditions and if the Court considers that the refusal is reasonable, the Court will make an order for the continuation of the employee's contract of employment and otherwise will make no order.

If, on the hearing of an application for interim relief, the employer fails to attend, or states an unwillingness to either reinstate or reengage the employee, the Court will make an order for the continuation of the employee's contract of employment and that order will continue the employment for the purposes of pay and benefits and seniority and pension rights and similar matters, and for the purpose of determining the period of continuous employment and the Court shall specify the amount which is to be paid by the employer to the employee by way of pay in respect of each normal pay period between the date of dismissal and the date of termination or settlement of the unfair dismissals claim. Any lump sum paid to the employee by the employer on or after dismissal which is wholly or part in lieu of wages will also be taken into account in determining the amount of the pay to be paid in those circumstances. Once an order is made, it is open to the employer and to the employee to apply to vary the order at any time up to the determination or settlement of the claim by reason of a relevant change of circumstances. A failure on the part of an employer to comply with an interim order for reinstatement or reengagement can result, on the application of the employee, in the making of a further order and an order for compensation.

Protection against penalisation (or threatened penalisation)

[29.19] Section 12 of the 2014 Act prohibits the penalisation by an employer of an employee for having made a protected disclosure.

Furthermore, an employer must not cause or permit any other person to penalise or threaten penalisation against an employee for having made a protected disclosure. Accordingly an employer can be vicariously liable for the actions of colleagues of the employee who made the protected disclosure.

If the penalisation in question constitutes the dismissal by the employer of the employee, the former employee's remedy is an unfair dismissal remedy rather than a penalisation remedy.

The term 'penalisation' is given a very wide meaning by s 3 of the 2014 Act.[16] Somewhat curiously, the definition refers to workers rather than employees although the statutory protection is available to employees only.

Where an employee claims to have been penalised or to have been the subject of a threat of penalisation by the employer or by any other person caused or permitted by the employer, he or she can make a complaint to the Rights Commissioner Service of the

---

16. Penalisation means any act or omission that affects a worker to the workers' detriment and includes suspension, layoff, dismissal, demotion, loss of opportunity for promotion, transfer of duties, change of work location, reduction in wages, change of working hours, the imposition or administration of any discipline or reprimand or other penalty including a financial penalty, unfair treatment, coercion, intimidation, harassment, discrimination, disadvantage, unfair treatment, injury, damage, loss and threat of reprisal.

Labour Relations Commission. If a complaint is upheld, the Rights Commissioner can declare that the complaint was well founded, can require the employer to take a specified course of action and require the employer to pay compensation of such amount (if any) as is just and equitable having regard to all the circumstances, but not exceeding 260 weeks (five years' remuneration). Again, if it is found that the investigation of the relevant wrongdoing concerned was not the sole or main motivation for making the disclosure, the amount of compensation that would otherwise have been just and equitable may be reduced by up to 25%. Complaints must be presented within six months of the contravention to which the complaint relates and that six-month period is extendable for up to another six months if the Rights Commissioner is satisfied that the failure to present the complaint in the first six-month period was due to exceptional circumstances. Uniquely, it is provided that if a delay in presenting a complaint is due to any misrepresentation by the employer, the first six-month period will not commence until the date on which the misrepresentation came to the employee's notice.

Either party to proceedings before a Rights Commissioner can appeal to the Labour Court from the decision of the Rights Commissioner within six weeks from the date on which the decision was communicated to the party concerned. The Labour Court is required to make procedures in relation to the conduct of those appeals, which procedures must include provision for the representation of the parties to such appeals. The Labour Court may refer questions of law to the High Court and the determination of the High Court is declared to be final and conclusive. Furthermore, a party to a Labour Court may appeal to the High Court from a determination of the Labour Court on a point of law, and again the determination of the High Court is stated to be final and conclusive. The Labour Court is empowered to take evidence on oath and to summon witnesses and documents. The Labour Court also has enforcement powers in respect of any decision of a Rights Commissioner which has not been carried out in accordance with its terms. The Circuit Court is given powers of enforcement in cases where employers fail to carry out a determination of the Labour Court.

Civil liability for detriment

[29.20] Section 13 of the 2014 Act, which is modelled on s 47B of the UK Act, and which is entitled 'Tort action for suffering detriment because of making a protected disclosure' provides that if a person causes detriment to another person because the other person, or a third person, made a protected disclosure, the person to whom the detriment is caused has a right of action in tort against the person by whom the detriment is caused.

It is noteworthy that the defendant is not necessarily the employer of the worker but can be any person who causes detriment to another person, or to a third person, by reason of the making of a protected disclosure. Accordingly, and by way of example, if one worker were to cause detriment to another worker or indeed to another person because of the making of a protected disclosure, the worker causing the detriment would incur civil liability on a personal basis. This opens up the possibility of liability on the part of colleagues, especially in circumstances where the employer may not have caused or permitted the imposition of the detriment concerned.

The term 'detriment' is defined as including coercion, intimation, harassment, discrimination, disadvantage or adverse treatment in relation to employment or prospective employment, injury, damage, loss and threat of reprisal.

The reference to prospective employment confirms that the detriment does not have to be caused during the working relationship but might be caused or suffered thereafter, possibly related to the giving of a negative reference by a previous employer which affects the worker's future prospects.

It is not open to a plaintiff to pursue a right of action for detriment and in respect of the same matter make a claim against the same person for unfair dismissal or penalisation.

In common with all other civil liability actions, claims of this type will be adjudicated upon by the District Court, Circuit Court or High Court depending on the amount of damages claimed. The period of limitations (of up to six years) will apply depending on the nature of the action.[17]

Immunity from civil liability

[29.21] Section 14 of the 2014 Act, which is modelled on s 18 of the New Zealand Act, and which is entitled 'Immunity from Civil Liability for making a protected disclosure', provides that no cause of action in civil proceedings, other than defamation, shall lie against a person in respect of the making of protected disclosure.

It also provides that a protected disclosure enjoys qualified privilege under the Defamation Act 2009; as a consequence of which, an action for defamation against a person who makes a protected disclosure will fail unless the plaintiff proves that the defendant, in making the protected disclosure, acted with malice.

Criminal law immunity

[29.22] Section 15 of the 2014 Act, which is also modelled on s 18 of the New Zealand Act, and which is entitled 'Making protecting disclosure not to constitute criminal offence', provides that, in the prosecution of a person for any offence prohibiting or restricting the disclosure of information, it is a defence for the person to show that, at the time of the alleged offence, the disclosure was or was reasonably believed by the person to be a protected disclosure.

This, therefore, is an exception to the general rule that disclosures are presumed to be protected disclosures unless the contrary is shown.

Protection of identity

[29.23] Section 16 of the 2014 Act, which is modelled on s 19 of the New Zealand Act, and which is entitled 'Protection of identity of maker of protected disclosure', prohibits a person to whom a protected disclosure is made, and any person to whom a protected

---

17. Section 3(1) of the Statute of Limitations (Amendment) Act 1991 as amended by s 7 of the Civil Liability and Courts Act 2004.

disclosure is referred in the performance of that person's duties, from disclosing to another person any information that might identify the person by whom the protected disclosure was made.

The protection is afforded to workers only, because only workers can make protected disclosures. However, the duty to protect the identity is not confined to employers. It extends to any person to whom a protected disclosure is made and any person to whom that protected disclosure is referred by the disclosee in the performance of the disclosee's duties. Accordingly, an individual to whom a protected disclosure is made is personally liable if they inappropriately disclose the identity of the worker by whom the protected disclosure was made. By necessary implication, it is of course permissible for a disclosee to refer a protected disclosure (including the identity of the worker making that protected disclosure) to another person in the discharge of the disclosee's duties.

Unlawful disclosure of the identity of a worker making a protected disclosure is actionable at the suit of the worker who made the protected disclosure if the worker suffers any loss by reason of the disclosure of his/her identity.

Section 16 sets out circumstances in which the protection of the identity of the worker who made the protected disclosure does not apply, and they are as follows:

(i)   If the person to whom the protected disclosure was made or referred shows that he/she took all reasonable steps to avoid disclosing information that might identify the worker who made the protected disclosure.

(ii)   If it is shown that the person to whom the protected disclosure was made or referred reasonably believes that the worker who made the protected disclosure does not object to the disclosure of information that might identify him or her.

(iii)   If the person to whom the protected disclosure was made or referred reasonably believes that disclosing information that might identify the worker who made the protected disclosure is necessary for:

(a)   the effective investigation of the relevant wrongdoing concerned;

(b)   the prevention of serious risks to the security of the State or public health or public safety or the environment; or

(c)   the prevention of crime or prosecution of a criminal offence.

(iv)   If it is shown that the disclosure is otherwise necessary in the public interest or is required by law.

A worker who made a protected disclosure and who claims that his/her identity was unlawfully disclosed may institute proceedings in the District Court, Circuit Court or High Court, depending on the amount of damages claimed, and the usual civil liability periods of limitation (generally up to six years but two years from the date the cause of action accrues in the case of a personal injury claim)[18] will apply.

It seems likely that an action under s 16 of the 2014 Act will often be accompanied by an action for causing detriment under s 13 because there is a substantial overlap.

---

18.   Section 3(1) of the Statute of Limitations (Amendment) Act 1991 as amended by s 7 of the Civil Liability and Courts Act 2004.

No contracting out

[29.24] Section 23 of the 2014 Act provides that any provision in any agreement is void in so far as it purports to prohibit or restrict the making of a protected disclosure, exclude or limit the operation of any provision of the 2014 Act, preclude a person from bringing any proceedings under or by virtue of the 2014 Act or preclude a person from bringing proceedings for breach of contract in respect of anything done in consequence of the making of a protected disclosure.

Public body protected disclosure/whistleblowing procedures

[29.25] Section 21 of the 2014 Act, which is modelled on s 11 of the New Zealand Act, obliges every public body to establish and maintain procedures for the making of protected disclosures by workers who are or were employed by the public body and for dealing with such disclosures. The Minister for Public Expenditure and Reform is empowered to issue guidance for the purpose of assisting public bodies accordingly and public bodies must have regard to any such guidance in the performance of their functions.

Section 22 of the 2014 Act obliges public bodies to publish, not later than 30 June each year, a report in relation to the immediately preceding year (in a form that does not enable the identification of the persons involved) containing information relating to the number of protected disclosures made to the public body, the actions if any taken in response to those protected disclosures and such other information relating to the protected disclosures, and the action taken, as may be requested by the Minister.

Employers in the private sector are not required by law to publish procedures for the making of protected disclosures but it is advisable that they should do so. There is also a statutory incentive on employers to do so because under s 10 of the 2014 Act one of the factors taken into account in deciding whether a disclosure to another person is or can be a protected disclosure, is the worker's adherence to the employer's procedure if the worker made an internal disclosure previously.

Special cases

[29.26] Four special cases are catered for in ss 17, 18, 19 and 20 of the 2014 Act as follows:

(i)   **Law enforcement**: s 17 provides that disclosures relating to law enforcement and related matters as described therein will not be protected disclosures unless they are made to the worker's employer, to a prescribed person (if any) or to a legal advisor or, if it is to be made to another person under s 10, it must first be made to a prescribed person and, following a passage of time the worker must reasonably believe that no or no adequate action has been taken and the disclosure must then made to the Comptroller and Auditor General (taxpayer information) or otherwise to a member of the Oireachtas. If there is no prescribed person, the worker must make the disclosure to his or her employer or to a member of the Oireachtas if the disclosure is to the effect that there has been an unlawful criminal investigation or unlawful prevention, detection, apprehension or prosecution process.

(ii) **Security, Defence, International Relations and Intelligence:** s 18 provides that disclosures relating to security, defence, international relations and intelligence will be protected only if made to the worker's employer, to the relevant Minister (public body related wrongdoing only), to the worker's legal adviser or to a Disclosures Recipient, which office is provided for in Sch 3. Section 10 is otherwise disapplied.

(iii) **Garda Síochána Ombudsman Commission:** s 19 amends the Garda Síochána Act 2005 by empowering the Garda Síochána Ombudsman Commission to investigate, as a prescribed person, protected disclosures made to it by workers who are members of the Garda Síochána.

(iv) **Defence Forces Ombudsman:** s 20 amends the Ombudsman (Defence Forces) Act 2004 empowering the Defence Forces Ombudsman to investigate complaints of penalisation of members of the Defence Forces for making a protected disclosure.

Existing sectoral protected disclosure provisions

[29.27] Schedule 4 to the 2014 Act lists all of the existing sectoral protected disclosure provisions (of which there are 18 in total) and provides that where a protected disclosure is made under any of those provisions and is also a protected disclosure under the 2014 Act, the protections created by the 2014 Act will apply to the person making such a protected disclosure.[19]

---

19. Those 18 provisions are as follows:
   Protections for Persons Reporting Child Abuse Act 1998, s 3;
   Prevention of Corruption (Amendment) Act 2001, s 8A;
   Standards in Public Office Acts 2001, s 5;
   Competition Act 2002, s 50;
   Communications Regulation Act 2002, s 24A;
   Health Act 2004, s 55A–55T;
   Employment Permits Act 2006, s 26;
   Consumer Protection Act 2007, s 87;
   Chemicals Act 2008, s 25;
   Charities Act 2009, s 61;
   National Asset Management Agency Act 2009, s 222;
   Inland Fisheries Act 2010, s 37;
   Criminal Justice Act 2011, s 20;
   Property Services (Regulation) Act 2011, s 67;
   Protection of Employees (Temporary Agency Work) Act 2012, s 21;
   Further Education and Training Act 2013, s 34;
   Central Bank (Supervision and Enforcement) Act 2013, s 38;
   European Communities (Occurrence Reporting in Civil Aviation) Regulations 2007, reg 5.

Obligation to make a disclosure

[29.28] The 2014 Act creates circumstances in which a worker becomes entitled to make a disclosure which will become a protected disclosure. There is nothing in the 2014 Act which imposes any obligation on a worker to make a disclosure. Likewise, in the majority of sectoral statutory disclosure provisions, the statutory provision is permissive, as distinct from mandatory, in that persons contemplated by the statutory provision are entitled, but not obliged, to make a disclosure. There are, however, four statutory provisions that impose on workers a statutory duty to make a disclosure or report.

Section 59 of the Charities Act 2009 applies to auditors and trustees of a charitable organisations, investment business firms advising a charitable organisation and persons involved in the preparation of the annual report of a charitable organisation who, in the course of and by virtue of carrying out their duties in relation to the charitable organisation, come into the possession of information that causes them to form the opinion that there are reasonable grounds for believing that an offence under the Criminal Justice (Theft and Fraud Offences) Act 2001 has been or is being committed, and imposes on them an obligation, as soon as may be, to notify the Charities Regulatory Authority in writing of that opinion and to provide the Authority with a report in writing of the particulars of the grounds on which the opinion was formed. Sections 60, 61 and 62 of the 2014 Act go on to provide a defence of qualified privilege, protection from civil liability and protection from penalisation of persons who make those reports to the Authority.

Section 19 of the Criminal Justice Act 2011 provides that a person shall be guilty of an offence if he or she has information which he or she knows or believes might be of material assistance in preventing the commission by any other person of a relevant offence, or of securing the apprehension or prosecution or conviction of any other person for a relevant offence, and fails without reasonable excuse to disclose that information, as soon as it is practicable to do so, to a member of the Garda Síochána. Relevant offences are specified in Schedule 1 to the Act and in summary are banking and investment offences, company law offences, money laundering and terrorist offences, theft and fraud offences, bribery and corruption offences, consumer protection offences and criminal damage to property offences. Section 20 of the Criminal Justice Act prohibits penalisation of employees for disclosing information relating to relevant offences.

Section 38(2) of the Central Bank (Supervision and Enforcement) Act 2013 provides that a person appointed to perform a pre-approval controlled function (PCF) in a regulated financial institution shall, as soon as it is practicable to do so, disclose to the Central Bank information relating to financial services offences or contraventions of financial services legislation or the destruction or likely destruction or concealment of evidence relating to same. The obligation does not arise if the person has a reasonable excuse. The privilege against self incrimination constitutes a reasonable excuse, as does knowledge on the part of the person concerned that the information has already been disclosed to the Central Bank by another person. Sections 40, 41 and 42 of the 2013 Act go on to confer protection from civil liability, protection of employees against penalisation and impose a tortious liability in respect of victimisation of persons who make those reports. Holders of controlled functions (CFs) are entitled to make those disclosures and avail of those protections, but they are not obliged to do so.

Regulation 5 of the European Communities (Occurrence Reporting in Civil Aviation) Regulations 2007[20] provides for mandatory reporting by pilots; designers manufacturers and maintainers of aircraft; air traffic controllers and flight information officers; airport managers; State air navigation installers and maintainers; and ground handling service providers, of occurrences which endanger or which, if not corrected, would endanger an aircraft or its occupants or any other person. Reports are made to the Irish Aviation Authority. Regulation 11 of the 2007 Regulations confers protection from civil liability on persons who make such.

Flowchart

[29.29] A Flowchart is set out overleaf which summarises the channels of disclosure and the tests that determine the circumstances in which each can be used.

---

20.   SI 285/2007.

PROTECTED DISCLOSURES ACT 2014: FLOWCHART

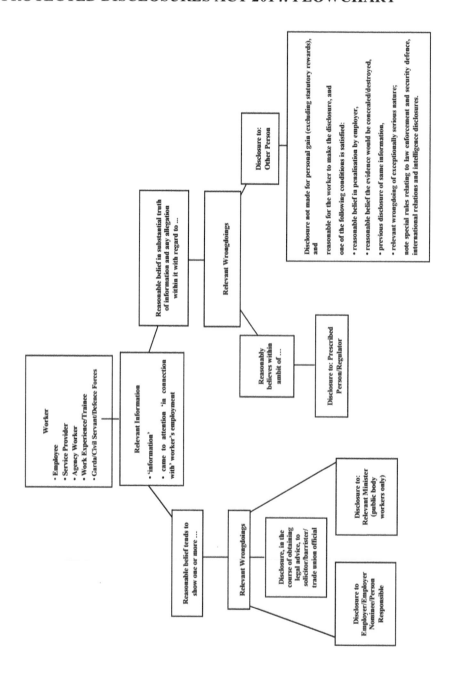

Chapter 30

WORKING TIME

TIME LIMITS

[30.01] *E Smith School T/A The High School v McDonnell[1] – Labour Court – appeal of decision of Rights Commissioner – Organisation of Working Time Act 1997, s 28(1) – entitlement to remuneration in respect of public holidays – time limits for making complaint – extension of time for making claim – factors to be taken into account when determining redress – just and equitable compensation*

This appeal arose from a claim for pay for public holidays under the Organisation of Working Time Act 1997. On querying his entitlement to pay in respect of public holidays, a part-time lecturer was told by the principal of the school in which he was working that he had no entitlement to a benefit in respect of public holidays. On each occasion when a public holiday occurred, the school closed and the claimant did not work. The claimant was not paid for these days. The claimant normally claimed social welfare benefits in respect of periods during which the school was closed and for which he was not paid. In January 2013 an official of the Department of Social Protection informed him that he could not claim benefits in respect of public holidays because he was entitled to payment from his employer for those days. He raised the matter again, this time with the bursar of the school, who undertook to clarify the position and, on doing so, he became satisfied that the claimant did have the entitlement which he claimed. The bursar undertook to pay the claimant in respect of public holidays falling thereafter. This did not satisfy the claimant and he made a complaint under the 1997 Act in June 2013. The respondent subsequently paid the claimant the sum of €1,108.12, which represented a day's pay for each of the public holidays that fell in the 18 months preceding the lodgement of his complaint.

The respondent submitted that the cognisable period for the purpose of the claim is the six-month period which ended on the claimant lodging the claim on 13 June 2013. Section 27(4) of the 1997 Act provides that:

> A rights commissioner shall not entertain a complaint under this Section if it is presented to the commissioner after the expiration of the period of 6 months beginning on the date of the contravention to which the complaint relates.

That subsection is qualified by s 27(5), which provides that:

> Notwithstanding subsection (4), a rights commissioner may entertain a complaint under this Section presented to him or her after the expiration of the period referred to in subsection (4) (but not later than 12 months after such expiration) if he or she is satisfied that the failure to present the complaint within that period was due to reasonable cause.

---

1.   *E Smith School T/A The High School v McDonnell* DWT1411.

The Labour Court noted that the test for deciding if reasonable cause has been shown for an extension of time under s 27(5) of the 1997 Act is well settled in a line of previous decisions of the Labour Court, starting with the decision in *Cementation Skanska (formerly Kvaerner Cementation) v Carroll*,[2] in which the Labour Court stated that:

> ... if reasonable cause exists, it is for the claimant to show that there are reasons which both explain the delay and afford an excuse for the delay. The claimant's failure to present the claim within the six-month time limit must have been due to the reasonable cause relied upon. Hence there must be a causal link between the circumstances cited and the delay and the claimant should satisfy the Court, as a matter of probability, that had those circumstances not been present he would have initiated the claim in time.

The claimant submitted that he had raised the question of his entitlement to public holidays with the respondent some three years previously. He said that he had been told in emphatic terms that he had no such entitlement having regard to the contractual basis upon which he was employed. The claimant accepted what he was told and did not pursue the matter further at that time. The respondent denies that the 1997 Act was contravened. It contended that, by paying the claimant the monetary value of the public holidays which fell in the 18 months prior to the date on which the claim was lodged, it had complied with the 1997 Act.

The Court accepted that the reason advanced by the claimant for not initiating his claim before 13 June 2013 both explained the delay and afforded a justifiable excuse for the delay. The Labour Court extended the time for bringing the complaint by a period of 12 months beyond the period specified in s 27(4) to 14 December 2011.

The Labour Court referred to the decision of the High Court in *Royal Liver Assurance Ltd v Macken*[3] in which Lavan J considered the nature of an employer's obligation under s 21(1) of the 1997 Act and the date on which a contravention arising from a failure to discharge that obligation accrues:

> The requisite infringement for the purposes of s 21(1) would arise in contexts where the employer has failed to elect between the various entitlements of an employee under s 21(1) or, where an employer fails to comply with a request made by an employee under s 21(2), where the employer fails to give a paid day off on the public holiday or an additional day's pay, as the case may be. In each case, it seems the infringement would arise on the date of the public holiday itself.

The Labour Court held that in this case the claimant did have a day off on each of the public holidays in issue because the school was closed on those days, but that the respondent was obliged by statute to pay the claimant for those days as they occurred. The Labour Court held that by reference to the *Royal Liver Assurance* decision, the 1997 Act was infringed on the date of each of the public holidays concerned, and accordingly the claimant's complaint was well founded as s 21 of the 1997 Act was separately contravened on each public holiday in the period cognisable for the purpose of this claim up to January 2013, at which point the respondent agreed to comply with the 1997 Act.

---

2.   *Cementation Skanska (formerly Kvaerner Cementation) v Carroll* WTC0338.
3.   *Royal Liver Assurance Ltd v Macken* [2002] 4 IR 427.

The Labour Court noted that the redress available to a successful claimant under the 1997 Act is governed by s 27(3) of the 1997 Act and provides that an employer may be required to pay an employee compensation of an amount that is just and equitable (but not exceeding two years' remuneration) if determined by the Court. The Labour Court noted that this subsection of the 1997 Act makes it clear that the claimant is not limited to recovering the economic or monetary value of the payments withheld, and all the circumstances include both aggravating and mitigating factors, it was appropriate for the Labour Court to take into account the duration over which the claimant's rights were infringed, the circumstances in which the claimant was deprived of his right to payment for public holidays, the response of the respondent when the claim was first raised and the degree of inconvenience suffered by the claimant in vindicating his rights. The Labour Court noted, however, that it could not award redress for those infringements of the claimant's rights that occurred outside the statutory time limit.

In addition to the arrears of wages already paid to him, the Labour Court was satisfied that the claimant was entitled to an award of general compensation, and measured the amount that was just and equitable at €1,500. The Labour Court stated that this should not be treated as remuneration for the purposes of tax. The decision of the Rights Commissioner decision was set aside and substituted with the terms of the Labour Court determination.

[30.02] *Sword Risk Services Ltd v O'Dwyer[4] – Labour Court – appeal of decision of Rights Commissioner – Organisation of Working Time Act 1997 – time limits running from contravention of Act – whether reasonable cause for extension of time*

The claimant, a former employee of the respondent, presented a claim to the Rights Commissioner on 15 March 2013 that the respondent failed to provide any or adequate rest intervals at work in accordance with s 12 of the 1997 Act.

A preliminary matter for determination by the Labour Court related to the time period in which the contravention of the Act was alleged to have occurred. The Labour Court noted that s 27(4) of the 1997 Act provides that a Rights Commissioner may not entertain a complaint under a relevant provision of the 1997 Act if it is presented to the Rights Commissioner after the expiration of the period of six months beginning on the date of the contravention to which the complaint relates. The Labour Court noted that as the complaint was presented to the Rights Commissioner on 15 March 2013, the cognisable period for the purpose of the claim was that commencing on 16 September 2012. Furthermore, as the claimant's employment with the respondent terminated on 1 October 2012, it was only the period from 16 September 2012 to 1 October 2012 which could be reviewed for the purposes of compliance with the 1997 Act. The claimant submitted that notwithstanding s 27(4) of the 1997 Act, s 27(5) of the 1997 Act provides that a Rights Commissioner (and the Labour Court on appeal) may extend the time for bringing a complaint specified in the Act by up to a further 12 months where reasonable cause is shown.

---

4.   *Sword Risk Services Ltd v O'Dwyer* DWT1410.

The claimant gave evidence that he suffered emotional upset from his partner's difficult pregnancy and the health problems affecting his newborn daughter. The claimant also stated that he had considered making a claim while he was still in the employment of the respondent but that he had decided against doing so because he believed that the respondent would retaliate by either reducing his hours or by dismissing him. The claimant submitted that these factors combined to prevent him from considering if he should initiate a claim under the 1997 Act.

The Labour Court noted that the test for deciding if reasonable cause has been shown for an extension of time under s 27(5) of the 1997 Act is settled in a line of previous decisions of the Labour Court, starting with the decision in *Cementation Skanska (formerly Kvaerner Cementation) v Carroll.*[5]

The Labour Court also considered relevant case law in the High Court, including the decision in *O'Donnell v Dun Laoghaire Corporation,*[6] in which it was pointed out that a Court should not extend a statutory time limit merely because the applicant subjectively believed that he or she was justified in delaying the institution of proceedings. In the *O'Donnell* case, Costello J pointed out that the reason relied upon must excuse the delay on an objective standard. The Labour Court also considered the decision of the High Court in *Minister for Finance v Civil and Public Services Union and Ors,*[7] in which a number of civil servants claimed that the absence of actual knowledge concerning their legal rights excused their failure to make a claim under the Employment Equality Act 1977 within the statutory time limit of six months. The High Court held that the absence of subjective knowledge on the part of the respondents concerning their constitutional or legal rights, or that an action is likely to be successful, does not prevent a cause of action accruing and time running under the 1977 Act. The High Court found that a failure to pursue a claim which had crystallised, until a legal precedent was in place which clarifies the law and indicates that the claim is likely to be successful, does not constitute 'reasonable cause' within the meaning of s 19(5) of the 1977 Act.

The Labour Court accepted the claimant's evidence that he had suffered emotional upset from his partner's difficult pregnancy and the health problems affecting his daughter. However it had difficulty in accepting that these factors explained the claimant's failure to pursue a claim under the 1997 Act within the time limits or that these reasons excused the delay. The Labour Court noted that the claimant's belief that the respondent would retaliate to his making a claim whilst still in employment was purely subjective and no evidence was proffered to establish any objective grounds to support that belief. The Labour Court held it was clear that the claimant was not prevented from making his claim in time, but that he chose not to do so. The Labour Court accordingly refused the application for an extension of time and affirmed the decision of the Rights Commissioner.

The Labour Court noted that the result of the decision on the preliminary point meant that the cognisable period for the purposes of the claim commenced on 16

---

5.   *Cementation Skanska (formerly Kvaerner Cementation) v Carroll* WTC 0338, see extract in **[30.01]**.

6.   *O'Donnell v Dun Laoghaire Corporation* [1991] ILRM 301.

7.   *Minister for Finance v Civil and Public Services Union and Ors* [2007] 18 ELR 36.

September 2012 and ended on 1 October 2012. The claimant had alleged that during this period he was deprived of 30-minute breaks from work on two occasions. This contention was based on the proposition that the claimant's employment came within the ambit of the Organisation of Working Time (Breaks at Work for Shop Employees) Regulations 1998. The Rights Commissioner found that these Regulations were inapplicable because the claimant was at all times employed as a security worker and not as a shop worker. The Labour Court noted that this aspect of the claim was not fully argued before it, and even if the claimant succeeded in convincing the Labour Court that the Rights Commissioner was incorrect in her conclusion on this point, the total reckonable loss for which he could recover amounted to one hour. The Labour Court stated that it would be prepared, if requested to do so, to consider further submissions from the parties on the applicability of the 1998 Regulations to the claimant, and if applicable, whether they had been contravened.

EXCEPTIONAL CIRCUMSTANCES/EMERGENCY – A NARROW DEFENCE FOR EMPLOYERS

[30.03] *Nurendale Ltd T/A Panda Waste v Suvac[8] – Labour Court – appeal of Rights Commissioner decision – Organisation of Working Time Act 1997, s 28(1) – whether s 5 of 1997 Act offered complete defence in circumstances where fire had destroyed major part of plant necessitating quick rebuilding of facility – circumstances where derogation in s 5 will apply*

The claimant alleged that he did not receive the statutory entitlements owing to him under the 1997 Act in respect of breaks, rest periods between shifts, notice periods in terms of finishing times of work, appropriate payment for Sunday working hours and sufficient payment for annual leave. The Rights Commissioner found in favour of the claimant and awarded him compensation for certain breaches on the part of the respondent. The claimant appealed against the quantum of the award,[9] claiming it was inadequate having regard to the gravity of the contraventions.

Section 5 of the Organisation of Working Time Act 1997 Act provides:

> Without prejudice to Section 6, an employer shall not be obliged to comply with Section 11, 12, 13, 16 or 17 where due to an exceptional circumstance or in emergency (including an accident or the imminent risk of an accident), the consequences of which could not have been avoided, despite the exercise of all due care and otherwise to the occurrence of unusual and unforeseeable circumstances beyond the employer's control, it would not be practical for the employer to comply with the section concerned.

In the hearings before the Labour Court and the Rights Commissioner, the respondent sought to rely on s 5 of the 1997 Act and referenced a fire which had occurred at the

---

8. *Nurendale Ltd T/A Panda Waste v Suvac* DWT1419.
9. €1,500 for breaches of s 11 of the 1997 Act, €700 for breaches of s 12, €208 for breaches of s 14(1), €1,500 for breaches of s 15(1), €500 for breaches of s 17, and €334 for breaches of s 20(1).

premises and destroyed a major part of the plant and which was an uninsured loss. The respondent contended that it was imperative that the plant be rebuilt as quickly as possible and suggested there were broader social imperatives associated with restoring its waste disposal facility as quickly as possible. The claimant was employed as a fitter and was engaged in the demolition and rebuilding of the plant. It was submitted on behalf of the respondent that the exigencies of the work required the claimant to continue working so as to complete certain tasks which could not be interrupted and the respondent alleged that the claimant undertook this work willingly and without demur. It was submitted by the respondent that s 5 of the 1997 Act operates to provide it with 'a complete defence'. In the alternative, the respondent suggested that the circumstances were a mitigating factor to be considered by the Court.

The Labour Court noted that s 5 of the 1997 Act gave effect to art 17(1)(g) of the Directive,[10] which provides for a derogation from the Directive. The Labour Court concluded that s 5 'is intended to apply in circumstances which it is not practicable to comply with the Act in order to undertake work in the immediate aftermath of an accident, or where there is an imminent risk of an accident. That suggests a close temporal nexus between the accident and the work in question.'

The Labour Court noted that the fire occurred in June 2012, but the contraventions complained of occurred between October 2012 and February 2013. Noting that the derogation in s 5 must be construed narrowly, the Court did not accept that the exigencies of the business or the broader social implication of the plant's operation could come within the intention of s 5 of the 1997 Act so as to relieve the respondent of liability.

In determining quantum, the Labour Court noted that the respondent had undoubtedly organised the claimant's working time with little or no regard to its legal duty under the 1997 Act. It also noted the claimant participated in this illegality by willingly working excessive hours. It was noted that the claimant at no stage took any action during his employment to assert his rights under the 1997 Act. The Labour Court determined these were matters of relevance in measuring the amount of compensation. The Labour Court ultimately varied the decision of the Rights Commissioner and awarded slightly more compensation to the claimant.

THE PROVISION OF REST FACILITIES ON SITE

[30.04] *Stasaitis v Noonan Services Group Ltd and the Labour Court[11] – High Court – Organisation of Working Time Act 1997, s 28 – Rules of the Superior Courts 1986, Ord 84C – whether Labour Court erred in law in finding respondent had complied with Organisation of Working Time Act 1997, s 12 and Organisation of Working Time (General Exemptions) Regulations 1998 (SI 21/1988) – where employer provides facilities in security hut on site for employee to take breaks during periods of inactivity*

---

10. Directive 2003/88/EC of the European Parliament and of the Council of 4 November 2003 concerning certain aspects of the organisation of working time.

11. *Stasaitis v Noonan Services Group Ltd and the Labour Court* [2014] IEHC 199.

This High Court point of law appeal arose from a Labour Court decision affirming a decision of a Rights Commissioner. The appellant was employed by the respondent as a security officer and was based at the premises of a third party company near Dublin Airport. The site was a warehouse facility and various vehicles entered and left the premises. The appellant's function was to monitor this traffic. He was based in a security hut, at the entrance to the site and it was common case that he worked in eight hour shifts and that during the shifts he was not permitted to leave the security hut, except to check vehicles entering and leaving the premises. He worked alone in performing these duties. It was also accepted by both parties that the respondent had not scheduled any specific breaks for the appellant over the course of the shift, but left it to the appellant to take breaks during periods of inactivity that occurred during the shift and he was provided with kitchen facilities in the security hut.

In his claim before the Rights Commissioner, the appellant asserted that the respondent was in breach of the statutory requirements to provide him with specific rest break periods. This claim was rejected by a Rights Commissioner and the appellant brought an appeal which was disallowed by the Labour Court. The Labour Court noted that the appellant had not made any complaints regarding his working time during his three years of employment and, on the balance of probabilities, concluded that the appellant had been told that he could take breaks during periods of inactivity during his shift. The Labour Court was further satisfied that the presence of kitchen facilities in the security hut must have made it clear to the appellant that he could avail of breaks while at work.

The Labour Court found that the respondent had come within the exemption provisions in regs 4 and 5 of the 1998 Regulations.[12]

It was submitted to the High Court on behalf of the appellant that the time he was required to remain in the security hut could only be classified as working time and that it was not possible for an employee to be considered to be working and at the same time to be enjoying the benefit of a rest period. It was further submitted that it was open to the High Court to intervene in a point of law appeal if it found that the Labour Court had based its decision on an unsustainable finding of facts. It was further asserted that the findings made by the Labour Court were erroneous and that the periods of inactivity experienced by the appellant in the course of his duties were neither a rest period nor a break. The appellant asserted that the inferences drawn by the Labour Court from the presence of cooking equipment in the security hut were unsustainable, having regard to the fact that the appellant was, at all times while he was in the hut, required to be available to discharge work duties as they might arise. The appellant asserted that he was afforded no breaks pursuant to regs 4 and 5 of the 1998 Regulations and thus the respondent was not entitled to rely upon the exemptions set out in reg 3 of the Regulations which must, it asserted, be strictly construed as a derogation from a European law right.

It was submitted by the respondent that there had been no error of law in circumstances where arrangements for breaks for the appellant had been put in place which were, at the very least, equivalent to the breaks referred to in the 1997 Act. It was

---

12.   Organisation of Working Time (General Exemptions) Regulations 1998, SI 21/1998.

further submitted that there had been no unsustainable findings of fact. The Labour Court had correctly determined the respondent was entitled to rely on the exemptions set out in the 1998 Regulations subject to compliance with reg 5.

Kearns P noted the agreement of both parties that the principles of strict construction must be extended to any derogation which in this case operates to exempt the employer from strict statutory obligations. Kearns P stated that he was satisfied that any arrangements put in place must satisfy the criteria of equivalence and compensation. Kearns P noted that on a purely factual basis it was difficult to see how it could be argued that the appellant was less well off by virtue of the arrangements put in place for compensatory rest in this case as when he was not required to operate the barrier or check vehicles he could move to an area of the security hut where he had available to him kitchen and other facilities, although he was not able to leave the hut.

Kearns P noted that the issue of the High Court jurisdiction in this type of case was comprehensively addressed by Hedigan J in *An Post v Monaghan*.[13] Kearns P noted the following statement of Hedigan J:

> This is an appeal on a point of law from a decision of the Labour Court. I will deal first with the role of the Court in such an appeal. It is plainly a limited role. The Court may only intervene where it finds that the Tribunal based its decision on an identifiable error of law or on the unsustainable finding of fact. The Court should be slow to interfere with the decisions of the Labour Court because it is an expert administrative Tribunal.

Kearns P concluded that there was no unsustainable finding of fact by the Labour Court and that it was perfectly entitled to hold that the arrangements put in place under which the appellant could obtain rest during periods of inactivity at work provided a sound factual basis for its findings. He further noted that the Labour Court was entitled to find that the arrangements either met the statutory requirements or satisfied a test that they complied with the requirements of equivalence and compensation in lieu thereof. Kearns P noted that while there was no set definition of 'break', it must be interpreted in the particular circumstances of this case to mean that the employer must ensure that the employee is afforded the compensatory breaks as per the derogations under the Regulations.

Kearns P noted that, in relation to s 6 of the 1997 Act, the appellant had stated that he was not provided with a compensatory or equivalent rest period or break in circumstances where he was not entitled to the ordinary rest period or break under ss 11, 12 or 13 of the 1997 Act. Kearns P noted that under s 6(2)(b) 'the employer has an obligation to make such arrangements as respect to the employee's conditions of employment as will compensate the employee'. The High Court noted that such compensatory arrangements cannot be of any material benefit, but that the requirement under s 6(2) may be met where the employee is provided with better physical conditions or amenities or services whilst at work as per s 6(3)(b). Kearns P noted that in this case the appellant was provided with kitchen facilities and an area in which to take breaks during periods of inactivity. Furthermore, the appellant was permitted to take such

---

13.   *An Post v Monaghan* [2013] IEHC 404. See *ACELY 2013* at [11.21].

breaks as he wanted during periods of inactivity and was provided with the amenities and facilities to do so. Therefore, the requirement to provide compensatory rest periods in relation to the derogation from the statutory rest periods and/or breaks must have been deemed to have been complied with. The appeal was dismissed.

REST BREAKS

[30.05] *HSE National Ambulance Service v O'Connor[14] – Labour Court – appeal against Rights Commissioner decision – Organisation of Working Time Act 1997, s 28(1) – whether employer in breach of ss 11 and 12 – whether claimant afforded adequate compensatory requirements in respect of s 11 – requirement on employers to justify each failure to provide break of 11 hours between shifts on objective grounds – right to 11 hour break fundamental right in EU law*

The claimant was an advanced Paramedic Team Leader in the National Ambulance Service. He submitted complaints that the respondent was in breach of s 11 of the Organisation of Working Time Act 1997 (the 1997 Act) on two occasions and of s 12 of the 1997 Act. The Rights Commissioner considered both complaints and determined they were not well-founded, which determination was appealed by the claimant.

The Labour Court noted that the claimant was employed to work in the service on a 585 hour roster spread over a 15-week period with a number of specified shifts. It was accepted that the nature of the emergency service provided by the respondent results in circumstances where it is not possible for the claimant to avail of the breaks and rest periods set out in the 1997 Act. However, the claimant in this case has asserted that he has not been provided with compensatory rest periods as required by s 6(2) of the 1997 Act.

The claimant stated that exigencies of the job required him to work beyond the end of his rostered shift and when this occurred, he should not have to recommence his next shift without the benefit of a break of 11 hours. He gave two examples within the reference period of where his shift had run over the expected end point. It was submitted by the respondent that the nature of the service provided rendered it impossible for it to determine the precise finish time of a shift. The respondent noted that the 1997 Act made special provision for emergency services and that it acted in accordance with those provisions. The respondent submitted that the claimant was provided with compensatory rest periods when it could not afford an 11-hour rest period between consecutive shifts and made reference to the LRC Code of Practice in relation to compensatory rest.[15] The respondent argued that the station in which the complainant is based had several restrooms, entertainment including multichannel TV, recreational exercise equipment, and catering and other rest facilities available for staff. It further noted that the claimant could avail of HSE staff canteen facilities in all other hospitals and community based locations. It further noted that when the claimant's shift ran over by three hours or more,

14. *HSE National Ambulance Service v O'Connor* DWT1484.
15. Organisation of Working Time (Code of Practice on Compensatory Rest and Related Matters) (Declaration) Order 1998 (SI 44/1998).

the guidelines in place provided that the claimant could be afforded an extended rest period to ensure his need for rest and relaxation was not compromised.

In its findings, the Labour Court noted the guidelines that were in force in the National Ambulance Service regarding compensatory rest, which stated that

> The shortening of an eleven hour rest period because of an emergency/urgent call to anywhere at or near the end of the shift does not automatically confer an entitlement to any defined rest period. In such circumstances, the crew are expected to report on time for their next shift.
>
> In relation to health and safety concerns that may arise where there is a significant (three hours or more) reduction of any rest period then common sense applies.

The Labour Court noted that this policy was relied upon by the respondent to justify its requirement that staff report for work at their scheduled shift commencement time, despite the absence of an eleven hour break between shifts. The Court held that such a standing instruction was not permitted under the 1997 Act. The claimant was entitled to an 11-hour break between shifts, except where, for objective reasons, such a break was not possible. The Court noted that objective reasons must be assessed in the context of each individual circumstance that arises and cannot be dealt with by way of a standing instruction in the nature set out in the guidelines quoted above. The 1997 Act places an obligation on the respondent to provide the claimant with a break of 11 hours between shifts and where it failed to do so, to justify the failure on objective grounds on each and every occasion in the context of the circumstances then prevailing. The Court further held that an inconvenience to rosters or cost to the service do not amount to an objective justification. The Court held that the entitlement to an 11-hour break is a fundamental right in EU law and any departure from it must be justified in the context of an individual breach. A standing order did not meet that requirement.

The Labour Court ordered the respondent to bring its policy into line with the terms of the 1997 Act in respect of the curtailment of an entitlement to an 11-hour break between its consecutive shifts.

In relation to the alleged breach of s 12, it was submitted by the claimant that he was at all times subject to an emergency callout at 90-second notice and he was required to attend to administrative and supervisory duties and was not in a position to avail of a rest period on any days. The respondent argued that the claimant had ample time over the course of the day to schedule a rest break. The Labour Court did not accept the claimant's arguments and noted that in the normal course of events, a break consists of a free period of time, the duration of which is known to the worker before the break commences. The Court noted that in an emergency service, it would be disproportionate to impose such a condition in an absolute manner. What the Court must weigh is whether the duration and frequency of callouts is such that a worker is prevented from availing of such breaks during working hours. The Court examined the working time records and after making allowances for the criticism of those records by the claimant, it found that he had adequate opportunity to take breaks from work in the course of each of the days. He noted that the claimant was, on each occasion, involved in administrative work with the ambulance base and could have scheduled time to take a break while engaged in those tasks. The Court did not uphold that portion of the complaint.

POINT OF LAW APPEALS ON QUANTUM

[30.06] *Bryszewski v Fitzpatricks and Hanleys Ltd T/A Caterway and the Labour Court (Notice Party)[16] – High Court[17] – appeal under Organisation of Working Time Act 1997, s 28(1) – whether amount of compensation awarded by Labour Court was inadequate – whether Labour Court departed from legal principles binding upon it – whether Labour Court failed to have regard to and apply principles of effectiveness, deterrence and proportionality as derived from European law and in particular the judgment of Von Colson and Kamann[18]*

The appellant was employed by the respondent, a company involved in the wholesale supply of fruit and vegetables to the catering industry. During the period that formed the basis of this complaint, the appellant worked as a relief driver for 18 weeks. Arising from his unhappiness with the arrangements available to him for taking rest breaks, the appellant brought a claim to a Rights Commissioner, who concluded that there had been a relatively small number of occasions when the appellant did not receive his proper break entitlements in breach of s 12 of the 1997 Act. The Rights Commissioner did not accept there had been any breach of s 17 of the 1997 Act. The appellant was awarded €300 in compensation, which he appealed to the Labour Court. Evidence was given in the Labour Court by the respondent that there were normally interruptions in work during which employees took breaks. However, the Labour Court concluded that, while the appellant did avail of some rest during these work interruptions, this did not adequately meet the requirements of s 12 of the 1997 Act. In relation to s 17 of the 1997 Act, the Court concluded that there was some element of non-compliance, but it was minor and inconsequential. The Labour Court decided that an award of compensation in the amount of €600 was fair and equitable and varied the decision of the Rights Commissioner accordingly.

On a point of law appeal to the High Court it was submitted on behalf of the appellant that, notwithstanding that the amount of compensation awarded to him had been doubled, it was so low that it could not be said to be effective, proportionate or dissuasive and could only be regarded as a nominal amount.

Birmingham J noted that an affidavit sworn by a director of the respondent made reference to the fact that subsequent to the appellant's claims, more detailed terms and conditions of employment were furnished to the appellant with reference to his break entitlements and also the respondent had installed a digital clocking-in system which recorded working times and daily rest periods at a cost of over €6,000. The High Court noted the principles enunciated in the *Von Colson and Kamann* case[19] and noted that the factual background to that case meant that, in accordance with German law, only nominal compensation in the amount of 7.02 deutschmarks could be awarded to the

---

16. *Bryszewski v Fitzpatricks and Hanleys Ltd T/A Caterway and the Labour Court (Notice Party)* [2014] IEHC 263.

17. This case was heard together with *Ruskys v Genpact Foods Ltd and Labour Court* [2014] IEHC 262, as both cases involved appeal pursuant to s 28(1) of the 1997 Act.

18. *Von Colson and Kamann v Land Nordrhein Westfalen* (Case C–14/83) [1984] ECR 1891.

19. *Von Colson and Kamann* (Case C–14/83) [1984] ECR 1891.

claimant in respect of the expenses incurred by her in applying for a post which she was refused because of her gender. Birmingham J contrasted that case with the outcome in this case in the award made by the Labour Court which Birmingham J stated was not a large one by any standards, but could be seen as a modest one. The High Court found that the award could not be regarded as nominal in the context of the *Von Colson and Kamann* case.

The High Court noted that the circumstances in which breaches of the 1997 Act occur are likely to vary significantly and that while some will involve breaches that are major, deliberate and egregious in nature, on the other end of the spectrum there may be breaches which are unintentional, minor, rectified and, in practice, of little consequence. The High Court noted that the Labour Court division was composed of persons of experience representing both sides of industry and thus was particularly well positioned to make an assessment of how a particular breach is to be categorised.

The High Court noted that while this was an appeal on a point of law, in essence it was an appeal in relation to quantum and the Court noted the well-established line of jurisprudence requiring it to exercise a degree of restraint and indeed deference when confronted with decisions of specialist tribunals. Birmingham J noted the comments of Clarke J in *Ashford Castle Ltd v SIPTU*:[20]

> Precisely what is fair and reasonable in the context of terms and conditions of employment is a matter upon which the Labour Court has great expertise and in my view, the Labour Court is more than entitled to bring its expertise to bear on those sort of issues which arise in this case.

> For those reasons, it does seem to me that a very high degree of deference indeed needs to be applied to decisions which involve the exercise by a statutory body, such as the Labour Court, of an expertise which the Court does not have.

The Court further noted similar comments by Hamilton CJ in *Henry Denny & Sons (Ireland) Ltd v The Minister for Social Welfare*,[21] where Hamilton CJ commented that courts should be slow to intervene with the decisions of expert administrative bodies. Birmingham J held that where an assessment of quantum is involved, which must inevitably involve an element of deciding where on the spectrum particular breaches are to be placed, a body such as the Labour Court is particularly well-positioned to undertake the task and it is certainly a case where the courts should be slow to intervene.

Birmingham J noted that there was no reason whatsoever to believe that the Labour Court was unaware of the *Von Colson and Kamann* line of jurisprudence and particularly noted that it had been raised in submissions before that Court. Birmingham J then went on to consider a number of Labour Court cases which had been cited by the appellant to suggest that the decision in this case was out of line with earlier precedents. Birmingham J stated that it was abundantly clear from the case law that the Labour Court takes breaches of the 1997 Act seriously, but that as is to be expected, awards in individual cases diverge to a significant extent. In the High Court's view, the Labour Court did scale breaches and identified where on the scale a particular breach falls. The

---

20.   *Ashford Castle Ltd v SIPTU* [2006] IEHC 201.
21.   *Henry Denny & Sons (Ireland) Ltd v The Minister for Social Welfare* [1998] 1 IR 34.

High Court concluded that there was no basis whatsoever in interfering with the Labour Court determination in this case and the appeal failed.

[30.07] *Ruskys v Genpact Ltd and Anor[22] – High Court – Organisation of Working Time Act 1997, s 28(1) – failure to receive full annual leave entitlements or compensate for Sunday working – failure to observe maximum weekly working hours and to afford adequate rest breaks*

This case was heard in conjunction with the previous case, **[30.06]**.

In this case, the appellant commenced employment as a general operative employed on the national minimum wage. He subsequently lodged complaints with the Rights Commissioner service that his employer was in breach of a number of provisions of the Organisation of Working Time Act 1997 and had also failed to comply with the requirements to supply him with written terms of employment contrary to the Terms of Employment (Information) Act 1994. The substance of the appellant's complaint was that he had not received his full annual leave entitlements, he had not received compensation for working on Sundays and that he had been required to work regularly in excess of the maximum 48-hour average working weekly limit and there were a number of specific occasions when he was not afforded a minimum daily rest break of 11 hours between shifts. The Rights Commissioner upheld in part the claim under the Act of 1997 and awarded the appellant €2,500 in compensation. This was appealed by the appellant and a subsequent hearing took place. The Labour Court concluded that ss 11, 15 and 19 of the 1997 Act had been contravened, but that the breaches of ss 11 and 19 were minor and technical. The Labour Court found that the other breach of s 15 of the Act was at the lower end of the scale. The Labour Court awarded compensation of €1,000 to the appellant and an appeal to the High Court followed. The High Court noted, for reasons outlined in the previous case,[23] that the Labour Court is particularly well-placed to identify where on the scale of seriousness a breach lies and, in this case, the Labour Court concluded that it was at the lower end of seriousness and this was a finding that could not be interfered with and thus the appeal was disallowed.

MOBILE ROAD TRANSPORT ACTIVITIES

[30.08] *First Direct Logistics Ltd v Stankiewicz[24] – Labour Court – Industrial Relations Acts 1946 to 2012 – s 19 of 2012 Regulations (SI 36/2012)[25] – whether respondent breached regs 5(a), 5(b), 8(3), 10, 11 and 12 of the 2012 Regulations*

This was an appeal from a decision of a Rights Commissioner by the claimant employee. The claimant submitted evidence as to the hours worked by him for a number

---

22. *Ruskys v Genpact Foods Ltd and Labour Court* [2014] IEHC 262.
23. See **[30.66]**.
24. *First Direct Logistics Ltd v Stankiewicz* RTD 141.
25. European Communities (Road Transport) (Organisation of Working Time of Persons Performing Mobile Road Transport Activities) Regulations (SI 36/2012).

of identified weeks and the respondent acknowledged that there had been a contravention of the Regulations, but that the average hours worked by the claimant were less than claimed. The Labour Court examined the evidence and preferred the claimant's evidence and awarded the claimant €2,000 in relation to the contravention. The Labour Court further found that the respondent was in breach of reg 8(3) in relation to breaks from work, reg 10 in relation to night working, reg 11 in relation to the obligation to notify a driver of Regulations and also the obligation to maintain records under reg 12. The Labour Court directed the respondent to pay the claimant total compensation of €4,500.

ZERO HOUR CONTRACTS

[30.09] *Ticketline T/A Ticketmaster v Mullen*[26] *– Labour Court – appeal of decision of Rights Commissioner – s 28(1) Organisation of Working Time Act 1997 – zero hours contract of employment – whether respondent in breach of s 18 of the 1997 Act*

This appeal to the Labour Court was brought by the claimant who was employed as a box office assistant under a contract of employment styled as a 'zero hours contract'[27]. The claimant had a fixed rate of pay and her hours varied from week to week and were assigned by the respondent on an 'as needs' basis. Evidence was given by the claimant that she was informed by her supervisor on commencing employment that it was a condition of her employment that she keep herself available to work any hours and all shifts offered to her. The claimant asserted that she did so over the course of her employment and worked in various venues at the discretion of the respondent. From January 2013, other than two hours' work assigned to her, she was offered no further work, her employment was not terminated and she did not receive a P45. The claimant wrote to her supervisor querying why she had not been given any work in the previous month. In this letter, the claimant referenced her zero hours contract and stated her entitlement under s 18 of the 1997 Act to be given work or be compensated with a payment equal to 25% of the hours that she had been required to be available for work. This letter was not replied to and so she sent a subsequent reminder. Correspondence ultimately followed from the respondent which disputed this.

It was alleged by the claimant that the respondent was in breach of s 18 of the 1997 Act which provides:

> … where a person is engaged under a contract of employment to be available to work a number of hours or as and when the employer requires, or a combination of both, and the employer does not require an employee to work at least 25% of the hours for which such work had been done in the week, then the employee shall be entitled to be paid by the employer the pay which they would have received if they had worked for the employer in that week either the percentage of hours or fifteen hours, whichever is less.

---

26.   *Ticketline T/A Ticketmaster v Mullen* DWT1434.
27.   The original complaint came before a Rights Commissioner, which, because of the non-attendance of the claimant, was dismissed for want of prosecution.

It was common case that the contract of employment did not require the claimant to make herself available for work any time she was required by the respondent. However, the claimant gave evidence that the manner in which the contract was administered was such that she was so required and this was advised to her by her supervisor. The Labour Court noted that the claimant's view had been set out by her in correspondence with the respondent on two separate occasions and that her supervisor did not respond to those letters, nor did she attend the hearing or otherwise contradict the claimant's assertions in this regard. The Court noted that while contradictory evidence was put forward by another manager of the respondent, he was not party to the discussions that took place between the claimant and her manager and was thus not in a position to give evidence.

The Labour Court therefore found, on the basis of the uncontroverted evidence of the claimant, that her contract of employment was administered as though she was required to be available for work at all times. The Court noted the provisions of s 18 of the 1997 Act and held that as the claimant was required to work at the respondent's request and to keep herself available for work as required, she came within the scope of s 18 of the Act.

The Labour Court found that the claimant was entitled, in accordance with s 18(2)(b) of the 1997 Act, to at least 25% of the hours for which such work had been done in the week, but as the claimant was not required to work in the relevant week, the Court was required to apply s 18(4) of the Act.[28] The Court found that the respondent had infringed s 18 of the 1997 Act and, the Court declared the complaint to be well-founded and required the respondent to pay to the complainant compensation in the sum of €3,000.

'SLEEP IN' NIGHT SHIFTS

[30.10] *Esparon T/A Middle West Residential Care Home v Slavikovska*[29] *– UK Employment Appeal Tribunal – National Minimum Wage Regulations 1999 (SI 1999/ 584) (UK) – whether claimant entitled to be paid in accordance with national minimum wage in circumstances where she was required to work a number of 'sleep in' night shifts at a residential care home – whether time spent during night shift amounted to working time*

This was an appeal by the respondent of a decision of a UK Employment Tribunal which found that the respondent had failed to pay the claimant a payment in accordance with the National Minimum Wage Regulations 1999 for hours spent on a night shift and had thus made unlawful deduction from her wages.

The respondent traded as a residential care home for residents with learning difficulties. The claimant was employed on a basic hourly rate with 'sleep in' duty at a

---

28. 'The references at Section 2(b) to the hours for which work of the type referred to in that provision has been done in the week concerned shall be construed as a reference to the number of hours of such work done in that week by another employee of the employer concerned or, in the case that the employer has required two or more employees to do such work for him or her in that week and the number of hours of such work done by each of them in that week is not identical, whichever number of hours of such work done by one of those employees in that week is the greatest.'

29. *Esparon T/A Middle West Residential Care Home v Slavikovska* [2014] UK EAT 0217/12.

fixed rate per shift. Evidence was given by the claimant that she was not allowed to sleep during night shifts and that she was required to work between 9pm and 10pm and from 7am to 9am but the night shift lasted from 9pm until 7am the following morning. The claimant's most recent contract of employment provided that she was resident at the care home and worked during the day, she had a tenancy agreement for her flat and paid rent and worked a sleep in shift from 9pm until 7am for which she was paid £25. The contractual provision of relevance in her contract stated that 'to comply with regulatory requirements you are required to provide back up in emergency situations'. Evidence was given by the claimant that she was not allowed to sleep on the night shift and did a variety of duties during the shift, to include checking residents every 40 minutes to one hour depending on their medical condition, ironing, changing incontinence pads and training new staff at night. This was denied by the respondent who said there were sleeping facilities and that the claimant was able to sleep on site but be available for emergency purposes. It should be noted that there were separate claims for unfair dismissal and harassment.

The UK EAT noted that there was no issue in principle as to whether the claimant was entitled to the benefit of the national minimum wage if, during her 'sleep in' shifts, she was carrying out 'time work'. The EAT noted that reg 15 related to 'time work' where a worker is available at or near a place of work for the purposes of doing 'time work' or by arrangement sleeps at or near a place of work and is provided with facilities for sleeping.

The UK EAT considered in detail the prevailing case law in this area and found that the claimant was engaged in 'time work' on two separate but independent bases. The EAT noted that the Employment Tribunal had found the claimant actually worked and carried out duties during the 'sleep in' sessions and was required to do so. The claimant was required to undertake the night shifts quite separately to her day job. The claimant's job, when she was required to sleep in on the premises, was one where she was entitled to be paid simply for being on the premises, regardless of whether she worked or not or whether she carried out her regular duties. She was paid simply to be there.

The respondent was obliged by the Regulations to have staff available on the premises at all times and the claimant was there to fulfil that obligation. She was required to undertake night shifts under the obligations placed on the respondent and it was essential she was there, even if she did nothing. The EAT noted that there was no authority for the proposition that the Regulations did not apply if the work in question is not the employee's main job or an adjunct to it and has to be core hours.

The EAT stated that the proper focus must be on the task actually carried out and that in the present case the claimant was paid to be on the premises and also carried out time work and thus was entitled to be paid at the rate of the national minimum wage and the respondent's appeal must be dismissed.

The EAT noted that in each of the cases it had considered employees were required to be on the premises 'just in case' and in that sense, on call. The EAT considered how it could be distinguished between those 'at work' cases where the employee is paid simply to be there 'just in case' and those 'on-call' cases where the employee is required to be there on-call and is not deemed to be working the whole time. The EAT suggested that an important consideration must be why the employer required the employee to be on the premises. If the employer requires the employee to on the premises pursuant to a statutory requirement to have a suitable person on the premises 'just in case', that in the view of the EAT would be a powerful indicator that the employee is being paid simply to be there and thus deemed to be working regardless of whether work is actually carried out.

ENTITLEMENT TO RECEIVE COMMISSION PAYMENTS WHILE ON ANNUAL LEAVE

[30.11] *ZJR Lock v British Gas Trading plc[30] – Directive 2003/88/EC[31] – CJEU – whether art 7 of Directive requires that Member States take measures to ensure that worker paid for periods of annual leave – reference to commission payments he would have earned during that period had he not taken leave as well as basic pay*

This was a request for a preliminary ruling referred by an Employment Tribunal in the United Kingdom arising from a claim brought by an internal energy sales consultant with British Gas. The claimant's remuneration had two main components; a fixed basic salary and a monthly variable commission payment. The commission payment was calculated by reference to sales achieved, specifically the number and type of new contracts concluded by British Gas. Commission was payable on conclusion of the sales contract with British Gas.

It was common case that the claimant went on paid annual leave from 19 December 2011 to 3 January 2012, during which time his remuneration for December 2011 was composed of his basic pay entitlement and a commission payment which he had earned over previous weeks. On average, the claimant's commission amounted to 60% of his monthly income. It was accepted that, as the claimant did not carry out work during his period of annual leave, he was not in a position to make any new sales or follow up on potential sales during that period and thus was not able to generate commission during that period. As this had an adverse effect on the salary he received during the months following annual leave, he decided to bring an action before the Employment Tribunal for outstanding holiday pay in respect of the period from 19 December 2011 to 3 January 2012. The Employment Tribunal decided to make a reference to the Court of Justice of the European Union (CJEU), specifically:

1. whether art 7 of Directive 93/104/EC, as amended by Directive 2003/88, required Member States to take measures to ensure that a worker is paid in respect of periods of annual leave by reference to commission payments he would have earned during that period had he not taken leave as well as his basic pay;

2. what are the principles which inform the answer to question 1?

3. if the answer to question 1 is yes, what principles, if any, are required to be adopted by Member States in calculating the sum that is payable to the worker by

---

30.   *ZJR Lock v British Gas Trading plc* (Case C–539/12).
31.   Directive 2003/88/EC concerning Certain Aspects of Organisation of Working Time.

reference to commission that the worker would or might have earned if he had not taken annual leave?

In its judgment, the CJEU noted that the entitlement of every worker to annual leave must be regarded as a particularly important principle of the EU social laws from which there can be no derogations. Further, the CJEU noted that it had already been established that the term 'paid annual leave' in art 7(1) of Directive 2003/88 meant that for the duration of annual leave within the meaning of that Directive, remuneration must be maintained and that in other words, workers must receive their normal remuneration for that period of rest.

The CJEU noted that Directive 2003/88 treats entitlement to annual leave and to a payment on that account as being two aspects of a single right. The main purpose of providing payment for that leave is to put the worker, during such leave, in a position which is as regards to salary comparable to periods of work. It was asserted on behalf of the respondent and the UK Government that this was achieved as the claimant had received, during his period of paid annual leave, a salary comparable to that earned during periods of work as he received not only his basic salary, but also commission resulting from sales which he had achieved during the weeks preceding his period of holiday. The CJEU was not willing to accept this argument.

The CJEU stated that, notwithstanding the remuneration received by a worker during the period in which he actually takes his annual leave, he may be deterred from exercising his right to annual leave, given the financial disadvantage which, although deferred, is nonetheless genuinely suffered by him during a period following that of his annual leave. The CJEU noted the concession by the respondent that the claimant did not generate any commission during the period of annual leave and thus in the period following his annual leave, the claimant was paid only reduced remuneration comprising his basic salary. The CJEU found that that adverse financial impact may deter a worker from actually taking leave which, as had been referred to in the Advocate General's opinion[32] was all the more likely in a situation such as in this case where the commission represented on average over 60% of the remuneration received by the claimant.

The CJEU found that such a reduction in a worker's remuneration in respect of paid annual leave was liable to deter him from actually exercising his right to take leave and this was contrary to the objective pursued by art 7 of the Directive. The CJEU found the fact that the reduction in remuneration occurs after the period of annual leave to be irrelevant. The CJEU concluded that the answer to the first and second questions raised was that art 7(1) of Directive 2003/88 must be interpreted as precluding national legislation and practice under which a worker whose remuneration consists of a basic salary and commission, the amount of which is fixed by reference to the contracts entered into by the employer as a result of sales achieved by that worker is entitled, in respect of his paid annual leave, to remuneration composed exclusively of his basic salary.

With regard to how such remuneration is to be calculated, the CJEU found that such determination of normal remuneration required a specific analysis. The CJEU stated

---

32.   Opinion of Advocate General Blot (Case–539/12).

that any inconvenient aspect which is linked intrinsically to the performance of the tasks which the worker is required to carry out under his contract of employment and in respect of which a monetary amount is provided and included in the calculation of the worker's total remuneration, must necessarily be taken into account for the purpose of calculating the amount to which the worker is entitled during his annual leave. The CJEU also noted its previous findings that all components of total remuneration relating to the professional and personal status of the worker must continue to be paid during his paid annual leave to include any allowances relating to seniority, length of service and professional qualifications. The CJEU noted that there is an intrinsic link between the commission received each month by the claimant and the performance of the task he is required to carry out under his contract of employment and thus such commission must be taken into account in the calculation of total remuneration to which a worker is entitled in respect of his annual leave. The CJEU determined that the answer to question 3, being the methods of calculation of the commission to which the claimant is entitled in respect of annual leave, must be assessed by the national court or tribunal on the basis of the rules and criteria set out by the CJEU's case law in light of the objective pursued by art 7 of the Directive.

ENTITLEMENT TO PAID ACCRUED BUT UNTAKEN ANNUAL LEAVE ON DEATH

[30.12] *Bollacke v K+K Klaas and Kock BV & Co AG[33] – CJEU – request for preliminary ruling – whether Directive 2003/88/EC precludes national legislation which provides that entitlement to paid annual leave is lost where employee dies whilst in employment – whether receipt of such allowance depends on prior application by applicant*

This request for a preliminary ruling came from a higher Labour Court in Germany in the context of proceedings between a widow and the former employer of her late husband, the respondent company. Mr Bollacke was seriously ill since 2009 and was unfit to work for more than eight months during that year. He was then again unable to work from 11 October 2010 until the date of his death on 19 November 2010. It was common case that he had a minimum of 140.5 days of annual leave outstanding at the date of his death. His widow subsequently applied to his employer for an allowance in lieu of those days of annual leave outstanding, but this was rejected by his employer on the grounds that there were doubts that an inheritable entitlement could exist. The Court of First Instance also rejected the application on grounds that under case law of the federal Labour Court, an entitlement to an allowance in lieu of paid annual leave outstanding at the end of the employment relationship does not arise where the relationship is terminated by the death of the employee. On appeal, the higher Labour Court decided to stay the proceedings and to refer the matter to the CJEU as to whether art 7 of Directive 2003/88 precluded national legislation which provided that the entitlement to paid annual leave is lost without conferring entitlement to an allowance in

---

33. *Bollacke v K+K Klaas and Kock BV & Co AG* (Case C–118/13).

lieu of leave outstanding where the employment relationship is terminated by the death of the employee and furthermore, the CJEU was asked whether receipt of such an allowance depends on a prior application by the applicant.

In its judgment, the CJEU noted that the entitlement of every worker to paid annual leave must be regarded as a particularly important principle of EU social law from which there can be no derogation. The CJEU further noted that the Directive treats the entitlement to annual leave and to payment on that account as being two aspects of a single right. The CJEU noted its previous finding that where the employment relationship has terminated and it is no longer possible to take annual leave, art 72 of the Directive 2003/88 provides that the worker is entitled to an allowance in lieu. The CJEU stated that it was in light of that case law that it must be established whether, when the event that terminated the employment relationship is the worker's death, such an event may preclude entitlement to paid annual leave being transformed into an entitlement to an allowance in lieu. The CJEU noted that receipt of financial compensation if the employment relationship has ended by reason of the worker's death is essential to ensure the effectiveness of the entitlement to paid annual leave granted to the worker under Directive 2003/88. The CJEU noted that if the obligation to paid annual leave were to cease with the end of the employment relationship because of the worker's death, the consequences would be an unintended occurrence beyond the control of both the worker and the employer, retroactively leading to a total loss of the entitlement to paid annual leave itself as affirmed in art 7 of the Directive. The CJEU concluded that, for those reasons, the provision of Directive 2003/88 cannot therefore be interpreted as meaning that the entitlement may be lost because of a worker's death. Since the Directive did not impose any condition for entitlement to an allowance in lieu, other than that relating to the fact that the employment relationship has ended, it must be held that receipt of such an allowance should not be made subject to an existence of a prior application for the purpose.

The CJEU concluded that art 7 of Directive 2003/88 must be interpreted as precluding national legislation or practice such as those at issue in the proceedings which provide that the entitlement to paid annual leave is lost without confirming entitlement to an allowance in lieu of leave outstanding where the employment relationship is terminated by the death of the worker. Receipt of such an allowance is not to be dependent on a prior application by the interested parties.

ACCRUAL OF ANNUAL LEAVE DURING SICK LEAVE

[30.13] An amendment has been made at the report stage to the Workplace Relations Bill 2014[34] to propose that s 19 of the Organisation of Working Time Act 1997 be amended to provide that employees may accrue annual leave while on certified sick leave,

The proposed amendment provides that accrued annual leave untaken in a leave year because of certified sick leave can be taken within the period of 15 months after the end of that leave year.

---

34.   See **[23.09]**.

Chapter 31

EMPLOYMENT MEDIATION

Mary Redmond

Consultant, Arthur Cox

INTRODUCTION

[31.01] Mediation is increasingly used to resolve disputes in many areas of life. It is one of the processes within alternative dispute resolution (ADR) and involves a neutral third party bringing two or more sides together with the aim of reaching an agreement all 'can live with'. Ireland, like the UK, has been a leader in using mediation to resolve conflict.

Mediation is no stranger to employment law but its scope will widen significantly when the Workplace Relations Bill 2014 (WRB) becomes law.[1] The Bill, when enacted, will apply mediation to employment rights disputes. For employment law, mediation's core values have great appeal: it is voluntary, confidential, speedy, inexpensive, it allows for flexible outcomes and self-determination of conflict.

This chapter considers the fertile background against which mediation in the WRB is being introduced. It then considers the relevant provisions in the WRB and in particular queries why the mediation option is apparently not being made available for unfair dismissal and redundancy claims. It makes suggestions to ensure that mediation will become the parties' option of choice, at least in the first instance. Finally, now as never before, mediation needs to be integrated into the workplace where its core values arguably have even greater appeal. This requires, as part of the stock in trade of employment documentation, a 'Mediation Policy and Guidelines', and appropriate mediation clauses in the contract of employment.

BACKGROUND: GENERALLY AND IN EMPLOYMENT LAW

[31.02] The Commercial Court established in 2004[2] kickstarted the successful promotion in Ireland of mediation through court referrals. Order 56A, r 2 of the Rules of the Superior Courts 1986[3] provides that when the court considers it appropriate in light

---

1. WRB as amended in the Select Committee on Jobs, Enterprise and Innovation, 6 November 2014.
2. Pursuant to the Rules of the Superior Courts (Commercial Proceedings) (SI 2/2004).
3. Inserted by the Rules of the Superior Courts (Mediation and Conciliation) (SI 502/2010). See *Fitzpatrick v Board of Management of St Mary's Touraneena National School* [2013] IESC 57, a personal injuries case involving bullying and harassment, where MacMenamin J made specific comments regarding efforts he felt should have been made to address the issues with ADR and referred to SI 502/2010. (contd .../)

of all the circumstances of the case, it may, on the judge's own initiative, or the application of any of the parties, invite the parties to use an ADR process to settle or determine the proceedings or issue. While Ireland has not introduced compulsory mediation prior to litigation, art 5(2) of EU Directive[4] allows for mediation to be compulsory or subject to incentives or sanctions provided the parties are not prevented from exercising their right of access to the courts. Order 56A has encouraged mediation by establishing costs sanctions for an unreasonable refusal to consider mediation. Other Acts inviting the parties to consider using mediation include the Civil Liability and Courts Act 2004 and the Enforcement of Court Orders (Amendment) Act 2009.

A broadly-based Mediation Bill is currently being drafted by the Department of Justice and Equality which will introduce an obligation on solicitors and barristers to advise any person wishing to commence court proceedings to consider mediation as a means of resolving a dispute before embarking on such proceedings. It will also provide that a court may, following the initiation of such proceedings, on its own initiative invite parties to consider mediation and suspend the proceedings to facilitate the mediation process. The Bill is eagerly awaited, the Draft General Scheme having first appeared in 2012.

For employers, employees, and trade unions, there are statutory mediation and conciliation processes for collective disputes within, for example, the Labour Relations Commission and the Labour Court under Industrial Relations legislation. Detailed statutory Codes of Practice have been developed providing guidance on processes to settle specific forms of grievances and other matters in industrial relations and employment.

Mediation has also been part of the statutory landscape of the Equality Tribunal under Employment Equality Acts and Equal Status Acts for many years. It must be said, however, that notwithstanding general satisfaction with the approach to such disputes, the statutory scheme has belied a core value of mediation, namely, its speed, with a waiting time of several months before the mediation meeting. Not least because of the functions of the Workplace Relations Commission described in s11 of the WRB, this will need to be reduced if mediation is to be broadened to cover employment rights disputes. If effected successfully, the new legislation will signal significant social and cultural change within the workplace.

There is an overwhelming business case for mediation: it will always be cheaper, most always successful, a powerful tool for management change and an holistic offering. Moreover, many established dispute resolution agencies in Ireland have come under huge strain with the individualisation of employment rights and the increase in employees pursuing claims, particularly in non-union workplaces.

---

3.   (contd) English cases endorsing the role of mediation in workplace disputes include *Vahidi v Fairstead House School Trust Ltd* [2005] EWCA Civ 06 and *McMillan Williams v Range* [2004] EWCA Civ 294.

4.   Given effect in the Rules of the Superior Courts (European Communities (Mediation) Regulations 2011 (SI 357/2012). And see the Law Reform Commission, *Alternative Dispute Resolution: Mediation and Conciliation* (LRC 98–2010), 92, in particular Ch 5.

THE WORKPLACE RELATIONS BILL

[31.03] The provisions on mediation in the WRB mirror those in the Equality Acts. However, the scope of the WRB is far wider and, as ever, one must avoid complacency. Parties will need encouragement if they are to choose the unfamiliar route of mediation for employment rights disputes.

Disputes or complaints under employment rights law have for years been addressed by means of adjudication by a Rights Commissioner, the Employment Appeals Tribunal, an Equality Tribunal, the Labour Court, or by means of National Employment Rights Authority (NERA) inspection. Under the WRB, there will be a choice: mediation or adjudication.

The WRB will replace the existing complex system of five different bodies with a two-tier system for employment rights and industrial relations disputes. It will transfer all existing functions of the Labour Relations Commission, including workplace mediation, to the Workplace Relations Commission (WRC). The services of the Equality Tribunal including mediation will come under the remit of the WRC.

MEANING OF MEDIATION IN THE WORKPLACE RELATIONS BILL

[31.04] 'Mediation' is not defined in the Bill and arguably should be,[5] if only because some employees, employers and their advisors are still unsure as to what it means and because mediation is a process with its own nuances. For example, there are different types of mediation: facilitative, evaluative, transactional, transformative, and directive. Will the first of these be used under the new law, the most common in this country, or will the approach be evaluative at times, given the fact that the WRB will be applying mediation to employment rights disputes where the legal rights of the parties within an anticipated reach of tribunal and court outcomes must surely feature? Transactional mediation encourages compromise and is also a likely candidate under the WRB. It is probably unlikely that the remaining forms of mediation will be used: transformational mediation which encourages the parties to take control of the process or directive mediation which involves suggestions from the mediator.

SERVICE AKIN TO EMPLOYMENT EQUALITY MEDIATION

[31.05] Sections 38 and 39 of the WRB provide for the appointment of mediation officers to the WRC and the provision of a mediation service to facilitate the resolution of employment rights disputes where possible at an early stage and without recourse to adjudication. As the Explanatory Memorandum to the WRB says, the service will be akin to the mediation service currently provided under equality legislation (but without,

---

5.   The Law Reform Commission, *Alternative Dispute Resolution: Mediation and Conciliation* (LRC 98–2010), fn 3 contains a draft Mediation and Conciliation Bill which defines mediation in s 4(1).

one might hope, the delays that characterise it at the moment). According to the Explanatory Memorandum it is envisaged that mediation (unlike the Early Resolution Service) will be offered to parties in more complex disputes 'such as cases under ... the Unfair Dismissals Acts requiring face-to-face mediation'.

COMPLAINTS VERSUS DISPUTES

[31.06] The WRB distinguishes between 'complaints' and 'disputes'. The Director General under s 40(1)(a) and (b) of the WRB may, where he or she is of the opinion that a complaint or dispute is capable of being resolved by mediation, refer the dispute (the subsection inadvertently fails to add a 'complaint' as well) for mediation by a mediation officer although not if either of the parties to the complaint or dispute objects to its being so referred. Section 40(9) of the WRB provides that for purposes of the section, a 'complaint' means a complaint presented to the Director General of the WRC under s 42. Likewise, s 40(9) of the WRB provides that a 'dispute' means a dispute referred to the Director General under s 42. A 'complaint' under s 42 of the WRB is a complaint that a provision specified in Part 1 or 2 of Sch 5 has been contravened in relation to the complainant. Part 1 of Sch 5 to the WRB specifies provisions under statute such as those under the Part-time, Fixed-Term, and Temporary Agency Work Acts while Part 2 of Sch 5 concerns statutory instruments, for example, on transfer of undertakings. A 'dispute' is one as to the entitlements of the employee under an enactment specified in Part 3 of Sch 5. Examples in Part 3 include maternity, adoptive, parental and carer's leave entitlements. Fixed-term legislation is referred to here as well as in Part 1. In the case of a complaint or a dispute so defined the Director General shall refer the complaint or dispute for adjudication by an adjudication officer 'subject to sections 39 [Case Resolution without reference to adjudication officer] and 40 [mediation]'.

UNFAIR DISMISSALS

[31.07] Inexplicably the Unfair Dismissals Acts do not appear in Parts 1, 2 or 3 of Sch 5. One is forced to look elsewhere in the WRB for a link, if any, to the mediation option.

Section 81 of the WRB deals with amendment of the Unfair Dismissals Act 1977 (the Act of 1977). Does this supply the missing link? Apparently not. On the contrary, adjudication seems to be the only route. Section 81(1)(c)(ii) substitutes the following for subs (1) of s 8 of the Act of 1977:

> A claim by an employee against an employer for redress under this Act for unfair dismissal may be referred by the employee to the Director General and, where such a claim is so referred, the Director General shall refer the claim to an adjudication officer for adjudication by the adjudication officer.

The new subsection mandates referral for adjudication and does not qualify the obligation on the Director General as being 'subject to sections 39 or 40 [the mediation sections]'. Even if it did, bearing in mind the precise boundaries in ss 40(9) and 42 of the

WRB and the principles of statutory construction, it must be doubtful whether that could include claims under the Act of 1977 for potential mediation.

Section 81(1)(d) applies the provisions of the WRB to claims for redress under the Act of 1977. Sections 43 and 44 of the WRB concern themselves with a complaint or dispute referred to an adjudication officer under s 42 of the Bill, and enforcement of adjudication officer's decisions, the reference to s 42 to be construed as a reference to s 8 of the Act of 1977. Self-evidently, under s 8, the claim will have been referred for adjudication.

Nor is the Redundancy Payments Act 1967 (the Act of 1967) specified in Sch 5. Section 77 of the WRB amends the Act of 1967. Subsection (1)(b)(ii) of s 77 of the WRB refers to the insertion in subs (2A) of s 24 of the Act of 1967 of the words:

> 'adjudication officer to whom the claim has been referred under section 39, if he is satisfied' for 'Tribunal, if it is satisfied …'.

but s 39 of the WRB does not include claims under the Act of 1967. Redundancy could be said to be distinguishable from unfair dismissals law, of course, the issues being mechanical and on the whole more suited to adjudication.

The most striking and inexplicable anomaly is the omission of unfair dismissals as a mediation option. It needs and will doubtless receive clarification at the earliest opportunity.

WHERE OPINION IS THAT MEDIATION APPROPRIATE UNDER THE WRB

[31.08] Where the Director General is of the opinion that mediation is appropriate, as earlier described, and the parties do not object, the complaint or dispute is referred for mediation to a mediation officer who may convene a mediation conference for the purpose of resolving the complaint or dispute. Participation in the service will be voluntary for both sides and parties availing of mediation will not lose the right to have their issues dealt with by means of a hearing. Nor will they be disadvantaged in relation to their waiting time for inspection or a hearing. If mediation is successful, resulting in compromise, settlement or withdrawal of the complaint, the outcome will be recorded in writing by the mediation officer, signed by the parties, be binding on them and enforceable in court.

As might be expected, confidentiality is protected. The terms of a resolution under s 39(7) of the WRB shall not be disclosed by a mediation officer or by either party in any court proceedings, other than in proceedings in respect of the contravention of the terms of the resolution, 'or otherwise'. All communications during a mediation conference and all records and notes held for the purposes of resolving any matter shall be confidential (presumably, although not spelled out, to the mediation officer and the parties) and not disclosed in court proceedings, other than in proceedings in respect of a contravention of the terms of a resolution agreed during the mediation conference, 'or otherwise': s 39(8) WRB.

In 2013 the Minister for Jobs, Enterprise and Innovation stated that in 2011, overall, 62% of cases referred to mediation were closed as a result of the mediation process. In

2012 that figure was 56%. One outcome from mediation that can be helpful and is not available in court, is an apology from one side to another. This healing mechanism can be most effective in helping parties to move forward.

It would be helpful if a written statement were required explaining why a party had declined mediation in circumstances where the Director General has formed the opinion that the dispute or complaint is capable of being resolved by mediation. Perhaps an obligation for the parties 'to consider mediation' in such circumstances might be included. This would require full information about the process, and perhaps attending an information session. Although a code of practice might cover such matters, they would be better included in the legislation or in regulations. It is important that all is done to ensure the success of introducing mediation into employment rights disputes. If this does not happen, the concept may be damaged.

When does mediation begin? The WRB could be specific as to when the clock starts and stops in mediation relative to other routes under legislation. It is specific as to time limits in relation to adjudication. In s 42(5) it says:

> Subject to subsection (7), an adjudication officer shall not entertain a complaint referred to him or her under this section if it has been presented to the Director General after the expiration of the period of 6 months beginning on the date of the contravention to which the complaint relates.

Subsection (7) of s 42 provides an exception where the adjudication officer is satisfied that the failure to present the complaint or refer the dispute within that period was due to reasonable cause. There appears to be no similar temporal restriction on mediation officers in relation to complaints referred to them by the Director General.

The qualifications for mediators will also be important given the sole emphasis in the Bill on employment legislation and statutory instruments. Equality mediation officers received impressive training in this form of ADR but equality is but a small part of employment rights. It is inconceivable, in the interests of quality assurance, that mediators should not have a minimum level of legal training or knowledge of the system. It would also be inconceivable given the likely need for evaluative as well as facilitative mediation.

MEDIATION IN THE WORKPLACE: NON-STATUTORY DISPUTE RESOLUTION MECHANISMS

[31.09] When the WRB is enacted into law, mediation will enter the domain of employment law. A culture change will follow, whereby the Win:Lose mindset will give way to one that explores solutions with which all sides 'can live'. As mediation is likely to play a leading role in employment rights disputes, employers would be well advised to begin introducing the same culture change within their employment. The Law Reform Commission said similarly:

> While the Commission acknowledges and commends the contribution of the statutory bodies which are responsible for the resolution of employment grievances and disputes outside of the court system, non-statutory dispute resolution mechanisms for resolving workplace disputes should also be available

for the resolution of workplace disputes and such mechanisms should be established internally within organisations.[6]

And it recommended that:

> ... organisations should consider designing and implementing internal dispute handling systems which incorporate mediation and conciliation processes so as to promote the early resolution of employment disputes.[7]

In the workplace, the scope for mediation is greater than that of the WRB given the iceberg nature of much workplace conflict. Nor would the employee's choice be mediation or adjudication as under the WRB. The objective would always be to explore solutions, to pursue dialogue.

What might this mean?

[31.10] To begin with, employment documentation should be explicit that mediation is the employer's preferred way of resolving all complaints, disputes and conflict relating to the employment. The WRB is confined to employment rights disputes: that is, disputes arising under statute or statutory instrument. Not all disputes arise in this way. Nor is the reach of mediation in the workplace confined to disputes: it can assist in relation to coaching, chairing, difficult or tough communications, inter-departmental territorial clashes, disagreements over corporate policy and practice, disputed allocation of reward in projects, divergence of expectations and understandings, investigations and assessments – often after a formal investigation where no fault has been found. It is also used in relation to contractual disputes including termination, grievances, discrimination, bullying and harassment, personality clashes, redundancies including collective redundancies and relational difficulties or breakdowns. It can be appropriate in some disciplinary matters such as non-performance. Mediation is not the default option for all disputes. It may be inappropriate where an employee has learning difficulties, or criminal activity may have been involved, or a party is insisting, perhaps intransigently, on having his/her grievance investigated and adjudicated.

In relation to all issues, the employer's procedures and agreements should:

(i) enable it to require the parties to a dispute to consider mediation particularly before those in dispute contemplate any adversarial or legal action which will result in substantial costs for both sides;

(ii) have a Mediation Policy and Mediation Guidelines which assimilate mediation into the employment environment;

---

6. Law Reform Commission, *Alternative Dispute Resolution: Mediation and Conciliation* (LRC 98–2010), fn 2 at para 5. 24.

7. Law Reform Commission, *Alternative Dispute Resolution: Mediation and Conciliation* (LRC 98–2010) at para 5. 21. See, also, Fitzgerald, 'The growing importance of workplace mediation in Ireland' IRN 20, 2014 and Sheehan, 'Mediation: new researach shows that "Talking" does work' IRN 32, 2014.

(iii) cross-refer to other employment policies and documents to which mediation may be linked.

Employers who undertake a mediation proofing exercise will find the effort fully repaid. The employer's environment may extend to customer/user complaints procedures where mediation may have a role, as well as to commercial disputes with partners, contractors and so on.

MEDIATION IS VOLUNTARY

[31.11] There is misunderstanding, even among some lawyers, about mediation's voluntary nature. An employer cannot force anyone to mediate. The key, as indicated earlier, is that the employer can make it *obligatory* for employees to *consider mediation*. In order for employees to 'consider mediation' and to arrive at an informed decision, the employer would need to provide timely information. This could mean compulsory attendance at a mediation information session, to be distinguished from compulsory participation in mediation. Often sufficient information is found in the Mediation Policy and Guidelines. There the employee will be reassured to learn that any agreement reached in mediation comes from those in dispute, not from the mediator. The mediator commonly is another employee trained by the employer or is from an external mediation service in charge of the process. Generally, but not always, parties are not represented.

CONFIDENTIALITY

[31.12] The parties should be asked to sign a mediation agreement beforehand ensuring matters such as confidentiality. And, like the scheme in the WRB, where there is a jointly resolved outcome, they should be asked to sign an agreement after the process to ensure the outcome is legally binding.

There can also be misunderstanding concerning mediation of employment matters and confidentiality. Anything said during the mediation is confidential to the parties and cannot be used in future legal proceedings. The outcome of mediation is also confidential to the parties. However, this may be unworkable in an ongoing employment relationship. Hence the parties may choose to reveal some or all of what has occurred during the mediation to colleagues, or their managers, on condition always that all agree. Agreement would be unnecessary in limited circumstances as where a potentially unlawful act had been committed or there was a serious risk to health and safety.

NAMES OF MEDIATORS AND COSTS OF MEDIATION

[31.13] The Mediation Policy will generally specify that the parties in dispute who opt for mediation may be asked to propose the names of external accredited mediators to each other. The contract will generally provide that in default of agreement a designated officer or organisation (such as CEDR) whose nomination will be final and binding will be asked to nominate a mediator.[8]

Payment for mediation needs to be clarified and costs need to be monitored. The costs to the employee of their own advisor's costs are distinguishable from those of the mediation. There are no set rules. Often it is thought undesirable that the employer should pay all costs of the mediation and preferable that costs be shared between the parties. But if procedures have been exhausted and mediation is an attempt to reach a settlement prior to legal proceedings the policy may say that the employer may agree to meet the whole or greater part of the cost of the mediation.

This and other matters are for discussion and advice between employers and their advisors. They are steps on the way to making mediation a sustainable part of the employer's culture. Let it be said finally that culture change and promotion of the process are also essential in the lawyer's toolkit for conflict resolution. There is a dawning realization by some experienced jurists that mediation has much to offer companies solve their conflicts. They realise the future will belong to ADR, and in employment disputes, to mediation. The pace of 'creative lawyering' should speed up more generally in employment law in this jurisdiction if, but only if, the WRB gets it right.

A personal postscript: if only the first step in attempting to create a world-class system for employment law had been to consolidate Ireland's employment rights legislation. As it is, practitioners have enough amendments, deletions, substitutions and insertions to festoon a balloon, or several of them. Quite apart from constitutional considerations concerning access to justice, complexity is not a value associated with world-class systems.

---

8. If not in the Mediation Policy, employers are not obliged to appoint an external mediator to resolve employment matters. In *Our Lady's Children's Hospital v A Worker* AD131000, the Labour Court rejected the claimant's argument that an external mediator should have been appointed and upheld the decision of the Rights Commissioner that the respondent's offer of mediation should be accepted by all parties.

INDEX